Guide to
Shakespeare

About the Author

David M. Zesmer is currently Professor of English at Illinois Institute of Technology. He received his B.A., M.A., and Ph.D. degrees from Columbia University. Dr. Zesmer is the author of *Guide to English Literature from Beowulf through Chaucer and Medieval Drama* (Barnes & Noble, 1961), the editor of *Dryden: Poetry, Drama, and Prose* (Bantam, 1967) and a contributor ("John Dryden") to *The Reader's Encyclopedia of Shakespeare*. He is at present working on a book, *John Milton as Educator*.

Guide to Shakespeare

David M. Zesmer

BARNES & NOBLE BOOKS

A DIVISION OF HARPER & ROW, PUBLISHERS

New York, Hagerstown, San Francisco, London

FOR SUE

Designed by Dianne Pinkowitz

First BARNES & NOBLE BOOKS edition published 1976

LIBRARY OF CONGRESS CATALOG CARD NUMBER: 73–34590

ISBN: 0 –06 –460164 –1

   79   80   5   4   3

Contents

Preface

This book provides a survey of all the dramatic and nondramatic works of Shakespeare and indicates some of the directions of recent scholarship and criticism. It is intended for undergraduate and graduate students and for other readers who may wish to explore Shakespeare with greater appreciation and understanding. I say "readers" because this *Guide,* while touching here and there upon the acting and staging of Shakespeare, makes no systematic attempt to deal with the plays in performance, a subject that has engaged such scholars as Arthur Colby Sprague, John Russell Brown, and Daniel Seltzer. In assessing various critical opinions, I have often stated or implied my own. But the object at all times is to open, not close, discussion.

I have included bibliographical footnotes along the way. In addition to documenting and reinforcing views expressed in the text, the notes (which appear at the end of each chapter) direct attention to other studies that may develop, qualify, or dispute such views. This arrangement enables the interested reader to pursue a particular issue as it comes up: Shakespeare and Tudor historiography, the motivation of Iago, the authorship of *Pericles,* and so on. In a deliberate effort to acquaint the reader with more recent scholarship, I may have occasionally slighted older studies of established value. One should redress the balance by consulting the standard bibliographies and bibliographical guides that are noted at the end of this volume. Rather than offer yet another extensive bibliography, I have listed a handful of books that I consider, for one reason or another, to be especially significant. They encompass a wide range of Shakespeare scholarship.

Several friends and scholars have read portions of the manuscript and made helpful suggestions: Thelma N. Greenfield, Robert A. Colby, Louis Marder, and especially Matthew W. Black. I have received valuable assistance from my daughter Sarah, Robert Cohen, Jeff Tobin, and Nina Halpern, all of whom spent countless hours checking the accuracy of quotations and footnotes. In this regard, Patricia McGeough has been indispensable. Mischa Rubin and Jura Scharf helped substantially with the proofreading. I am grateful to the staff of the Newberry Library for many services cheerfully and efficiently provided. A number of editors have worked with the manuscript over the years, and their labors are appreciated: Samuel Smith, Roger Walterhouse, Marian Arkin, Frances Caplan, and Libby Siegel. Most of all, I am indebted to Nancy Cone, editor and friend, whose patience has been inexhaustible. She truly understands Cassius's remark to Brutus, "A friend should bear his friend's infirmities."

Just about every student in my generation came to know and love Shakespeare in the great one-volume edition of George Lyman Kittredge. I am pleased that this landmark edition, unwithered by age and unstaled by custom, has furnished the text for all my quotations from Shakespeare.

1
Shakespeare and the Elizabethan Scene

Shortly before his death in September 1592, the Elizabethan playwright and pamphleteer Robert Greene addressed an anguished letter to three fellow dramatists and friends—most probably Christopher Marlowe, George Peele, and either Thomas Nashe or Thomas Lodge. Sick and penniless, Greene felt bitter at being deserted by the very people who should have helped him, namely, the actors. These "puppets," who cannot speak or move except by the grace of the playwright, Greene condemns as an ungrateful lot. One of them, in fact, presumes to think he can write plays himself:

> For there is an upstart Crow, beautified with our feathers, that with his *Tygers hart wrapt in a Players hyde*, supposes he is as well able to bombast out a blanke verse as the best of you: and beeing an absolute *Johannes fac totum* [Jack of all trades], is in his owne conceit the onely Shake-scene in a countrey.[1]

Greene entreats his learned friends to abandon the stage in favor of less treacherous employment, "& let those Apes imitate your past excellence, and never more acquaint them with your admired inventions."

Whatever its motivation, Greene's outburst enjoys the distinction of being the first recorded piece of Shakespearean criticism. The identity of the "upstart Crow" is clear from the pun "Shake-scene" as well as the phrase, "Tygers hart wrapt in a Players hyde," which parodies a line from Shakespeare's *3 Henry VI* (I, 4, 137), "O tiger's heart wrapp'd in a woman's hide!" The attack was at one time construed to mean that Greene was accusing Shakespeare of plagiarism, but this interpretation is unlikely. Two years before, Greene had used the figure of "Aesop's crow, being prancked with the glory of others' feathers" to disparage the acting profession: "Of thyself thou canst say nothing, and if the cobbler

1

hath taught thee to say 'Ave Caesar', disdain not thy tutor because thou pratest in a king's chamber."[2] A man of university education, Greene was perhaps jealous of Shakespeare, a nobody who at twenty-eight had already won substantial success.

Greene's tirade seems to have aroused quick resentment, for in December 1592 his literary executor Henry Chettle issued an apology. Without mentioning Shakespeare by name, Chettle says that he found the offended party to be extremely civil; moreover, "divers of worship [people of high standing] have reported his uprightnes of dealing, which argues his honesty, and his facetious grace in writting, that aprooves [confirms] his Art."[3] Six years later, in 1598, the clergyman and critic Francis Meres ranks Shakespeare with Ovid as a poet and with Plautus and Seneca, respectively, as a comic and tragic dramatist. Meres recalls the fancy that if the Muses spoke Latin they would speak with the tongue of Plautus: "So I say that the Muses would speak with Shakespeares fine filed phrase, if they would speake English."[4] Included in the First Folio (1623), the first collection of Shakespeare's plays, is an elegy from the pen of the playwright Ben Jonson—To the Memory of My Beloved, the Author, Mr. William Shakespeare, and What He Hath Left Us—containing the celebrated line, "He was not of an age, but for all time!" To the Restoration poet John Dryden, so different from Shakespeare in temperament and literary style, "he was the man who of all modern, and perhaps ancient poets, had the largest and most comprehensive soul."[5] And in the nineteenth century Coleridge, with characteristic enthusiasm, observed "with what armour clothed and with what titles authorized Shakespeare came forward as a poet to demand the throne of fame, as the dramatic poet of England."[6] One could produce endless evidence to the effect that Shakespeare, beginning in his own lifetime and continuing almost without interruption down to the present day, has held an unassailable position as the most popular dramatist of the English-speaking world and one of the supreme poets of all time.[7]

SHAKESPEARE'S LIFE

Inevitably, a vast legend has accumulated around Shakespeare the man and sometimes distorted our view of Shakespeare the artist. One formidable task of Shakespearean biography has been to test the legend against the known facts and the most reliable traditions.[8] As a result, the old image of Shakespeare the untutored genius "warbling his native woodnotes wild" has been drastically revised. "What emerges beyond reasonable doubt is the picture of a hard-reading man of letters engaged upon poetry and the drama, exploring literature for subjects and material to his taste or suitable for the demands of his company."[9]

The precise date of Shakespeare's birth is not known, but he was baptized on April 26, 1564, in Trinity Church, Stratford-on-Avon.[10] His father was John Shakespeare, a prosperous tanner and glover who became high bailiff (mayor) in 1568 and chief alderman in 1571; his mother was Mary Arden Shakespeare, daughter of a wealthy gentleman from Wilmecote. The social and economic position of the Shakespeare family makes it probable that the poet attended the local grammar school, where he would have received rigorous instruction in religion, Latin and Greek grammar (particularly Latin), rhetoric, and Latin literature.[11] Ben Jonson wrote in his elegy that Shakespeare had "small Latin and less Greek," but Jonson judged from the perspective of a classical scholar.

On November 28, 1582, Shakespeare married Anne Hathaway, an event that has led to intense speculation, some of it wildly imaginative. The license, issued the preceding day, was made out to "Willelmum Shaxpere *et* Annam Whateley *de* Temple Grafton." Biographers have been hard put to account for the discrepancy in the name of the bride. The most sensible explanation seems to be that a clerk inadvertently wrote "Whateley" for "Hathaway," possibly because on the same day he had been taking testimony in which a Whateley was involved. Some think, however, that two different William Shakespeares are meant. Others have suggested that we are dealing with only one Shakespeare but with two Annes. Shakespeare, according to this fanciful view, was getting ready to marry his truelove, Anne Whateley, when Anne Hathaway stormed in to assert a prior claim: Three months earlier Shakespeare had got her pregnant. Consequently, Anne Whateley retired from the field with a broken heart.[12] Shakespeare's bequest to Anne Hathaway of his "second best bed" is sometimes seen as proof that he did not love his wife, but we have no evidence to warrant any conclusions about the circumstances surrounding his marriage or the intimate details of his married life. The couple had three children: Susanna, baptized May 26, 1583; and twins, Hamnet and Judith, baptized February 2, 1585.

Apart from the mere mention of his name in a lawsuit brought by his father against a John Lambert in 1589, there is no trace of Shakespeare from 1585 until 1592, when Greene attacked the "Shake-scene" in London. These so-called lost years have inspired a great deal of research and conjecture, but no evidence can be found about what Shakespeare was doing all that time. Here are a few of the theories: He joined the army; he served as clerk in a law office; he was a physician's apprentice; he traveled to Italy; he sailed the seas with Sir Francis Drake. More plausible, though resting upon dubious authority, is the tradition that, for some of those years at any rate, he was a schoolmaster. There is the unsubstantiated rumor that he had to get away from Stratford because he had been caught poaching deer. According to another attractive story, Shakespeare came to London and held horses outside the theater until his acting talent was one day discovered. One ought to remember, however, that acting was a competitive profession and that success on the London stage generally presupposed long experience in lesser theaters in the provinces. Shakespeare may well have left Stratford to learn his craft as an actor.[13]

For the next twenty years or so, until about 1612, Shakespeare was an important figure in the literary and theatrical life of London. When the public theaters were closed (1592–1593) because of an outbreak of the plague, he apparently turned his attention to narrative poetry. *Venus and Adonis* was listed in the Stationers' Register on April 18, 1593 (evidence of imminent publication), and on May 9, 1594, *The Rape of Lucrece* was similarly registered.[14] Both poems are dedicated to Henry Wriothesley, earl of Southampton.

Shakespeare had evidently become a member of the Lord Chamberlain's Men by the time the company performed before the queen during the Christmas season of 1594–1595, for he is among the three actors named in the record of court payment. He seems to have continued with the Lord Chamberlain's Men (the company was called the King's Men after the accession of James I in 1603) for the rest of his professional career. This company regularly performed just north of London in the Theatre, built by James Burbage (see p. 8). When the lease expired in 1597 and prolonged negotiations failed to produce a renewal, the troupe dismantled the building (December 28, 1598), carried the wood and timber southward across the Thames, and used the old materials to build a famous new home—the Globe Theater. The playhouse was owned by the seven leading actors in the company: Richard and Cuthbert Burbage (sons of James Burbage) owned half interest; the other half was shared by Shakespeare, Augustine Phillips, Thomas Pope, John Heminge, and William Kempe. When Kempe withdrew from the company, Shakespeare's share was increased. In 1608 the King's Men took over an indoor theater, the Blackfriars, for winter use. Shakespeare's literary activity apparently stopped after the burning of the Globe in 1613.

Shakespeare spent his last years at Stratford, where in 1597 he had purchased New Place, then one of the town's most impressive houses. Such documents as have survived indicate that he was a good businessman who prospered in his theatrical ventures as well as other transactions, particularly real estate. He died in 1616 on what tradition has taken to be his birthday, April 23. The story that he died of a fever contracted after drinking too hard with Ben Jonson and the poet Michael Drayton is scarcely reliable. By 1661–1663, when this anecdote was recorded, Shakespeare had already become a legend.[15]

The most fantastic myth of all is the one that the plays of Shakespeare were written not by "the man from Stratford" but by somebody else. More than fifty different candidates have been proposed: Sir Francis Bacon, Sir Walter Raleigh, the Earl of Essex, the Earl of Derby, the Earl of Oxford, Christopher Marlowe, Queen Elizabeth I, and so on.

Although individual arguments vary, the anti-Stratfordians generally rest their case upon the altogether false assumption that the man from Stratford must have been ignorant, if not illiterate, while the author of the plays had to be an educated gentleman with an intimate knowledge of court life. They point to discrepancies in the spelling of Shakespeare's name as evidence of illiteracy, despite the fact that Elizabethan spelling, even among the aristocracy, was not standardized. Those who champion Essex have had to play fast and loose with the accepted chronology of Shakespeare's plays, many of which appeared long after 1601, when Essex was executed. A more recent notion is that Marlowe's death in 1593, which is a matter of public record, was faked so that he could escape to the Continent and secretly write plays that, for political reasons, were issued in Shakespeare's name. Some claim that the plays are too great to have been written by any one individual but were produced by a syndicate of Elizabethan dramatists. Many anti-Stratfordians, in particular the Baconians, insist that the real author preserved his identity for posterity, at least for the privileged few, through pictorial symbols and ciphers cleverly introduced into the texts of the plays. These arguments have been demolished by expert cryptographers.[16] According to one view, after writing Shakespeare's plays (as well as those of Greene and Marlowe), Bacon retired to a retreat in rural England and published under a succession of pseudonyms: John Bunyan, John Milton, Thomas Hobbes, Jonathan Swift, Thomas Carlyle.[17]

In *No Bed for Bacon,* a delightful spoof of some of the clichés about Elizabethan England, Shakespeare has at one point been left alone in the theater to attend to important business: He must decide once and for all how to spell his name; he must oblige the actor Burbage with a new play about a melancholy Prince of Denmark and a gravedigger; and he must get on with his never-to-be-finished task of writing a play that Francis Meres ascribed to him, "Love's Labour's Won" (see p. 44). But his solitude is interrupted by a visit from his good friend Francis Bacon, who pulls a sheaf of papers from his pocket and lays them on the desk. " 'By the way, Will,' he said. 'I almost forgot. When you've got a moment to spare, you might polish up this essay.' "[18]

SHAKESPEARE'S THEATER

Each generation exercises the privilege of interpreting Shakespeare, as it interprets all great writers, in the light of its own beliefs and attitudes. In recent years, however, scholars have increasingly directed our attention to the fact that Shakespeare lived and worked in Elizabethan England, and they have attempted to recover for twentieth-century readers and playgoers something of the atmosphere in which he flourished. It is hazardous to generalize about any era, particularly when dealing with someone of Shakespeare's stature. The artist always reserves the right to remold or transcend the values he shares with his contemporaries. Nevertheless, there are several features of the Elizabethan scene that ought to be considered if one is to gain a fuller understanding of Shakespeare's art: the theater for which he wrote; the English language as he knew it and used it; and the body of traditional thought about man and the universe that makes up what has conveniently been termed "the Elizabethan world picture."[19]

We know quite a bit about the theatrical organization of Shakespeare's London,[20] and we have obtained a reasonably clear picture of the composition and behavior of Elizabethan audiences.[21] It is also our good fortune that Philip Henslowe, the most famous theater owner of the time, kept an account book that furnishes illuminating details of the day-by-day financial operations of an Elizabethan playhouse.[22] Yet specific information about the actual staging of Shakespeare's plays is disappointingly scarce. The various reconstructions of the Globe and other playhouses have been for the most part conjectural. Scholars may agree on a few essentials, but ironically there is considerable controversy surrounding the most interesting problem confronting the Elizabethan theatrical historian: the appearance and use of the stage itself.[23]

It is certain that the Elizabethan stage evolved in some fashion from the medieval stage. The formal drama of the Middle Ages originated in embellishments upon the liturgy and was initially acted in churches as a supplement to the regular service. When the scenes became more elaborate and audiences more unwieldy, the drama moved out into the churchyards and streets. There were three major types of plays: miracles, or mysteries, which dramatized scriptural history; moralities, allegorical plays about man's spiritual struggles; and interludes, lighter plays often introduced between the acts of miracles and moralities. The actors, who at first were not professionals in the modern sense but members of various trade guilds, mounted the plays on horse-drawn floats (pageants) or on fixed stages in a field.[24] As plays came to be produced for diversified audiences throughout the country, the actors, in the manner of professional minstrels, roamed far and wide, performing in public streets, open fields, taverns, and baronial houses. Such was the troupe that visited the court of Denmark and acted, at Hamlet's request, "The Murder of Gonzago."[25]

There is little doubt that in the first half of the sixteenth century, innyards were used for dramatic presentations. The innyard provided a large court in which a wooden platform could be constructed, thereby furnishing a stage and a sizable pit where spectators could stand. The stables could serve as dressing rooms, and the several tiers of surrounding galleries would have been ideal for seating prosperous patrons. Moreover, a number of innkeepers in London and elsewhere would have found it profitable to lease their yards exclusively to theatrical companies.

But recent scholarship has challenged the long-accepted notion that Shakespeare's theater derived from the innyard. C. Walter Hodges has cogently argued that both the innyard and the permanent Elizabethan theater employed the traditional booth stage of the old street theater; and Glynne Wickham has marshaled impressive evidence that the inn was merely one of several possible locales for acting and that when a performance did occur at an inn it was given indoors, not in the yard. In another important study, Richard Southern suggests that Elizabethan stage practices may be traced directly to traditions developed by interlude players in the great Tudor halls.[26] We are a long way from either certainty or uniformity. "Every theatre," it has been observed, "is a patchwork quilt, made up of bits and pieces from the Miracle arenas, the Mystery pageants, the mountebank scaffolds, the innyards, the animal rings, the Court halls, from any place in short which had been used for drama in the previous hundred years."[27]

Although the theater was very much alive during the early years of Elizabeth I, the London acting companies were continually harassed by two implacable foes: Puritan agitators, like Stephen Gosson, who denounced theaters as inciting to sin; and the lord mayor and his council, who thought that the mobs congregating in the innyards and elsewhere were a hazard to public health and law enforcement. On December 6, 1574, a crisis was reached when the council, under the leadership of the lord mayor (Sir James Hawes), issued an order that made the continuance of theatrical performances in London all but impossible. The document (which Chambers prints in its entirety) may be quoted here in part, for it summarizes so well the hostility of both Puritans and municipal authorities:

Whearas hearetofore sondrye greate disorders and inconvenyences have benne found to ensewe to this Cittie by the inordynate hauntyinge of greate multitudes of people, speciallye youthe, to playes, enterludes, and shewes, namelye occasyon of ffrayes and quarrelles, eavell practizes of incontinencye in greate Innes, havinge chambers and secrete places adioyninge to their open stagies and gallyries, inveglynge and alleurynge of maides, speciallye orphanes and good Cityzens Children under Age, to previe and unmete Contractes, the publishinge of unchaste uncomelye and unshamefaste speeches and doynges, withdrawinge of the Queenes Maiesties Subiectes from dyvyne service on Sonndaies and hollydayes, at which Tymes suche playes weare Chefelye used, unthriftye waste of the moneye of the poore and fond persons, sondrye robberies by pyckinge and Cuttinge of purses, utteringe of popular busye and sedycious matters, and manie other Corruptions of youthe and other enormyties, besydes that allso soundrye slaughters and mayhemynges of the Quenes Subiectes have happened by ruines of Skaffoldes, fframes, and Stagies, and by engynes, weapons, and powder used in plaies; And whear[as] in tyme of goddes visitacion by the plaigue suche assemblies of the people in thronge and presse have benne verye daungerous for spreadinge of Infection. . . . 28

For these and other reasons the council decreed that henceforth no kind of play could be performed within the city unless it was first approved by the lord mayor and the court of aldermen. Moreover, plays would be exhibited only at such times and places as the lord mayor and aldermen should deem appropriate.

In 1576 an enterprising businessman, James Burbage, ingeniously evaded the decree. He built what has sometimes been called (misleadingly) the first permanent playhouse in London and named it simply the Theatre, erecting it in the priory of Holywell, between Shoreditch High Street and Finsbury Fields, just north of the city and outside the jurisdiction of the municipal authorities. The Curtain (1577) was built in the same general area. In 1600 Henslowe, together with his leading tragic actor Edward Alleyn, built the Fortune, also north of the city but west of the Shoreditch area. The Red Bull, built around 1605, completes the list of theaters in the northern district. A second and more important theatrical district was Bankside (the south bank of the Thames), likewise out of the control of the lord mayor and his council. Bankside was the home of the Rose (c. 1587), the Swan (c. 1595), the Hope (1613), and, of course, the Globe (1599), owned and operated by Shakespeare's company, the Lord Chamberlain's Men. (The professional companies were sponsored, but not financed, by prominent nobles.) Chief rival to the Lord Chamberlain's Men was the Lord Admiral's Men, later called Prince Henry's Men and Elector Palatine's Men. Its principal actor was Alleyn, who created the role of Tamburlaine in Marlowe's tragedy. In addition to Marlowe, the Lord Admiral's Men included on its roster of playwrights Thomas Heywood, Thomas Dekker, and Michael Drayton, as well as lesser figures (Anthony Munday, Henry Chettle, John Day, and others) sometimes characterized unfairly as "Henslowe's hacks."

What did Shakespeare's theater look like? Firsthand sources are limited to a few allusions in books of the period, a drawing or two (including one of the interior of the Swan), and building contracts for the Hope and the Fortune. Some contemporary scholars have raised fundamental doubts about matters of Elizabethan stagecraft that used to be taken for granted. Hence, one should allow for flexibility in theater design and refrain from making extravagant claims for any single hypothesis.29

The Elizabethan playhouse was generally round or polygonal, although the Fortune seems to have been rectangular. The stage, a bare platform with no front curtain, jutted out into an unroofed yard or pit. On either side of the stage were long, narrow spaces that may have been used by the actors for entrances and exits, but one cannot be sure that all theaters had such passageways. The groundlings stood in the pit, but gallants often crowded onto the stage and, according to contemporary accounts, behaved in a rowdy manner. There were usually three tiers of gallery seats, which were sold for an additional fee. Estimates as to the size of an Elizabethan audience vary, but 2,500 seems a reasonable figure for the capacity of the Rose and about 2,300 for the Fortune and the Globe. Johannes de Witt, the visitor from Utrecht who made the sketch of the Swan in 1596, said that the Swan could *seat* 3,000; and there is no evidence to the contrary.[30]

At the rear of the platform stage was a place called the tiring-house, where the actors dressed; it was part of the main building separated from the spectators by a wall. At the stage level of the tiring-house façade were two doorways through which the actors could pass and possibly a central opening. It has often been maintained that this central alcove (if it indeed existed) was an inner stage large enough to serve as a study, bedroom, or cave. Some scholars, however, doubt that any extended action would have been staged at a point so remote from most of the spectators and reject the notion of a large inner stage in favor of a temporary upper stage jutting out from the tiring-house wall and resembling the familiar curtained booth of the street theater.[31]

The upper stage is also a debatable point. According to the older view, there was a sizable curtained area on the level of the second gallery that could be used for interior scenes and scenes requiring elevation. There Brutus and Antony may have stood while addressing the Roman populace at Caesar's funeral, and there Juliet could have heard Romeo's outpouring of love in the balcony scene. But J. W. Saunders would limit the upper stage at the Globe to a mere window and would stage the orations of Brutus and Antony on a simple prop (a chair or box).[32] To repeat, no two theaters were identical, and even the same play could have been staged differently if moved from one theater to another. Overhanging the main platform was a roof canopy, the so-called heavens, which furnished shelter during light rains. Under the stage was the hell or cellarage from which devils and ghosts could rise through a trapdoor. "You hear this fellow in the cellarage," Hamlet says to his friends (I, 5, 151) when the Ghost cries out from below.

Because plays were generally acted beneath an open sky in midafternoon, the Elizabethan dramatist could not avail himself of the myriad scenic and lighting effects at the disposal of the modern playwright.

Since his audience was not supplied with printed programs, he had to create setting and mood almost exclusively with words. On the simplest level, Rosalind declares, "Well, this is the Forest of Arden" (*As You Like It,* II, 4, 15); and Richard III says, "Here pitch our tent, even here in Bosworth field" (*Richard III,* V, 3, 1). Both are speaking for the benefit of the spectators. Horatio's comment at the end of the first scene of *Hamlet,* "But look, the morn, in russet mantle clad, / Walks o'er the dew of yon high eastward hill" (I, 1, 166–167), is justly celebrated for its lyricism; but its chief function is simply to inform the audience that an eventful night has passed. Shakespeare often makes a virtue of necessity, imparting information with subtle artistry. As Duncan approaches Macbeth's castle anticipating warm hospitality, he speaks thus of Inverness:

> This castle hath a pleasant seat. The air
> Nimbly and sweetly recommends itself
> Unto our gentle senses.
> (*Macbeth,* I, 6, 1–3)

To a spectator who has just heard Lady Macbeth's invocation to the forces of darkness, Duncan's unintended irony would be evident. Later, Macbeth, having murdered Duncan and arranged for the murder of Banquo, impatiently awaits the coming of night:

> Light thickens, and the crow
> Makes wing to th' rooky wood.
> Good things of day begin to droop and drowse,
> Whiles night's black agents to their preys do rouse.
> (*Macbeth,* III, 2, 50–53)

Here Shakespeare not only supplies the setting, but he uses poetry to characterize Macbeth and to create a sinister atmosphere.

It can be seen that the Elizabethan stage, open at three sides and almost devoid of scenery, was much simpler than our own; and its very simplicity made it possible for the drama to move forward swiftly and continuously. A few words from the playwright and a bit of imagination on the part of the spectators—these were sufficient to convert Venice into Cyprus, Rome into Alexandria. The Chorus speaks in *Romeo and Juliet* of "the two hours' traffic of our stage" (I, Prologue, 12), a reasonable approximation of the time normally required for an Elizabethan play to be acted (*Hamlet,* of course, took longer). In addition to encouraging mobility and speed, the design of the theater established an extraordinary intimacy between actors and spectators, and the dramatist took full advantage of this relationship. A stage direction in an old miracle play reads: "Here Herod rages in the pageant and in the street also." One can imagine how exciting the swordplay of Macbeth and Macduff must have seemed to a groundling at the Globe Theater, separated from the action by no more than a few feet. The physical closeness also lent special force to the aside and the soliloquy.[33]

We have thus far been concerned with the Elizabethan "public" playhouse, where the Lord Chamberlain's Men and the other professional companies in Shakespeare's London performed. But the public theaters met recurrent competition from the "private" theaters, where different artistic and moral traditions prevailed. Although Shakespeare himself rarely, if ever, wrote for these private theaters, he was interested in them and may have been influenced by some of their practices.

The private theaters were occupied not by adult actors, but by specially trained children (not to be confused with the professional boy actors who took female roles in the public playhouses). It had become an established procedure in the London singing schools to "take up" potential choirboys and develop them into expert actors who could be exploited on the commercial stage. From a number of firsthand accounts, one gathers that this sometimes amounted to kidnapping. At the time (1576) when Burbage was building the Theatre, Richard Farrant, master of Windsor Chapel, leased a hall in the precinct of Blackfriars for use by the Windsor and the Chapel Royal boys. Blackfriars and Whitefriars (c. 1605) were both within the city limits, but they came under the jurisdiction of the crown rather than the lord mayor. Although anyone could attend the private theaters, the higher admission fees guaranteed a more affluent audience than that which regularly attended the public theaters. The private theaters were roofed, well heated, and artificially lighted so that they could be used in bad weather. Shakespeare's company, it will be recalled, held winter performances in Blackfriars after 1608. Over the years the private theaters attracted a distinguished group of playwrights, including John Lyly, Ben Jonson, George Chapman, Thomas Middleton, and John Marston, some of whom also wrote for public playhouses. The rivalry seems to have been intense. When Hamlet asks why the players visiting Elsinore have left the city, Rosencrantz answers (anachronistically) that they are victims of a "late innovation" (II, 2, 347) that has hurt their business:

But there is, sir, an eyrie [nest] of children, little eyases [nestling hawks], that cry out on the top of question and are most tyrannically clapp'd for't. These are now the fashion, and so berattle the common stages (so they call them) that many wearing rapiers are afraid of goose-quills and dare scarce come thither.

(*Hamlet*, II, 2, 354–360)

In other words, many gentlemen will not attend the newly unfashionable "common stages," or public theaters, lest they be satirized by dramatists writing for the children's companies.

The reader may wonder why Shakespeare wrote for the public theater. Would he not have felt more at home with the witty and genteel clientele that frequented the private theater? The answer, most probably, is no. The Elizabethan public theater was a national institution embracing a vast and heterogeneous audience. The private theater catered essentially to a small coterie that demanded a cynical and sometimes morbid dramatization of the seamy side of life. Shakespeare's warmth, his soundness, his abiding faith in the dignity of man—these qualities would have allied him with the diversified audience that came to the Globe.[34]

One final point: It has recently been suggested that, from 1574 on, performances in public were regarded chiefly as rehearsals for performances at court and that this fact had a significant effect upon the staging of Elizabethan and Jacobean plays. Perhaps future research into the dramaturgical conventions of the Tudor and Stuart courts will add to our knowledge of Shakespeare's stagecraft.[35]

SHAKESPEARE'S LANGUAGE

Elizabethan English was a flexible idiom, unencumbered by rigid ideas of correctness and not yet standardized in grammars and dictionaries. In addition to employing the standard language of his day, Shakespeare frequently uses language in ways distinctively his own. In this section we consider several facets of Shakespeare's English: pronunciation, grammar, vocabulary, wordplay, and imagery.

Pronunciation. From a study of Shakespeare's rhymes and metrical patterns, together with an examination of spelling variants in the printed books of the time, it is possible to gather some fairly reliable information concerning the pronunciation of Elizabethan English. Scholars are not in full agreement as to the details of Shakespeare's pronunciation, but the work of Helge Kökeritz has received favorable attention.[36] According to Kökeritz (and others), the *ea* in *seal* was pronounced approximately like the *a* in *sale;* hence, for *speak* and *dream* Shakespeare said *spake* and *drame.* Our *get* and *seldom* he pronounced *git* and *sildom.* He said *etarnal* and *vartue* instead of *eternal* and *virtue, nater* and *natral* instead of *nature* and *natural,* and *trone* instead of *throne.* Some words could be pronounced in more than one way: The noun *wind* could rhyme with either *kind* or *sinned, ear* with either *hear* or *hair, love* with either *prove* or *above.* The words *line* and *loin* were homonyms; *one* and *own,* also homonyms, could rhyme with *alone, gone,* and *none.*

One could cite many more examples of how Shakespeare's pronunciation differed from our own, but it would be more helpful to observe passages in the plays where these differences have a bearing upon the meaning. In *1 Henry IV* (II, 4, 261 ff.) Falstaff responds wittily to Poins's insistence that he furnish a "reason" (pronounced *raison*) for having run away at Gadshill. "Give you a reason on compulsion?" the fat rogue demands. "If reasons [raisins] were as plentiful as blackberries, I would give no man a reason upon compulsion." Similarly, an angry criticism of Caesar by Cassius depends for its effect upon our recognizing that *Rome* and *room* were homonyms:

> When could they say (till now) that talk'd of Rome
> That her wide walls encompass'd but one man?
> Now is it Rome indeed, and room enough,
> When there is in it but one only man!
> (*Julius Caesar*, I, 2, 154–157)[37]

Another aspect of Shakespeare's pronunciation that may temporarily confuse the modern reader is his placing of accent in particular words. Shakespeare, for example, said *antique, charácter, cómmendable, demónstrate,* and *revénue.* He could, when he wished, make two syllables out of *-tion,* or add a syllable to *Eng[e]land* or *rememb[e]rance.* He frequently, of course, made a distinct syllable out of final *-ed,* as in Antony's remark (*Julius Caesar*, III, 2, 82), "The good is oft interred with their bones." The funeral oration also provides interesting evidence of Shakespeare's flexibility:

> Ambition should be made of sterner stuff.
> Yet Brutus says he was ambitious.
> (III, 2, 98–99)

Ambition has three syllables; *ambitious,* in the very next line, has four. Yet despite differences between Elizabethan and modern pronunciation, it has been rightly said that "we should probably have little more difficulty in understanding Shakespeare's pronunciation than we experience in listening to a broad Irish brogue."[38]

Grammar. By present-day standards Shakespeare's grammar seems even more inconsistent than his pronunciation. The modern grammarian might be appalled at his apparent violations of principles of good usage. Juliet ignores the agreement of subject and verb (*Romeo and Juliet*, III, 2, 127). "Where *is* [italics mine] my father and my mother, nurse?" Romeo is just as guilty:

Heaven is here,
Where Juliet lives; and every cat and dog
And little mouse, every unworthy thing,
Live [italics mine] here in heaven and may look on her;
But Romeo may not.

(*Romeo and Juliet*, III, 3, 29–33)

Benedick says of Beatrice (*Much Ado about Nothing*, II, 1, 268–269), "So indeed all disquiet, horror, and perturbation *follows* [italics mine] her."[39] To express outrage at the wound Brutus dealt Caesar, Mark Antony chooses a double superlative (*Julius Caesar*, III, 2, 188), "This was the most unkindest cut of all." Although the double negative was losing favor in Shakespeare's day,[40] respectable characters use it frequently. Mercutio (*Romeo and Juliet*, III, 1, 58) refuses to leave the public streets. "I will not budge for no man's pleasure, I." Distinctions between the nominative and objective cases are not always preserved. "All debts are clear'd between you and I," Antonio writes to Bassanio (*The Merchant of Venice*, III, 2, 318–319), and Othello (*Othello*, IV, 2, 3) tells Emilia, "Yes, you have seen Cassio and she together." Such irregularities by no means indicate a lack of refinement on the part of Shakespeare or his characters.

In most cases Shakespeare's irregularities in grammar do not affect our understanding of the text, but in a few instances we cannot be certain. For example, distinctions between indicative and subjunctive mood may or may not be significant. When Slender (*The Merry Wives of Windsor*, I, 1, 298 ff.) asks, "*Be* [italics mine] there bears i' th' town?" he receives an answer, "I think there *are* [italics mine], sir." Here the indicative and subjunctive seem interchangeable. But what if the subjunctive is understood to imply contingency or doubt? Othello (*Othello*, III, 3, 384) declares to Iago, "I think my wife be honest, and think she is not"—a subtle indication, perhaps, that the seed of suspicion has taken root.[41] Another puzzle is the so-called colloquial possessive. Bottom (*A Midsummer Night's Dream*, I, 2, 95 ff.) recites to his fellow craftsmen a list of beards available for his portrayal of Pyramus in the forthcoming play: "I will discharge it in either your straw-colour beard, your orange-tawny beard, your purple-in-grain beard, or your French-crown-colour beard, your perfit yellow." He does not literally mean *your* as a possessive any more than we do today when we say something like, "Your shot of whiskey is your best cure for a cold." But when Hamlet says (*Hamlet*, I, 5, 166–167), "There are more things in heaven and earth, Horatio, / Than are dreamt of in your philosophy," he may be speaking of philosophy in general or criticizing Horatio's philosophy in particular.[42]

Perhaps the most striking feature of Shakespeare's grammar is the boldness with which he interchanges parts of speech. He may use an adjective for a verb, as when Andromache (*Troilus and Cressida*, V, 3, 84) "shrills her dolours forth"; a noun for an adjective, as in Cleopatra's allusion (*Antony and Cleopatra*, I, 5, 73–74) to her "salad days," when she "was green in judgment, cold in blood." From the noun *sky* he derives (*Measure for Measure*, I, 4, 34) the adjective *enskied,* a more interesting word than the customary *exalted.* Nouns can serve as compact verbs; the Archbishop of York (*2 Henry IV*, IV, 1, 203) says that the King will try to forget anything "that may repeat and history his loss," and Lucio (*Measure for Measure*, III, 2, 100) comments that, in the absence of the regular Duke of Vienna, Angelo "dukes it well." Shakespeare may add an unusual prefix to a noun, creating a fresh verb *unpeople* to replace the more orthodox *depopulate* or producing a new coinage like Hamlet's "out-herods Herod" (*Hamlet*, III, 2, 15). He can even parody the practice. In *The Merry Wives of Windsor* (I, 1, 222, 234), for example, the Welsh parson says, "I will description the matter to you," and, "But can you affection the oman [woman]?" To be sure, Shakespeare was not the only writer to take liberties with the parts of speech. John Donne in "Loves Deitie" (1. 20) would "ungod" the god of love.[43] But Shakespeare seems to have been unusually responsive to this literary trend. He was, as George Gordon has aptly said, "in the first rank of the advance, and of all its members the most exuberant; an experimenter always, though in the diction of his time; making his language as he went along."[44]

Vocabulary. A major challenge for Elizabethan writers was that of augmenting their language to keep pace with the ever-expanding horizons of Renaissance life. A number of new technical fields were coming to the fore and demanding a vocabulary that did not as yet exist in the vernacular. Moreover, with the rediscovery of classical literature came the realization that works in the modern languages in many respects did not match the richness of the Greek and Latin masterpieces. Translators often had difficulty finding English equivalents for words and concepts in their classical sources. Consequently, Elizabethan men of letters undertook to enlarge the English language by large-scale borrowings and adaptations from Greek, French, Italian, Spanish, and especially Latin.

There was a good deal of opposition to such use of foreign words, called inkhorn terms by their critics. The rhetorician Thomas Wilson, in a work published in 1553 and often reprinted during Shakespeare's lifetime, defends "plainnesse" and illustrates "outlandish English" with an imaginary letter from a man requesting a benefice:

Now therefore being accersited [brought] to such splendente renoume, and dignitie sp[l]endidious: I doubt not but you will adjuvate [aid] such poore adnichilate [reduced to nothing, i.e., *ad nihil*] orphanes, as whilome [formerly] ware condisciples [fellow students] with you, and of antique familiaritie in Lincolneshire. Among whom I being a Scholasticall panion [companion], obtestate [call upon] your sublimitie, to extoll mine infirmitie . . . . I obtestate your clemencie, to invigilate [be watchful] thus much for me . . . . But now I relinquish to fatigate your intelligence, with any more frivolous verbositie . . . . [45]

In *Strange News* (1592) Thomas Nashe assembles a list of so-called inkhornisms from the works of Gabriel Harvey, scholar and friend of Edmund Spenser. Among Harvey's abuses are *conscious, canicular, putative, fantasticality, addoulce, negotiations, polymechany,* and *extensively employed.*[46] Ben Jonson, in *The Poetaster* (1601), brings on the stage a character representing John Marston, feeds him an emetic, and purges him of offensive words: *retrograde, reciprocal, incubus, glibbery, lubrical, spurious, turgidous, oblatrant, prorumped, obstupefact,* and several others.[47]

If one examines the words proscribed by Wilson, Nashe, and Jonson, he soon realizes that the pejorative term *inkhorn* was applied to a number of words that are now perfectly acceptable. As Gordon points out, linguistic innovation sometimes caught on and sometimes failed, and the results were unpredictable:

You tried a thing to see what happened. The process might be fortunate, or it might not. It produced *turgidous*; but it also produced, and by exactly similar means, both *strenuous* and *conscious*. It supplied, from "domus," as a new word for mansion, the unnecessary *dome*; but this misfortune is amply compensated by such admirable discoveries as *orb* and *event*. It was responsible for *obstupefact,* but by precisely the same method achieved *degenerate* and *defunct*. Even the failures played their part, as in genuine experiment they so often do.[48]

Shakespeare was one of the most audacious inventors of words—some adapted from other languages, some developed from native English sources or resurrected from an earlier period. So vast was his range that one can merely suggest a few words and phrases that probably originated with him: *auspicious, assassination, countless, disgraceful, dwindle, foregone conclusion, gloomy, on purpose, laughable, savagery.* In addition to coining new words, Shakespeare developed fresh combinations. Once again it is Gordon who has best suggested our debt to him:

So far as history can yet tell us, he was the first of our writers to speak of "cudgeling one's brain," "falling to blows," "breathing" a word, and "breathing" one's last . . . . The stirring people of his plays "drink healths" and "pledges," say "done!" to a bargain, "lay odds" and play "the ten," "grovel" or "hedge," are "spiritless" and stare on "vacancy," or "reel" along the street . . . . They were the first public characters to call the world "dull," to speak of the "acts" of a play, to find speeches "flowery" and plain faces "homely," to be "fond" of each other . . . . No earlier writer is yet known to have spoken of a man's toes "looking through" his shoes . . . of an "abrupt" answer; of "men of note" and of sending a "note"; of "the minute" drawing on . . . of "catching" a person up, or "catching" a meaning or a cold . . . of being "bright" and cheerful, or of being "sick" of a thing; of "sealing" one's lips; of "returning" thanks, or a present, or an answer; of "getting" information, or "getting" an ailment; of "getting clear" of debt, or of a ship, or "getting" aboard, or back, or off, or on ("Get on thy boots").[49]

Like other writers of the age, Shakespeare invented words that did not last, among them *congree* ("agree together"), *definement* ("description"), *disliken* ("disguise"), and *solicity* ("courtship"). But there is scarcely a page that does not reflect his enormous contribution to the enrichment of the language.

The modern reader will not likely be deterred by Shakespeare's borrowings from other languages or by his experiments with the verbal resources of English. In most cases his innovations have been absorbed into the language, and when they have not, we can usually get at their meaning with little difficulty. More troublesome are the changes in meaning that some words have undergone since Shakespeare used them. Moreover, words that were familiar to Elizabethans may have disappeared from active use. Among the tasks imposed upon modern Shakespeare scholars is that of recovering the English language as it was generally spoken and understood in the sixteenth and seventeenth centuries.[50]

Recent investigations have shown that in order to determine what a word or phrase meant to Shakespeare, it is sometimes necessary to search for evidence among linguistic sources of a nonliterary nature, such as wills, deeds, court records, and popular proverbs.[51] For example, *trammel,* in Macbeth's soliloquy on his proposed murder of Duncan (*Macbeth,* I, 7, 3), seems to have meant not only "catch in a net," but also "bind up a corpse within the shroud"; *relative,* in Hamlet's "I'll have grounds / More relative than this" (*Hamlet,* II, 2, 631–632), denotes "able to be related" and therefore "able to be believed"; Hotspur's refusal (*1 Henry IV,* I, 3, 214) to surrender his Scottish prisoners to the King ("By God, he shall not have a Scot of them!") echoes an English proverb, "We will not lose a Scot," that is, "We will lose nothing." To an Elizabethan audience the word *honor,* extolled by Hotspur and ridiculed by Falstaff, would probably have suggested a series of cheaply patriotic tracts (published between 1589 and 1597) that idealized the maraudings of English soldiers and sailors; the character Pistol (*2 Henry IV* and *Henry V*) would have evoked by his name the image of a sixteenth-century weapon that was notoriously loud and inaccurate.[52] And one is continually discovering how much of Shakespeare's meaning can be clarified by reference to what has been euphemistically described as "the less decent language" of his day. In fact, on the basis of sexual innuendoes that the Elizabethans detected in such words as *nose, pen, table,* and *green,* Hilda Hulme would reject Theobald's famous emendation in *Henry V* (see p. 43), "and 'a babbled of green fields," and restore the First Folio reading, "a Table of greene fields."[53] Individual interpretations may be debated, but the application of the methods of linguistic research should in general add a new dimension to our appreciation of Shakespeare's artistry.

Wordplay. "Wordplay," it has been observed, "was a game the Elizabethans played seriously."[54] On her arrival at the Forest of Arden (*As You Like It,* II, 4, 9 ff.), a weary Celia says to her companions, "I pray you bear with me; I cannot go no further" (double negative!), to which Touchstone replies, "For my part, I had rather bear with you than bear you. Yet I should bear no cross if I did bear you, for I think you have no money in your purse." This retort, chosen almost at random, plays with at least three meanings of *bear:* "carry," "tolerate," and "produce children"; it also puns on *cross,* which in this context means both "affliction" and "coin." Similar games are played almost everywhere in Shakespeare. Note the following exchange between Hamlet and the Gravedigger:

> *Hamlet:* I think it [i.e., the grave] be thine indeed, for thou liest in't.
> *Clown:* You lie out on't, sir, and therefore 'tis not yours. For my part, I do not lie in't, yet it is mine.
> *Hamlet:* Thou dost lie in't, to be in't and say it is thine. 'Tis for the dead, not for the quick [living]; therefore thou liest.
> *Clown:* 'Tis a quick lie, sir; 'twill away again from me to you.
> (*Hamlet,* V, 1, 131–140)

Feste, the irrepressible clown in *Twelfth Night,* seems to epitomize the spirit of the game when, after a verbal duel with Viola, he remarks (III, 1, 13–15), "A sentence is but a chev'ril [soft, elastic leather] glove to a good wit. How quickly the wrong side may be turn'd outward!"

The pun must be viewed as one expression of the intoxication that Elizabethan writers felt with their language. Its use was not confined to comedy or even to comic moments in tragedy. After Duncan has been murdered, Lady Macbeth takes the blood-soaked daggers from her husband's hands and prepares to enter the dead man's chamber:

> If he do bleed,
> I'll *gild* [italics mine] the faces of the grooms withal,
> For it must seem their *guilt* [italics mine].
> (*Macbeth,* II, 2, 55–57)

The dying John of Gaunt (*Richard II,* II, 1, 73 ff.) puns upon his name for eleven lines ("Old Gaunt indeed, and gaunt in being old . . . . Gaunt am I for the grave, gaunt as a grave . . . . "). King Richard himself yields to no man when it comes to wordplay, for in the deposition scene he gazes into a looking glass and rings the changes on *face:*

> Was this face the face
> That every day under his household roof
> Did keep ten thousand men? Was this the face
> That like the sun did make beholders wink?
> Was this the face that fac'd so many follies
> And was at last outfac'd by Bolingbroke?
> A brittle glory shineth in this face.
> As brittle as the glory is the face,
>> [*Dashes the glass to the floor.*]
> For there it is, crack'd in a hundred shivers.
> Mark, silent king, the moral of this sport—
> How soon my sorrow hath destroy'd my face.
>> (*Richard II,* IV, 1, 281–291)

Mercutio dies (*Romeo and Juliet,* III, 1, 101–102) with a sardonic "Ask for me to-morrow, and you shall find me a grave man."

So thoroughly had the pun, or quibble, fallen into disfavor by the eighteenth century that Dr. Johnson in a famous passage maintained that it was Shakespeare's incurable vice:

> A quibble is to Shakespeare, what luminous vapours are to the traveller; he follows it at all adventures, it is sure to lead him out of his way, and sure to engulf him in the mire. It has some malignant power over his mind, and its fascinations are irresistible . . . . A quibble is the golden apple for which he will always turn aside from his career, or stoop from his elevation. A quibble, poor and barren as it is, gave him such delight, that he was content to purchase it, by the sacrifice of reason, propriety and truth. A quibble was to him the fatal *Cleopatra* for which he lost the world, and was content to lose it.[55]

Although there is some justice in Johnson's criticism, the occasions on which Shakespeare puns out of sheer devilment are not so numerous. Moreover, the pun has been restored to a place of eminence in life and letters; in James Joyce's *Ulysses* it was elevated to a form of art.

The quibble, which Dr. Johnson deplored, actually performs a number of functions in Shakespeare. Often it is little more than a game of "mis-taking the word," which comic characters play for its own sake. Sometimes, however, wordplay acts as a protective screen, as between young lovers like Beatrice and Benedick (in *Much Ado about Nothing*), who do not wish to make a public commitment to each other. In the case of Romeo and Mercutio, who pun incessantly, it helps define a youthful audacity whereby almost the whole of human experience is seen as a proving ground for wit. With Richard II wordplay partially suggests the King's passion for ceremony and ritual. For Hamlet words are two-edged swords, cutting away at pretensions and revealing the abhorrent contradictions between what people say and what they really mean. His speech abounds in bitterly paradoxical quibbles: "A little more than kin, and less than kind" (*Hamlet*, I, 2, 65); "Conception is a blessing, but not as your daughter may conceive" (II, 2, 185–187); "Ay [answering Ophelia's query as to whether the Player will tell what the show meant], or any show that you'll show him. Be not you asham'd to show, he'll not shame to tell you what it means" (III, 2, 154–156).[56] The pun in somewhat altered context becomes the malapropism (or so-called Dogberryism, after the oafish constable in *Much Ado about Nothing*), with its special kind of wisdom: "Is our whole dissembly appear'd?" (IV, 2, 1); "By this time our sexton hath reformed Signior Leonato of the matter" (V, 1, 261–263); "Dost thou not suspect my place? Dost thou not suspect my years?" (IV, 2, 77–78).

Thus wordplay need not be just a game but can also serve as a means of communicating simultaneously on two or more different and perhaps contradictory levels. In skillful hands it can provide the reader or listener with an ironic vision not otherwise accessible. "Shakespearean criticism today recognizes wordplay as a major poetic device, comparable in its effectiveness with the use of recurrent or clustered images."[57]

Imagery. One of the most noteworthy developments in modern literary criticism has been the intensification of interest in imagery, roughly defined as "the little word-picture used by a poet or prose writer to illustrate, illuminate, and embellish his thought."[58] It is not surprising that Shakespeare's imagery should have provided a fruitful field for investigation. No attempt will be made here to offer anything like a complete survey of the various approaches to this aspect of Shakespeare's art, but a few suggestions may be in order concerning the range and implications of some influential twentieth-century studies.

G. Wilson Knight was one of the first modern critics to emphasize that Shakespeare's similes, metaphors, and analogies conform to certain patterns. A play, Knight argued, must be seen in space as well as in time:

> By this I mean that there are throughout the play a set of correspondences which relate to each other independently of the time-sequence which is the story . . . . This I have sometimes called the play's "atmosphere" . . . . Perhaps it is what Aristotle meant by "unity of idea." Now if we are prepared to see the whole play laid out, so to speak, as an area, being simultaneously

aware of these thickly-scattered correspondences in a single view of the whole, we possess the unique quality of the play in a new sense.[59]

Thus, the atmosphere of *Hamlet* is one of death. "From the first scene to the last the shadow of death broods over this play."[60] *Macbeth* reveals "the murk and nightmare torment of a conscious hell . . . . a desolate and dark universe where all is befogged, baffled, constricted by the evil."[61] There is in the play a "disorder-symbolism" that is expressed in many ways, including recurring images involving fierce and ugly animals— tigers, ravens, owls, bats, scorpions. Knight would regard each play "as a visionary unit bound to obey none but its own self-imposed laws . . . as an expanded metaphor, by means of which the original vision has been projected into forms roughly correspondent with actuality."[62]

Caroline Spurgeon sought to amass, classify, and tabulate all of Shakespeare's images in the hope of obtaining a clearer understanding of the poet himself. She noted, for example, the preponderance in his works of nature images, especially images relating to growing things in gardens and orchards, and concluded from this and other data that Shakespeare was "a countryman through and through." "What he loves most," she says, "is to walk and saunter in his garden or orchard, and to note and study the flight and movements of the wild birds."[63] Professor Spurgeon also discovered a repeating, or iterative, imagery in individual plays: light and dark in *Romeo and Juliet*, disease in *Hamlet*, gardens in *Richard II*, animals in action in *Othello*, and so on.

It remained for Wolfgang Clemen, in a book originally published in German (1936), to stress that imagery cannot be separated from other elements in a play:

> An isolated image, an image viewed outside of its context, is only half the image. Every image, every metaphor gains full life and significance only from its context. In Shakespeare, an image often points beyond the scene in which it stands to preceding or following acts; it almost always has reference to the whole of the play. It appears as a cell in the organism of the play, linked with it in many ways.[64]

Clemen distinguished, for example, between Othello, to whom images come easily and spontaneously whenever he speaks, and Iago, for whom they are "a conscious and studied device by which he wishes to influence those to whom he is speaking."[65] In an effort to uncover some principle of artistic growth, Clemen treated Shakespeare's imagery chronologically. He concluded that in the early plays imagery is generally ornamental but that it becomes an integral part of the later plays, in which Shakespeare is said to have moved from rhetoric into the higher realm of poetry:

Only little by little did Shakespeare discover the possibilities which imagery offers to the dramatist. In his hands metaphors gradually develop into more and more effective instruments: at first fulfilling only a few simple functions, they later often serve several aims at one and the same time and play a decisive part in the characterization of the figures in the play and in expressing the dramatic theme. The image eventually becomes the favorite mode of expression of the later Shakespeare.[66]

Without minimizing the contribution that studies of imagery have made to Shakespearean criticism, one may voice a few reservations. In the first place, excessive preoccupation with imagery may make the critic lose sight of the fact that plays are written to be performed before live audiences and are inevitably shaped by historical and dramaturgical conditions.

A second problem is that the interpretation of images can be subjective. It is sometimes difficult to judge whether or not a given expression constitutes an image, whether it is a significant image, and whether it has a favorable or unfavorable connotation. For example, Clemen observes that the dragon, the eagle, the steed, the tiger, and the bear, which are all used as metaphors for Coriolanus, can be interpreted as "brave and noble animals" symbolic of a heroic nature.[67] This may be true for *Coriolanus*. But we have seen that the tiger and the bear are among the hideous creatures Knight discerns as part of the "disorder-symbolism" in *Macbeth*. Moreover, the critic in search of a pattern of imagery may attach undue importance to casual verbal similarities or may overlook or explain away images that do not readily fit his scheme.

Finally, a study of Shakespeare's imagery may lead to the belief that the complex images in the later plays are somehow better than the simple images in the earlier ones, an assumption that takes too narrow a view of his dramatic art. In the early works, where the images are often decorative, Shakespeare is adhering to established classical principles of adornment and amplification. To the Elizabethans, *rhetoric* was not a dirty word to be distinguished from a greater thing called *poetry*. The proper distinction would have been between *good* rhetoric, which was delightful, and *bad* rhetoric, which was not.[68] To measure the *Henry VI* plays according to aesthetic principles derived from *The Tempest* would be like evaluating an opera by Bellini, the early Verdi, or even Mozart by appealing to the practice of Wagner. One operatic style deliberately cultivates arias, set pieces, and embellishments; the other just as deliberately aims at making each note part of a distinctive dramatic context. Of course, *The Tempest* is greater than *Henry VI*, but not because Shakespeare by the end of his career had improved his understanding of imagery.

Despite the foregoing cautionary note, however, it cannot be denied that studies of Shakespeare's imagery, when undertaken with reasonableness and tact, can enrich our enjoyment of the plays.[69]

THE ELIZABETHAN WORLD PICTURE

This chapter concludes with a brief survey of some important concepts that formed part of the intellectual heritage of Shakespeare and his contemporaries. To what extent Elizabethans accepted these ideas literally, it is impossible to say, but they surely would have appreciated their power as poetic and dramatic metaphor.[70]

Renaissance England was fundamentally Christian in its view of the universe. It was generally believed that God created the world according to a perfect plan and assigned a special function to each of his creations, from the lowest stone to the most exalted of angels. So long as this order is preserved, the universe operates with marvelous beauty and efficiency. To quote from Richard Hooker's monumental opus defending the Anglican church, "For we see the whole world and each part thereof so compacted, that as long as each thing performeth only that work which is natural unto it, it thereby preserveth both other things and also itself."[71] If this universal order were disturbed at any point in the hierarchy, the resulting chaos would be terrifying beyond belief:

Now if nature should intermit her course, and leave altogether though it were but for a while the observation of her own laws; if those principal and mother elements of the world, whereof all things in this lower world are made, should lose the qualities which now they have; if the frame of that heavenly arch erected over our heads should loosen and dissolve itself; if celestial spheres should forget their wonted motions, and by irregular volubility turn themselves any way as it might happen; if the prince of the lights of heaven, which now as a giant doth run his unwearied course, should as it were through a languishing faintness begin to stand and to rest himself; if the moon should wander from her beaten way, the times and seasons of the year blend themselves by disordered and confused mixture, the winds breathe out their last gasp, the clouds yield no rain, the earth be defeated of heavenly influence, the fruits of the earth pine away as children at the withered breasts of their mother no longer able to yield them relief: what would become of man himself, whom these things now do all serve? See we not plainly that obedience of creatures unto the law of nature is the stay of the whole world?[72]

This principle of order enunciated by Hooker and other Renaissance thinkers appears again and again in Shakespeare, notably in Ulysses's speech on degree in *Troilus and Cressida* (I, 3, 75–137).

Not only does the whole universe manifest an orderly and unchanging hierarchy, but a clearly defined chain of command operates within each individual realm of existence. God is the ruler of the cosmos; the sun governs the planets; the king holds sway over the body politic; the husband is the sovereign in the family; the head commands obedience from the other parts of the body; and so on. Such a scheme provides poets with a rich supply of metaphor. Observe, for example, the frequent use in *Richard II* of the king–sun analogy or, in a lighter work, the lecture on wifely submission that the tamed shrew Katherine reads to rebellious women (including her sister): "Thy husband is thy lord, thy life, thy keeper, / Thy head, thy sovereign" (*The Taming of the Shrew*, V, 2, 146–147). Bolingbroke's usurpation of the English throne, Macbeth's murder of Duncan, the Trojans' abduction of Helen from her lawful husband, the casting out of Lear by his daughters—these acts become more terrible because they violate the order of nature and are thus sins against God.

This hierarchical world view also underlies the generally accepted psychology, or moral philosophy, of Shakespeare's day. Renaissance writers, following Aristotle, divide the soul into three faculties: the *vegetal,* the *sensible,* and the *rational.* The vegetal faculty, which is shared by all living creatures, is responsible for the nourishment, growth, and generation of the organic body. Higher in the scale is the sensible faculty, possessed by animals and human beings alike. This faculty is the source of all feeling and motion. After external impressions have been received by the five senses, they are sorted out by what is termed the *common sense* and then passed through the imagination (*phantasy*), to be ratified by reason. But occasionally, notably during illness, imagination gets out of hand and invents things on its own. This also occurs, as Mercutio demonstrates, during sleep, when reason has relaxed its vigilance and Queen Mab is free to gallop through the brain dispensing her dreams (*Romeo and Juliet,* I, 4, 53–103). Signs of an unruly imagination are readily discernible in the erratic behavior of lunatics, lovers, and poets; this point is made by Theseus in *A Midsummer Night's Dream* (V, 1, 4–22) and delightfully exemplified by the doting lovers in Shakespearean comedies.

The vegetal and sensible faculties are both subordinated to the rational faculty, that part of the soul which distinguishes man from all other creatures and confers upon him a measure of divinity. In the rational faculty are lodged the powers of reflection and judgment. In order to choose a wise and moral course of action, one must preserve the proper hierarchical organization within this highest of faculties: Reason must command will. But since the Fall of Man the will has grown corrupt and, rather than obey reason, has yielded to its own subordinate—appetite. Take away degree, Shakespeare's Ulysses warns the Greek leaders, and men will live only to satisfy their passions:

> Then everything includes itself in power,
> Power into will, will into appetite;
> And appetite, an universal wolf,
> So doubly seconded with will and power,
> Must make perforce an universal prey,
> And last eat up himself.
>   (*Troilus and Cressida*, I, 3, 119–124)

These are the terms Milton uses in *Paradise Lost* to account for the disruptive suspicion and hate that Adam and Eve experience after the Fall:

> For Understanding rul'd not, and the Will
> Heard not her lore, both in subjection now
> To sensual Appetite, who from beneathe
> Usurping over sovran Reason claimd
> Superior sway.
>   (9. 1127–1131)[73]

As suggested earlier, each area of activity within the universe is linked analogically with every other. Man is a microcosm, a little world, whose physical and moral state may correspond to conditions in the body politic or in the macrocosm, the great world. Just as the macrocosm is composed of the four elements (fire, air, water, earth), so is man compounded of four humors (choler, blood, phlegm, melancholy), which must be blended in exactly the right proportions. This doctrine lies behind Antony's final tribute to Brutus:

> His life was gentle, and the elements
> So mix'd in him that Nature might stand up
> And say to all the world, "This was a man!"
>   (*Julius Caesar*, V, 5, 73–75)

In *Richard II* Shakespeare draws a parallel between the dying John of Gaunt and an England wasting away under Richard's misrule. Elsewhere, Henry IV, oppressed by civil war, speaks to the Earl of Warwick about the nation's sickness:

> Then you perceive the body of our kingdom,
> How foul it is; what rank diseases grow,
> And with what danger, near the heart of it.
>   (*2 Henry IV*, III, 1, 38–40)

Warwick immediately picks up the metaphor, although the note he sounds is more hopeful:

> It is but as a body yet distempered,
> Which to his former strength may be restor'd
> With good advice and little medicine.
> (*2 Henry IV*, III, 1, 41–43)

It is characteristic of Shakespeare to use the figure of the microcosm to enlarge the dimensions of his tragic heroes. The storm that accompanies Othello's arrival in Cyprus foreshadows the chaos that will rage in his soul, and the madness of Lear acquires universal significance when it is reflected in cataclysmic rains and winds in nature. The death of Antony, that "triple pillar of the world" (*Antony and Cleopatra*, I, 1, 12), inspires Cleopatra to magnificent poetry in which her lover becomes the great world itself:

> His face was as the heav'ns, and therein stuck
> A sun and moon, which kept their course and lighted
> The little O, the earth.
> (*Antony and Cleopatra*, V, 2, 79–81)

She compares Antony's voice to "the tuned spheres" (V, 2, 84), an allusion to the familiar idea of the "music of the spheres" inherited from classical astronomy.[74] In *The Comedy of Errors* (III, 2, 116–143), Shakespeare employs the figure of the microcosm for a lighter purpose. Dromio of Syracuse describes the fat kitchen wench who is pursuing him. "She is spherical, like a globe. I could find out countries in her." Ireland stands in her buttocks, England in her chin, America on her nose. "Where stood Belgia, the Netherlands?" he is asked. "O, sir, I did not look so low."

Although the preceding discussion has stressed elements of unity and stability, it should not be inferred that Shakespeare lived in an uncomplicated age. England was rapidly changing from a feudal economy with an entrenched nobility to an economy based on private enterprise. Meanwhile, through a combination of legitimate maritime operations and some fortunate excursions into piracy, the country was beginning to build an overseas empire. Fresh opportunities for amassing wealth produced a new and influential middle class, such as Shakespeare depicts in *The Merry Wives of Windsor*. Political affairs were turbulent. Queen Elizabeth put off a decision on the fate of Mary Stuart, whose claim to the throne had enlisted considerable sympathy. She tolerated and even encouraged the reckless Earl of Essex until his rebellion caused her to order his execution. All Europe waited for Elizabeth to make up her mind about a husband and, more important, a successor; but she skillfully avoided commitments that could have had devastating consequences at home and abroad. Augmenting these tensions was the delicate task of keeping the Church of England poised between Roman Catholicism on the one hand and extreme Protestantism on the other.[75]

Eventually, of course, political and religious questions would bring about a civil war, and a crowned king, God's deputy on earth, would die on the scaffold—a grim commentary on the alleged inviolability of natural and divine law.

NOTES

1. *Greenes Groats-worth of Wit* (1592), in Edmund K. Chambers, *William Shakespeare: A Study of Facts and Problems*, 2 vols. (Oxford: Clarendon, 1930), 2: 188.

2. *Greene's Never too Late*, quoted in Walter W. Greg, *The Editorial Problem in Shakespeare*, 3d ed. (Oxford: Clarendon, 1954), p. 51. For the view that Shakespeare was indeed being accused of plagiarism, see John Dover Wilson, "Malone and the Upstart Crow," *Shakespeare Survey* 4 (1951): 56–68.

3. Chambers, *William Shakespeare*, 2: 189.

4. Ibid., p. 194.

5. John Dryden, "An Essay of Dramatic Poesy," in *Essays of John Dryden*, ed. W. P. Ker, 2 vols. (Oxford: Clarendon, 1900), 1: 79.

6. Samuel Taylor Coleridge, *Shakespearean Criticism*, ed. Thomas Middleton Raysor, rev. ed., 2 vols. (London: Dent, 1960), 1:187.

7. On Shakespeare's continuing impact, see Louis Marder, *His Exits and His Entrances: The Story of Shakespeare's Reputation* (Philadelphia: Lippincott, 1963).

8. For an exhaustive study of the origin and development of the Shakespeare myths, see Samuel Schoenbaum, *Shakespeare's Lives* (Oxford: Clarendon, 1970).

9. Charles J. Sisson, "Studies in the Life and Environment of Shakespeare since 1900," *Shakespeare Survey* 3 (1950): 6.

10. On Shakespeare and Stratford, see Mark Eccles, *Shakespeare in Warwickshire* (Madison: University of Wisconsin Press, 1961).

11. For a summary of Shakespeare's presumed grammar school training, see Virgil K. Whitaker, *Shakespeare's Use of Learning* (San Marino, Calif.: Huntington Library, 1953), pp. 14–44. The fullest study is Thomas W. Baldwin, *William Shakspere's Small Latine & Lesse Greeke*, 2 vols. (Urbana: University of Illinois Press, 1944).

12. See Ivor Brown, *Shakespeare* (Garden City, N.Y.: Doubleday, 1949), pp. 37–41. Some so-called anti-Stratfordians (see below) claim that Anne Whateley

recorded the progress of her romance with Shakespeare in one of her many literary works—*Shakespeare's Sonnets!*

13. On the nature and extent of theatrical activity in Shakespeare's England, see Alfred Harbage, *Shakespeare and the Rival Traditions* (New York: Macmillan, 1952), pp. 3–28. Harbage (p. 26) draws a useful analogy with organized baseball, with London corresponding to the major leagues.

14. The London Company of Stationers, incorporated in 1557, was an organization of printers and booksellers that attempted to regulate the book trade and thereby avoid interference by government officials. One of its functions was to exercise a kind of censorship; another was to register copyrights and protect its membership against unfair or dishonest competition. See Edmund K. Chambers, *The Elizabethan Stage*, 4 vols. (Oxford: Clarendon, 1923), 3: 160–162.

15. The indispensable book on virtually all matters pertaining to Shakespeare's life and work is Chambers, *William Shakespeare*. See also Edgar I. Fripp, *Shakespeare Man and Artist*, 2 vols. (London: Oxford University Press, 1938). Of the many excellent and reliable briefer treatments, see Gerald Eades Bentley, *Shakespeare: A Biographical Handbook* (New Haven: Yale University Press, 1961) and Roland Mushat Frye, *Shakespeare's Life and Times: A Pictorial Record* (Princeton: Princeton University Press, 1967). The Shakespeare documents have been reproduced and examined in Samuel Schoenbaum, *William Shakespeare: A Documentary Life* (Oxford: Clarendon, 1975).

16. See William F. and Elizebeth S. Friedman, *The Shakespearean Ciphers Examined* (Cambridge: Cambridge University Press, 1957).

17. For general surveys and critiques of the anti-Stratfordians, see Frank W. Wadsworth, *The Poacher from Stratford* (Berkeley: University of California Press, 1958); R. C. Churchill, *Shakespeare and His Betters* (Bloomington: Indiana University Press, 1959); and Marder, *His Exits and His Entrances*, pp. 166–188.

18. Caryl Brahms and S. J. Simon, *No Bed for Bacon* (Harmondsworth, Middlesex: Penguin, 1948), p. 23.

19. See E. M. W. Tillyard, *The Elizabethan World Picture* (New York: Macmillan, 1943).

20. See Chambers, *The Elizabethan Stage* (especially vol. 2).

21. See Alfred Harbage's three important studies: *Shakespeare's Audience* (New York: Columbia University Press, 1941); *As They Liked It: An Essay on Shakespeare and Morality* (New York: Macmillan, 1947); and *Shakespeare and the Rival Traditions* (New York: Macmillan, 1952). Harbage's conclusion that the audience was predominantly working-class has recently been questioned; see Ann Jennalie Cook, "The Audience of Shakespeare's Plays: A Reconsideration," *Shakespeare Studies,* ed. J. Leeds Barroll, 7 (1974): 283–305.

22. See Philip Henslowe, *Diary*, ed. Walter W. Greg, 2 vols. (London: A. H. Bullen, 1904–1908) and *Henslowe's Diary*, eds. R. A. Foakes and R. T. Rickert (Cambridge: Cambridge University Press, 1961).

23. For a reasoned summary of scholarship on the Elizabethan theater, see Andrew Gurr, *The Shakespearean Stage, 1574–1642* (Cambridge: Cambridge University Press, 1970). See also T. J. King, *Shakespearean Staging, 1599–1642* (Cambridge: Harvard University Press, 1971), pp. 119–132.

On the acting, see B. L. Joseph, *Elizabethan Acting,* rev. ed. (Oxford: Clarendon, 1964).

24. This view has been challenged by Alan H. Nelson, *The Medieval Stage: Corpus Christi Pageants and Plays* (Chicago: University of Chicago Press, 1974).

25. A classic study of the medieval stage is Edmund K. Chambers, *The Mediaeval Stage,* 2 vols. (Oxford: Clarendon, 1903); see also Hardin Craig, *English Religious Drama of the Middle Ages* (Oxford: Clarendon, 1955). Three "revolutionary" studies are Frederick M. Salter, *Mediaeval Drama in Chester* (Toronto: University of Toronto Press, 1955); Richard Southern, *The Medieval Theatre in the Round* (London: Faber, 1957); and Glynne W. Wickham, *Early English Stages 1300 to 1660. Volume One 1300 to 1576* (New York: Columbia University Press, 1959).

26. C. Walter Hodges, *The Globe Restored: A Study of the Elizabethan Theatre* (London: Benn, 1953), pp. 37–44 (see also the revised edition [London: Oxford University Press, 1968]); Glynne Wickham, *Early English Stages 1300–1660. Volume Two 1576 to 1660, Part I* (New York: Columbia University Press, 1963), pp. 186–196; Richard Southern, *The Staging of Plays before Shakespeare* (London: Faber, 1973), especially pp. 45–55. The arena stage has been championed by Leslie Hotson, *The First Night of Twelfth Night* (New York: Macmillan, 1954). Two pioneering works on the Elizabethan theater are Ashley H. Thorndike, *Shakespeare's Theater* (New York: Macmillan, 1916) and Joseph Quincy Adams, *Shakespearean Playhouses* (Boston: Houghton Mifflin, 1917).

27. J. W. Saunders, "Staging at the Globe, 1599–1613," *Shakespeare Quarterly* 11 (1960): 405.

28. Chambers, *The Elizabethan Stage,* 4: 273–274.

29. Until fairly recently the standard book on the Globe was John Cranford Adams, *The Globe Playhouse: Its Design and Equipment,* 2d ed. (New York: Barnes & Noble, 1961). Adams's view has been supported by Irwin Smith, *Shakespeare's Globe Playhouse: A Modern Reconstruction with Scale Drawings* (New York: Scribner, 1956). Breaking with Adams and Smith on a number of points is Hodges, *The Globe Restored* and *Shakespeare's Second Globe: The Missing Monument* (London: Oxford University Press, 1973). See also Richard Hosley, "The Origins of the So-Called Elizabethan Multiple Stage," *The Drama Review* 12:2 (1968): 28–50. In two controversial works, Frances A. Yates proposes that the engraving of the stage of a public theater shown in Robert Fludd's *Ars Memoriae* (1619) is part of an ancient architectural memory system and is based on the Globe: See *The Art of Memory* (Chicago: University of Chicago Press, 1966), pp. 342–367 and *Theatre of the World* (Chicago: University of Chicago Press, 1969), especially pp. 136–185.

30. See Harbage, *Shakespeare's Audience,* pp. 19–52.

31. See Hodges, *The Globe Restored,* pp. 53–62 (2d ed., pp. 47–63). Between pp. 90–91 of the second edition there is a conjectural reconstruction, including a curtained place behind the stage. See also Richard Hosley, "The Staging of Desdemona's Bed," *Shakespeare Quarterly* 14 (1963): 57–65. But J. C. Adams has reconstructed the original staging of *King Lear,* making extensive use of

the inner stage as an alternative acting area. See Appendix A to *The Globe Playhouse* (pp. 385–403).

32. Saunders, "Staging at the Globe, 1599–1613." See also Richard Hosley, "The Use of the Upper Stage in *Romeo and Juliet,*" *Shakespeare Quarterly* 5 (1954): 371–379.

33. See Warren D. Smith, *Shakespeare's Playhouse Practice: A Handbook* (Hanover, N.H.: University Press of New England, 1975).

34. In *Shakespeare and the Rival Traditions* Alfred Harbage discusses differences between the national and the coterie theater; Appendix B (pp. 343–350) lists the known repertoires of both from 1560 to 1613. See also Harbage's *As They Liked It,* as well as Henry S. Bennett, "Shakespeare's Audience," in *Studies in Shakespeare,* ed. Peter Alexander (London: Oxford University Press, 1964), pp. 56–70.

35. See Glynne Wickham, *Early English Stages 1300–1660. Volume Two 1576 to 1600, Part II* (New York: Columbia University Press, 1972).

36. See Helge Kökeritz, *Shakespeare's Pronunciation* (New Haven: Yale University Press, 1953); see also his *Shakespeare's Names: A Pronouncing Dictionary* (New Haven: Yale University Press, 1959). An indispensable study is ʻE. J. Dobson, *English Pronunciation, 1500–1700,* 2d ed., 2 vols. (Oxford: Clarendon, 1968).

37. Several interesting examples may be found in Karl J. Holzknecht, *The Backgrounds of Shakespeare's Plays* (New York: American Book, 1950), pp. 193–194.

38. Albert C. Baugh, *A History of the English Language,* 2d ed. (New York: Appleton, 1957), p. 283.

39. In Shakespeare's day the number of a verb could sometimes be determined by the singular or plural *idea* of its subject rather than by the singular or plural *form* of its subject. See George H. McKnight, *Modern English in the Making* (New York: Appleton, 1928), pp. 197–198.

40. See Margaret Schlauch, *The English Language in Modern Times (since 1400)* (Warsaw: Państwowe Wydawnictwo Nakowe, 1959), p. 53.

41. See Helge Kökeritz, "Shakespeare's Language," in *Shakespeare: Of An Age and For All Time,* ed. Charles Tyler Prouty (Hamden, Conn.: Shoe String, 1954), p. 42 and Schlauch, *The English Language in Modern Times,* p. 105.

42. The possessive case in general was not standardized in Elizabethan times. The apostrophe had not come into systematic use, nor had *its* replaced *his* as the possessive form of the indefinite pronoun *it.* Sometimes *it* stands for the possessive as well as for the nominative and objective. The Fool (*King Lear,* I, 4, 235–236) says, "The hedge-sparrow fed the cuckoo so long / That it had it head bit off by it young."

43. *The Poems of John Donne,* ed. Sir Herbert J. C. Grierson, 2 vols. (London: Oxford University Press, 1912), 1: 54.

44. George Gordon, "Shakespeare's English," in *Shakespearian Comedy and Other Essays* (London: Oxford University Press, 1944), p. 141. All quotations from this book have been reprinted by permission of the Oxford University Press, Oxford.

45. Thomas Wilson, *Wilson's Arte of Rhetorique* (1560), ed. G. H. Mair (Oxford: Clarendon, 1909), p. 163.

46. G. Gregory Smith, ed., *Elizabethan Critical Essays*, 2 vols. (Oxford: Clarendon, 1904), 2: 241–242.

47. C. H. Herford and Percy and Evelyn Simpson, eds., *Ben Jonson*, 11 vols. (Oxford: Clarendon, 1925–1950), 4: 312–313.

48. Gordon, "Shakespeare's English," p. 140.

49. Gordon, "Shakespeare's English," pp. 142–144. See also Holzknecht, *The Background of Shakespeare's Plays*, pp. 188–192 and McKnight, *Modern English in the Making*, pp. 188–190. For an excellent survey of the problem of enriching the vocabulary, see Baugh, *A History of the English Language*, secs. 157–172.

50. Most helpful is C. T. Onions, *A Shakespeare Glossary*, 2d ed., rev. (Oxford: Clarendon, 1958).

51. See Hilda M. Hulme, *Explorations in Shakespeare's Language* (London: Longmans, 1962) and Paul A. Jorgensen, *Redeeming Shakespeare's Words* (Berkeley: University of California Press, 1962). An earlier study, brief but illuminating, is F. P. Wilson, *Shakespeare and the Diction of Common Life* (Oxford: Clarendon, 1941).

52. These examples are found in Hulme, *Explorations in Shakespeare's Language*, pp. 20–24, 30–33, 68–72 and Jorgensen, *Redeeming Shakespeare's Words*, pp. 43–51, 70–74.

53. Hulme, *Explorations in Shakespeare's Language*, pp. 133–143. A standard work is Eric Partridge, *Shakespeare's Bawdy* (London: Routledge, 1947). See also E. A. M. Colman, *The Dramatic Use of Bawdy in Shakespeare* (London: Longmans, 1974).

54. M. M. Mahood, *Shakespeare's Wordplay* (London: Methuen, 1957), p. 9.

55. Samuel Johnson, "Preface to Shakespeare," in *Johnson on Shakespeare*, ed. Arthur Sherbo, Vols. 7 and 8 of The Yale Edition of the Works of Samuel Johnson (New Haven: Yale University Press, 1968), p. 74.

56. Wordplay, of course, is often bawdy; see, for example, Herbert A. Ellis, *Shakespeare's Lusty Punning in Love's Labour's Lost* (The Hague: Mouton, 1973).

57. Mahood, *Shakespeare's Wordplay*, p. 11.

58. Caroline F. E. Spurgeon, *Shakespeare's Imagery and What It Tells Us* (New York: Macmillan, 1935), p. 9.

59. G. Wilson Knight, *The Wheel of Fire*, 5th rev. ed. (Cleveland and New York: World Publishing, Meridian, 1957), p. 3. *The Wheel of Fire* was first published in 1930. Knight's other studies include *The Imperial Theme* (1931), *The Shakespearean Tempest* (1932), and *The Crown of Life* (1947)—all published in London by Oxford University Press.

60. Knight, *The Wheel of Fire*, p. 28.

61. Ibid., pp. 140–141.

62. Ibid., pp. 14–15.

63. Spurgeon, *Shakespeare's Imagery*, p. 204. Professor Spurgeon (pp. 16–29) uses Shakespeare's emphasis upon nature images to show, incidentally, that his mind differed radically from Sir Francis Bacon's.

64. Wolfgang H. Clemen, *The Development of Shakespeare's Imagery* (Cambridge: Harvard University Press, 1951), p. 3.

65. Ibid., pp. 120–121.

66. Ibid., p. 5. A similar point is made by Patrick Cruttwell, *The Shakespearean Moment* (London: Chatto & Windus, 1954).

67. Clemen, *Development of Shakespeare's Imagery*, p. 156.

68. On this point, see two lectures by Gladys D. Willcock: "Shakespeare and Rhetoric," *Essays and Studies* 29 (1944): 50–61 and "Language and Poetry in Shakespeare's Early Plays," in *Proceedings of the British Academy* 40 (1955): 103–117.

69. For an excellent survey of imagery studies through 1936, see Una Ellis-Fermor, *Some Recent Research in Shakespeare's Imagery* (London: Oxford University Press, 1937). A more recent review and critique is Kenneth Muir, "Shakespeare's Imagery—Then and Now," *Shakespeare Survey* 18 (1965): 46–57.

70. In addition to Tillyard's useful book, *The Elizabethan World Picture*, see Hardin Craig, *The Enchanted Glass* (New York: Oxford University Press, 1936; reprint ed., Oxford: Basil Blackwell, 1950); Herschel C. Baker, *The Dignity of Man* and *The Wars of Truth* (Cambridge: Harvard University Press, 1947 and 1952); Theodore Spencer, *Shakespeare and the Nature of Man*, 2d ed. (New York: Macmillan, 1949); Geoffrey Bush, *Shakespeare and the Natural Condition* (Cambridge: Harvard University Press, 1956); and W. Gordon Zeeveld, *The Temper of Shakespeare's Thought* (New Haven: Yale University Press, 1974).

71. Richard Hooker, *Of the Laws of Ecclesiastical Polity*, in *The Works of . . . Mr. Richard Hooker*, ed. Rev. John Keble, 3 vols. (Oxford: Clarendon, 1888), 1: 237.

72. Ibid., 207–208.

73. John Milton, *The Works of John Milton*, ed. Frank Allen Patterson, 20 vols. (New York: Columbia University Press, 1931–1940), 2: 300. The structure of the soul is described by countless Renaissance medical writers: Thomas Wright, André Du Laurens, Timothy Bright, and, most notably, Robert Burton. For good modern summaries, see Craig, *The Enchanted Glass*, pp. 113–138; Lily B. Campbell, *Shakespeare's Tragic Heroes: Slaves of Passion* (Cambridge: Cambridge University Press, 1930; reprint ed., with appendices, New York: Barnes & Noble, 1960), pp. 63–83; Ruth Leila Anderson, *Elizabethan Psychology and Shakespeare's Plays* (Iowa City: Iowa State University Press, 1927). For a detailed study of one phase of Elizabethan psychology, melancholy, see Lawrence Babb, *The Elizabethan Malady* (East Lansing: Michigan State University Press, 1951).

74. The heavenly bodies were said to be placed in an orderly series of concentric spheres that, in their revolutions, produce a sublime music. This music cannot be heard by man, living as he does in the corrupt region below the moon. (The notion was readily absorbed into the concept of the Fall of Man.) Poets delighted in the metaphorical possibilities of the figure. See, for example, *The Merchant of Venice*, V, 1, 54–65.

75. A venerable collection of essays on aspects of Elizabethan life is Walter Raleigh et al., eds., *Shakespeare's England: An Account of the Life and Manners of His Age*, 2 vols. (Oxford: Clarendon, 1916). See also the more recent collections: *Shakespeare in His Own Age,* which constitutes the whole of

Shakespeare Survey 17 (1964), and Kenneth Muir and S. Schoenbaum, eds., *A New Companion to Shakespeare Studies* (Cambridge: Cambridge University Press, 1971). Three outstanding histories of the period are Sir John Ernest Neale, *Queen Elizabeth I, A Biography* (Garden City, N. Y.: Doubleday, 1957); John B. Black, *The Reign of Elizabeth, 1558–1603*, 2d ed. (Oxford: Clarendon, 1959); and Stanley T. Bindoff, *Tudor England* (Baltimore: Penguin, 1962).

2
Text, Chronology, and Sources

To one who reads Shakespeare in modern editions, the text itself poses few problems. The plays are divided into acts and scenes, with entrances and exits duly noted; speeches are neatly laid out and distributed among the characters for whom they seem to have been intended; lines are not only numbered but also punctuated according to current practice; and, as an added convenience, one sometimes finds explicit stage directions. While the reader may now and then be puzzled by an awkward repetition or by a cryptic footnote (such as "*Hamlet,* III, ii, 262 must take your husbands [Pope]; must take your husband [Q1; White]; mistake your husbands [Q2]; mistake Husbands [F1]; mis-take husbands [Capell]"), it might not occur to him that his text does not coincide with Shakespeare's original or that there are variations from one edition to another.

Actually, the task of establishing a satisfactory, let alone definitive, Shakespearean text is enormously complex. In this chapter we shall discuss some of the difficulties besetting the modern editor, drawing special attention to conditions in Elizabethan theaters and printing houses that affected the quality of earlier texts. In addition, we shall focus on two somewhat related issues, which have engaged literary historians even though they may not be of major concern to playgoers and readers: the chronology of Shakespeare's plays and the sources from which they were derived. A full appreciation of Shakespeare's growth as an artist depends to some extent on a notion as to the order in which the poems and plays were written. And the study of sources can reveal one of the most fascinating aspects of Shakespeare's genius: his ability to fashion old and familiar materials into something rich and strange.

TEXT[1]

In 1623 two of Shakespeare's old associates in the theater, John Heminge and Henry Condell, collected thirty-six of his plays into a single volume, the First Folio. A *folio* was a sheet printed on both sides and folded once, forming two leaves (four pages); a *quarto* was a sheet folded twice to make four leaves (eight pages). (The terms *folio* and *quarto* came to be applied to books as well as to the paper folds utilized in making the books.) In a prefatory address "To the great Variety of Readers," Heminge and Condell regret the fact that Shakespeare, who had been dead for seven years, could not personally supervise the publication of his collected plays:

> It had bene a thing, we confesse, worthie to have bene wished, that the Author himselfe had liv'd to have set forth, and overseen his owne writings; But since it hath bin ordain'd otherwise, and he by death departed from that right, we pray you do not envie [begrudge] his Friends, the office of their care, and paine, to have collected & publish'd them; and so to have publish'd them, as where (before) you were abus'd with diverse stolne, and surreptitious copies, maimed, and deformed by the frauds and stealthes of injurious impostors, that expos'd them: even those, are now offer'd to your view cur'd, and perfect of their limbes; and all the rest, absolute in their numbers, as he conceived them.[2]

The editors of the First Folio overcame tremendous obstacles, and posterity is eternally in their debt. But they also created problems that still torment textual scholars.

Shakespearean Texts before the First Folio. A number of the problems growing out of the early texts can be traced to the generally unfavorable status of the theatrical profession during the Elizabethan period.[3] Writing for the stage was not considered a significant literary activity, and this prejudice was shared by the playwrights themselves. Although it was permissible, indeed mandatory, for fashionable gentlemen (like Sir Philip Sidney and Sir Walter Raleigh) to compose verses for their own amusement and their friends' entertainment, no person of quality would demean himself to write for publication. Such ignominy was reserved for professional writers, who were low in the social scale to begin with. Moreover, one acquired a literary reputation by producing lyric and narrative verse, not by grinding out plays for a popular audience. Most plays, in fact, remained unpublished even if they were successful. It has been observed that of the more than 280 plays mentioned in Henslowe's *Diary* as having been in some way connected with his companies between 1592 and 1603, only forty or so have survived in print.[4] Shakespeare had already written successful plays by 1593, but in the dedication of

Venus and Adonis, published in that year, he speaks of the poem as "the first heir of my invention"—an indication that the plays did not really count. "Comedies," the playwright John Marston stated in 1606, "are writ to be spoken, not read." As late as 1616 (the year of Shakespeare's death), when Ben Jonson presumed to publish his collected plays as *The Works of Ben Jonson,* there were many who resented his dignifying with the title "works" those trifles he had composed for the public stage.

Not only did Elizabethan dramatists feel that theirs was an ephemeral craft, but they also saw their manuscripts undergo harsh treatment while being prepared for stage production. The dramatists worked under terrific pressure, often in collaboration with other playwrights in their company. Sometimes they submitted only part of a manuscript and promised to supply the rest during rehearsal. When circumstances dictated quick action, the deadline could be met by resurrecting or adapting part of an older play or by parceling out unfinished work among the regular staff of writers who happened to be available. Before a work could be performed, the Master of the Revels examined it. If he found material offensive for moral or political reasons, he withheld approval until the necessary revisions were carried out. A key figure in the playhouse was the bookkeeper, or prompter, one of whose tasks was to convert the author's last complete draft (called foul papers) or fair copy into a clear and workable stage-copy, or book.[5] The bookkeeper would insert notes on costumes, cues, and stage business. More important, he made revisions and deletions to satisfy the Master of the Revels or to adjust to the conditions of a particular performance. He would probably not tamper with a text without consulting the author, but one cannot be sure that the author's wishes were invariably respected. In short, a play as finally acted may have borne little resemblance to the playwright's original conception, and sometimes the number of collaborators grew so large as to obscure a given author's unique contribution. Shakespeare, of course, may have been better treated, for he was a major playwright as well as a shareholder in his company. But it was ordinarily difficult for an Elizabethan dramatist to experience the feeling of personal pride traditionally associated with the creative artist. Under such conditions publication would not have been a prime objective.[6]

There were also practical reasons for not printing plays. If a play reached a wide reading public, it might lose some of its box-office appeal. A successful play could remain in the repertory for a long time and could be revived periodically. No shrewd theater manager would ordinarily part with a valuable commodity. Copyright was understood by the Elizabethans as protecting publishers against encroachments by other publishers; it did not protect the author himself or the company for which he wrote. Consequently, the printing of a play increased the risk of its falling into the hands of a rival acting troupe, a threat that existed even in the best of circumstances. Sometimes it was profitable to authorize publication of a play in order to stimulate business, recoup losses, block or counteract an unauthorized publication, or salvage something when a company was disbanding. But, on the whole, Elizabethan acting companies discouraged publication of their plays.

Nevertheless, a fairly sizable reading public began to develop for Elizabethan plays, and a number of pieces that had been written for the stage appeared individually in print, usually in quarto editions. Before 1623, the date of the First Folio, nineteen of Shakespeare's plays had been published in this manner, most of them more than once.[7] It was at one time assumed that all Shakespeare quartos were unauthorized versions, with virtually no claim to reliability. But, chiefly as a result of the pioneering studies of Alfred W. Pollard, scholars now distinguish between "good" quartos, printed from Shakespeare's own manuscripts or from playhouse copies of almost equal authority, and "bad" quartos, which were probably derived from texts that actors in London productions had reconstructed from memory in order to perform in the provinces. It was formerly believed that unscrupulous publishers made a habit of stealing plays by dispatching agents to the theater to take them down in shorthand, but this kind of piracy seems to have been rare in Elizabethan England.[8] Most of the quartos are of great importance to textual scholars.

In 1619 a publisher named Thomas Pavier attempted to capitalize on Shakespeare's growing reputation by issuing a collection of his plays in large quarto. Pavier assembled ten plays from various sources and in texts of varying quality. In fact, several of the plays are no longer considered part of the Shakespeare canon. However, he abandoned his project after a restraining order by the Lord Chamberlain (perhaps issued in response to an appeal from Shakespeare's company, the King's Men). At any rate, Pavier published the plays singly, not as a collection, and he took pains to conceal his part in the scheme by falsifying dates and imprints. The episode remains somewhat obscure, for Pavier was apparently a respectable businessman, as was William Jaggard, who was scheduled to do the printing for Pavier and whose firm actually did print the First Folio. Nevertheless, Pavier's collection indicates that the public was ready for a complete Shakespeare. Some scholars have gone so far as to suggest that the Pavier affair inspired Heminge and Condell to undertake the First Folio.

The First Folio and Its Successors. Under the date 8° Novembris 1623 is the following entry in the Stationers' Register:

Mr Blounte Isaak Jaggard. Entred for their Copie under the hands of Mr Doctor Worrall and Mr Cole, warden, Mr William Shakespeers Comedyes Histories, and Tragedyes soe manie of the said Copies as are not formerly entred to other men .... [9]

The entry goes on to record the names of sixteen of the eighteen plays being printed for the first time. Edward Blount and Isaac Jaggard (who succeeded his father, William Jaggard, as printer and bookseller) were the principal publishers; Jaggard was the printer. There is evidence that the book was intended for publication earlier. It was advertised in a catalog for the Frankfort book fair, in October 1622, and it seems to have been in the press in 1621, when it was laid aside for several months while Jaggard worked on other material. The First Folio finally reached the public in a printing of about 1200 copies—a modest debut for what has aptly been described as "the greatest contribution in a single volume to secular literature, and next to the Gutenberg Bible the most sought after by collectors."[10]

The title page of the Folio contains the legend "Mr. William Shakespeares Comedies, Histories, & Tragedies. Published according to the True Originall Copies." Below the title is the celebrated engraving of Shakespeare by Martin Droeshout, a Flemish artist. The portrait is not very accomplished, but it is one of only two representations of Shakespeare whose authenticity is unchallenged. (The other is the memorial bust in the Church of the Holy Trinity in Stratford.) Opposite the portrait are Ben Jonson's verses "To the Reader," advising that we look "Not on his Picture, but his Booke." The title page is followed by the dedicatory epistle to William and Philip Herbert, earls of Pembroke and Montgomery respectively; in it Heminge and Condell claim that they are collecting the plays (not editing them in the modern sense), "without ambition either of selfe-profit, or fame: onely to keepe the memory of so worthy a Friend, & Fellow alive, as was our SHAKESPEARE, by humble offer of his playes, to your most noble patronage."[11] The actual authorship of the dedication, like that of the ensuing address "To the great Variety of Readers" (see p. 35), has sometimes been attributed to Jonson himself. Next come two commendatory poems. One is by Hugh Holland; the other is Jonson's famous ode in which Shakespeare is called "the applause! delight! the wonder of our Stage!" and is said to be "not of an age, but for all time!" Completing the preliminary matter are a table of contents, which omits Troilus and Cressida; two more poems (one by Leonard Digges and one by an unidentified "I. [or J.] M."); and a list, "The Names of the Principall Actors in all these Playes." The inclusion of this list has been taken to indicate that Heminge and Condell wanted to impart theatrical emphasis to their project as a tribute to their company and to Shakespeare, their colleague and friend.[12] The thirty-six plays are printed in some 900 double-columned pages, with separate pagination for comedies, histories, and tragedies.[13]

As noted earlier, the Folio editors asserted that they were offering Shakespeare's plays "according to the True Originall Copies," hoping thereby to correct previous abuses in the form of "diverse stolne, and surreptitious copies." This protestation has given rise to speculation as to the truthfulness of the editors, for it has been established that very few of the early quartos were stolen. But contemporary scholars are convinced that after allowing for the fact that a dedicatory epistle "is an advertisement, rather than an affidavit,"[14] one must credit Heminge and Condell with a high degree of integrity. They acted honestly and, on the whole, wisely in two vital areas: the establishment of the Shakespeare canon and the selection of texts for the plays admitted into the canon.

The First Folio remains the most authoritative testimony as to the plays that are legitimately Shakespeare's. (That other Elizabethan dramatists may have contributed isolated passages to a few of the plays—the Hecate episode in *Macbeth,* for example—is a minor matter.) But the Folio creates at least two major problems. For one thing, the editors included *Henry VIII* among the thirty-six plays. There is no external evidence for doubting Shakespeare's authorship, and a number of responsible scholars argue that the very appearance of the play in the Folio is adequate reason for supposing him the sole author. Some authorities, however, believe that Shakespeare wrote only a few scenes of *Henry VIII* and assign the rest to John Fletcher. (Shakespeare seems to have collaborated with Fletcher on *The Two Noble Kinsmen,* which was not printed until 1634.)

A second source of confusion is the absence of *Pericles* from the First Folio, despite its having been published, along with several other doubtful plays, during Shakespeare's lifetime with his name on the title page. The present consensus is that Shakespeare wrote the last three acts of *Pericles* and that, even though the editors for some reason did not reprint it in 1623, the work deserves to be counted as the thirty-seventh play in the canon. Scholars have attempted to resolve some of these questions of authorship by means of metrical and linguistic tests (sometimes with the aid of electronic computers), but the results have so far been inconclusive.[15]

In selecting texts, the Folio editors had several alternatives (although in some cases their options must have been quite limited). If a play had already been published, they generally chose the best available quarto for their copy text, subject to the permission of the publisher who owned the copyright. A notable exception to this procedure was their apparent ignoring the good Second Quarto of *Hamlet* (1604) in favor of a different source. For texts of the eighteen plays not previously printed, they could choose either theatrical promptbooks or Shakespeare's own copies; and although present-day critics incline to the view that wherever possible the Folio editors turned to the author's manuscript rather than to a promptbook, neither source would have been entirely satisfactory. The "foul papers" presumably would have borne the marks of Shakespeare's deletions, second thoughts, interlinings, and general queries to be settled at rehearsal. Meanwhile, the promptbook, which corresponded closely to the play as acted, would reflect the revisions or excisions demanded by the Master of the Revels, as well as the almost inevitable abridgments that occur when a play is put on the stage. In several cases Heminge and Condell may have used copy prepared for Shakespeare's company by a scribe, Ralph Crane.[16] Finally, if reliable printed versions, manuscripts, or promptbooks were unobtainable, the Folio editors were obliged to resort to transcriptions or reconstructions of variable accuracy. Each play has a different textual history.[17]

The Folio was reprinted in 1632, in 1663–1664, and in 1685. These later Folios were not mere reprints but attempts on the part of the editors at a kind of textual criticism, with a number of corrections and emendations (not to mention a plentiful supply of fresh errors) successively introduced.[18] The Second Folio (1632) contains an epitaph on Shakespeare by the young John Milton. The Third Folio, which appeared in 1663 and was reissued in 1664, added in its second printing seven plays that had been ascribed to Shakespeare; of these, only *Pericles* retains any claim to authenticity.

The eighteenth and nineteenth centuries saw many editions of Shakespeare, some of which may be noted here. Shakespeare's first editor in the modern sense was Nicholas Rowe, whose edition appeared in 1709. Although Rowe made some effort to correct the Fourth Folio by referring to the quartos, he is primarily remembered for having provided lists of dramatis personae for each play and for having divided the plays into acts and scenes (in some cases for the first time). Rowe's arrangement, alien though it may be to the dramatic conventions of the Elizabethan stage, has become the standard of most modern editions. Alexander Pope produced an edition in 1725, but he played fast and loose with the text, relegating to footnotes or omitting altogether any readings that did not please him, including Macbeth's great line, "The multitudinous seas incarnadine" (*Macbeth,* II, 2, 62). The classical scholar Lewis Theobald, a brilliant emendator (see p. 43), exposed some of Pope's errors in 1726 and issued his own edition in 1734. Dr. Johnson's edition (1765) is memorable for its great preface, rich in critical insights, rather than for its value as a text. Edmund Malone's outstanding edition (1790) took a significant step in the direction of the modern position of such scholars as Pollard, McKerrow, Greg, and Dover Wilson, who insisted that the editor carefully evaluate the authority of particular texts. From the nineteenth century came two monumental editions, both containing elaborate textual variants and notes: the Cambridge Shakespeare (1863–1866; revised 1891–1893), edited by William George Clark, John Glover, and W. Aldis Wright; and the New Variorum Shakespeare, begun in 1871 by Howard H. Furness and still in progress (as of 1976) under the auspices of the Modern Language Association. And there are major twentieth-century editions either complete or in progress: the New Cambridge, the New Arden, and others. The editing of Shakespeare continues with undiminishable vigor.[19]

The Role of the Modern Editor. Inasmuch as the First Folio is esteemed by all Shakespeare scholars, one may indeed wonder what task remains for today's editor. Can he not simply tidy up the spelling and punctuation and reprint the Folio text? Better still, why not place the unedited Folio before the reader and let it speak for itself?

The problem does not permit so easy a solution. In the first place, there were probably as many as five distinct compositors at work, differing in competence as well as in habits of spelling and punctuation.[20] Then, too, no two copies of the Folio are identical throughout, and no single copy can properly be considered the correct copy. This confusing situation is due in large part to the proofreading methods followed in Elizabethan printing houses. As the printing was being run off, a sheet might be pulled out and examined. If errors were found, they would perhaps be corrected. But the printing had continued while the proofs were being read, and although the type may have been reset, the old incorrect sheets were used and bound along with the corrected ones. Consequently, among the various copies of the First Folio, one now discovers many combinations of good and bad text. And as Charlton Hinman observes, the proofreading was hit-or-miss at best:

> Yet we shall find that the proof-reading that was done for the Folio was in considerable measure confined to some six or eight plays in one section of the book, and especially to material set by a particular compositor. And we shall also find that it was not ordinarily concerned with the accuracy of the text— that it only rarely resulted in the correction of anything more than obvious typographical blemishes; and that, moreover, such changes as it did produce tended rather to corrupt than to recover and preserve what Shakespeare wrote.[21]

Not only is it impossible to find the definitive copy of the First Folio, but it is sometimes difficult to decide whether the Folio text of a given play is superior to an earlier quarto. As noted previously, many textual scholars believe the 1604 Second Quarto of *Hamlet* to be closer to Shakespeare's intentions than was the copy text used for the Folio; and other "good" quartos fall into the same category. Moreover, a "bad" or doubtful quarto (for example, the 1597 *Richard III* or the 1608 *King Lear*) may in isolated passages provide a better reading than does a generally more authoritative text. All texts, good and bad, contain their quota of misprints, improperly lined verses, obscure punctuation, old and somewhat ambiguous spellings, and frequently misdirected attempts on the part of the printer to improve what seemed to him defective. The modern editor has to approach each play as a unique textual problem. He must learn what kind of copy was used for each printed text; he must try to determine what changes were made in the copy by the Elizabethan censor, playhouse prompter, or editor; he must be able to judge what effect the compositors and proofreaders in the printing houses may have had on the copy they received. The editor should recognize the general features of Elizabethan handwriting, as well as the particular idiosyncrasies that might cause an author's handwriting to be misinterpreted by an editor or a compositor. (In this connection it should be noted that scholars have detected what they believe to be Shakespeare's hand in a small portion of the manuscript play *Sir Thomas More*.)[22]

In his dual capacity as detective and scholar, the editor must sometimes practice the art of emendation: That is, he must supply an acceptable reading whenever the text seems to make no sense (assuming, of course, that the defect actually exists and had been introduced inadvertently by the author, compositor, or proofreader). At the same time, the contemporary editor must recognize unwarranted emendations of earlier editors and restore what was there in the first place. There is no reason, in the case of *Romeo and Juliet* (II, 2, 43–44), to cling sentimentally to the bad First Quarto's "a Rose by any other *name* [italics mine] would smell as sweet" when the good Second Quarto reads "a rose by any other *word* [italics mine]."[23]

A few examples: Hamlet's first soliloquy (I, 2, 129–159) begins, in all four Folios, "O that this too too *solid* [italics mine] flesh would melt." The good Quarto (Q2, 1604) reads "sallied" for "solid." Because this reading did not appear to make sense, a number of editors chose to regard "sallied" as a corruption of "sullied" and emended the line to read, "O that this too too *sullied* [italics mine] flesh.... " Meanwhile, it has been argued that "sallied" is not a corruption at all, that it is a legitimate variant of "sullied," and that the Q2 "sallied" is what Shakespeare wrote and meant to write. Thus, there are three choices in this hotly contested matter: One may accept the Folio "solid," the Q2 reading as emended ("sullied"), or the Q2 reading as restored ("sallied").[24]

No less interesting in the case of *Othello* (II, 3, 164). After Montano has been wounded in a street fight with Cassio, he says, in the First Folio, "I bleed still, I am hurt to th' death. He dies." For years it was thought that "He dies" was a stage direction that got incorporated into the text by mistake, for the reliable First Quarto of *Othello* (1622) omits these two words altogether. Moreover, inasmuch as Montano clearly does *not* die, many editors accepted the emendation found in the Second Quarto (1630), in which the stage direction reads "[*He faints*]." It seems plausible, however, that no one had any reason to tamper with the First Folio reading to begin with; it makes good sense dramatically for Montano, rankling from his wounds, to cry out bitterly that he will retaliate against his enemy Cassio ("He dies!").[25]

One other example illustrates how errors can be introduced and compounded. Shylock exclaims, in the Folio, "Good news, good news! Ha, ha! Here in Genoa!" (*The Merchant of Venice,* III, 1, 111–112). This reading was rejected, logically enough, on the grounds that the speakers in the scene are not in Genoa but in Venice, and the text (following Rowe's lead) has usually been emended to read, "Good news, good news! Ha, ha! Where? in Genoa?" Here Shakespeare's own script can perhaps supply a clue. His final *e* and *d* were easily confused by compositors and proofreaders, and it is likely that the First Folio *here* was simply a misreading of the manuscript *herd*. Hence, Shylock may be saying *"heard* in Genoa!"[26]

No discussion of Shakespeare's text would be complete without a word about the most famous of all emendations, Theobald's inspired contribution to *Henry V.* As Mistress Quickly is describing the death of Sir John Falstaff, the Folio has the strange phrase "a Table of greene fields." Numerous attempts have been made to justify the phrase, perhaps as a stage direction or as a topical reference that is now obscure. But Theobald, in 1726, changed "a Table of greene fields" to " 'a [he] babbled of green fields," and few would be willing to give it up. The phrase, with its evocation of the green pastures of the Twenty-third Psalm, shows how emendation at its best can be bold and creative:

'A parted ev'n just between twelve and one, ev'n at the turning o' th' tide. For after I saw him fumble with the sheets, and play with flowers, and smile upon his fingers' ends, I knew there was but one way; for his nose was as sharp as a pen, and 'a babbled of green fields.

(Henry V, II, 3, 12–18)

CHRONOLOGY

Unfortunately, when Heminge and Condell issued the First Folio, they did not print the plays in chronological order. They merely grouped them (in some cases arguably) as comedies, histories, and tragedies, heading the collection with *The Tempest,* one of Shakespeare's last plays.

There are not many facts to help us determine the general sequence of the plays or fix precise dates for individual plays, and it is risky to draw conclusions from the meager evidence found in the works themselves or from subjective impressions of Shakespeare's emotional or stylistic development. The problem remains excruciatingly difficult.

It is impossible to consider in this chapter the facts and conjectures that lie behind the dating of each play. Nevertheless, a few things should be said concerning the kinds of information upon which inferences as to chronology have been based. And since there is no unanimity as to how such information should be interpreted, it will be convenient for the time being to present (with one or two qualifications) a working order that has gained fairly wide acceptance.

External Evidence. The most comprehensive single document in Shakespeare chronology is the *Palladis Tamia* of Francis Meres (see p. 2). Praising Shakespeare as the greatest English dramatist, Meres lists twelve plays known to him when he wrote in 1598 (his list need not have been complete). Although any play mentioned by Meres must have been produced by 1598, the list raises problems. Meres does not include *Henry VI,* probably a very early work, and he mentions *Henry IV* without specifying whether he means one or both parts. Furthermore, he lists immediately after *Love's Labour's Lost* a play called *Love labours wonne.* Scholars have expended many a lost labor in an effort to find such a play or, failing that, to identify it with some extant play of Shakespeare's—possibly *Much Ado about Nothing, The Taming of the Shrew, All's Well that Ends Well,* or *Troilus and Cressida.* We have not abandoned hope that this play may turn up; in fact, there is reason to believe that a play with that title was in print in 1603.[27]

Other external evidence may be helpful. There are some records of actual performances, valuable (like Meres's list) in that they furnish the latest possible dates for particular plays to have come into existence. For example, *The Comedy of Errors* was acted for the law students at Gray's Inn on December 28, 1594, and a performance of *Twelfth Night* (so the *Diary* of John Manningham tells us) occurred at the Middle Temple on February 2, 1602. We cannot be sure that such records refer to first performances, but Sir Henry Wotton's lively letter describing the burning of the Globe Theater (June 29, 1613) says that the fire took place during a performance of "a new play, called *All is True,* representing some principal pieces of the reign of Henry VIII,"[28] unquestionably Shakespeare's *Henry VIII.*

Topical allusions (which sometimes border on external evidence) are rare in Shakespeare, but there are exceptions. The last act of *Henry V* begins with the Chorus wishing the Earl of Essex a safe return from his military expedition to Ireland (March–September 1599), and as noted earlier (see p. 11), *Hamlet* includes a resentful comment on the resurgence of the children's acting companies (1599). Scholars are perhaps treading on more treacherous ground when they see in *A Midsummer Night's Dream* a specific allusion to the bad weather that plagued England in 1594, or when they detect in *King Lear* a specific reference to eclipses of the sun and moon that were observed in the fall of 1605.

Dates of publication are some help, but there could have been a long interval between a play's appearance on the stage and in print. To complicate matters further, a play might be registered with the Stationers' Company and not be printed for a good many years. *Troilus and Cressida* was registered in 1603 but apparently not printed until 1609; *As You Like It*, registered August 4, 1600, presumably was first published in the Folio twenty-three years later. External evidence, even when accurate, may be inconclusive.

Internal Evidence. Another sort of evidence is derived not from historical documents or from identifiable allusions, but from suppositions about Shakespeare's psychological and artistic development. Most of the so-called internal evidence takes for granted a fairly consistent and recognizable pattern in Shakespeare's growth. In a broad sense this generalization seems reasonable enough, for no one would deny that Shakespeare traveled a long road, both as a playwright and as a human being, from, say, *The Comedy of Errors* to *Macbeth*. But valid though this insight may be, it cannot be taken as primary evidence for a particular chronology. If one has learned something of the chronology of these two plays from factual sources, he may then find corroboration in the aesthetic judgment that *Macbeth* has greater scope than *The Comedy of Errors*. But a subtle circular argument could thus be set in motion: Shakespeare's maturity in a given play can lead all too easily into speculation about some maturing process in his inner life; this speculation can be quietly transformed into certainty; then it can be used as a basis for additional inferences about chronology.[29]

Similar restrictions apply to metrical tests. At one time scholars thought that Shakespeare's chronological development could be gauged by such measurable items as verbal parallels between one play and another, length of lines, ratio of blank verse to rhyme and to prose, and the relative frequency of end-stopped and run-on lines. But it is now thought that these tests were not conducted with sufficient accuracy and that they are useful, if at all, for confirming hypotheses that have been developed out of more solid external evidence.

In short, external evidence is almost always preferable to internal evidence in setting up a chronology. Although internal evidence may be illuminating in a general way when two plays, like *The Comedy of Errors* and *Macbeth*, seem to be widely separated in time and in magnitude, it is unlikely that we can effectively use it to fix the relative dates of *Macbeth* and *Othello,* which appear to be fairly close to each other in time and mood and are of comparable artistry. And to arrive at firm conclusions concerning the chronological relationship between two such different plays as *As You Like It* and *Hamlet,* each an authentic masterpiece in its own right, may be impossible on the basis of present knowledge.

Chronological Table for the Plays.[30] The following chronology is that recommended by Sir Edmund Chambers (*William Shakespeare,* 1: 270–271, by permission of the Oxford University Press, Oxford), but an occasional note has been added suggesting possible modifications in the light of more recent scholarship.[31] (There has been a trend in recent years toward an earlier dating of Shakespeare's plays.) The reader should constantly remind himself that Chambers's table, arranged according to theatrical seasons rather than calendar years, is intended simply as a working order; it does not claim to be definitive.

1590–1	*2 Henry VI* *3 Henry VI*
1591–2	*1 Henry VI*[32]
1592–3	*Richard III* *Comedy of Errors*[33]
1593–4	*Titus Andronicus*[34]
1594–5	*Taming of the Shrew* *Two Gentlemen of Verona* *Love's Labour's Lost*[35] *Romeo and Juliet*[36]
1595–6	*Richard II* *Midsummer Night's Dream*[37]
1596–7	*King John*[38] *Merchant of Venice*
1597–8	*1 Henry IV*[39]
1598–9	*2 Henry IV* *Much Ado About Nothing* *Henry V*
1599–1600	*Julius Caesar* *As You Like It* *Twelfth Night*[40]

1600–1	*Hamlet*[41]
	Merry Wives of Windsor[42]
1601–2	*Troilus and Cressida*
1602–3	*All's Well That Ends Well*
1603–4	———
1604–5	*Measure for Measure*
	Othello[43]
1605–6	*King Lear*
	Macbeth
1606–7	*Antony and Cleopatra*
1607–8	*Coriolanus*[44]
	Timon of Athens
1608–9	*Pericles*[45]
1609–10	*Cymbeline*
1610–11	*Winter's Tale*
1611–12	*Tempest*
1612–13	*Henry VIII*
	Two Noble Kinsmen

There is no external evidence for the dating of Shakespeare's contribution to *Sir Thomas More* (see p. 42), assuming that he had a share in the play. On the basis of the content and style of the passage thought to be in Shakespeare's hand, scholars have proposed 1600 or 1601 as a plausible date.

SOURCES

Like other Elizabethan dramatists, Shakespeare rarely invented his own plots, preferring to build his poems and plays out of familiar materials. This practice is sometimes explained on the grounds that the Elizabethan concept of originality differed from our own, that Shakespeare's contemporaries did not object if a writer retold an old story provided he did so in a novel and entertaining way.

But there was nothing unusual about this Elizabethan predilection for the familiar. After all, the artist in every age may want to reinterpret a well-known tale in the light of his own values. Aeschylus turned to a celebrated myth for his dramatization of the careers of Agamemnon, Orestes, and Electra; and half a century or so later, Sophocles and Euripides provided deeply personal insights into the same events. In the twentieth century, writers as distinctive as O'Neill, Sartre, and Giraudoux have reshaped the materials of that myth to fit a culture remote from classical Greece. None of these playwrights invented his own plots. A dramatist receives inspiration from any number of sources: a historical crisis, an episode in a real or fictitious war, a biblical story, an earlier literary treatment of a character or situation. The question of originality becomes almost irrelevant in Shakespeare's age as in our own.

But one should also realize that certain dramatic characterizations and themes, though traditional, need not be linked to specific literary sources. A blustering soldier (like Shakespeare's Pistol) does not necessarily owe his theatrical life to Plautus; the tricker tricked is so common a theme that we need not account for its presence in *The Merry Wives of Windsor* by invoking Italian comedy; and surely a writer at any time may contrast a loyal and a faithless friend (as Shakespeare does in *The Two Gentlemen of Verona*) without recourse to Boccaccio's tale of Titus and Gisippus.

It is all too easy to discover a "source" for a phrase or an idea that may have been a commonplace. When Benvolio urges Romeo to forget his mistress Rosaline and come with him to the Capulets' ball, he assures the distracted young lover that "one fire burns out another's burning" (*Romeo and Juliet*, I, 2, 46); and Proteus similarly announces the transfer of his affections from Julia to Silvia with the words

> Even as one heat another heat expels
> Or as one nail by strength drives out another,
> So the remembrance of my former love
> Is by a newer object quite forgotten.
> (*The Two Gentlemen of Verona*, II, 4, 192–195)

"One fire drives out another" and "One nail drives out another" were well-known proverbs used by a host of Renaissance writers,[46] and there is no justification for assuming that Shakespeare took these sayings from John Lyly or from any other particular source. Moreover, Shakespeare, like most of his contemporaries, probably collected certain traditional themes and formulas (called *topoi,* or topics) from classical authors and kept them available for ready reference. Consequently, to trace Jaques's "All the world's a stage" to a passage, say, in Du Bartas (1544–1590), which begins with the words, "*Le monde est un théâtre,*" is to ignore the fact that the world-as-a-stage metaphor descended from Plato through pagan and Christian channels, particularly the widely known *Policraticus* of John of Salisbury (c. 1120–1180), to become one of the most popular literary clichés of the Renaissance.[47] When a reader detects similarities between passages in different works, he may regard one as the source of the other. Actually, the similarities may be coincidental, or the authors may have independently assimilated a common cultural heritage.

Having noted some of the dangers of indiscriminate source hunting, one may profitably discuss the kinds of works Shakespeare normally consulted for details of plot and character: old plays; books of English history, especially Holinshed's *Chronicles;* classical biography such as North's translation of Plutarch's *Lives*; and English and Continental romance in verse and prose. This classification makes no attempt to deal with Shakespeare's philosophic ideas or with possible verbal echoes from books and contemporary plays, although these too have attracted considerable attention.[48]

Old Plays. Shakespeare may have begun his career as a rewriter of plays by other dramatists. The issue is complicated, however, by the fact that a number of plays he knew and possibly used have not survived in print, and their contents can only be guessed at from vague hints and allusions scattered through various Elizabethan documents. When a text *has* survived that we believe to be connected with a particular Shakespearean play, we cannot always determine whether he himself wrote it, either alone or in collaboration, as an early version; whether the text is a pirated edition or bad quarto of the Shakespearean play that we know; or whether somebody else wrote it completely, Shakespeare merely using it as a source.

The famous *Ur-Hamlet* is a case in point. One thing is certain: In all of early English literature there is, apart from Shakespeare's masterpiece, no extant play about Hamlet. And yet, on the basis of some tantalizing scraps of evidence (see p. 187), scholars have advanced the hypothesis that there was an earlier English Hamlet play and have assumed a line of development starting with the hypothetical *Ur-Hamlet*, extending through a series of revisions and translations and culminating in the full-blown Shakespearean *Hamlet* printed in the First Folio. But this same *Ur-Hamlet* is thought by some to be Shakespeare's earlier version of the mature *Hamlet*. Similarly, there is a minority opinion that *The Troublesome Reign of John King of England* and *The Famous Victories of Henry the Fifth,* which *are* extant and which have generally been considered sources for *King John* and *Henry IV–V* respectively, are early plays by Shakespeare, or at least pirated editions. A more vigorous controversy has developed concerning the anonymous early play entitled *A Pleasant Conceited History Called the Taming of a Shrew*. Although some authorities believe that this play is the source of *The Taming of the Shrew,* others claim that it should be classified as a bad quarto. The latter opinion seems to have gained the ascendancy.

In any case, Shakespeare never allowed himself to be rigidly governed by a play he was adapting. Observe some of the changes he saw fit to make when he was working with *The True Chronicle History of King Leir and His Three Daughters,* an anonymous play written about 1594 but not published until 1605. Shakespeare introduced the Fool into the dramatis personae, invented the gigantic spectacle of Lear's madness, and sensing that the traditional happy ending was not well-suited to the drama as he conceived it, caused the King and his devoted daughter to die soon after their reconciliation. Moreover, from another source, Sir Philip Sidney's *Arcadia,* he derived the subplot involving Gloucester and his two sons—a masterful piece of dramatic parallelism whereby the scope of Lear's tragedy is greatly enlarged.

One illustration will suffice to show how Shakespeare could appropriate the language of an old play and, with a bit of skillful rearranging and condensing, transform weakness into strength. *The Troublesome Reign of King John* concludes, somewhat lamely, with a patriotic speech of limited applicability (the passage is quoted in modernized spelling):

> Thus England's peace begins in Henry's [Henry III's] reign,
> And bloody wars are closed with happy league.
> Let England live but true within itself,
> And all the world can never wrong her State.
> Lewis, thou shalt be bravely shipped to France,
> For never Frenchman got of English ground
> The twentieth part that thou hast conquered.
> Dauphin, thy hand: to Worcester we will march:
> Lords all, lay hands to bear your sovereign
> With obsequies of honor to his grave:
> If England's peers and people join in one,
> Nor Pope, nor France, nor Spain can do them wrong.[49]

Shakespeare lifts the speech out of its specific historical context by substituting for the Pope, France, and Spain of the last line the more eloquent phrase, "the three corners of the world in arms." He also moves the third and fourth lines of the original to the end, transmuting them in the process into a ringing affirmation of his country's destiny:

> This England never did, nor never shall,
> Lie at the proud foot of a conqueror
> But when it first did help to wound itself.
> Now these her princes are come home again,
> Come the three corners of the world in arms,
> And we shall shock them. Naught shall make us rue
> If England to itself do rest but true.
>   (*King John,* V, 7, 112–118)[50]

The fact that Shakespeare made use of an old and graceless play did not prevent him from improving upon the dramatic structure and from breathing new life into the characters and verse.

English History: Holinshed. As England grew more powerful during the sixteenth century, patriotism began to flourish. England's national self-awareness took many forms of expression, including a tremendous outpouring of historical writing. Something will be said later (see chapter 5) about particular lessons of history as understood by the Elizabethans. For the time being, let it be noted that Elizabethan dramatists, Shakespeare included, found in medieval and Renaissance historical accounts a veritable mine of source material.

We know a number of the historical works that were of special interest to Shakespeare: Geoffrey of Monmouth's early *History of the Kings of Britain* (1137); *The Chronicle of Froissart,* as translated from the French (1523–1525) by Lord Berners; Edward Hall's *Union of the Two Noble and Illustre Famelies of Lancastre and Yorke* (1548); John Stow's *Chronicles of England* (1580); and others. But his most important single historical source was a huge project undertaken by the printer Reginald Wolfe as part of a universal history and cosmography: *Chronicles of England, Scotland, and Ireland,* chiefly the work of Raphael Holinshed. The first edition of Holinshed's *Chronicles* appeared in 1578; the second, which Shakespeare used, came out in 1587.

To Holinshed, Shakespeare was indebted for the basic design of the ten history plays, as well as for crucial elements in *Macbeth, King Lear,* and *Cymbeline.* But as was the case when he worked with old plays, Shakespeare frequently took extraordinary liberties with historical sources. If it suited his purposes, he would alter Holinshed's sequence. Sometimes he eliminated an episode entirely; occasionally he expanded the barest of hints into a full-bodied scene. He did not hesitate to change a character's age or to depart from the usual interpretation of motives and actions. John of Gaunt is made much older and is somewhat idealized in order to function as a respectful symbol of a dying era. Henry Percy (Hotspur), who was historically three years older than King Henry IV, becomes in Shakespeare's hands the same age as the King's madcap son. The contrast between Hotspur and Prince Hal, one of the main themes of *1 Henry IV*, is further emphasized by Shakespeare's departure from historical truth in having Hotspur killed by the Prince at the Battle of Shrewsbury. Richard III as Shakespeare conceived him is much more evil than he actually was. Shakespeare has sometimes been called to task for his disregard for historical accuracy, a seeming negligence accounted for on the grounds that he was either blindly partial to the House of Tudor or else simply ignorant. This criticism overlooks the fact that playwrights in all ages have taken liberties with history. Neither Shaw nor Anouilh nor

Maxwell Anderson dealt accurately with Joan of Arc. Schiller's *Mary Stuart* contains a meeting between Mary and Elizabeth that never took place. Similarly, Dryden's *All for Love* includes a scene in which Cleopatra and Octavia, the two fierce rivals for Antony's love, confront each other. Dryden defends his exercise of this "privilege of a poet":

> The French poets, I confess, are strict observers of these punctilios [nice details]: they would not, for example, have suffered Cleopatra and Octavia to have met . . . . This objection I foresaw, and at the same time contemned; for I judged it both natural and probable, that Octavia, proud of her new-gained conquest, would search out Cleopatra to triumph over her; and that Cleopatra, thus attacked, was not of a spirit to shun the encounter: and 'tis not unlikely, that two exasperated rivals should use such satire as I have put into their mouths; for, after all, though the one were a Roman, and the other a queen, they were both women.[51]

Like Dryden and other important dramatists, Shakespeare was a poet first and a historian second.

Space does not permit a full discussion of Shakespeare's handling of Holinshed, but a few examples from *Henry IV* will shed light upon his method. Holinshed reports that the Percys in the north were angered because the King had demanded the return of some Scottish prisoners. They "came to the king unto Windsore (upon a purpose to proove him) and there required of him, that either by ransome or otherwise, he would cause to be delivered out of prison Edmund Mortimer earle of March, their cousine germane [first cousin]."[52] In *1 Henry IV* the King himself, whom Shakespeare clearly intends to be the dominant figure, summons the Percys to account for their refusal to surrender the prisoners. Unable to obtain satisfaction, the Percys decide upon open rebellion. Here is Holinshed's brief version of the episode:

> The Persies with this answer and fraudulent excuse were not a little fumed, insomuch that Henrie Hotspur said openlie: Behold, the heire of the relme is robbed of his right, and yet the robber with his owne will not redeeme him. So in this furie the Persies departed, minding nothing more than to depose King Henrie from the high type of his royaltie, and to place in his seat their cousine Edmund earle of March.[53]

Out of this fragment Shakespeare builds a great scene, which includes Hotspur's impetuous tirade against the King for having warned him not to speak further of Mortimer:

> Speak of Mortimer?
> Zounds, I will speak of him, and let my soul
> Want mercy if I do not join with him!

Yea, on his part I'll empty all these veins,
And shed my dear blood drop by drop in the dust,
But I will lift the downtrod Mortimer
As high in the air as this unthankful king,
As this ingrate and cank'red Bolingbroke.

> (*1 Henry IV*, I, 3, 130–137)

. . . .

He said he would not ransom Mortimer,
Forbade my tongue to speak of Mortimer,
But I will find him when he lies asleep,
And in his ear I'll holloa "Mortimer."
Nay;
I'll have a starling shall be taught to speak
Nothing but "Mortimer," and give it him
To keep his anger still in motion.

> (I, 3, 219–226)

. . . .

All studies here I solemnly defy [reject]
Save how to gall and pinch this Bolingbroke;
And that same sword-and-buckler Prince of Wales—
But that I think his father loves him not
And would be glad he met with some mischance,
I would have him poisoned with a pot of ale.

> (I, 3, 228–233)

Shakespeare's Hotspur here emerges as a richly drawn character, but the initial concept is suggested, though faintly, by Holinshed.

At times Shakespeare reflects the actual language of the *Chronicles*. He takes from Holinshed the idea that Henry IV, in the last year of his reign, meant to lead an expedition to the Holy Land, "there to recover the citie of Jerusalem from the Infidels." Ironically, Henry does get to Jerusalem, but it is the Jerusalem chamber of his own palace, where he dies. Here is Holinshed's account:

> We find, that he was taken with his last sickenesse, while he was making his praiers at saint Edwards shrine. . . . He was so suddenlie and greevouslie taken, that such as were about him, feared least he would have died presentlie, wherfore to releeve him (if it were possible) they bare him into a chamber that was next at hand, belonging to the abbat of Westminster, where they laid him on a pallet before the fire, and used all remedies to revive him. At length, he recovered his speech, and understanding and perceiving himselfe in a strange place which he knew not, he willed to know if the chamber had anie particular name, whereunto answer was made, that it was called Jerusalem. Then said the king; Lauds be given to the father of heaven, for now I know that I shall die heere in this chamber, according to the prophesie of me declared, that I should depart this life in Jerusalem.[54]

In *2 Henry IV* Shakespeare makes the proposed pilgrimage to the Holy Land a recurring motif that suggests the King's troubled conscience and his desperate yearning for repentance. With a slight alteration the death scene is very similar to Holinshed's:

> *King:* Doth any name particular belong
> Unto the lodging where I first did swound?
> *Warwick:* 'Tis call'd Jerusalem, my noble lord.
> *King:* Laud be to God! Even there my life must end.
> It hath been prophesied to me many years,
> I should not die but in Jerusalem;
> Which vainly I suppos'd the Holy Land.
> But bear me to that chamber; there I'll lie.
> In that Jerusalem shall Harry die.
>   (*2 Henry IV*, IV, 5, 233–241)

Plutarch. One of the favorite books in Elizabethan England was Plutarch's *Lives of the Noble Grecians and Romans* (c. A.D. 75), translated into English by Sir Thomas North in 1579, from a French version by Jacques Amyot. It is easy to understand why Plutarch, especially in North's vigorous prose, appealed to Shakespeare; both writers were more concerned with the interpretation of character than with biographical minutiae. Shakespeare drew particularly upon four of Plutarch's accounts: "The Life of Julius Caesar," "The Life of Marcus Brutus," "The Life of Marcus Antonius," and "The Life of Caius Marcius Coriolanus." These provided most of the material for *Julius Caesar, Antony and Cleopatra,* and *Coriolanus.* "The Life of Marcus Antonius" also contains the story of Timon, the hero of *Timon of Athens.*

Shakespeare worked more closely with North's *Plutarch* than with Holinshed, sometimes doing little more than converting its prose into equivalent verse. For example, Coriolanus, banished from Rome because of his colossal pride, takes himself in disguise to Antium and the house of his longtime enemy Aufidius, the Volscian general. Aufidius is summoned by his servants to meet the strangely muffled visitor. Here is North's account:

> Tullus [Aufidius] rose presently from the board, and, coming towards him, asked him what he was, and wherefore he came. Then Martius [Coriolanus] unmuffled himself, and after he had paused a while, making no answer, he said unto him. "If thou knowest me not yet, Tullus, and, seeing me, dost not perhaps believe me to be the man I am in deed, I must of necessity bewray my self to be that I am. Im Caius Martius, who hath done to thy self particularly, and to all the Volsces generally, great hurt and mischief, which I cannot deny for my surname of Coriolanus that I bear. For I never

had other benefit nor recompense of all the true and painful service I have
done, and the extreme dangers I have been in, but this only surname: a good
memory and witness of the malice and displeasure thou shouldst bear me.
Indeed the name only remaineth with me: for the rest the envy and cruelty
of the people of Rome have taken from me, by the sufferance of the
dastardly nobility and magistrates, who have forsaken me, and let me be
banished by the people. This extremity hath now driven me to come as a
poor suitor to take thy chimney hearth, not of any hope I have to save my
life thereby. For if I had feared death, I would not have come hither to have
put my life in hazard: but pricked forward with spite and desire I have to
be revenged of them that thus have banished me."[55]

Shakespeare follows almost word for word:

Aufidius: Whence com'st thou? What wouldst thou? Thy name?
Why speak'st not? Speak, man. What's thy name?
Coriolanus: If, Tullus,   [*Unmuffles.*]
Not yet thou know'st me, and, seeing me, dost not
Think me for the man I am, necessity
Commands me name myself.
Aufidius: What is thy name?
Coriolanus: A name unmusical to the Volscians' ears
And harsh in sound to thine.

. . . .

My name is Caius Marcius, who hath done
To thee particularly and to all the Volsces
Great hurt and mischief. Thereto witness may
My surname Coriolanus. The painful service,
The extreme dangers, and the drops of blood
Shed for my thankless country are requitted
But with that surname—a good memory
And witness of the malice and displeasure
Which thou shouldst bear me. Only that name remains.
The cruelty and envy of the people,
Permitted by our dastard nobles, who
Have all forsook me, hath devour'd the rest
And suffer'd me by th' voice of slaves to be
Whoop'd out of Rome. Now this extremity
Hath brought me to thy hearth; not out of hope
(Mistake me not) to save my life; for if
I had fear'd death, of all the men i' th' world
I would have 'voided thee; but in mere spite,
To be full quit of those my banishers,
Stand I before thee here.

                    (*Coriolanus*, IV, 5, 58–89)

Even here, however, there is room for an original touch like, "by the voice of slaves to be / Whoop'd out of Rome" (IV, 5, 82–83).

In the most famous instance of his borrowing from North, the closeness of phraseology makes Shakespeare's touches of originality all the more striking. Here is the source of Shakespeare's description of Cleopatra:

> . . . . She disdained to set forward otherwise, but to take her barge in the river of Cydnus, the poop whereof was of gold, the sails of purple, and oars of silver, which kept stroke in rowing after the sound of the music of flutes, hautboys, citherns, viols, and such other instruments as they played upon in the barge. And now for the person of herself: she was laid under a pavilion of cloth of gold of tissue, apparelled and attired like the goddess Venus commonly drawn in picture: and hard by her, on either hand of her, pretty fair boys apparelled as painters do set forth god Cupid, with little fans in their hands, with the which they fanned wind upon her. Her Ladies and gentlewomen also, the fairest of them were apparelled like the nymphs Nereides (which are the mermaids of the waters) and like the Graces, some steering the helm, others tending the tackle and ropes of the barge, out of the which there came a wonderful passing sweet savour of perfumes, that perfumed the wharf's side, pestered with innumerable multitudes of people.[56]

Shakespeare preserves the details of his source, but he does much more. He casts the entire passage in a mood of playful hyperbole, suggesting that Cleopatra's beauty traps the very elements into amorous dotage. Moreover, he assigns the speech to the earthy and cynical Enobarbus so that we shall not make the mistake of taking it too seriously:

> The barge she sat in, like a burnish'd throne,
> Burn'd on the water. The poop was beaten gold;
> Purple the sails, and so perfumed that
> The winds were lovesick with them; the oars were silver,
> Which to the tune of flutes kept stroke, and made
> The water which they beat to follow faster,
> As amorous of their strokes. For her own person,
> It beggar'd all description. She did lie
> In her pavilion, cloth-of-gold of tissue,
> O'erpicturing that Venus where we see
> The fancy outwork nature.
>   (*Antony and Cleopatra*, II, 2, 196–206)

One could comment at length on the artistry of Shakespeare's additions. His Cleopatra is ever the queen, sitting here upon "a burnish'd throne." The poop is not simply gold, as in North, but "beaten gold," evoking the miraculous delicacy of John Donne's line, "Like gold to ayery thinnesse beate." Not content with North's straightforward comparison of Cleopatra to a picture of Venus, Shakespeare has his serpent of the Nile

> O'erpicturing that Venus where we see
> The fancy outwork nature.
> (II, 2, 205–206)

Especially brilliant is the conclusion. North describes the city emptying out to see the great spectacle. "So that in th' end, there ran such multitudes of people one after another to see her, that Antonius was left post alone in the market place in his Imperial seat to give audience." Shakespeare picks up the hint, places Antony (like Cleopatra) ironically upon a "throne," and ends with some more fun at the expense of the amorous air:

> From the barge
> A strange invisible perfume hits the sense
> Of the adjacent wharfs. The city cast
> Her people out upon her; and Antony,
> Enthron'd i' th' market place, did sit alone,
> Whistling to th' air; which, but for vacancy,
> Had gone to gaze on Cleopatra too,
> And made a gap in nature.
> (II, 2, 216–223)

English and Continental Romance. If the Elizabethans responded with enthusiasm to distinguished translations like North's *Plutarch,* they also hungered for sensational fiction from the Continent. In 1566–1567, William Painter published *The Palace of Pleasure,* a collection of 101 tales translated from such writers as Plutarch, Cinthio, Margaret of Navarre, and Boccaccio, but mostly from Bandello, by way of the French *Histoires Tragiques* of Pierre Boaistuau and François de Belleforest. Similar collections, more modest in scope, also appeared in England: Geoffrey Fenton's *Tragical Discourses* (1567), George Pettie's *Petite Palace of Pettie His Pleasures* (1576), Barnabie Riche's *Farewell to Military Profession* (1581), and George Whetstone's *Heptameron of Civil Discourses* (1582). From such works Shakespeare derived a number of plots. Boccaccio's story of Giletta of Narbonne, probably in Painter's translation, was the source of *All's Well that Ends Well;* Barnabe Riche's story of Apolonius and Silla, probably based on a version by Belleforest, furnished the main plot of *Twelfth Night;* and *Measure for Measure* was derived from Whetstone's *Promos and Cassandra,* which had appeared as both novella and play, with a probable debt to Cinthio's *Epitia* (which Shakespeare seems to have known in its Italian form).

Shakespeare may have first encountered the story of Romeo and Juliet in Painter's *Palace of Pleasure,* although his chief source was Arthur Brooke's poem *The Tragical History of Romeus and Juliet* (1562).

Shakespeare also made use of English fiction in verse and prose. He knew several versions of the story of Troilus and Cressida, including Chaucer's great narrative poem. *Pericles* shows an acquaintance with John Gower's version of the story of Apollonius of Tyre in his poem *Confessio Amantis* (1390); it is also related to a novel by Lawrence Twine (1576). *As You Like It* was adapted from Thomas Lodge's pastoral romance, *Rosalynde: Euphues Golden Legacie* (1590), and *The Winter's Tale* from Robert Greene's *Pandosto: The Triumph of Time* (1588). Shakespeare incorporated many details of plot from these sources, but he created works profoundly different in spirit and purpose.

Nowhere is Shakespeare's power to reshape his sources more effectively displayed than in *Othello.* He took his story from a sordid melodrama in Giraldi Cinthio's *Hecatommithi* (1565), which he probably read in the Italian (it had not yet been translated). In Cinthio's "Tale of the Moor" only "Disdemona" is given a name. She and her husband, although they had married against her family's wishes, have lived together harmoniously for a long time. By showing us the elopement in all its violence, Shakespeare sets the tone of the tragedy. In Cinthio's story there is no war to delay the couple's enjoyment of married love or to isolate Desdemona from her Venetian environment. Cinthio's evil Ensign has nothing of Iago's complex malignity. His wife knows what is going on but remains silent; Shakespeare's Emilia knows less but, ironically, becomes an unwitting accomplice in Desdemona's undoing by finding the crucial handkerchief (in Cinthio the Ensign himself steals it from Desdemona). Cinthio's Moor, his passions having been aroused, engages the Ensign to beat Desdemona with a stocking filled with sand, after which the two men together break her skull. Shakespeare's Othello takes upon himself the full responsibility of killing Desdemona, in what he would like to think is a sacrifice rather than a murder. And, of course, unlike Cinthio's lurid tale, *Othello* is steeped in poetry of the highest order.[57]

Table of Shakespeare's Sources. The following table lists the principal known sources of Shakespeare's plays and briefly categorizes them. It omits analogues and verbal or philosophic parallels, of which there are untold numbers.

Play	Sources
2 Henry VI	Holinshed, *Chronicles;* Hall, *The Union of . . .Lancaster and York* (prose histories)
3 Henry VI	Holinshed and Hall
1 Henry VI	Holinshed and Hall
Richard III	Holinshed and Hall
The Comedy of Errors	Plautus, *Menaechmi* and *Amphitruo* (Latin comedies)
Titus Andronicus	Not certain
The Taming of the Shrew	*Taming of a Shrew* (although this is probably a bad quarto) and Gascoigne, *Supposes* [?] (old plays)
The Two Gentlemen of Verona	Montemayor, *Diana Enamorada* (Spanish romance)
Love's Labour's Lost	Not known
Romeo and Juliet	Brooke, *The Tragical History of Romeus and Juliet* (poem)
Richard II	Holinshed; Froissart, *Chronicle* [?]
A Midsummer Night's Dream	Not known
King John	*The Troublesome Reign of King John* (old play); Holinshed
The Merchant of Venice	Ser Giovanni Fiorentino, *Il Pecorone* [?] (Italian novella)
1 Henry IV	Holinshed; *The Famous Victories of Henry the Fifth* (old play); Stow, *The Chronicles of England* [?] (prose history)
2 Henry IV	Holinshed; *The Famous Victories;* Hall [?]
Much Ado about Nothing	Bandello, *Timbreo and Fenecia* (Italian romance); Ariosto, *Orlando Furioso,* Book 5 [?] (romantic epic); Spenser, *The Faerie Queene,* Book 2, Canto 4 [?] (romantic epic)

Play	Sources
Henry V	Holinshed; Tacitus, *Annals* (Roman history); *The Famous Victories*
Julius Caesar	Plutarch, *Lives:* Julius Caesar, Marcus Brutus, Marcus Antonius (biography, North's translation)
As You Like It	Thomas Lodge, *Rosalynde: Euphues Golden Legacie* (pastoral romance); *Syr Clyomon and Clamydes* [?] (old play)
Twelfth Night	Barnabe Riche, *Riche His Farewell to Military Profession:* Tale of Apolonius and Silla (Italian novella of Bandello); *Gl'Ingannati* (Italian comedy)
Hamlet	Boaistuau and Belleforest, *Histoires Tragiques* (French version of Danish historical legend by Saxo Grammaticus); *Ur-Hamlet* [?] (old play [?])
The Merry Wives of Windsor	Not known
Troilus and Cressida	Chaucer, *Troilus and Criseyde* (narrative poem); Lydgate, *Siege of Troy* [?] (poem); Homer, *Iliad* (epic, Chapman's translation [?])
All's Well that Ends Well	Boccaccio, *Decameron:* Story of Giletta of Narbonne (Italian romance; retold in Painter, *The Palace of Pleasure*)
Measure for Measure	Whetstone, *Promos and Cassandra* (play; also in form of novel in Whetstone's *Heptameron of Civil Discourses*); Cinthio, "Epitia" (Italian story in Cinthio's *Hecatommithi;* also a play)
Othello	Cinthio, *Hecatommithi:* Tale of the Moor (Italian novella)

King Lear	*The True Chronicle History of King Leir and His Three Daughters* (old play); Geoffrey of Monmouth, *History of the Kings of Britain* (history); Holinshed; Sidney, *Arcadia*, Book 2, chapter 10: Story of the King of Paphlagonia (English romance)
Macbeth	Holinshed
Antony and Cleopatra	Plutarch, "Life of Marcus Antonius" (North's translation)
Coriolanus	Plutarch, "Life of Caius Marcius Coriolanus" (North's translation)
Timon of Athens	Plutarch, "Life of Marcus Antonius," "Life of Alcibiades"
Pericles	Gower, *Confessio Amantis:* Story of Apollonius of Tyre (poem); Twine, *The Pattern of Painful Adventure* (English novel)
Cymbeline	Holinshed; Boccaccio, *Decameron:* Story of Bernabo of Genoa
The Winter's Tale	Greene, *Pandosto: The Triumph of Time* (pastoral romance)
The Tempest	Not known
Henry VIII	Holinshed; John Foxe, *Book of Martyrs* (Protestant history)
The Two Noble Kinsmen	Chaucer, *The Knight's Tale* (verse romance)

NOTES

1. See T. H. Howard-Hill, *Shakespearian Bibliography and Textual Criticism: A Bibliography* (Oxford: Clarendon, 1971).
2. E. K. Chambers, *William Shakespeare: A Study of Facts and Problems*, 2 vols. (Oxford: Clarendon, 1930), 2: 230.

3. See Gerald Eades Bentley, *The Profession of Dramatist in Shakespeare's Time* (Princeton: Princeton University Press, 1971).

4. Karl J. Holzknecht, *The Backgrounds of Shakespeare's Plays* (New York: American Book, 1950), pp. 344–345. See also E. K. Chambers, *The Elizabethan Stage*, 4 vols. (Oxford: Clarendon, 1923), 3: 182.

5. It has been argued that the theater usually received a fair copy rather than foul papers; see Fredson Bowers, *On Editing Shakespeare* (Charlottesville: University Press of Virginia, 1966), pp. 13–19. Among Bowers's other important works in this area, see "Shakespeare's Text and the Bibliographical Method," *Studies in Bibliography* 6 (1954): 71–91; *Bibliography and Textual Criticism* (Oxford: Clarendon, 1964); and "Textual Criticism," *The Reader's Encyclopedia of Shakespeare*, eds. Oscar James Campbell and Edward G. Quinn (New York: T. Y. Crowell, 1966), pp. 864–869.

6. On the fate of manuscripts in Elizabethan playhouses, see Chambers, *William Shakespeare*, 1: 92–125 and W. W. Greg, *The Editorial Problem in Shakespeare*, 3d ed. (Oxford: Clarendon, 1954), pp. 22–48.

7. In counting nineteen, I include *Pericles*, which is now considered to be mainly by Shakespeare; *Othello*, which appeared in 1622, when the First Folio was well under way; and the two plays that are presumably unauthorized versions of *2* and *3 Henry VI* respectively, *The First Part of the Contention betwixt the Two Famous Houses of York and Lancaster* (1954) and *The True Tragedy of Richard Duke of York* (1595).

8. See, for example, W. W. Greg, *The Shakespeare First Folio: Its Bibliographical and Textual History* (Oxford: Clarendon, 1955), pp. 72–73. Two major contributions of Alfred W. Pollard are: *Shakespeare's Folios and Quartos: A Study in the Bibliography of Shakespeare's Plays* (London: Methuen, 1909) and *Shakespeare's Fight with the Pirates and the Problems of the Transmission of His Text*, 2d ed. (Cambridge: Cambridge University Press, 1920).

9. Chambers, *William Shakespeare*, 1: 138.

10. Holzknecht, *The Backgrounds of Shakespeare's Plays*, p. 366.

11. Chambers, *William Shakespeare*, 2: 228–229.

12. Gerald Eades Bentley, *Shakespeare: A Biographical Handbook* (New Haven: Yale University Press, 1961), pp. 188–189.

13. The most complete study of the printing of the Folio is Charlton Hinman, *The Printing and Proof-Reading of the First Folio of Shakespeare*, 2 vols. (Oxford: Clarendon, 1963). An older account, still valuable, is Edwin E. Willoughby, *The Printing of the First Folio of Shakespeare* (Oxford: Oxford University Press, 1932). See also John W. Shroeder, *The Great Folio of 1623: Shakespeare's Plays in the Printing House* (Hamden, Conn.: Shoe String, 1956).

14. Chambers, *William Shakespeare*, 1: 144.

15. On the role of computers, see two articles in R. A. Wisbey, ed., *The Computer in Literary and Linguistic Research* (Cambridge: Cambridge University Press, 1971): Harold Love, "The Computer and Literary Editing: Achievements and Prospects" (pp. 47–56) and R. L. Widmann, "The Computer in Historical Collation: Use of the IBM 360/75 in Collating Multiple Editions of *A Midsummer Night's Dream*" (pp. 57–63). See also L. Marder, "Computer Scholar-

ship," *A Reader's Encyclopedia of Shakespeare*, p. 137. For a practical application, with limited results, see Dolores M. Burton, *Shakespeare's Grammatical Style: A Computer-Assisted Analysis of Richard II and Antony and Cleopatra* (Austin: University of Texas Press, 1973).

16. See T. H. Howard-Hill's computer-assisted analysis, *Ralph Crane and Some Shakespeare First Folio Comedies* (Charlottesville: University Press of Virginia, 1972).

17. In addition to the various works of Pollard, Greg, Chambers, and Bowers, see two major studies by Ronald B. McKerrow: *An Introduction to Bibliography for Literary Students* (Oxford: Clarendon, 1927) and *Prolegomena for the Oxford Shakespeare: A Study in Editorial Method* (Oxford: Clarendon, 1939). An important but highly specialized study is Alice Walker, *Textual Problems of the First Folio* (Cambridge: Cambridge University Press, 1953), which argues that the Folio texts of *2 Henry IV*, *Hamlet*, and *Othello* were printed from annotated quarto copy. But J. K. Walton, *The Quarto Copy for the First Folio of Shakespeare* (Dublin: Dublin University Press, 1971), believes that these three Folio texts were all printed from a manuscript.

18. The later Folios have been carefully examined by Matthew W. Black and Matthias A. Shaaber, *Shakespeare's Seventeenth Century Editors, 1632–1685* (New York: Modern Language Association, 1937).

19. For a brief account of editors and editions, see Thomas Marc Parrott, *William Shakespeare: A Handbook*, rev. ed. (New York: Scribner, 1955), pp. 208–213. See also Allardyce Nicoll's informative essay, "The Editors of Shakespeare from First Folio to Malone," *Studies in the First Folio*, ed. Sir Israel Gollancz (London: Oxford University Press, 1924), pp. 157–178; and Arthur Brown, " 'The Great Variety of Readers,' " *Shakespeare Survey* 18 (1965): 11–22.

20. Hinman, *First Folio of Shakespeare*, 1: 180–226; 2: 504–529.

21. Ibid., 1: 227. Aided by an optical machine he devised to speed up the collation of texts as well as by an electronic computer, Professor Hinman compared most of the seventy-nine copies of the Folio that are in the Folger Library in Washington, D.C.

22. The classic statement of the case for Shakespeare's participation in the manuscript play is the joint effort of a number of scholars, including Sir E. M. Thompson, a distinguished handwriting expert. See Alfred W. Pollard, W. W. Greg, E. M. Thompson, J. Dover Wilson, and R. W. Chambers, *Shakespeare's Hand in the Play of Sir Thomas More* (Cambridge: Cambridge University Press, 1923). For a fascinating brief account, see John Dover Wilson, "The New Way with Shakespeare's Texts," *Shakespeare Survey* 9 (1956): 69–80.

23. See Bowers, *On Editing Shakespeare*, pp. 120–122. Specific emendations and restorations are the subject of C. J. Sisson's important book, *New Readings in Shakespeare*, 2 vols. (Cambridge: Cambridge University Press, 1956).

24. Sisson (*New Readings in Shakespeare*, 2: 208) prefers "solid."

25. See Peter Alexander, "Restoring Shakespeare: The Modern Editor's Task," *Shakespeare Survey* 5 (1952): 7.

26. Ibid., p. 5. The Montano and Shylock restorations are also discussed in Sisson, *New Readings in Shakespeare*, 2: 252 and 1: 138–139, respectively.

27. Thomas W. Baldwin, *Shakespere's Love's Labor's Won: New Evidence from the Account Books of an Elizabethan Bookseller* (Carbondale: Southern Illinois University Press, 1957).

28. Chambers, *William Shakespeare*, 2: 344.

29. A celebrated instance of this approach to Shakespeare is Edward Dowden, *Shakespeare: A Critical Study of His Mind and Art*, 6th ed. (London: Kegan Paul, 1882).

30. For the chronology of Shakespeare's nondramatic works, see pp. 66–67, 77, and 88.

31. See James G. McManaway, "Recent Studies in Shakespeare's Chronology," *Shakespeare Survey* 3 (1950): 22–33.

32. The first version of *1 Henry VI* has been put back to 1589–1590, with a possible revision in 1594, 1595, or 1598.

33. Although some scholars would move *The Comedy of Errors* back to the late 1580s, the fact that it was acted in 1594 in what may have been its first performance makes so early a date unlikely. Moreover, the maturity of its structure argues for a later date.

34. It is possible that *Titus Andronicus* was written, either all or in part by Shakespeare, in the late 1580s and reworked in 1593–1594.

35. Some say that *Love's Labour's Lost* was written in the late 1580s; others would make it 1593; and still others place it as late as 1596. The problem is exceptionally difficult.

36. *Romeo and Juliet* could plausibly be dated 1596.

37. If, as many believe, the play was written to celebrate a specific wedding, *A Midsummer Night's Dream* could be dated any year from 1590 to 1600, depending upon which wedding one happens to think Shakespeare was honoring. Of the alternatives to Chambers's 1595–1596, 1594 and 1596 seem the most acceptable. The dubious allusion to bad weather could apply to almost any year.

38. The problem with *King John* lies in its relationship with an earlier play, *The Troublesome Reign of John King of England*. If, as some believe, this earlier play was not merely Shakespeare's source but was actually written by him—it has even been suggested that *The Troublesome Reign* was a bad quarto of *King John*—then the date of *King John* would have to be set around 1591.

39. The first part of *Henry IV* may have been written a year sooner, in 1596.

40. A more likely date for *Twelfth Night* is 1601 or 1602.

41. Chambers himself later said that *Hamlet* could not have been produced before 1601. But the situation is confused by the so-called *Ur-Hamlet*, a play, not extant, which seems to have been in existence in 1589. There is also evidence that a Hamlet play was in the repertory in 1594.

42. This may be much earlier, a convincing case having been made that the play was first performed for the Feast of the Order of the Garter, April 23, 1597.

43. *Othello* may belong to the preceding season, 1603–1604.

44. *Coriolanus* may have been written in 1609.

45. The date of *Pericles* is complicated by the authorship question, but 1606–1607 is a possibility.

46. See nos. F277 and N17 in Morris Palmer Tilley, *A Dictionary of the Proverbs in England in the Sixteenth and Seventeenth Centuries* (Ann Arbor: University of Michigan Press, 1950), pp. 215–216, 489.

47. See Ernst Robert Curtius, *European Literature and the Latin Middle Ages*, trans. Willard R. Trask (New York: Pantheon, 1953), pp. 128–144.

48. The most complete collection of sources and analogues, together with good critical commentary, is Geoffrey Bullough's recently completed *Narrative and Dramatic Sources of Shakespeare*, 8 vols. (New York: Columbia University Press, 1957–1975). The reader may also consult John Payne Collier and W. Carew Hazlitt, eds., *Shakespeare's Library*, 2d ed., 6 vols. (London: Reeves and Turner, 1875); Kenneth Muir, *Shakespeare's Sources* (London: Methuen, 1957); W. G. Boswell-Stone, *Shakespere's Holinshed*, 2d ed. (London: Chatto & Windus, 1907); Richard Hosley, ed., *Shakespeare's Holinshed* (New York: Putnam, 1968); C. F. Tucker Brooke, ed., *Shakespeare's Plutarch*, 2 vols. (New York: Duffield & Company, 1909).

For a fascinating reconstruction of Shakespeare's mental processes during the composition of *King John, King Lear,* and other plays, see Jacob Isaacs, *Shakespeare's Earliest Years in the Theatre* (London: Geoffrey Cumberlege, 1953).

Several plays have recently been linked with English Catholic polemical pamphlets; see David Kaula, *Shakespeare and the Archpriest Controversy: A Study of Some New Sources* (The Hague: Mouton, 1975).

49. *The Troublesome Reign of King John,* Part 2, 11. 1185–1196, in Bullough, *Sources*, 4: 151.

50. On this passage, see Isaacs, *Shakespeare's Earliest Years in the Theatre*, p. 124.

51. John Dryden, *Essays*, ed. W. P. Ker (Oxford: Clarendon, 1900), 1: 192–193.

52. Bullough, *Sources*, 4: 184.

53. Ibid., p. 185.

54. Ibid., p. 278.

55. Brooke, ed., *Shakespeare's Plutarch*, 2: 177–178.

56. Ibid., pp. 38–39.

57. For some illuminating commentary upon Shakespeare's transformation of Cinthio, see Harley Granville-Barker, *Prefaces to Shakespeare*, 2 vols. (Princeton: Princeton University Press, 1946–1947), 2: 3–9. I have not personally seen Max Bluestone, *From Story to Stage* (The Hague: Mouton, 1974), which is said to be especially valuable for its discussion of *Othello* and *The Winter's Tale* and their narrative sources.

3
Narrative and Lyric Poems

Shakespeare's narrative and lyric verse ranks with the best of English poetry, although it does not match the achievement of his plays. Its volume is relatively small, totaling less than the number of lines in two plays of average length.[1] At one period in his life Shakespeare was probably better known for *Venus and Adonis* than for any of his works for the stage. In our own day, however, the sonnets (and a mere handful at that) are the only nondramatic poems that have managed to attract a substantial reading public; and even among specialists, this poetry is frequently dissected for supposed clues to Shakespeare's personal life rather than enjoyed for its own sake.

Nevertheless, there are reasons for taking serious notice of Shakespeare's nondramatic writings. For one thing, they are interesting in their own right. While remaining representative of the age in which they were produced, they are enlivened throughout by the author's special touch. These poems also reveal Shakespeare in the fascinating process of finding himself as an artist, and they point ahead to some of the paths he was to follow in the great plays of his maturity. It has often been observed that Shakespeare was a poet before he grew into a dramatist.[2] The seeds of the dramatist are to a large extent contained in the poet.

The works discussed in this chapter include the two Ovidian narratives, *Venus and Adonis* and *The Rape of Lucrece;* the *Sonnets;* and a curious poem generally considered part of the Shakespeare canon, *The Phoenix and Turtle.*

NARRATIVES: *VENUS AND ADONIS* AND
THE RAPE OF LUCRECE

The first of Shakespeare's works to appear in print was a long narrative poem called *Venus and Adonis,* which was both registered and printed (in quarto) in 1593. One year later a second long narrative, *The Rape of Lucrece,* was published (also in quarto). We do not know when either poem was actually written, but they are usually assigned to the two seasons during which the London theaters were shut down because of a plague: *Venus and Adonis* to 1592–1593 and *The Rape of Lucrece* to 1593–1594. In the dedication to *Venus and Adonis,* Shakespeare refers to the poem as "the first heir of my invention." Since he had undoubtedly written a number of plays before 1593, the phrase is ordinarily taken to mean simply that *Venus and Adonis* was his first work intended for publication. To some scholars, however, "the first heir of my invention" implies "the earliest work of all," in which case a date in the late 1580s could be correct for *Venus and Adonis* and possibly *The Rape of Lucrece* as well.[3] It has been suggested that Shakespeare probably did not write such fashionable poems until he came to London, where Ovidian narratives were the rage. But he could have arrived as early as 1585 or 1586. Moreover, Ovid was an integral part of every schoolboy's education during the Renaissance, and Shakespeare must have been well acquainted with his poetry before he left Stratford.

Ovid's influence upon Renaissance writers was perhaps stronger than that of any other classical author. Virgil had dominated the early Middle Ages. From the eleventh century on, however, Publius Ovidius Naso (c. 43 B.C.–A.D. 17) gained in popularity, both in England and on the Continent. Shakespeare and his contemporaries admired Ovid for his brilliance as a storyteller who infused the pagan myths with humor, sensuousness, and refinement. Not only were his works, particularly the *Metamorphoses,* frequently translated and paraphrased, but they were often interpreted along lines acceptable to Christian morality. A good deal of Ovid could be considered licentious, and the only way to make his fables suitable for educational purposes was to read them allegorically for the Christian truths that supposedly lay hidden under their cloak of wantonness. By Shakespeare's time the theological emphasis had been largely abandoned, but in many instances Ovid's tales were still read as moral, if not religious, allegories.[4]

As evidence of their esteem for Ovid's literary craftsmanship, Elizabethan writers produced a flood of narrative poems based upon episodes in the *Metamorphoses,* the *Amores,* the *Fasti,* and the *Tristia.* These adaptations include Thomas Lodge's *Scilla's Metamorphosis* (1589); Marlowe's *Hero and Leander* (1593), with its continuation by George Chapman (1598); and Michael Drayton's *Endimion and Phoebe* (1595). To this Ovidian tradition belong *Venus and Adonis* and, to a lesser degree, *The Rape of Lucrece.*

The story of Venus's love for Adonis is told in Ovid's *Metamorphoses* (10:519–559, 705–739). In Ovid's version Venus, the goddess of love, having inadvertently been grazed by one of Cupid's arrows, becomes smitten with the beauty of an incomparable mortal, offers herself to him, and abandons all other pastimes in order to remain his constant companion. She warns the courageous boy, who delights in hunting, to keep away from ferocious animals—the wild boar, the ravenous wolf, the bear, the lion—lest they take his life and leave her bereft. But Adonis ignores the advice, sets upon a boar with his hounds, and pierces him with a spear. The enraged boar pursues Adonis and gores him with his tusks. When Venus beholds her beloved lying dead in the sand, she sprinkles his blood with nectar and causes a red flower, the anemone, to spring up from it. There is no suggestion in Ovid, as there is in Shakespeare, that Adonis is unwilling to accept Venus's favors or indifferent to her torments. This element Shakespeare seems to have derived from two other episodes in the *Metamorphoses,* the tales of Salmacis and Hermaphroditus (4: 347–481) and of Echo and Narcissus (3: 427–452, 635–642).[5] He may also have been influenced by the Hippolytus myth, particularly as it reached him through Seneca's *Hippolytus.*

Venus and Adonis, written in six-line iambic pentameter stanzas rhyming *a b a b c c,* is dedicated to Henry Wriothesley, third earl of Southampton. Some have noted that its subject and style are tailored to the young patron's taste for elegant poetry in the Ovidian erotic tradition.[6] In fact, A. L. Rowse maintains that the situation depicted in the poem, that of a handsome youth who refuses to let a woman possess him, corresponds with Southampton's reluctance to marry and with a similar disinclination on the part of the mysterious friend to whom many of Shakespeare's sonnets are addressed. From this Rowse infers that Southampton (Adonis) is the friend.[7] There are, to be sure, parallels between the first seventeen sonnets, which urge the friend to marry, and the speech in which Venus attempts to persuade Adonis to partake of love and to leave a copy of his beauty for posterity:

> "Torches are made to light, jewels to wear,
> Dainties to taste, fresh beauty for the use,
> Herbs for their smell, and sappy plants to bear.
> Things growing to themselves are growth's abuse.
>   Seeds spring from seeds, and beauty breedeth beauty.
>   Thou wast begot; to get it is thy duty.
>
> "Upon the earth's increase why shouldst thou feed
> Unless the earth with they increase be fed?
> By law of nature thou art bound to breed,
> That thine may live when thou thyself art dead;
>   And so, in spite of death, thou dost survive,
>   In that thy likeness still is left alive."

(163–174)

But this theme appears again and again in Renaissance literature; for example, it is the argument used by Milton's Comus in his unsuccessful attempt to undermine the Lady's chastity. It would be a mistake to interpret either the passage or the poem as a whole on the basis of doubtful biographical inferences.

It would also be a mistake to insist (as some critics have done) that Shakespeare sympathizes with Venus. So far as Adonis is concerned, the goddess's passionate entreaties proceed not from love but from lust, and the young man makes a careful distinction, in expertly balanced clauses, between the two emotions:

> "Love comforteth like sunshine after rain,
> But Lust's effect is tempest after sun.
> Love's gentle spring doth always fresh remain;
> Lust's winter comes ere summer half be done.
>   Love surfeits not, Lust like a glutton dies;
>   Love is all truth, Lust full of forged lies."
>   (799–804)

When Venus kisses Adonis on the brow and cheek, she is compared to a predatory eagle that devours "till either gorge be stuff'd or prey be gone" (58). The good-night kiss, which she all but forces Adonis to grant, similarly points up her carnal appetite:

> Now quick desire hath caught the yielding prey,
> And glutton-like she feeds, yet never filleth.
> Her lips are conquerors, his lips obey,
> Paying what ransom the insulter willeth;
>   Whose vulture thought doth pitch the price so high
>   That she will draw his lips' rich treasure dry.
>
> And having felt the sweetness of the spoil,
> With blindfold fury she begins to forage.
> Her face doth reek and smoke, her blood doth boil,
> And careless lust stirs up a desperate courage,
>   Planting oblivion, beating reason back,
>   Forgetting shame's pure blush and honour's wrack.
>   (547–558)

Hardly a flattering portrait! Her animalistic wooing resembles Adonis's hunting of the boar.[8] It has been proposed, on the basis of the moralizing tradition behind the Renaissance reading of Ovid, that the poem is a Christian allegory, with Venus representing unbridled lust and Adonis unfallen man steadfast in his devotion to reason.[9] Such a view may be extreme, but it serves as a corrective to the equally one-sided notion that Adonis is a prig or a coquette[10] and that the poem is a celebration of sexual love. Far from arousing unmixed sympathy, Venus seems almost ridiculous in her lechery. Her sensuality is skillfully contrasted with Adonis's naive idealism.[11]

In any case, *Venus and Adonis* is a myth, not a psychological drama or moral treatise,[12] and it should not be taken too seriously. Shakespeare entertains his readers, in part with the hero's obtuse innocence but to a greater degree with the incongruous spectacle of all-powerful Venus as "the archetype of the romantic heroines who yearn to submit to their lovers."[13] The irony is stated most simply in some typical Shakespearean wordplay, "She's Love, she loves, and yet she is not lov'd" (610). Taking her cue from Renaissance poetry, Venus acts her unaccustomed role according to the rules. As she enfolds Adonis in her arms and "locks her lily fingers one in one" (228), she resorts to a florid image (with anatomical overtones) in the style of the Petrarchan sonneteer (see pp. 79–81):

> "Fondling," she saith, "since I have hemm'd thee here
> Within the circuit of this ivory pale,
> I'll be a park, and thou shalt be my deer;
> Feed where thou wilt, on mountain or in dale;
>   Graze on my lips; and if those hills be dry,
>   Stray lower, where the pleasant fountains lie.
>
> "Within this limit is relief enough,
> Sweet bottom-grass, and high delightful plain,
> Round rising hillocks, brakes obscure and rough,
> To shelter thee from tempest and from rain.
>   Then be my deer, since I am such a park.
>   No dog shall rouse thee, though a thousand bark."
>   (229–240)

The Petrarchan lover was expected to suffer a welter of conflicting emotions, and Venus conforms to the pattern:

> "O, where am I?" quoth she, "in earth or heaven,
> Or in the ocean drench'd, or in the fire?
> What hour is this? or morn or weary even?
> Do I delight to die, or life desire?
>   But now I liv'd, and life was death's annoy;
>   But now I died, and death was lively joy."
>   (493–498)

She is at first convinced that the boar did not see Adonis's face; if he had, he would have spared the youth. But later she reasons that the boar *did* see him and killed him accidentally while giving him a kiss.

" 'Had I been tooth'd like him, I must confess, / With kissing him I should have kill'd him first' " (1117–1118). Here Shakespeare laughs at romantic love and at the rhetoric in which it is conventionally expressed.[14] This, we shall see, is a major theme of the comedies, although one misses in *Venus and Adonis* the warmth that permeates *As You Like It* or *Twelfth Night*.

For most readers *Venus and Adonis* is memorable primarily for the way in which the sophisticated Ovidian erotic tradition has been freshened by a wealth of closely observed details from outdoor life: Adonis's steed catching sight of "a breeding jennet" (260) and tearing after her in high passion (a hint to Adonis!); "poor Wat," the frightened hare, pursued by hounds and turning frantically in a dozen different directions (679–708); the lark rising to awaken the morning (853–858). Particularly effective is the image of Venus's eyes withdrawing from the sight of the dead Adonis:

> Or as the snail, whose tender horns being hit,
> Shrinks backward in his shelly cave with pain,
> And there, all smooth'red up, in shade doth sit,
> Long after fearing to creep forth again;
>   So at his bloody view her eyes are fled
>   Into the deep-dark cabins of her head.
>   (1033–1038)

Coleridge, in a notable passage, analyzes the famous image that depicts Adonis's final departure from Venus, "Look how a bright star shooteth from the sky— / So glides he in the night from Venus' eye" (815–816):

> How many images and feelings are here brought together without effort and without discord—the beauty of Adonis—the rapidity of his flight—the yearning yet hopelessness of the enamoured gazer—and a shadowy ideal character thrown over the whole.[15]

There is almost too much music in *Venus and Adonis*. The young poet is sometimes intoxicated with images, spinning them out without due regard for narrative or dramatic context. Nevertheless, the poem in its very exuberance reveals Shakespeare's strength even as it offers evidence of his immaturity.

In the dedication to *Venus and Adonis* Shakespeare apologizes for his "unpolish'd lines" and promises to honor Southampton "with some graver labour." *The Rape of Lucrece*, published one year later in 1594, is probably the work he had in mind. The dedication to *Lucrece* is warmer than the earlier one, a fact that has led some scholars to postulate a deepening friendship between the poet and his patron, thereby reinforcing the claim that the "Mr. W. H." of the sonnets is Southampton. Once again we are in the realm of conjecture rather than verifiable fact.

The Rape of Lucrece, written in rhyme royal (stanzas of seven iambic pentameter lines, rhyming *a b a b b c c*), recounts one of the most familiar tales in classical literature. Found originally in Ovid's *Fasti* (2: 721–852) and in Livy's *Roman History* (Book 1, chapters 57–59), the story of Tarquin's assault upon the chaste Lucrece had been part of Chaucer's *Legend of Good Women* (c. 1386) and had appeared in several Renaissance collections—for example, William Painter's *Palace of Pleasure* (1566), where it closely follows Livy's narrative. Ovid may be considered the principal source, but the extent to which Shakespeare knew and utilized other versions has not been clearly established.[16]

The situation is essentially the same in most versions: While the Romans are besieging Ardea, the Emperor's son Sextus Tarquinius hears from Lucrece's husband Collatine of her incomparable chastity and resolves to visit her secretly in Rome. When Tarquin sees her, he becomes inflamed with lust. At night he steals into her bedchamber and, despite her pleas, ravishes her. Lucrece bemoans her fate, then summons Collatine home to inform him of the outrage. Rather than live in what to her is a state of defilement, she plunges a knife into her breast. Her body is borne in triumph through the streets of Rome; the Tarquins, father and son, are banished.

Shakespeare's *Lucrece* belongs in some respects to a literary genre known as the *complaint*.[17] In the typical complaint (for example, Samuel Daniel's *Complaint of Rosamond* [1592]) the ghost of some victim, often a wronged woman, appears before the poet and the world in order to reveal its unhappy fate. But Shakespeare dispenses with the ghost, preferring to tell his story in the third person. Consequently, he achieves dramatic effects that would not be possible in a first-person narrative and is able to provide vivid psychological insight into both Tarquin and Lucrece. Shakespeare handles the story almost as if he were writing for the stage.

If one considers the dramatic elements in the poem, then it is possibly Tarquin, not Lucrece, who occupies the central position. Like many of Shakespeare's tragic figures, Tarquin suffers both before and after his crime.[18] As he lights the torch that will guide him to Lucrece's bed, he experiences a fierce debate " 'tween frozen conscience and hot-burning will" (247). His words anticipate Othello's poignant "Put out the light, and then put out the light":

> "Fair torch, burn out thy light, and lend it not
> To darken her whose light excelleth thine!
> And die, unhallowed thoughts, before you blot

With your uncleanness that which is divine!
Offer pure incense to so pure a shrine.
    Let fair humanity abhor the deed
    That spots and stains love's modest snow-white weed."
                                        (190–196)

As Tarquin moves toward Lucrece's chamber, there are omens that
nature frowns upon his deed: A door grates; the wind almost extinguishes
his torch; a needle pricks his finger as he picks up Lucrece's glove (302–
322). But in his aroused emotional state Tarquin deliberately misinterprets
these warnings to heighten his lust. They are

"Like little frosts that sometime threat the spring
To add a more rejoicing to the prime
And give the sneaped [nipped with cold] birds more cause to sing."
                                        (331–333)

He confesses to Lucrece that his will is deaf to the promptings of reason—
a serious breach of Renaissance moral doctrine:

"I have debated even in my soul
What wrong, what shame, what sorrow I shall breed;
But nothing can affection's course control
Or stop the headlong fury of his speed.
I know repentant tears ensue the deed[,]
    Reproach, disdain, and deadly enmity;
    Yet strive I to embrace mine infamy."
                                        (498–504)

Once his lust is satisfied, Tarquin creeps away "like a thievish dog"
(736), hating his victory so despicably gained. He may not win our
sympathies, but he is in some respects a rough draft for Macbeth and,
even more, for the tormented Angelo in *Measure for Measure*, both of
whom are victims of passions they cannot control.

Although the presentation of Lucrece may be more stylized than that
of Tarquin, her conduct raises some interesting moral questions. According to the theology of St. Augustine and other medieval and Renaissance Christian writers, she is tainted. She should not have yielded to
Tarquin; or, if forced to submit, she should not have committed the
mortal sin of suicide but should have lived secure in the knowledge that
her chastity, as distinguished from her fleshly honor, remained undefiled.
Near the end of the poem Brutus upbraids Collatine for planning to
follow his wife's example of suicide:

"Why, Collatine, is woe the cure for woe?
Do wounds help wounds, or grief help grievous deeds?
Is it revenge to give thyself a blow

For his foul act by whom thy fair wife bleeds?
Such childish humour from weak minds proceeds.
  Thy wretched wife mistook the matter so,
  To slay herself that should have slain her foe."
                    (1821–1827)

However virtuous she may have been according to Roman doctrine,
Lucrece does not meet the standard demanded of the Christian wife, and
the reader should recognize the possibility that Shakespeare regarded
her behavior with this ambivalence.[19]

Whatever one's view of Lucrece's virtue, few would dispute the fact
that she has a flair for the rhetorical. Even in desperation, as when trying
to dissuade Tarquin, she enjoys turning a phrase. " 'This deed will make
thee only lov'd for fear; / But happy monarchs still are fear'd for love' "
(610–611). She smothers him with analogies; and when he speaks of
his "uncontrolled tide" (645) and of the "petty streams that pay a daily
debt / To their salt sovereign" (649–650), she simply will not let the
image alone:

"Thou art," quoth she, "a sea, a sovereign king;
And, lo, there falls into thy boundless flood
Black lust, dishonour, shame, misgoverning,
Who seek to stain the ocean of thy blood.
If all these petty ills shall change thy good,
  The sea within a puddle's womb is hearsed,
  And not the puddle in thy sea dispersed."
                    (652–658)

Lucrece later inveighs successively against Night, Opportunity, and
Time—the three impersonal forces that conspired with Tarquin to ruin
her. Her supply of metaphors is well-nigh inexhaustible:

"O comfort-killing Night, image of hell!
Dim register and notary of shame!
Black stage for tragedies and murthers fell!
Vast sin-concealing chaos! nurse of blame!
Blind muffled bawd! dark harbour for defame!
  Grim cave of death! whisp'ring conspirator
  With close-tongu'd treason and the ravisher!"
                    (764–770)

One is reminded of the deposition scene in *Richard II* (see p. 244) as
Lucrece ritualistically makes bequests of her soul and body, her resolution, her honor, her shame, and her fame (1177–1211); and she summons all her rhetorical energy to curse Tarquin:

"Let him have time to tear his curled hair,
Let him have time against himself to rave,
Let him have time of Time's help to despair,
Let him have time to live a loathed slave,
Let him have time a beggar's orts [scraps] to crave,
    And time to see one that by alms doth live
    Disdain to him disdained scraps to give."
                                        (981–987)

After several hundred lines of this kind of ingenious harangue, Lucrece brings her lamentation to a majestic climax by reflecting upon a painting of Troy and comparing her sorrows to those of Hecuba, the fallen Trojan queen. Then, as Lucrece identifies herself with King Priam, Tarquin (at first compared to Paris) is transformed into the villainous Sinon, who persuaded the Trojans to accept the wooden horse (*Aeneid* 2):

"For even as subtile Sinon here is painted,
So sober-sad, so weary, and so mild—
As if with grief or travail he had fainted—
To me came Tarquin armed; so beguil'd
With outward honesty, but yet defil'd
    With inward vice. As Priam him did cherish,
    So did I Tarquin; so my Troy did perish."
                                        (1541–1547)

The painting is a brilliant piece of moral heraldry, a pictorial emblem of the situation depicted in the poem.[20]

Shakespeare has prepared for this Trojan episode by using images of combat throughout the poem, which begins during a military siege. When Tarquin first sees Lucrece, he is captivated by the battle raging in her face between "Beauty's red and Virtue's white" (65), a war familiar to readers of Renaissance love poetry. He claims Affection as his captain. " 'And when his gaudy banner is display'd, / The coward fights and will not be dismay'd' " (272–273). Cheered on by his "drumming heart" (435), he *marches* to her bed; his hand on her breast is a battering ram assaulting "an ivory wall" (463–464). Before launching his attack, Tarquin tries to negotiate:

First like a trumpet doth his tongue begin
To sound a parley to his heartless foe:
Who o'er the white sheet peers her whiter chin,
The reason of this rash alarm to know.
                                        (470–473)

After the rape "troops of cares" are mustered to inquire as to the condition of "the spotted princess"—his soul: " 'She says her subjects with foul insurrection / Have batter'd down her consecrated wall'" (720–723). Meanwhile, Lucrece, "her mansion batter'd by the enemy," wants to die, to make a hole in her "blemish'd fort" (her body) so that her soul may find release (1170–1176). Thus, in the siege of Troy the poet has found an "objective correlative" for Lucrece's war with Tarquin. The painting reinforces her emotions even as it conventionalizes them.

The Rape of Lucrece, though coherent and impressive in design, is not a total success. As in the case of *Venus and Adonis*, there is too much moralizing. One also finds, as before, an accumulation of images, a heaping up of rhetorical extravagances, and a barrage of wordplay. But *Lucrece*, again like *Venus and Adonis*, may be enjoyed in part because it is so audaciously opulent.

SONNETS

In 1609 the publisher Thomas Thorpe, perhaps acting without authorization from the poet, issued a quarto containing 154 sonnets by Shakespeare. Thorpe supplied the following peculiarly worded dedication:

TO. THE. ONLIE. BEGETTER. OF.
THESE. INSVING. SONNETS.
M^R. W. H. ALL. HAPPINESSE.
AND. THAT. ETERNITIE.
PROMISED.
BY.
OVR. EVER-LIVING. POET.
WISHETH.
THE. WELL-WISHING.
ADVENTVRER. IN.
SETTING.
FORTH.
T. T.

Thorpe could scarcely have predicted that his little volume, with its obscure dedication, would arouse more controversy than almost any other book in the English language. But the problems it raises, interesting though they may be, should not stand in the way of our appreciation of the *Sonnets* as literature.

Problems. There are three major areas of debate concerning the sonnets: the date of their composition; the possible real-life identities of Mr. W. H. to whom they are dedicated and of the friend, the rival poet, and the dark lady who appear in the poems; and the extent to which the sonnets, either in their traditional sequence or in some rearrangement, tell a unified story that may be rooted in Shakespeare's personal experience.

Despite endless investigations into the subject, we simply do not know when the sonnets were written. Some—perhaps all—had to be in circulation by 1598, for Francis Meres mentions them in his *Palladis Tamia* of that year:

> As the soule of *Euphorbus* was thought to live in *Pythagoras:* so the sweete wittie soule of *Ovid* lives in mellifluous & hony-tongued *Shakespeare*, witnes his *Venus* and *Adonis*, his *Lucrece*, his sugred Sonnets among his private friends, &c.[21]

Scholars have searched the *Sonnets* for allusions to contemporary events, but with confusing results. Sonnet 107, for example, has been assigned to 1589, 1594, 1596, 1601, or 1603, according to whether the fifth line, "The mortal moon hath her eclipse endur'd," is taken to mean the defeat of the Armada; the execution of the Queen's physician, Dr. Lopez, who was accused of a plot to poison her; the Queen's recovery from an illness; the collapse of Essex's rebellion; or the release of the Earl of Southampton from prison following the accession of James I. As we have seen, verbal parallels can be found between the *Sonnets* and Shakespeare's narrative and dramatic verse of the 1590s, and some of the themes developed in the *Sonnets* are prominent in other poetry of the period.[22] Dispute continues, however, so that one must choose arbitrarily from among divergent and mutually incompatible theories, wait for the remote chance that incontestable proof may some day be forthcoming, or accept the *Sonnets* as "a miscellaneous collection of poems, written at different times, for different purposes, and with very different degrees of poetic intensity."[23]

Equally exasperating is the mystery of Mr. W. H. The situation is made more difficult by the ambiguous phrase, "onlie begetter," which seems to apply to him. Did Mr. W. H. inspire the poet to write the *Sonnets,* or did he merely give the manuscript to T. T., the printer Thomas Thorpe? And is Mr. W. H. the same person as the beautiful young friend who is addressed in so many of the sonnets? The two leading candidates for the role of Mr. W. H. are Henry Wriothesley, third earl of Southampton (1573–1620), to whom *Venus and Adonis* and *The Rape of Lucrece* had been dedicated, and William Herbert, third earl of Pembroke (1580–1630).[24] Oscar Wilde, taking up a suggestion originally made in the eighteenth century, produced a charming fantasy proving that Mr. W. H. was Willie Hughes, a nonexistent young actor in Shakespeare's company; and Leslie Hotson, in a display of virtuosity almost worthy of Sherlock Holmes, has followed a trail leading to William

Hatcliffe of Lincolnshire, who in 1588 presided as mock prince during festivities at Gray's Inn.[25] Hotson argues from the initial assumption that the sonnets were completed by the late 1580s. This reverses the usual procedure whereby a scholar first selects his favorite candidate, then ransacks the text of the *Sonnets* for allusions that might coincide with certain datable events in the man's life. Neither method is convincing.

Although the rival poet and the dark lady have attracted less attention than Mr. W. H., the confusion surrounding their identity is just as dense. Among the many nominees for the rival poet, who in several sonnets appears to have displaced the speaker from the affections of his friend, are Gervase Markham, Edmund Spenser, Christopher Marlowe, George Chapman, Ben Jonson, and John Donne, all contemporaries of Shakespeare. (But even Chaucer, who had been dead for 200 years, has been suggested!) The "dark lady," who is specifically referred to in twenty-six sonnets (127–152) but whose spirit hovers over several others, has usually been identified according to the critic's preference in the Mr. W. H. quarrel. Southamptionists generally incline to Mrs. John Davenant, mother of the Restoration poet and dramatist William Davenant. But if Pembroke is your man, the dark lady might be Mary Fitton, a young woman of doubtful respectability with whom the Earl of Pembroke was for a time infatuated.[26] According to A. L. Rowse, the dark lady was an Italian, Emilia Bassano, the wife of a musician (Will Lanier), who had previously been the mistress of the Lord Chamberlain (Henry Carey, first Lord Hunsdon); but this view has received little support.[27] These identifications are all based on guesswork.

The third problem, with its ramifications, is perhaps the most perplexing of all. Did Thorpe (in 1609) print the 154 sonnets in the order Shakespeare intended? For some, the answer is no, and attempts have been made, notably by Tucker Brooke, to rearrange the poems so as to present a coherent story.[28] Others defend the traditional order, arguing that each sonnet develops logically out of an earlier one and in most cases can be clearly connected with its immediate predecessor.[29] But it is possible, as some have suggested, that individual sheets got misplaced during the printing process, especially if Shakespeare did not personally supervise the undertaking. There is no external evidence one way or the other, and the original sequence at least has the virtues of familiarity and convenience.

Whether or not one accepts Thorpe's arrangement in the 1609 Quarto, speculation inevitably arises concerning the narrative structure of the *Sonnets* as a whole. Do the poems tell a continuous story? If so, does the story necessarily reflect real experiences in Shakespeare's life?

Whatever arrangement one may adopt for the *Sonnets*, the fact remains that the "plot" is thin. Sonnets 1–126 are generally said to be addressed to a young man of high social position with whom the poet develops a deep friendship. Sonnets 127–152 are written to or about the dark lady who captivates the poet, makes him a slave to lust, and then apparently casts her seductive spell upon the friend. (Sonnets 153 and 154, which conclude Thorpe's collection, are innocuous poems about Cupid, having little to do with the rest of the sequence.) The first seventeen sonnets urge the friend to marry and beget a child so that his incomparable beauty may be preserved for posterity. As the relationship between the two men progresses, there are fluctuations in situation and mood: The poet pledges to immortalize his friend in verse; they are separated on at least one occasion, during which time the poet is sustained by thoughts of their friendship; the poet chastises the young man for having robbed him of his mistress (perhaps the dark lady of the later sonnets), but forgives him; he becomes jealous because his friend seems to bestow patronage on other poets and on one rival poet in particular; they are reconciled; the poet contemplates old age and death, which will terminate the friendship. The action, such as it is, does not proceed smoothly, and there is no climax. Moreover, there is no substantial reason for assuming that all 154 poems refer to only one man and to only one woman. In fact, James Winny believes that the poet in the *Sonnets,* the friend, and the mistress are all imaginary, having been created out of Shakespeare's inner life rather than his actual experience.[30] Perhaps we should view the *Sonnets* as a loosely organized collection of quasi-dramatic situations that Shakespeare delineates from varied psychological and emotional perspectives.

Even if it could be shown conclusively that the sonnets tell a specific story, opinion would probably remain divided as to whether or not the story is autobiographical. Every piece of writing is in some way the author's personal revelation, the artistic synthesis of a host of conscious and unconscious recollections. But the true artist, particularly one with Shakespeare's gifts, comprehends a wider range of experience than he has directly undergone. Although critics frequently cite the sincerity of the sonnets to reinforce the claim that they are autobiographical, it seems that sincerity is communicated whenever an artist works with imagination and integrity. Sincerity is everywhere manifest in Shakespeare, perhaps to an even greater degree in the plays than in the *Sonnets.* Wordsworth was convinced that the sonnets were the key with which Shakespeare "unlocked his heart," but this romantic notion, like virtually all other speculations about the *Sonnets,* cannot be verified by any facts we now have.

The Sonnet Tradition. Behind the *Sonnets* of Shakespeare lies a literary tradition dating back to the Italian scholar and poet Francesco Petrarch (1304–1374). In addition to his copious writings in Latin, Petrarch composed well over 300 poems in Italian. Most are sonnets addressed to Laura, whom he may have known in real life, and they purport to record the inception and growth of his never-to-be-consummated love for her. These poems enjoyed enormous popularity in Italy and France, and they were eventually translated and imitated by English writers. During the Renaissance, particularly the sixteenth century, poets turned out thousands of sonnets, sometimes as independent lyrics but more often in sequences unified around a common story or theme.

The poets chiefly responsible for introducing the sonnet into England were Sir Thomas Wyatt (c. 1503–1542) and Henry Howard, earl of Surrey (c. 1517–1547), both of whom were published posthumously in an important anthology known as *Tottel's Miscellany* (1557). Thomas Watson's *Hecatompathia* (1582) is usually regarded as the first sonnet sequence in English, but the vogue reached its peak during the early 1590s with such works as Samuel Daniel's *Delia* (1592), Thomas Lodge's *Phyllis* (1593), and Michael Drayton's *Idea's Mirror* (1594). In addition to Shakespeare, two major poets produced sonnet sequences of rare distinction: Sir Philip Sidney (1554–1586), whose *Astrophel and Stella* (not published until 1591) tells the story of his love for Penelope Devereux, the wife of Lord Rich; and Edmund Spenser (c. 1552–1599), who celebrates in the *Amoretti* (1595) his love for Elizabeth Boyle (unusual in that it culminated in marriage). The sonnet continued in the mainstream of the English poetic tradition, as the works of Milton, Wordsworth, Keats, and Meredith (to name only a few) clearly attest. But, generally speaking, the sonnet sequence, as derived from Petrarch, did not survive the end of the sixteenth century.

From the sonnets of Petrarch and his disciples emerged the predominant pattern of Renaissance love poetry. The standard Petrarchan lover, whether he appears in lyric verse (like Sidney's Astrophel) or on the stage (like Romeo in the early scenes of *Romeo and Juliet*), worships at the shrine of a cruel-fair mistress, who is often the wife of another. Until Shakespeare's dark lady comes along to disrupt the stereotype, the mistress is customarily depicted with golden hair, eyes like the sun, lips of coral red, cheeks fair as roses, and teeth of pearly white. Upon encountering her divine beauty, the lover burns and freezes simultaneously; he scales the heights of exhilaration even as he is plunged into the depths of despair; he finds in the solitude of his bed nothing but an unremitting sleeplessness. His agonies may be expressed through recurring images: His heart may be compared to a fortress besieged by an invincible enemy or to a ship steered by a ruthless captain (Love) and tossed about on seas of indifference without hope of reaching port. By committing his grief to paper, the lover believes that he renders eternal his beloved's beauty as well as his own anguish, and to immortalize her physical charms he describes in detail her anatomical features. A Platonist of sorts, he identifies Love with Virtue, adoring his mistress because she is a copy of the ideal form of Beauty. But Virtue wages a running battle with Desire and makes him feel worse. Of these and other Petrarchan conventions, Shakespeare was thoroughly aware.[31]

In one respect Shakespeare departs radically from standard sonneteering: He addresses the bulk of his poems to a male friend rather than a female mistress. However, there is no reason to assume a homosexual element in their relationship. Although the sonnet literature of the Renaissance almost always celebrates the love of a man for a woman, writers in other genres regularly extol friendship between men as a worthier ideal. As we shall see, this bond (exemplified in the legendary Damon and Pythias) is at the root of Valentine's willingness, in *The Two Gentlemen of Verona*, to surrender to his friend all claim to his sweetheart. Furthermore, the term *lover* in Shakespeare's day did not have the exclusively sexual implication that it has today. Brutus's "Romans, countrymen, and lovers" (*Julius Caesar*, III, 2, 13) is identical in meaning with Mark Antony's "friends, Romans, countrymen." Shakespeare thus feels no hesitation in referring to his love for the young man or in using the vocabulary of Petrarchan love poetry to communicate his feeling. In one amusing sonnet (20) he suggests that Nature at first intended the friend to be a woman and gave him a woman's fair face, gentle heart, and bright eye. But Nature, herself a woman, fell in love with her creation and at the last minute made a slight addition, thereby precluding a physical relationship between the poet and his friend.

Although the term *sonnet* was often applied during the Renaissance to any short song, it is now generally defined more narrowly as a fourteen-line poem in iambic pentameter, conforming to certain specific structural and rhyming patterns. The Italian, or Petrarchan, sonnet is divided into two parts: the octave (eight lines) and the sestet (six lines), rhyming either *abbaabba cdcdcd* or *abbaabba cdecde*. The English sonnet (also called the Shakespearean, or Elizabethan, sonnet), which was popularized by Surrey, consists of three quatrains followed by a couplet; it rhymes *abab cdcd efef gg*. In a typical Shakespeare sonnet the quatrains state the subject, and the couplet summarizes what has been said, perhaps with a specific application to the poet's immediate situation. In a number of sonnets, however, Shakespeare also preserves the break in thought between what would be the octave and the sestet of the Italian sonnet, thus permitting himself, as far as poetic structure is concerned, to enjoy the best of both worlds.[32]

Literary Qualities. Many of Shakespeare's 154 sonnets must be reckoned among the very greatest lyrics in the English language. The full range of their artistry is revealed only in a close reading of the individual poems. The following discussion will be directed to some of their outstanding features.

The suffering lover does not loom large in Shakespeare's *Sonnets,* but his presence cannot be ignored. The poet sees himself as a slave (26, 57, 58), in bondage to the lord of his love:

> Being your slave, what should I do but tend
> Upon the hours and times of your desire?
> I have no precious time at all to spend,
> Nor services to do, till you require.
>
> (57)

He experiences the conventional sleeplessness of the Petrarchans (27, 28), a condition that evokes some of the familiar paradoxes dear to the hearts of Renaissance writers:

> When most I wink, then do mine eyes best see,
> For all the day they view things unrespected,
> But when I sleep, in dreams they look on thee
> And, darkly bright, are bright in dark directed.
>
> (43)

The couplet gives a final turn to the argument:

> All days are nights to see till I see thee,
> And nights bright days when dreams do show thee me.

In another sonnet (46) the eye and heart fight over how the spoils of battle should be divided:

> Mine eye and heart are at a mortal war
> How to divide the conquest of thy sight;
> Mine eye my heart thy picture's sight would bar,
> My heart mine eye the freedom of that right.

The verdict is rendered by a jury of thoughts impaneled for the purpose: The eye is awarded title to the beloved's outward beauty; the heart retains its rights to "thy inward love of heart."

On several occasions the poet rebels against the excesses of Petrarchism. He refuses to make the conventional comparison with sun, moon, or April flowers (21). While other poets resort to "strained touches" of rhetoric, he uses only "true plain words" (82). One of the most masterful sonnets (130) professes to repudiate poetic exaggeration:

My mistress' eyes are nothing like the sun;
Coral is far more red than her lips' red;
If snow be white, why then her breasts are dun;
If hairs be wires, black wires grow on her head.

About her face, voice, and carriage he has no illusions:

I grant I never saw a goddess go:
My mistress, when she walks, treads on the ground.

Then, with remarkable agility, the poet, having protested that his mistress is earthbound, in the very next line leaps verbally into the skies:

And yet, by heaven, I think my love as rare
As any she belied with false compare.

His mistress *is* divine, precisely because she is a real woman.[33]

"My Mistress' Eyes" has fun and warmth, qualities alien to the pessimistic mood of other "dark lady" sonnets. This creature is evil in that she arouses the poet's lust, "th' expense of spirit in a waste of shame" (129). As a symptom of this corruption, he plays lewdly with his first name (135, 136), which in Elizabethan English could mean "sexual desire":

Whoever hath her wish, thou hast thy Will,
And Will to boot, and Will in overplus.

(135)

In Sonnet 138 ("When My Love Swears That She Is Made of Truth") he argues that love thrives upon mutual deception, a point tellingly emphasized in the sexual punning of the couplet:

Therefore I lie with her and she with me,
And in our faults by lies we flattered be.

Elsewhere (147), when the poet speaks of the madness that her beauty has induced in him, an innocuous Petrarchan conceit is infused with new urgency:

Past cure I am, now reason is past care,
And frantic-mad with evermore unrest;
My thoughts and my discourse as madmen's are,
At randon [random] from the truth vainly express'd;
    For I have sworn thee fair; and thought thee bright,
    Who art as black as hell, as dark as night.

But she is irresistible. Through some strange power (150) she perverts his judgment "in the very refuse" of her deeds.

To counterbalance the ugly cynicism that permeates the dark lady sonnets, there are poems celebrating true love, or friendship. Men glory in a number of gifts (91)—high birth, skill, wealth, physical prowess, hawks and hounds. But the poet exults in his love, which consoles him amid the agonies of isolation and self-doubt. In the immortal Sonnet 29 ("When in Disgrace with Fortune and Men's Eyes"), the mere remembrance of his love lifts him out of despair:

> Yet in these thoughts myself almost despising,
> Haply I think on thee, and then my state,
> Like to the lark at break of day arising
> From sullen earth, sings hymns at heaven's gate. . . .

In a deft play on words, he would not change his "state" (condition) with the "state" (pomp, political domain) of kings. The equally famous Sonnet 116 ("Let Me Not to the Marriage of True Minds") asserts the eternal strength of love through an inspired variation on the Petrarchan ship metaphor:

> Love is not love
> Which alters when it alteration finds
> Or bends with the remover to remove.
> O, no! it is an ever-fixed mark
> That looks on tempests and is never shaken;
> It is the star to every wand'ring bark,
> Whose worth's unknown, although his highth be taken.

In Sonnet 106 ("When in the Chronicle of Wasted Time") the Platonic notion of ideal forms is treated with startling originality: The poet's beloved is not just another copy of Beauty, but the ideal form itself, the pattern of all the beautiful creatures of ages past and the inspiration for all the love songs poets have composed in their honor.

But earthly love and beauty cannot last forever, and some of the most memorable sonnets are those dealing with the ravages of time. In Sonnet 12 mutability is exhibited through a variety of images: "the clock that tells the time," "the violet past prime," "sable curls all silver'd o'er with white," trees "barren of leaves." Perceiving this evidence of decay, the poet is forced to realize that his beloved is also perishable:

> Then of thy beauty do I question make
> That thou among the wastes of time must go,
> Since sweets and beauties do themselves forsake
> And die as fast as they see others grow . . . .

With unremitting haste "the waves make towards the pebbled shore" (60), and human beings move inexorably towards death:

> Nativity, once in the main of light,
> Crawls to maturity, wherewith being crown'd,
> Crooked eclipses 'gainst his glory fight,
> And Time that gave doth now his gift confound.
> Time doth transfix the flourish set on youth
> And delves the parallels in beauty's brow,
> Feeds on the rarities of nature's truth,
> And nothing stands but for his scythe to mow.

Old age itself is described in the great Sonnet 73 ("That Time of Year Thou Mayst in Me Behold"), in which the central images—autumn, twilight, glowing fire—suggest a diminishing span of time. The very imminence of death enhances the urgency and strength of love:

> This thou perceiv'st, which makes thy love more strong,
> To love that well which thou must leave ere long.[34]

Nowhere is the threat of time more superbly communicated than in Sonnet 64 ("When I Have Seen by Time's Fell Hand Defaced"). The poet begins by impersonally recording evidence of destruction:

> When I have seen by Time's fell hand defaced
> The rich proud cost of outworn buried age;
> When sometime lofty towers I see down rased,
> And brass eternal slave to mortal rage . . . .

"Outworn buried age" alludes simultaneously to a specific tomb and to an entire epoch; the pun "down rased" (raised; razed) implies that tearing down is, ironically, the only constructive action of which time is capable and foreshadows the decay of man's loftiest monuments even as they are being erected; the equally effective pun on "mortal" (deadly; human) offers a mocking reminder that man's vaunted creations will be obliterated by the violence of human beings who are themselves transitory. The second quatrain depicts the ceaseless give-and-take between sea and land as a war between two kingdoms. This "interchange of state" (political empire; condition; pomp) leads in the third quatrain to a denial of the very concept of being—"state itself confounded to decay." Then the poet, after formulating the principle of cosmic ruin, is reminded of his own impending loss and, from one line to the next, shifts to a tone of heartbreaking simplicity:

Ruin hath taught me thus to ruminate,
That Time will come and take my love away.

Having begun in empirical observation, the argument has proceeded with
inexorable logic to a grand hypothesis and finally to a painful and
intensely personal conclusion:

This thought is as a death, which cannot choose
But weep to have that which it fears to lose.[35]

Although man cannot overcome the fact of his mortality, there are
ways of mitigating its damage. The first seventeen sonnets stress the
obligation of beauty to perpetuate itself through offspring:

From fairest creatures we desire increase,
That thereby beauty's rose might never die,
But as the riper should by time decease,
His tender heir might bear his memory . . . .
                    (1)

By not leaving an heir, the poet's friend commits a form of suicide:

For thou art so possess'd with murd'rous hate
That 'gainst thyself thou stick'st not to conspire,
Seeking that beauteous roof to ruinate
Which to repair should be thy chief desire.
. . . .
  Make thee another self for love of me,
  That beauty still may live in thine or thee.
                    (10)

If all men were of a mind to remain single, the world would be finished
after one generation (11). Beauties die as rapidly as others grow:

And nothing 'gainst Time's scythe can make defence
Save breed, to brave him when he takes thee hence.
                    (12)

There are "many maiden gardens" (16) waiting for the privilege of
bearing the friend's "living Flowers," the most effective means of making
war against "this bloody tyrant, Time."
   In an effort to win immortality, not just for themselves, but for those
they love, men also write poetry. "Shall I compare thee to a summer's
day?" the poet asks in the well-known Sonnet 18. He answers that the

beauty of summer is tragically brief but that his beloved, thanks to his verse, can live forever:

> But thy eternal summer shall not fade
> Nor lose possession of that fair thou ow'st [have],
> Nor shall Death brag thou wand'rest in his shade
> When in eternal lines to time thou grow'st.
>   So long as men can breathe or eyes can see,
>   So long lives this [poem], and this gives life to thee.

The couplet of Sonnet 19 has a defiant ring:

> Yet do thy worst, old Time! Despite thy wrong,
> My love shall in my verse ever live young.

Especially strong is the beginning of Sonnet 55, which insists that poems, unlike man's more material achievements, are themselves indestructible and that they act as a preservative against death and oblivion:

> Not marble nor the gilded monuments
> Of princes shall outlive this pow'rful rhyme;
> But you shall shine more bright in these contents
> Then unswept stone, besmear'd with sluttish time.

Brass, stone, earth, the boundless sea—all are at the mercy of "sad mortality" (65). Is there no way to prevent time from similarly despoiling fragile beauty?

> O, none! unless this miracle have might,
> That in black ink my love may still shine bright.

Let it be remembered that death, "that fell arrest / Without all bail" (74), can take away only the poet's body, "the dregs of life"; his soul survives in his poetry and in his love:

> When thou reviewest this, thou dost review
> The very part was consecrate to thee.
> The earth can have but earth, which is his due;
> My spirit is thine, the better part of me.

In Sonnet 146 ("Poor Soul, the Centre of My Sinful Earth") the poet expresses wonder that man, having so short a lease on his rapidly fading mansion (the body), should lavish wealth and ornament upon the "outward walls." He would be wise to provide nourishment for his soul and

thereby secure a long-term lease. Paradoxically, the soul flourishes only
as the body that encases it is allowed to decay:

> Then, soul, live thou upon thy servant's loss,
> And let that pine to aggravate [augment] thy store;
> Buy terms divine in selling hours of dross;
> Within be fed, without be rich no more.

Death, in the person of the hungry worm, devours man's body. But in
the life of the spirit, the soul will instead feed on death: "And Death
once dead, there's no more dying then." Although the sonnets are not
explicitly religious, this sonnet comes close to enunciating the traditional
Christian response to the tormenting threat of personal annihilation.[36]

THE PHOENIX AND TURTLE

In addition to *Venus and Adonis, The Rape of Lucrece,* and the
Sonnets, other nondramatic verse was ascribed to Shakespeare during
his lifetime. In 1599 an anthology of twenty short poems appeared under
the title *The Passionate Pilgrim,* with his name affixed. But although the
first two items in the volume are versions of Sonnets 138 and 144 and
three other poems are lyrics from *Love's Labour's Lost,* the remaining
fifteen items have generally been rejected from the Shakespeare canon.
Included in the 1609 Quarto of the *Sonnets* was a skillfully constructed
poem, *A Lover's Complaint,* the familiar lament of a fair maiden
seduced and abandoned by a fickle youth. Most authorities doubt that
Shakespeare wrote it.[37] About the authenticity of *The Phoenix and
Turtle,* however, there seems to be no question. This curious work
apparently was Shakespeare's contribution to a collection published in
1601, Robert Chester's *Love's Martyr: Or, Rosalins Complaint,* which
included poems by John Marston, George Chapman, and Ben Jonson.

The Phoenix and Turtle is a requiem sung at the funeral of two birds,
united in death as in life "in a mutual flame" (l. 24).[38] The phoenix
symbolizes beauty; the turtledove, truth or, more specifically, constancy
in love. Together they demonstrate a remarkable paradox: They manage
to fuse their identities into a perfect unity without surrendering their
uniqueness:

> So they lov'd as love in twain
> Had the essence but in one;
> Two distincts, division none:
> Number there in love was slain.

Hearts remote, yet not asunder;
Distance, and no space was seen
'Twixt this turtle and his queen;
But in them it were a wonder.
(25–32)

Each possesses, and is possessed by, its mate. "Either was the other's mine" (36). Because of their transcendent love, which surpasses reason and even creates a new form of intellectual discourse, the conventional concepts of property and number have to be annulled:

Property was thus appalled,
That the self was not the same;
Single nature's double name
Neither two nor one was called.
(37–40)

The birds have departed the world without leaving any posterity. Hence, the virtues they represent no longer have an authentic life on earth:

Truth may seem, but cannot be;
Beauty brag, but 'tis not she:
Truth and Beauty buried be.
(62–64)

Despite (or because of) its many obscurities, the poem has evoked a wealth of interpretive comment. It has been read simply as an occasional poem celebrating in allegorical form a personal event, perhaps the marriage of Chester's patron Sir John Salisbury, or Shakespeare's own estrangement from Southampton, or the death of the only son of Lucy, countess of Bedford. William H. Matchett has restated an older view that the phoenix and the turtle, whose relationship is imperfect, are allegorical representations of Elizabeth and Essex respectively.[39] But scholars in increasing numbers have concentrated on what they take to be the philosophic patterns emerging from the poem. J. V. Cunningham has argued that Shakespeare portrays the birds in terms borrowed from scholastic theology; their "essence" (divine substance) is One on the analogy of the Trinity. G. Wilson Knight suggests that Shakespeare's central purpose, here as in the *Sonnets,* is to exalt "a mystical love-union beyond sex." According to K. T. S. Campbell, the subject is poetry itself, which is paradoxically "simple and complex and contains within itself the fact of its own nothingness," a paradox Shakespeare reworks in the great tragedies.[40]

It seems reasonable to suppose that in this poem Shakespeare, whatever else he may have intended, deliberately cultivates some of the motifs of Renaissance Neoplatonism and that he does so in a "metaphysical" style akin to that of John Donne in, for example, *The Canonization* or *A Valediction: Forbidding Mourning*.[41] And Shakespeare, like Donne, may be less serious in his poem than many critics would like to believe. In any case, *The Phoenix and Turtle* remains a delightfully ingenious lyric that merits a secure place among Shakespeare's nondramatic works.

NOTES

1. Gerald Eades Bentley, *Shakespeare: A Biographical Handbook* (New Haven: Yale University Press, 1961), p. 159.

2. See, for example, George Rylands, "Shakespeare the Poet," in *A Companion to Shakespeare Studies* (1934), ed. Harley Granville-Barker and G. B. Harrison (Garden City, N.Y.: Doubleday, Anchor Books, 1960), pp. 89–115.

3. Leslie Hotson, *Mr. W. H.* (London: Rupert Hart-Davis, 1964), p. 104.

4. On medieval and Renaissance attitudes toward Ovid, see Douglas Bush, *Mythology and the Renaissance Tradition in English Poetry* (Minneapolis: University of Minnesota Press, 1932), chap. 4; Louis R. Zocca, *Elizabethan Narrative Poetry* (New Brunswick, N.J.: Rutgers University Press, 1950), pp. 209–218; Hallett Smith, *Elizabethan Poetry* (Cambridge: Harvard University Press, 1952), pp. 64–130; and Davis P. Harding, *Milton and the Renaissance Ovid* (Urbana: University of Illinois Press, 1946), pp. 11–26. Mythological allegory in Renaissance art as well as literature is discussed in Jean Seznec's monumental study, *The Survival of the Pagan Gods: The Mythological Tradition and Its Place in Renaissance Humanism and Art*, trans. Barbara F. Sessions (New York: Pantheon, 1953), pp. 84–121, 314–315.

5. These Ovidian texts, together with a helpful introduction, are reprinted in Geoffrey Bullough, *Narrative and Dramatic Sources of Shakespeare*, 8 vols. (New York: Columbia University Press, 1957–1975), 1: 161–176. See also the New Arden edition of Shakespeare's *Poems*, ed. F. T. Prince, 3d ed. (Cambridge: Harvard University Press, 1960), pp. 185–188.

6. See, for example, Smith, *Elizabethan Poetry*, p. 88.

7. A. L. Rowse, *William Shakespeare: A Biography* (New York: Harper & Row, 1963), pp. 150–151 and A. L. Rowse, ed., *Shakespeare's Sonnets* (London: Macmillan, 1964), pp. xiv–xv.

8. Muriel C. Bradbrook, *Shakespeare and Elizabethan Poetry* (London: Chatto & Windus, 1951), pp. 62–63.

9. See Robert P. Miller's two articles: "Venus, Adonis, and the Horses," *ELH* 19 (1952): 249–264 and "The Myth of Mars's Hot Minion in *Venus and Adonis*," *ELH* 26 (1959): 470–481.

10. See J. D. Jahn, "The Lamb of Lust: The Role of Adonis in Shakespeare's *Venus and Adonis*," *Shakespeare Studies*, ed. J. Leeds Barroll, 6 (1970): 11–25.

11. See Norman Rabkin, "*Venus and Adonis* and the Myth of Love," *Pacific Coast Studies in Shakespeare*, eds. Waldo F. McNeir and Thelma N. Greenfield (Eugene: University of Oregon Books, 1966), pp. 20–32.

12. See J. W. Lever, "Venus and the Second Chance," *Shakespeare Survey* 15 (1962): 81–88.

13. A. C. Hamilton, *The Early Shakespeare* (San Marino, Calif.: The Huntington Library, 1967), p. 145.

14. The comic elements are discussed in Eugene B. Cantelupe, "An Iconographical Interpretation of *Venus and Adonis,* Shakespeare's Ovidian Comedy," *Shakespeare Quarterly* 14 (1963): 141–151. According to Cantelupe, Shakespeare parodies the traditional presentation of the myth, which emphasized the Neoplatonic equation of love and beauty; in this version they are opposed and contradictory. See also Gordon Ross Smith, "Mannerist Frivolity and Shakespeare's *Venus and Adonis*," *Hartford Studies in Literature* 3 (1971): 1–11.

15. Samuel Taylor Coleridge, *Shakespearean Criticism*, ed. Thomas Middleton Raysor, rev. ed., 2 vols. (London: Dent, 1960), 1: 189.

16. See Bullough, *Sources,* 1: 179–199 and the New Arden *Poems*, pp. 189–201.

17. On the complaint and its relationship to so-called mirror literature, see Smith, *Elizabethan Poetry*, pp. 102–126.

18. See Sam Hynes, "The Rape of Tarquin," *Shakespeare Quarterly* 10 (1959): 451–453 and Harold R. Walley, "*The Rape of Lucrece* and Shakespearean Tragedy," *PMLA* 76 (1961): 480–487. There is a brief comment on the poem's tragic elements in the New Cambridge edition of Shakespeare's *Poems*, ed. J. C. Maxwell (Cambridge: Cambridge University Press, 1966), pp. xxiv–xxvi.

19. See Don Cameron Allen, "Some Observations on *The Rape of Lucrece*," *Shakespeare Survey* 15 (1962): 89–98. The Augustinian view is carefully explained and applied by Roy W. Battenhouse, "Shakespeare's Re-Vision of Lucrece," *Shakespearean Tragedy: Its Art and Its Christian Premises* (Bloomington: Indiana University Press, 1969), pp. 3–41.

20. See Bradbrook, *Shakespeare and Elizabethan Poetry*, pp. 104–116. Troy was allegorized during the Renaissance to mean the human body ravaged from within and without; see Allen, "Some Observations on *The Rape of Lucrece*."

21. E. K. Chambers, *William Shakespeare: A Study of Facts and Problems*, 2 vols. (Oxford: Clarendon, 1930), 2: 194.

22. An effort to date the *Sonnets* through establishing thematic links may be found in Claes Schaar, *Elizabethan Sonnet Themes and the Dating of Shakespeare's "Sonnets,"* Lund Studies in English 32 (Lund, Sweden: C. W. K. Gleerup, 1962).

23. L. C. Knights, "Shakespeare's Sonnets," *Scrutiny* 3 (1934): 134. Knights's excellent essay is reprinted in *Explorations* (London: Chatto & Windus, 1946), pp. 40–65.

24. The reversal of Southampton's initials, H. W., is not very encouraging to Southamptonists. A variant of the Southampton theory would retain Henry Wriothesley as the friend in the *Sonnets* and would credit Mr. W. H. as the man who released the *Sonnets* for publication, Sir William Harvey, who in 1598

or 1599 married young Southampton's mother. See Rowse, *William Shakespeare*, pp. 200, 295. Recent champions of Pembroke include John Dover Wilson, *An Introduction to the Sonnets of Shakespeare* (Cambridge: Cambridge University Press, 1963), pp. 59–74 and Oscar J. Campbell, ed., *Sonnets, Songs, and Poems of Shakespeare* (New York: Schocken, 1965).

25. Oscar Wilde, *The Portrait of Mr. W. H.* (London: Methuen, 1921, 1958); Leslie Hotson, *Mr. W. H.* (London: Rupert Hart-Davis, 1964).

26. Shaw made use of the Pembroke–Mary Fitton theory in his one-act play *The Dark Lady of the Sonnets.*

27. A. L. Rowse, *Shakespeare the Man* (New York: Harper & Row, 1973), pp. 87–113.

28. Tucker Brooke, ed., *Shakespeare's Sonnets* (London: Oxford University Press, 1936); see Introduction. It has more recently been proposed that Sonnets 100, 101, 63–68, 19, 21, and 105 form a unified sequence. See Brents Stirling, "A Shakespeare Sonnet Group," *PMLA* 75 (1960): 340–349; see also Stirling's *The Shakespeare Sonnet Order: Poems and Groups* (Berkeley: University of California Press, 1968).

29. See, for example, T. W. Baldwin, *On the Literary Genetics of Shakspere's Poems and Sonnets* (Urbana: University of Illinois Press, 1950).

30. James Winny, *The Master-Mistress: A Study of Shakespeare's Sonnets* (New York: Barnes & Noble, 1968), pp. 1–120. For a somewhat similar view, see J. W. Lever, *The Elizabethan Love Sonnet* (London: Methuen, 1956), pp. 162–277.

31. A standard work is Lisle C. John, *The Elizabethan Sonnet Sequences: Studies in Conventional Conceits* (New York: Columbia University Press, 1938). On Shakespeare's parallels with, and departures from, his classical and Renaissance predecessors, see J. B. Leishman, *Themes and Variations in Shakespeare's Sonnets* (London: Hutchinson, 1961). In an intriguing study, Katharine Wilson argues that Shakespeare deliberately parodies specific sonnets of his predecessors and contemporaries; see her *Shakespeare's Sugared Sonnets* (New York: Barnes & Noble, 1974). See also F. T. Prince, "The Sonnet from Wyatt to Shakespeare," in *Elizabethan Poetry*, eds. J. R. Brown and Bernard Harris, Stratford-upon-Avon Studies 2 (London: Edward Arnold, 1960), pp. 11–29.

32. An illuminating discussion of Shakespeare's artistic use of the sonnet form is to be found in Edward Hubler, *The Sense of Shakespeare's Sonnets* (Princeton: Princeton University Press, 1952), pp. 11–37.

33. On the parodic elements in Sonnet 130, see Wilson, *Shakespeare's Sugared Sonnets*, pp. 83–88.

34. For an excellent analysis of Sonnet 73, see Stephen Booth, *An Essay on Shakespeare's Sonnets* (New Haven: Yale University Press, 1969), pp. 118–130. Booth (pp. 15–28) writes brilliantly on the structural principle for individual sonnets, and on pp. 61–66 he discusses rhetorical structure.

35. For brief but penetrating remarks on Sonnet 64, see Michael Goldman, *Shakespeare and the Energies of Drama* (Princeton: Princeton University Press, 1972), p. 30.

36. Among recent editions and studies of the *Sonnets*, see (in addition to those

already cited) Hilton Landry, *Interpretations in Shakespeare's Sonnets* (Berkeley: University of California Press, 1963); *Shakespeare's Sonnets,* eds. W. G. Ingram and Theodore Redpath (New York: Barnes & Noble, 1965); Murray Krieger, *A Window to Criticism: Shakespeare's Sonnets and Modern Poetics* (Princeton: Princeton University Press, 1964); the New Cambridge edition of *Sonnets,* ed. John Dover Wilson (Cambridge: Cambridge University Press, 1966); *Sonnets,* ed. Douglas Bush (Baltimore: Penguin, 1970); and Philip J. T. Martin, *Shakespeare's Sonnets: Self, Love and Art* (Cambridge: Cambridge University Press, 1972).

A full and extremely useful bibliography, including a section on individual sonnets, is Tetsumaro Hayashi, *Shakespeare's Sonnets: A Record of Twentieth-Century Criticism* (Metuchen, N.J.: Scarecrow, 1972).

37. A case *for* Shakespeare's authorship has been made by Kenneth Muir, "*A Lover's Complaint:* A Reconsideration," in *Shakespeare 1564–1964,* ed. Edward A. Bloom (Providence: Brown University Press, 1964), pp. 154–166 and reluctantly seconded by Maxwell, New Cambridge *Poems,* pp. xxxiii–xxxvi.

38. The poem is ably summarized by Robert Ellrodt, "An Anatomy of *The Phoenix and the Turtle,*" *Shakespeare Survey* 15 (1962): 99–110.

39. William H. Matchett, *The Phoenix and the Turtle: Shakespeare's Poem and Chester's Loves Martyr* (The Hague: Mouton, 1965).

40. J. V. Cunningham, "'Essence' and the *Phoenix and Turtle,*" *ELH* 19 (1952): 265–276; G. Wilson Knight, *The Mutual Flame* (1955) (New York: Barnes & Noble, 1962), p. 199; K. T. S. Campbell, "*The Phoenix and the Turtle* as a Signpost of Shakespeare's Development," *British Journal of Aesthetics* 10 (1970): 177.

41. On the "metaphysical" qualities of the poem, see Murray Copland, "The Dead Phoenix," *Essays in Criticism* 15 (1965): 279–287. For a brief, though excellent, survey of twentieth-century studies, see J. W. Lever, "Twentieth-Century Studies in Shakespeare's Songs, Sonnets, and Poems: The Poems," *Shakespeare Survey* 15 (1962): 25–28. For a more complete review, see Richard Allen Underwood's book-length study, *Shakespeare's "The Phoenix and Turtle": A Survey of Scholarship,* Salzburg Studies in English, no. 15 (Salzburg: Universität Salzburg, 1974). Underwood suggests (pp. 299–300) that the phoenix represents imagination, the turtle form. Together they stand for the making of poetry.

4
Comedy

From *The Comedy of Errors* to *The Merry Wives of Windsor*

We do not know when Shakespeare began writing for the stage or whether his initial efforts were directed to comedy, history, or tragedy. From the outset, however, he displayed a remarkable affinity for comedy, and Dr. Johnson thought comedy was his natural calling: "His tragedy seems to be skill, his comedy to be instinct."[1] In any case, *Hamlet* and *King Lear* sprang from the same vision of life that had inspired *The Comedy of Errors* and *Twelfth Night*. As Dover Wilson observed, "The stuff of [Shakespeare's] 'mind and art' was first woven on the comic loom and it retained something of this comic texture right up to the end."[2]

Shakespearean comedy reflects a varied literary and social background, though opinion differs as to the relative significance of particular components. Shakespeare absorbed a classical tradition embracing Greek prose romances and the narrative poems of Ovid no less than the comedies of Plautus and Terence. He also had access to narrative and dramatic materials from Italy: the prose novella; the romantic epic; and the commedia del l'arte, a type of improvisational professional theater that originated during the Middle Ages and flourished in the sixteenth century. But the strongest ingredients in Shakespeare's literary heritage seem to have come from his native soil. In addition to drawing upon medieval English drama with its unabashed mixture of the serious and the comic (for example, the *Second Shepherds' Play*), Shakespeare was indebted to the plays of his immediate predecessors and his contemporaries, to the so-called artificial comedies of John Lyly as well as the popular comedies of George Peele, Robert Greene, and Thomas Nashe.[3] Scholars have also pointed out connections between the comedies and Elizabethan festivals—May games, for example, and customs centering upon the Lord of Misrule.[4] In view of the many traditions that were available to the dramatist, it might be well not to place too much stress upon any single factor in Shakespeare's background but to acknowledge that in comedy, as in everything else he undertook, he achieved a synthesis entirely his own.[5]

What Shakespeare attempted in the earlier comedies, and brought to perfection in *Much Ado about Nothing, As You Like It,* and *Twelfth Night* (see chapter 7), was the reconciliation of realism and romance. Roman dramatists, if they treated the subject of love at all, portrayed it as amusing sex intrigue, and the realistic laughter of classical comedy often led to an unfeeling cynicism. On the other hand, the authors of the chivalric romances idealized love as an ennobling emotion, an attitude that, if carried to extremes, could become irrational and humorless. In Shakespeare's world there is a wholesome interaction of rival forces. In the words of George Gordon, "The solemnity of Love is relieved by the generosity of Laughter, and the irresponsibility of Laughter by the seriousness of Love."[6] We continually step "from Illyria to the Buttery Hatch," from some lovers' romantic utopia to the pantry below the stairs.[7] Some of Shakespeare's most engaging characters are those well-balanced young people, usually women, who, like Rosalind in *As You Like It,* can live easily in both worlds, with sufficient sanity to see the comedy in their own romantic excesses.

The comedies may be conveniently divided into two categories: farce and romantic comedy.[8] Farce, as exemplified in *The Comedy of Errors,* ordinarily emphasizes the comic situation rather than the characters who become entangled in it; in romantic comedy, such as *The Two Gentlemen of Verona,* individual characters assume greater importance and to a large degree determine the direction of the plot. But there is considerable interweaving of the two types. The farces may have serious overtones arising out of Shakespeare's involvement with the human beings to whom he gave dramatic life, and the romantic comedies (like *A Midsummer Night's Dream* and *Twelfth Night*) receive continual nourishment from the wild imbroglios that are the hallmark of farce.

Three farces will be examined here: *The Comedy of Errors* and *The Taming of the Shrew,* both relatively early plays, and *The Merry Wives of Windsor,* a somewhat later work that has spiritual links with the early farces. Of the earlier romantic comedies, *The Two Gentlemen of Verona* and *Love's Labour's Lost* are uneven but highly promising. In *A Midsummer Night's Dream* and *The Merchant of Venice,* Shakespeare reached maturity as a comic dramatist.

THE COMEDY OF ERRORS

Although *The Comedy of Errors,* the shortest play in the canon (1,777 lines), was first printed in the 1623 Folio, it had been acted at Gray's Inn on the night of December 28, 1594. This may have been the first performance. But Dromio of Syracuse's description of Nell, the globelike kitchen wench (see p. 26), seems to contain a punning allusion to the French civil war between Henri IV and his opponents. France, Dromio says, is located in Nell's forehead, "arm'd and reverted, making war against her heir [hair]" (III, 2, 126–127). Because the war ended in a truce in 1593, some scholars would move the play back a few years, perhaps as far as the late 1580s. All we can say for sure is that *The Comedy of Errors* was written before the end of 1594.[9]

The main source is a Roman farce by Plautus called *Menaechmi*. In the Latin original Menaechmus, a traveler from Syracuse, arrives in Epidamnum not knowing that his long-lost twin brother lives there. The Menaechmi do not meet until the final scene, after they have repeatedly been mistaken for each other. Among those who confuse the brothers are their servants, a courtesan, and the wife of Menaechmus of Epidamnum, who is bewildered by her husband's seemingly erratic behavior. Shakespeare may also have adapted an incident from a second Plautine comedy, *Amphitruo:* Jupiter, in order to make love to Alcmena, disguises himself as her husband Amphitruo; meanwhile, the real husband is excluded from his own house by Mercury, disguised as Amphitruo's servant Sosia.[10]

If *The Comedy of Errors* belongs to Shakespeare's so-called apprenticeship, it reveals an incredible mastery of dramatic structure.[11] Shakespeare sets the action in Ephesus, names each brother Antipholus, and, as if Plautus's complications were not enough, provides the twin protagonists with twin servants, each named Dromio and kept ignorant of the other's existence. The chance of error is thus compounded, for each twin, in addition to furnishing other people in Ephesus with opportunities to mistake his identity, can now himself be fooled. Antipholus of Syracuse instructs his Dromio to deposit gold at the Centaur Inn for safekeeping, then beats the other Dromio for not having done so. Dromio of Ephesus complains to his master, Antipholus of Ephesus, who is furious with him for talking nonsense. Dromio of Syracuse faithfully deposits the gold, only to be beaten by Antipholus of Syracuse for having apparently pretended not to deposit it. More amusing is the misunderstanding that arises when Antipholus of Syracuse, who is unmarried, is warmly entertained by his brother's wife Adriana while the real husband is locked out. To make matters worse, Antipholus of Syracuse spurns Adriana, who believes him to be her husband, and openly makes love to her unmarried sister Luciana. Accompanying these entanglements is the kind of wordplay that Shakespeare was never to abandon. Adriana threatens to beat Dromio of Ephesus if he does not invite Antipholus to dinner: "Back, slave, or I will break thy pate across!"; the servant replies in one of those outrageous double puns: "And he will bless that cross with other beating, / Between you I shall have a holy head." (II, 1, 78–80).

In addition to demonstrating Shakespeare's expert manipulation of farcical intrigue, the play anticipates his later works.[12] In the relationship between Luciana and Antipholus of Syracuse, Shakespeare tentatively explores what will become a major theme in the romantic comedies: wooing, or courtship. He frames the comic action within a subplot that borders on the tragic, involving the Syracusan merchant Aegeon, separated from his wife and sons and sentenced to die for entering the hostile city of Ephesus. At the last minute the old man is reunited with his sons (the Antipholuses) and his wife, and is saved from death. Deliverance from evil and the restoration of the family are important motifs in the last plays, the dramatic romances. Finally, Shakespeare sometimes transcends pure farce in his conception of character, especially that of Adriana. In contrast with her sister Luciana, who sees the woman's role as one of submission to a husband, Adriana is a combination of jealous shrew, martyr, and clinging vine. Yet she is an independent woman with a distinctive and not unsympathetic point of view about the double standard in sexual morality.

Although *The Comedy of Errors* has been taken more seriously in recent years,[13] it is not a masterpiece by Shakespearean standards. The plotting and dialogue, however, are adroitly handled, and the play touches lightly upon issues of abiding interest. It makes us laugh, as a good farce should; but, to quote R. A. Foakes, "it also invites compassion, a measure of sympathy, and a deeper response to the disruption of social and family relationships which the action brings about."[14]

THE TAMING OF THE SHREW

A play called *The Taming of a Shrew* was acted and printed in 1594; *The Taming of the Shrew* as we know it first appeared in the 1623 Folio. The plays are closely linked, for the three main components of *A Shrew* are all found in *The Shrew*: (1) the folktale motif of the marriage and taming of an ill-tempered woman; (2) the intrigue, literary in origin, surrounding the wooing of a younger and more sought-after younger sister; (3) an induction (introductory scenes) in which, as a practical joke that has analogues in *The Arabian Nights,* a nobleman takes home a sleeping drunkard, persuades him when he wakes that he is a richly attired lord just recovered from a strange lunacy, and stages for his benefit a play within a play telling the stories of the two sisters.

According to some scholars, *A Shrew* and *The Shrew* are two different plays, each derived independently from an earlier play, now lost. Others regard *A Shrew,* which Shakespeare may or may not have

written, as an early version of *The Shrew*, which he did write. But the
present consensus is that only Shakespeare could have so skillfully integrated the three stories into a unified work and that *A Shrew* is
probably a bad quarto of *The Shrew,* in which case Shakespeare's play
could have been written almost any time before 1594. This view is
reinforced by Richard Hosley's investigation of sources and analogues
and by Jan Harold Brunvand's exhaustive comparison of *A Shrew* and
The Shrew with folktales incorporating the taming theme.[15]

Petruchio's taming of Katherine (Hosley thinks the source may be an
anonymous ballad, "A Shrewde and Curste Wyfe") sets off the dramatic
sparks. Despite a fearful disposition that frightens her would-be suitors,
Kate must find a husband before her father will consider bestowing the
more popular and seemingly more agreeable Bianca. Only Petruchio,
who has "come to wive it wealthily in Padua" (I, 2, 75), accepts the
challenge:

Have I not in my time heard lions roar?
Have I not heard the sea, puff'd up with winds,
Rage like an angry boar chafed with sweat?
Have I not heard great ordnance in the field,
And heaven's artillery thunder in the skies?
Have I not in a pitched battle heard
Loud 'larums, neighing steeds, and trumpets' clang?
                    (I, 2, 201–207)

Is such a man to be intimidated by a woman's tongue? "Fear [scare] boys
with bugs [bugabears]!" (I, 2, 211).

To subdue his foe, Petruchio employs a skillful combination of sarcasm,
perversity, and downright abuse carried out with robust humor and,
sometimes at least, romantic aplomb. He humiliates Kate by coming to
the wedding late and in an outlandish costume, by swearing so loud at
the ceremony that the priest drops his book, and by commanding Kate
to leave before the wedding feast. When they arrive at his country house,
Petruchio, having forced his ravenous bride to wade through the mud,
erupts with rage on the pretext that the supper is burnt and sends Kate
to bed. The next day he again refuses to let her eat, dismisses the
Haberdasher who has brought exactly the hat that had been ordered,
and pours out invective upon the poor Tailor, although Kate's gown is
faultless:

O monstrous arrogance! Thou liest, thou thread, thou thimble,
Thou yard, three-quarters, half-yard, quarter, nail!
Thou flea, thou nit, thou winter cricket thou!
Brav'd [defied] in mine own house with a skein of thread?
Away, thou rag, thou quantity, thou remnant ....
                    (IV, 3, 107–112)

He compels Kate to say that the sun is the moon, then upbraids her for lying. Her only recourse is to acquiesce in his every whim:

> Then God be bless'd, it is the blessed sun!
> But sun it is not when you say it is not,
> And the moon changes even as your mind.
> What you will have it nam'd, even that it is,
> And so it shall be so for Katherine.
>   (IV, 5, 18–22)

At the end of the play Petruchio wagers on his wife's superior obedience and wins. Kate publicly reprimands Bianca and all other women who do not submit to their masters:

> Such duty as the subject owes the prince,
> Even such a woman oweth to her husband;
> And when she is froward, peevish, sullen, sour,
> And not obedient to his honest will,
> What is she but a foul contending rebel
> And graceless traitor to her loving lord?
>   (V, 2, 155–160)

Kate's speech does not sit well with some modern critics. Shaw finds it "altogether disgusting to modern sensibility"; and Harold Goddard and Nevill Coghill, both sympathetic to Kate's situation, regard her apparent submission as a strategy to trick Petruchio into believing he has won. Ralph Berry argues that Kate and Petruchio are both playing the lovers' game, she by exaggerating the role of subordinate female, he by overstating his case for male supremacy.[16] One cannot be certain of Shakespeare's attitude, but Robert Heilman has reminded us that the play is essentially a straightforward farce and that Kate may have indeed been transformed into a more agreeable wife.[17]

The Bianca plot comes from a play by George Gascoigne, *The Supposes* (1566), itself a translation of a play by Ariosto. The prologue to Gascoigne's comedy explains that a *suppose* is "a mystaking or imagination of one thing for another."[18] Gascoigne's hero Erostrato (Lucentio) changes roles with his servant Dulipo (Tranio) and secures employment in the household of his beloved Polynesta (Bianca). Like Lucentio, Erostrato introduces a counterfeit who poses as his father, until the real father arrives and adds to the comic confusion. At another level Shakespeare's Bianca is a "suppose," for she appears to be compliant when she may in fact be more shrewish than her sister. It has been suggested that "supposes," not shrew taming, is the unifying idea behind the play, which is built upon the "interplay of love and illusion, and transformation on varying levels."[19]

The "supposes" theme is prominent in the Induction. Christopher Sly—

"old Sly's son of Burton Heath; by birth a pedlar, by education a card-maker, by transmutation a bearherd, and now by present profession a tinker" (Induction, 2, 19–22)—awakens from a drunken stupor to find himself in the guise and surroundings of a noble lord, with servants, a "wife," and a company of players at his disposal. His speech has an authentic Elizabethan ring:

> Ask Marian Hacket, the fat alewife of Wincot, if she know me not. If she say I am not fourteen pence on the score [on the books] for sheer ale, score me up for the lying'st knave in Christendom.

> (Induction, 2, 22–26)

While the Katherine-Petruchio "comonty" is being enacted for his benefit by the players of the nobleman prankster, Sly makes a memorable venture into dramatic criticism. "A good matter, surely," he comments. "Comes there any more of it?" (I, 1, 255–256). Although he soon drops out of the play (he remains in *A Shrew*),[20] Christopher Sly has been on the stage long enough to leave a vivid imprint. His earthiness helps root the play in reality.[21] A forerunner of Bottom and Dogberry, those wonderful clowns who remain blissfully self-assured even as they un-wittingly testify to their simplemindedness, Sly all but steals the show.

THE TWO GENTLEMEN OF VERONA

The Two Gentlemen of Verona, possibly Shakespeare's earliest ro-mantic comedy, was first printed in the 1623 Folio. Despite some con-fusion whereby Valentine leaves Verona for Milan but seems at one point to be in Padua and later back in Verona, the text is good and offers little support for the theory that it was abridged or mangled by non-Shakespearean hands. There is no external evidence for the date, which has been variously estimated between 1590 and 1595.[22]

The plot is largely derived from the episode of Felix and Felismena, in the Spanish chivalric romance *Diana Enamorada* (1542), by the Portuguese writer Jorge de Montemayor. (Some think the material reached Shakespeare by way of a lost English play, *Felix and Philiomena,* which was acted in 1585.)[23] In Shakespeare's version Valentine, im-patient with his friend, the lovesick Proteus, and eager to see the world, sets out for a visit to the court of the Duke of Milan, while Proteus stays in Verona to be near Julia. Once in Milan, Valentine falls in love with Silvia, the Duke's daughter. When Proteus is himself dispatched to Milan, he, too, is smitten with her and forgets his vows to Julia as well as his obligations to Valentine. Proteus informs the Duke of Valentine's intention to elope with Silvia and thereby brings about his friend's banishment from Milan. Valentine subsequently encounters a band of Robin Hood-type outlaws in the nearby forest, and they compel him to become their chief. Meanwhile, Proteus unsuccessfully tries to promote his own cause with Silvia on the pretext of helping Thurio, a clownish suitor favored by the Duke. Through a series of intrigues that defy summary, all the major characters end up in the forest, with Julia disguised as a page in the service of Proteus. At the climax of the play, Valentine leaps out of hiding to prevent Proteus from taking Silvia by force and, after hearing the would-be rapist's brief expression of remorse, makes a startling offer:

> Then I am paid;
> And once again I do receive thee honest.
> Who by repentance is not satisfied
> Is nor of heaven nor earth; for these are pleas'd;
> By penitence th' Eternal's wrath's appeas'd.
> And, that my love may appear plain and free,
> All that was mine in Silvia I give thee.
>   (V, 4, 77–83)

The play turns out well, of course, with Valentine marrying Silvia and the repentant Proteus reunited with Julia. Even the outlaws are granted amnesty.

The play has never been popular, largely because the last scene strikes many readers as outrageous: How could Valentine have been willing to sacrifice his Silvia to a brute like Proteus? Without presuming to justify his action, one may suggest, first, that the play is a comedy, governed by an unwritten law that the happy ending takes precedence over plausibility. Second, a Renaissance audience would have been familiar with the doctrine that friendship between men is nobler than love between a man and a woman. (Some even see the play as a parody both of courtly love and of the exaggerated code of friendship.)[24] Shakespeare may have adapted the specific situation from the story of Tito and Gisippo, in Boccaccio's *Decameron,* a tale best known to Elizabethans in a version appearing in Sir Thomas Elyot's *The Governour* (1531); but the conflicting claims of love and friendship were also examined in two famous works of John Lyly, the novel *Euphues* (1578) and the play *Endimion* (c. 1588).[25] Then, too, both young men are undergoing a painful process of self-discovery and should perhaps be viewed somewhat tolerantly.[26] Finally, it should be noted that in this episode Shakespeare may be chiefly concerned with forgiveness and reconciliation. Here he approaches the theme in a tentative or perfunctory manner; in later plays it will be a fundamental motif, not just in the comedies, but in *King Lear* and the dramatic romances as well.[27]

The Two Gentlemen of Verona contains other ingredients that find their way into Shakespeare's more mature plays. Julia, with her maid Lucetta (I, 2, 1–49), surveys the roster of her suitors with a gaiety not unlike Portia's in a more famous scene (*The Merchant of Venice*, I, 2). Like many other Shakespearean heroines, Julia dresses as a boy in order to be near her lover; and like Viola in *Twelfth Night,* she suffers in silence as she carries love messages to another woman. The forest in which Valentine takes refuge is a faint prophecy of the great Arden of *As You Like It,* and his words praising the "shadowy desert, unfrequented woods" (V, 4, 2) comprise a rough draft for the exiled Duke's speech on the sweet uses of adversity (*As You Like It,* II, 1, 1–18).

More important, Shakespeare, in this youthful play, begins his lifelong habit of laughing at lovers without diminishing our affection for them. In the later comedies, as previously suggested, this laughter is often conveyed by the self-aware lovers themselves. But in *The Two Gentlemen of Verona* the humor is suggested for the most part by Speed and Launce, the two comic servants of Valentine and Proteus respectively.[28] Speed twits Valentine upon observing in him the symptoms of love:

First, you have learn'd, like Sir Proteus, to wreathe your arms like a malecontent; to relish a love song like a robin redbreast; to walk alone like one that had the pestilence; to sigh like a schoolboy that had lost his A B C; to weep like a young wench that had buried her grandam; to fast like one that takes diet; to watch like one that fears robbing; to speak puling [whining] like a beggar at Hallowmas.

(II, 1, 18–27)

Immediately after Proteus and Julia part, having tearfully exchanged rings, Launce, who will accompany his master to Milan, enters with his dog Crab and burlesques the scene. In a comic monologue he complains that at *his* leave-taking one member of his family expressed no grief:

My mother weeping; my father wailing; my sister crying; our maid howling; our cat wringing her hands, and all our house in great perplexity—yet did not this cruel-hearted cur [Crab] shed one tear. He is a stone, a very pebble stone, and has no more pity in him than a dog.

(II, 3, 7–13)

One ought not conclude a discussion of *The Two Gentlemen of Verona* without calling attention to its most notable lines: the song "Who is Silvia?" (IV, 2, 39–53), famous in its setting by Franz Schubert. Shakespeare has placed this lovely serenade in an unusual dramatic context: Thurio hires musicians to soften Silvia's heart; Proteus appropriates the serenade for his own purposes; Silvia, appreciating the music but adamant in her loyalty to Valentine, refuses Proteus's suit and upbraids him for betraying both friend and sweetheart; Julia, in her disguise, looks on heartbroken. But at the end of this richly counterpointed scene, the old Host is singularly unmoved. "By my halidome," he confesses, "I was fast asleep" (IV, 2, 136). His remark constitutes yet another gentle satire of sentimental lovers.[29]

LOVE'S LABOUR'S LOST

The Quarto of *Love's Labour's Lost,* the copy used for the First Folio, was published in 1598, "as it was presented," the title page informs us, "before her Highnes this last Christmas. Newly corrected and augmented *By W. Shakspere.*" This last phrase has led to speculation that a lost "bad" quarto preceded the 1598 text, but the theory has not won much support. On the basis of stylistic affinities with other works, as well as possible topical allusions too intricate to be detailed here, the date of composition is usually set at 1593, 1594, or 1595, although a case has been made for an earlier performance by a company of children in 1588, followed by the enlarged version acted before the Queen in 1597 and printed in 1598.[30]

No literary source has been found, but Shakespeare's slender plot seems to make some use of contemporary topics familiar to an Elizabethan audience. In the play King Ferdinand of Navarre and his friends Longaville, Dumain, and Berowne resolve to overcome the frailties of the flesh and spend three years in scholarly seclusion. Almost immediately their precious Academe is assaulted by the Princess of France, who has come on a diplomatic mission accompanied by three beautiful attendants, Maria, Katherine, and Rosaline. Although the ladies are barred from the palace and forced to occupy a tent in the park outside (like an encampment of enemy troops), each of the four would-be scholars in quick turn falls in love, forswears his vows, and gets caught in the act of reading to himself a sonnet he has composed for his sweetheart. Unified in their determination to wage an active amatorial campaign, they now send gifts and woo the ladies disguised as Muscovites.[31] But the Princess and her attendants put on masks and trick each suitor into courting the wrong person. When the joke has been revealed and the ladies and gentlemen are being entertained by a pageant, a messenger arrives with news that the Princess's father is dead and that she must return to France. The gentlemen propose marriage, but each lady prescribes a year of penance before giving her answer. The play concludes with two fine songs, "When daisies pied" and "When icicles hang."

While the general reader's acquaintance with the play may be limited to these two songs, scholars have had a field day attempting to connect incidents and characters with possible real-life counterparts. No other play of Shakespeare's seems so dependent upon topicalities and private jokes, many of which are now lost. A case in point is the intriguing metaphor employed by the King in speaking of Berowne's dark-haired mistress Rosaline:

> O paradox! Black is the badge of hell,
> The hue of dungeons, and the school of night;
> And beauty's crest becomes the heavens well.
>
> (IV, 3, 254–256)

The phrase "school of night" may be a satiric reference to an academy formed by Sir Walter Raleigh, George Chapman, and others for philosophical and scientific discussions. This coterie was denounced by a hostile pamphleteer in 1592 as "Sir Walter Rauley's Schoole of Aetheisme," and its alleged heresies came under official investigation.[32] It is this sort of problem that disturbs readers and potential theatrical producers. As one actor-scholar has said, "Here is a fashionable play; now, by three hundred years, out of fashion."[33]

Yet there is enduring interest in this play, as recent successes on the stage have made clear. It is a satire on excess and a plea for moderation. From the beginning Berowne, the most intelligent of the votaries, is skeptical about a code that runs so contrary to human nature; and even as he subscribes to the "barren tasks, too hard to keep" (I, 1, 47), he predicts that the experiment will fail:

> Necessity will make us all forsworn
> Three thousand times within this three years' space;
> For every man with his affects is born,
> Not by might mast'red, but by special grace.
>
> (I, 1, 150–153)

With a sense of irony worthy of Benedick (in *Much Ado about Nothing*), he feigns astonishment at his surrender to the god of love:

> O—and I, forsooth, in love? I that have been love's whip,
> A very beadle to a humorous sigh,
> A critic, nay, a night-watch constable,
> A domineering pedant o'er the boy,
> Than whom no mortal so magnificent!
> This wimpled, whining, purblind, wayward boy;
> This senior junior, giant dwarf, Dan Cupid,
> Regent of love-rhymes, lord of folded arms,
> Th' anointed sovereign of sighs and groans ....
>
> (III, 1, 175–184)

Later his friends plead with him to justify their oath breaking, to come up with "some salve for perjury" (IV, 3, 289). Berowne obliges with a magnificent rationalization: Beauty is the noblest of scholarly studies, and it too has texts:

> From women's eyes this doctrine I derive.
> They sparkle still the right Promethean fire;
> They are the books, the arts, the academes,
> That show, contain, and nourish all the world.
>   (IV, 3, 350–353)

For all its charm, Berowne's rhetoric underscores a fundamental flaw that he shares with his companions, the inability to feel or to communicate honest emotion. After their intellectual pose at the beginning, the four men make a sudden shift into new roles, equally exaggerated and absurd, as romantic lovers. At both extremes they are preoccupied with artifice and illusion. They have not achieved the harmony of asceticism and worldliness that authentic love demands.[34] Their word games (charged, as is the play as a whole, with sexual imagery that mocks their ascetic pretensions),[35] the stylized choreography of their recantation scene, the comic formality of the wooing masquerade—all indicate that they cannot be taken seriously. Berowne realizes that literary artifice has poisoned his soul:

> Taffeta phrases, silken terms precise,
>   Three-pil'd hyperboles, spruce affectation,
> Figures pedantical—these summer flies
>   Have blown me full of maggot ostentation.
>   (V, 2, 406–409)

But he soon relapses. Rosaline, understandably, orders this "man replete with mocks" (V, 2, 852) to do penance in a hospital:

> You shall this twelvemonth term from day to day
> Visit the speechless sick and still converse
> With groaning wretches; and your task shall be,
> With all the fierce endeavour of your wit
> To enforce the pained impotent to smile.
>   (V, 2, 859–863)

The traditional happy ending is thus deferred. After their twelvemonth and a day—"That's too long for a play," Berowne tersely comments (V, 2, 887)—these callow youths may have grown up. "The moral," says J. J. Anderson, "is a very Shakespearian one, suggesting not that men should aim for spiritual perfection, but merely that they should be responsibly human."[36]

Other characters in the play also become objects of good-natured satire. The bombastic Spaniard Don Adriano de Armado describes in a letter how he caught the clown Costard with the country wench Jaquenetta, "a child of our grandmother Eve, a female, or, for thy more sweet understanding, a woman" (I, 1, 266–268):

> The time When? About the sixth hour, when beasts most graze, birds best peck, and men sit down to that nourishment which is called supper. So much for the time When. Now for the ground Which? which, I mean, I walk'd upon. It is ycliped [called] thy park. Then for the place Where? where, I mean, I did encounter that obscene and most prepost'rous event that draweth from my snow-white pen the ebon-coloured ink which here thou viewest, beholdest, surveyest, or seest.
>
> (I, 1, 237–249)

(The fact that Armado himself burns with lust for Jaquenetta and eventually marries her provides additional evidence for the powerful claims of nature that the academicians try to deny.) As ridiculous as Armado's florid style, but liberally garnished with the schoolmaster's arid Latin, is the speech of the village pedant Holofernes:

> The deer was, as you know, *sanguis*, in blood; ripe as the pomwater [apple], who now hangeth like a jewel in the ear of *coelo*, the sky, the welkin, the heaven, and anon falleth like a crab on the face of *terra*, the soil, the land, the earth.
>
> (IV, 2, 3–7)

" 'The preyful princess pierc'd and prick'd a pretty pleasing pricket' " (IV, 2, 58); thus the scholar demonstrates his "gift" for poetry (and, incidentally, his preoccupation with sexual wordplay). In the words of the sprightly page Moth, Holofernes and Armado "have been at a great feast of languages and stol'n the scraps" (V, 1, 39–40). To round out the gallery, Shakespeare gives us a dim-witted constable appropriately named Dull (the progenitor of Dogberry in *Much Ado about Nothing* and of Elbow in *Measure for Measure*) and the curate Nathaniel. After Nathaniel is hooted off the stage for his impersonation of Alexander in the pageant of the Nine Worthies, Costard gently explains: "He is a marvellous good neighbour, faith, and a very good bowler; but for Alisander—alas! you see how 'tis—a little o'erparted" (V, 2, 586–589). Many of the characters, like poor Nathaniel, are "o'erparted," having aspired to performances beyond their capacities.[37]

The play's most effective moment is the sudden appearance of Marcade, with his brief message that the King of France is dead. "The scene begins to cloud," Berowne says (V, 2, 730); and, indeed, many critics see in this unexpected development a chilling sign that the ultimate reality from which there is no escape has intruded upon the ivory tower.[38] In this context the concluding songs, with their crisp images of spring and winter, symbolize the end of affectation and reaffirm the great "going-on power of life."[39]

A MIDSUMMER NIGHT'S DREAM

The First Quarto of *A Midsummer Night's Dream* appeared late in 1600; the Second Quarto, a reprint published in 1619, was used for the Folio. The play, which appears in Francis Meres's list of 1598, may have been written for a private performance at some aristocratic wedding, and at least seven possible weddings, ranging from 1590 to 1600 (Meres notwithstanding), have been suggested. Titania's description of the miserable weather caused by Oberon's "brawls" (II, 1, 81–117) is often taken as an allusion to the summer of 1594. When Bottom warns his fellow amateur actors that it may be dangerous to bring a lion onto the stage (III, 1, 30–34), Shakespeare could be recalling a pageant honoring the baptism of the son of James VI of Scotland, in 1594. On this occasion a chariot that was to have been drawn by a lion was, in the interest of safety, drawn by a Moor instead. Such internal evidence points to a date around 1594 or 1595, but we cannot be sure. There is no definitive source, although Kenneth Muir has traced the "Pyramus and Thisby" story through several older versions that Shakespeare may have read.[40]

In *A Midsummer Night's Dream* Shakespeare achieves an exquisite blend of three diverse yet similar worlds held together by a single dramatic idea. Take the world of the two pairs of young lovers in the court of Theseus, Duke of Athens; the ethereal world of Oberon and Titania, King and Queen of the Fairies; the workaday world of Bottom the weaver and Snout the tinker. Transport these three groups somehow to a wood near Athens, where laws and inhibitions are temporarily suspended. Let loose the mischievous hobgoblin Puck, or Robin Good-fellow, "that merry wanderer of the night" (II, 1, 43), with a magical love-juice that he sprinkles upon the eyelids of unsuspecting sleepers.[41] Then look on in amazement as the madness called love scrambles the three worlds almost beyond recognition. The courtly lovers get entangled in what looks like a hopeless quadrangle: Helena in love with Demetrius in love with Hermia in love with Lysander in love with Helena; and the fairy queen dotes upon an ass head, worn by Bottom with imperturbable self-assurance. Of course, everything gets straightened out in time for a triple wedding, including the marriage of Theseus and Hippolyta, Queen of the Amazons. "Lord, what fools these mortals be!" (III, 2, 115), says Puck. And the fairies are just as foolish.

Caught inextricably in Cupid's net, the human lovers display a "drastic helplessness of will and mind."[42] Their movements have been likened to a figured ballet devoid of passion:

> The lovers quarrel in a dance pattern: first, there are two men to one woman and the other woman alone, then for a brief space a circular movement, each one pursuing and pursued, then a return to the first figure with the position of the women reversed, then a cross-movement, man quarrelling with man and woman with woman, and then, as finale, a general setting to partners, including not only the lovers but fairies and royal personages as well .... The harmony and grace of the action would have been spoilt by convincing passion.[43]

We have trouble, says a recent critic, remembering even important details about the lovers: Which girl is taller? Who is forbidden to marry whom? Who finally *does* marry whom? "Their names seem little more than labels, as interchangeable as their alliances in the wood."[44] At one point Helena seems to understand the irrationality of the lovers' behavior:

> Things base and vile, holding no quantity,
> Love can transpose to form and dignity.
> Love looks not with the eyes, but with the mind;
> And therefore is wing'd Cupid painted blind.
>   (I, 1, 232–235)

But such an insight belongs more properly to a Rosalind; coming from Helena it is out of character.

One mortal in the play rises above folly and becomes a detached observer of the immaturity surrounding him. To Theseus, who strongly resembles Chaucer's Theseus in *The Knight's Tale* (a probable source), Shakespeare assigns a pivotal speech:

> Lovers and madmen have such seething brains,
> Such shaping fantasies, that apprehend
> More than cool reason ever comprehends.
> The lunatic, the lover, and the poet
> Are of imagination all compact.
>   (V, 1, 4–8)

Theseus echoes the Renaissance notion, most fully expounded in Robert Burton's *Anatomy of Melancholy* (1621), that love is a derangement of the senses and that the lover's imagination distorts reality, forcing him to perceive beauty where none exists.[45] A seasoned lover himself, Theseus has already experienced passion, fickleness, and jealousy; he brings to his impending marriage a perspective that the novices have not yet acquired.[46] As suggested earlier, in Shakespeare's greatest comedies, the young lovers—Beatrice and Benedick, Rosalind, Viola—are capable simultaneously of folly and wisdom, with no loss of psychological consistency. Here, however, romantic folly is concentrated in the young people, while the wisdom to recognize it belongs to Theseus. His is a partial wisdom, some say, for it fails to perceive that illusion and imagination, as embodied in lovers and poets, may also constitute powerful forms of reality.[47]

In the play Shakespeare employs a skillful combination of verse and prose. His lovers, as if to emphasize their interchangeability, often speak in the stylized manner of the Petrarchan sonneteer:

> *Lysander:* How now, my love? Why is your cheek so pale?
> *Hermia:* Belike for want of rain, which I could well
>   Beteem them from the tempest of my eyes.
>   (I, 1, 128–131)

Frequently they resort to stichomythy (an antiphonal dialogue in rhyme consisting of balanced one-line statements and responses):

> *Hermia:* I frown upon him; yet he loves me still.
> *Helena:* O that your frowns would teach my smiles such skill!
> *Hermia:* I give him curses; yet he gives me love.
> *Helena:* O that my prayers could such affection move!
> *Hermia:* The more I hate, the more he follows me.
> *Helena:* The more I love, the more he hateth me.
>   (I, 1, 194–199)

In contrast with the lovers' posturings, the fairies have two predominant modes of expression. At times they invoke homely rustic images, as in Puck's account of the reaction of Snout and the other craftsmen to Bottom's transformation:

> As wild geese that the creeping fowler eye,
> Or russet-pated choughs [crows], many in sort,
> Rising and cawing at the gun's report,
> Sever themselves and madly sweep the sky;
> So at his sight away his fellows fly.
>   (III, 2, 20–24)

Or they can rise to rapturous lyricism. Oberon's description to Puck of the origin of the love philter (the speech is usually interpreted as a tribute to Queen Elizabeth) is sheer magic:

That very time I saw (but thou couldst not)
Flying between the cold moon and the earth
Cupid, all arm'd. A certain aim he took
At a fair Vestal, throned by the West,
And loos'd his love-shaft smartly from his bow,
As it should pierce a hundred thousand hearts.
But I might see young Cupid's fiery shaft
Quench'd in the chaste beams of the wat'ry moon,
And the imperial vot'ress passed on,   '
In maiden meditation, fancy-free.
Yet mark'd I where the bolt of Cupid fell.
It fell upon a little Western flower,
Before milk-white, now purple with love's wound,
And maidens call it love-in-idleness.

                                    (II, 1, 155–168)

Finally, there is the realistic prose of Bottom and his friends. "I must to the barber's, monsieur; for methinks I am marvail's hairy about the face; and I am such a tender ass, if my hair do but tickle me, I must scratch" (IV, 1, 25–28).[48]

In addition to these varied literary styles, Shakespeare makes brilliant use of parody, particularly in "Pyramus and Thisby," which has an organic relationship to the rest of the play. The story, out of Ovid, deals with lovers separated by parental decree. Shakespeare uses the tale to spoof Hermia and Lysander, but perhaps he also glances at his own *Romeo and Juliet,* which may have preceded *A Midsummer Night's Dream* and in a sense served as its tragic counterpart.[49] The wall through which Pyramus and Thisby converse by moonlight recalls the orchard wall that Romeo leaps. The Nurse in *Romeo and Juliet* bewails the heroine's presumed death in hyperbolic rhetoric:

O day! O day! O day! O hateful day!
Never was seen so black a day as this.
O woful day! O woful day!
    (*Romeo and Juliet,* IV, 5, 52–54)

Listen to Pyramus as Shakespeare burlesques the lament:

O grim-look'd night! O night with hue so black!
O night, which ever art when day is not!
O night, O night! alack, alack, alack,
I fear my Thisby's promise is forgot!
(*A Midsummer Night's Dream,* V, 1, 171–174)

Like Romeo, Pyramus kills himself in the belief that his sweetheart is dead; and Thisby, like Juliet, follows suit. In *A Midsummer Night's Dream* Helena is alarmed to discover Lysander asleep in the woods:

But who is here? Lysander! on the ground?
Dead, or asleep? I see no blood, no wound.
Lysander, if you live, good sir, awake.
                    (II, 2, 100–102)

Listen to Thisby as she stumbles upon the body of her lover:

    Asleep, my love?
    What, dead, my dove?
O Pyramus, arise!
    Speak, speak! Quiet dumb?
    Dead, dead? A tomb
Must cover thy sweet eyes.
                    (V, 1, 331–336)

Like Titania's fondling of the ass's ears, "Pyramus and Thisby" presents a devastating critique of sentimental romanticism.[50]

The star of "Pyramus and Thisby" is Nick Bottom, one of Shakespeare's great comic characters. Like Hamlet, Bottom enters enthusiastically into his theatrical production. But where Hamlet insists that the stage "hold, as 'twere, the mirror up to nature" (*Hamlet,* III, 2, 24–25) and help uncover truth, the engagingly literal-minded Bottom would have a prologue assure the audience that his play is *not* real, "that I Pyramus am not Pyramus, but Bottom the weaver" (III, 1, 22–23).[51] He would play all the parts from lovers to tyrants, including the roaringest lion the Duke ever heard. When Peter Quince the carpenter, the titular director, tries to quiet him with the tactful suggestion that he might prove *too* convincing and frighten the ladies, Bottom has a solution. "But I will aggravate my voice so that I will roar you as gently as any sucking dove; I will roar you an 'twere any nightingale" (I, 2, 83–86). He is equally at home with the simple tradesmen; in the arms of Titania, where he wants only to scratch and munch dry oats; or in the ducal court. When the Duke teasingly proposes that the wall, impersonated by Snout, should return Pyramus's curses, "Pyramus" steps out of character to set him straight:

No, in truth, sir, he should not. "Deceiving me" is Thisby's cue. She is to enter now, and I am to spy her through the wall. You shall see it will fall pat as I told you.
                    (V, 1, 185–188)

Wherever he is, Bottom takes command by remaining his undaunted and undauntable self. He stands for "the crude native matter of human instinct."[52] As he moves in and out of the various levels of the play, Bottom becomes, in the words of one critic, that vital "connecting link between the distant world of myth and fancy and the Elizabethan world of reality."[53]

THE MERCHANT OF VENICE

The First Quarto of *The Merchant of Venice*, the text used for the Folio, was printed in 1600; the Second Quarto, fraudulently dated 1600, was printed in 1619 as part of Thomas Pavier's abortive venture (see p. 37). The play is mentioned in Meres's *Palladis Tamia* (1598). There are two allusions that may bear on the date. The "wolf . . . hang'd for human slaughter" (IV, 1, 134) is sometimes read as a translated pun on the name of the Portuguese Jewish physician Roderigo Lopez (*lupus*, "wolf"), who was executed in 1594 for allegedly plotting to poison the Queen. The second passage, "And see my wealthy Andrew dock'd in sand" (I, 1, 27), may refer to the Spanish ship *St. Andrew*, captured in 1596 during an English expedition to Cadiz. Scholars generally date the play between 1596 and 1598.[54]

The principal source is the story of Giannetto, from a medieval Italian collection *Il Pecorone*, by Ser Giovanni Fiorentino. First printed in 1558, the tale has several elements very close to Shakespeare's: suitors competing for the hand of a wealthy widow at Belmonte; Giannetto's financing his successful courtship with funds borrowed by his godfather from a Jewish moneylender; the bond of a pound of flesh that is about to be forfeited when the heroine, disguised as a lawyer, arrives at the courtroom to insist that not a drop of blood be shed in its collection; the trick whereby the "lawyer" forces Giannetto to part with the ring she had given him and later accuses him of infidelity.

The story of the caskets is found in another medieval collection, the *Gesta Romanorum*, first translated from the Latin around 1524. Here the Emperor of Rome tests his prospective daughter-in-law by requiring her to choose from among three vessels: one gold, one silver, one lead. Like Bassanio, she chooses lead, thereby passing the test and receiving her reward of a happy marriage. (The tale was an allegory of God testing the Soul for his Son.) We do not know whether Shakespeare was the first to combine the pound of flesh and the casket stories or whether this had been done in an earlier play, *The Jew* (no longer extant), referred to in Stephen Gosson's *School of Abuse* (1579) as "representing the greediness of worldly choosers and the bloody minds of usurers." Shakespeare also knew Christopher Marlowe's popular play *The Jew of Malta* (c. 1589), which was in the repertory of the Admiral's Men.[55]

In an effort to unify the Belmont and Venice plots, Shakespeare makes important changes in Ser Giovanni's story. To win the widow, Giannetto must prove his love by not going to sleep, a test with clear sexual implications. In contrast, Bassanio wins Portia, a virgin, when he scorns gold and silver and accepts the challenge posed by the inscription on the lead casket: " 'Who chooseth me must give and hazard all he hath' " (II, 7, 16). This change points up a contrast between Belmont and Venice, where Bassanio's choice would not be understood (except, perhaps, by Antonio) because of that city's preoccupation with money and merchandise.[56] The heroine of *Il Pecorone* devises the competition herself, then tricks each suitor before Giannetto into failing the test. But Portia is faithful to the stringent conditions of her father's will, which provides an interesting parallel with the rigidity of Antonio's bond. This bond, contracted in Venice, enables Bassanio to seek Portia in Belmont and, in turn, makes it necessary for her to go to Venice to save Antonio. And she saves him by submitting to the full rigor of the original bond. Sigurd Burckhardt discerns a circular chain: The bond, an agent of destruction, is transformed into an instrument of deliverance, a process symbolized in the ring of love that Portia gives Bassanio.[57] Furthermore, W. Gordon Zeeveld has brilliantly demonstrated that the comic plot, with the rings that Bassanio and Gratiano wrongfully "give away" to the lawyers, parallels the serious pound-of-flesh plot. In both instances the principle of equity, "justice seasoned with mercy," is invoked, first by Portia in the courtroom, later by Bassanio in Belmont.[58]

Shakespeare's Belmont is filled with joy, and its mistress abounds in charm. In a lighthearted scene, Portia jests with her waiting woman Nerissa about the faults of her suitors. The Neapolitan prince is so proud of his ability to shoe his horse that Portia is "much afeard my lady his mother play'd false with a smith" (I, 2, 47–48). To escape the Duke of Saxony's nephew, she need only set a glass of wine on one of the wrong caskets. "For, if the devil be within and that temptation without, I know he will choose it" (I, 2, 105–107). As for the French lord Bon, "God made him, and therefore let him pass for a man" (I, 2, 60–61). Although we know Portia will get her heart's desire, we share her suspense. When Bassanio's turn comes, we listen approvingly as, with exquisite grace, she conveys a hint of her love:

I pray you tarry; pause a day or two
Before you hazard; for in choosing wrong
I lose your company. Therefore forbear awhile.
There's something tells me (but it is not love)
I would not lose you.

(III, 2, 1–5)

She makes a slip of the tongue, then, as Freud (expanding on an observation by Otto Rank) points out,[59] corrects it without really changing her meaning:

One half of me is yours, the other half yours—
Mine own, I would say; but if mine, then yours,
And so all yours!

                              (III, 2, 16–18)

This is one of those marvelously subtle Shakespearean touches.

While Portia and Bassanio are discovering their love, Belmont casts its spell on other lovers. Nerissa becomes the wife of Bassanio's witty friend Gratiano, and a third pair soon arrives: Lorenzo and Jessica, who have eloped from Venice. In Portia's moonlit garden, as they await news from Venice, Lorenzo begins a duet, "In such a night as this" (V, 1, 1); and, in alternation, he and Jessica playfully (or perhaps ominously?)[60] invoke classical lovers who ended in misfortune: Troilus and Cressida, Pyramus and Thisbe, Dido and Aeneas, Jason and Medea. Their game, which is interrupted just as they are beginning to ring the changes on their own situation, provides welcome relief from the tension of the courtroom scene and indicates that Lorenzo and Jessica are perhaps more fully realized characters than some might think. Lorenzo has the privilege of speaking some of the most luminous poetry that Shakespeare ever wrote:

How sweet the moonlight sleeps upon this bank!
Here will we sit and let the sounds of music
Creep in our ears. Soft stillness and the night
Become the touches of sweet harmony.
Sit, Jessica. Look how the floor of heaven
Is thick inlaid with patens of bright gold.

                              (V, 1, 54–59)

But the fun and melody that permeate this lovers' sanctuary cannot dispel the fearful impression made by Jessica's father, who, though appearing in only five of the play's twenty scenes, exerts an influence far too somber for the bright world of romance. After almost four centuries Shylock, who leaves the Venice courtroom in defeat at the end of Act IV, still dominates most discussions of the play and remains a challenge to actors and critics.

From his first entrance Shylock is depicted as an alien speaking a constricted language that is uniquely his. "Three thousand ducats— well.... For three months—well.... Antonio shall become bound— well.... Three thousand ducats for three months, and Antonio bound" (I, 3, 1–10). The usurer, with his relentless repetitions, is as parsimonious with words as with money. His clipped style becomes the perfect vehicle for expressing controlled but long-festering hatred:

You call me misbeliever, cutthroat dog,
And spet upon my Jewish gaberdine,
And all for use of that which is mine own.
Well then, it now appears you need my help.
Go to then, you come to me and you say,
"Shylock, we would have moneys." You say so—
You that did void your rheum upon my beard
And foot me as you spurn a stranger cur
Over your threshold. Moneys is your suit.
What should I say to you? Should I not say
"Hath a dog money? Is it possible
A cur can lend three thousand ducats?" or
Shall I bend low, and in a bondman's key,
With bated breath and whisp'ring humbleness,
Say this:
"Fair sir, you spet on me on Wednesday last;
You spurn'd me such a day; another time
You call'd me dog; and for these courtesies
I'll lend you thus much moneys?"

(I, 2, 112–130)

Later, after his daughter Jessica has taken his ducats and fled with a Christian, leaving him to bear the taunts of Bassanio's friends, Shylock delivers his immortal speech, a brilliant synthesis of self-pity, vindictiveness, and racial pride:

I am a Jew. Hath not a Jew eyes? Hath not a Jew hands, organs, dimensions, senses, affections, passions? fed with the same food, hurt with the same weapons, subject to the same diseases, healed by the same means, warmed and cooled by the same winter and summer as a Christian is? If you prick us, do we not bleed? If you tickle us, do we not laugh? If you poison us, do we not die? And if you wrong us, shall we not revenge? If we are like you in the rest, we will resemble you in that. If a Jew wrong a Christian, what is his humility? Revenge. If a Christian wrong a Jew, what should his sufferance be by Christian example? Why, revenge.

(III, 1, 61–74)[61]

Thus Shylock, who had called the pound of flesh a "merry bond" (I, 3, 174), comes to regard it as a symbol of retribution. He attempts to elevate personal revenge to the level of a moral and racial principle. What an inhuman figure he cuts in the courtroom! Insisting with grotesque logic that the pound of flesh is rightfully his, he whets his knife upon the sole of his shoe—a gesture that to this day chills spectators in the theater. Portia tries to reach him with her celebrated appeal:

The quality of mercy is not strain'd;
It droppeth as the gentle rain from heaven
Upon the place beneath. It is twice blest—
It blesseth him that gives, and him that takes.
. . . .
Though justice be thy plea, consider this—
That, in the course of justice, none of us
Should see salvation. We do pray for mercy,
And that same prayer doth teach us all to render
The deeds of mercy.

                                      (IV, 1, 184–202)

Shylock is not moved. He has brought a scale so as to weigh one pound
exactly; such meticulousness would have been prescribed in the bond.
But when Portia urges that a surgeon be ready to stop Antonio's wounds,
Shylock refuses. "Is it so nominated in the bond?" he asks. "I cannot
find it; 'tis not in the bond" (IV, 1, 259–262). At this point Shylock
must be subdued with his own weapons, and Portia can be as legalistic
as he.[62]

Except for Hamlet, Shylock has provoked more discussion than any
other character in Shakespeare, and the critic's task has been made more
difficult by the experience of European Jewry under Hitler. What attitude
should one take toward the repugnant Jew in the play and toward the
unfeeling Christians who rejoice in his suffering? Shakespeare obviously
did not think of anti-Semitism in the Nazi sense, and neither he nor his
fellow Elizabethans could have known many Jews at first hand.[63] Nevertheless, critical assessments of *The Merchant of Venice* seem ultimately
to hinge on the Jewish question.

It is impossible to do justice to the huge volume of commentary on
Shylock, but a few representative views may be summarized. E. E. Stoll
sees him unsentimentally as a Jew and a usurer, a character who would
have elicited only contempt from Shakespeare's audience. But James
Smith argues that Shakespeare need not have tailored his sympathies and
attitudes to fit those of a mass public. To Bernard Grebanier the Jewish
issue is irrelevant, but Shylock the usurer is cruel and unsympathetic.
The poet Heinrich Heine romanticizes Shylock. (One night, Heine reports, a "pale, fair Briton" stood beside him in a box at Drury Lane and,
after the fourth act, "fell to weeping passionately, several times exclaim-
ing, 'The poor man is wronged!' ") In Shylock, Heine says, "the Poet
vindicates an unfortunate sect, which for mysterious purposes, has been
burdened by Providence with the hate of the rabble both high and low,
and has reciprocated this hate—not always by love." H. B. Charlton
considers Shylock to be the composite product of Shakespeare the anti-
Semite and Shakespeare the dramatist and observes that the raving

demon of the courtroom scene has been largely created by his Christian tormentors. According to Tillyard, Shylock is neither comic nor joyless, but "the hero's enemy in the fairy-tale"; this echoes Granville-Barker's declaration that "there is no more reality in Shylock's bond and the Lord of Belmont's will than in Jack and the Beanstalk." Dover Wilson calls Shylock "a terrible old man . . . the inevitable product of centuries of racial persecution," but goes on to say that Shakespeare does not take sides and draws no moral. Finally, Nevill Coghill and Barbara Lewalski are among those who maintain that the play, in the tradition of medieval allegory, presents the conflict between Justice and Mercy, Jew and Gentile, the Old Law and the New—with the marriage of Jessica and Lorenzo symbolizing the harmony of the two themes. Coghill proposes that, however one may react today to Shylock's enforced conversion, an Elizabethan audience would have construed it as evidence of Antonio's mercifulness: The Jew is being offered salvation. Comic Shylocks, malevolent Shylocks, heroic Shylocks, allegorized Shylocks, and even a few Shylocks dwindled by critics to near insignificance—there is no end to the discussion.[64]

This radical disagreement concerning Shylock and his function in what is, after all, a comedy underscores a weakness in the play. Despite the structural relationships between the Belmont and the Venice plots, the materials of *The Merchant of Venice* are in the final analysis not completely integrated. In *A Midsummer Night's Dream* Shakespeare managed to unite three groups of characters—courtiers, fairies, tradesmen—around a cohesive dramatic theme, the irrationality of romantic love. But *The Merchant of Venice,* an "ironic comedy,"[65] presents two fundamentally discordant worlds with two irreconcilable life-styles: romantic Belmont, generously infused with delectable make-believe; and harsh, mercantile Venice, operating on the principle of economic gain and allowing no room for the delicate, the joyous, or the fanciful. Even so, Shakespeare might have solved the problem had he not created so powerful a Shylock to upset the balance. If Shylock were simply a monster, we would have no trouble. But, as Mark Van Doren says, he is instead "a man thrust into a world bound not to endure him."[66]

THE MERRY WIVES OF WINDSOR

Tradition has it that Shakespeare wrote a third Falstaff play at the command of Queen Elizabeth, who wanted to see the fat knight in love. Be that as it may, *The Merry Wives of Windsor* poses problems as to text, date, and occasion. First published in 1602 in a bad quarto, it was not reprinted until 1623, when a much longer and better version appeared in the First Folio.[67] Although scholars used to date the play around 1600 on the basis of its presumed relationship to *Henry IV* and *Henry V*, there is strong evidence for the view (originally set forth by Leslie Hotson in 1931) that it was first performed at Whitehall on April 23, 1597 (St. George's Day), at the Feast of the Order of the Garter.[68] There is no known source, but there are countless analogues.[69]

It is customary to denigrate the play on the grounds that its Falstaff is a dupe who lacks the wit of his incomparable namesake in *Henry IV*.[70] But as Dr. Johnson observed, "Falstaff could not love, but by ceasing to be Falstaff."[71] Shakespeare's only bourgeois play succeeds on its own terms as an ingenious and fast-moving farce, full of deception and counter-deception.[72]

In the main plot Sir John, who fancies himself a ladies' man (actually it is money he is after), sends duplicate love letters to Mrs. Ford and Mrs. Page. The merry wives resolve to teach him a lesson, and, assisted by the go-between Mistress Quickly, they arrange a tryst between Falstaff and Mrs. Ford at the latter's house. Meanwhile, Ford (disguised as "Brook") hears Falstaff boast of his impending amour and burns with jealousy. When Ford bursts in, hoping to catch his wife in the act, Falstaff is hurriedly stuffed into a basket of dirty linen and dumped into a ditch by the river Thames. At a second assignation, again interrupted by Ford, Falstaff disguises himself as the fat woman of Brainford, receives a vigorous beating from Ford, and finally escapes. Ford and Page are then let in on the fun, and all join forces to humiliate Falstaff again. A third rendezvous is arranged for Windsor Park, where Falstaff, disguised as Herne the hunter and wearing a buck's head, is pinched and burned by an assortment of characters disguised as satyrs, hobgoblins, and fairies.[73] Falstaff at last gets the point. "I do begin to perceive that I am made an ass" (V, 5, 124–125).

Despite the relative drabness of this imitation Falstaff, there are flashes of the old brilliance. Reflecting upon his sojourn in the river, Sir John laughs at himself: "And you may know by my size that I have a kind of alacrity in sinking. If the bottom were as deep as hell, I should down" (III, 5, 12–15). He is almost exuberant as he describes to the disguised Ford the sensation of being crammed in the laundry basket:

And then, to be stopp'd in, like a strong distillation, with stinking clothes that fretted in their own grease. Think of that—a man of my kidney!—think of that!—that am as subject to heat as butter; a man of continual dissolution and thaw.

(III, 5, 114–119)

Later, explaining to "Brook" how, as the fat woman of Brainford, he was thrashed by Ford, Falstaff reveals his old talent for equivocating:

I will tell you, he beat me grievously in the shape of a woman; for in the shape of man, Master Brook, I fear not Goliah [Goliath] with a weaver's beam, because I know also life is a shuttle.

(V, 1, 21–25)

Although Falstaff is the star, one can also respond to the gusto of the secondary plot: the elaborate deception whereby Anne Page marries her truelove Fenton, although her mother champions the Frenchman Dr. Caius while her father has promised her to the well-to-do Slender. Dr. Caius, together with the Welsh parson Hugh Evans, makes fritters of the English language, and Anne certainly does not want to marry him. "Alas, I had rather be set quick [alive] i' th' earth / And bowl'd to death with turnips!" (III, 4, 90–91). As for Slender, who exemplifies "intellect flickering with its last feeble glimmer,"[74] let his "proposal" to Anne speak for itself:

Slender: Now, good Mistress Anne—
Anne: What is your will?
Slender: My will? Od's heartlings [God's little heart], that's a pretty jest indeed! I ne'er made my will yet, I thank heaven. I am not such a sickly creature, I give heaven praise.
Anne: I mean, Master Slender, what would you with me?
Slender: Truly, for mine own part, I would little or nothing with you. Your father and my uncle hath made motions. If it be my luck, so; if not, happy man be his dole! They can tell you how things go better than I can.

(III, 4, 57–69)

"Good mother," Anne pleads (and we commiserate), "do not marry me to yond fool" (III, 4, 87).

There are other memorable characters. The bombastic Pistol speaks scarcely a word of intelligible English. The warmhearted Host of the Garter Inn is a "bully" Englishman whether laughing at the lovesick Fenton, who in love "smells April and May" (III, 2, 68–70), or averting a duel between the French body-curer and the Welsh soul-curer:

Shall I lose my doctor? No! he gives me the potions and the motions. Shall I lose my parson, my priest, my Sir Hugh? No! he gives me the proverbs and the no-verbs. Give me thy hand, terrestrial! so. Give me thy hand, celestial! so. . . . Your hearts are mighty, your skins are whole, and let burnt sack be the issue.

(III, 1, 104–112)

Finally, there is Mistress Quickly, who chastises Parson Evans for corrupting a young pupil with Latin demonstrative pronouns:

You do ill to teach the child such words. He teaches him to hick and
to hack, which they'll do fast enough of themselves, and to call *horum.* Fie
upon you!

(IV, 1, 67–70)

Verdi's opera *Falstaff,* which has been described as "the very best
commentary on *The Merry Wives* ever written,"[75] concludes with a
fugue in honor of laughter, an ensemble Falstaff himself initiates. All is
forgiven. The victim draws the social group together, and that is entirely
in the spirit of Shakespeare's happy comedy.[76]

NOTES

1. Samuel Johnson, "Preface to Shakespeare," in *Johnson on Shakespeare,* ed.
Arthur Sherbo, Vols. 7 and 8 of The Yale Edition of the Works of Samuel
Johnson (New Haven: Yale University Press, 1968), p. 69.
2. John Dover Wilson, *Shakespeare's Happy Comedies* (Evanston, Ill.: North-
western University Press, 1962), p. 16.
3. See Muriel C. Bradbrook, *The Growth and Structure of Elizabethan Comedy*
(London: Chatto & Windus, 1955), pp. 71–85 and Ernest William Talbert,
Elizabethan Drama and Shakespeare's Early Plays (Chapel Hill: University
of North Carolina Press, 1963), pp. 7–60. On Lyly's influence, see Marco
Mincoff, "Shakespeare and Lyly," *Shakespeare Survey* 14 (1961): 15–24 and
G. K. Hunter, *John Lyly: The Humanist as Courtier* (London: Routledge &
Kegan Paul, 1962), pp. 298–349. On Greene, see Norman Sanders, "The
Comedy of Greene and Shakespeare," in *Early Shakespeare,* eds. John Russell
Brown and Bernard Harris, Stratford-upon-Avon Studies 3 (London: Edward
Arnold, 1961), pp. 35–53.
4. See C. L. Barber, *Shakespeare's Festive Comedy* (Princeton: Princeton Uni-
versity Press, 1959). See also Northrop Frye, "The Argument of Comedy," in
English Institute Essays 1948, ed. D. A. Robertson, Jr. (New York: Columbia
University Press, 1949), pp. 58–73.
5. For a full description of classical, medieval, and Elizabethan traditions
inherited by Shakespeare (e.g., disguise and trickery, the judge-and-the-nun
motif, interrupted marriages), see Leo Salingar, *Shakespeare and the Traditions
of Comedy* (London: Cambridge University Press, 1974). This is an indispensable book, and the author promises a sequel to be devoted more directly
to Shakespeare's plays.
6. George Gordon, *Shakespearian Comedy and Other Studies* (Oxford: Oxford
University Press, 1944), p. 49.
7. More recently Alexander Leggatt has taken the view, similar to Gordon's,
that Shakespearean comedy is built upon various kinds of juxtapositions and
dislocations. See his excellent book *Shakespeare's Comedy of Love* (London:
Methuen, 1974).
8. John Russell Brown, in *Shakespeare and His Comedies,* 2d ed. (London:

Methuen, 1962), pp. 28–44, distinguishes between intrigue comedy and narrative comedy. A more recent distinction has been made on the assumption that, as he evolved as a comic dramatist, Shakespeare achieved an "increasingly complex depth of characterization"; see Larry S. Champion, *The Evolution of Shakespeare's Comedy: A Study in Dramatic Perspective* (Cambridge: Harvard University Press, 1970), p. 7. Champion accordingly sees three kinds of comedy: (1) comedy of *physical action;* (2) comedy of *identity,* in which a character's true nature is revealed to others or to himself; (3) comedy of *transformation of values,* involving sin, repentance, and sacrificial forgiveness. Champion's book contains important notes (pp. 189–233) that can be read virtually as a comprehensive guide to critical opinion on many salient points, including individual plays and characters.

9. On the text, see E. K. Chambers, *William Shakespeare: A Study of Facts and Problems,* 2 vols. (Oxford: Clarendon, 1930), 1: 305–312; W. W. Greg, *The Shakespeare First Folio: Its Bibliographical and Textual History* (Oxford: Clarendon, 1955), pp. 200–202; and the New Arden *The Comedy of Errors,* ed. R. A. Foakes, 5th ed. (Cambridge: Harvard University Press, 1962), pp. xi–xvi. On the date, see Sidney Thomas, "The Date of *The Comedy of Errors,*" *Shakespeare Quarterly* 7 (1956): 377–384 and the New Arden edition, pp. xvi–xxiii. The Elizabethan account of the Gray's Inn performance is reprinted in Chambers, 2: 319–320 and the New Arden edition, pp. 115–117.

10. On sources, see Geoffrey Bullough, *Narrative and Dramatic Sources of Shakespeare,* 8 vols. (New York: Columbia University Press, 1957–1975), 1: 3–54; Kenneth Muir, *Shakespeare's Sources* (London: Methuen, 1957), pp. 18–20; and the New Arden edition, pp. xxiv–xxxiv, 109–115.

11. Even in his apprenticeship, Shakespeare shows astonishing maturity and capacity for innovation, especially in comedy; see Robert Y. Turner, *Shakespeare's Apprenticeship* (Chicago: University of Chicago Press, 1974). On the structure of the play, see G. R. Elliott, "Weirdness in *The Comedy of Errors,*" *University of Toronto Quarterly* 9 (1939): 95–106. For an excellent analysis of I, 2, see Harold Brooks, "Themes and Structure in *The Comedy of Errors,*" in *Early Shakespeare,* eds. Brown and Harris, pp. 55–71.

12. See Peter G. Phialas, *Shakespeare's Romantic Comedies: The Development of Their Form and Meaning* (Chapel Hill: University of North Carolina Press, 1966), pp. 3–17.

13. Brown (*Shakespeare and His Comedies,* pp. 54–57) sees it as a study of *possessive* love versus *giving* love; Brooks ("Themes and Structure," pp. 55–71), as a search for personal identity. Brooks's view is shared by Michael Grivelet, "Shakespeare, Molière, and the Comedy of Ambiguity," *Shakespeare Survey* 22 (1969): 15–26; and by A. C. Hamilton, *The Early Shakespeare* (San Marino, Calif.: The Huntington Library, 1967), pp. 90–108.

14. R. A. Foakes, in the New Arden edition, p. 1. For another balanced appraisal, see Ralph Berry, *Shakespeare's Comedies: Explorations in Form* (Princeton: Princeton University Press, 1972), pp. 24–39.

15. See Richard Hosley, "Sources and Analogues of *The Taming of the Shrew,*" *The Huntington Library Quarterly* 27 (1963–1964): 289–308 and Jan Harold Brunvand, "The Folktale Origin of *The Taming of the Shrew,*" *Shakespeare*

Quarterly 17 (1966): 345–359. On the text, see Greg, *The Shakespeare First Folio*, pp. 210–216 and the New Cambridge *The Taming of the Shrew*, eds. A. Quiller-Couch and John Dover Wilson (Cambridge: Cambridge University Press, 1928), pp. 97–126.

16. Edwin Wilson, ed., *Shaw on Shakespeare* (London: Cassell, 1961), p. 180; Harold Goddard, *The Meaning of Shakespeare* (Chicago: University of Chicago Press, 1951), pp. 68–73; Nevill Coghill, "The Basis of Shakespearian Comedy," *Essays and Studies*, n. s. 3 (1950): 1–28, reprinted in *Shakespeare Criticism, 1935–1960*, ed. Anne Ridler (London: Oxford University Press, 1963), pp. 201–227; Berry, *Shakespeare's Comedies*, pp. 67–70.

Juliet Dusinberre, *Shakespeare and the Nature of Women* (New York: Barnes & Noble, 1975), makes a case for a strong feminist current in Elizabethan England. See also Carroll Camden, *The Elizabethan Woman* (London: Cleaver-Hune, 1952).

17. Robert B. Heilman, "*The Taming* Untamed, or, The Return of the Shrew," *Modern Language Quarterly* 27 (1966): 147–161.

18. In Bullough, *Sources*, 1: 112.

19. Cecil Seronsy, " 'Supposes' as the Unifying Theme in *The Taming of the Shrew*," *Shakespeare Quarterly* 14 (1963): 15–30.

20. There is disagreement as to whether Shakespeare's play originally had an epilogue. It did, says Peter Alexander, "The Original Ending of *The Taming of the Shrew*," *Shakespeare Quarterly* 20 (1969): 111–116; but it was later cut because of a personnel shortage in Shakespeare's company. It did not, says Richard Hosley, "Was There a Dramatic Epilogue to *The Taming of the Shrew?*" *Studies in English Literature, 1500–1900* 1, no. 2 (Spring 1961): 17–34.

21. See Thelma N. Greenfield, "The Transformation of Christopher Sly," *Philological Quarterly* 33 (1954): 34–42.

22. See the New Arden *Two Gentlemen of Verona*, ed. Clifford Leech, 2d ed. (Cambridge: Harvard University Press, 1969), pp. xxi–xxxv, where a case is made for composition on several strata. On the text, see pp. xiii–xxi; Chambers, *William Shakespeare*, 1: 329–331; and Greg, *The Shakespeare First Folio*, pp. 217–218.

23. See Bullough, *Sources*, 1: 203–266.

24. See Hereward T. Price, "Shakespeare as a Critic," *Philological Quarterly* 20 (1941): 390–399; Berry, *Shakespeare's Comedies*, pp. 40–53.

25. Earlier versions of the love-friendship theme are surveyed by Hamilton, *The Early Shakespeare*, pp. 114–127.

26. See Thomas E. Scheye, "Two Gentlemen of Milan," *Shakespeare Studies*, ed. J. Leeds Barroll, 7 (1974): 11–23; Peter Lindenbaum, "Education in *The Two Gentlemen of Verona*," *Studies in English Literature, 1500–1900* 15 (1975): 229–244.

27. See Phialas, *Shakespeare's Romantic Comedies*, pp. 53–55; Robert G. Hunter, *Shakespeare and the Comedy of Forgiveness* (New York: Columbia University Press, 1965), pp. 85–87; and Alan R. Velie, *Shakespeare's Repentance Plays: The Search for an Adequate Form* (Rutherford, N. J.: Fairleigh Dickinson University Press, 1972), pp. 17–35. The form, says Velie (pp. 91–113), was fully developed in *The Winter's Tale*.

28. Harold Brooks, "Two Clowns in a Comedy (to say nothing of the Dog)," *Essays and Studies*, n.s. 16 (1963): 91–100.

29. It has been shown that the play, in its use and criticism of the conventions of love poetry, has important links with the *Sonnets*. See Inga-Stina Ewbank, " 'Were man but constant, he were perfect': Constancy and Consistency in *The Two Gentlemen of Verona*," *Shakespearian Comedy*, eds. Malcolm Bradbury and David Palmer, Stratford-upon-Avon Studies 14 (London: Edward Arnold, 1972), pp. 31–57.

30. See Alfred Harbage, "*Love's Labour's Lost* and the Early Shakespeare," *Philological Quarterly* 41 (1962): 18–36. Evidence for the date is surveyed in the New Arden *Love's Labour's Lost,* ed. Richard David, 4th ed. (Cambridge: Harvard University Press, 1951), pp. xxvi–xxxii. On the text, see the New Arden edition, pp. xvii–xxvi; Chambers, *William Shakespeare*, 1: 331–338; Greg, *The Shakespeare First Folio*, pp. 219–224; the New Cambridge edition, eds. A. Quiller-Couch and John Dover Wilson (Cambridge: Cambridge University Press, 1923), pp. vii–xlii, 98–135.

31. On the possible significance of the Muscovite episode, see Bullough, *Sources*, 1: 431–433.

32. See the New Arden edition, pp. xliv–xlvi. Two major studies of Raleigh's presumed relationship to the play are Frances A. Yates, *A Study of Love's Labour's Lost* (Cambridge: Cambridge University Press, 1936) and Muriel C. Bradbrook, *The School of Night* (Cambridge: Cambridge University Press, 1936), especially pp. 151–178.

33. Harley Granville-Barker, *Prefaces to Shakespeare*, 2 vols. (Princeton: Princeton University Press, 1946–1947), 2: 413.

34. See Bobbyann Roesen, "*Love's Labour's Lost*," *Shakespeare Quarterly* 4 (1953): 411–426 and Paul E. Memmo, Jr., "The Poetry of the *Stilnovisti* and *Love's Labour's Lost*," *Comparative Literature* 18 (1966): 1–15.

35. See Herbert A. Ellis, *Shakespeare's Lusty Punning in Love's Labour's Lost* (The Hague: Mouton, 1973).

36. J. J. Anderson, "The Morality of *Love's Labour's Lost*," *Shakespeare Survey* 24 (1971): 55. See also E. M. W. Tillyard, *Shakespeare's Early Comedies* New York: Barnes & Noble, 1965), p. 151 and Herbert R. Coursen, Jr., "*Love's Labour's Lost* and the Comic Truth," *Papers on Language and Literature* 6 (1970): 316–322.

37. This is among the perceptive points made by Thomas M. Greene, "*Love's Labour's Lost:* The Grace of Society," *Shakespeare Quarterly* 22 (1971): 315–328.

38. Arguing that Marcade's entrance has been taken too seriously, Thomas McFarland believes that the pastoral world retains its serenity even in the face of death. See *Shakespeare's Pastoral Comedy* (Chapel Hill: University of North Carolina Press, 1972), pp. 61–63.

39. Barber, *Shakespeare's Festive Comedy*, p. 118. Among those who have written well on the relationship of the songs to the play as a whole, see Catherine McLay, "The Dialogues of Spring and Winter: A Key to the Unity of *Love's Labour's Lost*," *Shakespeare Quarterly* 18 (1967): 119–127; S. K. Heninger, Jr., "The Pattern of *Love's Labour's Lost*," *Shakespeare Studies*, ed.

J. Leeds Barroll 7 (1974): 25–53; and Malcolm Evans, "Mercury versus Apollo: A Reading of *Love's Labour's Lost*," *Shakespeare Quarterly* 26 (1975): 113–127.

40. See Kenneth Muir, "Pyramus and Thisbe: A Study in Shakespeare's Method," *Shakespeare Quarterly* 5 (1954): 141–153 and *Shakespeare's Sources*, pp. 31–47. See also Bullough, *Sources*, 1: 367–422. On the text, see the New Cambridge *A Midsummer Night's Dream,* eds. A. Quiller-Couch and John Dover Wilson (Cambridge: Cambridge University Press, 1924), pp. vii–viii, 77–100, 154–159 and Greg, *The Shakespeare First Folio*, pp. 240–247. The play's appropriateness for a wedding celebration has been shown by Paul A. Olson, "*A Midsummer Night's Dream* and the Meaning of Court Marriage," *ELH* 24 (1957): 95–119.

41. On Robin Goodfellow and Elizabethan fairy lore in general, see Minor White Latham, *The Elizabethan Fairies* (New York: Columbia University Press, 1930) and Katherine M. Briggs, *The Anatomy of Puck* (London: Routledge & Kegan Paul, 1959).

42. Barber, *Shakespeare's Festive Comedy*, p. 129.

43. Enid Welsford, *The Court Masque* (Cambridge: Cambridge University Press, 1927), pp. 331–332.

44. Stephen Fender, *Shakespeare: A Midsummer Night's Dream* (London: Edward Arnold, 1968), p. 14.

45. This theme is established in the very first scene of the play; see Frank Kermode's stimulating analysis, "The Mature Comedies," in *Early Shakespeare*, eds. Brown and Harris, pp. 214–220.

46. Theseus's reputation during the Renaissance was somewhat tainted; hence Shakespeare may have intended him to be viewed ironically. See D'Orsay W. Pearson, " 'Unkinde' Theseus: A Study in Renaissance Mythography," *English Literary Renaissance* 4 (1974): 276–298.

47. Several studies in one way or another address themselves to this point: Brown, *Shakespeare and His Comedies*, pp. 83–91; R. W. Dent, "Imagination in *A Midsummer Night's Dream*," *Shakespeare Quarterly* 15 (1964): 115–129; Fender, *Shakespeare: A Midsummer Night's Dream*; James L. Calderwood, *Shakespearean Metadrama* (Minneapolis: University of Minnesota Press, 1971), pp. 120–148; Marjorie B. Garber, *Dream in Shakespeare* (New Haven: Yale University Press, 1974), pp. 59–87; and an excellent book-length study of the play, David P. Young, *Something of Great Constancy: The Art of "A Midsummer Night's Dream"* (New Haven: Yale University Press, 1966), especially pp. 109–166.

48. See B. Ifor Evans, *The Language of Shakespeare's Plays* (London: Methuen, 1959), pp. 70–77.

49. See an important older study, Samuel B. Hemingway, "The Relation of *A Midsummer Night's Dream* to *Romeo and Juliet*," *Modern Language Notes* 24 (1911): 78–80.

50. For further remarks on "Pyramus and Thisby," *A Midsummer Night's Dream*, and *Romeo and Juliet*, see Barber's long note in *Shakespeare's Festive Comedy*, pp. 152–154; Kenneth Muir, "Shakespeare as Parodist," *Notes and Queries* 199 (1954): 467–468; and Madeleine Doran, "Pyramus and Thisbe

Once More," in *Essays on Shakespeare and Elizabethan Drama in Honor of Hardin Craig*, ed. Richard Hosley (Columbia: University of Missouri Press, 1962), pp. 149–161.

51. For perceptive commentary on Bottom's play and its relationship to the real world, see Anne Righter, *Shakespeare and the Idea of the Play* (London: Chatto & Windus, 1962), pp. 107–110, also interesting for its insights into *Love's Labour's Lost* and the play-within-a-play convention.

52. H. B. Charlton, *Shakespearian Comedy* (London: Macmillan, 1938), p. 119.

53. William B. Dillingham, "Bottom: The Third Ingredient," *Emory University Quarterly* 12 (1956): 230–237. That the play is a political allegory, with Bottom representing the Duke of Alençon (who was trying to negotiate a marriage with Queen Elizabeth) has been argued by Marion A. Taylor, *Bottom, Thou Art Translated* (Amsterdam: Rodopi NV, 1973), especially pp. 131–165.

54. Evidence for the date is assessed in the New Arden edition, ed. John Russell Brown, 7th ed. (Cambridge: Harvard University Press, 1955), pp. xxi–xxvii. On the text, see pp. xi–xxi; Greg, *The Shakespeare First Folio*, pp. 240–247; and the New Cambridge edition, eds. A. Quiller-Couch and John Dover Wilson (Cambridge: Cambridge University Press, 1926), pp. 91–119, 173–177.

55. On the sources, see the New Arden edition, pp. 140–174; Bullough, *Sources*, 1: 445–514; and Muir, *Shakespeare's Sources*, pp. 47–51.

56. Brown (*Shakespeare and His Comedies*, pp. 61–75) discusses the interrelationships between commerce and love in the play.

57. Sigurd Burckhardt, *"The Merchant of Venice:* The Gentle Bond," *ELH* 29 (1962): 239–262.

58. W. Gordon Zeeveld, *The Temper of Shakespeare's Thought* (New Haven: Yale University Press, 1974), pp. 149–159.

59. Sigmund Freud, "Introductory Lectures on Psycho-analysis: Lecture II ('Parapraxes')," *The Complete Psychological Works of Sigmund Freud*, ed. James Strachey, 24 vols. (London: Hogarth, 1966–1974), 15: 37–38.

60. The television version of the 1970 National Theatre production ends with Jessica alone on the stage and (like her father, played by Sir Laurence Olivier) excluded from the general merriment.

61. Alan C. Dessen suggests that the stage Jew was used as a stage device to expose Christian hypocrisy; see "The Elizabethan Stage Jew and Christian Example: Gerontus, Barabas, and Shylock, *"Modern Language Quarterly* 35 (1974): 231–245.

62. There have been numerous discussions of the courtroom scene by legal scholars. See, for example, George W. Keeton, *"Shylock* v. *Antonio,"* in his *Shakespeare's Legal and Political Background* (London: Pitman, 1967), pp. 132–150 and O. Hood Phillips, *Shakespeare and the Lawyers* (London: Methuen, 1972), pp. 91–118. Phillips includes an exhaustive survey of earlier opinions about the trial. The play may also reflect Shakespeare's deep, perhaps personal, involvement with legal issues of his day. See Mark Edwin Andrews, *Law versus Equity in The Merchant of Venice* (Boulder: Colorado University Press, 1965) and W. Nicholas Knight, "Equity, *The Merchant of Venice*, and William Lambarde," *Shakespeare Survey* 27 (1974): 93–104.

63. But see C. J. Sisson, "A Colony of Jews in Shakespeare's London," *Essays and Studies* 23 (1938): 38–51.

64. E. E. Stoll, "Shylock," *Journal of English and Germanic Philology* 10 (1911): 236–279, included in E. E. Stoll, *Shakespeare Studies* (New York: Macmillan, 1927); James Smith, *Shakespearian and Other Essays* (Cambridge: Cambridge University Press, 1974), pp. 58–61; Bernard Grebanier, *The Truth about Shylock* (New York: Random House, 1962); Heinrich Heine, *Sämmtliche Werke* (Philadelphia, 1856), 5: 324, quoted in the New Variorum *The Merchant of Venice*, ed. Horace H. Furness, 11th ed. (Philadelphia: Lippincott, 1888, 1916), pp. 449–450; Charlton, *Shakespearian Comedy*, pp. 123–160; Tillyard, *Shakespeare's Early Comedies*, p. 194; Granville-Barker, *Prefaces to Shakespeare*, 1: 335; Coghill, "The Basis of Shakespearian Comedy"; Barbara K. Lewalski, "Biblical Allusion and Allegory in *The Merchant of Venice*," *Shakespeare Quarterly* 13 (1962): 327–343.

There is a useful collection of recent essays: Sylvan Barnet, ed., *Twentieth-Century Interpretations of The Merchant of Venice* (Englewood Cliffs, N.J.: Prentice-Hall, 1970). For some vivid glimpses of Shylock as interpreted by famous actors of the eighteenth, nineteenth, and twentieth centuries, see John Russell Brown, "The Realization of Shylock," in *Early Shakespeare*, eds. Brown and Harris, pp. 187–209 and Toby Lelyveld, *Shylock on the Stage* (Cleveland: The Press of Western Reserve University, 1960).

In a lighter vein, see Leo Rockas's *tour de force* satirizing the symbolic readings of the play, " 'A Dish of Doves': *The Merchant of Venice*," *ELH* 40 (1973): 339–351.

65. It is so characterized in Anthony D. Moody's stimulating book, *Shakespeare: The Merchant of Venice* (London: Edward Arnold, 1964).

66. Mark Van Doren, *Shakespeare* (New York: Holt, 1939), p. 105. Patrick Swinden, in *An Introduction to Shakespeare's Comedies* (London: Macmillan, 1973), p. 76, sees Shylock as "a splendid gargoyle stuck to the edifice of a fairy palace." But James Smith (*Shakespearian and Other Essays*, pp. 43–68) writes well on the interaction of fairytale and realistic elements in the play.

67. On the text, see Greg, *The Shakespeare First Folio*, pp. 334–337 and the New Arden *The Merry Wives of Windsor*, ed. H. J. Oliver, 2d ed. (Cambridge: Harvard University Press, 1971), pp. viii–xiii.

68. See Leslie Hotson, *Shakespeare versus Shallow* (Boston: Little, Brown, 1931) and William Green, *Shakespeare's 'Merry Wives of Windsor'* (Princeton: Princeton University Press, 1962).

69. See Bullough, *Sources*, 2: 3–58 and the New Arden edition, pp. lviii–lxv. A. L. Bennett thinks Nicholas Udall's play *Ralph Roister Doister* might be a source; see *Renaissance Quarterly* 23 (1970): 429–433.

70. S. C. Sen Gupta says that the play "is a comedy of intrigue not character and this Falstaff has no character worth discussing." See his *Shakespearian Comedy* (London: Oxford University Press, 1950), pp. 271–275. In writing of Falstaff, Swinden (*An Introduction to Shakespeare's Comedies*, p. 77) disdains even to consider "the impostor in the buck-basket."

71. Sherbo, *Johnson on Shakespeare*, p. 341.

72. Alexander Leggatt places Shakespeare's play in the tradition of the citizen

comedy; see his *Citizen Comedy in the Age of Shakespeare* (Toronto: University of Toronto Press, 1973), especially pp. 146–149. On the "practices" (deceptions) in the play, see Bertrand Evans, *Shakespeare's Comedies* (Oxford: Clarendon, 1960), pp. 98–117.

73. This episode has been seen as a comic counterpart of the Actaeon myth as interpreted in Renaissance literature and iconography, the hunter Actaeon having been punished for lechery. See John M. Steadman, "Falstaff as Actaeon: A Dramatic Emblem," *Shakespeare Quarterly* 14 (1963): 231–244.

74. F. S. Boas, *Shakspere and His Predecessors* (1896; reprint ed., New York: Haskell House, 1968), p. 298.

75. Jeanne Addison Roberts, "Falstaff in Windsor Forest: Villain or Victim?" *Shakespeare Quarterly* 26 (1975): 8–15.

76. Ibid.

5
The Earlier History Plays

Of the thirty-six plays in the First Folio, ten were classified by Heminge and Condell, the Folio editors, as histories: two tetralogies dealing with "modern" English history, from the reign of Richard II (1377–1399) to the Battle of Bosworth and the accession of Henry VII (1485), and single plays about the reigns of King John (1199–1216) and Henry VIII (1509–1547), respectively.

The histories have traditionally been interpreted against a background of Tudor moral and political philosophy.[1] Renaissance chroniclers— Polydore Vergil (c. 1470–1555), Edward Hall (c. 1498–1547), and Raphael Holinshed (c. 1529–1580)—perceived in the stretch of history from Richard II to Henry VII a pattern of cause and effect, murder and revenge, sin and punishment. England's guilt was transmitted from generation to generation (as in Aeschylean tragedy) until it was expiated, according to divine plan, at the Battle of Bosworth, where the Earl of Richmond (the future Henry VII) defeated Richard III.[2] In his prayer on the eve of that memorable battle, Richmond sees himself as an agent of God's justice:

> O thou whose captain I account myself,
> Look on my forces with a gracious eye.
> Put in their hands thy bruising irons of wrath,
> That they may crush down with a heavy fall
> Th' usurping helmets of our adversaries.
> Make us thy ministers of chastisement,
> That we may praise thee in thy victory.
>   (*Richard III*, V, 3, 109–115)

Richmond's victory, which ended the civil war known as the Wars of the Roses, meant that God chose the Tudor monarchs (Henry VII and his descendants, including Elizabeth I) to be his exalted deputies on earth. Their inviolable supremacy would fortify the kingdom against invasion from without and civil war from within. Appealing to the principle of order as outlined by Hooker (see p. 23) and set forth in Ulysses' speech on degree (*Troilus and Cressida*, I, 3, 75–137), the Tudor government equated obedience to the king with obedience to God. The "Exhortation concerning Good Order and Obedience to Rulers and Magistrates" (1547), one of the Homilies (standardized sermons) compiled by the government and read throughout England, makes this point with unusual eloquence:

> Almighty God hath created and appointed all things, in heaven, earth and waters, in a most excellent and perfect order. In heaven he hath appointed distinct orders and states of archangels and angels. In the earth he hath assigned kings, princes, with other governors under them, all in good and necessary order. The water above is kept and raineth down in due time and season. The sun, moon, stars, rainbow, thunder, lightning, clouds, and all birds of the air, do keep their order. The earth, trees, seeds, plants, herbs, and corn, grass and all manner of beasts keep them in their order. All the parts of the whole year, as winter, summer, months, nights and days, continue in their order.... For where there is no right order, there reigneth all abuse, carnal liberty, enormity, sin, and Babylonical confusion. Take away kings, princes, rulers, magistrates, judges, and such states of God's order, no man shall ride or go by the highway unrobbed, no man shall sleep in his own house or bed unkilled, no man shall keep his wife, children, and possessions in quietness, all things shall be common, and there must needs follow all mischief and utter destruction, both of souls, bodies, goods and common wealths.[3]

If a subject presumed to pass judgment upon his king, he was challenging all authority, human and divine, and inviting national disaster.

But history was considered valuable for sovereigns no less than for their subjects. Just as Machiavelli found in Livy's history of Rome examples for Italian statesmen to imitate or avoid, so English monarchs might learn from the successes and failures of their predecessors. The popular poem *The Mirror for Magistrates* (1559, 1563, 1578, 1587) offered instructive historical parallels. In the words of the dedication:

> For here as in a loking glas, you shall see (if any vice be in you) howe the like hath bene punished in other heretofore, whereby admonished, I trust it will be a good occasion to move you to the soner amendment.[4]

The play *Gorboduc* (1561), based upon an episode in Geoffrey of Monmouth's *History of the Kings of Britain* (1137), was intended to point up the dangers inherent in a divided kingdom and an uncertain succession.[5] The "good" and "bad" kings portrayed by Shakespeare and other dramatists were traditional symbols of virtues and vices affecting the health of the body politic. If the Lord's Anointed was to fulfill his mission in a worthy manner, he could ignore these models only at extreme peril.

In recent years scholars have increasingly questioned the extent to which Shakespeare shared the Tudor assumptions about history. It has been argued that the histories consistently stress "a political rather than a providential interpretation of events"[6] and that Shakespeare and his contemporaries would have been appalled at the idea of an avenging God who extended his wrath for generations over a whole people.[7] Shakespeare, we are told, was tough and pragmatic, even with regard to so sacrosanct a matter as the legitimacy of a king. "Repeatedly," one critic says of *Henry VI*, "the question of Henry's right to rule turns on the question of whether he can rule."[8] Another goes so far as to suggest that between the writing of *Henry VI* and *Henry V* (the last play in the later tetralogy), Shakespeare came to terms with Machiavellianism, realizing that the successful king had to be devious and ruthless and that an effective ruler, even a usurper, was preferable to a weak king whose legitimacy was beyond question.[9]

It is not difficult to reconcile these views. Although Shakespeare's histories can be profitably studied in the context of Tudor political thought, one should not regard them as message plays that expound uncritically this or that moral idea. No doubt Shakespeare believed in orderly government and deplored rebellion. But A. P. Rossiter has rightly called attention to the ambivalence of the history plays. Shakespeare's intuitive sense of the fullness of experience transcended the narrow morality of the Tudor myth. Hence, although he may have used the myth as a frame, he also saw fit, in Rossiter's words, "to undermine it, to qualify it with equivocations: to vex its applications with sly or subtle ambiguities: to cast doubts on its ultimate human validity, even in situations where its principles seemed most completely applicable."[10] Shakespeare wrote the history plays for the living stage.

Shakespeare's first historical tetralogy—*Henry VI* (Parts One, Two, and Three) and *Richard III*—presents a continuous sequence of events, from the death of Henry V (1422) to the Battle of Bosworth (1485), which ended the reign of Richard III. While forming a comprehensive survey of events during the Wars of the Roses (1455–1485), the four plays may also be seen as the culmination of actions depicted in the more mature tetralogy that Shakespeare wrote several years later (see chapter 8). We learn in the earlier cycle that a long succession of English woes began in 1399 with the deposition and murder by Henry Bolingbroke of an anointed king, Richard II.[11] As Henry IV, Bolingbroke was plagued by internal rebellions. Under his son, Henry V, England enjoyed a resurgence of national glory, but the interlude was all too brief. At Henry V's death, the crown was inherited by the infant Henry VI. The court was rife with factionalism, and Henry VI when he came of age was powerless. England thus entered a new phase of foreign and domestic upheaval, climaxed by Richard III's blood-drenched rise to the throne.

The authorship of the *Henry VI* plays used to be in doubt, with Shakespeare generally considered one of several collaborators in a project that may have included Marlowe, Greene, and Nashe. Nowadays the prevailing opinion is that Shakespeare wrote all of Parts Two and Three and was responsible for much, perhaps all, of Part One. Indeed, Hereward T. Price has made so strong a case for the excellence of *1 Henry VI* as a dramatic structure that one is almost forced to acknowledge Shakespeare as its sole author.[12] Still unresolved is the relationship between Parts Two and Three and two other plays, *The First Part of the Contention betwixt the Two Famous Houses of York and Lancaster* (1594) and *The True Tragedy of Richard Duke of York* (1595). According to an older theory, recently revived, these are pre-Shakespearean source-plays that Shakespeare rewrote. Most scholars, however, endorse the view that they are bad quartos of *2* and *3 Henry VI*.[13]

From Greene's parody of a line from *3 Henry VI* (see p. 1), we know that Parts Two and Three existed in 1592. Part One may have been written later. But the present tendency is to assume that the plays were written in natural order: Parts One and Two in 1590, Part Three in 1590–1591. The principal sources for all three plays are Raphael Holinshed's *Chronicles of England, Scotland, and Ireland* (1587 ed.) and Edward Hall's *Union of the Two Noble and Illustre Families of Lancaster and York* (1548). As always, Shakespeare alters his source for dramatic effect. For example, the historic Joan of Arc was executed in 1431, but in *1 Henry VI* she is alive in 1451 to lead the French against Talbot and the English at Bordeaux.[14]

Each of the *Henry VI* plays has its dramatic focus, as will be apparent when we examine them individually, and it is quite proper that a recent study deliberately addresses itself to their discrete structures.[15] But a fundamental unity is provided in the person of King Henry, who never wanted the crown that had been thrust upon him in infancy. "Was never subject long'd to be a king / As I do long and wish to be a subject" (*2 Henry VI,* IV, 9, 5–6). He pleads when he should command, as when the servants of the bitter rivals Gloucester and Winchester skirmish with each other:

O, how this discord doth afflict my soul!
Can you, my Lord of Winchester, behold

My sighs and tears and will not once relent?
Who should be pitiful if you be not?
                    (*1 Henry VI*, III, 1, 106–109)

York, his most formidable enemy, upbraids him for his weakness:

King did I call thee? No! thou art not King,
Not fit to govern and rule multitudes,
Which dar'st not, no, nor canst not rule a traitor.
That head of thine doth not become a crown;
Thy hand is made to grasp a palmer's staff
And not to grace an awful princely sceptre.
                    (*2 Henry VI*, V, 1, 93–98)

This denunciation echoes a speech made earlier by Margaret of Anjou, Henry's impassioned queen:

But all his mind is bent to holiness,
To number Ave-Maries on his beads;
His champions are the prophets and apostles,
His weapons holy saws of sacred writ;
His study is his tiltyard, and his loves
Are brazen images of canonized saints.
I would the college of the Cardinals
Would choose him Pope and carry him to Rome
And set the triple crown upon his head!
That were a state fit for his holiness.
                    (*2 Henry VI*, I, 3, 58–67)

During the climactic action of Part Three, Henry yearns for the simple life of the shepherd (*3 Henry VI*, II, 5, 21–54), "a pitifully small thing compared with the majestic order he as a king should have been able to impose."[16]

Thus, the suffering of the King, which has something of a redemptive quality about it, is a major unifying theme of the *Henry VI* plays. But there are other effective structural devices. One scholar has shown how the three plays are both an embodiment and a criticism of heroic idealism, which gradually deteriorates between the Hundred Years' War and the accession of the House of York.[17] And the dominant imagery of the three plays—traps, predatory beasts, and cosmic chaos, respectively— has been related to England's progressive spiritual disintegration.[18] To be sure, the *Henry VI* plays do not represent the peak of Shakespeare's artistry, but if we take them seriously (and critics are beginning to do just that), they will repay our attention.

HENRY VI, PART ONE

1 Henry VI underscores the first phase of England's calamity: military defeat at the hands of the French. The play begins in 1422 at the funeral of Henry V, who had led his nation to victory at Agincourt (see chapter 8). But even as his spirit is invoked to bless the realm and "keep it from civil broils" (I, 1, 53), messengers announce, in rapid succession, that several French cities have been retaken, that France has crowned the Dauphin king, and that Lord Talbot, England's finest warrior, has been captured. In this scene, as elsewhere in the play, the heroic past is undermined by the bold intrusion of the present.[19] Talbot's eventual defeat at the siege of Bordeaux (IV, 5–7) crushes any hope of preserving the territories won by Henry V.

It is clear, however, that the English armies themselves are not responsible for their humiliation. Even the French Duke of Alençon, at first contemptuous of the famished English soldiers who "want their porridge and their fat bull-beeves" (I, 2, 9), changes his tune:

> For none but Samsons and Goliases
> It sendeth forth to skirmish. One to ten?
> Lean raw-bon'd rascals—who would e'er suppose
> They had such courage and audacity?
> (I, 2, 33–36)

The fault lies, rather, with selfish political leaders who, at the bier of Henry V, had already begun to claw at each other. Punishment comes in the person of Joan of Arc (Joan La Pucelle). Although despised by Britishers as a strumpet and witch, Joan feels sure that hers is a divine mission. "Assign'd am I to be the English scourge," she declares (I, 2, 129). But Talbot is defeated not so much by Joan's mystical strength as by the fact that the Earl of Somerset and the Duke of York are too busy wrangling with each other to send reinforcements.[20] As the loyal Sir William Lucy insists:

> The fraud of England, not the force of France,
> Hath now entrapp'd the noble-minded Talbot.
> Never to England shall he bear his life,
> But dies betray'd to fortune by your strife.
> (IV, 4, 36–39)

The internecine strife boils over initially in the play's most famous episode: the Temple Garden scene (II, 4). In this masterful scene, which Shakespeare invented, Richard Plantagenet (later Duke of York) engages in a furious argument with Somerset that leads to the alignment of the two rival factions. Each lord present in the garden plucks a rose to symbolize his allegiance, a white rose for York and a red one for Lancaster. As threat follows upon threat, Plantagenet swears undying hatred toward his foes:

> And, by my soul, this pale and angry rose,
> As cognizance of my blood-drinking hate,
> Will I for ever, and my faction, wear
> Until it wither with me to my grave
> Or flourish to the height of my degree.
>
> (II, 4, 107–111)

Significantly, the issue being disputed is obscured by personal rancor and name-calling; we see "natural nobility diverted to trivial ends."[21]

At the end of the scene, the Earl of Warwick makes the kind of dire prediction that is a hallmark of the histories:

> And here I prophesy: this brawl to-day
> Grown to this faction in the Temple Garden
> Shall send, between the Red Rose and the White,
> A thousand souls to death and deadly night.
>
> (II, 4, 124–127)

The way to this doom begins in various stratagems and treasons. York, learning that he has a claim to the throne, embarks upon a relentless quest for power. The Bishop (later Cardinal) of Winchester plots the overthrow of the good Humphrey, duke of Gloucester and Protector of the Realm. The Earl of Suffolk falls in love with Margaret of Anjou and (since he is already married) brings her home, without authorization, to be Henry's bride, hoping that he himself will control the kingdom through her. Henry decides to marry Margaret sight unseen, even though he had contracted for the daughter of the Earl of Armagnac (a marriage that might have repaired the breach with France). As *1 Henry VI* ends, new mischief is afoot.

There are many effective dramatic strokes in *1 Henry VI*: Shakespeare reinforces the theme of discord by introducing three women whose sexuality threatens to overthrow English manhood—Joan of Arc, the Countess of Auvergne (who unsuccessfully tries to seduce Talbot), and Margaret, whose evil influence will be highlighted in subsequent plays in the tetralogy.[22] Not only is the sight of the Talbots, father and son, fighting side by side touching in itself, but it provides an ironic contrast with the treachery in the English court.[23] And the language with which Suffolk courts Margaret and with which Henry reacts to her beauty parodies the conventions of Petrarchan love poetry—one more sign of the general decay.[24]

1 Henry VI has faults. Shakespeare has not differentiated the characters by giving each an individual style (although Talbot's speeches have an appropriate elegiac tone). He often allows a character to moralize at the cost of psychological consistency. And as in other works of the early period, he strains after rhetorical effects that sometimes seem overly ingenious. Despite these flaws, however, *1 Henry VI* is a strong play, solidly organized and crowded with life.

HENRY VI, PART TWO

In *2 Henry VI* dissension paralyzes constructive activity at home and engulfs the whole of English society. The play covers a span of ten years, from the arrival of Margaret of Anjou in England (1445) to the Duke of York's victory over the Lancastrian forces at the Battle of St. Albans (1455). In addition to depicting the rise of York, revealed by the imagery to be a man of action,[25] the drama focuses upon the downfall of Humphrey, duke of Gloucester, and his ambitious wife, as well as the retribution that begins to overtake those responsible for his death. We are also made vividly aware of the horrors of Jack Cade's rebellion.

From the beginning, Humphrey, traditionally an idealized figure, is destined for destruction.[26] Having incurred the enmity of Cardinal Beaufort, bishop of Winchester, he opposes the King's marriage with Margaret, especially as it involves turning over the duchies of Anjou and Maine to her father, King Reignier. Humphrey is grieved at this defilement of the memory of Henry V:

> O peers of England, shameful is this league!
> Fatal this marriage, cancelling your fame,
> Blotting your names from books of memory,
> Rasing the characters of your renown,
> Defacing monuments of conquer'd France,
> Undoing all as all had never been!
>   (I, 1, 98–103)

Naturally, this reproof does not sit well with Margaret and her lover, Suffolk, who join forces with the Cardinal and the Duke of York to destroy Humphrey. The weak King Henry, like the hero of a medieval morality play who chooses wrong over right, allows his faith in Humphrey to be undermined by evil counselors.[27] Humphrey views his own arrest and impending death as a prologue to further wickedness, and he so warns the King:

> Ah, gracious lord, these days are dangerous!
> Virtue is chok'd with foul ambition
> And charity chas'd hence by rancour's hand;

Foul subornation is predominant
And equity exil'd your Highness' land.
                    (III, 1, 142–146)

At Suffolk's instigation, Humphrey is murdered, but not until the aroused common people threaten to take justice into their own hands does the King understand the dreadful situation.

The murderers of course must be punished, although the most awesome of the conspirators, Margaret and York, are temporarily spared. The Cardinal, tormented by visions of Humphrey's ghost, dies in agony while his enemy Warwick jeers, "See how the pangs of death do make him grin!" (III, 3, 24). Suffolk is banished. The scene in which he takes leave of Margaret includes poetry of unusual tenderness. "Even now be gone!" the Queen bids him (III, 2, 352) as she tearfully kisses his hand. But then—

O, go not yet! Even thus two friends condemn'd
  Embrace, and kiss, and take ten thousand leaves,
  Loather a hundred times to part than die.
                    (III, 2, 353–355)

Suffolk's gentle response almost earns our forgiveness:

'Tis not the land I care for, wert thou thence.
A wilderness is populous enough,
So Suffolk had thy heavenly company;
For where thou art, there is the world itself
With every several pleasure in the world;
And where thou art not, desolation.
I can no more.
                    (III, 2, 359–365)

Captured by pirates and awaiting death at their hands, Suffolk achieves a new dignity. The proud nobleman refuses to humble himself before "these paltry, servile, abject drudges!" (IV, 1, 105):

                    No, rather let my head
Stoop to the block than these knees bow to any
Save to the God of heaven and to my king;
And sooner dance upon a bloody pole
Than stand uncover'd to the vulgar groom.
True nobility is exempt from fear.
                    (IV, 1, 124–129)

Perhaps Shakespeare intends a bit of irony as Suffolk, of all people, dies for God and King Henry. In any case, he should not be murdered by these brigands. Such an outrage could occur only in a topsy-turvy society.

It is appropriate that the death of Suffolk, with its implications of social disorder, should in Shakespeare's narrative be followed by Jack Cade's rebellion. Encouraged secretly by the Duke of York (who will one day seize the crown), the clothier Cade poses as heir to the throne and leads the rabble in an assault upon authority. His is the voice of anarchy, and it is frightfully comic: "There shall be in England seven halfpenny loaves sold for a penny; the three-hoop'd pot shall have ten hoops, and I will make it felony to drink small beer" (IV, 2, 70–74). "Away, burn all the records of the realm! My mouth shall be the parliament of England" (IV, 7, 16–17). "There shall not a maid be married but she shall pay to me her maidenhead ere they have it" (IV, 7, 129–130). Cade commands the execution of the clerk of Chatham, who is guilty of the sin of reading and writing, and he condemns Lord Say, who by erecting a grammar school "most traitorously corrupted the youth of the realm" and surrounded himself with men "that usually talk of a noun and a verb and such abominable words as no Christian ear can endure to hear" (IV, 7, 35–45). The rebellion, which anticipates the great mob scenes in *Julius Caesar* and *Coriolanus,* is aptly summarized in Cade's vaunt, "then are we in order when we are most out of order" (IV, 2, 199–200). But Cade and his cohorts are no worse than the aristocrats whose behavior they imitate. Cade's army has been described as an antimasque of York's rebellion, a parody of his pretension to the throne.[28]

Nevertheless, Cade has a splendid death scene. Deserted by the fickle mob, he stumbles into the garden of Alexander Iden and, though weak with hunger, engages Iden in a fight. Even dying, Cade is a blusterer, but this time he evokes compassion:

> O, I am slain! Famine and no other hath slain me. Let ten thousand devils come against me, and give me but the ten meals I have lost, and I'd defy them all.
>
> (IV, 10, 63–67)

In the Elizabethan view, Cade is a traitor, a threat to the peace, and a promulgator of ungodly moral and political doctrine. But Shakespeare never forgets that this complex figure, like Suffolk, is a man and, in his way, a hero.

HENRY VI, PART THREE

In *3 Henry VI* the feeble King, alone on a hillside while the battle rages about him, has a vision of "a *Son* that hath kill'd his Father" followed by "a *Father* that hath kill'd his Son"—complementary emblems of England's spiritual disintegration. The Father bitterly laments:

> O, pity, God, this miserable age!
> What stratagems, how fell, how butcherly,
> Erroneous, mutinous, and unnatural,
> This deadly quarrel daily doth beget!
> (II, 5, 88–91)[29]

There is a nightmarish quality about *3 Henry VI;* it is not a play so much as "a surrealistic montage of the faces of humanity twisted into expressions which reflect a primordial substratum of violence."[30] The inhuman struggle between Lancaster and York costs much English blood. Queen Margaret's partisan, Lord Clifford, kills York's son, young Rutland; then Clifford himself is killed. After Margaret gloats over York's distress, she is repaid by the stabbing of her only son, Prince Edward. Retribution matches outrage, and the pinnacle is reached when Henry is murdered in the Tower by that "indigested and deformed lump" (V, 6, 51) who will raise depravity to a fine art, York's ambitious son Richard, duke of Gloucester.

Henry submits to death peacefully because he has removed himself from the political arena in search of an ever elusive tranquillity. In I, 1, in a display of weakness that infuriates Margaret, he disinherits his son Edward and names York his heir. As Margaret takes personal command of the Lancastrian forces, the King withdraws and reflects enviously upon the shepherd's life (II, 5, 21–54). Later, after hiding in Scotland, he returns to England in disguise; wearing no crown, he proclaims:

> My crown is in my heart, not on my head;
> Not deck'd with diamonds and Indian stones,
> Nor to be seen. My crown is call'd content;
> A crown it is that seldom kings enjoy.
> (III, 1, 62–65)

Having been deposed by York's son (Edward IV) and imprisoned in the Tower, Henry lays his hand hopefully on the head of young Richmond, who will one day rise out of the ruins as Henry VII:

> If secret powers
> Suggest but truth to my divining thoughts,
> This pretty lad will prove our country's bliss.
> His looks are full of peaceful majesty,
> His head by nature fram'd to wear a crown,
> His hand to wield a sceptre, and himself
> Likely in time to bless a regal throne.
> (IV, 6, 68–74)

It is almost with relief that Henry, grown in dignity and self-knowledge, prepares for death at the hand of Richard, to whom he addresses his last words: "O, God forgive my sins and pardon thee!" (V, 6, 60).

The climactic episode in *3 Henry VI* is the Battle of Wakefield, where the two archenemies, York Senior and Margaret, meet and exult in their mutual hatred. York is captured, but Margaret prolongs his life in order to degrade and mock him:

> Where are your mess of sons to back you now?
> The wanton Edward, and the lusty George?
> And where's that valiant crookback prodigy,
> Dicky your boy, that with his grumbling voice
> Was wont to cheer his dad in mutinies?
> (I, 4, 73–77)

Where, she asks, is Rutland? In answer to her own question, she thrusts into York's face a handkerchief stained with the boy's blood. "And if thine eyes can water for his death, / I give thee this to dry thy cheeks withal" (I, 4, 82–83). Next she sets a paper crown upon his head. "Ay, marry, sir, now looks he like a king!" (I, 4, 96). York, himself a master of invective, responds in kind: "She-wolf of France, but worse than wolves of France, / Whose tongue more poisons than the adder's tooth!" (I, 4, 111–112). He denounces Margaret as the antithesis of every feminine virtue (including in this indictment the line Robert Greene parodied when he attacked the "Shake-scene" for his "tiger's heart wrapp'd in a player's hide!" [see p. 1]):

> O tiger's heart wrapp'd in a woman's hide!
> How couldst thou drain the lifeblood of the child,
> To bid the father wipe his eyes withal,
> And yet be seen to bear a woman's face?
> Women are soft, mild, pitiful, and flexible;
> Thou stern, obdurate, flinty, rough, remorseless.
> (I, 4, 137–142)

As noted earlier, in repudiating the gentle qualities traditionally expected of her sex, Margaret opens yet another breach in the principle of order expounded by Renaissance moral philosophers.

Although Henry, Margaret, and York generate considerable dramatic interest, the character who makes the greatest impact is Richard, duke of Gloucester, soon to reign as Richard III. "He's sudden if a thing comes in his head," says Edward (V, 5, 86) upon learning that his crookback brother is on his way to the Tower "to make a bloody supper" of King Henry. The brief glimpses of Richard in the *Henry VI* plays add up to a stunning portrait: his macabre promise that young Clifford "shall sup with Jesu Christ to-night" (*2 Henry VI,* V, 1, 214); the melodramatic flourish as he throws down Somerset's head and says, "Speak thou for me, and tell them what I did" (*3 Henry VI,* I, 1, 16); his sophism that York's oath to let Henry reign quietly is not binding because it was not taken before a magistrate "that hath authority over him that swears" (I, 2, 24); the simplicity with which he expresses loyalty to York (II, 1, 20): "Methinks 'tis prize enough to be his son." There is a hearty vulgarity in his asides to Clarence during their brother Edward's court-ship of Lady Grey (III, 2, 11–117), and delightful irony in his assurances to Edward that he does not disapprove of the match:

No, God forbid that I should wish them sever'd
Whom God hath join'd together! Ay, and 'twere pity
To sunder them that yoke so well together.
(IV, 1, 21–23)

Of course nothing would please Richard more than to see Edward—and Clarence, too—thoroughly "wasted, marrow, bones, and all" (III, 2, 125) so that his own path to the throne may be clear.

The full scope of Richard's villainy is revealed to the audience in two major soliloquies, arresting specimens of Shakespeare's early dramatic art. In the first, Richard confides that his deformity keeps him from finding "heaven in a lady's lap" (*3 Henry VI,* III, 2, 148). His pleasures must lie in the fulfillment of his ambition to be king:

I'll make my heaven to dream upon the crown
And, whiles I live, t' account this world but hell
Until my misshap'd trunk that bears this head
Be round impaled with a glorious crown.
(III, 2, 168–171)

"Why, I can smile, and murther whiles I smile," the arch-hypocrite proudly announces (III, 2, 182):

I can add colours to the chameleon,
Change shapes with Proteus for advantages,
And set the murtherous Machiavel to school.
Can I do this, and cannot get a crown?
Tut, were it farther off, I'll pluck it down.
(III, 2, 191–195)

In the second soliloquy, delivered right after he has stabbed Henry, Richard declares that his soul will be as deformed as his body:

The midwife wonder'd, and the women cried
"O, Jesus bless us! He is born with teeth!"
And so I was; which plainly signified
That I should snarl and bite and play the dog.
Then, since the heavens have shap'd my body so,
Let hell make crook'd my mind to answer it.
I have no brother, I am like no brother;
And this word "love," which greybeards call divine,
Be resident in men like one another,
And not in me! I am myself alone.

(V, 6, 74–83)

Richard thus withdraws from the community of men and becomes a lonely, pitiless demon.

3 Henry VI is a play of virtually unrelieved cruelty. With the exception of the ill-fated King Henry, the principal characters are propelled by an insatiable lust for power. Their ruthless energy is reflected in the harsh images that dominate their speech. In this play, for example, the sun, traditionally the symbol of majesty and of regeneration, is treated as man's deadly enemy: burning, scalding, shriveling, breeding flies, attracting gnats, parching the entrails. Another persistent motif, that of the tempest, receives its fullest expression in Margaret's elaborate ship metaphor:

We will not from the helm, to sit and weep,
But keep our course (though the rough wind say no)
From shelves and rocks that threaten us with wrack.
As good to chide the waves as speak them fair.
And what is Edward but a ruthless sea?
What Clarence but a quicksand of deceit?
And Richard but a ragged fatal rock?
All these the enemies to our poor bark.

(V, 4, 21–28)

Human beings, helpless inhabitants of a universe for whose violence they are in large part responsible, "are conceived as ships struggling against the tide or carried inertly before the gale, and the storm thus appears as the arbitrary instrument of the chaos which men's actions have created."[31]

RICHARD III

Richard III first appeared in 1597 and went through five additional printings before the 1623 Folio. The 1597 Quarto (Q1), a memorial reconstruction, is more highly regarded than it used to be, but the Folio text was probably based on Q3 (1602), possibly supplemented by Q6

(1622). The play is clearly a continuation of *3 Henry VI;* a feasible date
is 1592–1593.[32]

The source is the 1587 edition of Holinshed's *Chronicles,* much of
which came verbatim from Edward Hall. There is disagreement about
the character of the historical Richard; but the portrait that emerges in
Shakespeare's play is a creation of the Tudor myth, particularly as reflected in Sir Thomas More's *History of King Richard the Third* (c.
1513), where Richard is evil incarnate.[33] Shakespeare does not mitigate
Richard's alleged villainy; in fact, he makes it worse. As a result, *Richard
III* has sometimes been disparaged as crude melodrama. And yet audiences and actors are irresistibly drawn to the overwhelming personality
of its hero. Richard is the first of Shakespeare's truly great roles, and
its unabashed theatricality needs no apology.[34]

As early as 1785, Richard's essential quality was defined by Thomas
Whately in his *Remarks on Some of the Characters of Shakespeare.*
Distinguishing Richard from Macbeth, to whom he bears some resem-
blance, Whately wrote:

> Crimes are [Richard's] delight: but Macbeth is always in an agony when he
> thinks of them . . . . [Macbeth] is pensive even while he is enjoying the effect
> of his crimes; but Richard is in spirits merely at the prospect of committing
> them; and what is effort in the one, is sport to the other.[35]

Richard's outlandish crimes are indeed undertaken as a kind of sport,
and he shares the fun with us. Several critics have noted that Richard
is an actor par excellence. He quickly establishes a unique relationship
with the audience—as if he were the presenter, or master of ceremonies,
arranging a play within a play for our benefit and delight.[36] In his
opening soliloquy, delivered in a spirit of gaiety and self-satire, he
confides that the end of the war, with the Yorkists now installed on the
throne, has left him nothing to do. Not being cut out for amorous capers,
he will busy himself in intrigue:

> Why, I, in this weak piping time of peace,
> Have no delight to pass away the time,
> Unless to see my shadow in the sun
> And descant on mine own deformity.
> And therefore, since I cannot prove a lover
> To entertain these fair well-spoken days,
> I am determined to prove a villain
> And hate the idle pleasures of these days.
>   (I, 1, 24–31)

Once he is rid of his brothers—King Edward and George, Duke of
Clarence—the world will be free for him "to bustle in!" (I, 1, 152).

Supremely vital and intelligent, Richard catches his victims off guard. Clarence is led off to the Tower convinced that Richard will save him. He is just out of earshot when Richard muses ironically:

> Simple plain Clarence! I do love thee so
> That I will shortly send thy soul to heaven,
> If heaven will take the present at our hands.
> (I, 1, 118–120)

Even as he is about to be murdered at Richard's behest, Clarence clings to the illusion that his brother loves him. The misconception is all the more glaring because Clarence has just narrated a ghastly dream in which Richard tempts him from his shipboard cabin and pushes him overboard:

> O Lord! methought what pain it was to drown!
> What dreadful noise of water in mine ears!
> What sights of ugly death within mine eyes!
> Methoughts I saw a thousand fearful wracks;
> A thousand men that fishes gnaw'd upon;
> Wedges of gold, great anchors, heaps of pearl,
> Inestimable stones, unvalued jewels,
> All scatt'red in the bottom of the sea.
> (I, 4, 21–28)

Clarence envisions death and damnation as ghosts from his guilt-ridden past shriek, " 'Clarence is come—false, fleeting, perjur'd Clarence . . . . ' " (I, 4, 55). Moments later Clarence is dead, his body stuffed in a butt of malmsey wine; he has indeed been "drowned."[37]

Later in the play Hastings, who made the mistake of not supporting Richard's coronation with enough enthusiasm, gets an abrupt awakening. Having been greeted cordially by Richard, Hastings is pleased, not knowing that he is being set up for the kill:

> His Grace looks cheerfully and smooth this morning;
> There's some conceit [idea] or other likes him well
> When that he bids good morrow with such spirit.
> I think there's never a man in Christendom
> Can lesser hide his love or hate than he,
> For by his face straight shall you know his heart.
> (III, 4, 48–53)

"Thou art a traitor," Richard suddenly exclaims (III, 4, 74), on the palpably absurd pretext that the strumpet Jane Shore has cast a spell on his crooked body and that Hastings is her protector. Hastings had been too smug to perceive his danger; now his head is chopped off and presented to Richard, who seems sick with disillusionment. "So dear I lov'd the man that I must weep" (III, 5, 24).

In one of his most startling moves, Richard without warning turns against the Duke of Buckingham, "my other self, my counsel's consistory" (II, 2, 151). Why? Because he hesitates before consenting to Richard's most gruesome exploit, the murder of the two young princes in the Tower. When Buckingham claims the earldom of Hereford, promised him earlier, he gets a cutting rebuff: "I am not in the giving vein to-day" (IV, 2, 118).

Not all of Richard's energies are devoted to the forcible removal of relatives and friends. What a performance he delivers as a lover! As Lady Anne (I, 2) stands over the coffin of her father-in-law Henry VI, whom he has murdered, and bemoans the death of her husband Edward, whom he has also murdered, Richard approaches and, rising to the challenge, bombards her with a mixture of impudence and flattery. It was her beauty, he declares, that led him to commit murder, and he bids her plunge his sword into his breast. Anne finally stops cursing him and seems willing to become his wife. The scene, which has no historical warrant and is not even crucial for the plot, demonstrates Richard's almost diabolical power. We find our initial horror giving way to fascination, and "Anne's submission becomes ours."[38] When it is over, Richard has every right to crow:

Was ever woman in this humour woo'd?
Was ever woman in this humour won?
I'll have her, but I will not keep her long.
What? I that kill'd her husband and his father
To take her in her heart's extremest hate,
With curses in her mouth, tears in her eyes,
The bleeding witness of my hatred by,
Having God, her conscience, and these bars against me,
And I no friends to back my suit withal
But the plain devil and dissembling looks?
And yet to win her—all the world to nothing?
Ha!

(I, 2, 227–238)[39]

To conceive of Richard as a lover may be difficult; to imagine him in the role of the pious Christian staggers belief. And yet this is the character he assumes in the most audacious scene in the play, when the Lord Mayor of London leads a delegation to Baynard's Castle to persuade Richard to accept the crown (III, 7). Richard makes a flamboyant entrance, flanked by two bishops and holding a prayer book. Despite his seemingly profound reluctance, he is prevailed upon to be king. Then, having accepted the burden of reigning in the secular world, he turns to the bishops and leaves the stage with undiminished serenity. "Come, let us to our holy work again" (III, 7, 246).

It is artistically and historically right that Richard, for all his theatrical appeal, should ultimately be punished so that stability may be restored to a troubled England. On the eve of the Battle of Bosworth, he confesses, "I have not that alacrity of spirit / Nor cheer of mind that I was wont to have" (V, 3, 73–74). He has been said to suffer at this point from psychological attrition, a split in his personality induced by conscience and by the curses that have been heaped upon him.[40] Richard and Richmond, in a stylized sequence, withdraw to their tents and prepare for sleep. One by one the ghosts from Richard's past appear (the episode recalls Clarence's dream): Prince Edward; Henry VI; Clarence; Hastings; Buckingham; the two slaughtered young princes; wretched Anne, who never knew a quiet hour as Richard's wife. "Despair and die!" they cry out, while to Richmond they promise victory and long life. For the first time Richard experiences fear. Like Clarence's murderers (I, 4, 124–125), he must reckon with "some certain dregs of conscience":

My conscience hath a thousand several tongues,
And every tongue brings in a several tale,
And every tale condemns me for a villain.
Perjury, perjury, in the high'st degree,
Murther, stern murther, in the dir'st degree,
All several sins, all us'd in each degree,
Throng to the bar, crying all "Guilty! guilty!"
I shall despair. There is no creature loves me;
And if I die, no soul shall pity me.
(V, 3, 194–202)

In contrast, Richmond, who has been compared to Constantine dreaming of the Cross before his fateful battle with the Huns (A.D. 312),[41] enjoys "the sweetest sleep, and fairest-boding dreams / That ever ent'red in a drowsy head" (V, 3, 228–229). The symmetry continues as each leader sends his troops off to battle with a ringing oration. (Shakespeare reverses the traditional order; Richard speaks last, perhaps so as to retain our sympathy as long as possible.)[42] After Richard is slain, Richmond, soon to be crowned Henry VII, announces that the houses of York and Lancaster will be reunited through his marriage with Elizabeth, daughter of Edward IV:

And let their heirs (God, if thy will be so)
Enrich the time to come with smooth-fac'd peace,
With smiling plenty, and fair prosperous days!
(V, 5, 32–34)

Neither Richard's last-minute anguish nor Richmond's moralizing is dramatically convincing, but one must see the conclusion of *Richard III* as part of the Tudor view of history.

Richmond is not the only symbol of England's historical destiny. He shares this function with old Queen Margaret, that venerable "she-wolf of France" who roared her way through the *Henry VI* plays and is now brought on stage (in violation of historical accuracy) as the prophetic voice of an avenging nemesis.[43] "My hair doth stand an end to hear her curses," Hastings remarks (I, 3, 304). Although she calls down imprecations upon all her foes, she saves her choice gems for the "poisonous bunch-back'd toad" (I, 3, 246):

> Stay, dog, for thou shalt hear me.
> If heaven have any grievous plague in store
> Exceeding those that I can wish upon thee,
> O let them keep it till thy sins be ripe,
> And then hurl down their indignation
> On thee, the troubler of the poor world's peace!
> The worm of conscience still begnaw thy soul!
> . . . .
>
> No sleep close up that deadly eye of thine,
> Unless it be while some tormenting dream
> Affrights thee with a hell of ugly devils!
> Thou elvish-mark'd, abortive, rooting hog!
> (I, 3, 216–228)

The atrocities Margaret committed in *Henry VI* recede into the background, as she epitomizes the clamor for divine retribution that overtakes Richard.

Margaret's most impressive scene (IV, 4) follows the murder of the young princes. She is joined on the stage by Richard's mother (the Duchess of York) and Edward IV's widowed queen, Elizabeth. The three wronged and afflicted women sit down on the earth to embark upon an elaborate festival of lamentation.[44] As they chant their dirge and compare sorrows, Margaret's passion for revenge reaches new heights. Richard, "hell's black intelligencer" (IV, 4, 71), still lives, but she anticipates his terrible death:

> But at hand, at hand,
> Ensues his piteous and unpitied end.
> Earth gapes, hell burns, fiends roar, saints pray,
> To have him suddenly convey'd from hence.
> Cancel his bond of life, dear God, I pray,
> That I may live to say, "The dog is dead."
> (IV, 4, 73–78)

Before leaving for France, she bequeaths to the newly bereaved Elizabeth grim instructions in the art of cursing:

> Forbear to sleep the night, and fast the day;
> Compare dead happiness with living woe;
> Think that thy babes were sweeter than they were
> And he that slew them fouler than he is.
> Bett'ring thy loss makes the bad causer worse;
> Revolving this will teach thee how to curse.
>   (IV, 4, 118–123)

This great choric scene had begun with a fine image of decay. "So now prosperity begins to mellow / And drop into the rotten mouth of death" (IV, 4, 1–2). Much of the meaning of *Richard III* and of the tetralogy as a whole is compressed into this image. Richard, misshapen product of a distorted age, engineers his breathtaking rise to power and prospers for a time. But just as he attains his most fruitful success, God sends his "ministers of chastisement" to rid the land of a festering evil.

Nicholas Brooke makes the interesting point that Richard is cut down by the whole formal structure of the play, that tragedy (in the person of the brilliantly individualized hero) is destroyed by the "ritual of history, the swelling chorus of a more-than-human force."[45] Although his defeat may be imperative from the standpoint of Tudor historiography, an audience in the theater is likely to experience a more ambivalent reaction, summed up many years ago by Clarence V. Boyer. "[Richard's] audacity and demoniac energy fascinate us; our admiration is not willing but compelled."[46] Like the Vice in the medieval morality play from whom he is said to have descended,[47] Richard cavorts with such exuberance that we end up almost wanting him to win.

KING JOHN

First published in the 1623 Folio, *King John* could have been written almost any time before 1598; Meres mentions it among the tragedies. Dover Wilson thinks it was written c. 1590 and revised in 1594; E. A. J. Honigmann believes it was written once and for all in 1590–1591; and Robert A. Law makes a case for 1594–1596. The principal source was a play in two parts, first printed in 1591, *The Troublesome Reign of John King of England* (it is possible that this is a bad quarto of some version of Shakespeare's play). In any case, it is convenient to discuss *King John* with Shakespeare's early histories.[48]

Although we tend to remember the historical King John primarily for having been forced by his rebellious barons to grant Magna Charta (1215), the Elizabethans were more concerned with other problems arising during his reign (1199–1216). After the death of his brother Richard I, John occupied the throne; but his title was fiercely contested by Arthur (son of John's older brother Geoffrey), who enjoyed the military support of Philip II of France. In 1203 Arthur died in captivity, amid rumors that John had ordered his murder. John also had trouble with the Church. When Pope Innocent III wanted Stephen Langton installed as Archbishop of Canterbury (1206), the King defied him. In 1208 the Pope placed England under interdict and excommunicated John. Five years later John capitulated by surrendering his crown to the papal legate and receiving it back again as a symbol that he held England in fief from the Pope. Following the signing of Magna Charta, John fought anew with the English barons, who were aided by France. John died in 1216, with the campaign still in progress, and was succeeded by his nine-year-old son Henry III. Shakespeare used all these episodes, making an adjustment here and there to produce a unified dramatic effect.

John presented an ambiguous image to subsequent generations. Medieval chroniclers, writing from a Roman Catholic view, regarded him as a usurper, murderer, and heretic; in the sixteenth century, however, he was looked on as a Protestant martyr and heroic champion of English nationalism. Both attitudes are depicted in Shakespeare's play.[49] But in his "drama of ideas,"[50] Shakespeare, exploring with unusual subtlety the intricate realities of the world of politics, departs from the antipapal didacticism of his more immediate sources[51] and by and large reverts to the medieval assessment of John, portraying him as almost totally unsympathetic.

Shakespeare's John is clearly a usurper, a point made in the first scene. When Chatillon, the French ambassador, addresses him as England's "borrowed majesty" (I, 1, 4) and states Arthur's case in careful detail, John can reply only with an angry threat. He bids Chatillon return to his king bearing word of England's determination to fight:

> Be thou as lightning in the eyes of France;
> For ere thou canst report I will be there,
> The thunder of my cannon shall be heard.
>   (I, 1, 24–26)

John boasts that "our strong possession and our right" (I, 1, 39) will see him through, whereupon his mother Elinor confides the truth:

> Your strong possession much more than your right,
> Or else it must go wrong with you and me.
> So much my conscience whispers in your ear,
> Which none but heaven and you and I shall hear.
>   (I, 1, 40–43)

Similarly, when King Philip of France confronts John before the town of Angiers and charges that England by right belongs to Arthur (II, 1, 89–109), no rational answer is forthcoming. John's title is not legitimate; he is a de facto king who governs by sheer might.

Shakespeare is more direct than his sources in revealing the King's active complicity in the death of Arthur. John wishes his chamberlain, Hubert, to sense his evil intention and quietly put it into effect. Reassured of Hubert's loyalty, he speaks plainly:

> *King John:* Good Hubert, Hubert, Hubert, throw thine eye
> On yon young boy. I'll tell thee what, my friend,
> He is a very serpent in my way;
> And wheresoe'er this foot of mine doth tread,
> He lies before me. Dost thou understand me?
> Thou art his keeper.
> *Hubert:* And I'll keep him so
> That he shall not offend your Majesty.
> *King John:* Death.
> *Hubert:* My lord?
> *King John:* A grave.
> *Hubert:* He shall not live.
> *King John:* Enough.
> I could be merry now. Hubert, I love thee.
> Well, I'll not say what I intend for thee.
> (III, 3, 59–68)

In a scene heavy with pathos but in its own way moving (IV, 1), Arthur persuades Hubert to spare his life. However, in attempting to escape, the boy leaps from a high wall and is killed. No amount of repentance can alter the fact that John is guilty.

Why, one may ask, does Shakespeare go out of his way to make John so unappealing? Perhaps because he wishes to show that, no matter how dubious his title or how loathsome his crimes, as England's king, John is entitled to the loyalty of his subjects. After the death of Arthur is made known, the Earl of Salisbury is "stifled with this smell of sin" (IV, 3, 113) and joins the rebellion; later, however, he returns to the fold (at an opportune moment, when the tide is turning in the King's favor and continued revolt is imprudent):

> We will untread the steps of damned flight
> And, like a bated and retired flood,
> Leaving our rankness and irregular course,
> Stoop low within those bounds we have o'erlook'd
> And calmly run on in obedience
> Even to our ocean, to our great King John.
> (V, 4, 52–57)

To Philip Faulconbridge, the King's most zealous partisan, the killing of Arthur is "a damned and a bloody work" (IV, 3, 57), and he is deeply distressed:

> I am amaz'd, methinks, and lose my way
> Among the thorns and dangers of this world.
> . . . .
> From forth this morsel of dead royalty
> The life, the right, and truth of all this realm
> Is fled to heaven . . . .
>   (IV, 3, 140–145)

Nevertheless, he tells Hubert that they must continue to serve their king, and upon John's death (he has been poisoned by a monk for reasons that are not made explicit) Faulconbridge pledges that he will just as faithfully support the new king, Henry III.

It is this Philip Faulconbridge, illegitimate son of Richard the Lion-Hearted, who emerges as the most attractive character in the play, particularly as the robust spokesman for English nationalism. In the early scenes we are impressed primarily by his coarseness and vitality. He is delighted to learn from his mother that a great hero was his sire:

> Madam, I would not wish a better father.
> Some sins do bear their privilege on earth,
> And so doth yours.
>   (I, 1, 260–262)

When a citizen of Angiers proposes that England's quarrel with France be settled by a marriage between Lady Blanch and the Dauphin and threatens a fight to the death should the match be declined, Faulconbridge explodes:

>   Here's a large mouth indeed,
> That spits forth death, and mountains, rocks and seas;
> Talks as familiarly of roaring lions
> As maids of thirteen do of puppy-dogs!
> What cannoneer begot this lusty blood?
> He speaks plain cannon-fire and smoke and bounce;
> He gives the bastinado [blow] with his tongue.
> Our ears are cudgell'd; not a word of his
> But buffets better than a fist of France.
> Zounds! I was never so bethump'd with words
> Since I first call'd my brother's father dad.
>   (II, 1, 457–467)

During the course of the action, Philip the Bastard becomes much more than a blustering soldier. He assumes the complex role of choric commentator. At the end he has been transfigured almost into pure symbol as we hear from his lips that magnificent affirmation of England's historic destiny:

> This England never did, nor never shall,
> Lie at the proud foot of a conqueror
> But when it first did help to wound itself.
> Now these her princes are come home again,
> Come the three corners of the world in arms,
> And we shall shock them. Naught shall make us rue
> If England to itself do rest but true.
> (V, 7, 112–118)[52]

It is sometimes objected that Philip remains outside the play, but Shakespeare has prepared us to accept his final identification with England by packing his speech from the beginning with energetic pictures of Elizabethan life—eelskins, puppy dogs, toasting irons, the traveler with "his toothpick at my worship's mess" (I, 1, 190), and many more. As one critic has astutely observed, "He speaks of England before fate calls him to speak for England."[53] Like Richard III, the Bastard is a descendant of the morality Vice, but by the end he has been transformed into an equally allegorical figure, the Patriot.[54]

For all his idealism, Faulconbridge is not a mere dreamer. His patriotic fervor grows from his sensitivity to the requirements of practical politics. This is the significance of his famous speech (II, 1, 561–598) on "commodity" (expediency) after the marriage of Blanch and the Dauphin is arranged. At first he resents the match, but he soon realizes that France and England have both acted in obedience to "this Commodity, / This bawd, this broker, this all-changing word . . . . " (II, 1, 581–582). Perhaps he too should adopt commodity, that is, if given the chance:

> Not that I have the power to clutch my hand
> When his fair angels [coins] would salute my palm,
> But for my hand, as unattempted yet,
> Like a poor beggar, raileth on the rich.
> . . . .
> Since kings break faith upon commodity,
> Gain, be my lord, for I will worship thee!
> (II, 1, 589–598)

The speech is not simple, and it is perhaps ironic. It has been described as an inversion of Ulysses' speech on degree (see pp. 298–299), evidence that the cherished ideal of order has broken down and been supplanted by a new cynicism.[55] Another critic sees in the speech the Bastard's amoral awakening to materialistic realism.[56] James Calderwood interprets the play as a dramatic crucible in which are tested two opposing principles, commodity and honor: that is, scheming self-interest versus loyalty to the good of England. The Bastard matures to the point where he can synthesize these two ideals, incorporating the techniques of commodity into the service of honor.[57] In any case, the Bastard's allegiance to John (like Salisbury's compliance) should not be explained simply on the basis of Tudor political theory. Its justification rests also on the pragmatic consideration that John is the most efficient instrument for England's preservation. In this respect, *King John* may be a turning point in Shakespeare's thinking, a work in which he begins to appreciate the kind of creative Machiavellianism that will be embodied in Henry V.[58] The play is a dramatic essay on realpolitik. John's legal claim becomes irrelevant, and even the removal of Arthur, whose situation has been said to parallel that of Mary Stuart,[59] may prove conducive to the public good.

While admiring *King John* for its brilliant, if perhaps cynical, analysis of man's accommodation to political necessity, one should not forget that the play's characters include a woman of awesome power—Constance, the widowed mother of young Arthur. Like Margaret of Anjou, Constance seethes with bitterness and is a skillful wielder of curses. Although much of her vituperation is monotonously high-keyed, she has several fine moments. When John tries to bribe Arthur into relinquishing his title, the King's mother, Elinor, says invitingly, "Come to thy grandam, child." Constance retaliates by sarcastically adopting the tone of the nursery:

> Do, child! go to it [its] grandam, child!
> Give grandam kingdom, and it grandam will
> Give it a plum, a cherry, and a fig.
> There's a good grandam!
>
>   (II, 1, 160–163)

Learning of the proposed marriage between Blanch and the Dauphin, she seats herself on the ground, proclaiming that only the huge earth can support her misery. "Here I and sorrows sit; / Here is my throne, bid kings come bow to it" (III, 1, 73–74). She mourns extravagantly when her son is imprisoned, so that the King of France admonishes her: "You are as fond of grief as of your child" (III, 4, 92). Her answer reveals that she is capable of tenderness:

Grief fills the room up of my absent child:
Lies in his bed, walks up and down with me,
Puts on his pretty looks, repeats his words,
Remembers me of all his gracious parts,
Stuffs out his vacant garments with his form.
                    (III, 4, 93–97)

Then, tearing her hair, Constance—"this wildest of Shakespeare's widows, this queen of all his wailing women, this wonderful and terrible poetess who is so amazingly accomplished in the dialectic of grief"[60]— makes her final exit.

King John has never been popular in the theater. In fact, Robert Ornstein (among others) regards it as a hack assignment that Shakespeare undertook without any real enthusiasm.[61] But it deserves to be better known. Adrien Bonjour has made a cogent defense of its structure, arguing that as John declines, the Bastard rises; the King, driven by commodity in the worst sense, succumbs to criminal temptation in order- ing the death of Arthur, while Faulconbridge, morally revolted, wins our interest and sympathy in the second part of the play.[62] And while the play endorses the traditional Tudor doctrine on the relationship between king and subjects, it attempts to reconcile that doctrine with the em- pirical choices demanded of a free nation. *King John* must be ranked among Shakespeare's most sophisticated achievements.

NOTES

1. See especially E. M. W. Tillyard, *Shakespeare's History Plays* (New York: Macmillan, 1946) and Lily B. Campbell, *Shakespeare's "Histories": Mirrors of Elizabethan Policy* (San Marino, Calif.: The Huntington Library, 1947).

2. See Ronald S. Berman, "Fathers and Sons in the Henry VI Plays," *Shake- speare Quarterly* 13 (1962): 487–497.

3. Quoted in Max M. Reese, *The Cease of Majesty: A Study of Shakespeare's History Plays* (London: Edward Arnold, 1961), pp. 37–38. The first three chapters of this book (pp. 1–88) provide an excellent summary of Tudor his- toriography.

4. Lily B. Campbell, ed., *The Mirror for Magistrates* (1938) (New York: Barnes & Noble, 1960), pp. 65–66.

5. On *Gorboduc* and other pre-Shakespearean history plays, see Irving Ribner, *The English History Play in the Age of Shakespeare*, rev. ed.(London: Methuen, 1965), pp. 30–91 and David Bevington, *Tudor Drama and Politics* (Cam- bridge: Harvard University Press, 1968).

6. Moody E. Prior, *The Drama of Power: Studies in Shakespeare's History Plays* (Evanston, Ill.: Northwestern University Press, 1973), p. 37.

7. See especially Henry Angsar Kelly, *Divine Providence in the England of Shakespeare's Histories* (Cambridge: Harvard University Press, 1970), pp. 297–306. See also J. P. Brockbank, "The Frame of Disorder—*Henry VI*," in *Early Shakespeare*, eds. John Russell Brown and Bernard Harris, Stratford-upon-Avon Studies 3 (London: Edward Arnold, 1961), pp. 73–99; David Riggs, *Shakespeare's Heroical Histories: Henry VI and Its Literary Tradition* (Cambridge: Harvard University Press, 1971), especially pp. 29–33; Robert Ornstein, *A Kingdom for a Stage: The Achievement of Shakespeare's History Plays* (Cambridge: Harvard University Press, 1972), pp. 1–32; and A. L. French, "The Mills of God and Shakespeare's Early History Plays," *English Studies* 55 (1974): 313–324.

8. Prior, *The Drama of Power*, p. 117.

9. Michael Manheim, *The Weak King Dilemma in the Shakespearean History Play* (Syracuse, N.Y.: Syracuse University Press, 1973).

10. Arthur P. Rossiter, *Angel with Horns and Other Shakespeare Lectures* (New York: Theatre Arts Books, 1961), p. 59.

11. Scholars now tend to play down the importance of Bolingbroke's usurpation for an understanding of the *Henry VI* plays. See Brockbank, "The Frame of Disorder," p. 98 and Prior, *The Drama of Power*, p. 353, n. 1.

12. Hereward T. Price, *Construction in Shakespeare*, The University of Michigan Contributions to Modern Philology no. 17 (Ann Arbor: University of Michigan Press, 1951), pp. 20–21, 24–37.

13. See Peter Alexander, *Shakespeare's Henry VI and Richard III*, with introduction by Alfred W. Pollard (Cambridge: Cambridge University Press, 1929) and Madeleine Doran, *Henry VI, Parts Two and Three: Their Relation to the "Contention" and the "True Tragedy"* (Iowa City: University of Iowa Press, 1928). The New Arden editor is Andrew S. Cairncross, 3d ed. (Cambridge: Harvard University Press, 1962 [Part 1], 1957 [Part 2], 1964 [Part 3]). Cairncross believes Shakespeare the sole author of all three plays. The New Cambridge editor is John Dover Wilson (Cambridge: Cambridge University Press, 1952). Dover Wilson argues for multiple authorship, with Shakespeare (and Nashe) merely revising the work of Greene, who initially wrote all three parts.

14. On the date, see the New Arden editions: 1, pp. xxxv–xxxviii; 2, pp. xlv–xlvi; 3, pp. xliii–xlv and J. G. McManaway, "Recent Studies in Shakespeare Chronology," *Shakespeare Survey* 3 (1950): 23. On sources, see Geoffrey Bullough, *Narrative and Dramatic Sources of Shakespeare*, 8 vols. (New York: Columbia University Press, 1957–1975), 3: 23–217.

15. Don M. Ricks, *Shakespeare's Emergent Form: A Study of the Structures of the Henry VI Plays* (Logan: Utah State University Press, 1968). Elizabethan theaters, Ricks says (p. 39), were not likely to be producing trilogies and tetralogies; each play had to stand as an independent work.

16. Tillyard, *Shakespeare's History Plays*, p. 153.

17. Riggs, *Shakespeare's Heroical Histories*, pp. 93–139. See also Wayne L. Billings, "Ironic Lapses: Plotting in *Henry VI*," *Studies in the Literary Imagination* 5 (1972): 27–49.

18. Carol McGinnis Kay, "Traps, Slaughter, and Chaos: A Study of Shake-

speare's Henry VI Plays," *Studies in the Literary Imagination* 5 (1972): 1–26.

19. See John W. Blanpied, "'Art and Baleful Sorcery': The Counterconsciousness of *Henry VI, Part I*," *Studies in English Literature, 1500–1900* 15 (1975): 213–227.

20. On this point, see A. L. French, "Joan of Arc and *Henry VI*," *English Studies* 49 (1968): 425–429.

21. Riggs, *Shakespeare's Heroical Histories*, p. 111. On the Temple Garden scene, see also Prior, *The Drama of Power*, pp. 104 ff. and Robert Y. Turner, *Shakespeare's Apprenticeship* (Chicago: University of Chicago Press, 1974), pp. 38 ff. Turner emphasizes Shakespeare's balance and neutrality in the scene, as opposed to his partisan treatment of the Talbot–Joan confrontation.

22. See David M. Bevington, "The Domineering Female in *1 Henry VI*," *Shakespeare Studies,* ed. J. Leeds Barroll, 2 (1967): 51–58.

23. See Robert B. Pierce, *Shakespeare's History Plays: The Family and the State* (Columbus: Ohio State University Press, 1971), p. 43.

24. See Riggs, *Shakespeare's Heroical Histories,* pp. 112–113.

25. See James L. Calderwood, "Shakespeare Evolving Imagery: *2 Henry VI*," *English Studies* 48 (1967): 481–493.

26. Samuel M. Pratt, "Shakespeare and Humphrey Duke of Gloucester: A Study in Myth," *Shakespeare Quarterly* 16 (1965): 201–216.

27. On the moralitylike process in *2 Henry VI,* see Ernest William Talbert, *Elizabethan Drama and Shakespeare's Early Plays* (Chapel Hill: University of North Carolina Press, 1963), pp. 185–209.

28. See Ornstein, *A Kingdom for a Stage,* p. 51. On Cade, see also Ricks, *Shakespeare's Emergent Form,* p. 73 and Brockbank, "The Frame of Disorder," pp. 87–90. A good study of Shakespeare and the mob is Brents Stirling, *The Populace in Shakespeare* (New York: Columbia University Press, 1949).

29. On the father-son tableau, see Pierce, *Shakespeare's History Plays,* pp. 68 ff.; Inga-Stina Ewbank, "'More Pregnantly than Words': Some Uses and Limitations of Visual Symbolism," *Shakespeare Survey* 24 (1971): 15.

30. Ricks, *Shakespeare's Emergent Form,* p. 96.

31. Reese, *The Cease of Majesty,* p. 193. On the sea imagery, see also F. E. Halliday, *The Poetry of Shakespeare's Plays* (New York: Barnes & Noble, 1964), pp. 57–58; Alvin B. Kernan, "A Comparison of the Imagery in *3 Henry VI* and *The True Tragedie of Richard Duke of York*," *Studies in Philology* 51 (1954): 431–442; Kay, "Traps, Slaughter, and Chaos"; and Paul A. Jorgensen, "A Formative Shakespearean Legacy: Elizabethan Views of God, Fortune, and War," *PMLA* 90 (1975): 222–233.

32. On the text, see Alice Walker, *Textual Problems of the First Folio* (Cambridge: Cambridge University Press, 1953), pp. 13–36; the New Cambridge *Richard III,* ed. John Dover Wilson (Cambridge: Cambridge University Press, 1954), pp. vii–xi, 140–160; J. K. Walton, *The Copy for the Folio Text of Richard III,* Auckland University College Monograph Series, no. 1 (Auckland, N.Z., 1955); and E. A. J. Honigmann, "The Text of *Richard III*," *Theatre Research Recherches Théâtrales* 7 (1965): 48–55. See also *The Tragedy of King Richard III: Parallel Texts of the First Quarto and the First Folio with Variants of the Early Quartos,* ed. Kristian Smidt (New York: Humanities, 1969).

33. On the historical Richard, his possible role in the murder of the young princes, and his reputation in Tudor England, see Paul Murray Kendall, *Richard the Third* (London: Allen and Unwin, 1955), especially pp. 393–418. A valuable survey of Richard as he was portrayed in chronicles, poetry, and drama is George B. Churchill, *Richard the Third up to Shakespeare* (Berlin: Mayer & Müller, 1900). See also Bullough, *Sources,* 3: 221–349.

34. On *Richard III* in the theater, see Arthur Colby Sprague, *Shakespeare's Histories: Plays for the Stage* (London: The Society for Theatre Research, 1964), pp. 123–141.

35. D. Nichol Smith, ed., *Shakespeare Criticism: A Selection,* 2d ed. (London: Oxford University Press, 1946), pp. 130–131.

36. See Nicholas Brooke, *Shakespeare's Early Tragedies* (London: Methuen, 1968), pp. 56–58; Anne Righter, *Shakespeare and the Idea of the Play* (London: Chatto & Windus, 1962), pp. 95–100; and Wolfgang Clemen, *A Commentary on Shakespeare's Richard III,* trans. Jean Bonheim (London: Methuen, 1968), pp. 150–157 and passim. Clemen's book, with its scene-by-scene commentary on the action, is indispensable.

37. On Clarence's dream, see Marjorie B. Garber, *Dream in Shakespeare* (New Haven: Yale University Press, 1974), pp. 21–26.

38. A. C. Hamilton, *The Early Shakespeare* (San Marino, Calif.: The Huntington Library, 1967), p. 192.

39. For a superb analysis of the wooing scene and its counterparts in pre-Shakespearean drama, see Clemen, *A Commentary on Shakespeare's Richard III,* pp. 22–42. Persuasion scenes are also discussed in Turner, *Shakespeare's Apprenticeship,* pp. 75–78. See also Denzell S. Smith, "The Credibility of the Wooing of Anne in *Richard III,*" *Papers on Language and Literature* 7 (1971): 199–202 and John Palmer, *Political and Comic Characters in Shakespeare* (New York: St. Martin, 1965), pp. 81–85.

40. See William B. Toole, "The Motif of Psychic Division in *Richard III,*" *Shakespeare Survey* 27 (1974): 21–32.

41. Emrys Jones, "Bosworth Eve," *Essays in Criticism* 25 (1975): 38–54.

42. Philip Williams, "*Richard the Third:* The Battle Orations," *English Studies in Honor of James Southall Wilson,* University of Virginia Studies, vol. 4 (Charlottesville, 1951), pp. 125–130.

43. Margaret returned to France in 1475 and died in 1482, three years before the Battle of Bosworth.

44. The scene is analyzed by Pierce, *Shakespeare's History Plays,* pp. 89–124, where the ritual grief of the family is associated with nemesis. See also Clemen, *A Commentary on Shakespeare's Richard III,* pp. 176–188 and Brooke, *Shakespeare's Early Tragedies,* pp. 50–52. An older treatment of the pattern of nemesis in *Richard III* is in R. G. Moulton, *Shakespeare as a Dramatic Artist* (Oxford: Oxford University Press, 1892), p. 115.

45. Brooke, *Shakespeare's Early Tragedies,* p. 52.

46. Clarence V. Boyer, *The Villain as Hero in Elizabethan Tragedy* (New York: Dutton, 1914), p. 92.

47. Bernard Spivack, *Shakespeare and the Allegory of Evil* (New York: Columbia University Press, 1958), pp. 386–407.

48. On the text, see W. W. Greg, *The Shakespeare First Folio: Its Bibliographical and Textual History* (Oxford: Clarendon, 1955), pp. 248–255; the New Cambridge *King John,* ed. John Dover Wilson (Cambridge: Cambridge University Press, 1936), pp. vii–xlvii passim, 91–94; the New Arden *King John,* ed. E. A. J. Honigmann, 4th ed. (Cambridge: Harvard University Press, 1954), pp. xxxiii–xliii. On the date, see the New Cambridge edition, pp. xlviii–lvii; the New Arden edition, pp. xliii–lviii; and Robert Adger Law, "On the Date of *King John,*" *Studies in Philology* 54 (1957): 119–127. On sources, see the New Cambridge edition, pp. xvii–xxxiv; the New Arden edition, pp. xi–xxxiii; and Bullough, *Sources,* 4: 1–151. The most complete study of *The Troublesome Reign* is Virginia Mason Carr, *The Drama as Propaganda: A Study of The Troublesome Raigne of King John,* Salzburg Studies in English Literature no. 28 (Salzburg, Austria: Universität Salzburg, 1974), which contains (pp. 1–20) a good survey of the textual dispute concerning this play and *King John.*

49. John R. Elliot, "Shakespeare and the Double Image of King John," *Shakespeare Studies,* ed. J. Leeds Barroll, 1 (1965): 64–84 and Carr, *The Drama as Propaganda,* pp. 21–41.

50. S. C. Sen Gupta, *Shakespeare's Historical Plays* (London: Oxford University Press, 1964), p. 111.

51. See L. C. Knights, *William Shakespeare: The Histories* (London: Longmans, 1962), pp. 26–31.

52. For a comparison of this passage with its prototype in *The Troublesome Reign,* see above (p. 50).

53. Reese, *The Cease of Majesty,* p. 279.

54. Julia C. Van de Water, "The Bastard in *King John,*" *Shakespeare Quarterly* 11 (1960): 137–146.

55. Sigurd Burckhardt, "*King John:* The Ordering of This Present Time," *ELH* 33 (1966): 133–153.

56. Ronald Berman, "Anarchy and Order in *Richard III* and *King John,*" *Shakespeare Survey* 20 (1967): 51–59.

57. James L. Calderwood, "Commodity and Honour in *King John,*" *University of Toronto Quarterly* 29 (1960): 341–356.

58. Manheim, *The Weak King Dilemma,* pp. 129–160.

59. Campbell, *Shakespeare's "Histories,"* pp. 136–149.

60. Mark Van Doren, *Shakespeare* (New York: Holt, 1939), p. 113.

61. Ornstein, *A Kingdom for a Stage,* pp. 83–101.

62. Adrien Bonjour, "The Road to Swinstead Abbey: A Study of the Sense and Structure of *King John,*" *ELH* 18 (1951): 253–274.

6
Tragedy

From *Titus Andronicus* to *Hamlet*

For most playgoers and readers Shakespeare's tragedies rank among the supreme masterpieces of world literature. Although innumerable volumes have been written about them, one work marked a milestone in modern criticism: A. C. Bradley's *Shakespearean Tragedy* (1904). Many scholars continue to make the refutation or defense of Bradley the focus of their own critical approaches to the tragedies. Some may quarrel with his general method or with his comments on specific characters and dramatic situations; but Bradley's initial lecture in particular ("The Substance of Shakespearean Tragedy") is a penetrating analysis of Shakespeare's tragic conception, especially as it is expressed in *Hamlet, Othello, King Lear,* and *Macbeth.*[1]

According to Bradley, Shakespearean tragedy presents a tale of suffering and calamity leading to the death of an exceptional man. His misfortunes proceed from acts or omissions for which he himself is largely responsible, and they convey with unmistakable clarity "the sense of causal connection of character, deed, and catastrophe" (p. 15). While the plot may hinge upon an external conflict, we are primarily caught up in the moral struggle within the hero's soul. Because of his uncompromising intellect and will, the protagonist poses a grave threat to the natural order and hence must be destroyed. But in purging itself of the evil he embodies, the universe must bring about the ruin of much good that he also embodies. This produces the impression of waste that lends poignancy to his downfall. In Bradley's view the hero's defeat exemplifies a painful and all-encompassing mystery. " 'What a piece of work is man,' we cry; 'so much more beautiful and so much more terrible than we knew! Why should he be so if this beauty and greatness only tortures itself and throws itself away?' " This contradiction is, for Bradley, the very essence of tragedy:

Everywhere, from the crushed rocks beneath our feet to the soul of man, we see power, intelligence, life and glory, which astound us and seem to call for our worship. And everywhere we see them perishing, devouring one another and destroying themselves, often with dreadful pain, as though they came into being for no other end.[2]

Like everything else Shakespeare wrote, the tragedies have no genuine antecedents or counterparts, but they make use of several literary and philosophic traditions. Shakespeare, like many of his predecessors and contemporaries in the theater, was influenced, directly and indirectly, by the Roman dramatist Lucius Annaeus Seneca (c. 4 B.C.–A.D. 65). The tragedies of Seneca (for example, *Medea, Agamemnon,* and *Thyestes*) exploited a number of sensational elements that were to become staples of the Elizabethan stage: adultery; incest; murder and revenge; ghosts and other supernatural visitants; madness, real as well as simulated. These motifs, all of which are found in *Hamlet,* may have reached Shakespeare to a large extent through the plays of Thomas Kyd (1558–1594), notably *The Spanish Tragedy* (c. 1589).[3]

A second legacy, one that Shakespeare adapted from medieval tragedy, was the concept of "the fall of princes," a phrase derived from a famous Latin work by Boccaccio, *De Casibus Virorum et Feminarum Illustrium* (On the Falls of Illustrious Men and Women; c. 1363). In this collection of narratives, the ghosts of great personages tell frightening tales of how, from their eminence atop Fortune's wheel, they were abruptly cast down into the depths of misery. The Middle Ages and Renaissance produced a number of translations and imitations of *De Casibus.* Among them were *The Monk's Tale,* from Chaucer's *Canterbury Tales* (1386–1400); John Lydgate's *Fall of Princes* (1431–1438); and *The Mirror for Magistrates* (see p. 129). At his best, Boccaccio goes beyond the conventional medieval view of tragedy, which enshrines Fortune as an all-powerful and arbitrary force; he begins to explore the relationship between character and destiny, one of Shakespeare's major concerns.

Finally, Shakespeare was well acquainted with the English morality play (for example, *The Castle of Perseverance* [c. 1425], *Mankind* [c. 1475], and *Everyman* [c. 1500]). Although the genre had been secularized by the time Shakespeare wrote, the great Christian theme of death, which the morality play had emphasized, never lost its hold on the imagination of Elizabethan playwrights. Shakespeare's tragic heroes are bound up in the world, each in an individual way. Yet they also take on the characteristics of Everyman. In their sin and in their suffering— sometimes, perhaps, in their redemption—these tortured souls emerge as prototypes of humanity.[4]

TITUS ANDRONICUS

The First Quarto of *Titus Andronicus,* undiscovered until 1904 (when a copy turned up in the house of a Swedish post office clerk), was published in 1594 and reprinted with minor changes in 1600 and 1611. The 1611 Quarto was the basis for the text used in the 1623 Folio, except for a few lines and one whole scene (III, 2) that were probably copied from some version no longer extant. From Henslowe's *Diary* (see p. 6), we know that a performance took place on January 24, 1594. This may not have been the premiere but a revision of a play written by Shakespeare or someone else, perhaps as early as 1589.[5] The date of *Titus Andronicus* remains a mystery. If Shakespeare used a single source, it could have been some earlier version of an eighteenth-century chapbook (discovered in 1936) containing a ballad on Titus and a novel, *The History of Titus Andronicus.*[6] In any case, he was clearly indebted to Ovid's tale of the rape of Philomela, in book 6 of the *Metamorphoses;* and the climax of the play, in which Titus executes his fiendish revenge, may have been derived from Seneca's *Thyestes.* The slaying of Alarbus (I, 1, 96–144) was possibly influenced by the scene of the "Slaughter of the Innocents," in the Coventry Mystery Cycle.[7]

The plot is a veritable extravaganza of blood and revenge. Victorious over the Goths, Titus Andronicus returns to Rome with prisoners. Among them are the Gothic Queen Tamora; her sons, Alarbus, Demetrius, and Chiron; and her lover Aaron the Moor. Despite the Queen's tearful entreaties, Titus orders Alarbus slaughtered as a sacrifice to the shades of his twenty-one dead sons. Tamora and her two remaining sons resolve to avenge Alarbus's murder. Meanwhile, Saturninus and Bassianus, sons of the late Emperor, are rivals for the succession. Titus himself is offered the imperial throne but declines:

> Give me a staff of honour for mine age,
> But not a sceptre to control the world.
> Upright he held it, lords, that held it last.
>   (I, 1, 198–200)

He throws his support to Saturninus, the less worthy of the two, who wants to marry Titus's daughter Lavinia while at the same time lusting after Tamora. When Lavinia is abducted by Bassianus, Titus explodes with rage and tries to pursue them. He even kills his own son Mutius for blocking his path and, to make matters worse, refuses to allow his dead son an honorable burial in the family tomb. At long last, however, the father begrudgingly changes his mind, and Mutius is buried. Saturninus now resents Titus's influence in Rome and allows himself to become a pawn in the evil designs of Tamora and her two sons.

From this point on, horror is piled upon horror. Demetrius and

Chiron, encouraged by their mother and Aaron, stab Bassianus and prepare to rape Lavinia in a wonderfully macabre setting. "Drag hence her
husband to some secret hole," Chiron suggests, "And make his dead
trunk pillow to our lust" (II, 3, 129–130). They throw Bassianus's body
into a pit (this has been seen as a visual symbol of the descent into hell),[8]
ravish Lavinia, and, to keep her from identifying them, cut off her
tongue and hands. Next, Aaron tricks Martius and Quintus, sons of
Titus, into the selfsame pit and convinces Saturninus that they were the
murderers of Bassianus. When Martius and Quintus are condemned to
death, a third son of Titus, Lucius, tries to rescue them and is banished.
As an additional treat, Aaron informs Titus that the Emperor will spare
his sons if their father, as a gesture of goodwill, agrees to give up his right
hand. Titus accepts the offer, and Aaron chops off the hand on the spot—
only to send it back with a messenger a few minutes later, along with the
dissevered heads of Martius and Quintus.

The victims now get *their* chance. In a grotesque scene, Lavinia turns
the pages of Ovid with her stumps until she finds the story of Philomela,
whose tongue had similarly been cut off after she had been raped by
Tereus. Urged to give more signs, she places a staff in her mouth and
with her stumps traces in the sand the names of her assailants. To
initiate his revenge, Titus slits the throats of Demetrius and Chiron while
Lavinia holds a basin between her stumps to catch the blood. Next
Titus, partly insane and partly feigning insanity, invites Tamora to a
banquet and, in the attire of a cook, places a dish before his guests. To
end Lavinia's shame, he kills her and then names Demetrius and Chiron as
her defilers. He next informs Tamora that she has been feasting on the flesh
of her sons baked in a pie. The play ends with a further round of slayings:
Titus kills Tamora; Saturninus kills Titus; Lucius, back in Rome at the
head of a Gothic army, kills Saturninus. Lucius is hailed as the new
Emperor, in which capacity he orders that Aaron be half-buried and left
to starve and that Tamora's corpse be thrown to the birds and beasts.

It is difficult to take all this seriously, and Dover Wilson thinks the play
is intended as a parody: "*The Most Lamentable Romaine Tragedie of
Titus Andronicus* seems to jolt and bump along like some broken-down
cart, laden with bleeding corpses from an Elizabethan scaffold, and driven
by an executioner from Bedlam dressed in cap and bells."[9] The problem
is not so much that the violence is excessive, for the atrocities in *King
Lear* are almost as outrageous. What robs *Titus Andronicus* of tragic
stature is its failure to evoke real sympathy. We remain aloof, surprised,
and perhaps even amused as one atrocity follows another, but never
genuinely involved. There is an emblematic, pageantlike quality about
the play, and the effect of its hyperbolic scenes of suffering is, in the
words of one critic, "that of a living picture rather than of life itself."[10]

This emotional distance is reinforced by an artificial literary style. The ornamental imagery bears no organic relationship to what is happening on the stage. When Martius falls into the pit and beholds Bassianus's corpse, he indulges in staggeringly incongruous embellishments:

> Upon his bloody finger he doth wear
> A precious ring that lightens all this hole,
> Which, like a taper in some monument,
> Doth shine upon the dead man's earthy cheeks
> And shows the ragged entrails of the pit.
> So pale did shine the moon on Pyramus
> When he by night lay bath'd in maiden blood.
>   (II, 3, 226–232)

But the prize for inappropriateness has to go to Marcus for his outburst shortly after that most bizarre of stage directions, *"Enter . . . Lavinia, her hands cut off, and her tongue cut out, and ravish'd"*:

> Speak, gentle niece. What stern ungentle hand
> Hath lopp'd and hew'd and made thy body bare
> Of her two branches—those sweet ornaments
> Whose circling shadows kings have sought to sleep in
> And might not gain so great a happiness
> As half thy love? Why dost not speak to me?
> Alas, a crimson river of warm blood,
> Like to a bubbling fountain stirr'd with wind,
> Doth rise and fall between thy rosed lips,
> Coming and going with thy honey breath.
>   (II, 4, 16–25)

The contrast between the horror of the situation and the playfulness of the imagery creates an absurd effect inconsistent with the purposes of tragedy.[11]

Even Aaron the Moor, the most arresting figure in the play, becomes ludicrous in the end. Earlier, exulting in his passion for Tamora, he achieves a grandeur reminiscent of Marlowe's heroic figures, notably Tamburlaine:

> Upon her wit doth earthly honour wait,
> And virtue stoops and trembles at her frown.
> Then, Aaron, arm thy heart and fit thy thoughts
> To mount aloft with thy imperial mistress . . . .
> . . . .
> Away with slavish weeds and servile thoughts!
> I will be bright and shine in pearl and gold.
> To wait upon this new-made emperess.

To wait, said I? To wanton with this queen,
This goddess, this Semiramis, this nymph . . . .
(II, 1, 10–22)[12]

And the villain displays a touch of Richard III's laconic wit when he suddenly silences forever the nurse who was witness to the birth of his and Tamora's black child. "Weeke, weeke!—So cries a pig prepared to the spit" (IV, 2, 146). But in his exuberant recapitulation of a life devoted to evil, Aaron runs the gamut from appalling crimes to naughty pranks. "Art thou not sorry for these heinous deeds?" he is asked. "Ay, that I had not done a thousand more," comes the answer:

Even now I curse the day (and yet I think
Few come within the compass of my curse)
Wherein I did not some notorious ill:
As kill a man, or else devise his death;
Ravish a maid, or plot the way to do it;
Accuse some innocent, and forswear myself;
Set deadly enmity between two friends;
Make poor men's cattle break their necks;
Set fire on barns and haystacks in the night
And bid the owners quench them with their tears.
Oft have I digg'd up dead men from their graves
And set them upright at their dear friends' door . . . .
(V, 1, 123–136)

The net result of this series of anticlimaxes is to render his terrible career almost comic. Aaron is indeed a far cry from the truly depraved Iago, to whom he has been compared.

Yet it would be wrong to write *Titus* off as a weird joke; there are several features that make it well worth studying. For one thing, Shakespeare presents a comprehensive summary of Roman political institutions: free commonwealth, elected monarch, and (Titus's preference) hereditary monarchy.[13] In the second place, following Renaissance commentators who interpreted Ovid allegorically, Shakespeare sets forth in Ovidian symbols the theme of order versus chaos found in the *Metamorphoses*.[14] In the preface to his famous translation of Ovid (1567), Arthur Golding observes that when the state falls into disorder and vice it changes itself and its people "to eagles, tigers, bulls, and bears." This statement finds an echo in Titus's brilliant metaphor "Rome is but a wilderness of tigers" (III, 1, 54), as well as in the epithet "that ravenous tiger" (V, 3, 195), which Lucius applies to Tamora. Indeed, the play has been characterized as a study of the "emergence of the beast in man,"[15] and the savage rape and dismemberment of Lavinia, like the Ovidian rape of Lucrece (to which Shakespeare twice refers in the play), may be seen as a central symbol of moral and political disorder.[16] Finally, despite Shakespeare's hit-or-miss characterization, Titus himself partially embodies a tragic conception that was to be more fully developed in the later plays. To quote one scholar, "In the pride in his own recititude that blinds him to other moral values, Titus offers a real prophecy of the great tragic heroes, especially of Brutus."[17]

It has been suggested that Shakespeare had a collaborator for Titus; Thomas Kyd and, more frequently, George Peele have been thought likely candidates.[18] This idea seems to have sprung up for no better reason than that many readers, in their revulsion at the subject matter, are eager to shift the blame away from Shakespeare. But the play was included in the First Folio, and none of Shakespeare's contemporaries seems to have doubted his authorship. It is among the tragedies ascribed to him by Francis Meres. More important, Titus Andronicus, whatever its faults, attests to a mastery of theatrical construction beyond the reach of any other Elizabethan dramatist.[19]

ROMEO AND JULIET

The First Quarto (Q1) of Romeo and Juliet appeared in 1597; the Second Quarto (Q2), in 1599. Although Q1 is a bad quarto and Q2 a good one, the relationship between the two texts has been the subject of considerable debate, as yet unresolved. (It has been demonstrated that Q1 offers a superior version of the famous Queen Mab speech.)[20] It is likely that Q1, corrected and augmented by a scribe with access to Shakespeare's foul papers, provided the copy for Q2 and, subsequently, for the 1623 Folio. But Q2 may have been set up directly from the foul papers.[21] The date is also unsettled, and the "evidence" is purely internal. In I, 3, 23, the Nurse (whose memory need not be infallible) recalls the day Juliet was weaned: " 'Tis since the earthquake now eleven years," a remark often read as an allusion to the London earthquake of 1580. But 1591 is almost certainly too early. The play is usually linked with Shakespeare's so-called lyrical period, which includes Richard II and A Midsummer Night's Dream; and in view of the possible parody of Romeo and Juliet in "Pyramus and Thisby" (A Midsummer Night's Dream, V. 1; see pp. 110–111), a date near 1595 seems plausible.

About sources one can speak with more assurance. The play is taken directly from Arthur Brooke's long narrative poem, The Tragicall Historye of Romeus and Juliet (1562), which in turn is based on Matteo Bandello's Italian prose version of 1554, although Brooke probably used the work in Pierre Boaistuau's French translation (1559). But the main ingredients of this popular Renaissance love story were already present in Masuccio Salerintano's Il Novellino (1476) and Luigi da Porto's Istoria novellamente ritrovata di due Nobili Amanti (c. 1530). It is difficult to determine to what extent Shakespeare may have been acquainted with any of these pre-Brooke renderings of the tale, but he must have read a later translation of Boaistuau included in William Painter's *Palace of Pleasure* (1567). At any rate, it was Brooke who supplied nearly all the details of Shakespeare's plot and who in fact furnished the dramatist with many actual words and phrases. The finest touches, however, are original with Shakespeare. For example, to emphasize the tragic conflict between the old and the young, Shakespeare lowers Juliet's age to fourteen. He telescopes the time of the action from three months to four days, thereby intensifying the sense of urgency experienced by the lovers and the audience. With unerring theatrical instinct, he introduces the superb meeting of Romeo and Paris in the Capulet tomb. And he transforms two minor figures into major personalities: the Nurse, whose character is suggested but not developed in Brooke, and Mercutio, previously little more than a name.[22]

Before the play begins, the Chorus enters and speaks the celebrated Prologue:

Two households, both alike in dignity,
  In fair Verona, where we lay our scene,
From ancient grudge break to new mutiny,
  Where civil blood makes civil hands unclean.
From forth the fatal loins of these two foes
  A pair of star-cross'd lovers take their life;
Whose misadventur'd piteous overthrows
  Doth with their death bury their parents' strife.
                    (I, Prologue, 1–8)

Not only do these lines provide a concise summary of the plot, but they call attention to one of the underlying themes of the tragedy: the paradoxical relationship between love and hate. The love of Romeo and Juliet gains poignancy and strength precisely because it must somehow survive in the deadly atmosphere generated by the hostility of their families. Yet at the end of the play old Capulet beholds the dead bodies of Romeo and Juliet, the "poor sacrifices of our enmity" (V, 3, 304), and takes the hand of his bitter foe Montague. Ironically, the Capulet tomb has become the symbol of the continuity of family and social life.[23] The interaction of love and hate is complete; the reconciliation of the elders has been accomplished through the deaths of the children.

This fundamental ambiguity is reinforced by the succession of misadventures that speed the "star-cross'd lovers" to catastrophe. Shortly after their marriage, Romeo enters the street full of goodwill toward the Capulets, only to be taunted by Juliet's hotheaded cousin Tybalt. When Romeo refuses the challenge, Mercutio interprets his behavior as "calm, dishonourable, vile submission" (III, 1, 76) and draws his own sword on Tybalt. With the best of intentions Romeo tries to separate the two, but Mercutio is fatally wounded under his friend's arm. Now obliged to fight, Romeo kills Tybalt in the ensuing clash, thereby bringing on his banishment from Verona. "O, I am fortune's fool!" (III, 1, 141), he exclaims. Friar Laurence, friend and confidant to the lovers, prepares a potion that gives Juliet the appearance of death. The plan calls for Romeo, after Juliet's "burial," to return from exile in Mantua and join Friar Laurence in the Capulet vault to wait for her to awaken, whereupon the lovers are to go back to Mantua and remain there while the Friar tries to reunite their families. But the Friar's letter explaining the complicated scheme is never delivered to Romeo because its bearer happens to be placed under quarantine. Meanwhile, Romeo, hearing that Juliet is dead, purchases a dram of poison and hastens to the tomb. He arrives a moment too soon (the effect of the sleeping potion has not yet worn off) and resolves to die with Juliet:

> Here, here will I remain
> With worms that are thy chambermaids. O, here
> Will I set up my everlasting rest
> And shake the yoke of inauspicious stars
> From this world-wearied flesh.
>
> (V, 3, 108–112)

Fearing the worst, Friar Laurence rushes to the vault, seconds too late to prevent Romeo from swallowing the poison. When Juliet opens her eyes and finds him dead, she stabs herself. The Friar had cautioned Romeo against acting rashly. "Wisely, and slow. They stumble that run fast" (II, 3, 94). But the warning has wider application. *All* the characters run too fast, and the mood of the play is one of terrible explosiveness.[24]

At virtually every turn the characters in the play are victimized by an ironic reversal. *Romeo and Juliet* is often described as a tragedy of accident rather than character, and it is indeed difficult to distinguish actions that are creditable from those that are blameworthy. A case in point is Friar Laurence, whose well-meaning efforts turn out to be ruinous, as he himself acknowledges:

> And here I stand, both to impeach and purge
> Myself condemned and myself excus'd.
>
> (V, 3, 226–227)

Even in his first speech, a soliloquy delivered as he holds a basket of flowers, he reflects that good and evil frequently reside within a single plant:

For naught so vile that on the earth doth live
But to the earth some special good doth give;
Nor aught so good but, strain'd from that fair use,
Revolts from true birth, stumbling on abuse.
Virtue itself turns vice, being misapplied,
And vice sometime's by action dignified.
Within the infant rind of this small flower
Poison hath residence, and medicine power.

(II, 3, 17–24)

This is a play in which good intentions often lead to disaster. There are no villains.

If individual actions begin well and turn out badly, the play as a whole initially promises to be a comedy and, about halfway through, abruptly changes. At first the feud seems little more than a bawdy exchange between Montague and Capulet servants, with both sides too cowardly to draw blood. When Capulet calls for his long sword, his wife quickly reminds him that his fighting days are over. "A crutch, a crutch! Why call you for a sword?" (I, 1, 83). However testily he may behave later, Capulet for the time being is an innocuous old man who delivers stale witticisms at the Capulets' ball and looks back nostalgically to his youthful capers, when he was quite a gallant:

I have seen the day
That I have worn a visor and could tell
A whispering tale in a fair lady's ear,
Such as would please. 'Tis gone, 'tis gone, 'tis gone!

(I, 5, 23–26)

When we are introduced to Romeo, this somewhat absurd young man is languishing in unrequited love for Rosaline with scarcely a cliché of the Petrarchan sonneteer omitted from his arsenal. He steals into the woods before sunrise to augment the dew with tears and the clouds with sighs. His speech is saturated with those amusing contradictions, or oxymorons, which Renaissance love poets found appealing:

O heavy lightness! serious vanity!
Misshapen chaos of well-seeming forms!
Feather of lead, bright smoke, cold fire, sick health!
Still-waking sleep, that is not what it is!
This love feel I, that feel no love in this.

(I, 1, 185–189)

Rosaline, who inspires this outburst, never appears on the stage; she is, in effect, a poetic fabrication. At a more serious level, to be sure, Romeo's oxymorons are the rhetorical counterpart of the paradoxes that suffuse the dramatic action, and later, along with his and Juliet's verbal quibbling, they help convey the lovers' mental anguish.[25] But in the early scenes both Romeo and Rosaline are portrayed in part as comic stereotypes.

The comic perspective is chiefly supplied by Mercutio and the Nurse. Mercutio, the cynic, views love as fair game for satire. The Nurse, with a zest for life that recalls Chaucer's Wife of Bath and foreshadows Falstaff, believes that sexual pleasure is everything. Although Shakespeare conceives both characters as foils for the romanticism of the lovers and endows each with a highly individualized point of view and style, they ultimately prove too shallow to command our total sympathy. Neither is capable of understanding Romeo and Juliet's all-encompassing commitment to each other.

To Mercutio everything is a joke, as he demonstrates in his sparkling account of how the fairy Queen Mab,[26] in a chariot of empty hazelnut, whisks through our imaginations as we sleep and fills our dreams with secret fantasies:

> And in this state she gallops night by night
> Through lovers' brains, and then they dream of love;
> O'er courtiers' knees, that dream on cursies straight;
> O'er lawyers' fingers, who straight dream on fees;
> O'er ladies' lips, who straight on kisses dream,
> Which oft the angry Mab with blisters plagues,
> Because their breaths with sweetmeats tainted are.
> Sometime she gallops o'er a courtier's nose,
> And then dreams he of smelling out a suit;
> And sometime comes she with a tithe-pig's tail
> Tickling a parson's nose as 'a lies asleep,
> Then dreams he of another benefice.
>
> (I, 4, 70–81)

Not caring, or even knowing, that his friend Romeo has shifted from Rosaline to Juliet, he twits him unmercifully.[27] When Romeo climbs over the wall into the Capulets' orchard, Mercutio playfully tries to "conjure" him:

> Romeo! humours! madman! passion! lover!
> Appear thou in the likeness of a sigh;
> Speak but one rhyme, and I am satisfied!
> Cry but "Ay me!" pronounce but "love" and "dove . . . . "
>
> (II, 1, 7–10)

Receiving no answer, he summons him in the name of specific parts of Rosaline's anatomy, spicing his mock incantation with brazen sexual innuendoes that undermine the romantic tradition. In a later scene, when Romeo joins in the repartee, Mercutio is delighted:

Why, is not this better now than groaning for love? Now art thou sociable, now art thou Romeo; now art thou what thou art, by art as well as by nature.

(II, 4, 92–95)

Even his own impending death furnishes material for a bitter jest. "The hurt cannot be much," Romeo reassures him. Mercutio offers a grim rejoinder:

No, 'tis not so deep as a well, nor so wide as a church door; but 'tis enough, 'twill serve. Ask for me to-morrow, and you shall find me a grave man. I am peppered, I warrant, for this world. A plague o' both your houses!

(III, 1, 98–103)

It is with the death of this gallant spirit that the mood of the play suddenly darkens and we enter the realm of tragedy.

Unlike Mercutio, who masks his feelings behind a smoke screen of wit, the Nurse unblushingly reveals herself in almost every line she speaks. One of her happiest recollections is of the time that Juliet, not yet three, fell on her face, prompting an earthy comment:

And then my husband (God be with his soul!
'A was a merry man) took up the child.
"Yea," quoth he, "dost thou fall upon thy face?
Thou wilt fall backward when thou hast more wit;
Wilt thou not, Jule?" and, by my holidam,
The pretty wretch left crying, and said "Ay."
To see now how a jest shall come about!
I warrant, an I should live a thousand years,
I never should forget it. "Wilt thou not, Jule?" quoth he,
And, pretty fool, it stinted [stopped], and said "Ay."

(I, 3, 39–48)[28]

She delights in her role of go-between because it permits her to parcel out news of Romeo to the impatient Juliet and to enjoy vicariously the pleasures of the wedding night. With the banishment of Romeo, however, the Nurse's pragmatic sexuality dictates that Juliet obey her parents and marry the County Paris:

O, he's a lovely gentleman!
Romeo's a dishclout to him. An eagle, madam,
Hath not so green, so quick, so fair an eye
As Paris hath. Beshrew my very heart,
I think you are happy in this second match,
For it excels your first; or if it did not,
Your first is dead—or 'twere as good he were
As living here and you no use of him.

(III, 5, 220–227)

Even while trying to rouse Juliet from her deathlike sleep, she licks her lips:

> What, not a word? You take your pennyworths now!
> Sleep for a week; for the next night, I warrant,
> The County Paris hath set up his rest
> That you shall rest but little. God forgive me!
> Marry, and amen.
>
> (IV, 5, 4–8)

In the words of the actor-scholar Harley Granville-Barker, the Nurse "needs no critical expanding, she expounds herself on all occasions; nor explanation, for she is plain as daylight; nor analysis, lest it lead to excuse; and she stays blissfully unregenerate."[29]

But the fact remains that the Nurse deserts Juliet in her hour of need, provoking the angry soliloquy, "Ancient damnation! O most wicked fiend!" (III, 5, 237). Together with the death of Mercutio, the Nurse's about-face breaks all remaining ties between the lovers and the world and leaves them, except for the ineffectual Friar Laurence, irretrievably alone.[30] Yet, through the intensity of their love, Romeo and Juliet manage to build for themselves a radiant inner world that outlasts the accidents and betrayals that curtail their lives.

From their first awkward meeting to the final desperate kiss that Juliet plants on Romeo's dead lips, their passion is invested with a sanctity incomprehensible to everyone else. Romeo attends the ball expecting to confirm Rosaline's supreme beauty, but when he catches sight of Juliet, his reaction is instantaneous. "O, she doth teach the torches to burn bright!" (I, 5, 46). To quote Rosalie Colie's arresting term, the love-at-first-sight convention is "unmetaphored": A literary device is made part of the reality of the play itself.[31] Romeo approaches Juliet in the only style he knows, that of the Petrarchan lover, and his first words to her form the opening quatrain of a sonnet:

> If I profane with my unworthiest hand
> This holy shrine, the gentle fine is this:
> My lips, two blushing pilgrims, ready stand
> To smooth that rough touch with a tender kiss.
>
> (I, 5, 95–98)

Juliet picks up the religious image, playfully admonishing him that pilgrims and saints must use lips only for prayer. They complete the sonnet with a kiss. "You kiss by th' book," Juliet says (I, 5, 112), with charming insight into Romeo's previous emotional life. The scene is a perfect blend of the light and the serious; it suggests that the old infatuation with Rosaline is forgotten and that something new and wonderful is about to take its place. Thus the sonnet itself has lost its artificiality and has been transfigured into the "formal embodiment of valid feeling."[32]

They next meet in Capulet's orchard, where love shuts out hatred. Always fresh is Juliet's rapturous declaration from her balcony that only Romeo's name, "Montague," is her enemy:

> O, be some other name!
> What's in a name? That which we call a rose
> By any other name [*word* in Q2] would smell as sweet.
> So Romeo would, were he not Romeo call'd,
> Retain that dear perfection which he owes [possesses]
> Without that title. Romeo, doff thy name;
> And for that name, which is no part of thee,
> Take all myself.
>
> (II, 2, 42–49)

Here Juliet feels at one with Romeo, and she speaks with a simplicity absent from the earlier rhetoric associated with Rosaline as well as from the verbal games she herself occasionally plays.[33] When Juliet fervently repeats his name, Romeo responds with similar straightforwardness and lyricism:

> It is my soul that calls upon my name.
> How silver-sweet sound lovers' tongues by night,
> Like softest music to attending ears!
>
> (II, 2, 166–168)

But the sweet sorrow of parting cannot be postponed:

> *Juliet:* Romeo!
> *Romeo:*   My dear?
> *Juliet:*   At what o'clock to-morrow
>   Shall I send to thee?
> *Romeo:*   By the hour of nine.
> *Juliet:* I will not fail. 'Tis twenty years till then.
>   I have forgot why I did call thee back.
> *Romeo:* Let me stand here till thou remember it.
> *Juliet:* I shall forget, to have thee still stand there,
>   Rememb'ring how I love thy company.
> *Romeo:* And I'll still stay, to have thee still forget,
>   Forgetting any other home but this.
>
> (II, 2, 169–177)

"This," a critic has said, "is the commonplace made marvelous."[34]

After the brief marriage scene in Friar Laurence's cell (II, 6), the lovers are separated. Romeo gets embroiled with Mercutio and Tybalt, and Juliet waits breathlessly for night to bring her husband to her arms:

> Gallop apace, you fiery-footed steeds,
> Towards Phoebus' lodging! Such a wagoner
> As Phaëton would whip you to the West
> And bring in cloudy night immediately.
> Spread thy close curtain, love-performing night,
> That runaway eyes may wink, and Romeo
> Leap to these arms untalk'd of and unseen.
> . . . .
> O, I have bought the mansion of a love,
> But not possess'd it; and though I am sold,
> Not yet enjoy'd. So tedious is this day
> As is the night before some festival
> To an impatient child that hath new robes
> And may not wear them.
>   (III, 2, 1–31)

She stands on the threshold of womanhood, eager for the consummation of her love but in full command of her emotions. Meanwhile, the more impulsive Romeo learns from Friar Laurence of his impending banishment and refuses the comfort of "adversity's sweet milk, philosophy":

> Hang up philosophy!
> Unless philosophy can make a Juliet,
> Displant a town, reverse a prince's doom,
> It helps not, it prevails not. Talk no more.
>   (III, 3, 55–60)

He throws himself on the ground, then brandishes a dagger with which he threatens to take his own life. Eventually Friar Laurence calms him down.

The lovers are together once more, at Juliet's window the morning after their glorious experience as man and wife.[35] As in the early scene in Capulet's orchard, they attempt to delay the inevitable. For a while Juliet seeks to maintain the illusion that it is still night:

> Wilt thou be gone? It is not yet near day.
> It was the nightingale, and not the lark,
> That pierc'd the fearful hollow of thine ear.
> Nightly she sings on yond pomegranate tree.
> Believe me, love, it was the nightingale.
>   (III, 5, 1–5)

"It was the lark, the herald of the morn," Romeo answers (III, 5, 6). Before long, however, he acquiesces in the deception:

Let me be ta'en, let me be put to death.
I am content, so thou wilt have it so.
I'll say yon grey is not the morning's eye,
'Tis but the pale reflex of Cynthia's [the moon's] brow;
Nor that is not the lark whose notes do beat
The vaulty heaven so high above our heads.
I have more care to stay than will to go.
Come, death, and welcome! Juliet wills it so.
How is't my soul? Let's talk; it is not day.

(III, 5, 17–25)

"It is, it is!" Juliet finally insists, for she knows in her heart that reality cannot be wished away. "It is the lark that sings so out of tune" (III, 5, 26–27). In the earlier balcony scene Juliet had declared with childlike innocence that the name "Montague" was her enemy, and Romeo, dagger in hand, had later offered to cut his hateful name out of his anatomy (III, 3, 105–108). Both had somehow felt that by merely changing the name they could make everything right. But in this second balcony scene, a painfully altered echo of the first,[36] Romeo reluctantly tears himself away, and they realize, with a maturity beyond their years, that they must accept reality with all its heartbreak. That which we call a lark by any other name remains a lark.

As suggested previously, *Romeo and Juliet* may not qualify as a tragedy in the strict sense. The hostile forces are not clearly defined, and the relationship between fate and individual responsibility becomes somewhat obscured. One is aware of what has been called "a kind of moral schizophrenia," with the lovers being crossed by the stars, by their families, and by themselves.[37] In the words of Donald Stauffer, a sympathetic critic, the play "may fail as serious tragedy because Shakespeare blurs the focus and never makes up his mind entirely as to who is being punished, and for what reason."[38] Indeed, a number of critics would place much of the blame on the lovers. Romeo and Juliet, some say, make rash choices and are unduly stubborn. Romeo has even been condemned for idolatry; at the very least, it is argued, his passionate devotion to Juliet must be censured as alien to the teachings of Christianity. According to James Seward, an Elizabethan audience could have seen the manifestations of Romeo and Juliet's romantic love as "mere exhalations of lust," and Francis Fergusson has made an illuminating comparison between the lovers and Paolo and Francesca, the passionate sinners in Dante's *Inferno* (Canto 5, 73–142).[39]

Those who hold such moralistic views sometimes seem to regard the play primarily as a poetic text to be studied rather than a drama to be experienced. They thus run the risk of emphasizing critical reflection at the expense of an audience's immediate emotional response to the characters in their tragic predicament. "In *Romeo and Juliet*," Caroline

Spurgeon writes, "the beauty and ardour of young love are seen by Shakespeare as the irradiating glory of sunlight and starlight in a dark world."[40] When that light is finally quenched, we feel the pain too keenly to sit in judgment.

JULIUS CAESAR

The only authoritative text of *Julius Caesar,* that printed in the 1623 Folio, is excellent. External evidence points to 1599 as the date. In *The Mirror of Martyrs,* published in 1601 but, according to the dedication, ready for the printer "some two yeares agoe," the poet John Weever alludes to Shakespeare's Forum scene (III, 2):

> The many-headed multitude were drawne
> By *Brutus* speech, that *Caesar* was ambitious,
> When eloquent *Mark Antonie* had showne
> His vertues, who but *Brutus* then was vicious?

Moreover, the Swiss doctor Thomas Platter records that on September 21, 1599, during a visit to London, he crossed the water to attend, evidently at the Globe, a performance of the tragedy of the first emperor, *Julius Caesar.*[41] Platter is mistaken, of course, about Caesar's being the first emperor, but he is probably referring to Shakespeare's play. *Julius Caesar* is not listed in Meres's *Palladis Tamia* (1598); this is further corroboration, perhaps, for the 1599 date.[42]

The major source was Plutarch's *Lives of the Noble Grecians and Romans* (c. A.D. 75) in Sir Thomas North's famous translation of 1579. Shakespeare draws heavily upon the lives of Caesar, Antonius, and Brutus; but he is ever alert to the possibility of rearranging or inventing episodes in the interest of theatrical effectiveness. He compresses into a single day Caesar's triumph, the Feast of the Lupercal, and the disrobing of Caesar's images by the Tribunes, thereby suggesting the confused moral and political atmosphere of Rome. By placing Antony's funeral oration right after Brutus's speech and by bringing it to a climax with the reading of Caesar's will, Shakespeare brilliantly underscores the contrasting styles of the two antagonists and at the same time provides a demonstration of the mob's instability. He introduces the mention of Portia's death into the quarrel scene (IV, 3)—a delicate touch that seals the reconciliation of Brutus and Cassius. Shakespeare may have used other sources: Appian's *Auncient Historie and Exquisite Chronicle of the Romanes Warres,* translated in 1578; Thomas Kyd's *Cornelia* (1594), a translation of Robert Garnier's French Senecan tragedy; and *Caesar's Revenge,* an anonymous English play published in 1607 but probably composed several years before *Julius Caesar*. But his indebtedness to Plutarch cannot be overstated.[43]

The assassination of Caesar in 44 B.C. exerted a profound influence on medieval and Renaissance men of letters. Although individual writers took sides on personal or political grounds, the prevailing opinion was that the principal actors in that momentous drama were complicated human beings whose behavior, private as well as public, should evoke both admiration and reproof. This ambivalence is reflected in Shakespeare. If we are sometimes hard put to decide just who in *Julius Caesar* lays largest claim to our sympathy, the reason is that Shakespeare himself devotes almost equal attention to Caesar, Brutus, and Mark Antony (not to mention Cassius, for whom, especially in performance, a compelling argument can also be made). Shakespeare establishes what one critic describes as a "mood of ironic contemplation, of disinterested reflection upon the great persons and happenings of an age that had vanished . . . ."[44] Rather than involve us deeply in the anguish of a single protagonist torn asunder by cataclysmic error, as is often the case in the later tragedies, he bids us stand dispassionately aside in order to observe—in victim, conspirators, and avenger alike—the discrepancy, in the words of Derek Traversi, "between what men propose and what, as political beings, they in fact achieve."[45] Or, as Nicholas Brooke demonstrates, we are presented with a picture of what men do, not what they ought to do.[46]

Although "the foremost man of all this world" (IV, 3, 22) appears only briefly in the play that bears his name, Shakespeare manages to suggest in a few well-chosen details something of Caesar's magnitude. With superb efficiency Caesar dismisses the Soothsayer who warns him to beware the ides of March. "He is a dreamer. Let us leave him. Pass" (I, 2, 24). His slightest whim has the ring of an ultimatum:

> Let me have men about me that are fat,
> Sleek-headed men, and such as sleep a-nights.
> Yond Cassius has a lean and hungry look.
> He thinks too much. Such men are dangerous.
> (I, 2, 192–195)

Having become a legend in his own eyes, Caesar often refers to himself in the third person, as if, to quote from Edward Dowden's classic study, he were speaking "of some power above and behind his consciousness."[47] He insists on going to the Capitol on the fateful ides of March, having rationalized the bad dreams of his wife Calphurnia and the omens described by the augurers:[48]

> No, Caesar shall not [stay home]. Danger knows full well
> That Caesar is more dangerous than he.

We are two lions litter'd in one day,
And I the elder and more terrible,
And Caesar shall go forth.

(II, 2, 44–48)

Even as the conspirators close in on him, Caesar is in the act of refusing to revoke his banishment of Publius Cimber and is thereby asserting his godlike inflexibility:

I could be well mov'd, if I were as you;
If I could pray to move, prayers would move me:
But I am constant as the Northern Star,
Of whose true-fix'd and resting quality
There is no fellow in the firmament.

(III, 1, 58–62)

He does, indeed, "bestride the narrow world / Like a Colossus" (I, 2, 135–136).

But Caesar is "a Colossus with clay feet."[49] Following Plutarch, Shakespeare makes a point of his infirmities. Cassius recalls the time Caesar challenged him to a swimming, match and then, tiring before the race was over, cried: " 'Help me, Cassius, or I sink!' " (I, 2, 111). Just as Aeneas had borne his aged father from the flames of Troy, so Cassius carried Caesar from the Tiber. "And this man," says Cassius, "Is now become a god" (I, 2, 115–116). Cassius also remembers how Caesar, shaking with the fever in Spain, called for water like a sick girl. From Casca we hear that just after refusing the crown for the third time, Caesar suffered an epileptic seizure in the marketplace and foamed at the mouth. As leading members of the conspiracy, Cassius and Casca are prejudiced witnesses. But from Caesar's own lips we learn of another weakness (not mentioned in any of the sources). The revelation is particularly striking because it occurs at the end of an arrogant statement to Antony about why men like Cassius are dangerous:

I rather tell thee what is to be fear'd
Than what I fear; for always I am Caesar.
Come on my right hand, for this ear is deaf,
And tell me truly what thou think'st of him.

(I, 2, 211–214)

In its context, as Maurice Charney observes, the disclosure is "an ironic comment on Caesar's omnipotent and superhuman claims."[50] There are two Caesars. Beneath the bravado of the public hero is an ailing and faltering man.[51]

If Caesar falls short of his godlike self-image, Shakespeare nevertheless portrays him as an extraordinary statesman who dominates the scene while he is alive and whose spirit continues to shape Rome's destiny after his death. Whatever their reasons for destroying Caesar and the principles he embodies, the conspirators cannot fill the power vacuum caused by his removal. This deficiency is especially true of Brutus and Cassius. While Shakespeare does not share Dante's judgment that the two are frozen, along with Judas Iscariot, in the ninth and deepest circle of hell (*Inferno,* Canto 34, 28–69), he considers them guilty of a terrible mistake, perhaps even a crime.[52] The conspiracy fails because its architects, in Shakespeare's view, lack the political intelligence to understand or control the chaotic forces they set in motion.

Brutus occupies a special position in Shakespeare's development: He is the first of a long line of tragic heroes in whom internal action predominates over external action.[53] He loves Caesar yet fears that his friend is ambitious. In a fascinating soliloquy ("It must be by his death" [II, 1, 10–34]), a model of fallacious reasoning, he concedes that Caesar has so far given no indication that he will abuse the power he seeks. However, "It is the bright day that brings forth the adder, / And that craves [requires] wary walking" (II, 1, 14–15). Once he reaches the top of the ladder, Caesar may turn his back on everything below:

> Then lest he may, prevent. And since the quarrel
> Will bear no colour for the thing he is,
> Fashion it thus: that what he is, augmented,
> Would run to these and these extremities;
> And therefore think him as a serpent's egg,
> Which, hatch'd, would as his kind grow mischievous,
> And kill him in the shell.
>
> (II, 1, 28–34)

Brutus reluctantly joins the conspiracy in the hope that the murder of Caesar, itself an evil act, will bring forth good in the form of a liberated Rome. He tortures himself because he cannot reconcile the claims of public policy and personal friendship.[54] After the assassination he appears in the Forum to deliver his eloquent self-justification to the Plebeians:

> Not that I lov'd Caesar less, but that I lov'd Rome more. Had you rather Caesar were living, and die all slaves, than that Caesar were dead, to live all freemen? As Caesar lov'd me, I weep for him; as he was fortunate, I rejoice at it; as he was valiant, I honour him; but—as he was ambitious, I slew him .... With this I depart, that, as I slew my best lover [friend] for the good of Rome, I have the same dagger for myself when it shall please my country to need my death.
>
> (III, 2, 23–52)

All the other conspirators, Mark Antony observes in his epitaph, were motivated by envy of Caesar; Brutus alone acted out of idealism.

The conspiracy, as Cassius soon realizes, needs the moral tone Brutus can lend to it. Yet, ironically, it is Brutus's apparent idealism that is in large measure responsible for the failure of the cause and for the civil disorder that subsequently engulfs Rome. When Cassius makes the practical suggestion that Antony, "a shrewd contriver" (II, 1, 158), be killed with Caesar, Brutus recoils at the prospect of shedding excessive blood:

> Let us be sacrificers, but not butchers, Caius.
> We all stand up against the spirit of Caesar,
> And in the spirit of men there is no blood.
> O that we then could come by Caesar's spirit
> And not dismember Caesar!
>
> (II, 1, 166–170)

This insensitivity to the threat posed by Antony is again evident when Brutus, despite Cassius's warning, makes the fatal error of permitting him to speak at Caesar's funeral. He later shows faulty military judgment by insisting on taking the offensive against Antony's army at Philippi. Republicanism is doomed to failure, largely because of the imperfect vision of its leading advocate.[55]

If Brutus were simply the naive intellectual forced into the uncongenial world of political action, one could perhaps be more sympathetic to him. But his idealism is flawed.[56] His absolute sense of honor helps produce a subtle kind of moral insensibility that blinds him to questions of good and evil.[57] No doubt he is sincere in wanting to avoid unnecessary bloodshed, and he would genuinely prefer to kill Caesar's spirit without damaging Caesar's body—as though it were possible to commit murder and remain free of the murderer's stain. But this same Brutus comes up with a shocking suggestion:

> Stoop, Romans, stoop,
> And let us bathe our hands in Caesar's blood
> Up to the elbows and besmear our swords.
> Then walk we forth, even to the market place,
> And waving our red weapons o'er our heads,
> Let's all cry "Peace, freedom, and liberty!"
>
> (III, 1, 105–110)

In proposing this ritualistic bloodbath, Brutus blurs the distinction between sacrificers and butchers. "Having accepted republicanism as an honorable end," one critic writes, "he sets out to dignify assassination, the means, by lifting it to a level of rite and ceremony."[58] He needs to make his conduct coincide with his exalted image of himself, thereby betraying an egoism very similar to Caesar's. The play is so constructed that the tragedies of Caesar and Brutus are complementary.[59]

Unlike Brutus, Cassius, who sparks the plot against Caesar, does not indulge in self-examination. He wants Rome to be a republic, but he is also fired by personal animosity. Why pay homage, he asks, to a mere man who is no better than anyone else?

> "Brutus," and "Caesar." What should be in that "Caesar"?
> Why should that name be sounded more than yours?
> Write them together: yours is as fair a name.
> Sound them: it doth become the mouth as well.
> Weigh them: it is as heavy. Conjure with 'em:
> "Brutus" will start a spirit as soon as "Caesar."
> Now in the names of all the gods at once,
> Upon what meat doth this our Caesar feed
> That he is grown so great?
>
> (I, 2, 142–50)[60]

While Brutus generally moves on a lofty plane and views human nature in the best possible light, Cassius reacts with a frankness that borders on the cynical. There is a refreshing candor in his terse remarks to Antony after the assassination, particularly since they follow Brutus's high-minded rhetoric:

> Your voice shall be as strong as any man's
> In the disposing of new dignities.
>
> (III, 1, 177–178)

Cassius has clearly sized up the enemy with penetrating accuracy, and while he and Brutus prepare for battle at Philippi, he is not above chiding his friend with an "I-told-you-so" for allowing Antony to live and bandy words with them in the prebattle parley:

> Now, Brutus, thank yourself!
> This tongue had not offended so to-day
> If Cassius might have rul'd.
>
> (V, 1, 45–47)

He denounces Antony to his face as "a masker and a reveller"; Octavius Caesar, who will eventually emerge as the real power in Rome, he dismisses as "a peevish schoolboy" (V, 1, 61–62). That Cassius is impetuous, quick to anger, and, even to his friends, thoroughly exasperating, he himself would be the first to admit. Yet, in the words of Granville-Barker, "the man is lovable, as those which are spendthrift of themselves can be, and as—for all his virtues—Brutus is not."[61]

In the famous quarrel scene, Shakespeare brings Cassius to Brutus's tent near Sardis and with uncommon artistry permits us to observe in detail the two contrasting personalities interacting with each other.

Brutus, who in his own words is "arm'd so strong in honesty" (IV, 3, 67),
chastises Cassius for having "an itching palm" (IV, 3, 10). A heated
argument ensues in which Brutus, losing for the moment his habitual self-
control, lashes out at his comrade:

Go show your slaves how choleric you are
And make your bondmen tremble. Must I budge?
Must I observe you? Must I stand and crouch
Under your testy humour? By the gods,
You shall digest the venom of your spleen,
Though it do split you; for from this day forth
I'll use you for my mirth, yea, for my laughter,
When you are waspish.

                              (IV, 3, 43–50)

"A friend should bear his friend's infirmities," Cassius tells him (IV, 3,
86); then, complaining like a child that Brutus does not love him any
more, he unleashes a torrent of self-pity:

Come, Antony, and young Octavius, come!
Revenge yourselves alone on Cassius.
For Cassius is aweary of the world;
Hated by one he loves; brav'd by his brother;
Check'd like a bondman; all his faults observ'd,
Set in a notebook, learn'd and conn'd by rote
To cast into my teeth. O, I could weep
My spirit from mine eyes! There is my dagger,
And here my naked breast . . .
. . . .
Strike as thus didst at Caesar; for I know,
When thou didst hate him worst, thou lov'dst him better
Than ever thou lov'dst Cassius.

                              (IV, 3, 93–107)

At this point Brutus's anger subsides, and the two men once again join
hands and hearts in unstinting affection. A few moments later comes the
beautifully understated revelation of Brutus's heartfelt grief:

Cassius: I did not think you could have been so angry.
Brutus: O Cassius, I am sick of many griefs.
Cassius: Of your philosophy you make no use
    If you give place to accidental evils.
Brutus: No man bears sorrow better. Portia is dead.
Cassius: Ha! Portia?
Brutus: She is dead.
Cassius: How scap'd I killing when I cross'd you so?
    O insupportable and touching loss!

                              (IV, 3, 143–151)

Harmony is restored, and the friends bury unkindness in a bowl of wine. Just before the final battle, Brutus rises to the height of Stoic dignity to bid Cassius farewell:

> But this same day
> Must end that work the ides of March begun,
> And whether we shall meet again I know not.
> Therefore our everlasting farewell take.
> For ever and for ever farewell, Cassius!
> If we do meet again, why, we shall smile;
> If not, why then this parting was well made.
>   (V, 1, 112–118)

Cassius echoes the refrain:

> For ever and for ever farewell, Brutus!
> If we do meet again, we'll smile indeed;
> If not, 'tis true this parting was well made.
>   (V, 1, 119–121)

They do not meet again. Faced with impending military defeat, Cassius orders his servant Pindarus to stab him to death, and Brutus runs on his own sword.

Although they differ markedly in temperament and outlook, Brutus and Cassius share an abiding commitment to the libertarian principles for which they thought they were striking a blow on the ides of March. Almost immediately after Caesar's death, however, they are confronted with a new menace in the person of Caesar's devoted friend Mark Antony, a clever opportunist with no particular attachment to any political ideology. "Shakespeare," it has been said, "keeps him in ambush throughout the first part of the play."[62] Then, as the action unfolds, Antony slowly comes into his own as a character of major dramatic interest.

Before the assassination Antony speaks only thirty-three words, and our first impression of him afterward is derived from the disarming but somewhat cryptic message he dispatches with his servant:

> Brutus is noble, wise, valiant, and honest;
> Caesar was mighty, bold, royal, and loving.
> Say I love Brutus and I honour him;
> Say I fear'd Caesar, honour'd him, and lov'd him.
> If Brutus will vouchsafe that Antony
> May safely come to him and be resolv'd
> How Caesar hath deserv'd to lie in death,
> Mark Antony shall not love Caesar dead
> So well as Brutus living.
>   (III, 1, 126–134)

This carefully worded communication prepares for Antony's entrance and for the double role he is for the time being obliged to play. He must seem sincerely grief-stricken for his murdered friend while putting on a convincing show of goodwill toward the murderers. "Let each man render me his bloody hand," he says (III, 1, 184) in what looks like a gesture of fellowship but also may be interpreted as ironic counterritual to the ceremony Brutus had prescribed following the assassination.[63] Left alone after obtaining permission to speak in the Forum, Antony begs forgiveness of Caesar's corpse for consorting with these butchers and predicts that civil strife, blood, and destruction will descend upon Rome. Mingled with his love for Caesar, however, is a lust for power. When the general insurrection has been launched, Antony coldly ticks off to the other members of the triumvirate the names of those he wishes to condemn:

> *Antony:* These many, then, shall die; their names are prick'd.
> *Octavius:* Your brother too must die. Consent you, Lepidus?
> *Lepidus:* I do consent—
> *Octavius:*   Prick him down, Antony.
> *Lepidus:* Upon condition Publius shall not live,
>   Who is your sister's son, Mark Antony.
> *Antony:* He shall not live. Look, with a spot I damn him.
>   (IV, 1, 1–6)

No sooner is Lepidus out of earshot than Antony suggests to young Octavius that he has outlived his usefulness to them and ought to be put out to pasture like an old horse. "You may do your will," Octavius declares (IV, 1, 27). Antony has succeeded in turning his real devotion to Caesar to personal advantage.

Nowhere is Antony's skill as a tactician more apparent than in his brilliant oratorical performance at Caesar's funeral, the high point of the play. Knowing that the Plebeians have been reconciled to the assassination and will tolerate no disparagement of Brutus, Antony begins in a low key to deal with the argument that Caesar was ambitious. Before long, he has transformed the innocent phrase "For Brutus is an honourable man" (III, 2, 88) into devastating irony. Out of loyalty to the "honourable men" who stabbed Caesar, he will resist the temptation to incite the Plebeians against them:

> O masters! If I were dispos'd to stir
> Your hearts and minds to mutiny and rage,
> I should do Brutus wrong, and Cassius wrong,
> Who, you all know, are honourable men.
> I will not do them wrong. I rather choose
> To wrong the dead, to wrong myself and you,
> Than I will wrong such honourable men.
>   (III, 2, 127–133)

Therefore, he will not read Caesar's will. " 'Tis good you know not that you are his heirs," he says. "For if you should, O, what would come of it?" (III, 2, 151–152). Naturally, they snap at the bait. "They were villains, murderers! The will! Read the will!" (III, 2, 161). Before proceeding, however, Antony steps down from the pulpit and displays every bloody rent in Caesar's robe, saving for the climax the hole made by Brutus's dagger, "the most unkindest cut of all" (III, 2, 188). Pretending to calm the Plebeians, he insidiously keys them up:

> Good friends, sweet friends, let me not stir you up
> To such a sudden flood of mutiny.
> They that have done this deed are honourable.
>
> (III, 2, 215–217)

He is no orator like Brutus; he is just "a plain blunt man" who loves his friend (III, 2, 223–224):

> But were I Brutus,
> And Brutus Antony, there were an Antony
> Would ruffle up your spirits, and put a tongue
> In every wound of Caesar that should move
> The stones of Rome to rise and mutiny.
>
> (III, 2, 231–235)

So successful are his incitements to mob action that he must remind his audience to hear the will he had not intended to read.[64] As the Plebeians rush away from the Forum to burn and pillage, Antony can indeed survey his handiwork with deep satisfaction:

> Now let it work. Mischief, thou art afoot.
> Take thou what course thou wilt.
>
> (III, 2, 265–266)

Not only does the Forum scene provide a demonstration of Antony's immense talent for demagoguery, but it gives sharp emphasis to one of Shakespeare's central themes: the inability of the masses to act in a politically responsible manner. In this one scene, and on a purely emotional basis, they switch their allegiance from Caesar to Brutus and back again, although their loyalty at the end is not so much to Caesar as to some course of anarchic action they have adopted in his name. Their behavior serves as an ironic commentary on the republican ideal.

There is nothing surprising in the Plebeians' wild response to Antony's oration, for Shakespeare has made clear from the very beginning that they are fickle. As the play opens, the Tribunes are upbraiding the people for having deserted their old favorite Pompey:

You blocks, you stones, you worse than senseless things!
O you hard hearts, you cruel men of Rome!
Knew you not Pompey? Many a time and oft
Have you climb'd up to walls and battlements,
To tow'rs and windows, yea, to chimney tops,
Your infants in your arms, and there have sat
The livelong day, with patient expectation,
To see great Pompey pass the streets of Rome.

                                          (I, 1, 40–47)

And now they are strewing flowers in the path of Caesar, "that comes in triumph over Pompey's blood" (I, 1, 56). In the next scene the conspirator Casca offers a characteristically cynical account of Caesar's rejection of the crown, including a fanciful explanation of his epileptic fit that does scant credit to the admiring multitudes:

And still as he refus'd it, the rabblement hooted, and clapp'd their chopt [chapped] hands, and threw up their sweaty nightcaps, and uttered such a deal of stinking breath because Caesar refus'd the crown that it had, almost, chok'd Caesar; for he swoonded and fell down at it. And for mine own part, I durst not laugh, for fear of opening my lips and receiving the bad air.

                                          (I, 2, 245–252)

Much more serious, of course, is the rampage that follows the Forum scene. The mob, completely out of control, sets upon the wrong man and kills him:

1st Plebeian: Tear him to pieces! He's a conspirator.
Cinna: I am Cinna the poet! I am Cinna the poet!
4th Plebeian: Tear him for his bad verses! Tear him for his bad verses!
Cinna: I am not Cinna the conspirator.
4th Plebeian: It is no matter; his name's Cinna! Pluck but his name out of his heart, and turn him going.

                                          (III, 3, 30–39)

This senseless murder recalls those grimly comic scenes in *Henry VI, Part Two,* depicting the uprising of Jack Cade and his English rabble (see p. 137). Like the early histories, *Julius Caesar* presents a disturbing picture of the social disintegration that follows political upheaval.[65]

Julius Caesar has been the work most often chosen to introduce young students to Shakespeare, but let no one infer on that account that the play is lacking in artistic or intellectual subtlety. To be sure, it is not metaphysical like *Othello, King Lear,* and *Macbeth;* and no character in it can boast the infinite variety of a Hamlet or a Cleopatra. But its virtues are solid. The action is swift, clear, and, for all its turns and counterturns, strongly organized so as to develop a consistent theme. Not only are the characters interesting and diverse as individuals, but they interact superbly with each other. Finally, the moral and political issues raised by the assassination and its consequences are both significant and timeless.[66]

HAMLET

The world's most enthralling literary work begins as the Ghost of the King of Denmark appears at midnight on the battlements of Elsinore with a message for his son, who already wears the "inky cloak" (I, 2, 77) of profound melancholy. If the young man ever loved his father, he must "revenge his foul and most unnatural murther" (I, 5, 25). The Ghost identifies the murderer as his brother Claudius, the present King, an "incestuous and adulterate beast" (I, 5, 42) who poisoned him and then seduced and married the widowed Queen. The son is not to harm his mother, but "leave her to heaven" (I, 5, 86) and to the thorns of conscience. The Prince's obligation would seem to be quite clear. Yet, before the play is over, eight people, including two entire families, have been wiped out: King Claudius; Queen Gertrude; the Prince's former sweetheart, Ophelia, along with her father Polonius and brother Laertes; two old friends, Rosencrantz and Guildenstern; and, of course, the tortured Prince of Denmark himself.

Bradley has engagingly put into words the probable reaction of anyone hearing the story for the first time. " 'What a sensational story! Why, here are some eight violent deaths, not to speak of adultery, a ghost, a mad woman, and a fight in a grave!' " And then comes that inevitable question. " 'But why in the world did not Hamlet obey the Ghost at once, and so save seven of those eight lives?' "[67] Indeed, the history of *Hamlet* criticism, for better or for worse, is essentially the record of thousands of attempts to cope with this deceptively innocent question. But *Hamlet* poses difficulties at almost all levels, and before considering the problem of interpretation, let us glance at some of the baffling circumstances surrounding the text, date, and genealogy of the play.

There are three extant texts of *Hamlet:* the bad First Quarto (Q1) of 1603, the good Second Quarto (Q2) of 1604, and the version included in the 1623 Folio (F1). The prevailing opinion is that Q1 is an imperfect and badly truncated reconstruction from memory of some other text.[68] Some would argue, however, that Q1 is a complete play in its own right, perhaps an early effort by Shakespeare himself. Polonius is called Corambis in Q1; and the text, as the following quotation will attest, often differs substantially from that with which we are familiar:

To be, or not to be, I there's the point,
To Die, to sleepe, is that all? I all:
No, to sleepe, to dreame, I mary there it goes,
For in that dreame of death, when wee awake,
And borne before an euerlasting Iudge,
From whence no passenger euer retur'nd,
The vndiscouered country, at whose sight
The happy smile, and the accursed damn'd
But for this, the joyfull hope of this,
Whol'd beare the scornes and flattery of the world,
Scorned by the right rich, the rich curssed of the poore?
The widow being oppressed, the orphan wrong'd,
The taste of hunger, or a tirants raigne,
And thousand more calamities besides,
To grunt and sweate vnder this weary life,
When that he may his full *Quietus* make,
With a bare bodkin, who would this indure,
But for a hope of something after death?
Which pusles the braine, and doth confound the sence,
Which makes vs rather beare those euilles we haue,
Than flie to others that we know not of.
I that, O this conscience makes cowardes of vs all,
Lady in thy orizons, be all my sinnes remembred.[69]

The First Quarto is an extremely interesting work, even though it lacks the authority of Q2 and F1.

When it comes to choosing between the two good texts, the modern editor is in a quandary. Q2 contains about 200 lines not found in F1, notably the soliloquy "How all occasions do inform against me" (IV, 4, 32–66). On the other hand, F1 supplies several important passages missing from Q2, including Hamlet's colloquy with Rosencrantz and Guildenstern in which he characterizes Denmark as a prison (II, 2, 244–276) and the discussion of the War of the Theaters (II, 2, 352–379), from which we learn how the children's companies, "little eyases, that cry out on the top of question and are most tyranically clapp'd for't," threaten to put the adult actors out of business (see p. 11). The textual problem continues to fascinate scholars, and it would not be feasible within the compass of this brief discussion to attempt an evaluation of the rival theories.[70]

The play in its present form belongs somewhere between 1598 and 1602. The earlier limit is based on two considerations: (1) *Hamlet* is not listed in Meres's *Palladis Tamia* of 1598; (2) the reference to the War of the Theaters would not have made sense before that year, for that was when the Children of the Chapel Royal began to perform at the Blackfriars. The later limit is fixed by the entry of *Hamlet* in the Stationers' Register in July 1602.

It may be possible, however, to narrow the date from both ends. First, just before the "little eyases" passage (perhaps a later interpolation), Rosencrantz comments on the "inhibition" of the traveling players as probably resulting from the "late innovation" (II, 2, 346–347); this is presumably an allusion to a decree issued by the Privy Council on June 22, 1600, severely restricting the number of playhouses in London. Second, there is a marginal note on *Hamlet* in Gabriel Harvey's copy of a 1598 edition of Chaucer; this note also contains a reference to the Earl of Essex and appears to have been written before February 1601 (when Essex was executed). But we cannot be more precise. "All in all," in the words of one who has assessed the various pieces of evidence, "we may say that *Hamlet* seems to have been written after late 1599 and before the summer of 1601, perhaps before February 1601; and the most likely date of composition seems to be late 1599 to early 1600."[71]

The task of determining the date of the play in its present form is further complicated by a tantalizing literary mystery, that of the *Ur-Hamlet* (*Ur* is a German prefix meaning primitive or original). There seems to have been an earlier Hamlet play on the Elizabethan stage, for Thomas Nashe makes a punning reference to such a work in his *Epistle* to Robert Greene's *Menaphon,* published in 1589. Attacking certain translators and would-be dramatists, Nashe observes that "English Seneca," if you ask him nicely on a frosty morning, "will affoord you whole Hamlets, I should say handfuls of Tragicall speeches."[72] Nashe goes on to speak of "the Kidde in Æsop," a remark that has led some scholars to attribute the lost *Ur-Hamlet* to Thomas Kyd, author of *The Spanish Tragedy,* a drama of revenge that resembles Shakespeare's play in several important respects. It is conceivable that Shakespeare himself wrote the *Ur-Hamlet* very early in his career and drastically revised it around 1600. In any case, a play *Hamlet*—by Kyd, Shakespeare, or somebody else—is listed in Philip Henslowe's *Diary* (see p. 6) as having been acted at Newington Butts on June 11, 1594. Moreover, a character in Thomas Lodge's *Wit's Miserie* (1596) is said to look as pale as "the Visard of the ghost which cried so miserably at the Theator, like an oister wife, Hamlet, revenge."[73] Yet another ingredient in the puzzle is a German play, *Der bestrafte Brudermord* ("Fratricide Punished"). Though not printed until 1781 (from a 1710 manuscript), *Der bestrafte Brudermord* may be based on a German Hamlet play known to have been acted in Dresden in 1626. This work may in turn have been derived from the *Ur-Hamlet* or some other older acting version or from the First Quarto.

Although Shakespeare's main source seems to have been that elusive *Ur-Hamlet,* the story can be traced back several centuries. Long a part of Scandinavian folk tradition, the tale of "Amleth" first assumes literary form in the *Historia Danica* (c. 1200) of the Danish historian Saxo

Grammaticus. Most of the elements of Shakespeare's *Hamlet* are contained in Saxo: the death of Amleth's father at the hands of his brother Feng; the murderer's marriage with Amleth's mother Geruth, the widowed Queen; Amleth's pretense of madness to protect himself from his uncle; a confrontation between mother and son in Geruth's bedroom, at which time Amleth kills one of Feng's spies; Amleth's departure for England with two companions who bear secret instructions from Feng ordering the King of England to have him killed; the hero's discovery of the plot and his forging of substitute instructions sending the two envoys to their doom; Amleth's return from England and his subsequent revenge upon Feng and his henchmen. Saxo's story reappears in the fifth volume of François de Belleforest's *Histoires Tragiques,* published in French in 1576 and translated into English in 1608. If one looks beyond the direct sources and attempts to track down the major ideas and attitudes that are reflected in *Hamlet,* one has to take into account virtually the whole of Renaissance culture: Timothy Bright's *Treatise of Melancholy,* Reginald Scot's *Discovery of Witchcraft,* Christopher Marlowe's *Dido Queen of Carthage,* Erasmus's *Moriae Encomium* (Praise of Folly), Castiglione's *Courtier,* John Lyly's *Euphues,* and countless other literary and nonliterary works. One may indeed agree that "the richness of interaction between *Hamlet* and Renaissance culture is almost infinite."[74]

Aside from an occasional dissenting voice, notably that of T. S. Eliot, everyone acknowledges that in *Hamlet* Shakespeare successfully transmutes the materials of primitive melodrama into a sublime work of art.[75] Critics have focused their commentary on the character of the hero, who has stimulated more controversy than any other figure in literature. To return to Bradley's question: "But why in the world did not Hamlet obey the Ghost at once, and so save seven of those eight lives?" E. E. Stoll explains Hamlet's delay as a common convention of Elizabethan revenge tragedy.[76] But most critics have sought psychological explanations. It may be helpful to touch briefly upon some representative theories—with the caution that, where Hamlet's personality is concerned, no bona fide student of literature, including the author and the reader of this book, should be satisfied with any opinion but his own.[77]

In *Wilhelm Meisters Lehrjahre* (1795), Goethe takes the position that Hamlet is too sensitive to kill Claudius. "A lovely, pure, noble, and most moral nature, without the strength of nerve which forms a hero, sinks beneath a burden which it cannot bear and must not cast away." Echoing Goethe, George Bernard Shaw declares that Hamlet is too humane to murder in cold blood. Shaw praises the performance (1897) of Forbes Robertson, who portrayed "a man whose passions are those which have produced the philosophy, the poetry, the art, and the state-

craft of the world, and not merely those which have produced its weddings, coroners' inquests, and executions." A. P. Rossiter views the
central conflict in the play as "the clash between what we feel for the
intelligence, generosity, fineness of Hamlet, and the fortuitousness,
meanness and clumsiness of the forces by which he is destroyed." Peter
Alexander, disputing the notion that Hamlet has a tragic flaw, draws an
interesting analogy between Hamlet and the Raymond Chandler detective
hero who fights corruption. With these so-called Goethian critics who see
Hamlet as essentially too good for his fate, one may include Eleanor
Prosser, who regards the Ghost as a malevolent creature sent by the
Devil to tempt the hero into what he as a Christian had to view as a
sin.[78]

To the nineteenth century we are indebted for the introspective Hamlet,
a conception associated with Samuel Taylor Coleridge, who has been
called "the most influential critic of *Hamlet* that has ever lived."[79]
Coleridge builds his theory upon Hamlet's most famous soliloquy:

> Thus conscience does make cowards of us all,
> And thus the native hue of resolution
> Is sicklied o'er with the pale cast of thought,
> And enterprises of great pith and moment
> With this regard their currents turn awry
> And lose the name of action.
>
> (III, 1, 83–88)

Coleridge's Hamlet suffers from an imbalance between action and meditation. "Hence great, enormous, intellectual activity, and a consequent
proportionate aversion to real action . . . . " Of the hundreds of critics
who have accepted or adapted this portrait of a Hamlet preoccupied
with his inner world and out of touch with the external world, two may
be mentioned here. D. G. James observes that *Hamlet* "is a tragedy
not of excessive thought but of defeated thought. Hamlet does not know,
and he knows of no way of knowing," because he "has come to no clear
and practised sense of life." In a similar vein, L. C. Knights comments
upon Hamlet's inadequacy in coping with an evil and corrupt world.
"Hamlet is a man who in the face of life and death can make no
affirmation." [80]

It should come as no surprise that critics have often interpreted
Hamlet's behavior in the light of a formal theory of psychology. Drawing
upon a vast body of Elizabethan writings on psychology and moral
philosophy (like Timothy Bright's *Treatise of Melancholy* and Thomas
Wright's *Passions of the Mind*), Lily B. Campbell discusses *Hamlet* as
a "tragedy of grief"; more specifically, she sees the play as "the story of
three young men—Hamlet, Fortinbras, and Laertes—each called upon

to mourn the death of a father, each feeling himself summoned to revenge wrongs suffered by his father," and each reacting according to his individual temperament. On the other hand, Dr. Ernest Jones, friend and disciple of Freud, has examined the character of Hamlet from the point of view of modern psychiatry and psychoanalysis. He finds the hero to be struggling with an unresolved Oedipus complex: He cannot kill Claudius because Claudius, in murdering Hamlet's father, carried out the wish that Hamlet himself had subconsciously harbored. However one chooses to respond to specific details of Jones's essay, the fact remains that his Freudian approach has left its mark upon subsequent studies, particularly insofar as it has led to a more intense concentration, in the theater as well as the classroom, on the strange relationship between Hamlet and his mother and, of course, between Hamlet and Ophelia.[81]

With so many plausible, and sometimes mutually contradictory, explanations to choose from, some critics have decided that there is no single answer to the question of Hamlet's delay. "There are many answers," says Alfred Harbage, "or rather many combinations of answers, with each member in each combination susceptible to innumerable degrees of emphasis." Shakespeare has left the hero "an enduring moral enigma," thereby achieving "the most astonishing balancing feat in literature." Mark Van Doren proposes that Shakespeare restricts our view of Hamlet. "In any situation only the relevant portion of the person speaks; the whole man never does, except in the play as a whole, which can be thought of as his body speaking, or rather his life." Van Doren's Hamlet "is an intellectual seen altogether from the outside. We know him as one from the way he behaves, not from the things he says he believes."[82]

But, as Nicholas Brooke observes, "to throw all the play into an analysis of Hamlet's psychology would be absurd."[83] There are an increasing number of studies that in one way or another object to the traditional preoccupation with the hero at the expense of the drama as a whole. Several writers (for example, Spurgeon, Clemen, Altick) have concentrated on this or that aspect of the play's imagery (although Kenneth Muir cautions that the imagistic structure of *Hamlet* is too complex for any one image or group of images to be isolated).[84] J. K. Walton feels that the question of "character" has been allowed to obscure the equally important issue of dramatic structure. Too often, according to the classicist H. D. F. Kitto, *Hamlet* is treated as though it were draped around the hero for no other purpose than to display his personality. Kitto asserts that *Hamlet* is a religious drama in the Greek sense of concern with "the natural working-out of sin" and that its hero has been created "in order to show how he, like the others, is inevitably engulfed by the evil that has been set in motion, and how he himself becomes the cause of further ruin." Similarly, G. Wilson Knight feels that the shadow of "mental and spiritual death" hovers over the play from first scene to last. In a well-known lecture, C. S. Lewis takes exception to what he calls "the orthodox line of *Hamlet* criticism" (Goethe, Coleridge, and their followers) and urges a broader perspective. "I believe," Lewis says, "that we read Hamlet's speeches with interest chiefly because they describe so well a certain spiritual region through which most of us have passed and anyone in his circumstances might be expected to pass, rather than because of our concern to understand how and why this particular man entered it." In the view of Nigel Alexander, Hamlet is battling both himself and the external world, and the audience is "conscripted, by the fact of their human birth, to fight in the same war."[85]

Thus theories about the prince as well as the poem continue to flourish, and it is obviously impossible to arrive at a definitive interpretation. The remainder of this chapter will focus upon a few crucial aspects of Hamlet's character in the hope of enhancing the reader's understanding of the hero and of the unfolding tragic situation in which he is reluctantly involved.

As noted earlier, Hamlet is suffering from an all-encompassing melancholy even before the Ghost reveals his harrowing tale. He gives expression to this feeling in the first of his great soliloquies:

> O God! God!
> How weary, stale, flat, and unprofitable
> Seem to me all the uses of this world!
> Fie on't! ah, fie! 'Tis an unweeded garden
> That grows to seed; things rank and gross in nature
> Possess it merely [utterly]. That it should come to this!
> (I, 2, 132–137)

Denmark, he tells Rosencrantz and Guildenstern, is to him a prison. He has of late lost all his mirth:

> And indeed, it goes so heavily with my disposition that this goodly frame, the earth, seems to me a sterile promontory; this most excellent canopy, the air, look you, this brave o'erhanging firmament, this majestical roof fretted with golden fire—why, it appeareth no other thing to me than a foul and pestilent congregation of vapours. What a piece of work is a man! how noble in reason! how infinite in faculties! in form and moving how express and admirable! in action how like an angel! in apprehension how like a god! the beauty of the world, the paragon of animals! And yet to me what is this quintessence of dust? Man delights not me . . . .
> (II, 2, 309–323)

The change is poignantly described by Ophelia after Hamlet has apparently rejected her and denounced women in general:

O, what a noble mind is here o'erthrown!
The courtier's, scholar's, soldier's, eye, tongue, sword,
Th' expectancy and rose of the fair state,
The glass of fashion and the mould of form,
Th' observ'd of all observers—quite, quite down!
And I, of ladies most deject and wretched,
That suck'd the honey of his music vows,
Now see that noble and most sovereign reason,
Like sweet bells jangled, out of tune and harsh;
That unmatch'd form and feature of blown [blooming] youth
Blasted with ecstasy [madness]. O, woe is me
T' have seen what I have seen, see what I see!

                                        (III, 1, 158–169)

A man of transcendent gifts, the personification of the Renaissance prince as delineated by Castiglione, has undergone a saddening transformation.

One sympton of Hamlet's depression is that a normally exuberant wit has been converted into a caustic weapon that spares only Horatio. The hero gives a sarcastic reason for his mother's speedy remarriage:

Thrift, thrift, Horatio! The funeral bak'd meats
Did coldly furnish forth the marriage tables.
                                        (I, 2, 180–181)

Against the meddling Polonius, who will "loose" his daughter to him in an effort to learn the cause of his madness, Hamlet unleashes a barrage of abuse. "Do you know me, my lord?" the old man asks. "Excellent well," Hamlet replies. "You are a fishmonger" (II, 2, 173–174)—a devastating insult since *fishmonger* is a term of contempt and also Elizabethan slang for pimp. Ophelia must not walk in the sun. "Conception is a blessing, but not as your daughter may conceive" (II, 2, 185–187). He batters Ophelia with his avowed loathing for the human race. "Get thee to a nunnery!" he savagely reiterates, lest she become "a breeder of sinners" (III, 1, 122–123); the word *nunnery* sometimes connoted brothel to Shakespeare's audience. He condemns all women as hypocrites, with a pun on the word *face:*

I have heard of your paintings too, well enough. God hath given you one face, and you make yourselves another.... I say, we will have no moe marriages. Those that are married already—all but one—shall live; the rest shall keep as they are.

                                        (III, 1, 148–157)

At the play scene his speech abounds in sexual innuendo:

Hamlet: Lady, shall I lie in your lap?
Ophelia: No, my lord.
Hamlet: I mean, my head upon your lap?
Ophelia: Ay, my lord.
Hamlet: Do you think I meant country matters?
Ophelia: I think nothing, my lord.
Hamlet: That's a fair thought to lie between maids' legs.
Ophelia: What is, my lord?
Hamlet: Nothing.

(III, 2, 119–128)

The death of Polonius, whom he has mistakenly killed instead of Claudius, he dismisses with a grim joke:

King: Now, Hamlet, where's Polonius?
Hamlet: At supper.
King: At supper? Where?
Hamlet: Not where he eats, but where he is eaten. A certain convocation of politic worms are e'en at him. Your worm is your only emperor for diet . . . . Your fat king and your lean beggar is but variable service—two dishes, but to one table.

(IV, 3, 17–26)

When he is ordered to England, Hamlet bids a cryptic good-bye to Claudius:

Hamlet: Farewell, dear mother.
King: Thy loving father, Hamlet.
Hamlet: My mother! Father and mother is man and wife; man and wife is one flesh; and so, my mother.

(IV, 3, 51–55)

The quip points simultaneously to the ideal relationship that should have bound Gertrude to his true father and to the shame of her present physical union with Claudius.[86]

If Hamlet is cruel to others, he is equally hard on himself, particularly for his failure to respond to the demands imposed upon him by the Ghost:

The time is out of joint. O cursed spite
That ever I was born to set it right!

(I, 5, 189–190)

It amazes him that an actor can work himself into a frenzy while reciting the mythical sorrows of the Queen of Troy:[87]

                    And all for nothing!
For Hecuba!
What's Hecuba to him, or he to Hecuba,
That he should weep for her? What would he do,
Had he the motive and the cue for passion
That I have?

                    (II, 2, 583–588)

In the most celebrated speech in dramatic literature, he attempts to
justify life or death. "To be, or not to be—that is the question" (III, 1,
56–88). Life may be intolerable, but, he reasons, the bad dreams that
possibly await us in the sleep of death "must give us pause":

    Who would these fardels [burdens] bear,
    To grunt and sweat under a weary life,
    But that the dread of something after death—
    The undiscover'd country, from whose bourn
    No traveller returns—puzzles the will,
    And makes us rather bear those ills we have
    Than fly to others that we know not of?

                    (III, 1, 76–82)[88]

Hamlet later observes the Norwegian soldiers, under the command of
young Fortinbras, exposing themselves to danger "even for an eggshell"
(IV, 4, 53). For a mere "fantasy and trick of fame" (IV, 4, 61), they
fight for a worthless piece of land that the Poles defend with equal
ferocity. But Hamlet, with excellent reasons to spur him on, lets all
sleep, not knowing why he still lives to say, " 'This thing's to do' " (IV,
4, 44). Neither the Player weeping for Hecuba nor the soldiers marching
to their graves think "too precisely on th' event" (IV, 4, 41). They do
what is expected of them in a professional manner. Hamlet, in contrast,
luxuriates in introspection and self-reproach.

A number of factors contribute to Hamlet's dejection, and he himself
does little to discourage the various hypotheses advanced by other characters in the play. He is said to be grief-stricken over the death of his
father, resentful of his mother's "o'erhasty" marriage with his uncle,
angered at being cheated by Claudius out of his rightful succession to
the Danish throne, sick with love for Ophelia, who has been instructed
by her father to rebuff him. It has indeed been argued in a famous study
that the play scene set up to catch the conscience of Claudius is a
"multiple mousetrap," in which Hamlet cleverly performs all the roles
expected of him by the different characters.[89] But whatever validity
these impressions may hold individually or in combination, the roots of
Hamlet's spiritual malaise lie much deeper.

Almost from his very first words Hamlet reveals a serious concern with the disparity between appearance and reality.[90] If death is "common" to all living things, then why, his mother asks, "seems it so particular with thee?" (I, 2, 72–75). In his reply Hamlet, while purporting to insist upon his own sincerity, makes a guarded allusion to Gertrude's dissembling:

> Seems, madam? Nay, it is. I know not "seems."
> 'Tis not alone my inky cloak, good mother,
> Nor customary suits of solemn black,
> Nor windy suspiration of forc'd breath,
> No, nor the fruitful river in the eye,
> Nor the dejected haviour of the visage,
> Together with all forms, moods, shapes of grief,
> That can denote me truly. These indeed seem,
> For they are actions that a man might play;
> But I have that within which passeth show—
> These but the trappings and the suits of woe.
>   (I, 2, 76–86)

His mother, he later reflects, "seemed" to love his father; and the observation betokens Hamlet's preoccupation with her sexuality:

>   Why, she would hang on him
> As if increase of appetite had grown
> By what it fed on.
>   (I, 2, 143–145)

She followed the corpse with a show worthy of one of the prodigious mourners of classical mythology, "like Niobe, all tears" (I, 2, 149); and yet, her eyes still red, she proceeded "to post / With such dexterity to incestuous sheets!" (I, 2, 156–157). Deception is a way of life in Denmark. Polonius lovingly gives his son Laertes permission to return to France (armed with a collection of banal, if well-intentioned, maxims), then directs his servant to elicit information about his behavior by devious means. From the Ghost, Hamlet learns that a man "may smile, and smile, and be a villain" (I, 5, 108). He feels betrayed by Ophelia, who allows herself to be used against him; again Polonius is the principal contriver. Rosencrantz and Guildenstern are only too willing to serve as spies for Claudius, to the point of carrying Hamlet's death warrant to the King of England. Finally, Laertes, though professing to accept Hamlet's offer of love with an open heart, enters into a conspiracy with Claudius to kill him in the fencing match with a poisoned foil. Except for Hamlet's friendship with Horatio, virtually every human relationship in the court of Denmark has been corroded by falsehood.

In view of Hamlet's avowed loathing for hypocrisy, it is significant that he himself should resort to stratagems of which dissimulation is a major component. He puts on an "antic disposition" (I, 5, 172), deluding everyone around him as to the cause of his methodic madness. He "stages" a rebuke to the King's sycophants Rosencrantz and Guildenstern by calling for recorders and demanding that Guildenstern play. When the latter protests that he is unskilled, Hamlet is quick with the moral:

> Why, look you now, how unworthy a thing you make of me! You would play upon me; you would seem to know my stops; you would pluck out the heart of my mystery; you would sound me from my lowest note to the top of my compass; and there is much music, excellent voice, in this little organ, yet cannot you make it speak. 'Sblood, do you think I am easier to be play'd on than a pipe? Call we what instrument you will, though you can fret me, you cannot play upon me.
>
> (III, 2, 379–389)[91]

It is fitting that Hamlet should seek to entrap Claudius through a theatrical performance.[92] In his advice to the players, he insists that art must illuminate real life, that the purpose of acting, "was and is, to hold, as 'twere, the mirror up to nature; to show virtue her own feature, scorn her own image, and the very age and body of the time his form and pressure" (III, 2, 24–28). He thoroughly enjoys his "mousetrap," and when its success proves the Ghost's reliability, he boasts to Horatio that the production should win him a partnership in a troupe of actors. Hamlet always dramatizes himself and his surroundings.[93]

You may select your favorite symptoms and diagnose Hamlet's disease, but when you think you have him figured out, he shifts before your eyes. He is thirsty for the King's blood after the "mousetrap." But finding the villain at the one moment when Claudius smells the rankness of his offense and is apparently praying, Hamlet freezes into one of the many stop-action tableaux that are a feature of the play.[94] Revenge on Claudius, he says, would be incomplete were he "to take him in the purging of his soul" (III, 3, 85). He would rather catch him in an act "that has no relish of salvation in't" (III, 3, 92):

> Then trip him, that his heels may kick at heaven,
> And that his soul may be as damn'd and black
> As hell, whereto it goes.
>
> (III, 3, 93–95)

What kind of man, we wonder, so desperately needs to damn a soul as well as kill a body?[95] Hamlet loves his mother and believes her innocent of murder. Yet he relentlessly sets up a "glass" wherein she can see her shame vividly reflected:

> Nay, but to live
> In the rank sweat of an enseamed bed,
> Stew'd in corruption, honeying and making love
> Over the nasty sty!
>
> (III, 4, 91–94)

Hamlet feels sorry for having stabbed Polonius, but he cynically proceeds to "lug the guts into the neighbour room" (III, 4, 212). He is responsible for Ophelia's madness, with its complicated erotic fantasies,[96] and for her suicide; yet he leaps into her grave with Laertes, protesting that forty thousand brothers could not match his love for her.[97] If he is scrupulous about taking a human life, he has no qualms about forging a new commission to the King of England guaranteeing the execution of Rosencrantz and Guildenstern. "They are not near my conscience" (V, 2, 58), he tells Horatio; his attitude, says Kenneth Muir, "shows how far he has himself been corrupted in the course of the play."[98] Hamlet is a mass of contradictions, a fragmented and deeply troubled soul.

Nevertheless, after a painful struggle with the demons that torment him, Hamlet ultimately arrives at an inner peace. The change is first apparent in the graveyard scene, which is said to be a semiallegorical summing up of the whole theme of the play.[99] Here he philosophizes over the skull of the King's jester Yorick, whose "flashes of merriment . . . were wont to set the table on a roar" (V, 1, 210–211). Where are his jokes now? And if the mighty Alexander and Julius Caesar return to clay and serve merely to stop a beer barrel or keep out the wind, then how significant is any human endeavor? As one critic observes, Hamlet "moves now to a wholly new sort of serenity, which allows him to see himself in relation to his world, to both its good and its evil."[100] Having believed all along that the universe was somehow waiting for him to decide, or not decide, upon his course of action against Claudius, Hamlet learns from the death of Polonius, which he did not intend, and from his own fortuitous escape from death in England that neither he nor any other mortal can control his destiny:

> Let us know,
> Our indiscretion sometime serves us well
> When our deep plots do pall; and that should learn us
> There's a divinity that shapes our ends,
> Rough-hew them how we will—
>
> (V, 2, 7–11)

In rejecting Horatio's advice to cancel the fencing match with Laertes, he calmly accepts the will of a higher power:

There's a special providence in the fall of a sparrow. If it be now, 'tis not to come; if it be not to come, it will be now; if it be not now, yet it will come: the readiness is all. Since no man knows aught of what he leaves, what is't to leave betimes? Let be.

(V, 2, 230–235)[101]

"The readiness is all." Having mastered this difficult lesson, Hamlet is now prepared for any eventuality. In the hectic final scene he is stabbed with the foil that Claudius and Laertes have poisoned; the Queen sips the poisoned drink intended for Hamlet; in an exchange of weapons Hamlet secures the poisoned foil and, without any agonizing self-examination, attacks and fatally wounds Laertes and the King. Then, to make his revenge doubly sure, he forces the poisoned drink into Claudius's mouth. He forgives Laertes and finds sufficient strength to frustrate Horatio's suicide attempt with a touching request:

> If thou didst ever hold me in thy heart,
> Absent thee from felicity awhile,
> And in this harsh world draw thy breath in pain,
> To tell my story.

(V, 2, 357–360)

Hamlet's last act is eminently practical: He gives his dying voice in behalf of Fortinbras's succession to the throne. At last he is the "whole man" Van Doren speaks of, and his behavior at the end is spontaneous as it had never been before.

If much of the play remains ambiguous, does it matter? "But what would *Hamlet* be," one critic asks, "without its puzzles: the eternal piquancy of its imperfection?" The hero himself continues to resist our most persistent efforts to "play upon" him. "All that humanity is, all that humanity might be, seem figured in him. It is no wonder if we find it a task of some difficulty to pluck out all the mysteries of his soul."[102] Perhaps Kenneth Muir has said the last word: "In the theater the problems which baffle the critics do not arise. An audience may argue about the play, but it never doubts the reality of the hero."[103]

NOTES

1. A. C. Bradley, *Shakespearean Tragedy,* 2d ed. (London: Macmillan, 1905), pp. 5–39. For an assessment of Bradley and his impact, see Katharine Cooke, *A. C. Bradley and His Influence in Twentieth-Century Shakespeare Criticism* (Oxford: Clarendon, 1972).
2. Ibid., p. 23.
3. On Seneca's formal influence, see John W. Cunliffe, *The Influence of Seneca*

on Elizabethan Tragedy (New York: Macmillan, 1893), especially pp. 66–88 and H. B. Charlton, *The Senecan Tradition in Renaissance Tragedy* (1921; reprint ed., Manchester: Manchester University Press, 1946), pp. 138–200. On Seneca's philosophy (as opposed to his theatrical devices), see R. J. Kaufmann, "The Senecan Perspective and the Shakespearean Poetic," *Comparative Drama* 1 (1967): 182–198. Seneca's influence has been minimized by Howard Baker, *Induction to Tragedy* (University: Louisiana State University Press, 1939).

4. See Willard Farnham, *The Medieval Heritage of Elizabethan Tragedy* (1936; reprint ed., New York: Barnes & Noble, 1957). See also Baker, *Induction to Tragedy*, pp. 154–179.

5. This conjectural play is discussed in W. Braekman, *Shakespeare's Titus Andronicus: Its Relationship to the German Play of 1620 and to Jan Vos's Aran en Titus* (Ghent: University of Ghent, 1969), especially pp. 109–116.

6. On the chapbook, see Ralph M. Sargent, "The Source of *Titus Andronicus*," *Studies in Philology* 46 (1949): 167–183.

7. On the text, see the New Cambridge *Titus Andronicus*, ed. John Dover Wilson (Cambridge: Cambridge University Press, 1948), pp. vii, 91–99 and the New Arden edition, ed. J. C. Maxwell, 3d ed. (Cambridge: Harvard University Press, 1961), pp. xv–xxiv. On the date, see the New Cambridge, pp. xxxiv–l and the New Arden, pp. xx–xxx. On sources, see the New Arden, pp. xxx–xxxv; Geoffrey Bullough, *Narrative and Dramatic Sources of Shakespeare*, 8 vols. (New York: Columbia University Press, 1957–1975), 6: 3–79; Nancy L. Harvey, "*Titus Andronicus* and *The Shearmen and Taylors' Play*," *Renaissance Quarterly* 22 (1969): 27–31. Baker, *Induction to Tragedy*, pp. 121 ff., doubts the influence of *Thyestes*.

8. On the symbolism of the pit, see A. C. Hamilton, *The Early Shakespeare* (San Marino, Calif.: The Huntington Library, 1967), pp. 82 ff. and Albert H. Tricomi, "The Aesthetics of Mutilation in *Titus Andronicus*," *Shakespeare Survey* 27 (1974): 17–18.

9. Dover Wilson, in the New Cambridge edition, p. xii. See also Mark Van Doren, *Shakespeare* (New York: Holt, 1939), pp. 42–43.

10. Muriel C. Bradbrook, *Shakespeare and Elizabethan Poetry* (London: Chatto & Windus, 1951), p. 105. See also Jack E. Reese, "The Formalization of Horror in *Titus Andronicus*," *Shakespeare Quarterly* 21 (1970): 77–84.

11. See Wolfgang H. Clemen, *The Development of Shakespeare's Imagery* (Cambridge: Harvard University Press, pp. 25–26).

12. See Nicholas Brooke, "Marlowe as Provocative Agent in Shakespeare's Early Plays," *Shakespeare Survey* 14 (1961): 34–44.

13. T. J. B. Spencer, "Shakespeare and the Elizabethan Romans," *Shakespeare Survey* 10 (1957): 27–38. There may also be political significance in the relationship between the Romans and the Goths, whom Elizabethans considered to be a civilizing influence. See Ronald Broude, "Roman and Goth in *Titus Andronicus*," *Shakespeare Studies*, ed. J. Leeds Barroll, 6 (1972): 27–34. For a different estimate of the qualities of the Romans and Goths, see W. Gordon Zeeveld, *The Temper of Shakespeare's Thought* (New Haven: Yale University Press, 1974), pp. 206–207.

14. For an excellent discussion of Ovid's influence, see Hamilton, *The Early Shakespeare*, pp. 63–89 passim. Ovid's myth of the four ages of man may also be reflected in *Titus*; see Michael Payne, *Irony in Shakespeare's Roman Plays*, Salzburg Studies in English Literature 19 (Salzburg, Austria: Universität Salzburg, 1974), pp. 1–28.

15. Nicholas Brooke, *Shakespeare's Early Tragedies* (London: Methuen, 1968), p. 46. See also Alan Sommers, " 'Wilderness of Tigers': Structure and Symbolism in *Titus Andronicus*," *Essays in Criticism* 10 (1960): 275–289.

16. See Eugene M. Waith, "The Metamorphosis of Violence in *Titus Andronicus*," *Shakespeare Survey* 10 (1957): 39–49. See also Tricomi, "The Aesthetics of Mutilation in *Titus Andronicus*."

17. Virgil K. Whitaker, *The Mirror up to Nature: The Techniques of Shakespeare's Tragedies* (San Marino, Calif.: The Huntington Library, 1965), p. 97.

18. Dover Wilson (New Cambridge edition, pp. xxv–xxxiv) believes the play was written by Peele and revised by Shakespeare. According to Maxwell (New Arden edition, pp. xxvi–xxx), Peele may have had a hand in Act I.

19. The structural unity of the play has been defended from several points of view. See Hereward T. Price, "The Authorship of *Titus Andronicus*," *Journal of English and Germanic Philology* 42 (1943): 55–81; T. J. B. Spencer, *William Shakespeare: The Roman Plays* (London: Longmans, 1963), pp. 9–14; and John P. Cutts, "Shadow and Substance: Structural Unity in *Titus Andronicus*," *Comparative Drama* 2 (1968): 161–172.

20. Sidney Thomas, "The Queen Mab Speech in *Romeo and Juliet*," *Shakespeare Survey* 25 (1972): 73–80.

21. On the text, see the New Cambridge *Romeo and Juliet*, eds. John Dover Wilson and George I. Duthie (Cambridge: Cambridge University Press, 1955), pp. xiv–xvi, 112–118; J. Dover Wilson, "The New Way with Shakespeare's Texts: II. Recent Work on the Text of *Romeo and Juliet*," *Shakespeare Survey* 8 (1955): 81–99; Harry R. Hoppe, *The Bad Quarto of Romeo and Juliet: A Bibliographical and Textual Study* (Ithaca, N.Y.: Cornell University Press, 1948), pp. 57–73; and *The Most Excellent and Lamentable Tragedie of Romeo and Juliet: A Critical Edition*, ed. George Walton Williams (Durham, N.C.: Duke University Press, 1964), pp. xi–xvi, 142–149.

22. See Kenneth Muir, *Shakespeare's Sources* (London: Methuen, 1957), pp. 21–30; Bullough, *Sources*, 1: 269–363; Olin H. Moore, *The Legend of Romeo and Juliet* (Columbus: Ohio State University Press, 1950), especially good on Boccaccio (pp. 21–27) and da Porto (pp. 111–118). For the verbal parallels with Brooke, see the notes to the New Cambridge edition, pp. 119–221 passim. Also useful is Virgil K. Whitaker, *Shakespeare's Use of Learning* (San Marino, Calif.: The Huntington Library, 1953), pp. 106–117.

23. See G. K. Hunter, "Shakespeare's Earliest Tragedies: *Titus Andronicus* and *Romeo and Juliet*," *Shakespeare Survey* 27 (1974): 8.

24. See Brents Stirling, *Unity in Shakespearian Tragedy* (New York: Columbia University Press, 1956), pp. 10–25 and Michael Goldman, *Shakespeare and the Energies of Drama* (Princeton: Princeton University Press, 1972), pp. 33–44.

25. On the oxymoron as key to the play's structure, see Robert O. Evans, *The Osier Cage: Rhetorical Devices in Romeo and Juliet* (Lexington: University of Kentucky Press, 1966), pp. 18–41. See also M. M. Mahood, *Shakespeare's Wordplay* (London: Methuen, 1957), p. 70 and John Lawlor, "*Romeo and Juliet*," in *Early Shakespeare*, eds. John Russell Brown and Bernard Harris, Stratford-upon-Avon Studies 3 (London: Edward Arnold, 1961), pp. 132–133.

26. On the Queen Mab speech and its context, see Herbert McArthur, "Romeo's Loquacious Friend," *Shakespeare Quarterly* 10 (1959): 35–44 and Marjorie B. Garber, *Dream in Shakespeare* (New Haven: Yale University Press, 1974), pp. 35–47.

27. The play has been called a tragedy of unawareness; Mercutio, like the other characters, does not know the workings of fate. See Bertrand Evans, "The Brevity of Friar Laurence," *PMLA* 65 (1950): 841–865.

28. The dramatic relevance of the Nurse's speech is discussed by Barbara Everett, "*Romeo and Juliet:* The Nurse's Story," *The Critical Quarterly* 14 (1972): 129–139.

29. Harley Granville-Barker, *Prefaces to Shakespeare*, 2 vols. (Princeton: Princeton University Press, 1946–1947), 2: 331.

30. The progressive isolation of the lovers from their environment is discussed in T. J. B. Spencer's excellent introduction to his edition; see *Romeo and Juliet* (Harmondsworth, Middlesex: Penguin, 1967), pp. 24–30.

31. Roslie Colie, *Shakespeare's Living Art* (Princeton: Princeton University Press, 1974), p. 145. Similarly, the *hortus conclusus* ("walled garden"), a metaphor of virginity, is unmetaphored in the balcony scene when Romeo leaps over the orchard wall.

32. Brooke, *Shakespeare's Early Tragedies*, p. 96.

33. See Harry Levin, "Form and Formality in *Romeo and Juliet*," *Shakespeare Quarterly* 11 (1960): 3–11.

34. Granville-Barker, *Prefaces*, 2: 346.

35. Colie (*Shakespeare's Living Art*, p. 145) sees this scene as an unmetaphoring of the literary convention of the *aubade*, the "dawn song."

36. See James Black, "The Visual Artistry of *Romeo and Juliet*," *Studies in English Literature, 1500–1900* 15 (1975):245–256.

37. Whitaker, *The Mirror up to Nature*, p. 119.

38. Donald A. Stauffer, *Shakespeare's World of Images: The Development of His Moral Ideas* (New York: Norton, 1949), p. 56.

39. See James H. Seward, *Tragic Vision in Romeo and Juliet* (Washington, D. C.: Consortium, 1973), p. 31; Francis Fergusson, "Romantic Love in Dante and Shakespeare," *Sewanee Review* 83 (1975): 253–266. See also Paul N. Siegel, "Christianity and the Religion of Love in *Romeo and Juliet*," *Shakespeare Quarterly* 12 (1961): 371–392 (reprinted in his *Shakespeare in His Time and Ours* [Notre Dame, Ind.: University of Notre Dame Press, 1968], pp. 69–107) and Franklin M. Dickey, *Not Wisely But Too Well: Shakespeare's Love Tragedies* (San Marino, Calif.: The Huntington Library, 1957), pp. 63–117. There are two pertinent articles in *Pacific Coast Studies in Shakespeare*, eds. Waldo F. McNeir and Thelma N. Greenfield (Eugene: University of

Oregon Books, 1966), pp. 33–46 and 47–67, respectively: Douglas L. Peterson, *"Romeo and Juliet* and the Art of Moral Navigation," and Stanley Stewart, "Romeo and Necessity."

40. Caroline F. E. Spurgeon, *Shakespeare's Imagery and What It Tells Us* (New York: Macmillan, 1935), p. 310.

41. E. K. Chambers, *William Shakespeare: A Study of Facts and Problems,* 2 vols. (Oxford: Clarendon, 1930), 2: 199, 322.

42. On the text, see the New Cambridge *Julius Caesar,* ed. John Dover Wilson (Cambridge: Cambridge University Press, 1949), pp. 92–97 and the New Arden edition, ed. T. S. Dorsch, 6th ed. (Cambridge: Harvard University Press, 1955), pp. xxiii–xxvi. On the date, see the New Cambridge, pp. viii–xi and the New Arden, pp. vii–viii.

43. See the New Arden, pp. xii–xix; Muir, *Shakespeare's Sources,* pp. 187–200; Bullough, *Sources,* 5: 3–211; J. Leeds Barroll, "Shakespeare and Roman History," *Modern Language Review* 53 (1958): 327–343.

44. Harold S. Wilson, *On the Design of Shakespearian Tragedy* (Toronto: University of Toronto Press, 1957), p. 87.

45. Derek Traversi, *Shakespeare: The Roman Plays* (Stanford, Calif.: Stanford University Press, 1963), p. 22.

46. Brooke, *Shakespeare's Early Tragedies,* pp. 138–162.

47. Edward Dowden, *Shakspere: A Critical Study of His Mind and Art,* 6th ed. (London: Kegan Paul, 1882), p. 285.

48. Marjorie Garber (*Dream in Shakespeare,* pp. 47–58) sees the misinterpreted dream as an important motif in the play, illustrating how the rational mind blinds itself to the great irrational powers.

49. Ernest Schanzer, *The Problem Plays of Shakespeare: A Study of Julius Caesar, Measure for Measure, Antony and Cleopatra* (1963; reprint ed., New York: Schocken, 1965), p. 26.

50. Maurice Charney, *Shakespeare's Roman Plays: The Function of Imagery in the Drama* (Cambridge: Harvard University Press, 1961), p. 73.

51. See J. I. M. Stewart, *Character and Motive in Shakespeare* (London: Longmans, 1949), pp. 46–55 and Norman Sanders's fine introduction to *Julius Caesar* (Harmondsworth, Middlesex: Penguin, 1967), pp. 7–41. Caesar (like Brutus and the republicans) indulges in unconscious role playing; see John W. Velz, " 'If I were Brutus Now . . . ': Role-playing in *Julius Caesar,*" *Shakespeare Studies,* ed. J. Leeds Barroll, 4 (1969): 149–159.

52. See D. S. Brewer, "Brutus's Crime: A Footnote to *Julius Caesar,*" *Review of English Studies,* n.s., 3 (1952): 51–54.

53. Whitaker, *The Mirror up to Nature,* pp. 123–132.

54. The complex, and sometimes ironic, relationship of public and private values is ably discussed by L. C. Knights in "Shakespeare and Political Wisdom: A Note on the Personalism of *Julius Caesar* and *Coriolanus,*" *Sewanee Review* 61 (1953): 43–55.

55. On the idea of the commonwealth and the failure of republicanism, see Zeeveld, *The Temper of Shakespeare's Thought,* pp. 74–98. See also David Bevington, *Tudor Drama and Politics* (Cambridge: Harvard University Press, 1968), pp. 248–250.

56. See Spencer, *William Shakespeare: The Roman Plays,* p. 27.

57. See Alexander Welsh, "Brutus Is an Honorable Man," *Yale Review* 64 (1975): 496–513 and Norman Council, *When Honour's at the Stake: Ideas of Honour in Shakespeare's Plays* (London: Allen and Unwin, 1973), pp. 60–74.

58. Stirling, *Unity in Shakespearian Tragedy,* p. 41. On the blood imagery, see also Leo Kirschbaum, "Shakespeare's Stage Blood and Its Critical Significance," *PMLA* 64 (1949): 517–529 and Charney, *Shakespeare's Roman Plays,* pp. 48–59.

59. Adrien Bonjour, *The Structure of Julius Caesar* (Liverpool: Liverpool University Press, 1958), p. 3. J. L. Simmons, *Shakespeare's Pagan World: The Roman Tragedies* (Charlottesville: University Press of Virginia, 1973), pp. 86–94, maintains that Brutus is the reverse image of Caesar.

60. R. A. Foakes writes perceptively on the symbolic values attached to names in this play; see "An Approach to *Julius Caesar,*" *Shakespeare Quarterly* 5 (1954): 259–270.

61. Granville-Barker, *Prefaces,* 2: 362.

62. Ibid., p. 366.

63. Stirling, *Unity in Shakespearian Tragedy,* p. 49.

64. For a close reading of Antony's speech, see Traversi, *Shakespeare: The Roman Plays,* pp. 52–57.

65. See Brents Stirling, *The Populace in Shakespeare* (New York: Columbia University Press, 1949).

66. An exceptionally good collection is Leonard F. Dean, ed., *Twentieth Century Interpretations of Julius Caesar* (Englewood Cliffs, N.J.: Prentice-Hall, 1968).

67. Bradley, *Shakespearean Tragedy,* p. 89.

68. Q1 may be a memorial reconstruction of an official abridgment (for use at the Globe) of F1. See J. M. Nosworthy, *Shakespeare's Occasional Plays: Their Origin and Transmission* (New York: Barnes & Noble, 1965), pp. 186–215.

69. *Shakespeare's Hamlet: Collotype Reproduction of the Quarto of 1603* (Cambridge: Harvard University Press, 1931), D4–E1. See also G. B. Harrison's edition for the Elizabethan and Jacobean Quartos series: *The Tragicall Historie of Hamlet Prince of Denmarke 1603* (New York: Barnes & Noble, 1966), pp. 28–29.

70. See Chambers, *William Shakespeare,* 1: 408–425; Greg, *The Shakespeare First Folio: Its Bibliographical and Textual History* (Oxford: Clarendon, 1955), pp. 299–333; G. I. Duthie, *The "Bad" Quarto of Hamlet* (Cambridge: Cambridge University Press, 1941); Nosworthy, *Shakespeare's Occasional Plays,* pp. 128–185. For an excellent survey of the vast literature on the texts, see Clifford Leech, "Studies in *Hamlet,* 1901–1955," *Shakespeare Survey* 9 (1956): 4–7.

71. E. A. J. Honigmann, "The Date of *Hamlet,*" *Shakespeare Survey* 9 (1956): 24–34 (quotation from p. 33).

72. E. K. Chambers, *The Elizabethan Stage,* 4 vols. (Oxford: Clarendon, 1923), 4: 235.

73. See Chambers, *William Shakespeare,* 1: 411.

74. Joseph Satin, *Shakespeare and His Sources* (Boston: Houghton Mifflin, 1966), p. 383. See also Muir, *Shakespeare's Sources,* pp. 110–122; Bullough, *Sources,* 7: 3–189; Frank McCombie, *"Hamlet* and the *Moriae Encomium,"* *Shakespeare Survey* 27 (1974): 59–69. A classic study is Sir Israel Gollancz, *The Sources of Hamlet* (London: Oxford University Press, 1926).

75. Following the lead of J. M. Robertson, Eliot argues that Shakespeare was unable to impose his own dramatic concern, Hamlet's reaction to his mother's guilt, upon the "intractable" materials of the old revenge play; nor could he find in the external world of the play an adequate equivalent, or "objective correlative," for the hero's intense emotions. The play is thus "most certainly an artistic failure." See T. S. Eliot, "Hamlet and His Problems," first printed in *The Sacred Wood* (1920) and included in his *Selected Essays: 1917–1932* (New York: Harcourt, 1932), pp. 121–126.

76. Elmer Edgar Stoll, *Hamlet: An Historical and Comparative Study,* Studies in Language and Literature, no. 7 (Minneapolis: University of Minnesota Press, 1919).

77. For a useful (if sometimes arbitrary) grouping of different schools of criticism, see Paul Gottschalk, *The Meanings of Hamlet* (Albuquerque: University of New Mexico Press, 1972). *Hamlet* criticism, with its problems and implications for criticism as a whole, has been perceptively analyzed by Morris Weitz, *Hamlet and the Philosophy of Literary Criticism* (Chicago: University of Chicago Press, 1964).

78. On Goethe, see Paul S. Conklin, *A History of Hamlet Criticism: 1601–1821* (New York: King's Crown, 1947), pp. 105–109. See also Edwin Wilson, ed., *Shaw on Shakespeare* (London: Cassell, 1961), pp. 75–95 (quotation from p. 82); A. P. Rossiter, *Angel with Horns and Other Shakespeare Lectures* (New York: Theatre Arts Books, 1961), pp. 171–188 (quotation from p. 180); Peter Alexander, *Hamlet Father and Son* (Oxford: Clarendon, 1955), p. 170 ff.; Eleanor Prosser, *Hamlet and Revenge* (Stanford, Calif.: Stanford University Press, 1967).

79. Conklin, *Hamlet Criticism,* p. 133.

80. Samuel Taylor Coleridge, *Shakespearean Criticism,* ed. Thomas Middleton Raysor, rev. ed., 2 vols. (London: Dent, 1960), 1:16–40, 2:150–155, 223–226 (quotation from 1:34); D. G. James, *The Dream of Learning* (Oxford: Clarendon, 1951), pp. 33–68 (quotation from pp. 42, 47); L. C. Knights, *Some Shakespearean Themes and an Approach to Hamlet* (Stanford, Calif.: Stanford University Press, 1966), pp. 151–233 (quotation from p. 197). See also R. A. Foakes's revolutionary new edition of *Coleridge on Shakespeare: The Text of the Lectures of 1811–12* (London: Routledge & Kegan Paul, 1971), pp. 124–128.

81. See Lily B. Campbell, *Shakespeare's Tragic Heroes: Slaves of Passion* (Cambridge: Cambridge University Press, 1930; New York: Barnes & Noble, 1960), pp. 109–147; Ernest Jones, *Hamlet and Oedipus* (New York: Norton, 1949; Garden City, N. Y.: Doubleday, Anchor Books, 1954). Jones's book is an elaboration of a view he first presented much earlier. On Hamlet's treatment of Ophelia, see Harold Jenkins, "Hamlet and Ophelia," *Proceedings of the British Academy* 49 (1963): 135–151.

According to Erik Erikson, Hamlet is in delayed adolescence and is suffering from "identity diffusion" as he searches for something or somebody to be true to; see "Youth: Fidelity and Diversity," *Daedalus* 91 (1962):5–27. For a summary of psychoanalytic views, see Norman N. Holland, *Psychoanalysis and Shakespeare* (New York: McGraw-Hill, 1964), pp. 163–206.

82. Alfred Harbage, *As They Liked It: An Essay on Shakespeare and Morality* (New York: Macmillan, 1947), pp. 103–104; Van Doren, *Shakespeare,* p. 196.

83. Brooke, *Shakespeare's Early Tragedies,* p. 186.

84. Spurgeon, *Shakespeare's Imagery,* pp. 316–320, 367–371; Clemen, *Shakespeare's Imagery,* pp. 106–118; Richard D. Altick, "*Hamlet* and the Odor of Mortality," *Shakespeare Quarterly* 5 (1954):167–176; Kenneth Muir, *Shakespeare: Hamlet* (London: Edward Arnold, 1963), pp. 13–19.

85. J. K. Walton, "The Structure of *Hamlet,*" in *Hamlet,* eds. John Russell Brown and Bernard Harris, Stratford-upon-Avon Studies 5 (London: Edward Arnold, 1963), pp. 44–89; H. D. F. Kitto, *Form and Meaning in Drama: A Study of Six Greek Plays and of Hamlet* (New York: Barnes & Noble, 1957), p. 330; G. Wilson Knight, "The Embassy of Death: An Essay on *Hamlet,*" *The Wheel of Fire,* 5th rev. ed. (Cleveland: World Publishing, Meridian Books, 1957), p. 28; C. S. Lewis, "Hamlet: The Prince or the Poem?", *Proceedings of the British Academy* 28 (1942): 139–154 (quotation from p. 151), frequently reprinted; Nigel Alexander, *Poison, Play, and Duel: A Study in Hamlet* (London: Routledge & Kegan Paul, 1971), p. 60.

86. Claudius is ably (and somewhat sympathetically) discussed by Maynard Mack, Jr., *Killing the King: Three Studies in Shakespeare's Tragic Structure* (New Haven: Yale University Press, 1973), pp. 108–117. Claudius is "a fallen angel, who, though darkened, yet shines" (p. 109).

87. For a brilliant analysis of the Player's speech, see Harry Levin, *The Question of Hamlet* (New York: Oxford University Press, 1959), pp. 138–164.

88. On the "To be or not to be" speech, see Brooke, *Shakespeare's Early Tragedies,* pp. 192–197; Muir, *Shakespeare: Hamlet,* pp. 33–36; Nigel Alexander, *Poison, Play, and Duel,* pp. 73–76; Vincent F. Petronella, "Hamlet's 'To be or not to be' Soliloquy: Once More into the Breach," *Studies in Philology* 71 (1974):72–88.

89. John Dover Wilson, *What Happens in Hamlet,* 3d ed. (Cambridge: Cambridge University Press, 1951), pp. 138–197.

90. The appearance-reality theme has been discussed by numerous critics, notably Maynard Mack, "The World of *Hamlet,*" *Yale Review* 41 (1952): 502–523. See also Lee Sheridan Cox, *Figurative Design in Hamlet: The Significance of the Dumb Show* (Columbus: Ohio State University Press, 1973) and Terence Hawkes, *Shakespeare and the Reason* (New York: Humanities, 1965), pp. 1–71.

91. The passage abounds in musical puns: "play," "stops," "pluck," "sound," "note," "compass" (musical range), "organ," and "fret," which means "irritate" and is also a term for the metal ridge placed across the finger board of a stringed instrument.

92. "The Murder of Gonzago" has been subtly analyzed by Alexander (*Poison, Play, and Duel,* pp. 101 ff.), who sees it as an ethical act of memory for the whole court and not just as a rhetorical device.

93. On Hamlet's interest in the theater and the theater symbolism of the play

in general, see Charles R. Forker, "Shakespeare's Theatrical Symbolism and Its Function in *Hamlet*," *Shakespeare Quarterly* 14 (1963), 215–229 and Maurice Charney, *Style in Hamlet* (Princeton: Princeton University Press, 1969), pp. 137–153.

94. See Goldman, *Shakespeare and the Energies of Drama*, pp. 74–93.

95. Stoll (*Hamlet*, pp. 51–62) argues that not killing the King at prayer is entirely appropriate for the hero of an Elizabethan revenge tragedy.

96. Ophelia displays the symptoms of what the Elizabethans called *erotomania* (erotic melancholy); see Carroll Camden, "On Ophelia's Madness," *Shakespeare Quarterly* 15 (1964):247–255.

97. Salvador de Madariaga, who considers Hamlet a contemptible egocentric, argues that he has seduced and abandoned Ophelia; see his provocative book *On Hamlet* (London: Hollis & Carter, 1948), pp. 31–73. But Jenkins ("Hamlet and Ophelia") believes that Hamlet has condemned her (like Jephtha's daughter; see II, 2, 422–431) to virginity, thereby denying her life's fulfillment.

98. Muir, *Shakespeare: Hamlet*, p. 30.

99. See G. R. Elliott, *Scourge and Minister: A Study of Hamlet as Tragedy of Revengefulness and Justice* (Durham, N. C.: Duke University Press, 1951), p. 162.

100. Derick R. C. Marsh, *Shakespeare's Hamlet* (Sydney, Australia: Sydney University Press, 1970), p. 102.

101. On Hamlet's acceptance of providence, see Fredson Bowers, "Hamlet as Minister and Scourge," *PMLA* 70 (1955): 740–749; Bertram Joseph, *Conscience and the King: A Study of Hamlet* (London: Chatto & Windus, 1953), pp. 130–151; Roy Walker, *The Time is out of Joint: A Study of Hamlet* (London: Andrew Dakers, 1948), pp. 141–153. For a vigorous dissent from the view that Hamlet accepts his role in a providential scheme, see Roy W. Battenhouse, *Shakespearean Tragedy: Its Art and Its Christian Premises* (Bloomington: Indiana University Press, 1969), pp. 249–250.

102. A. J. A. Waldock, *Hamlet: A Study in Critical Method* (Cambridge: Cambridge University Press, 1931), pp. 97, 99.

103. Muir, *Shakespeare: Hamlet*, p. 61. There are several collections of essays on *Hamlet*. See, for example, the Norton critical edition of *Hamlet*, ed. Cyrus Hoy (New York: Norton, 1963) and David Bevington, ed., *Twentieth Century Interpretations of Hamlet* (Englewood Cliffs, N. J.: Prentice-Hall, 1968).

The reader should consult Edward Quinn et al., eds., *The Major Shakespearean Tragedies: A Critical Bibliography* (New York: Free Press, 1973), pp. 1–76. This work is particularly valuable because it contains full summaries and rather detailed critical evaluations of the items presented.

7
Comedy

Much Ado about Nothing
As You Like It
Twelfth Night

In *Much Ado about Nothing, As You Like It,* and *Twelfth Night* Shakespeare reached his peak as a comic dramatist. The three plays have much in common: They are filled with gaiety (even *Much Ado,* where villainy for a time threatens to win); like the romantic comedies that preceded them, they are concerned with the psychology of lovers; they rely heavily upon deception and disguise, not simply as theatrical expedients (which they usually were in the earlier comedies), but as important elements of theme and texture. Never content merely to repeat himself, Shakespeare created a distinctive atmosphere for each of these comedies. Later, having perfected romantic comedy, he proceeded to modify its conventions for the different artistic objectives of his so-called problem plays and dramatic romances. Throughout his career, he continued to experiment.

MUCH ADO ABOUT NOTHING

The Folio text (1623) of *Much Ado about Nothing* was printed from the only earlier text, the 1600 Quarto. The play is not mentioned in Francis Meres's *Palladis Tamia* (1598), although some would identify it as the *Love's Labour's Won* that Meres numbers among the comedies. Moreover, the text occasionally assigns speeches to Kempe instead of Dogberry, and we know that the actor Will Kempe, who created the role, left the Lord Chamberlain's Men late in 1599. Thus the play can probably be dated 1598–1599.[1]

There are two principal plots: One involves Claudio and Hero; the other, Beatrice and Benedick. The Claudio-Hero story could have been derived from the tale of Ginevora and Ariodante, which the Italian poet

Ariosto had included in his epic *Orlando Furioso* (1516), a work well
known to Elizabethans in John Harington's translation (1591). It could
also have reached Shakespeare from Matteo Bandello's tale of Sir
Timbreo and Fenicia in a collection, *Novelliere* (1554). But the story
existed in many dramatic and nondramatic versions. On the other hand,
the Beatrice-Benedick plot was probably Shakespeare's own invention.[2]

The Claudio-Hero plot barely escapes tragedy. While visiting Messina,
Claudio, a young Florentine noble, falls in love with Hero, daughter of
the governor Leonato. On the very eve of their intended wedding,
Claudio is tricked by the evil Don John (bastard brother of Don Pedro,
Prince of Arragon) into believing that he sees Hero conducting an
amorous intrigue with Borachio; the person involved is really Hero's
gentlewoman Margaret, who has been beguiled into impersonating her
mistress. The next day, in a powerful scene, Claudio publicly repudiates
Hero at the altar:

> There, Leonato, take her back again.
> Give not this rotten orange to your friend.
> She's but the sign and semblance of her honour.
> Behold how like a maid she blushes here!
> . . . .   ,
>   Would you not swear,
> All you that see her, that she were a maid
> By these exterior shows? But she is none:
> She knows the heat of a luxurious [lecherous] bed;
> Her blush is guiltiness, not modesty.
>
>   (IV, 1, 32–43)

"This looks not like a nuptial" (IV, 1, 69), Claudio's friend Benedick
tersely comments. Claudio stalks out of the church, and Hero swoons.[3]
In order to bring Claudio to remorse, Friar Francis has Leonato circulate
the report that Hero is dead. Meanwhile, the evildoers are exposed when
two members of the watch overhear Borachio boasting of his part in the
conspiracy. Claudio, now crushed with grief, hangs an epitaph on Hero's
tomb restoring her good name, and he agrees to marry Leonato's niece.
When he takes her hand, the niece unmasks and turns out to be Hero
herself. Many critics consider Claudio unworthy of so lovely a bride,
some even feeling that Shakespeare made a serious miscalculation in his
portrait of him. "A hard deposit of unpleasantness," Patrick Swinden
writes, "crystallises around Claudio and sinks the centre of the play."[4]
But Claudio, after all, is the hero of a comedy and must be endured,
repentance and all.[5]

While this serious action nears its climax, another sort of conspiracy
is being hatched. Benedick and Beatrice, Hero's cousin, "never meet but
there's a skirmish of wit between them" (I, 1, 63–64). Because both

are, in addition, outspoken in their commitment to the single life, Don Pedro undertakes the Herculean labor of bringing the two warriors "into a mountain of affection th' one with th' other" (II, 1, 382–383). Conspiring with Claudio and Leonato, he arranges for Benedick to overhear a trumped-up conversation to the effect that Beatrice secretly languishes for him. Almost immediately thereafter, Hero and her two attendants, Margaret and Ursula, play the identical trick on Beatrice, having her overhear that Benedick is pining for *her*. The contrivance is a spectacular success. Beatrice and Benedick, while still relishing their membership in the "college of wit-crackers" (V, 4, 101–102), declare their love; and at the end of the play, with Claudio and Hero reunited and with Don John captured and facing punishment, they joyously prepare for marriage.

It is evident that the Beatrice and Benedick plot is not, as some would have it, a mere diversion that Shakespeare dreamed up in order to distend what otherwise would have been a flimsy play. On the contrary, it bears an organic relationship to the Claudio-Hero story. Both actions are based on deception, which may serve either pernicious or wholesome purposes. They are further connected in that the victimizers in the one case—Hero, Claudio, Margaret, and even Leonato—are the victims in the other. Claudio enters enthusiastically into the fun of duping Benedick, unaware that he himself is to be duped by Don John. And Don Pedro, the genial mastermind of the comic deception, is among the deluded spectators to Hero's supposed wantonness. One critic has noted at least eight "practices" (deceptions) in the play. "No crowd of characters in a Shakespearian world exhibits more universal predilection for the game, such readiness to exchange and then exchange again the roles of deceiver and deceived."[6]

While the two main events do not get under way until the second act is nearly over, Shakespeare presents some preliminary contests that quickly establish the motif of deception and its frequent companion, eavesdropping.[7] At a masquerade, Don Pedro agrees to impersonate Claudio and win Hero for him. A servant overhears the plan and mistakenly informs Leonato that Don Pedro loves Hero. Meanwhile, Borachio, who was also eavesdropping, reports the conversation accurately to Don John. The latter, sensing an opportunity to sow discord, pretends to mistake Claudio for Benedick and urges "Benedick" to dissuade Don Pedro from loving Hero. Claudio falls for the trick. "The Prince wooes for himself" (II, 1, 181), he bitterly reflects, and his suspicion is reinforced moments later when the real Benedick tells him, "The Prince hath got your Hero . . . . But did you think the Prince would have served you thus?" (II, 1, 199–203). Although the error is rectified, the seed of mistrust has been planted, and Claudio is now primed for Don John's machinations. At the same time, Don Pedro, having tested his wings, is ready for his more ambitious "practice" on Beatrice and Benedick.

Claudio and Hero have been described as "plot-ridden" characters: conventionalized figures who, barring a lively touch here and there, are kept artificial.[8] Such is decidedly not the case with Beatrice and Benedick, who must be ranked among Shakespeare's most dazzling personages. Almost before we know it we are caught up in their merry war:

> *Beatrice:* I wonder that you will still be talking, Signior Benedick. Nobody marks you.
> *Benedick:* What, my dear Lady Disdain! are you yet living?
> *Beatrice:* Is it possible Disdain should die while she hath such meet food to feed it as Signior Benedick? Courtesy itself must convert to disdain if you come in her presence.
>
> (I, 1, 119–124)

And so it goes, with Beatrice usually getting the last word. "You have put him down, lady," Don Pedro tells her on one occasion; "you have put him down." "So I would not he should do me, my lord, lest I should prove the mother of fools" (II, 1, 292–295)—a snappy retort from a lady who doth possibly protest too much. Benedick similarly gives himself away when Claudio declares Hero to be the loveliest creature he has ever seen. Not so, says Benedick. "There's her cousin, an [if only] she were not possess'd with a fury, exceeds her as much in beauty as the first of May doth the last of December" (I, 1, 192–195).

Like earlier heroes (Valentine in *The Two Gentlemen of Verona* and Berowne in *Love's Labour's Lost*), Benedick begins as "an obstinate heretic in the despite of beauty" (I, 1, 236–237) and ends as one of Cupid's devout, though satirical, worshipers. Laughing at the lovesick Claudio, he vows that *he* shall never look pale with love. "With anger, with sickness, or with hunger, my lord; not with love" (I, 1, 251–252). In Leonato's orchard, just before his own downfall, he laments the fact that Claudio, a soldier, has gone soft and vows that it could not happen to *him*:

> I will not be sworn but love may transform me to an oyster; but I'll take my oath on it, till he have made an oyster of me he shall never make me such a fool. One woman is fair, yet I am well; another is wise, yet I am well; another virtuous, yet I am well; but till all graces be in one woman, one woman shall not come in my grace.
>
> (II, 3, 24–32)

A few minutes later, the friendly mischief having been transacted, this sworn enemy of love makes a superb about-face. "Love me? Why, it must be requited" (II, 3, 231–232). He will be "horribly in love" with

Beatrice, even though his friends will make a few jokes at the former bachelor's expense:

> But doth not the appetite alter? A man loves the meat in his youth that he cannot endure in his age. Shall quips and sentences and these paper bullets of the brain awe a man from the career of his humour? No, the world must be peopled. When I said I would die a bachelor, I did not think I should live till I were married.

> (II, 3, 247–253)

In the tradition of the romantic lover, Benedick tries to write poetry, but he gives up. "No, I was not born under a rhyming planet, nor I cannot woo in festival terms" (V, 2, 39–41). He returns to the language of wit. Let no one, he declares at the end of the play, flout at him for having spoken against marriage, "for man is a giddy thing, and this is my conclusion" (V, 4, 109–110).

While Benedick is adjusting to the idea of marriage, Beatrice, "born to speak all mirth and no matter" (II, 1, 343–344), experiences parallel development. Grateful that she has no husband, she intends never to have one—not, at any rate, "till God make men of some other metal than earth . . . . Adam's sons are my brethren, and truly I hold it a sin to match in my kin[d]red [marry a relative]" (II, 1, 62–68). According to the proverb, an old maid is supposed to lead apes to hell, but Beatrice will go no farther than the gate:

> And there will the devil meet me like an old cuckold with horns on his head, and say "Get you to heaven, Beatrice, get you to heaven. Here's no place for you maids." So deliver I up my apes, and away to Saint Peter—for the heavens. He shows me where the bachelors sit, and there live we as merry as the day is long.

> (II, 1, 45–52)

"Will you have me, lady?" Don Pedro playfully asks. "No, my lord," she quips, "unless I might have another for working days: your Grace is too costly to wear every day" (II, 1, 339–342). From her hiding place in the arbor she hears that she is inordinately proud, that, in Hero's fine phrase, "Disdain and scorn ride sparkling in her eyes" (III, 1, 51). Unaware of her own precarious situation, Hero offers to talk Benedick out of his reported passion by devising "some honest slanders" on Beatrice's reputation (III, 1, 84–85). Left alone, Beatrice emerges from the arbor. Although her customary medium is prose of unequaled buoyancy, she now expresses her complex emotions in formal rhymed verse (as if holding something in reserve for her next meeting with Benedick himself):

What fire is in mine ears? Can this be true?
  Stand I condemn'd for pride and scorn so much?
Contempt, farewell! and maiden pride, adieu!
  No glory lives behind the back of such.
And, Benedick, love on; I will requite thee,
  Taming my wild heart to thy loving hand.
If thou dost love, my kindness shall incite thee
  To bind our loves up in a holy band;
For others say thou dost deserve, and I
Believe it better than reportingly.
                                 (III, 1, 107–116)[9]

Her capitulation, like Benedick's, is swift because there was never any genuine resistance. Leonato may be right when he exclaims, "O Lord, my lord! if they were but a week married, they would talk themselves mad" (II, 1, 368–369). But does anybody really doubt that Beatrice and Benedick will make up the happiest and sanest marriage in all Shakespeare?

The game of wit that Beatrice and Benedick play serves an important psychological and dramatic purpose. It enables them to fence through a screen of trenchant words, thereby hiding their real emotions from everyone else, from each other, and perhaps even from themselves. Through their raillery they can cling to their self-delusion as long as they wish, and when the subterfuge is no longer convincing, they can succumb to their true feelings without losing face:

Benedick: They swore that you were almost sick for me.
Beatrice: They swore that you were well-nigh dead for me.
Benedick: 'Tis no such matter. Then you do not love me?
Beatrice: No, truly, but in friendly recompense.
                                 (V, 4, 80–83)

The damaging evidence is produced; each has written a "halting sonnet of his own pure brain" (V, 4, 87):

Benedick: A miracle! Here's our own hands against our hearts. Come, I will have thee; but, by this light, I take thee for pity.
Beatrice: I would not deny you; but, by this good day, I yield upon great persuasion, and partly to save your life, for I was told you were in a consumption.
Benedick: Peace! I will stop your mouth.

                                            [*Kisses her.*]
                                            (V, 4, 91–98)

But the wit of Beatrice and Benedick can be intensely serious, too. It quickens their perceptions and clarifies their insights. Of all the lords and ladies in Messina, only Beatrice and Benedick have the right instincts about Don John. "How tartly that gentleman looks!" Beatrice comments. "I never can see him but I am heart-burn'd an hour after" (II, 1, 3–5). When Hero is humiliated in the church, Benedick knows where to fix blame: "The practice of it lives in John the bastard" (IV, 1, 189). Welded into a new unity by their comprehension of the evil in their midst and by their genuine sympathy for Hero, Beatrice and Benedick now converse with unaccustomed depth of feeling, though still with an admixture of wit. Beatrice hints that she would be most thankful to the man who would right her cousin's wrong. Her ensuing dialogue with Benedick builds to a startling climax:

Benedick: By my sword, Beatrice, thou lovest me.
Beatrice: Do not swear, and eat it.
Benedick: I will swear by it that you love me, and I will make him eat it that says I love not you.
Beatrice: Will you not eat your word?
Benedick: With no sauce that can be devised to it. I protest I love thee.
Beatrice: Why then, God forgive me!
Benedick: What offence, sweet Beatrice?
Beatrice: You have stayed me in a happy hour. I was about to protest I loved you.
Benedick: And do it with all thy heart.
Beatrice: I love you with so much of my heart that none is left to protest.
Benedick: Come, bid me do anything for thee.
Beatrice: Kill Claudio.

(IV, 1, 276–291)

Here is surely one of the world's great theatrical moments. "A reader or audience is shocked," one critic says, "as Benedick is shocked. He had not anticipated that the claims of love could extend quite so far into the territory of bitterness."[10]

At the opposite extreme from this mercurial pair of lovers, Shakespeare has enriched *Much Ado* with some of his most memorable low comedy characters, the thickheaded constable Dogberry and his inept crew of watchmen. Dogberry murders the language with such gems as "Comparisons are odorous" (III, 5, 18) and "Is our whole dissembly appear'd?" (IV, 2, 1), and he gives outrageous instructions to the "most senseless and fit" men who make up the watch (III, 3, 23). They are to "comprehend all vagrom men" (III, 3, 26), but they must let thieves alone, for "they that touch pitch will be defil'd" (III, 3, 60). Dogberry's finest hour comes when Conrade, one of Don John's followers, calls him an ass after the departure of the learned sexton, who had been recording the proceedings. Dogberry is frustrated:

Dost thou not suspect my place? Dost thou not suspect my years? O that he were here to write me down an ass! But, masters, remember that I am an ass. Though it be not written down, yet forget not that I am an ass. No, thou villain, thou art full of piety, as shall be prov'd upon thee by good witness . . . . O that I had been writ down an ass!

(IV, 2, 77–91)

How beautifully ironic that Dogberry and his fellow simpletons should be the ones to unravel Don John's knavery! "What your wisdoms could not discover," Borachio confesses to Don Pedro, "these shallow fools have brought to light" (V, 1, 239–240). In this respect Dogberry is curiously linked with Beatrice and Benedick; in fact, the Dogberryism is an inverted form of their wordplay. Dogberry's stubbornly wrongheaded fascination with words reinforces the play's general theme of *hubris* (pride). "For," as A. P. Rossiter has observed, "in their pride or conceit, all the principals in some degree mistake themselves: as they mistake or wrongly take situations, and mistake or wrongly take words, on purpose and wittily or accidentally and absurdly."[11]

Dogberry also resembles Beatrice and Benedick in that he helps keep the travails of Claudio and Hero in comic perspective. His crew uncovers Don John's villainy before the scheduled wedding, and it is only Dogberry's splendid "tediousness" that prevents Leonato from learning of it in time to set things right. But even as Claudio is shaming Hero in the church, the audience remains comfortable in the knowledge that the "aspicious" Conrade and Borachio have been duly "comprehended" and are in jail awaiting "excommunication." Between Dogberry on the one hand and Beatrice and Benedick on the other, we cannot become much concerned with the fleeting clouds.[12]

Much Ado about Nothing is a substantial play, one of Shakespeare's best; and critics have begun to interpret it (as they have other comedies) along serious lines. For John Russell Brown its theme is the quest for "love's truth." According to Ralph Berry, the play is concerned with problems of knowing. William G. McCollom sees it as a study of true wit (Beatrice and Benedick) versus false wit, or pretentious wisdom (Claudio). Emphasizing the Claudio-Hero plot, Paul and Miriam Mueschke focus upon the concept of feminine honor, of which Hero is the supreme embodiment. And Barbara Lewalski identifies the main theme as love, in the Neoplatonic and Christian sense, reaching its highest manifestation in Hero's redemptive sacrifice, her feigned death, and "return to life."[13]

All these views may be valid in part. But perhaps the special quality of this play, with its unique mingling of the grave and the gay, is best captured by Beatrice after Don Pedro has praised her wit:

Pedro: Your silence most offends me, and to be merry best becomes you, for out o' question you were born in a merry hour.

Beatrice: No, sure, my lord, my mother cried; but then there was a star danc'd, and under that was I born.

(II, 1, 345–350)[14]

AS YOU LIKE IT

As You Like It was first published in the 1623 Folio, but it was probably written in 1599–1600. It is one of four plays (three of them Shakespeare's) cited in the Stationers' Register under the date August 4, 1600, with instructions that they not be printed. This was a common method of protecting plays from unauthorized publication. *As You Like It* is not listed in *Palladis Tamia* (1598), unless, as is most unlikely, it is the ubiquitous *Love's Labour's Won*. The famous line, "Who ever lov'd that lov'd not at first sight?" (III, 5, 82), is a quotation from Marlowe's *Hero and Leander,* which remained unpublished until 1598.[15]

The play owes much to the pastoral tradition. Shepherds and country life had been idealized by Greek poets as early as the third century B.C. In the pastoral world of poetic imagination, innocent shepherds tend their flocks and fall in love with beautiful lasses to whom they write anguished verse. Pastoralism was in particular vogue during the Renaissance, and although the genre is more commonly associated with lyric poetry, its practitioners included many dramatists and prose writers. In some cases, notably Edmund Spenser's poem *The Shepheardes Calender* (1579) and Sir Philip Sidney's prose epic *Arcadia* (1590), the pastoral tradition produced major literary works. More often, however, it merely provided courtly readers with elegant escapist entertainment overlaid with conventional moralizing and, on occasion, personal, political, and religious satire. Among the most influential pastorals was Montemayor's *Diana Enamorada* (1542), the major source of *The Two Gentlemen of Verona* (see p. 59).[16]

The source of *As You Like It* is Thomas Lodge's pastoral romance *Rosalynde: Euphues Golden Legacie* (1590), which in turn was derived from *The Tale of Gamelyn,* an anonymous fourteenth-century poem. In the play, Orlando, son of the deceased Sir Rowland de Boys, is mistreated by his older brother Oliver, who withholds his inheritance. When Orlando challenges the wrestler Charles at the court of Duke Frederick, Oliver hopes his brother will be maimed or killed. But Orlando defeats Charles, to the chagrin of Oliver but to the relief and delight of two young women: Frederick's daughter Celia and her cousin Rosalind. The latter is the daughter of Frederick's brother Duke Senior, the rightful ruler, who lives in exile in the Forest of Arden. Fearful of his niece's popularity, Duke Frederick banishes Rosalind, who has fallen in love with Orlando as Orlando has with her. Rosalind adopts the male disguise of Ganymede and sets out for Arden Forest, accompanied by Celia, in the role of Ganymede's sister Aliena, and by the court jester Touchstone. Meanwhile, Orlando, together with the old servant Adam, has fled from Oliver; and he too shows up in Arden.

From that point on, marvelous things happen: "Ganymede" undertakes to cure Orlando of love by pretending to be Rosalind; the shepherdess Phebe, disdainful of the doting swain Silvius, falls in love with Ganymede; Oliver, arriving at Arden in search of his brother, repents his villainy when Orlando rescues him from a lioness; Rosalind reveals her identity and is restored to her father; word comes that Duke Frederick has arrived at Arden, undergone a religious conversion, and withdrawn from the world. The play ends with a quadruple wedding. Orlando pairs off with Rosalind; Oliver with Celia; Silvius with Phebe, cleansed of her pride and of her passion for Ganymede; and Touchstone with the country wench Audrey, "a poor virgin, sir, an ill-favour'd thing, sir, but mine own" (V, 4, 60–61). Duke Senior and his retinue (with one notable exception, Jaques) return to the court and prosperity.[17]

Shakespeare follows Lodge closely, but his modifications are significant. For one thing, the violence is either toned down or discarded. Lodge's Saladyne (Oliver) at one point puts Rosader (Orlando) in chains. The wrestler in *Rosalynde* has his neck broken, whereas Shakespeare's Charles merely suffers a decisive beating. Lodge's usurper, Torismond (Frederick), is not converted but is killed in battle with Gerismond (Duke Senior); moreover, by making the two men brothers (in Lodge they are not), Shakespeare creates a parallel with the Oliver-Orlando situation. Then, too, Orlando is gentler than Rosader, a crude blusterer; in fact, some see Shakespeare's hero as a Hercules-Christ figure and note the element of Christian forgiveness in his behavior toward Oliver.[18] Shakespeare's Arden has no room for heroes who cannot be civilized or villains who cannot repent. Finally, of course, there are characters in *As You Like It* who have no counterparts in Lodge's pastoral: the rustics Audrey and William and two of Shakespeare's most memorable creations, Touchstone and Jaques.[19]

Shakespeare makes of Arden Forest a sweet little pastoral retreat where "many young gentlemen . . . fleet the time carelessly as they did in the golden world" (I, 1, 123–125).[20] In Arden, however, Shakespeare also delicately satirizes the pastoral ideal in a manner analogous to Cervantes's treatment of chivalry in *Don Quixote:* It is not a parody but, as David Young points out, "a more searching look at the ideal through an intensive examination of its distance from the real."[21] We can admire the values of the exiled Duke, who wishes to establish harmony with the natural world. But when we first meet him, he is expounding to his followers on the uses of adversity. How lucky we are, he says, to be freezing, for the icy blasts of winter are a better medicine for the soul than were the comforts of court life:

> And this our life, exempt from public haunt,
> Finds tongues in trees, books in the running brooks,
> Sermons in stones, and good in everything:
> I would not change it.
>
> (II, 1, 15–18)

His attendant Amiens praises him on his ability to translate authentic misery into pleasant rhetoric. Right after that, as an ironic comment upon Duke Senior's speech, we are told that a deer weeping profusely into a stream provided Jaques with the occasion for ludicrous moralizing. So much for those "books in the running brooks"! And the only tongues to be found in the trees will be the rotten love poems Orlando places there. "Truly the tree yields bad fruit" (III, 2, 123), Touchstone wryly observes.

As soon as Rosalind and her companions arrive at Arden, they stumble upon clichés of pastoral romance. Silvius, a stereotype of the lovesick shepherd dreamed up in books, describes his agonies to an old shepherd, Corin, who in his youth must have "sigh'd upon a midnight pillow" (II, 4, 26) even as Silvius is sighing now:

> If thou rememb'rest not the slightest folly
> That ever love did make thee run into,
> Thou hast not lov'd.
> Or if thou hast not sat as I do now,
> Wearing [tiring] thy hearer in thy mistress' praise,
> Thou hast not lov'd.
> Or if thou hast not broke from company
> Abruptly, as my passion now makes me,
> Thou hast not lov'd. O Phebe, Phebe, Phebe!
>
> *Exit.*
> (II, 4, 33–41)

This strikes a sympathetic chord in Rosalind, who is herself in love, but it purports to remind Touchstone of how *he* acted as a lover:

> I remember, when I was in love I broke my sword upon a stone and bid him take that for coming a-night to Jane Smile; and I remember the kissing of her batlet [bat used to pound clothes during washing], and the cow's dugs that her pretty chopt [chapped] hands had milk'd; and I remember the wooing of a peascod instead of her, from whom I took two cods, and

giving her them again, said with weeping tears, "Wear these for my sake." We that are true lovers run into strange capers.

(II, 4, 44–54)

Meeting the shepherdess whose cruelty has reduced Silvius to wretchedness, Ganymede offers advice that betokens a practicality unusual in such an idyllic setting: "Sell when you can! you are not for all markets" (III, 5, 60). As we can see, Arden Forest abounds in "dislocating confrontations," or "juxtapositions," that Alexander Leggatt identifies as a central ingredient of Shakespearean comedy.[22]

Shakespeare also ridicules the pastoral tradition through the bumpkins Audrey and William. "Truly," Touchstone confides to Audrey, "I would the gods had made thee poetical" (III, 3, 15–16). "I do not know what poetical is," she answers. "Is it honest in deed and word? Is it a true thing?" (III, 3, 17–18). In winning her from the monosyllabic William, Touchstone entertains no illusions as to his motive. "As the ox hath his bow, sir, the horse his curb, and the falcon her bells, so man hath his desires; and as pigeons bill, so wedlock would be nibbling" (III, 3, 80–83). And he is happy to get married, to "press in here . . . amongst the rest of the country copulatives" (V, 4, 57–58). Audrey and William provide down-to-earth contrast to the artificial shepherds invented by urbane courtiers and poets.

Among Arden's most interesting residents is the melancholy Jaques, who takes upon himself the burden of cleansing "the foul body of th' infected world" (II, 7, 60). Like the others in Duke Senior's party, he professes a loathing for the court, and he enjoys Amiens's bittersweet songs ("Under the Greenwood Tree" and "Blow, Blow, Thou Winter Wind"). "I can suck melancholy out of a song as a weasel sucks eggs. More, I prithee more!" (II, 5, 12–14). His malady, he claims, is derived from extensive travel and experience. This assertion evokes from Ganymede a cutting reproof:

Farewell, Monsieur Traveller. Look you lisp and wear strange suits, disable all the benefits of your own country, be out of love with your nativity and almost chide God for making you that countenance you are; or I will scarce think you have swam in a gundello [gondola].

(IV, 1, 33–38)

To Jaques, nothing has purpose or value, and his most famous speech, "All the world's a stage" (II, 7, 139–166), is—quite properly for him—a detached chronicle of man's futility as he lives through the seven ages. To be sure, Jaques invokes images of sharp humor:

Then the whining schoolboy, with his satchel
And shining morning face, creeping like snail

Unwillingly to school. And then the lover,
Sighing like furnace, with a woful ballad
Made to his mistress' eyebrow.

(II, 7, 145–149)

But as Leggatt shrewdly observes, "Behind the pose of melancholy we detect a genial interest in humanity. His lecture ... has a light, jocular tone that works against the cynicism of its content."[23] He is himself a performer par excellence, playing to the hilt his role of brooding cynic.

It is the realist Touchstone who puts Jaques in his place most consistently. Is it not ironic that Jaques should boast of having met a fool in the forest without realizing that the fool was laughing at *him?* Touchstone impresses him with a platitudinous discourse on time. " 'It is ten o'clock' " (II, 7, 22), he says with intense seriousness:

"Thus we may see," quoth he, "how the world wags.
'Tis but an hour ago since it was nine,
And after one hour more 'twill be eleven;
And so, from hour to hour, we ripe and ripe,
And then, from hour to hour, we rot and rot;
And thereby hangs a tale."

(II, 7, 23–28)

Here Touchstone catches and mocks the spirit of the ages-of-man speech. His parody of Jaques's hollow rhetoric becomes explicit in a punctilious lecture on the seven degrees of quarreling: Retort Courteous, Quip Modest, Reply Churlish, Reproof Valiant, Countercheck Quarrelsome, Lie Circumstantial, and Lie Direct (V, 4, 71–108). Some critics hear in Jaques the voice of Shakespeare; others regard him as a hateful misanthrope. It seems more likely that he is simply another subject for good-natured laughter. He is also a little sad, and by no means unattractive, as he blesses the restored Duke and the four married couples, knowing that his disposition excludes him from their earthly pleasures. He has been seen as the "fool scapegoat" whose exclusion "purges Arden of discordant emotions."[24] Jaques chooses to join Frederick in holy meditation; from the converts, he says, "there is much matter to be heard and learn'd" (V, 4, 191).

Touchstone performs a function different from that of the clowns in earlier comedies. Scholars generally believe that this is the result of a personnel change in the Lord Chamberlain's Men, namely, the departure of Will Kempe in 1599 and the arrival of Robert Armin.[25] Kempe specialized in broad humor of the Bottom and Dogberry type; Armin's talent lay chiefly in witty repartee. In *As You Like It* the emphasis shifts from doltish buffoonery to sophisticated raillery, with Touchstone the first in a line of court jesters that includes Feste in *Twelfth Night* and leads to the poignant Fool in *King Lear*. "He uses his folly like a stalking horse," Duke Senior says of Touchstone, "and under the presentation of that he shoots his wit" (V, 4, 111–113). (This, interestingly, is also Hamlet's technique: He puts on an "antic disposition" so that, as a "fool," he may speak freely and with immunity.) [26]

When we first meet the irreverent Touchstone, he is demonstrating to Celia and Rosalind that a knight can swear by his honor to an untruth and yet not be forsworn. Just as the girls cannot swear by their non-existent beards, the knight cannot swear by his nonexistent honor (I, 2, 63–85). "O Jupiter," Rosalind exclaims on arriving at Arden Forest, "how weary are my spirits!" The fool responds, "I care not for my spirits if my legs were not weary . . . . Ay, now am I in Arden, the more fool I! When I was at home, I was in a better place" (II, 4, 1–17). But he is shrewd enough to know that, however one might idealize life in the court or in the country, there is little to choose between the two. When Corin asks how he likes the shepherd's life, Touchstone replies:

> Truly, shepherd, in respect of itself, it is a good life; but in respect that it is a shepherd's life, it is naught. In respect that it is solitary, I like it very well; but in respect that it is private, it is a very vile life. Now in respect it is in the fields, it pleaseth me well; but in respect it is not in the court, it is tedious. As it is a spare life, look you, it fits my humour well; but as there is no more plenty in it, it goes much against my stomach.
>
> (III, 2, 13–22)

Also going much against his stomach are Orlando's verses to Rosalind, and he launches into a parody that gets progressively more outspoken in its sexuality:

> If a hart do lack a hind,
> Let him seek out Rosalinde.
> If the cat will after kind,
> So be sure will Rosalinde.
> . . . .
> Sweetest nut hath sourest rind,
> Such a nut is Rosalinde.
> He that sweetest rose will find
> Must find love's prick, and Rosalinde.
>
> (III, 2, 107–118)

"The detachment of his wit," Mark Van Doren observes, "gives everything perspective, including himself," and that is why he can, incongruously, marry the unpoetical Audrey. "He is intellect afield; contemptuous of what he sees so far from home, but making the thin best of what is there."²⁷ Ralph Berry takes a stronger view; he sees Touchstone's various encounters (with Corin, Orlando, Audrey, Jaques, and even Rosalind) as illustrations of his will to master his social superiors and inferiors, an inclination shared by most of the major characters in the play. (The wrestling match thus becomes an important visual image.)²⁸ In any case, Touchstone thoroughly enjoys the vigorous give-and-take of debate, and he almost always wins.

The last word belongs not to Touchstone, with his dry intellect, but to Rosalind, perhaps the most charming and witty heroine in all literature. Her characteristic note is sounded in a speech to Orlando in which she challenges the venerable myth of dying for love:

> The poor world is almost six thousand years old, and in all this time there was not any man died in his own person, videlicet [to wit], in a love cause . . . . Men have died from time to time, and worms have eaten them, but not for love.
>
> (IV, 1, 95–108)

As Ganymede-Rosalind delivers this harangue to Orlando, she hopes with all her heart that he will not believe her. This is the essence of Rosalind's witchcraft: the ability to view romantic sentiment, including her own, from a comic perspective. To her ear the tedious lovers' litany initiated by Phebe may sound "like the howling of Irish wolves against the moon" (V, 2, 118–119), but she herself remains an enthusiastic howler. She has the vitality of Portia and Beatrice, fortified by the wisdom of Duke Theseus.

Rosalind positively sparkles. When Celia bids her be merry despite her father's banishment, she responds flippantly: "From henceforth I will, coz, and devise sports. Let me see. What think you of falling in love?" (I, 2, 26–28). Almost before she knows it, Rosalind is playing the game in earnest,²⁹ as she hints to Orlando after his victory. "Sir, you have wrestled well, and overthrown / More than your enemies" (I, 2, 265–266). Her femininity continually creeps through the male disguise. She deplores Phebe's abuse of Silvius because it discredits her sex. As Celia teasingly parcels out the news that Orlando is in the forest, Rosalind explodes in impatience: "Dost thou think, though I am caparison'd [dressed] like a man, I have a doublet and hose in my disposition?" (III, 2, 204–206). Learning that Orlando is indeed nearby, she bombards her cousin with questions for which Celia, a lively match, has a clever answer:

> *Rosalind:* Alas the day! what shall I do with my doublet and hose? What did he when thou saw'st him? What said he? How look'd he? Wherein went he? What makes he here? Did he ask for me? Where remains he?

How parted he with thee? and when shalt thou see him again? Answer
me in one word.

Celia: You must borrow me Gargantua's mouth first; 'tis a word too great
for any mouth of this age's size.

(III, 2, 231–240)

When Oliver produces a handkerchief stained with Orlando's blood (he
had been wounded slightly by the lioness), Ganymede swoons; but she
recovers, insisting that the fainting spell was "counterfeited." Let Ganymede counterfeit to be a *man,* Oliver chides. "So I do; but, i' faith, I should
have been a woman by right" (IV, 3, 176–177).

Rosalind excels in her scenes as Ganymede with Orlando. Some
foolish lover, says Ganymede, is ruining the forest carving "Rosalind"
on the barks of trees. But it could not be Orlando, for he does not
exhibit the proper symptoms:

A lean cheek, which you have not; a blue [i.e., weary looking] eye and
sunken, which you have not; an unquestionable [gloomy] spirit, which you
have not; a beard neglected, which you have not.... Then your hose should
be ungarter'd, your bonnet unbanded, your sleeve unbutton'd, your shoe
untied, and everything about you demonstrating a careless desolation.

(III, 2, 392–401)

The offer to purge Orlando by impersonating Rosalind (a minor episode
in Lodge) produces some of Shakespeare's most inspired comedy, and
the fun is augmented when we recall that on the Elizabethan stage
Rosalind would have been acted by a boy. The masquerade would thus
be compounded: the boy actor playing the girl Rosalind playing the boy
Ganymede imitating Rosalind.

When Orlando shows up late for his appointment, Ganymede appears
implacable:

Break an hour's promise in love? He that will divide a minute into a
thousand parts and break but a part of the thousand part of a minute in the
affairs of love, it may be said of him that Cupid hath clapp'd him o' th'
shoulder, but I'll warrant him heart-whole.

(IV, 1, 44–49)

The next minute she dissolves enticingly into a young woman in love.
Then, when the situation begins to get out of control, she returns to
the game:

Rosalind: Come, woo me, woo me! for now I am in a holiday humour and
like enough to consent. What would you say to me now, an I were your
very very Rosalind?

Orlando: I would kiss before I spoke.

Rosalind: Nay, you were better speak first; and when you were gravell'd [grounded on gravel; stuck] for lack of matter, you might take occasion to kiss. Very good orators, when they are out, they will spit; and for lovers, lacking (God warn us!) matter, the cleanliest shift is to kiss.

(IV, 1, 68–78)

After forcing Celia to "marry" her to Orlando, she can barely wait for him to leave so that she can give vent to her ecstasy:

O coz, coz, coz, my pretty little coz, that thou didst know how many fathom deep I am in love! But it cannot be sounded. My affection hath an unknown bottom, like the Bay of Portugal.... I'll tell thee, Aliena, I cannot be out of the sight of Orlando. I'll go find a shadow, and sigh till he come.

(IV, 1, 209–223)

As David Young has said, "She steers a course between the excessive subjectivity that cuts Jaques off from the immediate situation, and the excessive objectivity in Touchstone that threatens to destroy all personal emotion."[30] That is why she is the soul of the play.

In Rosalind, with her exquisite blend of idealism and good sense, Shakespeare has created his perfect woman and raised her almost to the level of a symbol—a force that can bind up wounds, reconcile estranged brothers, and unite lovers in the holy joys of marriage.[31] But the radiance of Shakespeare's vision transcends even the glow generated by this incomparable heroine. Of all his works *As You Like It* is "the one which is most consistently played over by a delighted intelligence. It is Shakespeare's most Mozartian comedy."[32]

TWELFTH NIGHT

The earliest text of *Twelfth Night*, an excellent one, is that of the First Folio (1623). The play was probably written sometime between 1600 and 1602 (and possibly revised around 1606). John Manningham (d. 1622), lawyer and diarist, records that he saw it acted at Middle Temple on February 2, 1602. According to Leslie Hotson, the first performance took place ("in the round") at court in 1601 on January 6, which as Epiphany, or Twelfth Night, celebrated the coming of the Magi.[33] Some favor 1600 as a more likely date for the premiere. When Maria (III, 2, 83–85) reports that Malvolio "does smile his face into more lines than is in the new map with the augmentation of the Indies," Shakespeare is alluding to a map published in 1600 in Richard Hakluyt's *Voyages;* the song "Farewell, Dear Heart" (II, 3, 110–121) was borrowed from Robert Jones's *First Booke of Songs and Ayres,* also published in 1600.[34]

It is generally believed that the main plot comes from the story of Apolonius and Silla, in Barnabe Riche's *Farewell to Militarie Profession* (1581). But the popular tale existed in several versions going back to the anonymous Italian play *Gl'Ingannati* ("The Deceived Ones"), first performed in 1531 and published in 1537. A strong case has been made for Shakespeare's indebtedness to the commedia del l'arte (see p. 94), particularly Giambattista Della Porta's play *La Cintia* (acted before 1591 and printed in 1601).[35] As *Twelfth Night* opens, Orsino, Duke of Illyria, is languishing for the Countess Olivia, who, in mourning for a brother, has abjured the company of men for seven years. But one of the Duke's emissaries, Cesario, finally gains admittance, and Olivia is smitten. "Even so quickly may one catch the plague?" (I, 5, 314), she muses—a particularly bad plague at that, inasmuch as Cesario is really Viola, a young woman in male disguise who has been separated by shipwreck from her presumably dead brother Sebastian. Once again we have an impossible tangle: Orsino loves Olivia; Olivia loves Cesario; and, inevitably, Cesario, whose true sex cannot be revealed, loves Orsino. But Sebastian, Viola's identical twin, has also been rescued; and when he turns up, the complications multiply. The situation is resolved according to the formula of romantic comedy: Olivia marries Sebastian, a carbon copy of the Cesario who stole her heart; Orsino, having lost Olivia, transfers his devotion to Viola, a woman once more.

Like the Forest of Arden, Illyria is a haven for lovers, but its prevailing mood is one of cloying sentimentality, as is reflected in the Duke's celebrated opening speech:

> If music be the food of love, play on,
> Give me excess of it, that, surfeiting,
> The appetite may sicken, and so die.
> That strain again! It had a dying fall;
> O, it came o'er my ear like the sweet sound
> That breathes upon a bank of violets,
> Stealing and giving odour! Enough, no more!
> 'Tis not so sweet now as it was before.
>
> (I, 1, 1–8)

The sound indeed echoes the sense, for, as John Hollander has shown, the Duke's lush poetry immediately establishes a crucial theme of the play: self-discovery through surfeiting. That is, the characters are to indulge in excessive feasting, physically or emotionally, to the point that "the appetite may sicken, and so die." In Larry Champion's terminology, *Twelfth Night* is Shakespeare's most perfect "comedy of identity." Its major characters discover that they have assumed false or unnatural positions and begin to perceive the truth about themselves.[36]

Orsino basks in his romantic conception of himself. He does not care for the cheerful ditties of his own time; he fancies old-fashioned songs about love's innocence chanted by "the spinsters and the knitters in the sun" (II, 4, 45). The clown Feste obliges with a haunting lyric based upon the death-from-a-broken-heart cliché Rosalind had demolished in *As You Like It*:

> Come away, come away, death,
>   And in sad cypress let me be laid.
> Fly away, fly away, breath;
>   I am slain by a fair cruel maid.
>   (II, 4, 52–55)

Interestingly, Alan Downer sees the song as a parody of the innocent lyric the Duke has described.[37] Be that as it may, Orsino regards himself as the epitome of constancy and bristles at Cesario's suggestion that a woman's love might be as strong as his:

> There is no woman's sides
> Can bide the beating of so strong a passion
> As love doth give my heart; no woman's heart
> So big to hold so much; they lack retention.
> . . . .
>   Make no compare
> Between that love a woman can bear me
> And that I owe Olivia.
>   (II, 4, 96–106)

But the Duke's mind, Feste says, is "a very opal" (II, 4, 77), and he later seems more than willing to settle for Viola, thereby demonstrating that he never truly loved Olivia but was merely luxuriating in the posture of being in love as prescribed in the orthodox literary documents. In this respect he is akin to Silvius in *As You Like It* and Romeo in the pre-Juliet days.

More important, the Duke's inexplicable shift from Olivia to Viola (like Olivia's hasty exchange of Cesario for Sebastian) exemplifies what many believe to be the play's central idea: the instability of love, of Illyria, and of human life in general. *Twelfth Night* is a study of the "protean, contradictory nature of love,"[38] and the havoc it creates has implications far beyond the immediate situation of Olivia and Orsino. "Nothing," says D. J. Palmer, "is fixed or still in Illyria: an impression of capricious and elaborate artifice in the plot is directly related to a major theme of the play, the theme of mutability."[39] This is the essence of Feste's famous song "O Mistress Mine, Where Are You Roaming?" (II, 3, 40–53). Although it is a jaunty invitation to pleasure (aimed indirectly at Olivia), the song is based on the premise that time inevitably destroys love and beauty:

> What is love? 'Tis not hereafter;
> Present mirth hath present laughter;
>   What's to come is still unsure:
> In delay there lies no plenty;
> Then come kiss me, sweet and twenty!
>   Youth's a stuff will not endure.
>   (II, 3, 48–53)[40]

Olivia's grief is as excessive as Orsino's sentimentality, and her unnatural vow reminds us of the academicians in *Love's Labour's Lost*. Her uncle Sir Toby Belch has no patience with such nonsense. "What a plague means my niece to take the death of her brother thus? I am sure care's an enemy to life" (I, 3, 1–3). Olivia is also a bit sardonic, as shown in her reply when Cesario pleads on the Duke's behalf that she marry and leave the world a copy of her graces:

> O, sir, I will not be so hard-hearted. I will give out divers schedules of my beauty. It shall be inventoried, and every particle and utensil labell'd to my will:—as, item, two lips, indifferent red; item, two grey eyes, with lids to them; item, one neck, one chin, and so forth.
>
>   (I, 5, 262–267)

We are pleased when she succumbs to Cesario, partly because we already know that Sebastian is waiting in the wings to provide her with a way out of her dilemma. Meanwhile, Sebastian, the bewildered beneficiary of the passion unintentionally stirred up by Cesario, takes his good fortune without asking too many questions:

> For though my soul disputes well with my sense
> That this may be some error, but no madness,
> Yet doth this accident and flood of fortune
> So far exceed all instance, all discourse,
> That I am ready to distrust mine eyes
> And wrangle with my reason, that persuades me
> To any other trust but that I am mad,
> Or else the lady's mad.
>
>   (IV, 3, 9–16)

He rushes off to marry Olivia, thereby showing himself to be a pragmatic young man without the romantic delusions that suffuse the Illyrian atmosphere.

Of the characters in Illyria, it is Viola who achieves the truest perspective. Within the limits imposed by her disguise and her commission from Orsino, she manages to make fun of her rival. "Is't not well done?" Olivia asks as she removes her veil. Viola cannot resist. "Excellently done, if God did all" (I, 5, 253–255). As Viola begins to grasp the strange predicament, she is both amused and perplexed by her doubly ironic role:

> What will become of this? As I am a man,
> My state is desperate for my master's love.
> As I am a woman (now alas the day!),
> What thriftless sighs shall poor Olivia breathe!
> O Time, thou must untangle this, not I;
> It is too hard a knot for me t' untie!
>
> (II, 2, 37–42)

Another facet of her personality is revealed when, to refute Orsino's contention that women cannot love as deeply as men, she tells him of her father's daughter who loved a man just as Cesario might love the Duke if Cesario were a woman. The charming little fiction leads to one of the great passages in the play: Viola's poignant description, in the third person, of her own enforced silence. What, Orsino asks, is the story of that sister?

> A blank, my lord. She never told her love,
> But let concealment, like a worm i' th' bud,
> Feed on her damask cheek. She pin'd in thought;
> And, with a green and yellow melancholy,
> She sat like Patience on a monument,
> Smiling at grief.
>
> (II, 4, 113–118)

Viola, in Harold Jenkins's words, "represents a genuineness of feeling against which the illusory can be measured."[41]

Although Viola in many ways resembles Rosalind, G. K. Hunter makes an important distinction between the two heroines: "Rosalind is able to use her disguise as a genuine and joyous extension of her personality. Viola suffers constriction and discomfiture in *her* role."[42] Perhaps that is one of the reasons why Viola's wit so often finds an outlet in half-concealed sexual quips. When Feste expresses the hope that Jove will some day reward Cesario with a beard, she responds, "By my troth, I'll tell thee, I am almost sick for one, though I would not have it grow on my chin" (III, 1, 52–54). Maneuvered into a fight with Sir Andrew Aguecheek, Cesario displays a shocking lack of virility. "Pray God defend me!" she exclaims in a double-entendre addressed to the audience. "A little thing would make me tell them how much I lack of a man" (III, 4, 331–333). If she cannot quite match Rosalind's unparalleled vivacity, Viola is nonetheless endowed with a special delicacy that in its own way is enormously appealing.

While the lovers are attending to the usual business of romantic comedy, a perpetual carouse goes on in the pantry. Chief revelers are Olivia's uncle, Sir Toby Belch, and his protégé, Sir Andrew Aguecheek, whom he has taken under his wing ostensibly to be a suitor for Olivia but actually to subsidize his recreations. Sir Toby has been compared to Falstaff, but, as Feste all too accurately puts it, Olivia's kinsman "has a most weak pia mater [brain]" (I, 5, 122–123), and one might add, a touch of the Dogberry:

> *Olivia:* Cousin, cousin, how have you come so early by this lethargy?
> *Sir Toby:* Lechery? I defy lechery.

(I, 5, 131–133)

Sir Andrew, a prize fool, laments his misspent education. "I would I had bestowed that time in the tongues that I have in fencing, dancing, and bear-baiting. O, had I but followed the arts!" (I, 3, 97–99). The foppish knight is also a first-class coward. "For Andrew," Sir Toby observes, "if he were open'd, and you find so much blood in his liver as will clog the foot of a flea, I'll eat the rest of th' anatomy" (III, 2, 64–67). It is good fun, therefore, when Sir Toby manipulates him into challenging his purported rival Cesario, and Sir Andrew is naturally grateful to this fellow coward for the opportunity to put the sword away.

Sir Toby and Sir Andrew are joined in their high jinks by Olivia's pert gentlewoman, Maria, "as witty a piece of Eve's flesh as any in Illyria" (I, 5, 30–31), who alternately chides them and enters wholeheartedly into their festivities. They also receive regular visits from Feste, for, as he says, foolery "does walk about the orb like the sun; it shines everywhere" (III, 1, 43–44). This jolly crew in the buttery, reflecting a philosophy very different from the lugubriousness of Orsino and Olivia, likes nothing better than to "rouse the night owl in a catch" (II, 3, 60), a lively round in which the melody is hurled rapidly from one singer to the next.

To one pair of ears, however, the music produced by the merrymakers is most disagreeable:

> Have you no wit, manners, nor honesty, but to gabble like tinkers at this time of night? Do ye make an alehouse of my lady's house, that ye squeak out your coziers' [cobblers'] catches without any mitigation or remorse of voice?

(II, 3, 94–98)

These harsh accents belong to Olivia's steward Malvolio, who is "sick of self-love" and tastes "with a distemper'd appetite" (I, 5, 97–98). Sir Toby meets Malvolio's grating intrusion with memorable indignation: "Art any more than a steward? Dost thou think, because thou art virtuous, there shall be no more cakes and ale?" (II, 3, 122–125). Although Sir Toby labels him a Puritan, Maria sees through Malvolio's hypocrisy:

> The devil a Puritan that he is, or anything constantly but a time-pleaser [opportunist]; an affection'd [affected] ass ... the best persuaded of himself; so cramm'd, as he thinks, with excellencies that it is his grounds of faith that all that look on him love him.
>
> (II, 3, 159–165)

In his stupendous conceit he imagines himself Count Malvolio, the husband of Olivia, richly attired in a "branch'd [embroidered] velvet gown" (II, 5, 54) and playing with a precious jewel as he uses his authority to reprimand Sir Toby. As Maria observes, "He has been yonder i' the sun practising behaviour to his own shadow this half hour" (II, 5, 18–20).

The Elizabethans, says one critic, would have viewed Malvolio's ambition as a threat to the class structure and would have welcomed his being put in his place.[43] In any case, his presumption is exploited by Maria in the hilarious subplot. She places in his path a cryptic letter in what looks like Olivia's handwriting. " 'I may command where I adore .... M. O. A. I. doth sway my life' " (II, 5, 115–118). "If I could make that resemble something in me!" (II, 5, 131–132), he declares, then decides that Olivia is the author and he the intended recipient since all the letters are in "Malvolio." He reads on with increasing smugness:

> "In my stars I am above thee; but be not afraid of greatness. Some are born great, some achieve greatness, and some have greatness thrust upon 'em. Thy Fates open their hands; let thy blood and spirit embrace them ...."
>
> (II, 5, 155–160)

Maria has not only skillfully caught up Malvolio's own thoughts and ambitions, but she has also captured his literary style so as to sustain the illusion that Olivia's feelings coincide with his own. " 'Let thy tongue tang arguments of state; put thyself into the trick of singularity' " (II, 5, 163–164). The stroke is indeed brilliant. "Both the thoughts and words in the letter are so expressive of Malvolio's being that they produce instant conviction."[44]

Malvolio carries out all the instructions contained in the letter. He appears before Olivia cross-gartered, in yellow stockings, and smiling insipidly. When he supplements these eccentricities with impudent speech, he is taken away as a madman and locked up in a dark room. To add to his torment, Feste, still rankling from Malvolio's earlier insults, visits him alternately as himself and as the curate Sir Topas, come to exorcise the "hyperbolical fiend" (IV, 2, 28) that vexes the lunatic. Meanwhile, "Sir Topas" finds further "evidence" that Malvolio is deranged:

> *Feste:* Say'st thou that house is dark?
> *Malvolio:* As hell, Sir Topas.
> *Feste:* Why, it hath bay windows transparent as barricadoes [barricades], and the clerestories [windowed walls] toward the south north are as lustrous as ebony; and yet complainest thou of obstruction?
> *Malvolio:* I am not mad, Sir Topas. I say to you the house is dark.
> *Feste:* Madman, thou errest. I say there is no darkness but ignorance, in which thou art more puzzled than the Egyptians in their fog [i.e., during the ninth plague, darkness].

(IV, 2, 37–49)

The trick works so well that Sir Toby marries the resourceful wench who devised it. When the truth comes to light, Malvolio is not disposed to forgive. His exit speech sounds a jarring note. "I'll be reveng'd on the whole pack of you!" (V, 1, 386). There is a hint that he will be brought back into the company, but we cannot be sure. One critic views him as a scapegoat who must be "sacrificed" so that comedy may live.[45]

Some may sympathize with Malvolio (Charles Lamb even saw in him a tragic dignity),[46] but Olivia's self-righteous steward never reaches anything like the level of awareness that the heroes of tragedy struggle to achieve. Shakespeare did not repeat the mistake made in *The Merchant of Venice* of creating a villain too big to be absorbed into the sunny atmosphere of comedy. Like Shylock, Malvolio is excluded at the end of the play; but unlike Shylock, he remains a target of satire with no implications outside himself. As one critic points out, "Malvolio rejects the challenge to alter himself, and grotesquely continues to defy his antagonists, who are not villains of great power, but jovial tipplers. The struggle is unworthy as well as unheroic."[47]

Malvolio's real nemesis is that joyous spirit appropriately named Feste. Like Touchstone in *As You Like It,* Feste, in Olivia's words, is "an allow'd fool" (I, 5, 101–102), privileged to speak out with impunity. Sometimes he makes bawdy wordplay. "My lady will hang thee for thy absence," Maria tells him. "Let her hang me!" he replies. "He that is well hang'd in this world needs to fear no colours" (I, 5, 3–6). Feste also engages in mild satire. As he dons the gown and beard to impersonate the curate, he comments wryly: "And I would I were the first that ever dissembled in such a gown" (IV, 2, 6–7). Most important, he examines the weaknesses of the other characters under the hard light of logic. Witness his remarkable "proof" that *Olivia* is the fool. "Take the fool away," Olivia orders. "Do you not hear, fellows?" Feste retorts. "Take away the lady" (I, 5, 41–43). And he begins his catechism:

> *Clown:* Good madonna, why mourn'st thou?
> *Olivia:* Good fool, for my brother's death.
> *Clown:* I think his soul is in hell, madonna.
> *Olivia:* I know his soul is in heaven, fool.
> *Clown:* The more fool, madonna, to mourn for your brother's soul, being in heaven. Take away the fool, gentlemen.
>
> (I, 5, 72–78)

When Viola remarks that she saw him recently at Orsino's, Feste makes the reply, quoted earlier, that foolery, like the sun, shines everywhere. "I would be sorry, sir, but the fool should be as oft with your master as with my mistress" (III, 1, 44–46).

Although Feste performs essentially the same function as Touchstone, there are interesting differences. Touchstone, despite his commitment to the goat-girl Audrey, remains intellectually detached from his surroundings; Feste can get aroused to active involvement. If Touchstone's forte is highly sophisticated parody, Feste's is a plain speaking that is almost free of "ironic counterstatement."[48] There are songs in *As You Like It,* but Touchstone does not sing them; Feste is a consummate musician whose catches and lyrics embrace a wide range of human experience. He is softer than Touchstone, just as Orsino is milder than Orlando and Viola gentler than Rosalind.[49]

Thus *Twelfth Night* is not merely a recapitulation of motifs from previous comedies. To be sure, there are the identical twins separated by shipwreck, an echo of *The Comedy of Errors.* The heroine dresses as a boy and carries love messages to her rival, as Julia did in *The Two Gentlemen of Verona;* and she is solicited by a deluded woman, as Rosalind was wooed by Phebe. Like Benedick in *Much Ado about Nothing,* Malvolio is tricked into believing that he is loved. He is as alien to Illyria as Shylock was to Belmont in *The Merchant of Venice.* But the mood of this comic masterpiece is unique. There is, Clifford Leech suggests, an "ultimate drawing back from a secure sense of harmony." Or, as Anne Barton puts it, one feels that the exclusiveness at the end of *Twelfth Night* contrasts sharply with the "various and crowded dance that brings *As You Like It* to a festive close."[50]

Not surprisingly, critics have seen in *Twelfth Night* anticipations of more somber plays: *King Lear* and, more recently, the so-called dark comedy *All's Well that Ends Well.*[51] And the final song is indeed a strange mixture of seriousness and nonsense. Left alone on the stage, Feste, in words that mysteriously seem to recall St. Paul's "When I was a child" (1 Cor. 13: 11),[52] reminds the audience that the play is done:

> When that I was and a little tiny boy,
>   With hey, ho, the wind and the rain,
> A foolish thing was but a toy,
>   For the rain it raineth every day.
>   (V, 1, 398–401)

On one level Feste presents a jaunty, perhaps obscene, history of love and its tribulations. But the song also has a bittersweet quality suggesting a harsh world beyond Touchstone's ken. Illyria seems a shade more melancholy, and more fragile, than the Forest of Arden.[53]

NOTES

1. On the text, see the New Cambridge *Much Ado about Nothing*, eds. A. Quiller-Couch and John Dover Wilson (Cambridge: Cambridge University Press, 1923), pp. vii–xiii, 89–107; W. W. Greg, *The Shakespeare First Folio: Its Bibliographical and Textual History* (Oxford: Clarendon, 1955), pp. 277–281; and J. H. Smith, "The Composition of the Quarto of *Much Ado about Nothing*," *Studies in Bibliography* 16 (1963): 9–26.

2. The fullest study of sources, with interesting commentary, is Charles T. Prouty, *The Sources of Much Ado about Nothing* (New Haven: Yale University Press, 1950). See also Geoffrey Bullough, *Narrative and Dramatic Sources of Shakespeare,* 8 vols. (New York: Columbia University Press, 1957–1975), 2:61–139 and Kenneth Muir, *Shakespeare's Sources* (London: Methuen, 1957), pp. 52–55.

3. The visual power of the church scene (as well as other scenes in the play) is discussed by J. R. Mulryne, *Shakespeare: Much Ado about Nothing* (London: Edward Arnold, 1965).

4. Patrick Swinden, *An Introduction to Shakespeare's Comedies* (London: Macmillan, 1973), p. 100.

5. Referring to *Much Ado* and other plays, Richard Levin warns against ascribing to Shakespeare ironic or inconclusive endings. See "Refuting Shakespeare's Endings," *Modern Philology* 72 (1974–1975):337–349.

6. Bertrand Evans, *Shakespeare's Comedies* (Oxford: Clarendon, 1960), p. 69.

7. Paul A. Jorgensen, *Redeeming Shakespeare's Words* (Berkeley: University of California Press, 1962), pp. 22–42, observes how the title plays with multiple meanings of *nothing* and *noting:* observing, eavesdropping, recording, reporting. *Nothing* could also mean the female genitalia—appropriate in a play about misinterpreted sexual behavior.

8. Leo Kirschbaum, *Character and Characterization in Shakespeare* (Detroit: Wayne State University Press, 1962), p. 129. See also Josephine Waters Bennett, ed., *Much Ado about Nothing* (Baltimore: Penguin, 1958), pp. 20–24.

9. See Muriel C. Bradbrook, *Shakespeare and Elizabethan Poetry* (London: Chatto & Windus, 1951), p. 182.

10. Mulryne, *Shakespeare: Much Ado about Nothing*, p. 31.

11. A. P. Rossiter, *Angel with Horns* (New York: Theatre Arts Books, 1961), p. 78. Dogberry's comic *hubris* is perceptively discussed in James Smith, "*Much Ado about Nothing*: Notes from a Book in Preparation," *Shakespearian and Other Essays* (London: Cambridge University Press, 1974), pp. 24–42. See also John A. Allen, "Dogberry," *Shakespeare Quarterly* 24 (1973): 35–53.

12. For a discussion of how Shakespeare blocks our involvement and guarantees a detached perspective, see Larry S. Champion, *The Evolution of Shakespeare's Comedy: A Study in Dramatic Perspective* (Cambridge: Harvard University Press, 1970), pp. 67–81.

13. John Russell Brown, *Shakespeare and His Comedies,* 2d ed. (London: Methuen, 1962), pp. 109–123; Ralph Berry, *Shakespeare's Comedies: Explorations in Form* (Princeton: Princeton University Press, 1972), pp. 154–174; William G. McCollom, "The Role of Wit in *Much Ado about Nothing*," *Shakespeare Quarterly* 19 (1968): 165–174; Paul and Miriam Mueschke, "Illusion and Metamorphosis in *Much Ado about Nothing*," *Shakespeare Quarterly* 18 (1967): 53–65; Barbara K. Lewalski, "Love, Appearance, and Reality: Much Ado about Something," *Studies in English Literature, 1500–1900* 8 (1968): 235–251.

14. A good anthology of criticism is Walter R. Davis, ed., *Twentieth Century Interpretations of Much Ado about Nothing* (Englewood Cliffs, N. J.: Prentice-Hall, 1969).

15. On the text, see the New Cambridge *As You Like It*, eds. A. Quiller-Couch and John Dover Wilson (Cambridge: Cambridge University Press, 1926), pp. 93–108 and Greg, *The Shakespeare First Folio,* pp. 293–295. I have not seen the New Arden edition (1975), ed. Agnes Latham.

16. On the pastoral tradition, see W. W. Greg's classic *Pastoral Poetry and Pastoral Drama* (London: A. H. Bullen, 1906); William Empson, *Some Versions of Pastoral* (London: Chatto & Windus, 1935); Frank Kermode, *English Pastoral Poetry from the Beginnings to Marvell* (London: Harrap, 1952); and S. K. Heninger, Jr., "The Renaissance Perversion of Pastoral," *Journal of the History of Ideas* 22 (1961): 254–261. See also David Young, *The Heart's Forest: A Study of Shakespeare's Pastoral Plays* (New Haven: Yale University Press, 1972), pp. 1–37 and Thomas McFarland, *Shakespeare's Pastoral Comedy* (Chapel Hill: University of North Carolina Press, 1972), pp. 20–24. Indispensable for the classical background is Thomas G. Rosenmeyer, *The Green Cabinet: Theocritus and the European Pastoral Lyric* (Berkeley: University of California Press, 1969).

17. For a helpful scene-by-scene analysis, with good commentary, see Michael Jamieson, *Shakespeare: As You Like It* (London: Edward Arnold, 1965).

18. See Richard Knowles, "Myth and Type in *As You Like It*," *ELH* 33

(1966): 1–22 and René E. Fortin, " 'Tongues in Trees': Symbolic Patterns in *As You Like It*," *Texas Studies in Literature and Language* 14 (1972–1973): 569–582.

19. On Shakespeare and his sources, see Muir, *Shakespeare's Sources*, pp. 55–66; Bullough, *Sources*, 2: 143–266; and Marco Mincoff, "What Shakespeare Did to *Rosalynde*," *Shakespeare-Jahrbuch* 96 (1960): 78–89.

20. See two interesting studies of the time imagery in the play: Jay L. Halio, " 'No Clock in the Forest': Time in *As You Like It*," *Studies in English Literature, 1500–1900* 2 (1962): 197–207 and Rawdon Wilson, "The Way to Arden: Attitudes Toward Time in *As You Like It*," *Shakespeare Quarterly* 26 (1975): 16–24. While both critics agree that the court is characterized by a "time consciousness," for Halio, Arden represents "timelessness"; whereas for Wilson it represents subjective time (or feeling) as opposed to objective time.

An important book on the golden age is Harry Levin, *The Myth of the Golden Age in the Renaissance* (London: Faber, 1969). "The myth of the Golden Age is a nostalgic statement of man's orientation in time, an attempt at transcending the limits of history" (p. xv). On *As You Like It*, see pp. 121–123. See also Erwin Panofsky's classic essay on Poussin's famous painting, "*Et in Arcadia Ego:* On the Conception of Transience in Poussin and Watteau," in *Philosophy and History: Essays Presented to Ernst Cassirer*, eds. Raymond Klibansky and H. J. Paton (Oxford: Clarendon, 1936), pp. 223–254. Even in Poussin's Arcadia, death holds sway.

21. Young, *The Heart's Forest*, p. 40. See also Harold Jenkins, "*As You Like It*," *Shakespeare Survey* 8 (1955): 40–51 and Albert R. Cirillo, "*As You Like It:* Pastoralism Gone Awry," *ELH* 38 (1971): 19–39.

22. Alexander Leggatt, *Shakespeare's Comedy of Love* (London: Methuen, 1974), pp. 85–219.

23. Ibid., pp. 200–201. In William Charles Macready's famous production of the play in 1842–1843 at Drury Lane, Jaques was stripped of some of his best invective and made (for the Victorian audience) "noble, loving wise, and fatherly tender." See Charles H. Shattuck's handsome book, *Mr. Macready Produces As You Like It; A Prompt-Book Study* (Urbana: University of Illinois Press, 1962), p. 40.

24. See Alice Lotvin Birney, *Satiric Catharsis in Shakespeare* (Berkeley: University of California Press, 1973), p. 16; see also pp. 79–98. More seriously, McFarland (*Shakespeare's Pastoral Comedy*, pp. 98–121) finds the exclusion of Jaques and Frederick, like the Cain and Abel motif that clouds the earlier part of the play, alien to the comic vision.

25. See Leslie Hotson, "Robert Armin, Shakespeare's Fool," in his *Shakespeare's Motley* (1952; reprint ed., New York: Haskell House, 1971), pp. 84–128.

26. See Enid Welsford, *The Fool: His Social and Literary History* (London: Faber, 1935); on Touchstone, see pp. 249–251. See also S. L. Bethell, *Shakespeare and the Popular Dramatic Tradition* (Durham, N. C.: Duke University Press, 1944), pp. 111–116 and Robert Hillis Goldsmith, *Wise Fools in Shakespeare* (East Lansing: Michigan State University Press, 1955), pp. 47–51. For a criticism of Touchstone as fool and man, see Harold C. Goddard,

The Meaning of Shakespeare (Chicago: University of Chicago Press, 1951), pp. 285–291.

27. Mark Van Doren, *Shakespeare* (New York: Holt, 1939), p. 156. Similarly, John Palmer notes that Touchstone "puts all things and every person in the play, including himself, to the comic test." See John Palmer, *Political and Comic Characters of Shakespeare* (London: Macmillan, 1965), p. 383.

28. Berry, *Shakespeare's Comedies*, pp. 175–195.

29. On the thematic importance of the game, see D. J. Palmer, *"As You Like It* and the Idea of Play," *Critical Quarterly* 13 (1971): 234–245.

30. Young, *The Heart's Forest*, p. 67.

31. See Peter G. Phialas, *Shakespeare's Romantic Comedies* (Chapel Hill: University of North Carolina Press, 1966), pp. 239–255 and Harold Jenkins, *"As You Like It,"* *Shakespeare Survey* 8 (1955): 50–51.

32. Helen Gardner, *"As You Like It,"* in *More Talking of Shakespeare,* ed. John Garrett (London: Longmans, 1959), p. 18. A useful collection is Jay L. Halio, ed., *Twentieth Century Interpretations of As You Like It* (Englewood Cliffs, N. J.: Prentice-Hall, 1968).

33. Barbara K. Lewalski finds in the play Christian reverberations appropriate to the spirit of Epiphany; see her "Thematic Patterns in *Twelfth Night,"* *Shakespeare Studies,* ed. J. Leeds Barroll, 1 (1965): 168–181.

34. On the date, see Leslie Hotson, *The First Night of Twelfth Night* (New York: Macmillan, 1955). On the text and date, see also the New Cambridge *Twelfth Night,* eds. A. Quiller-Couch and John Dover Wilson, 2d ed. (Cambridge: Cambridge University Press, 1930, 1949), pp. vii–x, 89–101; the New Yale edition, ed. William P. Holden (New Haven: Yale University Press, 1954), pp. 137–138; Greg, *The Shakespeare First Folio,* pp. 296–298; *Twelfth Night,* ed. Charles T. Prouty (Baltimore: Penguin, 1958), pp. 15–25; and *Twelfth Night,* ed. S. Musgrove (Berkeley: University of California Press, 1969), pp. 1–12. Robert K. Turner, Jr., "The Text of *Twelfth Night,"* *Shakespeare Quarterly* 26 (1975): 128–138, argues that the text is derived from the scribal copy of a manuscript, not a promptbook. I have not seen the New Arden edition (1975), edited by J. M. Lothian and T. W. Craik.

35. Robert C. Melzi, "From Lelia to Viola," *Renaissance Drama* 9 (1966): 67–81. On sources, see also Bullough, *Sources,* 2: 269–372; Muir, *Shakespeare's Sources,* pp. 66–77; the New Cambridge edition, pp. x–xvii.

36. See John Hollander, *"Twelfth Night* and the Morality of Indulgence," *Sewanee Review* 67 (1959): 220–238 and Champion, *The Evolution of Shakespeare's Comedy,* pp. 81–95.

37. Alan Downer, "Feste's Night," *College English* 13 (1951–1952): 258–265.

38. See Leo G. Salingar's masterful essay, "The Design of *Twelfth Night,"* *Shakespeare Quarterly* 9 (1958): 117–139.

39. D. J. Palmer, "Art and Nature in *Twelfth Night,"* *Critical Quarterly* 9 (1967): 201–212.

40. On this song and its relationship to the theme of death, see Charles R. Lyons, *"Twelfth Night:* The Illusion of Love's Triumph and the Accommodation of Time," in his *Shakespeare and the Ambiguity of Love's Triumph* (The Hague: Mouton, 1971), pp. 44–68.

41. Harold Jenkins, "Shakespeare's *Twelfth Night*," *Rice Institute Pamphlet* 45:4 (January 1959): 30.

42. G. K. Hunter, *William Shakespeare: The Late Comedies* (London: Longmans, 1962), p. 45.

43. John W. Draper, *The Twelfth Night of Shakespeare's Audience* (Stanford, Calif.: Stanford University Press, 1950), pp. 86–112. According to Draper, several major characters are upwardly mobile in search of "social security" (pp. 251 ff.).

44. Phialas, *Shakespeare's Romantic Comedies*, p. 264; see also Van Doren, *Shakespeare*, p. 168. For an illuminating analysis of the letter scene, see Leggatt, *Shakespeare's Comedy of Love*, pp. 239–241.

45. Melvin Seiden, "Malvolio Reconsidered," *University of Kansas City Review* 28 (1961): 105–114.

46. Lamb's famous discussion, "On Some of the Old Actors," in his *Essays of Elia*, is frequently anthologized; see, for example, *Lamb's Criticism*, ed. E. M. W. Tillyard (London: Cambridge University Press, 1923), pp. 53–55. See also Joan Coldwell, "The Playgoer as Critic: Charles Lamb on Shakespeare's Characters," *Shakespeare Quarterly* 26 (1975): 184–195.

47. Sylvan Barnet, "Charles Lamb and the Tragic Malvolio," *Philological Quarterly* 33 (1954): 178–188 (quotation from p. 181).

48. C. L. Barber, *Shakespeare's Festive Comedy* (Princeton: Princeton University Press, 1959), p. 253.

49. On Feste, see (in addition to the discussions by Downer and Barber) Welsford, *The Fool*, pp. 251–253 and Goldsmith, *Wise Fools in Shakespeare*, pp. 51–57.

50. Clifford Leech, *Twelfth Night and Shakespearian Comedy* (Toronto: University of Toronto Press, 1965), p. 38; Anne Barton, "*As You Like It* and *Twelfth Night*: Shakespeare's Sense of an Ending," in *Shakesperian Comedy*, eds. Malcolm Bradbury and David Palmer, Stratford-upon-Avon Studies 14 (London: Edward Arnold, 1972), pp. 160–180.

51. See Julian Markels, "Shakespeare's Confluence of Tragedy and Comedy: *Twelfth Night* and *King Lear*," *Shakespeare Quarterly* 15: (1964): 75–88; Roger Warren, " 'Let Summer Bear It Out': A Note on *Twelfth Night* and *All's Well*," *Notes and Queries*, n. s. 20 (1973): 136–138.

52. See Lewalski, "Thematic Patterns in *Twelfth Night*."

53. On Feste's final song, see Brown, *Shakespeare and His Comedies*, p. 182 and Hunter, *William Shakespeare: The Later Comedies*, pp. 54–55. A particularly good essay on the play is Joseph H. Summers, "The Masks of *Twelfth Night*," *University of Kansas City Review* 22 (1955): 25–32. A helpful anthology is Walter N. King, ed., *Twentieth Century Interpretations of Twelfth Night* (Englewood Cliffs, N. J.: Prentice-Hall, 1968).

8
The Later History Plays

Shakespeare's second historical tetralogy begins with a portrayal of those events in the reign of Richard II (1377–1399) that lead to his deposition by Bolingbroke and his subsequent murder. It continues with Bolingbroke's troubled reign as Henry IV (1399–1413). After his death the crown passes to his son Henry V, whose brief reign (1413–1422) is highlighted by military victory over the French. The action concludes as the hero prepares to marry Princess Katherine, daughter of the king of France. While working on the second cycle, Shakespeare wanted his audience to remember the *Henry VI* plays and *Richard III*. The epilogue to *Henry V* looks ahead to ground covered in the earlier tetralogy:

> Henry the Sixth, in infant bands crown'd King
>> Of France and England, did this king succeed;
> Whose state so many had the managing
>> That they lost France and made his England bleed;
> Which oft our stage hath shown . . . .
>> *(Henry V, Ep., 9–13)*

The rest is familiar: the Wars of the Roses; the emergence of Richard III; the Battle of Bosworth, which ended the civil war and placed Henry Tudor, earl of Richmond, on the throne as Henry VII.[1]

The *Richard II–Henry V* cycle belongs to the 1590s, but it is convenient to include in this chapter the last of the history plays, *Henry VIII*, probably first staged in 1613.

RICHARD II

Richard II, the two parts of *Henry IV*, and *Henry V* make up a closely linked sequence. In these four plays, each a masterpiece in its own right,

Shakespeare presents a consistent political theme, establishes readily discerned patterns of cross-reference and verbal echo, creates vivid characters who develop as the cycle unfolds, and sustains remarkable contrasts in style from character to character and from play to play.

Richard II was entered in the Stationers' Register on August 29, 1597, and published in quarto that same year. Although two additional quartos (Q2 and Q3) appeared in 1598, the famous deposition scene (IV, 1) was not included until Q4 (1608). Its omission from printed versions (it was probably performed on the stage) may have been due to censorship either by the publisher Andrew Wise or by the official censor. During Elizabeth's lifetime, the queen was identified with Richard and the Earl of Essex with Bolingbroke.[2] In fact, on February 7, 1601, the day before Essex's unsuccessful rebellion, the Lord Chamberlain's Men revived *Richard II* presumably at the request of the earl's followers. By 1608, with Essex long since tried and executed and with the queen dead for five years, the entire play, deposition scene and all, would have been "safe." The Folio text (1623) was probably printed from Q3 (1598), perhaps augmented by Q5 (1615). *Richard II* is dated 1593–1596; it may have been written after Samuel Daniel's *First Four Books of the Civil Wars* (1595).[3]

Shakespeare's main source was the 1587 edition of Raphael Holinshed's *Chronicles*. In addition, he was probably indebted to Daniel's *Civil Wars* and may have resorted on occasion to Edward Hall's *Union of . . . Lancaster and York* (1548) and to several French chroniclers, notably Jean Froissart. *Richard II* was also modeled after Christopher Marlowe's *Edward II* (c. 1592), in which a weak king is deposed. We are not certain that Shakespeare knew and used the anonymous play *Thomas of Woodstock* (c. 1591–1594), but A. L. French argues persuasively that *Richard II* is built on the assumption that Richard was indeed responsible for the murder of his uncle, Woodstock—a point the older play makes explicit.[4] Shakespeare departs from his sources in a number of instances. He idealizes John of Gaunt, a ruthless opportunist in Holinshed, and expands the role of Northumberland, who in this play conspires against Richard, later rebels against Henry IV, and then is said to have become "crafty-sick" (*2 Henry IV,* Induction, 37) before the crucial Battle of Shrewsbury. Shakespeare adds the allegorical scene (III, 4) suggesting that Richard is a poor gardener who allows England, "our sea-walled garden" (III, 4, 43), to become choked with weeds and overrun with caterpillars. There is a superb scene (V, 1) in which Richard bids farewell to his queen as he is led off to prison and as she prepares to depart for France. Shakespeare is entirely responsible for the tragic Richard who emerges in the last two acts.[5]

In the first half of the play, Richard is depicted in an unfavorable light. As noted earlier, he has been involved in the murder of Woodstock, Lord Protector of the Realm. He is willful, irresponsible, and arbitrary in the exercise of his inherited—and in his view inalienable—power.[6] Spurning the counsel of his uncles, John of Gaunt (Duke of Lancaster) and Edmund of Langley (Duke of York), he surrounds himself with young flatterers who indulge in a riot of extravagance. In the opening scene he is caught in the middle of a quarrel between Thomas Mowbray, Duke of Norfolk, and Gaunt's son Henry Bolingbroke, Duke of Hereford. Later, having banished them both, he greedily waits for old Gaunt to die in order to confiscate the wealth that by right should pass to Bolingbroke. To compound the injustice, Richard uses Gaunt's estate to help finance the ill-advised Irish wars. Bolingbroke takes advantage of Richard's absence in Ireland to return from exile with strong supporters, among them the Earl of Northumberland and his son Henry Percy, the Hotspur of *1 Henry IV*. Finally confronted by Bolingbroke and his allies, Richard abdicates without resistance. Almost every step he takes turns out to be ruinous to himself and to England.

Richard is "the last king of the old medieval order,"[7] enamored of the ceremonies of kingship but unwilling to acknowledge (as Henry V *will* acknowledge) that ceremony is the "outward expression of inward responsibility."[8] A master stylist, Richard stages a lavish tournament between Mowbray and Bolingbroke (I, 3) and then, at the last minute, throws down his warder (truncheon) and prevents them from fighting. Unable to comprehend the essence of royalty, he clings pathetically to its symbols. Listen to his chant as Northumberland, representing Bolingbroke, approaches him at Flint Castle:

> What must the King do now? Must he submit?
> The King shall do it. Must he be depos'd?
> The King shall be contented. Must he lose
> The name of king? A God's name, let it go!
> I'll give my jewels for a set of beads,
> My gorgeous palace for a hermitage,
> My gay apparel for an almsman's gown,
> My figur'd goblets for a dish of wood,
> My sceptre for a palmer's walking staff,
> My subjects for a pair of carved saints,
> And my large kingdom for a little grave,
> A little little grave, an obscure grave . . . .
> (III, 3, 143–154)

It is not enough that he simply be deposed; he must one by one divest himself of all his accoutrements:

I give this heavy weight from off my head
And this unwieldy sceptre from my hand,
The pride of kingly sway from out my heart.
With mine own tears I wash away my balm,
With mine own hands I give away my crown,
With mine own tongue deny my sacred state,
With mine own breath release all duty's rites.
                            (IV, 1, 204–210)

Richard brings dignity to his concept of a king's prerogatives, but he
counts upon a feudal loyalty that is already obsolescent. When threatened
by the purposeful energy of an opportunist like Bolingbroke, he is
helpless.[9]

A key figure in the moral and political structure of the play is old
John of Gaunt, who embodies the good counsel that the impetuous king
sees fit to reject. Interestingly enough, however, the two are kindred
spirits, at least insofar as rhetorical style is concerned. The dying Gaunt
plays with his name:

O, how that name befits my composition!
Old Gaunt indeed, and gaunt in being old.
Within me grief hath kept a tedious fast;
And who abstains from meat that is not gaunt?
. . . .
Gaunt am I for the grave, gaunt as a grave,
Whose hollow womb inherits naught but bones.
                            (II, 1, 73–83)

Richard indulges in a similar game when at Flint Castle he is asked to
come down to the "base court" (the lower court):

In the base court? Base court, where kings grow base,
To come at traitors' calls and do them grace!
In the base court? Come down? Down court! down king!
For night owls shriek where mounting larks should sing.
                            (III, 3, 180–183)

It has been said that Richard consistently demonstrates an "inability
to square circumstances with his own emotional distortion of them."[10]
A similar deficiency underlies Gaunt's advice to his son to transform the
misery of his exile into poetic metaphor:

Suppose the singing birds musicians,
The grass whereon thou tread'st the presence strow'd,

The flowers fair ladies, and thy steps no more
Than a delightful measure or a dance.

(I, 3, 288–291)

Bolingbroke's answer is that of the consummate realist:

O, who can hold a fire in his hand
By thinking of the frosty Caucasus?
Or cloy the hungry edge of appetite
By bare imagination of a feast?
Or wallow naked in December snow
By thinking on fantastic summer's heat?

(I, 3, 294–299)[11]

Gaunt's big moment, of course, is his renowned panegyric to England. Maynard Mack, Jr., rightly observes that in this speech (II, 1, 31–68) Gaunt depicts an ideal of kingship firmly rooted in the traditions of Christian heroic service.[12] In its context, however, Gaunt's tribute is artificial almost to the point of irony. The faithful public servant waits for Richard to come to his deathbed and hear a final word of advice. ("Pray God we may make haste, and come too late!" says Richard [I, 4, 64].) With the stage set for Gaunt to exercise the dying man's time-hallowed privilege of delivering a solemn valedictory, but with his intended audience not yet arrived, he goes ahead anyway with his "aria":

This royal throne of kings, this scept'red isle,
This earth of majesty, this seat of Mars,
This other Eden, demi-paradise,
This fortress built by Nature for herself
Against infection and the hand of war,
This happy breed of men, this little world,
This precious stone set in the silver sea . . .
. . . .
This blessed plot, this earth, this realm, this England . . . .

(II, 1, 40–50)

Unfortunately, Gaunt's string of metaphors, in style as well as in content, is little more than a ceremonious tribute to a bygone age. How dramatically appropriate it is that Gaunt, this venerable symbol of an outworn political order, should sicken and die before a third of the play is over! His style then becomes the exclusive property of King Richard.[13]

The play is intensely political,[14] and its central problem is that Richard, the duly anointed ruler of England, is unfit to rule. Early in the play,

Gaunt is urged to avenge the murder of his brother Woodstock, but he refuses:

> God's is the quarrel; for God's substitute,
> His deputy anointed in his sight,
> Hath caus'd his death; the which if wrongfully,
> Let heaven revenge; for I may never lift
> An angry arm against his minister.
>
>   (I, 2, 37–41)

"What subject can give sentence on his king?" the Bishop of Carlisle demands (IV, 1, 121) before Richard enters Westminster Hall to be deposed. Bolingbroke, Carlisle charges, is a traitor to God's earthly steward, and his usurpation must bring disaster:

> And if you crown him, let me prophesy,
> The blood of English shall manure the ground
> And future ages groan for this foul act . . . .
> . . . .
> Disorder, horror, fear, and mutiny
> Shall here inhabit, and this land be call'd
> The field of Golgotha and dead men's skulls.
>
>   (IV, 1, 136–144)

It is Richard himself, however, who asserts the idea most eloquently, when he upbraids Northumberland for neglecting to bow in the presence of majesty:

> We are amaz'd; and thus long have we stood
> To watch the fearful bending of thy knee,
> Because we thought ourself thy lawful king.
> And if we be, how dare thy joints forget
> To pay their awful duty to our presence?
> If we be not, show us the hand of God
> That hath dismiss'd us from our stewardship.
>
>   (III, 3, 72–78)

"Not all the water in the rough rude sea," Richard solemnly declares, "can wash the balm off from an anointed king" (III, 2, 54–55).

A crisis arises, however, when the anointed king who governs badly is challenged by a usurper who governs well. It has been argued that Richard abuses his trust and compromises his divine right.[15] Perhaps so. But this does not solve the problem facing the Duke of York, that "figure of comic pathos,"[16] who, as a prototype of the English people, reluctantly shifts allegiance from Richard to Bolingbroke. Shakespeare subtly explores a complex political and philosophical issue but refuses to provide a simple answer.

Of equal interest to playgoers and readers is the personal fate of the hero. The public Richard is a failure; the private Richard manages to attain as a man the stature that eluded him while he wore the crown.[17] And as his kingship disintegrates, this human being becomes increasingly vulnerable and, for all his foolishness, immensely sympathetic.[18]

In a classic analysis of the hero's character, Coleridge points out that Richard "makes a merit of his resignation. He scatters himself into a multitude of images, and in conclusion endeavours to shelter himself from that which is around him by a cloud of his own thoughts."[19] Indeed, *Richard II* is the first of Shakespeare's plays in which the chief character uses simile and metaphor as the natural expression of his mind and temperament; or, to put it another way, there is in this play a superb union of character and style.[20] Richard is a poet, a great minor poet, Van Doren calls him, whose preoccupying theme is himself and his sufferings.[21]

When he returns from Ireland and arrives on the coast of Wales, Richard dramatically addresses his native soil:

> As a long-parted mother with her child
> Plays fondly with her tears and smiles in meeting,
> So weeping, smiling, greet I thee, my earth,
> And do thee favours with my royal hands.
> (III, 2, 8–11)[22]

His allies having been defeated, he can only lament the disintegration of kingship:

> Of comfort no man speak!
> Let's talk of graves, of worms, and epitaphs,
> Make dust our paper, and with rainy eyes
> Write sorrow on the bosom of the earth.
> Let's choose executors and talk of wills.
> ....
>
> For God's sake let us sit upon the ground
> And tell sad stories of the death of kings!
> (III, 2, 144–156)

The fall of a king, he says, demands an eloquence beyond his powers. "O that I were as great / As is my grief, or lesser than my name!" (III, 3, 136–137). There is one almost comic occasion when, imprisoned in Pomfret Castle, he tries to compare his prison to the world but is momentarily stumped:

And, for because the world is populous,
And here is not a creature but myself,
I cannot do it.

                    (V, 5, 3–5)

"Yet I'll hammer it out," he vows. And he does![23]

He reaches dizzy histrionic heights in the deposition scene, where he assumes the role of Christ betrayed. Forcing Bolingbroke to grasp the crown on one side while he holds the other, Richard invokes a poignant image:

Now is this golden crown like a deep well
That owes [owns] two buckets, filling one another,
The emptier ever dancing in the air,
The other down, unseen, and full of water.
That bucket down and full of tears am I,
Drinking my griefs whilst you mount up on high.

                    (IV, 1, 184–189)

As noted earlier (see p. 19), he calls for a mirror (the episode is not in Holinshed) in which he may read the sorrows in his face. After playing with the word *face*, he hurls the glass to the floor. "How soon my sorrow hath destroy'd my face," he moralizes (IV, 1, 291). Bolingbroke corrects him. "The shadow of your sorrow hath destroy'd / The shadow of your face" (IV, 1, 292–293). Richard is delighted that his enemy has improved on the metaphor:

                    Say that again.
The shadow of my sorrow? Ha! let's see!
'Tis very true: my grief lies all within;
And these external manners of laments
Are merely shadows to the unseen grief
That swells with silence in the tortured soul.

                    (IV, 1, 293–298)

Bolingbroke has shown fine insight into Richard's dramatic posturing, his inability to distinguish between form and substance. But, more important, Richard at this moment understands himself. Through the device of the mirror, traditionally associated with both vanity and truth telling, Shakespeare beautifully conveys his transformation from self-conceit to humility, from King to Man.[24]

A fundamental question remains: Who is responsible for Richard's removal? Holinshed clearly states that Bolingbroke intended to become king from the moment he returned from banishment, and several critics share that view. Moody Prior sees Bolingbroke's silence as part of a sophisticated plan to get the throne without seeming to circumvent the law. He is, in the words of R. F. Hill, "a schemer who does not soliloquize," a man who does not let us know the silent workings of his mind. Others, notably A. L. French, feel that Richard deposed himself—a reading that would seriously undercut the theory that Shakespeare's history plays were in large part conceived as Tudor propaganda. Bolingbroke, says Robert Ornstein, made no conscious decision; he was, according to A. R. Humphreys, "carried into usurpation." For L. C. Knights the play demonstrates how power, almost without premediation, "must necessarily fill a vacuum caused by the withdrawal of power." John Palmer takes the similar but harsher position that Bolingbroke is "that most dangerous of all climbing politicans, the man who will go further than his rivals because he never allows himself to know where he is going." A third possibility is that Richard is not all that innocent. According to Harold Folland and Lois Potter (among others), he skillfully manipulates Bolingbroke into the role of usurper by employing rhetorical weapons. Richard goes out, to quote Nicholas Brooke, "not as a weeping Narcissus, but as a man conscious of moral victory."[25]

In any case, Richard dominates the action with his powerful verbal and visual imagery. But it is York who produces what is perhaps the most significant image in _Richard II:_ that of Richard and Bolingbroke as actors in a theater.[26] York reports that Richard followed Bolingbroke into London. " 'God save thee, Bolingbroke!' " everyone shouted (V, 2, 11), but the appearance of Richard was regarded as an anticlimax:

> As in a theatre the eyes of men,
> After a well-grac'd actor leaves the stage,
> Are idly bent on him that enters next,
> Thinking his prattle to be tedious,
> Even so, or with much more contempt, men's eyes
> Did scowl on gentle Richard. No man cried "God save him!"
> No joyful tongue gave him his welcome home,
> But dust was thrown upon his sacred head.
>
> (V, 2, 23–30)[27]

Shakespeare's full-fledged tragic heroes—Hamlet, Othello, Lear, Macbeth—are all to some extent actors and poets like Richard, but theirs is a fuller music. [28]

HENRY IV, PARTS ONE AND TWO

Henry IV, Part One was published in quarto (Q1) in 1598 (four leaves survive from an earlier edition [Qo] of the same year), and five more quartos appeared before the 1623 Folio, which was set up from Q5 (1613). Part Two was printed in 1600, with a scene (III, 1) omitted; except for a reissue of this text (probably the same year) with the missing scene restored, the play was not printed again until its publication in the First Folio. _Henry IV_ is listed in Francis Meres's _Palladis_

Tamia (1598), but no parts are specified. If, as seems logical, the plays followed closely upon *Richard II*, then 1596 would be about right for Part One and early 1597 for Part Two. Shakespeare may have written *The Merry Wives of Windsor*, his third Falstaff play, before Part Two, in which case Part Two could plausibly be dated a few months later.[29] We do not know whether the two parts were conceived from the beginning as a single work or whether Part Two was an afterthought or a sequel that Shakespeare devised on the strength of the tremendous popularity of Part One.[30]

No other play of Shakespeare's offers more varied delights than *1 Henry IV* (and Part Two is on almost as high a level). The King, shaken and "wan with care" (One, I, 1, 1), approaches the dignity of a tragic hero. Two young men, Prince Hal and Hotspur, provide a brilliant study in contrasting personalities. Above all, *Henry IV* contains among its dramatis personae a fat and rascally old man of nimble wit who reigns as the king of all comic figures: "that swoll'n parcel of dropsies, that huge bombard of sack, that stuff'd cloakbag of guts" (One, II, 4, 496–498). Who but Sir John Falstaff? To make Shakespeare's achievement even more astonishing, these diverse elements are welded together to form a political commentary of considerable subtlety.[31]

The chief sources are Holinshed's *Chronicles* (1587 ed.) and an anonymous play, *The Famous Victories of Henry the Fifth*, printed in 1589. (The suggestion that *The Famous Victories* is Shakespeare's, perhaps a bad quarto, has received virtually no support.)[32] Shakespeare probably made use of Daniel's *Civil Wars* (1595) and possibly drew upon Edward Hall's *Union of . . . Lancaster and York* (1548) and John Stow's *Chronicles of England* (1580). From Sir Thomas Elyot's *Governour* (1531) he may have derived the popular episode, described in Part Two (V, 2, 68–101), of Prince Hal's imprisonment for boxing the ears of the Lord Chief Justice. In addition to the legend of Wild Prince Hal and his reconciliation with his father Henry IV, the sources provided the main outline of the Percys' rebellion and Hotspur's role therein,[33] as well as (in *The Famous Victories*) a faint sketch of Jockey Oldcastle, the prototype of Falstaff.

As usual, Shakespeare's changes are profoundly important. The historical Hotspur was twenty-three years older than Hal and two years older than Henry IV; Shakespeare makes Hotspur and Hal the same age in order to place them in military and philosophical contrast. Mistress Quickly, hostess of the Boar's Head, scarcely exists in the sources; in Shakespeare she is a fully developed character. In Holinshed the trick whereby the rebels at Gaultree Forest are persuaded to disperse after being promised peace and redress of grievances is attributed to Westmoreland alone; in *2 Henry IV* (IV, 2) it is masterminded by Prince John, Hal's brother, perhaps, as Richard Beck observes, to demonstrate that deception is "almost hereditary" in the royal family. "It is a family characteristic to employ means that are dubious morally to achieve ends that are successful politically."[34] And, of course, Jockey Oldcastle notwithstanding, there is no real precedent for the magnificent Sir John (although Falstaff's name was Sir John Oldcastle in Shakespeare's early versions of the *Henry IV* plays).[35]

In *1* and *2 Henry IV*, King Henry, the crafty Bolingbroke of *Richard II,* is afflicted by a number of disturbances. His major political problem is continuous civil war. In Part One the northern barons, who had helped depose Richard, are led in rebellion by the Earl of Northumberland (who later withdraws) and his son Henry Percy (Hotspur). Together with the Welsh under Owen Glendower and the Scots under Douglas, they plan to strike against "this thorn, this canker, Bolingbroke," who had been planted in place of "Richard, that sweet lovely rose" (One, I, 3, 175–176). In Part Two, with Hotspur dead and the first wave of the insurrection crushed, the Archbishop of York sparks a new uprising to help purge the land of a burning fever. Even as he musters his forces, however, the Archbishop deplores the fickleness of the multitude, formerly enthusiastic in support of Bolingbroke, but now nostalgic for Richard:

> O thou fond Many! with what loud applause
> Didst thou beat heaven with blessing Bolingbroke
> Before he was what thou wouldst have him be!
> And being now trimm'd in thine own desires,
> Thou (beastly feeder) art so full of him
> That thou provok'st thyself to cast him up.
> So, so (thou common dog) didst thou disgorge
> Thy glutton bosom of the royal Richard;
> And now thou wouldst eat thy dead vomit up,
> And howl'st to find it.
>
> (Two, I, 3, 91–100)

To underscore the wildness that overruns the nation, Shakespeare introduces Part Two with a prologue spoken by Rumour, who spreads the false report that Hotspur has defeated the King's armies at Shrewsbury and killed Prince Hal.

Although the King, by fair means or foul, can handle the two rebellions, his conscience is a tougher adversary. During most of Part Two he is sick and, like Macbeth, obsessed by sleeplessness:

> O sleep, O gentle sleep!
> Nature's soft nurse, how have I frighted thee,
> That thou no more wilt weigh my eyelids down
> And steep my senses in forgetfulness?
>
> (Two, III, 1, 5–8)

The lowliest of his subjects, even a humble sailor in the midst of raging storms, can enjoy repose. But not the King! "Uneasy lies the head that wears a crown" (Two, III, 1, 31). Try as he may to preserve the diplomatic fiction that he did not intend to seize the throne but historical necessity so ordered events "that I and greatness were compell'd to kiss" (Two, III, 1, 74), he confesses to Hal on his deathbed that he sinned:

> God knows, my son,
> By what bypaths and indirect crook'd ways
> I met this crown; and I myself know well
> How troublesome it sat upon my head.
> To thee it shall descend with better quiet,
> Better opinion, better confirmation;
> For all the soil of the achievement goes
> With me into the earth.
> (Two, IV, 5, 184–191)

He plans a crusade to the Holy Land to expiate his crime, although he is enough of a politician to know that keeping his enemies occupied abroad would allow them no time to foment a domestic revolution.[36] But, ironically, the only Jerusalem he is permitted to see is the Jerusalem Chamber in his own palace, the room where he dies.

Not the least of King Henry's worries is the conduct of his son (Prince Hal) the Prince of Wales, who has been interpreted as belonging to the prodigal son tradition.[37] We learned in *Richard II* that Henry's "unthrifty son" frequents the London taverns "with unrestrained loose companions" (V, 3, 1–7). In the first scene of *1 Henry IV* the unhappy King expresses his envy of Northumberland, whose son Hotspur "is the theme of honour's tongue" (I, 1, 81):

> O that it could be prov'd
> That some night-tripping fairy had exchang'd
> In cradle clothes our children where they lay,
> And call'd mine Percy, his Plantagenet!
> Then would I have his Harry, and he mine.
> (One, I, 1, 86–90)

He sees Hal repeating the mistake that Richard, "the skipping King" (One, III, 2, 60), had made: He is too much in the public eye. Bolingbroke, on the other hand, had created a more desirable image by rationing his appearances:

> Thus did I keep my person fresh and new,
> My presence, like a robe pontifical,
> Ne'er seen but wond'red at; and so my state,

Seldom but sumptuous, show'd like a feast
And won by rareness such solemnity.
(One, III, 2, 55–59)

While Hal debases himself with low associates, Hotspur is a veritable "Mars in swathling clothes" (One, III, 2, 112), adding luster to the Percy name. The King is so discouraged that he half expects his son to join the insurgents.

Although Hal's performance at the Battle of Shrewsbury brings a temporary reconciliation, Part Two finds father and son again estranged. In a great scene during which so many of the play's interconnected conflicts, public and private, seem to reach a climax,[38] the dying King is deeply grieved when the Prince, thinking him already dead, removes the crown and places it on his own head. Henry berates him in magnificent verse:

Thou hid'st a thousand daggers in thy thoughts,
Which thou hast whetted on thy stony heart
To stab at half an hour of my life.
What, canst thou not forbear me half an hour?
Then get thee gone and dig my grave thyself,
And bid the merry bells ring to thine ear,
That thou art crowned, not that I am dead.
Let all the tears that should bedew my hearse
Be drops of balm to sanctify thy head.
Only compound me with forgotten dust;
Give that which gave thee life unto the worms.
(Two, IV, 5, 107–117)

With such an ingrate on the throne, all order will be dissolved; thieves and murderers will be elevated to high office:

For the Fifth Harry from curb'd license plucks
The muzzle of restraint, and the wild dog
Shall flesh his tooth on every innocent.
(Two, IV, 5, 131–133)

England will again be a wilderness, "peopled with wolves, thy old inhabitants!" (Two, IV, 5, 138). But Prince Hal's explanation (or is it, as John Palmer thinks, part of his consistent pattern of self-justification?)[39] is that he removed the crown to symbolize his father's release from the burdens of kingship. Hal pledges that he will be a worthy sovereign. The King can now face death with a measure of consolation.

The Prince is truly a chip off the old block, and his father need not have worried about him. At the earliest opportunity Hal speaks the famous soliloquy reassuring the audience that he will reform:

I know you all, and will awhile uphold
The unyok'd humour of your idleness.
Yet herein will I imitate the sun,
Who doth permit the base contagious clouds
To smother up his beauty from the world,
That, when he please again to be himself,
Being wanted, he may be more wond'red at
By breaking through the foul and ugly mists
Of vapours that did seem to strangle him.

                              (One, I, 2, 219–227)

It is good strategy, he says, to pay a debt one has not promised; his reformation, coming as a surprise, will be all the more attractive (One, I, 2, 232–241). In a tough-minded analysis of the speech, Robert Ornstein observes that Hal, for tactical purposes, creates the myth of the reckless prince and conceals his assets. "Like a clever Elizabethan shopkeeper, Hal knows how to display the merchandise of his behavior in such a light that it appears richer than it is."[40]

But there is more to Hal's youthful escapades than Machiavellian image making. The Earl of Warwick tells the King that mixing with the riffraff is part of Hal's education:

The Prince but studies his companions
Like a strange tongue, wherein, to gain the language,
'Tis needful that the most immodest word
Be look'd upon and learnt; which once attain'd,
Your Highness knows, comes to no further use
But to be known and hated.

                              (Two, IV, 4, 68–73)

Hal thus demonstrates a political astuteness worthy of a Bolingbroke. From the start, Tillyard says, he maintains toward his tavern friends and others an "ironic detachment"[41] altogether proper for a king who will one day mean business. Moreover, from his tavern adventures he gains an understanding that his father lacked, a quality that will endear him to his subjects and enhance his effectiveness. On the night before the Battle of Agincourt (*Henry V*, IV, 1) he will wander in disguise among his troops, once again exposing himself to the thoughts and feelings of ordinary Englishmen.

The young man to whom the Prince is regularly, and for the most part adversely, compared is one of Shakespeare's most appealing characters. When we first meet Hotspur in *1 Henry IV* (he had appeared in *Richard II*), he is explaining to the King his reason for not surrendering his Scottish prisoners as ordered. (The episode is barely mentioned in

Holinshed.) He is angry because the King sent as his emissary a dandy
who took offense at the sight and smell of a corpse:

> I then, all smarting with my wounds being cold,
> To be so pest'red with a popingay [parrot],
> Out of my grief and my impatience
> Answer'd neglectingly [carelessly], I know not what—
> He should, or he should not; for he made me mad
> To see him shine so brisk, and smell so sweet,
> And talk so like a waiting gentlewoman
> Of guns and drums and wounds—God save the mark!—
> . . . .
> . . . . and but for these vile guns,
> He would himself have been a soldier.
>
>   (One, I, 3, 49–64)

With Lady Percy, his spirited wife, Hotspur playfully pretends that softness is outside his range:

> Away,
> Away, you trifler! Love? I love thee not;
> I care not for thee, Kate. This is no world
> To play with mammets [dolls] and to tilt with lips [kiss].
> We must have bloody noses and crack'd crowns,
> And pass them current too. Gods me, my horse!
>
>   (One, II, 3, 92–97)

Completely lacking in diplomacy, he almost ruins a military conference
by antagonizing Owen Glendower. This colorful Welsh warrior claims
that he is "not in the roll of common men" (One, III, 1, 43), insisting
that at his birth the heavens were on fire and the earth shook with fear.
"Why, so it would have done at the same season," Hotspur replies,
"if your mother's cat had but kitten'd, though you yourself had never
been born" (One, III, 1, 18–20). Glendower's chatter about devils and
prophecies and clip-winged griffins he dismisses as "skimble-skamble
stuff" (One, III, 1, 154) that taxes his patience:

>   O, he is as tedious
> As a tired horse, a railing wife;
> Worse than a smoky house. I had rather live
> With cheese and garlic in a windmill far
> Than feed on cates [delicacies] and have him talk to me
> In any summer house in Christendom.
>
>   (One, III, 1, 159–164)

"In Hotspur," says Mark Van Doren, "Shakespeare has learned at last to make poetry as natural as the human voice."[42] One cannot help liking this volatile and impertinent youth.

But Hotspur, for all his spirit, borders on the ridiculous, as he pursues honor with exaggerated zeal:

> By heaven, methinks it were an easy leap
> To pluck bright honour from the pale-fac'd moon,
> Or dive into the bottom of the deep,
> Where fadom line could never touch the ground,
> And pluck up drowned honour by the locks,
> So he that doth redeem her thence might wear
> Without corrival [partner] all her dignities.
>
> (One, I, 3, 201–207)

(This famous speech is quoted [inaccurately] in Francis Beaumont's satirical play *The Knight of the Burning Pestle* [1607?] as a specimen of "huffing," or blustering.) In the "I know you all" soliloquy, Hal exploits the code of honor as a means to other ends; for Hotspur, honor is valuable in itself.[43]

Mortally wounded at Shrewsbury, Hotspur finally realizes that nothing can endure, not even time itself:

> O Harry, thou hast robb'd me of my youth!
> I better brook the loss of brittle life
> Than those proud titles thou hast won of me.
> They wound my thoughts worse than thy sword my flesh.
> But thoughts the slaves of life, and life time's fool [sport],
> And time, that takes survey of all the world,
> Must have a stop.
>
> (One, V, 4, 77–83)

Insight comes late to Hotspur; one is forced to grant him "the indulgence allowed to those who refuse to grow up."[44]

Several characters point out Hotspur's limitations. For example, Northumberland loses his temper as his son persists in fuming about the prisoners the King took away:

> Why, what a wasp-stung and impatient fool
> Art thou to break into this woman's mood,
> Tying thine ear to no tongue but thine own!
>
> (One, I, 3, 236–238)

Prince Hal offers a parody of his rival:

I am not yet of Percy's mind, the Hotspur of the North; he that kills me some six or seven dozen of Scots at a breakfast, washes his hands, and says to his wife, "Fie upon this quiet life! I want work." "O my sweet Harry," says she, "how many hast thou kill'd to-day?" "Give my roan horse a drench [dose of medicine]," says he, and answers "Some fourteen," an hour after, "a trifle, a trifle."

(One, II, 4, 114–122)

Later, over Hotspur's lifeless body, Hal pronounces an epitaph in which praise is qualified by reproof; the valiant warrior was, after all, a traitor:

> Fare thee well, great heart!
> Ill-weav'd ambition, how much art thou shrunk!
> When that this body did contain a spirit,
> A kingdom for it was too small a bound;
> But now two paces of the vilest earth
> Is room enough. This earth that bears thee dead
> Bears not alive so stout a gentleman.
> ....
> Adieu, and take thy praise with thee to heaven!
> Thy ignominy sleep with thee in the grave,
> But not rememb'red in thy epitaph!

(One, V, 4, 87–101)[45]

And Lord Bardolph notes that Hotspur made a tragic miscalculation at Shrewsbury. He

> lin'd himself with hope,
> Eating the air on promise of supply,
> Flatt'ring himself in project of a power
> Much smaller than the smallest of his thoughts,
> And so, with great imagination,
> Proper to madmen, led his powers to death
> And, winking, leapt into destruction.

(Two, I, 3, 27–33)

Hotspur's most uncompromising, though indirect, critic, is in no hurry to rush into death, with or without honor:

What need I be so forward with him that calls not on me? Well, 'tis no matter; honour pricks me on. Yea, but how if honour prick me off when I come on? How then? Can honour set to a leg? No. Or an arm? No. Or take away the grief of a wound? No. Honour hath no skill in surgery then? No. What is honour? A word. What is that word honour? Air. A trim reckoning! Who hath it? He that died a Wednesday.

(One, V, 1, 129–138)

Inasmuch as the dead can neither feel it nor hear it and since detraction will not suffer it in the living, "therefore I'll none of it" (One, V, 1, 142). This remarkable catechism is a sample of the mind and speech of what Dr. Johnson called the "unimitated, unimitable" Sir John Falstaff.[46] To overrate honor is, for Falstaff, to underrate the most precious of all values, life. "There's honour for you!" he laconically remarks (One, V, 3, 33) over the corpse of the brave Sir Walter Blunt:

> I like not such grinning honour as Sir Walter hath. Give me life; which if I can save, so; if not, honour comes unlook'd for, and there's an end.
>
> (One, V, 3, 62–65)

To Falstaff, war is an abomination. When fighting with Douglas, he falls and pretends to be dead. But did he really dissemble? No, he says. The only way to dissemble is to be a corpse:

> Counterfeit? I lie; I am no counterfeit. To die is to be a counterfeit; for he is but the counterfeit of a man who hath not the life of a man; but to counterfeit dying when a man thereby liveth, is to be no counterfeit, but the true and perfect image of life indeed. The better part of valour is discretion; in the which better part I have saved my life.
>
> (One, V, 4, 113–122)

He has been told that to assemble the pitiful band of rascals who make up his recruits, he must have unloaded the gibbets and impressed the dead bodies into service:

> Tut, tut! good enough to toss [i.e., for cannon fodder]; food for powder, food for powder. They'll fill a pit as well as better. Tush, man, mortal men, mortal men.
>
> (One, IV, 2, 71–74)

They *do* fill a pit. "I have led my rag-of-muffins where they are pepper'd. There's not three of my hundred and fifty left alive; and they are for the town's end, to beg during life" (One, V, 3, 36–40). Against such deflation of military glory Hotspur's heroics cannot stand up. Yet, as Clifford Leech astutely observes, Falstaff and Hotspur, though polar opposites, are alike "in standing away from the cold calculations of the other major figures in the play."[47] That is one reason we find them both so refreshing.

Falstaff's wit holds nothing and nobody sacred, himself and his huge bulk least of all. Before the Gadshill robbery Prince Hal orders "fat-guts" (One, II, 2, 33) to lie down and listen for the footsteps of the intended victims. "Have you any levers to lift me up again, being down?" (One,

II, 2, 36–37). When he is reprimanded for his incessant lying and indebtedness, he protests that Adam's Fall in the state of innocence surely extenuates poor Jack Falstaff's crimes in the days of villainy. "Thou seest I have more flesh than another man, and therefore more frailty" (One, III, 3, 185–189). "God keep lead out of me!" he prays when he finds Sir Walter Blunt dead. "I need no more weight than mine own bowels" (One, V, 3, 35–36). Witty himself, he is also "the cause that wit is in other men," including his tiny page, to whom he remarks, "I do here walk before thee like a sow that hath overwhelm'd all her litter but one" (Two, I, 2, 11–14).

One of Falstaff's outstanding talents is for a special kind of misrepresentation that his enemy the Lord Chief Justice calls "wrenching the true cause the false way" (Two, II, 1, 120–121). Often this takes the form of the corrupter pretending that it is *he* who has been corrupted:

> Thou hast done much harm upon me, Hal—God forgive thee for it! Before I knew thee, Hal, I knew nothing; and now am I, if a man should speak truly, little better than one of the wicked.
>
> (One, I, 2, 102–106)

Life is trying for one whose voice has become cracked from singing anthems (Two, I, 2, 212–213). "Is there no virtue extant?" (One, II, 4, 132) he tearfully asks:

> Go thy ways, old Jack, die when thou wilt; if manhood, good manhood, be not forgot upon the face of the earth, then am I a shotten herring [a herring without its roe]. There lives not three good men unhang'd in England; and one of them is fat, and grows old. God help the while! A bad world, I say.
>
> (One, II, 4, 141–147)

We have no business liking Falstaff, but the fat rogue charms us. In the robbery at Gadshill, itself a parody of the "heroic" action depicted in the main plot, Falstaff behaves really badly: He and three others rob a band of travelers, only to be set upon, stripped, and put to ignominious flight by Prince Hal and Ned Poins, who are disguised. The Prince and Poins anticipate with delight how at the Boar's Head Falstaff will embellish the episode, and Sir John does not disappoint them. He displays his hacked sword and pierced doublet, and to demonstrate his prodigious courage, he exaggerates the number and strength of his "assailants." When it is revealed that the four had been overcome by a meager two, Falstaff agilely shifts his ground to transform retreat into moral victory:

By the Lord, I knew ye as well as he that made ye. Why, hear you, my masters. Was it for me to kill the heir apparent? Should I turn upon the true prince? Why, thou knowest I am as valiant as Hercules; but beware instinct. The lion will not touch the true prince. Instinct is a great matter. I was now a coward on instinct. I shall think the better of myself, and thee, during my life—I for a valiant lion, and thou for a true prince.

(One, II, 4, 295–304)

He displays similar resourcefulness when, after defaming the Prince to the whore Doll Tearsheet, he learns that the Prince overheard him. "I disprais'd him before the wicked," he explains, "that the wicked might not fall in love with him; in which doing, I have done the part of a careful friend and a true subject.... No abuse, Hal." (Two, II, 4, 346–350).

All the wit in the world, however, cannot save Falstaff from repudiation when Prince Hal becomes Henry V. For better or for worse, perpetual holiday is unthinkable in a king; sensuality must yield to discipline.[48] Hal has been likened to the folk hero who expels his antitypes and absorbs their strength,[49] and D. J. Palmer has argued that the "I know you all" soliloquy, like the play as a whole, is rich in biblical allusions to the casting out of the Old Adam and the re-creation of the Prince as New Man.[50]

Shakespeare paves the way for Falstaff's banishment, not simply in the "I know you all" speech, but in the structure of the play itself. In an extemporaneous dramatic skit at the Boar's Head, Falstaff assumes the role of Henry IV while the Prince plays himself. In a superb parody of the highly polished Elizabethan prose style known as euphuism,[51] Falstaff warns his "son" against all his companions but one, a fat, virtuous man of noble carriage:

And now I remember me, his name is Falstaff. If that man should be lewdly given, he deceiveth me; for, Harry, I see virtue in his looks. If then the tree may be known by the fruit, as the fruit by the tree, then, peremptorily I speak it, there is virtue in that Falstaff.

(One, II, 4, 467–473)

But when the two change roles, we get a foretaste of what will happen. Acting the part of his father, Prince Hal condemns the "old white-bearded Satan"; Falstaff has to plead for mercy:

No, my good lord. Banish Peto, banish Bardolph, banish Poins; but for sweet Jack Falstaff, kind Jack Falstaff, true Jack Falstaff, valiant Jack Falstaff, and therefore more valiant being, as he is, old Jack Falstaff, banish not him thy Harry's company, banish not him thy Harry's company. Banish plump Jack, and banish all the world!

(One, II, 4, 520–527)

"I do, I will" (One, II, 4, 528) is Hal's ominous reply.[52]

There are other omens. In the last act of Part One, Hal stands over the body of Hotspur, who is really dead, and over the body of Falstaff, who is pretending. This is a remarkable tableau of Hal and "the two half-men whom he has transcended."[53] After pronouncing his epitaph for Hotspur, he spies Falstaff and delivers a second valediction:

> What, old acquaintance? Could not all this flesh
> Keep in a little life? Poor Jack, farewell!
> I could have better spar'd a better man.
> O, I should have a heavy miss of thee
> If I were much in love with vanity!
> (One, V, 4, 102–106)

Here again is a private rehearsal for one of Henry V's first public actions. In Part Two, while the fat knight's capers are as funny as in Part One, the Prince no longer participates. The characters, especially Hal and Falstaff, become increasingly isolated and self-enclosed.[54] Shakespeare turns moral necessity into artistic virtue by surrounding Falstaff with a variety of new comic foils: the earthy Doll Tearsheet; Pistol, full of swagger and bombast, that roguish exaggeration (says Leslie Hotson) of every man's fantasy that he is eloquent and bold;[55] and old Justice Shallow. But there is a dark quality about Part Two (there is no young Hotspur to generate excitement), and the atmosphere seems to affect Falstaff himself.[56] Shallow constantly offers his rambling recollections of youthful adventures that probably never happened, memories that Falstaff compresses into a bittersweet "We have heard the chimes at midnight, Master Shallow" (Two, III, 2, 228–229).

Hal's final rejection of Falstaff is one of the most famous moments in all literature, and it evokes a mixed reaction. There is something both funny and sad in the spectacle of the old reprobate tearing himself away from dinner with Justice Shallow, saddling his horse, and rushing off to the new king filled with expectation. "I am Fortune's steward," he declares:

> I know the young king is sick for me. Let us take any man's horses; the laws of England are at my commandment. Blessed are they that have been my friends, and woe to my Lord Chief Justice!
> (Two, V, 3, 136–144)

But when Falstaff arrives breathless at the King's train, he is instead spurned, preached at, and sentenced to prison by a Hal who no longer chooses to recognize him:

I know thee not, old man. Fall to thy prayers.
How ill white hairs become a fool and jester!
I have long dreamt of such a kind of man,
So surfeit-swell'd, so old, and so profane;
But being awak'd, I do despise my dream.
Make less thy body, hence, and more thy grace;
Leave gormandizing. Know the grave doth gape
For thee thrice wider than for other men.
Reply not to me with a fool-born jest.
Presume not that I am the thing I was;
For God doth know (so shall the world perceive)
That I have turn'd away my former self;
So will I those that kept me company.

                    (Two, V, 5, 51–63)

The welfare of England demands that Henry V rid himself of "the tutor and the feeder of my riots" (Two, V, 5, 66), and Shakespeare, as we have seen, dutifully prepares us along the way to accept Falstaff's public humiliation. But not even Shakespeare can make us like it.

In 1774 Maurice Morgann, in a work of deep affection, argued that Falstaff was really not a coward but a hero. Many critics (notably Bradley) have followed Morgann in idealizing the fat knight and deploring his banishment. Falstaff, says Michael Goldman, somehow embodies the English glory that he undermines; he is also our own body, in all its vulnerability, and we are protective toward him. "There we feel," John Bailey writes, "but for the grace of God, and but for our own inherent weakness and stupidity, go we." Clifford Leech declares that "to send Falstaff to the Fleet [prison] is to put human nature in chains that must be broken." "It is we who have been rejected," Richard Beck observes. Roy Battenhouse identifies Falstaff with the tradition of the Christian Fool. W. H. Auden goes even further, viewing Falstaff as "a comic symbol for the supernatural order of charity."[57]

Other critics have been less sympathetic. "No man," Dr. Johnson wrote (1765), "is more dangerous than he that with a will to corrupt, hath the power to please." In reacting against Morgann's position, scholars have linked Falstaff with certain comic stereotypes, many of them more or less contemptible, that were a familiar part of the literary tradition in which Shakespeare flourished. For example, Dover Wilson and Bernard Spivack trace Falstaff's ancestry to the morality Vice. E. E. Stoll regards him as the *miles gloriosus,* or braggart soldier, of Roman comedy. For C. L. Barber, he is the Lord of Misrule and, in the end, the Scapegoat carrying off bad luck for the community. Like Battenhouse, Walter Kaiser examines him against the background of the wise Fool, particularly Stultitia, in Erasmus's *Praise of Folly* (1509), although, unlike Stultitia (according to Kaiser), Falstaff is not endowed with Christian significance.[58]

One may venture the suggestion that many critics, whether they approach Falstaff admiringly or moralistically, do so too solemnly. To be sure, Shakespeare inherited the tradition that Henry V led a wild life before ascending the throne, when his responsibilities as king no doubt required him to cast off the excesses of youth. It is equally true that Shakespeare was familiar with a wide range of comic characters in classical and early English drama and that Falstaff incorporates a number of well-established theatrical conventions. But as was his wont, Shakespeare created neither a moral abstraction nor a bloodless stage type but a complex human being. No matter how one interprets Falstaff, the fact remains that he dominates the action, and we care for him more than for the efficient politicians like Prince John, or perhaps even Prince Hal, who carry the day. In the words of a contemporary editor, "he blows through the play like a great gust of laughter and comes within an ace of turning Shakespeare's history of Henry IV into the comedy of Falstaff."[59]

HENRY V

A bad quarto of *Henry V* appeared in 1600 and was twice reprinted; the full text was not published until the 1623 Folio. The date can be fixed with some certainty, for the Chorus preceding Act V contains an explicit reference to the Earl of Essex's departure for Ireland in March 1599.[60] The epilogue to *2 Henry IV* promises a continuation of the story (with Falstaff in it), and *Henry V* must have followed fairly soon after that play. In addition to the ubiquitous Holinshed, Shakespeare probably used *The Famous Victories of Henry V* (see p. 246), possibly a corrupt version of an earlier lost play.[61]

It may come as a surprise that much of the important action in *Henry V* is narrated by a chorus that appears before each act and at the conclusion of the play. But *Henry V* may be viewed as a bold experiment in which Shakespeare applies to the stage a number of literary techniques traditionally associated with epic poetry.[62] Although the subject in general may lend itself to this treatment, Shakespeare's commitment to the epic manner means that he must sometimes forgo the opportunity to develop the drama through the interaction of characters.

The epic note is first sounded in the Prologue, which, like the opening of the *Iliad* or the *Aeneid,* is a magnificent invocation of supernatural aid:

O for a Muse of fire, that would ascend
The brightest heaven of invention,
A kingdom for a stage, princes to act,
And monarchs to behold the swelling scene!
                        (Prologue, 1–4)

The Elizabethan playhouse cannot encompass the exalted events:

> Can this cockpit hold
> The vasty fields of France? Or may we cram
> Within this wooden O the very casques
> That did affright the air at Agincourt?
> (Prologue, 11–14)

"Play with your fancies," we are later urged (III, Chorus, 7), not, as some (among them Granville-Barker) would have us believe, because Shakespeare feels the need to apologize,[63] but because he has adopted the long-standing ritual whereby the epic poet acknowledges his subject to be above his mortal powers. Michael Goldman has characterized the tone of the Chorus and Henry as one of constant straining, a quality appropriate in a play about a king rousing himself and his people to superhuman efforts.[64]

Throughout the play the Chorus sustains the epic mood, describes what has happened or is about to happen, and offers interpretations designed to shape our responses. A case in point is the Chorus at the beginning of Act II. After reporting with pride that "all the youth of England are on fire" (II, Chorus, 1) for battle, it laments the fact that three of Henry's close associates have been corrupted and are plotting his death (II, Chorus, 20–30). This prepares us for the fine scene (II, 2) in the council chamber (in Southampton) where the King dramatically confronts and sentences the traitors. The Chorus preceding Act IV draws a contrast between "the confident and over-lusty French" (IV, Chorus, 18) and "the poor condemned English" (IV, Chorus, 22) who are outnumbered. But it is filled with admiration for the noble "Harry," who in one of the play's most memorable scenes (IV, 1) will move about incognito among his troops:

> O, now, who will behold
> The royal captain of this ruin'd band
> Walking from watch to watch, from tent to tent,
> Let him cry "Praise and glory on his head!"
> For forth he goes and visits all his host,
> Bids them good morrow with a modest smile
> And calls them brothers, friends, and countrymen.
> . . . .
> That every wretch, pining and pale before,
> Beholding him, plucks comfort from his looks.
> A largess universal, like the sun,
> His liberal eye doth give to every one,
> Thawing cold fear. Then, mean and gentle all,
> Behold, as may unworthiness define,
> A little touch of Harry in the night.
> (IV, Chorus, 28–47)

Henry V resembles a narrative poem, with the Chorus providing continuity for the plot and with the individual episodes that are dramatized on the stage reinforcing points already made. The classical epic plunges *in medias res* (in the middle of things) and, in the course of its story, looks backward and forward. By employing the Chorus as he does, Shakespeare approximates the method of Homer, Virgil, the *Beowulf* poet, and Milton.

Further evidence that *Henry V* is the dramatic equivalent of an epic may be found in the character of the King himself. Henry's conduct is in large measure derived from precepts found in Renaissance military books.[65] He is frequently idealized as the "mirror of all Christian kings" (II, Chorus, 6), the "Star of England" (Epilogue, 6) who guides his country through a brief interlude of glory between two long stretches of civil war and shame.[66] While tragic heroes are usually tormented by doubts, Harry impresses us as "a man of action who is uncritical about his own assumptions."[67] Unlike Shakespeare's other royal protagonists, he is preeminently successful. He wants to do everything right; or, perhaps more accurately, he wishes at all times to appear just. Henry invades France only after the Archbishop of Canterbury's involved discourse on the Salique Law (I, 2, 33–114) has convinced him and his courtiers that he may "with right and conscience" (I, 2, 96) lay claim to the French throne. Before condemning the three traitors to death, he pardons a drunk who had railed against his person (II, 2, 39–43). Not until the French violate the law of arms and kill the English boys does he order his men to kill their prisoners (IV, 7, 58–68). Moreover, he tries to expiate his father's sin against God's anointed deputy Richard II, and on the eve of the Battle of Agincourt he humbly prays:

> Not to-day, O Lord,
> O, not to-day, think not upon the fault
> My father made in compassing the crown!
> I Richard's body have interred new;
> And on it have bestowed more contrite tears
> Than from it issued forced drops of blood.
> (IV, 1, 309–314)

Henry takes kingship seriously, as is revealed in the soliloquy spoken after he, disguised as "Harry le Roy," mingles with his men:

> Upon the King! Let us our lives, our souls,
> Our debts, our careful wives,
> Our children, and our sins, lay on the King!
> We must bear all. O hard condition,
> Twin-born with greatness, subject to the breath
> Of every fool, whose sense no more can feel
> But his own wringing! What infinite heart's-ease
> Must kings neglect that private men enjoy!
> (IV, 1, 247–254)

Unlike Richard II, who was aware only of the trappings of kingship, Henry accepts the responsibilities of his sacred office without over-valuing the "idol ceremony" that is his due (IV, 1, 257).[68]

It may be difficult for us to warm up to Henry, partly, as Alfred Harbage has put it, "because we are not sixteenth-century Englishmen convinced of the heavenly obligation to reduce France to a shambles."[69] Nevertheless, Shakespeare intends to portray him as a good king in peace as in war. This is one of the themes of Henry's stirring exhortation at Harfleur:

> Once more unto the breach, dear friends, once more;
> Or close the wall up with our English dead!
> In peace there's nothing so becomes a man
> As modest stillness and humility;
> But when the blast of war blows in our ears,
> Then imitate the action of the tiger:
> Stiffen the sinews, summon up the blood,
> Disguise fair nature with hard-favour'd rage;
> Then lend the eye a terrible aspect . . . .
> . . . .
> Now set the teeth and stretch the nostril wide,
> Hold hard the breath and bend up every spirit
> To his full height!
>
>   (III, 1, 1–17)

Henry credits his success at Agincourt to God alone:

>   O God, thy arm was here!
> And not to us, but to thy arm alone,
> Ascribe we all! When, without stratagem,
> But in plain shock and even play of battle,
> Was ever known so great and little loss
> On one part and on th' other? Take it, God,
> For it is only thine!
>
>   (IV, 8, 111–117)

It is an additional sign of his exemplary rule that he was able to unite English, Welsh, Irish, and Scottish forces (represented respectively by Gower, Fluellen, Macmorris, and Jamy) into a single national army with a firm purpose. As E. E. Stoll has astutely commented, Henry fulfills the English people's "notion of their hero king."[70]

But is he Shakespeare's hero king? Although Henry has been stoutly defended as warrior and statesman,[71] there are those who feel that the dramatist views him with ambivalence, if not outright disapproval. It has been suggested that the Archbishop's public justification of Henry's claim to the French throne was contrived by the King as sanction for the invasion of France, an immoral course of action that he has already decided to adopt.[72] Similar doubts have been expressed concerning Henry's decision to kill the French prisoners: The text leaves unanswered the question of whether he acts out of military necessity or out of a savage lust for revenge.[73] And the speech he delivers to the citizens of Harfleur, in which he threatens to destroy the city if they do not yield, is barbaric, even if construed as a rhetorical ploy:

> ... why, in a moment look to see
> The blind and bloody soldier with foul hand
> Defile the locks of your shrill-shrieking daughters;
> Your fathers taken by the silver beards,
> And their most reverend heads dash'd to the walls;
> Your naked infants spitted upon pikes,
> Whiles the mad mothers with their howls confus'd
> Do break the clouds, as did the wives of Jewry
> At Herod's bloody-hunting slaughtermen.
>   (III, 3, 33–41)[74]

Even the courtship scene, which one would assume to be a comic and lighthearted aftermath to the terrible war,[75] raises problems. Shakespeare may indeed be extracting humor from the discomfort of King Henry, the epitome of the vigorous English soldier, trying to speak the language of love to the sophisticated Princess Katherine of France, particularly in view of the language barrier between them. But what is one to make of the following exchange?

> *Katherine:* Is it possible dat I sould love de ennemie of France?
> *King Henry:* No, it is not possible you should love the enemy of France, Kate; but in loving me you should love the friend of France; for I love France so well that I will not part with a village of it—I will have it all mine.
>   (V, 2, 178–184)

Hugh Richmond detects in Henry's tone a curious echo of Richard's insidious seduction of Anne (*Richard III,* I, 2), and Manheim sees the courtship as yet another Machiavellian stratagem.[76] It is entirely possible, as several critics have pointed out, that *Henry V* starts out as a patriotic play but ends up as a satire on war and heroism. More likely, however, the play is another superb example of Shakespeare's sense of the complexity of human experience. He can depict a great warrior king without losing sight of the horrors of war or of the irony inherent in the conduct of the hero himself.[77] That too is in keeping with the spirit of the Homeric epic.

The comedy in the play—aside from Princess Katherine's delightful English lesson (III, 4), with its bawdy innuendoes, and the wooing scene—is provided chiefly by the fiery Welsh officer Fluellen, who laments in his special brand of fractured English that modern soldiers ignore true military discipline. Deploring loud talk, he assures Captain Gower that Pompey the Great faithfully preserved "the true and aunchient prerogatifes and laws of the wars . . . . You shall find, I warrant you, that there is no tiddle taddle nor pibble pabble in Pompey's camp" (IV, 1, 67–72). With an amazing show of logic (what a parody of scholarly research!) he argues that Henry V is like "Alexander the Pig [Big]" (IV, 7, 14). Was not Alexander born in Macedon and Henry in Monmouth, Wales?

> I tell you, Captain, if you look in the maps of the orld, I warrant you sall find, in the comparisons between Macedon and Monmouth, that the situations, look you, is both alike. There is a river in Macedon, and there is also moreover a river at Monmouth. It is call'd Wye at Monmouth; but it is out of my prains what is the name of the other river. But 'tis all one; 'tis alike as my fingers is to my fingers, and there is salmons in both.
>
> (IV, 7, 24–33)

Fluellen further recalls that, just as Alexander killed his best friend Cleitus "being in his ales and his cups," so Henry, "being in his right wits and his good judgments, turn'd away the fat knight with the great belly doublet" (IV, 7, 47–51); Fluellen has forgotten his name.

As noted above, Falstaff himself is not a character in *Henry V*, although the epilogue to *2 Henry IV* had promised the audience that he *would* be "if you be not too much cloy'd with fat meat" (*2 Henry IV*, Epilogue, 27–28). Perhaps Shakespeare felt that his presence in France would detract from the King's achievements. Nevertheless, Falstaff's death, as reported by Mistress Quickly, is one of the peaks of dramatic literature; and Shakespeare may have included it to remind us that, in the words of one critic, "to avoid being the weak king, Henry had to muffle his human qualities."[78] "The King has kill'd his heart," Mistress Quickly says of the ailing Sir John (II, 1, 92–93), and with customary pomposity the braggart Pistol agrees that Falstaff's heart is "fracted and corroborate" (II, 1, 130). In Mistress Quickly's account of how Falstaff in his last minutes on earth fumbled with the sheets and "babbled of green fields" (see p. 43), Shakespeare maintains just the right balance between tenderness and humor:

> "How now, Sir John?" quoth I. "What, man? be o' good cheer." So 'a cried out, "God, God, God!" three or four times. Now I, to comfort him, bid him 'a should not think of God; I hop'd there was no need to trouble himself with any such thoughts yet. So 'a bade me lay more clothes on his

feet. I put my hand into the bed and felt them, and they were as cold as any stone. Then I felt to his knees, and so upward and upward, and all was as cold as any stone.

(II, 3, 18–28)

"They say he cried out of [repented] sack," says Corporal Nym. "Ay, that 'a did," Mistress Quickly agrees. "And of women," Bardolph suggests. "Nay, that 'a did not," she indignantly *dis*agrees, certain that for this vice Falstaff could never have felt regret. "Yes, that 'a did," a young boy insists, "and said they were devils incarnate." Mistress Quickly changes the subject with a pun. " 'A could never abide carnation; 'twas a colour he never lik'd" (II, 3, 29–36). And off go Pistol, Nym, and Bardolph to the wars. Life continues as usual, which is just the way Falstaff would have wanted it.

HENRY VIII

The only text of *Henry VIII*, a very good one, is that in the 1623 Folio. The principal sources are the 1587 edition of Holinshed's *Chronicles* and John Foxe's *Acts and Monuments* (1597), a popular book about Protestant martyrdom. At what may have been the first performance of this play, perhaps Shakespeare's final work for the stage, the Globe playhouse burned to the ground. Sir Henry Wotton, who was present on that occasion (June 29, 1613), wrote about it in a letter to his nephew, Sir Edmund Bacon (July 2, 1613):

The King's players had a new play, called *All is True*, representing some principal pieces of the reign of Henry VIII, which was set forth with many extraordinary circumstances of pomp and majesty.... Now, King Henry making a masque at the Cardinal Wolsey's house, and certain chambers being shot off at his entry, some of the paper, or other stuff, wherewith one of them was stopped, did light on the thatch, where being thought at first but an idle smoke, and their eyes more attentive to the show, it kindled inwardly, and ran round like a train, consuming within less than an hour the whole house to the very grounds. This was the fatal period [end] of that virtuous fabric, wherein yet nothing did perish but wood and straw, and a few forsaken cloaks.[79]

One man "had his breeches set on fire, that would perhaps have broiled him, if he had not by the benefit of a provident wit put it out with bottle ale." There is little doubt that the play referred to is *Henry VIII*. Three times the prologue insists upon the "truth" of what is to follow, and *All Is True* was probably an alternative title.[80]

Henry VIII has received insufficient attention from critics; scholarship has been concerned almost exclusively with the so-called authorship problem. The play was included without comment in the Folio, and there is no external evidence for supposing that Shakespeare did not write it in its entirety. Nevertheless, the prevailing opinion, at least until fairly recently, has been that *Henry VIII* is largely the work of John Fletcher (1570–1625), with Shakespeare receiving credit for only a few sections: I, 1 and 2; II, 3 and 4; III, 2, 1–203; and V, 1. This is not the place to take a stand on an issue that is still debated, although the pendulum seems to be swinging back to a belief in Shakespeare's undivided authorship. But it may be noted that the arguments advanced for collaboration with Fletcher (for example, the higher incidence in the Fletcherian scenes of feminine endings, of *'em* as opposed to *them*, and of *has* rather than *hath*) amount to little more than vague impressions reinforced by statistical tabulations of questionable value. Moreover, a number of passages allegedly written by Fletcher (Cranmer's prophecy [V, 5, 15–63] at the christening of the infant Queen Elizabeth is a case in point) reveal a level of poetic mastery perhaps beyond the reach of any Elizabethan dramatist other than Shakespeare.[81]

A major theme of the play is "mutability in high places."[82] The prologue promises tragedy in the medieval tradition, whereby men of high renown are suddenly plummeted to ruin:

> Think you see them great,
> And follow'd with the general throng, and sweat
> Of thousand friends. Then, in a moment, see
> How soon this mightiness meets misery.
> (Prologue, 27–30)

Much of the action consists of an "anthology of falls" in the tradition of Boccaccio's *De Casibus* (see p. 159) and *The Mirror for Magistrates*.[83] First to be undermined is the Duke of Buckingham, caught in the net of Cardinal Wolsey's intrigue while preparing to expose him to the King. But the two most impressive victims are the unfortunate Katherine of Aragon, whom Henry, with Wolsey's support, divorces to marry Anne Bullen (Boleyn); and, finally, Wolsey himself, who alienates the King by plotting to thwart the new marriage.

Katherine exhibits a strong character. She speaks out against the unjust taxes for which Wolsey is responsible (I, 2, 18–29) and denounces the corrupt surveyor who, at Wolsey's instigation, accuses Buckingham of treason (I, 2, 171–176). At her trial, convened so that her marriage with Henry may be nullified, she boldly challenges Wolsey's authority; as her enemy, the man who has blown the coal of dissension between husband and wife, the Cardinal dare not act as her judge:

> Y'are meek and humble-mouth'd;
> You sign your place and calling, in full seeming,

With meekness and humility; but your heart
Is cramm'd with arrogancy, spleen, and pride.
                    (II, 4, 107–110)

Upon learning from the gentleman usher, Griffith, that Wolsey has been overthrown and that in his downfall he "found the blessedness of being little" (IV, 2, 66), she summons the strength to forgive him:

Whom I most hated living, thou [Griffith] hast made me,
With thy religious truth and modesty,
Now, in his ashes honour. Peace be with him!
                    (IV, 2, 73–75)

Unlike the proud figures in Shakespeare's earlier histories who go down to defeat with a curse on their lips, Katherine—and, for that matter, Buckingham and Wolsey, too—can accept with equanimity whatever fate may decree. Katherine dies without rancor:

                Remember me
In all humility unto his Highness.
Say his long trouble now is passing
Out of this world. Tell him in death I bless'd him,
For so I will. Mine eyes grow dim. Farewell,
My lord.
. . . .
                Although unqueen'd, yet like
A queen, and daughter to a king, inter me.
I can no more.
                    (IV, 2, 160–173)

"Nothing but death," she had said earlier, "shall e'er divorce my dignities" (III, 1, 141–142), and, indeed, she remains a queen to the end.

It is Wolsey, however, who learns most from personal disaster and who manages to achieve rare heights of eloquence.[84] When the King has found him out, Wolsey realizes his doom:

I have touch'd the highest point of all my greatness,
And from that full meridian of my glory
I haste now to my setting. I shall fall
Like a bright exhalation in the evening,
And no man see me more.
                    (III, 2, 223–227)

His soliloquy on his fall is justly famous:

Farewell, a long farewell to all my greatness!
This is the state of man: to-day he puts forth
The tender leaves of hopes; to-morrow blossoms
And bears his blushing honours thick upon him;
The third day comes a frost, a killing frost,
And when he thinks, good easy man, full surely
His greatness is a-ripening, nips his root,
And then he falls, as I do. I have ventur'd,
Like little wanton boys that swim on bladders,
This many summers in a sea of glory;
But far beyond my depth.

>   (III, 2, 351–361)

But he assures his servant Cromwell that now he is truly happy:

I know myself now, and I feel within me
A peace above all earthly dignities,
A still and quiet conscience. The King has cur'd me—
I humbly thank his Grace—and from these shoulders,
These ruin'd pillars, out of pity taken
A load would sink a navy—too much honour.

>   (III, 2, 378–383)

In his final speech Wolsey, who throughout his career had amassed earthly possessions, leaves everything to his sovereign:

There take an inventory of all I have
To the last penny. 'Tis the King's. My robe,
And my integrity to heaven, is all
I dare now call mine own. O Cromwell, Cromwell!
Had I but serv'd my God with half the zeal
I serv'd my king, he would not in mine age
Have left me naked to mine enemies.

>   (III, 2, 451–457)

Having gained the inestimable prize of self-knowledge, Wolsey approaches the stature of a Shakespearean tragic hero.

Despite the catastrophes that overtake its great personages, *Henry VIII* is chiefly memorable not as a tragedy but as a "series of magnificent shows."[85] The pageantry reaches a climax in the birth of Elizabeth, England's finest daughter. Consequently, Henry and Anne, whatever view historians may take of their romance, are portrayed sympathetically in Shakespeare's play. Henry is an able king, aware of his responsibilities to his subjects and apparently sincere when he professes a bad conscience regarding the propriety of his marriage to Katherine (II, 4, 170–209). Anne, for her part, is depicted not as an opportunist but as a simple girl summoned by powers beyond her control to fulfill a lofty destiny. Early in the play the Lord Chamberlain predicts that Anne may bring glory to England:

> Beauty and honour in her are so mingled
> That they have caught the King; and who knows yet
> But from this lady may proceed a gem
> To lighten all this isle?
>
> (II, 3, 76–79)

This hope comes to fruition with the birth of Elizabeth, who even in the cradle gives promise of "a thousand thousand blessings" (V, 5, 20) for generations to come. There are few speeches in Shakespeare to match the inspired tribute offered by Archbishop Cranmer at her baptism, and it is fitting that on this auspicious occasion the words should echo the beautifully simple cadences of the Bible:

> Truth shall nurse her,
> Holy and heavenly thoughts still counsel her.
> She shall be lov'd and fear'd. Her own shall bless her;
> Her foes shake like a field of beaten corn
> And hang their heads with sorrow. Good grows with her.
> In her days every man shall eat in safety
> Under his own vine what he plants, and sing
> The merry songs of peace to all his neighbours.
>
> (V, 5, 29–36)

Cranmer's prophecy extends beyond the lifetime of Elizabeth to include her successor, James I:

> Nor shall this peace sleep with her; but as when
> The bird of wonder dies, the maiden phoenix,
> Her ashes new create another heir
> As great in admiration as herself,
> So shall she leave her blessedness to one
> (When heaven shall call her from this cloud of darkness)
> Who from the sacred ashes of her honour
> Shall starlike rise, as great in fame as she was,
> And so stand fix'd. Peace, plenty, love, truth, terror,
> That were the servants to this chosen infant,
> Shall then be his and like a vine grow to him.
>
> (V, 5, 40–50)[86]

Having presented in a series of histories what has seemed an almost continuous record of disorder and bloodshed, Shakespeare at long last envisions redemption. This is a fitting note on which to end his survey of English history.[87]

There has been a growing tendency in recent years to link *Henry VIII* with Shakespeare's dramatic romances rather than with his histories. Here (as in *Pericles, Cymbeline, The Winter's Tale,* and *The Tempest*) one detects a strong element of masque and processional; a movement toward the symbolic; a major emphasis upon such themes as restoration, justice and injustice, the regeneration of the old by the new, forgiveness, and patience in adversity. According to some critics, Shakespeare, having progressed from the time-bound concerns of history to the timeless world of romance, now chooses to turn back to history so that he may give a new substance to the moral values expounded in the romances. In the words of Howard Felperin, *Henry VIII* thus becomes "a Christian history play," "a metaphysical drama being enacted before men's eyes."[88] In any case, Shakespeare has created a history play with a difference. "Perhaps," to quote the New Arden editor, "*Henry VIII* should be thought of as the last innovation of a mind forever exploring."[89]

NOTES

1. For a discussion of Shakespeare and Tudor historiography, see the introduction to chapter 5 (pp. 128–130).
2. On the political allegory, see Lily B. Campbell, *Shakespeare's "Histories": Mirrors of Elizabethan Policy* (San Marino, Calif.: The Huntington Library, 1947), pp. 169–181.
3. On the text, see the New Cambridge *Richard II,* ed. John Dover Wilson (Cambridge: Cambridge University Press, 1939), pp. vii–x, 107–114; Richard E. Hasker, "The Copy for the First Folio *Richard II,*" *Studies in Bibliography* 5 (1952–1953): 53–72; the New Variorum edition, ed. Matthew W. Black (Philadelphia: Lippincott, 1955), pp. 355–391; and the New Arden edition, ed. Peter Ure (Cambridge: Harvard University Press, 1956), pp. xiii–xxix. On the date, see E. K. Chambers, *William Shakespeare: A Study of Facts and Problems,* 2 vols. (Oxford: Clarendon, 1930), 1:351 ff., 2: 323–327; the New Variorum, pp. 393–395; and the New Arden, pp. xxix–xxx.
4. A. L. French, "*Richard II* and the Woodstock Murder," *Shakespeare Quarterly* 22 (1971): 337–344. *Woodstock,* which has been edited by A. P. Rossiter (London: Chatto & Windus, 1946), clarifies several points that are obscure in Shakespeare. For example, Richard becomes "landlord of England" (II, 1, 113) by farming out the realm to his favorites; they assume power of taxation in exchange for paying the king a monthly rental of £7,000. Richard also issues "blank charters": Tax returns would be signed "blank" so that the collector could fill in the income. See I, 4, 42–52.
5. See R. A. Law, "Deviations from Holinshed in *Richard II,*" *Texas Studies*

in English 29 (1950): 91–101; the New Variorum, pp. 405–505; the New Arden, pp. xxx–li; Geoffrey Bullough, *Narrative and Dramatic Sources of Shakespeare*, 8 vols. (New York: Columbia University Press, 1957–1975), 3: 353–491.

6. But Nicholas Brooke, *Shakespeare's Early Tragedies* (London: Methuen, 1968), pp. 107–137, argues that Richard is a strong king at first and that his weakness emerges later.

7. E. M. W. Tillyard, *Shakespeare's History Plays* (London: Chatto & Windus, 1944), p. 253.

8. W. Gordon Zeeveld, *The Temper of Shakespeare's Thought* (New Haven: Yale University Press, 1974), p. 41. Zeeveld (pp. 1–73) discusses the political and ecclesiastical background of ceremony in the *Richard II–Henry V* plays.

9. See Derek Traversi, *Shakespeare: From Richard II to Henry V* (Stanford, Calif.: Stanford University Press, 1957), pp. 12–48 passim.

10. Donald A. Stauffer, *Shakespeare's World of Images: The Development of His Moral Ideas* (New York: Norton, 1949), p. 93.

11. On the Gaunt-Bolingbroke scene, see James Winny, *The Player King: A Theme of Shakespeare's Histories* (New York: Barnes & Noble, 1968), pp. 70–72.

12. Maynard Mack, Jr., *Killing the King: Three Studies in Shakespeare's Tragic Structure* (New Haven: Yale University Press, 1973), pp. 15–19.

13. But one should remember that in the early plays mental and emotional anguish is always accompanied by rhetorical heightening and wordplay; see R. F. Hill, "Dramatic Techniques and Interpretation in *Richard II*," in *Early Shakespeare*, eds. John Russell Brown and Bernard Harris, Stratford-upon-Avon Studies 3 (London: Edward Arnold, 1961), pp. 101–121.

14. John R. Elliott, Jr., "History and Tragedy in *Richard II*," *Studies in English Literature, 1500–1900* 8 (1968): 253–271.

15. See Robert Rentoul Reed, Jr., *Richard II: From Mask to Prophet,* The Pennsylvania State University Studies no. 25 (University Park, 1968), p. 29. For a good discussion of divine right and legitimacy, see Moody E. Prior, *The Drama of Power: Studies in Shakespeare's History Plays* (Evanston, Ill.: Northwestern University Press, 1973), pp. 139–155.

16. A. R. Humphreys, *Shakespeare: Richard II* (London: Edward Arnold, 1967), p. 45. York's dilemma is ably described by Robert Ornstein, *A Kingdom for a Stage: The Achievement of Shakespeare's History Plays* (Cambridge: Harvard University Press, 1972), pp. 114–124.

17. The twin nature of kingship, a medieval notion, is the subject of Ernst H. Kantorowicz, *The King's Two Bodies: A Study in Medieval Political Theology* (Princeton: Princeton University Press, 1957); see pp. 24–41 for a perceptive analysis of *Richard II* from this point of view. See also Reed, *Richard II,* pp. 33–57 and Humphreys, *Shakespeare: Richard II,* pp. 34–38.

18. See Karl F. Thompson, "Richard II, Martyr," *Shakespeare Quarterly* 8 (1957): 159–166 and Michael Manheim, *The Weak King Dilemma in the Shakespearean History Play* (Syracuse, N. Y.: Syracuse University Press, 1973), pp. 53–66.

19. Samuel Taylor Coleridge, *Shakespearean Criticism,* ed. Thomas Middleton

Raysor, rev. ed., 2 vols. (London: Dent, 1960), 1: 128–141; 141–150, 229–235 (quotation is from 2: 146).

20. Wolfgang H. Clemen, *The Development of Shakespeare's Imagery* (Cambridge: Harvard University Press, 1951), pp. 54–55 and Madeleine Doran, "Imagery in *Richard II* and *Henry IV*," *Modern Language Review* 37 (1942): 113–122. Among other important studies of the play's imagery are Richard D. Altick, "Symphonic Imagery in *Richard II*," *PMLA* 62 (1947): 339–365; Paul Jorgensen, "Vertical Patterns in *Richard II*," *Shakespeare Association Bulletin* 23 (1948): 119–134; and S. K. Heninger, Jr., "The Sun-King Analogy in *Richard II*," *Shakespeare Quarterly* 11 (1960): 319–327.

21. Mark Van Doren, *Shakespeare* (New York: Holt, 1939), p. 89.

22. It is interesting, in view of this mother-child image, that Coleridge (*Shakespearean Criticism*, 1: 134–135; 2: 145) should have noted in Richard a feminine quality, "misplaced in a man, and altogether unfit for a king."

23. For interesting commentary on the Pomfret Castle soliloquy, see Winny, *The Player King*, pp. 65–68.

24. See Peter Ure, "The Looking-Glass of *Richard II*," *Philological Quarterly* 44 (1955): 219–224. See also Ure's comments in the New Arden *Richard II*, pp. lxxxi–lxxxiii.

25. Prior, *The Drama of Power*, pp. 150–151; Hill, "Dramatic Techniques," p. 115; A. L. French, "Who Deposed Richard the Second?" *Essays in Criticism* 17 (1967): 411–433; Ornstein, *A Kingdom for a Stage*, p. 115; Humphreys, *Shakespeare: Richard II*, p. 43; L. C. Knights, *William Shakespeare: The Histories* (London: Longmans, 1962), p. 31; John Palmer, *Political and Comic Characters of Shakespeare* (New York: St. Martin, 1965), p. 134; Harold F. Folland, "King Richard's Pallid Victory," *Shakespeare Quarterly* 24 (1973): 390–399; Lois Potter, "The Antic Disposition of Richard II," *Shakespeare Survey* 27 (1974): 33–41; Brooke, *Shakespeare's Early Tragedies*, p. 133.

26. In the 1973 production by the Royal Shakespeare Company this point was subtly underscored by having the two principal actors alternate as Richard and Bolingbroke from performance to performance, a device that also suggested the cyclical nature of history.

27. On the theater imagery, see Georges A. Bonnard, "The Actor in Richard II," *Shakespeare-Jahrbuch* 87 (1952): 87–101; Leonard Dean, "*Richard II:* The State and the Image of the Theater," *PMLA* 67 (1952): 211–218; and Anne Righter, *Shakespeare and the Idea of the Play* (London: Chatto & Windus, 1962), pp. 122–127. Righter is particularly good on the subject of Richard as player-king, as is Winny, *The Player King*, pp. 48–85.

28. Several good essays are collected in Paul M. Cubeta, ed., *Twentieth Century Interpretations of Richard II* (Englewood Cliffs, N.J.: Prentice-Hall, 1971).

29. The New Cambridge editor is John Dover Wilson (Cambridge: Cambridge University Press, 1946). The New Arden editor is A. R. Humphreys (Cambridge: Harvard University Press [6th ed.] 1960 [Part One]; [rev. ed.] 1966 [Part Two]). On the text, see the New Cambridge Part One, pp. 103–108; the New Cambridge Part Two, pp. 115–123; the New Arden Part One, pp. lxvi–lxxviii; the New Arden Part Two, pp. lxviii–lxxxvi; and W. W. Greg, *The*

Shakespeare First Folio: Its Bibliographical and Textual History (Oxford: Clarendon, 1955), pp. 262–276. On the date, see the New Arden Part One, pp. xi–xv; and the New Arden Part Two, pp. xi–xvii.

30. Arguing for the unity of the two parts are, among others, Tillyard, *Shakespeare's History Plays,* pp. 264–304 passim; Dover Wilson, New Cambridge Part One, pp. vii–xiii; and Humphreys, New Arden Part Two, pp. xxi–xxviii. Among the dissenters are R. A. Law, "Structural Unity in the Two Parts of *Henry IV*," *Studies in Philology* 24 (1927): 223–242; M. A. Shaaber, "The Unity of *Henry IV*," in *Joseph Quincy Adams Memorial Studies,* eds. Giles Dawson and Edwin E. Willoughby (Washington, D.C.: Folger Shakespeare Library, 1948), pp. 217–227; and Harold Jenkins, *The Structural Problem in Shakespeare's Henry the Fourth* (London: Methuen, 1956). Jenkins thinks one play grew into two.

31. On the complex interrelationships between the serious and comic elements in the play, see especially Gareth Lloyd-Evans, "The Comical-Tragical-Historical Method: *Henry IV*," in *Early Shakespeare,* eds. J. R. Brown and Bernard Harris, pp. 145–163 and Harold E. Toliver, "Falstaff, the Prince, and the History Play," *Shakespeare Quarterly* 16 (1965): 63–80.

32. See Seymour M. Pitcher, *The Case for Shakespeare's Authorship of The Famous Victories* (Albany: State University of New York, 1961).

33. For examples of Shakespeare's use and transformation of the Percy material, see above (pp. 51, 52–53).

34. Richard J. Beck, *Shakespeare: Henry IV* (London: Edward Arnold, 1965), p. 34. See also Paul A. Jorgensen, "The 'Dastardly Treachery' of Prince John of Lancaster," *PMLA* 76 (1961): 488–492.

35. On the sources, see the New Arden Part One, pp. xxi–xxxix, 167–195; New Arden Part Two, pp. xxix–xliii, 189–242; Bullough, *Sources,* 4: 155–343.

36. This was considered sound policy; see G. R. Waggoner, "An Elizabethan Attitude toward Peace and War," *Philological Quarterly* 33 (1954): 20–33.

37. See John Dover Wilson, *The Fortunes of Falstaff* (Cambridge: Cambridge University Press, 1944), pp. 15–35 and Robert B. Pierce, *Shakespeare's History Plays: The Family and the State* (Columbus: Ohio State University Press, 1971), pp. 171 ff.

38. See John W. Blanpied, " 'Unfathered heirs and loathly birds of nature': Bringing History to Crisis in *2 Henry IV*," *English Literary Renaissance* 5 (1975): 212–231; Pierce, *Shakespeare's History Plays,* pp. 206–210; and Traversi, *From Richard II to Henry V,* pp. 149–156.

39. Palmer, *Political and Comic Characters,* pp. 185–187.

40. Ornstein, *A Kingdom for a Stage,* p. 138.

41. Tillyard, *Shakespeare's History Plays,* p. 274.

42. Van Doren, *Shakespeare,* p. 125; see also Doran, "Imagery in *Richard II* and *Henry IV*."

43. See Norman Council, *When Honour's at the Stake: Ideas of Honor in Shakespeare's Plays* (London: Allen and Unwin, 1973), pp. 36–59.

44. Max M. Reese, *The Cease of Majesty* (London: Edward Arnold, 1961), p. 305.

45. Perhaps the lines "This earth that bears thee dead / Bears not alive so

stout a gentleman" (92–93) are an oblique reference to fat John Falstaff, who is playing possum a few feet away. If so, the tribute to Hotspur is still more ambivalent.

46. *Johnson on Shakespeare*, ed. Arthur Sherbo, Vols. 7 and 8 of The Yale Edition of the Works of Samuel Johnson (New Haven: Yale University Press, 1968), p. 523.

47. Clifford Leech, *William Shakespeare: The Chronicles* (London: Longmans, 1962), p. 26.

48. See C. L. Barber, "Rule and Misrule in *Henry IV*," *Shakespeare's Festive Comedy* (Princeton: Princeton University Press, 1959), pp. 192–221 and Jonas A. Barish, "The Turning Away of Prince Hal," *Shakespeare Studies*, ed. J. Leeds Barroll, 1 (1965): 9–17.

49. Toliver, "Falstaff, the Prince, and the History Play."

50. D. J. Palmer, "Casting off the Old Man: History and St. Paul in *Henry IV*," *Critical Quarterly* 12 (1970): 267–283.

51. Named for John Lyly's *Euphues* (1578), the style featured alliteration, balanced clauses, rhetorical questions, illustrative examples from history, similes from "unnatural natural history," proverbs, and other devices.

52. On the play extempore and its relation to the drama, see Richard L. McGuire, "The Play-within-the Play in *1 Henry IV*," *Shakespeare Quarterly* 18 (1967): 47–52. That the entire scene (II, 4), including the extemporaneous play, duplicates in miniature the structure of the entire play is ably argued by Waldo F. McNeir, "Structure and Theme in the First Tavern Scene (II, iv) in *1 Henry IV*," *Pacific Coast Studies in Shakespeare*, eds. Waldo F. McNeir and Thelma N. Greenfield (Eugene: University of Oregon Books, 1966), pp. 89–105.

53. Pierce, *Shakespeare's History Plays*, p. 195.

54. Ornstein, *A Kingdom for a Stage*, pp. 152–174 passim and Muriel C. Bradbrook, *"King Henry IV,"* in *Stratford Papers on Shakespeare, 1965–67*, ed. B. A. W. Jackson (Shannon, Ireland: Irish University Press; McMaster University Library Press, 1969), pp. 168–185.

55. Leslie Hotson, "Ancient Pistol," in *Shakespeare's Sonnets Dated and Other Essays* (London: Rupert Hart-Davis, 1949), pp. 57–75.

56. The somberness of Part Two has been frequently noted. See Clifford Leech, "The Unity of *2 Henry IV*," *Shakespeare Survey* 6 (1953): 16–24; Leech, *William Shakespeare: The Chronicles*, pp. 28–30; John Pettigrew, "The Mood of *Henry IV, Part 2*," *Stratford Papers on Shakespeare, 1965–67*, pp. 145–167.

57. *Morgann's Essay "On the Dramatic Character of Sir John Falstaff,"* ed. William Arthur Gill (London: Henry Frowde, 1912); A. C. Bradley, "The Rejection of Falstaff," in *Oxford Lectures on Poetry* (London: Macmillan, 1909), pp. 247–275; Michael Goldman, *Shakespeare and the Energies of Drama* (Princeton: Princeton University Press, 1972), pp. 45–57; John Bailey, "A Note on Falstaff," in *A Book of Homage to Shakespeare*, ed. Israel Gollancz (London: Oxford University Press, 1916), p. 150; Leech, *William Shakespeare: The Chronicles*, p. 31; Beck, *Shakespeare: Henry IV*, p. 58; Roy Battenhouse, "Falstaff as Parodist and Perhaps Holy Fool," *PMLA* 90 (1975): 32–52;

W. H. Auden, *The Dyer's Hand and Other Essays* (New York: Random House, 1962), p. 198.

Morgann's essay has been frequently reprinted; see especially Maurice Morgann, *Shakespearian Criticism,* ed. Daniel A. Fineman (Oxford: Clarendon, 1972), which contains Morgann's longer revisions.

58. Sherbo, ed., *Johnson on Shakespeare,* p. 523. Dover Wilson, *The Fortunes of Falstaff,* pp. 15–35; Bernard Spivack, "Falstaff and the Psychomachia," *Shakespeare Quarterly* 8 (1957): 449–459; E. E. Stoll, "Falstaff," *Shakespeare Studies* (New York: Macmillan, 1927), pp. 403–490; Barber, *Shakespeare's Festive Comedy,* pp. 192–221; Walter Kaiser, *Praisers of Folly* (Cambridge: Harvard University Press, 1963), pp. 193–275.

59. *Henry IV, Part One,* ed. M. A. Shaaber (Baltimore: Penguin, 1957), p. 24.

Two useful collections are James Sanderson, ed., *Twentieth Century Interpretations of Henry IV, Part One* (Englewood Cliffs, N.J.: Prentice-Hall, 1969) and, by the same publisher, David Young, ed., *Twentieth Century Interpretations of Henry IV, Part Two* (1968).

60. Assuming that the reference was not a later interpolation, as is argued by Warren D. Smith, "The *Henry V* Choruses in the First Folio," *Journal of English and Germanic Philology* 53 (1954): 38–57.

61. On the text, see Greg, *The Shakespeare First Folio,* pp. 282–288; the New Cambridge *Henry V,* ed. John Dover Wilson (Cambridge: Cambridge University Press, 1947), pp. 111–118; the New Arden *Henry V,* ed. J. H. Walter (Cambridge: Harvard University Press, 1954), pp. xxxviii–xliii. On the date, see the New Arden edition, pp. xi–xii. On sources, see the New Arden, pp. xxxiv–xxxviii, 159–167; Bullough, *Sources,* 4: 347–432; Pitcher, *The Famous Victories.*

62. See Walter, in the New Arden edition, pp. xiv–xviii.

63. Harley Granville-Barker, "From *Henry V* to *Hamlet,*" *Proceedings of the British Academy, 1924–25* 11 (1926): 283–309, reprinted in *More Prefaces to Shakespeare* (Princeton: Princeton University Press, 1974), pp. 135–167. See also Van Doren, *Shakespeare,* pp. 170–179.

64. Goldman, *Shakespeare and the Energies of Drama,* pp. 58–73.

65. See Paul A. Jorgensen, *Shakespeare's Military World* (Berkeley: University of California Press, 1956), pp. 86–100.

66. James Winny (*The Player King,* pp. 173–176) sees Henry not as an ideal king so much as a figure of folklore.

67. S. C. Sen Gupta, *Shakespeare's Historical Plays* (London: Oxford University Press, 1964), p. 141.

68. Zeeveld, *The Temper of Shakespeare's Thought,* pp. 1–73.

69. Alfred Harbage, *William Shakespeare: A Reader's Guide* (New York: Noonday, 1963), p. 171.

70. E. E. Stoll, "*Henry V,*" in *Poets and Playwrights* (Minneapolis: University of Minnesota Press, 1930), p. 42.

71. See, for example, Charles Williams, "*Henry V,*" in *Shakespeare Criticism, 1919–35,* ed. Anne Bradby (London: Oxford University Press, 1936), pp. 180–188; Dover Wilson, *The Fortunes of Falstaff,* pp. 6–7, 60–81, 123 ff. and passim; Reese, *The Cease of Majesty,* pp. 317–332. In *The Frontiers of*

Drama, 2d ed. (London: Methuen, 1964), pp. 34–55, Una Ellis-Fermor acknowledges Henry's virtues as the ideal statesman king, but she notes that he is morally and intellectually "insufficient."

72. See Traversi, *Shakespeare: From Richard II to Henry V,* p. 169; J. C. Maxwell, "Simple or Complex? Some Problems in the Interpretation of Shakespeare," *Durham University Journal* 46, n.s. 15 (1953–1954): 112–115; Manheim, *The Weak King Dilemma,* p. 168. Manheim compares the scene to *Richard III,* III, 7, where Richard is "persuaded" to assume the throne.

73. Maxwell, "Simple or Complex?"

74. On this speech (which was omitted in Olivier's celebrated film *Henry V*), see Allan Gilbert, "Patriotism and Satire in *Henry V*," in *Studies in Shakespeare,* eds. Arthur D. Matthews and Clark M. Emery (Coral Gables, Fla.: University of Miami Press, 1953), pp. 40–64 and Ornstein, *A Kingdom for a Stage,* pp. 175–202.

75. See Jorgensen, *Shakespeare's Military World,* pp. 248–259.

76. Hugh M. Richmond, *Shakespeare's Political Plays* (New York: Random House, 1967), p. 177; Manheim, *The Weak King Dilemma,* pp. 180–181.

77. See C. H. Hobday, "Imagery and Irony in *Henry V*," *Shakespeare Survey* 21 (1968): 107–114; Roy W. Battenhouse, "The Relation of *Henry V* to *Tamburlaine*," *Shakespeare Survey* 27 (1974): 71–79; Gilbert, "Patriotism and Satire in *Henry V*"; Ornstein, *A Kingdom for a Stage,* pp. 175–202; and Gordon Ross Smith, "Shakespeare's *Henry V:* Another Part of the Critical Forest," *Journal of the History of Ideas* 37 (January–March 1976): 3–26. Jorgensen believes that Shakespeare intended to glorify Henry but did not succeed because of his own divided mind and uncertain hand; see Paul A. Jorgensen, "Accidental Judgments, Casual Slaughters, and Purposes Mistook: Critical Reactions to Shakespeare's *Henry the Fifth*," *Shakespeare Association Bulletin* 22:2 (1947): 51–61.

Several good studies are collected in Ronald S. Berman, ed., *Twentieth Century Interpretations of Henry V* (Englewood Cliffs, N.J.: Prentice-Hall, 1968).

78. Manheim, *The Weak King Dilemma,* p. 177.

79. Chambers, *William Shakespeare,* 2: 343.

80. On the text and date, see the New Cambridge *Henry VIII,* ed. J. C. Maxwell (Cambridge: Cambridge University Press, 1962), pp. ix–xxviii, 113–117 and the New Arden edition, ed. R. A. Foakes, 3d ed. (Cambridge: Harvard University Press, 1964), pp. xv–xxxv. On the sources, see the New Arden, pp. xxxv–xxxix, 183–215 and Bullough, *Sources,* 4: 435–510.

81. The collaborationist theory, which goes back at least as far as James Spedding (1850), has been forcefully restated by J. C. Maxwell; see the New Cambridge edition, pp. ix–xxviii. See also Marco Mincoff, "*Henry VIII* and Fletcher," *Shakespeare Quarterly* 12 (1961): 239–260. The most vigorous defense of Shakespeare's sole authorship, a view reintroduced by Peter Alexander, "Conjectural History, or Shakespeare's *Henry VIII*," *Essays and Studies, 1930* 16 (1931): 85–120, is to be found in a study primarily concerned with another play in which collaboration with Fletcher is said to be involved: Paul Bertram, *Shakespeare and The Two Noble Kinsmen* (New Brunswick,

N.J.: Rutgers University Press, 1965), pp. 124–179. R. A. Foakes, though believing that Shakespeare's case is strong on the basis of the play's structural unity, thinks that the truth lies between the two extreme positions; that is, Shakespeare wrote considerably more of *Henry VIII* than the Fletcherians would give him credit for. See the New Arden edition, pp. xv–xxviii.

82. Leech, *William Shakespeare: The Chronicles*, p. 35.

83. See Frank Kermode, "What is Shakespeare's *Henry VIII* About?" *Durham University Journal*, n.s. 9 (1948): 48–55 and Eugene M. Waith, *The Pattern of Tragicomedy in Beaumont and Fletcher* (New Haven: Yale University Press, 1952), pp. 117–124.

84. On Wolsey's reputation in Shakespeare's day, see Paul L. Wiley, "Renaissance Exploitation of Cavendish's *Life of Wolsey*," *Studies in Philology* 43 (1946):121–146.

85. Waith, *The Pattern of Tragicomedy*, p. 119.

86. It has been argued that Cranmer's prophecy is tacked on to the play, that it does not logically or dramatically resolve the moral ambiguities Shakespeare has presented in the actions that precede it. See Lee Bliss, "The Wheel of Fortune and the Maiden Phoenix of Shakespeare's *King Henry the Eighth*," *ELH* 42 (1975): 1–25.

87. An indispensable commentary on the play (though perhaps extravagant in its enthusiasm) is G. Wilson Knight, "*Henry VIII* and the Poetry of Conversion," *The Crown of Life: Essays in Interpretation of Shakespeare's Final Plays* (London: Methuen, 1948), pp. 256–336.

88. Howard Felperin, "Shakespeare's *Henry VIII*: History as Myth," *Studies in English Literature, 1500–1900* 6 (1966): 225–246. For a similar view, see Hugh M. Richmond, "Shakespeare's *Henry VIII*: Romance Redeemed by History," *Shakespeare Studies*, ed. J. Leeds Barroll, 4 (1969): 334–349; Ronald Berman, "*King Henry VIII*: History and Romance," *English Studies* 48 (1967): 112–121; and the New Arden *Henry VIII*, ed. R. A. Foakes, pp. xxxix–xlvii.

89. Foakes, in the New Arden *Henry VIII*, p. lxiv.

9
Problem Plays

All's Well that Ends Well
Measure for Measure
Troilus and Cressida

The term *problem play* was originally associated with the social dramas produced around the end of the nineteenth century by such playwrights as Ibsen, Galsworthy, and Shaw. It was F. S. Boas, writing in 1896, who first applied the term to certain works of Shakespeare: *All's Well that Ends Well, Measure for Measure, Troilus and Cressida,* and *Hamlet;* and while *Hamlet* has in most discussions been restored to its traditional place among the tragedies, the others have by and large retained membership in the "problem" group.[1] Boas argued that in these plays we are exposed to "artificial" communities where intricate issues are raised— issues that "preclude a completely satisfactory outcome" and leave us with unanswered questions. "Dramas so singular in theme and temper," he went on to say, "cannot be strictly called comedies or tragedies. We may therefore borrow a convenient phrase from the theatre of to-day and class them together as Shakspere's problem-plays."[2] One often hears the trio (with *Hamlet* excluded) referred to as dark or bitter comedies, to distinguish them from romantic comedies, such as *Much Ado about Nothing, As You Like It,* and *Twelfth Night.*

Scholars and general readers alike disagree as to the tone, intent, and artistic merit of the problem plays. Dover Wilson believes that around 1600 Shakespeare entered into a protracted period of "gloom and dejection." W. W. Lawrence, using the tools of literary history, demonstrates that Shakespeare was adapting familiar medieval stories that his Elizabethan audience would have accepted with little fuss and certainly without the intense philosophic questionings that a twentieth-century audience might entertain. According to some critics, notably G. Wilson Knight, all three plays are allegorical; and *All's Well* and *Measure for Measure* are in effect Christian parables. E. M. W. Tillyard finds common to these plays (and *Hamlet*) an interest on Shakespeare's part in speculative thought for its own sake, sometimes at the expense of the drama. A. P. Rossiter regards the problem plays, including *Hamlet* and to some extent *Othello,* as embodiments of the "tragicomic view of man," which employs the "art of inversion, deflation, and paradox." In these plays, says R. A. Foakes, the dramatist experiments with "discontinuities and contradictions in character and action, withdrawing from the basic commitment to romantic love and to common ethical attitudes shown in the earlier comedies." And H. B. Charlton offers the novel opinion that the problem plays, whose chronology is uncertain at best, were actually written before the great romantic comedies, that they constitute steps along the road to Shakespeare's discovery of "the true sources of nobility in man and of joy in life."[3]

"The best way to treat the conception of the so-called 'dark comedies'," one scholar suggests, "is to explain it away."[4] The proposal makes excellent sense, for putting the plays in a separate category assumes more resemblances than may actually exist.[5] *All's Well* and *Measure for Measure* are romantic comedies where, whatever the complications, Robin Goodfellow's promise is eventually fulfilled:

> Jack shall have Jill;
> Naught shall go ill;
> The man shall have his mare again, and all shall be well.
> (*A Midsummer Night's Dream,* III, 2, 461–463)

Measure for Measure is, however, a more serious play that raises profound and disturbing questions about the nature of justice and morality. And in *Troilus and Cressida* Jack gets no Jill; there is no ending at all, either happy or unhappy. *Measure for Measure* and *Troilus and Cressida* are somewhat alike in that both depict a decaying society. In *Measure for Measure,* however, the rottenness provides the background for a remarkable story about individual human beings, whereas in *Troilus and Cressida* the disintegration of the community itself seems to be Shakespeare's major preoccupation.

The three problem plays have been linked together for so long that it is useful to devote a special chapter to them. But one should bear in mind that the grouping is perhaps more arbitrary than any other in the realm of Shakespeare criticism.[6]

ALL'S WELL THAT ENDS WELL

All's Well that Ends Well was first printed in the 1623 Folio. The text has many imperfections, and some editors have therefore assumed that it is a hasty revision, possibly by someone other than Shakespeare, of an

earlier work. Like a number of Shakespeare's plays, *All's Well* has been
identified with the *Love's Labour's Won* mentioned in Meres's *Palladis
Tamia* (1598), but there is no solid clue as to its date of composition or
any record of a performance during Shakespeare's lifetime. If the role of
Lavatch was created for Robert Armin, the comic star who played
Touchstone and Feste, *All's Well* would have been written after he joined
the Lord Chamberlain's Men, that is, not before the latter part of 1599.
The play is often assigned to 1602–1604, for no reason other than its
alleged similarity to *Measure for Measure*, which is usually dated 1604.[7]

The source of *All's Well* is the tale of Beltramo de Rossiglione and
Giglietta di Nerbone, which is the ninth novella of the third day in
Boccaccio's *Decameron*. It was well known to Elizabethans in William
Painter's translation in *The Palace of Pleasure* (1566).[8] Shakespeare's
plot falls into two segments. In the first part of the play, the King of
France is dying of a fistula (an ulcerous sore) that baffles the skill of
his learned doctors. Helena, an orphaned gentlewoman living in the
household of the Countess of Rossillion, travels to Paris hoping to help
him with special remedies that she learned from her father, the celebrated
physician Gerard de Narbon. The journey also gives her an excuse to
follow the Countess's son Bertram, whom she loves but, because of his
superior rank, despairs of marrying. To the amazement of the court she
cures the King, who promises her any husband she wishes. When Helena
chooses Bertram, the latter is indignant and has to be forced to go through
with the marriage by the King himself. Right after the wedding, however,
Bertram escapes to join the army of the Duke of Florence, accompanied
by his associate, the braggart Parolles. When Helena returns to Rossillion,
Bertram sends a letter announcing that he will not recognize her as a
wife unless she meets two conditions during their separation: She must
obtain the ring from his finger, and she must conceive and beget his
child. So ends the first part of the action, which focuses upon the ancient
folk motif of the revival of the ailing King.

The second part of the plot deals with Helena's relentless efforts to
reclaim her husband. Disguised as a pilgrim, she sets out for the shrine
of Saint Jaques le Grand. On her arrival at Florence, she learns that
Bertram is attempting to seduce a virtuous young woman appropriately
named Diana. Helena convinces Diana and her mother that she is
Bertram's lawful wife, then persuades them to help her win him back.
Diana agrees to yield her body to Bertram on condition that he give
her his ring. When the midnight rendezvous takes place, Helena substitutes herself in bed for Diana without Bertram's knowledge and gets
his ring in exchange for a ring that the King had given her. Word later
reaches Rossillion that Helena is dead. Just as Bertram is about to accept
in marriage the daughter of the old lord Lafew, the King notices the

ring that the Count had acquired at his assignation with the presumed Diana and has him arrested for Helena's murder. Meanwhile, Diana arrives with her mother and accuses Bertram of having seduced her and broken his promise to marry her. Bertram attempts to answer her charges with equivocations and outright lies. But when Diana replies in riddles to questions about the rings and about her chastity, the King orders her arrested. At this point Helena steps forward to explain what has happened and prove that she has fulfilled Bertram's prerequisites for a reconciliation. The hero seems repentant and ready to love her forever.

If *All's Well* is compared to Boccaccio's story, one is struck by the fact that Shakespeare makes Bertram much more unattractive than Beltramo. The young Count quickly forfeits our good will when he derides Helena's humble origin:

> *King:* Thou know'st she has rais'd me from my sickly bed.
> *Bertram:* But follows it, my lord, to bring me down
>   Must answer for your raising? I know her well.
>   She had her breeding at my father's charge.
>   A poor physician's daughter my wife? Disdain
>   Rather corrupt me ever!
>
>   (II, 3, 118–123)

The King reads him a lecture on one of the main themes of the play. True nobility is measured by deeds rather than birth, and by such a standard the poor physician's daughter is the epitome of virtue and honor:

> The property by what it is should go,
> Not by the title. She is young, wise, fair;
> In these to nature she's immediate heir;
> And these breed honour.
> . . . .
>   Honours thrive
> When rather from our acts we them derive
> Than our foregoers.
>   (II, 3, 137–144) [9]

When Bertram, unlike Boccaccio's Beltramo, remains defiant, the King asserts his authority:

>   Here, take her hand,
> Proud scornful boy, unworthy this good gift,
> That dost in vile misprision [contempt; mistake] shackle up
> My love and her desert . . . .
> . . . .

          that wilt not know,
It is in us to plant thine honour where
We please to have it grow.

                                    (II, 3, 157–164)

Lafew numbers Bertram among the nation's "unbak'd and doughy youth" (IV, 5, 3–4); and the Countess herself, who loves Helena as a daughter, condemns her arrogant son as a "rash and unbridled boy" (III, 2, 30) who must somehow achieve maturity and regain his lost honor.[10] Meanwhile, Bertram runs the gamut of loathsome behavior. He is a snob, a husband who forsakes his wife, a seducer and would-be adulterer, and a liar. In addition, he falls under the influence of Parolles.[11]

By blackening the character of Bertram, Shakespeare departs radically from his sources. As several scholars have observed, the emphasis is very different from that in earlier versions of the tale. "Instead of a clever wench who must prove herself worthy of an aristocratic husband, we have an unworthy husband who must be made worthy of his wife."[12] The change is crucial to Shakespeare's dramatic structure, for Helena can thereby unify the two main actions in the play. As the great restorative force, she first heals the King, then administers the cure to Bertram, this time on a spiritual level.

There is ample warrant in the text for stressing the allegorical nature of Helena's role. Both cures are linked through religious imagery.[13] Helena tells the Countess that her remedies involve more than mere medical skill, and she presents her credentials to the King in language rich in scriptural allusion:

He that of greatest works is finisher
Oft does them by the weakest minister.
So holy writ in babes hath judgment shown
When judges have been babes; great floods have flown
From simple sources, and great seas have dried
When miracles have by the greatest been denied.
                                    (II, 1, 139–144)

"Of heaven, not me, make an experiment" (II, 1, 157), Helena implores. The King finally concedes that she may be the agent of a higher power:

Methinks in thee some blessed spirit doth speak
His powerful sound within an organ weak;
And what impossibility would slay
In common sense, sense saves another way.
                                    (II, 1, 178–181)

The Countess goes so far as to suggest that Bertram's salvation requires the intercession of the Virgin Mary:

> What angel shall
> Bless this unworthy husband? He cannot thrive
> Unless her prayers, whom heaven delights to hear
> And loves to grant, reprieve him from the wrath
> Of greatest justice.
>
> (III, 4, 25–29)

In the words of Clifford Leech, "Helena in her curing of the King is a dispenser of divine grace, and in her definitive subjection of Bertram she is setting his foot on the path of Christian virtue."[14] Some would interpret *All's Well* as a morality play, with Helena representing "heavenly grace" and Bertram "natural, unredeemed man," who is temporarily ensnared by Vice, in the person of Parolles, much as Prince Hal is supposedly in the toils of Falstaff.[15]

It would be misleading, however, to emphasize Helena's symbolic or theological function at the expense of her flesh-and-blood femininity. On a realistic level one may deplore the object of her devotion, but there is no denying that she loves him with uncompromising fervor. Lafew consoles Helena on the loss of her father, but the moment she is alone on the stage she lets us know that her father is not on her mind:

> I have forgot him. My imagination
> Carries no favour in't but Bertram's.
> I am undone! There is no living, none,
> If Bertram be away. 'Twere all one
> That I should love a bright particular star
> And think to wed it, he is so above me.
> In his bright radiance and collateral [secondary] light
> Must I be comforted, not in his sphere.
>
> (I, 1, 93–100)

After some brief but delightful verbal fencing with the Countess ("the most beautiful old woman's part ever written"),[16] Helena acknowledges her love with unusual passion:

> Then I confess
> Here on my knee before high heaven and you,
> That before you, and next unto high heaven,
> I love your son.
> . . . .
> I know I love in vain, strive against hope;
> Yet in this captious [ready to take] and intenible [unable to retain] sieve

I still pour in the waters of my love
And lack not to lose still. Thus, Indian-like,
Religious in mine error, I adore
The sun, that looks upon his worshipper
But knows of him no more.

(I, 3, 197–213)

She pursues her goal with unflagging energy, too busy shaping her destiny to find time for tears. We are capable, she says, of more than we imagine:

Our remedies oft in ourselves do lie,
Which we ascribe to heaven. The fated sky
Gives us free scope; only doth backward pull
Our slow designs when we ourselves are dull.
. . . .
Impossible be strange attempts to those
That weigh their pains in sense, and do suppose
What hath been cannot be. Who ever strove
To show her merit that did miss her love?

(I, 1, 231–242)

Helena, it has been said, "has body as well as mind,"[17] and Shakespeare makes a special point of her sexuality. Early in the play she indulges in a robust dialogue with Parolles, who perceives that she is "meditating on virginity" (I, 1, 121). Like Chaucer's Wife of Bath, Parolles argues that virginity must be lost if the race is to be preserved. In fact, "there was never virgin got till virginity was first lost" (I, 1, 139–140). How, Helena asks, may a girl "lose it to her own liking"? Parolles is ready with an answer:

Let me see. Marry, ill, to like him that ne'er it likes. 'Tis a commodity will lose the gloss with lying; the longer kept, the less worth. Off with't while 'tis vendible; answer the time of request.

(I, 1, 163–169)

When Lafew first announces to the King that there is a "Doctor She" who may be able to cure him, he does so in language brimful of sexual innuendo:

I have seen a medicine
That's able to breathe life into a stone,
Quicken a rock, and make you dance canary
With sprightly fire and motion; whose simple touch
Is powerful to araise King Pepin [Charlemagne's son], nay,
To give great Charlemaine a pen in's hand,
And write to her a love-line.

(II, 1, 75–81)[18]

Moreover, Lafew introduces her to the King with a ribald allusion to himself as "Cressid's uncle" (II, 1, 100), the notorious go-between Pandarus.

There is nothing prudish about Helena. Without implying that she is in any way vulgar or promiscuous, Shakespeare makes certain that we pay full attention to her physical charms. This is especially appropriate in a play dominated by kindly old people—the King, Lafew, and the Countess—who now live in a world of reminiscences. Like the ailing sovereign himself, the older generation is enfeebled; and the instrument of its rebirth must be a beautiful young woman who, while retaining her purity, can exemplify love in all its aspects, secular as well as spiritual. In Shakespeare's last plays—*Pericles, The Winter's Tale, The Tempest,* and even *Henry VIII*—the motif of the redemptive power of youth receives full development. But in *All's Well* Shakespeare is content merely to sketch what will become a preoccupying theme in the dramatic romances.[19]

Thus Helena becomes the embodiment of several interesting and important ideas. For one thing, she offers convincing proof that moral virtue does not depend upon the accident of birth. Secondly, she conveys the awesome power of womanhood and feminine love. Through her extraordinary femininity, she exercises her miraculous gifts as a physical and spiritual healer. Finally, Helena, essentially because of her attractiveness as a young woman, can bring renewal to a dying generation. She is bold and assertive in all her endeavors, and the sublimity of her goals is refreshingly united with a pragmatic view of human accomplishment:

> All's well that ends well. Still the fine's the crown.
> Whate'er the course, the end is the renown.
> (IV, 4, 35–36)

Yet all has decidedly not been well in the judgment of a substantial body of readers who are disquieted, or even repelled, by the play. They object to the sordidness of the story, especially to that old standby of popular literature, the so-called bed trick. The poetry, they claim, is often perfunctory, as though Shakespeare had lost interest in what he was doing. They criticize the clown Lavatch as a feeble imitation of those great jesters Touchstone and Feste. Most important, they dislike both the hero and the heroine. Even interpreted symbolically, Bertram is too accomplished a scoundrel to qualify as anybody's ideal husband. He has been ably defended on the grounds that he is immature rather than vicious and that he is, after all, loved by an unusual woman who deserves marriage, the traditional happy ending of comedy.[20] But Helena's interest in him has been taken to indicate that she must be an opportunist eager to get her man and climb the social ladder at any cost. Neither

Bertram nor Helena is blessed with the mirthfulness of Shakespeare's more memorable young lovers: Bassanio and Portia, Benedick and Beatrice, Orlando and Rosalind.[21]

Some of these objections have been dealt with implicitly in the foregoing discussion, and others are perhaps unanswerable. The principal weakness is that in *All's Well* (and to a lesser extent in *Measure for Measure*) Shakespeare, in the words of Ifor Evans, "found himself engaged with themes and problems that were too strong for the stories that tried to contain them."[22] In the first half of the play Bertram and Helena are brilliantly depicted, but in the second part they are forced to meet the awkward demands imposed by the folktale that Shakespeare inherited. Helena's role in the salvation of Bertram, as well as the hero's actual conversion, is hinted at rather than worked out dramatically. To be sure, Robert Y. Turner has examined Bertram in the context of the prodigal son tradition and shown how Shakespeare deliberately substitutes an intense trial scene for the usual scene of purgation.[23] Nevertheless, while we understand Shakespeare's intention, we do not enjoy the satisfaction of seeing it fulfilled in an aesthetically convincing manner. In brief, Shakespeare does not sustain to the end the tone of high seriousness; and although we may be absorbed in the expertly managed mechanics of the comic intrigue, the intrigue itself comes as a disappointment following the intensity of the play's beginning.

If *All's Well* does not entirely succeed as a drama, the fault may be partially ours. Perhaps we approach the play with preconceptions derived from other, better-known examples of Shakespearean comedy. Josephine Bennett praises *All's Well* as a masterful study of the follies of young love as seen "from the oblique angle of maturity,"[24] but some of us may expect to be transported to Arden or Illyria, an idyllic never-never land where beautiful young people fall ecstatically in love and await the last-minute development that will smooth away the obstacles to their happiness. It is inconceivable that Orlando should despise his Rosalind or that, having married her, he should churlishly refuse to take her into his bed. In fact, as noted earlier, *All's Well* is emphatically, perhaps startlingly, concerned with sex; whereas there is virtually no sexuality in the romantic comedies (apart from the puns and double-entendres that Shakespeare always delights in).

In short, we have not been prepared for the kind of realism Shakespeare explores in *All's Well* and therefore cannot adequately appreciate the depth of his characterization. The repentant Bertram and the noble but determined Helena, far from attesting to any erosion of Shakespeare's artistic powers, deserve to be ranked among his most original and lifelike portrayals.[25] This is the major reason that *All's Well that Ends Well*, despite its deficiencies, is an arresting play.

MEASURE FOR MEASURE

Measure for Measure was first printed, with many errors, in the 1623 Folio. As is generally the case when a text is defective, scholars (for example, the New Cambridge editors) have raised the possibility of an earlier version that Shakespeare or someone else in the company may have hastily reworked. It is unlikely, however, that there is any significant hand other than Shakespeare's in *Measure for Measure*. The play was acted on December 26, 1604 (St. Stephen's Night), at the court of James I, but we know nothing further about its early stage history. There is no record of another production before 1662, when William Davenant's hybrid *The Law against Lovers*, containing bits of *Measure for Measure* and *Much Ado about Nothing*, briefly held the stage. The New Arden editor assigns *Measure for Measure* to the summer of 1604.[26]

The main source is George Whetstone's play *Promos and Cassandra* (1578), in turn derived from a prose tale in Giraldi Cinthio's *Hecatommithi* (1565), the collection from which Shakespeare also took the plot of *Othello*. Whetstone later produced a prose version that was included in his *Heptameron of Civill Discourses* (1582); and Cinthio, conversely, adapted his own story as a play, *Epitia* (published 1583). In these earlier accounts, all of which Shakespeare probably knew, the heroine (Cassandra in Whetstone, Epitia in Cinthio) is given the opportunity to save her condemned brother's life by yielding her body to the lust of the wicked judge. And she does just that. As Cinthio tells the story, the brother is executed all the same, but Whetstone has the jailer conveniently substitute the head of a recently executed felon. In both cases the judge eventually confesses his guilt to the Emperor. He is first forced to marry the woman he has wronged and then sentenced to death. The heroine successfully pleads for his life, and husband and wife live happily ever after.[27] Shakespeare follows his sources rather carefully, although, as we shall see, he cannot reconcile the conventional ending with his own artistic design. Therefore, among other changes, he invents the character of Mariana in order to use the ever-popular bed trick.

Measure for Measure is set in Vienna, where vice runs rampant and the laws have been allowed to sleep for many years. Duke Vincentio absents himself on some mysterious business, leaving behind his trusted minister Angelo with instructions to enforce discipline as he sees fit. The deputy fixes upon an old law that makes fornication a capital offense, and the first victim is young Claudio, who has had sexual relations with Juliet. This act, strictly speaking a sin in Shakespeare's Vienna, is somewhat extenuated by the fact that the couple intend to be married as soon as the dowry can be arranged. At Claudio's request, his friend Lucio induces the condemned man's sister Isabella to intercede with Angelo. The latter, smitten with her beauty and virtue, offers to free Claudio if Isabella submits to his lust, a proposal that makes Angelo guilty of the very sin he is bent on punishing. At first, Isabella refuses, and Claudio seems doomed. But a Friar Lodowick, in reality the Duke in disguise, saves the situation. Angelo, he confides, has a skeleton in his own closet in the person of Mariana, whom he had long ago contracted to marry but had jilted because her dowry had miscarried. Inasmuch as their betrothal would have been considered a verbal contract, legally and morally binding in the future,[28] Isabella is persuaded to agree to an assignation at which Mariana, without Angelo's knowledge, can be substituted in his bed to consummate their old marriage vows. But Angelo, after enjoying the presumed Isabella, breaks his promise. He orders Claudio's execution and demands to see the victim's severed head. Through a series of maneuvers engineered by the Duke-Friar, proceedings of which Isabella is unaware, the head of the pirate Ragozine, who has conveniently died in prison of a fever, is substituted for that of Claudio. The Duke returns in his proper guise and brings events to a happy conclusion: Angelo acknowledges his guilt, marries the long-suffering Mariana, and, at Isabella's behest, is pardoned and saved from death. Claudio, believed dead by everyone, reappears and is married to Juliet. And as a final touch, the Duke hints that he himself wants to marry Isabella.

Shakespeare alters the traditional story in a number of ways. He changes the brother's original offense from rape to fornication, thereby mitigating its gravity. Isabella is not portrayed as simply a virtuous woman caught in a dilemma, but as a devout Christian called to her brother's aid just as she is becoming a novice in the strict Sisterhood of Saint Clare. This greatly intensifies her emotional conflict. As already noted, there is no Mariana in the earlier accounts. Shakespeare needs her in order to spare Isabella the indignity of prostituting herself to Angelo as well as to free her from the moral and psychological absurdity of having to marry him. Lucio is also a new character, an irreverent cynic who provides comic relief while embodying the moral depravity that permeates the city. Then, too, the role of the Duke has been so expanded that he is often regarded as the play's central character.

Many readers would rank the first half of *Measure for Measure* among Shakespeare's greatest achievements. His poetic imagination is fired by the pressures exerted upon the major characters, particularly Isabella, whose spiritual commitment must withstand excruciating tests. Her compassion is pitted against Angelo's self-righteousness and harsh standard of justice. Then, when he proposes a way to save Claudio, she has to deal with the vexing question of whether the end ever justifies the means. Once this issue is seemingly resolved in her mind, she receives a fresh jolt when Claudio fails to support her. A final test, perhaps the most difficult of all, occurs at the end of the play, when Isabella, still believing that Angelo has had her brother killed, is called upon to forgive him. Isabella is on the rack, as are Angelo and Claudio, and from the agonies of these three human beings Shakespeare extracts superb drama.

A key issue in the play is the relationship between freedom, or natural impulse (particularly the sexual instinct), and restraint, whether self-imposed or enforced by law.[29] Angelo expounds a rigorous theory of government that leaves no room for weakness:

> We must not make a scarecrow of the law,
> Setting it up to fear the birds of prey,
> And let it keep one shape till custom make it
> Their perch, and not their terror.
>
> (II, 1, 1–4)

He grants that offenders sometimes go undetected and that a jury may contain one or two thieves "guiltier than him they try" (II, 1, 21). But he can punish only the criminal who gets caught. Nor should the judge's own faults, Angelo argues with unintentional irony, extenuate those of Claudio or any other criminal:

> But rather tell me,
> When I that censure him do so offend,
> Let mine own judgment pattern out my death,
> And nothing come in partial [without partiality].
>
> (II, 1, 28–31)

He reminds Isabella of his obligation to condemn not just the sin, which already stands condemned, but the sinner. Moreover, "pity" has a more profound meaning than she comprehends:

> I show it [pity] most of all when I show justice;
> For then I pity those I do not know,
> Which a dismiss'd offence would after gall,
> And do him right that, answering one foul wrong,
> Lives not to act another.
>
> (II, 2, 100–104)

But Isabella, arguing on a different plane, is even more convincing. She begins hesitantly, for she must plead in behalf of a vice she abhors. However, with Lucio in the background to prod her, she warms to her task. In words that recall Portia's famous plea to Shylock in *The Merchant of Venice,* Isabella extols the Christian concept of mercy above that of justice. "Your brother is a forfeit of the law" (II, 2, 71), Angelo declares. So is everybody else, she answers:

> Why, all the souls that were were forfeit once,
> And he that might the vantage best have took
> Found out the remedy. How would you be
> If he which is the top of judgment should
> But judge you as you are? O, think on that!
> And mercy then will breathe within your lips
> Like man new made.

> (II, 2, 73–79)

Men should learn from Almighty God that the truly powerful abstain from the indiscriminate exercise of power. Isabella's language rings with passion:

> Could great men thunder
> As Jove himself does, Jove would ne'er be quiet,
> For every pelting [paltry] petty officer
> Would use his heaven for thunder—nothing but thunder!
> Merciful heaven,
> Thou rather with thy sharp and sulphurous bolt
> Split'st the unwedgeable and gnarled oak
> Than the soft myrtle. But man, proud man,
> Drest in a little brief authority,
> Most ignorant of what he's most assur'd
> (His glassy essence), like an angry ape,
> Plays such fantastic tricks before high heaven
> As make the angels weep . . . .

> (II, 2, 110–122)

"Go to your bosom," she bids him. "Knock there, and ask your heart what it doth know / That's like my brother's fault" (II, 2, 136–138).

Ironically, it is Isabella herself who unwittingly encourages Angelo's lust, not only through her beauty and purity, but also by innocuous words that reinforce his subconscious impulses. "We cannot weigh our brother with ourself." "Hark how I'll bribe you!" "Heaven keep your honour safe!" (II, 2, 126, 145, 157). The austere Angelo—Lucio says that his blood is "snow-broth" (I, 4, 58) and that he urinates "congeal'd ice" (III, 2, 118)—begins to feel strange yearnings, which he conveys to the audience in an aside rich in sexual implication. Isabella, he says, speaks "such sense that my sense breeds with it" (II, 2, 142). Although Angelo cannot be corrupted by the tricks of the experienced wanton, he is irresistibly drawn to Isabella's innocence, perhaps because it betokens an ideal that ultimately eludes his grasp:

> Having waste ground enough,
> Shall we desire to raze the sanctuary,
> And pitch our evils there? O, fie, fie, fie!

What dost thou? or what art thou, Angelo?
Dost thou desire her foully for those things
That make her good?
                    (II, 2, 170–175)

Virtue, he discovers, poses for him a more dangerous temptation than overt evil. How painful to Angelo is the sudden realization that he, too, is a sinner. Like Hamlet's uncle, the guilt-ridden Claudius, he makes a futile effort to pray:

                    Heaven hath my empty words,
Whilst my invention [thought], hearing not my tongue,
Anchors on Isabel. Heaven in my mouth,
As if I did but only chew his name,
And in my heart the strong and swelling evil
Of my conception!
                    (II, 4, 2–7)

It has been effectively argued that Angelo has been seduced, not "by a phantom of his imagination, but by the woman in Isabella" and that she herself is fearful of her power, not entirely inadvertent, to arouse his sexuality.[30] In any case, ensnared by a passion he has never dared acknowledge, Angelo forgets his responsibility to the law and thinks only of satisfying his unholy desire.

When Angelo makes his offer to save Claudio, Isabella at first does not understand his conditions. She agrees that sinning to save a brother's life constitutes a kind of charity. Angelo becomes more explicit. What would she do, he asks hypothetically, if she could save Claudio by giving up her body to someone influential with the judge? "As much," she answers, "for my brother as myself"; and her imagery calls to mind Leavis's fine phrase about her "sensuality of martyrdom":

That is, were I under the terms of death,
Th' impression of keen whips I'ld wear as rubies,
And strip myself to death as to a bed
That longings have been sick for, ere I'ld yield
My body up to shame.
                    (II, 4, 99–104)[31]

She would gladly die for him, but not at the price of eternal damnation. Nor should Claudio feel any differently:

Better it were a brother died at once
Than that a sister, by redeeming him,
Should die for ever.
                    (II, 4, 106–108)

Isabella draws a distinction between "lawful mercy," which she asks of
Angelo, and "foul redemption," which he demands of her (II, 4, 111–
113). When she finally grasps his meaning, she threatens to expose him,
only to be frustrated by the realization that no one will believe her. "More
than our brother is our chastity" (II, 4, 185), she asserts after Angelo
has left the stage. Modern readers sometimes regard Isabella's decision
as priggish, or even uncharitable. But behind her choice lay a long and
glorious tradition of Christian martyrdom.

Claudio, too, faces a complex moral choice. In his prison cell he allows
the Duke-Friar to prepare him for the inevitable:

> Be absolute for death. Either death or life
> Shall thereby be the sweeter. Reason thus with life:
> If I do lose thee, I do lose a thing
> That none but fools would keep.

> (III, 1, 5–8)

With apparently no hope of reprieve, Claudio can accept this stoical
comfort and announce to Isabella his defiance of death, which he couches
in language appropriate to his sensuous nature:

> If I must die,
> I will encounter darkness as a bride
> And hug it in mine arms.
> (III, 1, 83–85)

"There spake my brother!" (III, 1, 86), Isabella exults. But when Claudio
learns that it is in her power to save him, he instinctively snatches at
the chance for life. "O Isabel!" "What says my brother?" "Death is a
fearful thing" (III, 1, 115–116). This is a fine Shakespearean touch—a
young man's sudden, simple reflection that he is not geared to martyrdom.
In the vein of Hamlet's most famous speech, Claudio elaborates on the
terrors of the unknown:

> Ay, but to die, and go we know not where;
> To lie in cold obstruction and to rot;
> This sensible warm motion to become
> A kneaded clod; and the delighted spirit
> To bathe in fiery floods, or to reside
> In thrilling region of thick-ribbed ice,
> To be imprison'd in the viewless winds
> And blown with restless violence round about
> The pendent world; or to be worse than worst
> Of those that lawless and incertain thought
> Imagines howling!

> (III, 1, 118–128)

"Sweet sister, let me live!" (III, 1, 133), he implores; but the uncompromising Isabella lashes him verbally until he repents his lapse of courage. The action is at an impasse: Human justice cannot resolve the legal and moral problems raised in the first part of the play, and some sort of divine intervention would seem to be necessary.[32]

From this point on, the Duke-Friar takes over completely, and tension eases as the play moves toward the inevitable happy ending. As is the case with *All's Well that Ends Well,* the intrigue in the second half of *Measure for Measure* is brilliantly managed. The focus, however, shifts from the great moral and philosophical issues embodied in Angelo, Isabella, and Claudio to the antics of the man Lucio describes as "the old fantastical Duke of dark corners" (IV, 3, 163–164). The Duke-Friar, who has been characterized as a pompous figure presiding over a farce, just happens to produce a substitute bride and then a substitute corpse, thereby converting potential tragedy into "joyous, playful, mocking comedy."[33] If the solution does not ring true, one should bear in mind, as one critic has said, that "tragi-comedy is notorious for its shifts: for the trick of balancing its accounts by discovering sixpence at the back of the drawer."[34]

One may marvel at Shakespeare's skill in bringing about the comic denouement and still find *Measure for Measure* in some respects disturbing. The role of the Duke is not clearly defined. Although he conforms to the literary tradition of the Disguised Ruler,[35] no satisfactory reason is given for his temporary abdication; we do not know whether he intends from the outset to unmask and reform Angelo. The Duke could assert his identity at any time and free Claudio from prison, but he elects to play devious games and allows the young man to arrive at the very brink of death before stepping in. He also engages in a cat-and-mouse game with Isabella, concealing the fact that Claudio is alive and thus causing her needless anguish.

Critics have advanced a host of theories to account for the Duke's mystifying and capricious behavior. For W. W. Lawrence, he is simply an artificial "stage Duke" required for the working out of the plot. But Clifford Leech notes contradictions between his dramatic function and his personal qualities, citing several instances of his indifference or insensitivity to the feelings of the other characters. D. R. C. Marsh finds his concept of justice unacceptable and believes that Shakespeare's wry and clear-sighted exposure of human vanity (in Marsh's view, the main theme of the play) embraces the Duke no less than Angelo and Isabella. All three, says Jocelyn Powell, undertake a spiritual journey during which they learn that true virtue requires more than textbook knowledge. Other critics idealize the Duke in one way or another. Mary Lascelles equates him with Prospero, that stage manager par excellence in *The Tempest,* and therefore with Shakespeare himself. Josephine Bennett and David Stevenson detect parallels between the Duke and James I (the work, we recall, was acted before His Majesty). According to Lawrence Hyman, the Duke challenges the rigidity of both Angelo and Isabella and affirms the value of life with all its sinfulness. Wilson Knight and Roy Battenhouse are among those for whom the Duke is a Christ symbol; he guides Isabella along the road to charity until, in Knight's words, she "bows to a love greater than her own saintliness." R. W. Chambers similarly speaks of him as "an earthly Providence" who must torture Isabella until she forgives. The Duke has been equated with God, and Nevill Coghill has observed that the role of Lucio is analogous to that of Satan in the Book of Job.[36] That each of these interpretations has been cogently challenged and just as cogently defended may indicate that Shakespeare himself could not—or, at any rate, did not—resolve the inconsistencies in the Duke's character.

Misgivings about Isabella are also widespread. As implied earlier, she has been accused of acting as legalistically as Angelo.[37] Some readers have difficulty understanding her commitment to chastity when her brother's life is at stake, and they become outraged when she then acquiesces in a scheme to sacrifice someone else's virginity. Moreover, they argue, if chastity means so much to her, how can she compromise her religious convictions by marrying the Duke? In an effort to make the marriage seem more plausible, some have read it allegorically as the union of Justice and Truth, much like the marriage of the Red Cross Knight and Una in Book 1 of Spenser's *Faerie Queene.*[38]

One need not invoke allegory, however, to explain Isabella. Shakespeare's contemporaries celebrated chastity as the noblest ideal of womanhood, and they would have understood the heroine's judgment that it is sinful to prolong earthly life by forfeiting eternal salvation. Moreover, the substitution in Angelo's bed of Mariana for Isabella would be acceptable because it not only restores Mariana to her rights and saves Claudio's life, but it turns out to be the instrument of Angelo's repentance and regeneration.[39] As Jocelyn Powell has observed, we suspend critical judgment here (as elsewhere in the play); there is a theatrical logic whereby the audience is more concerned with righting Angelo's two wrongs than with Isabella's participation in the intrigue.[40] And there is nothing unseemly in Isabella's possible marriage to the Duke, for, according to most Christian writers in the Renaissance, chastity attains its highest fulfillment in the holy love that unites husband and wife. In any case, Shakespeare's audience would have expected the heroine to get married at the end of a comedy. Interestingly, Isabella herself says nothing to the Duke's delicately worded proposal, thereby permitting us merely to surmise (if we wish) that their wedding will take place. Much depends, of course, on how the ending is interpreted and staged in a given production. But one may suggest that by playing down the marriage, Shakespeare manages to send the spectators home happy while preserving Isabella's integrity as "a thing enskied and sainted" (I, 4, 34).

Superficially, then, *Measure for Measure* is a romantic comedy, leading to a trio, or quartet, of marriages at the final curtain (even Lucio is forced to take a wife). Like other romantic comedies, the play offers a rich assortment of low characters. Elbow, a simple constable in the mold of Dogberry, brings before the bar of justice "two notorious benefactors . . . void of all profanation in the world that good Christians ought to have" (II, 1, 50–56) and angrily denies that he "respected" with his wife before marriage (II, 1, 170–188). The tapster Pompey is more than willing to abandon pimping in order to enter the "more penitent trade" (IV, 2, 53) of hangman. Mistress Overdone, keeper of a brothel, is concerned over dwindling profits. "Thus, what with the war, what with the sweat [sweating sickness], what with the gallows, and what with poverty, I am custom-shrunk [short of customers]" (I, 2, 83–85). To be sure, the vitality of Pompey and Mistress Overdone contrasts sharply with the strictness of Angelo and Isabella.[41] But these comic characters, together with Lucio, also attest to a corruption that gnaws away at society, a foulness that has no counterpart in Arden or Illyria. And the artificial machinery whereby the plot is unraveled does not harmonize with the grave issues that are explored at the beginning.

Thus *Measure for Measure* is a "problem play" both in structure and overall tone. It has a number of paradoxes that remind some critics of John Donne and other Metaphysical poets.[42] It may well be that Shakespeare intends to stimulate us by continually shifting his perspective of the characters and their situations, a technique that makes it virtually impossible to categorize the play.[43] Shakespeare certainly extends the scope of comedy far beyond its traditional frontier.

Whatever questions it may leave unanswered, *Measure for Measure* remains one of his wisest and most engrossing plays. Much of its wisdom is contained in the lines from the Sermon on the Mount to which Shakespeare's title alludes: "Judge not, that ye be not judged. For with what measure ye mete, it shall be measured to you again" (Matthew 7:2). But a second scriptural quotation, though not explicitly invoked, is equally significant for an understanding of the play: "As I live, saith the Lord God, I have no pleasure in the death of the wicked; but that the wicked turn from his way and live" (Ezekiel 33:11).[44]

TROILUS AND CRESSIDA

Troilus and Cressida was entered in the Stationers' Register under the date February 7, 1603, but we know of no printed text before 1609,

when the play appeared in quarto. During the course of its printing, the
publishers, Richard Bonian and Henry Walley, substituted a new title
page. According to the 1603 entry, as well as the earlier title page, the
play was acted by Shakespeare's company at the Globe, but the later
title page contains an epistle to the reader claiming that the work was
"never stal'd with the Stage, never clapper-clawd with the palmes of the
vulgar." Perhaps the play had indeed been acted before 1609, but at a
private gathering at one of the inns of court rather than at a public
theater.[45] More likely, however, a private performance (if there was
one) would have come after the public performance.[46] The Folio text
(1623), a good one, may have been based upon the Quarto, but in some
instances the Quarto is superior. On the strength of possible allusions to
Ben Jonson's *Cynthia's Revels* (1600) and, in the prologue, to his play
The Poetaster (1601), together with the 1603 entry in the Stationers'
Register, *Troilus* is dated around 1601–1602. But the problems surrounding the text, date, circumstances of composition, and original staging
are complex.[47]

Like Chaucer's *Troilus and Criseyde* (c. 1385), to which it is indebted,[48]
Shakespeare's play is a love story acted out against the background of
the siege of Troy. After seven long years the war has not been settled.
Helen, the wife of the Greek chieftain Menelaus, sleeps untroubled in
the bed of her lover Paris, who had carried her off (not unwillingly)
to Troy and set in motion the Greek military expedition to win her back.
While the Trojans debate and reject the possibility of ending the costly
war by returning Helen to Menelaus, the Greeks are in disarray. Their
greatest hero Achilles sulks in his tent with his friend Patroclus and
ridicules the rest of his comrades. When Hector issues a challenge to
single combat, expecting Achilles to accept, the Greeks, at the suggestion
of the cunning Ulysses, decide to select their representative by lot. In
the hope of goading Achilles into action, they rig the lottery so that the
choice falls upon Ajax, "who wears his wit in his belly and his guts
in his head" (II, 1, 79–80). Hector and Ajax fight briefly but stop
when it turns out that they are kinsmen. Eventually Patroclus dies at
the hands of Hector, whereupon Achilles enters furiously into battle.
He kills Hector while the latter is unarmed and drags the dead body
around the city. At the end of the play the war is still in progress.

Meanwhile, we are involved in what seems to be a love story. Troilus,
the youngest son of King Priam of Troy and second in valor only to his
brother Hector, becomes infatuated with Cressida, a Trojan woman
whose father, the priest Calchas, has joined the Greeks. While the military
and diplomatic maneuvering is afoot, Troilus, with Cressida's uncle
Pandarus as go-between, is virtually thrown into his beloved's bed. Having
satisfied their intense desire, the lovers swear to be eternally faithful. But

almost immediately thereafter, in an exchange of prisoners, Cressida is returned to the Greek camp, escorted by the Greek captain Diomedes. With only token resistance from her, Diomedes becomes Cressida's new lover. During a temporary truce Ulysses conducts Troilus to Calchas's tent, where they watch Cressida make love to Diomedes and bestow upon him the very sleeve Troilus had given her to signify their deathless devotion. The next day, enraged by Cressida's betrayal, the young man rushes into battle determined to kill his rival; but although Troilus and Diomedes skirmish, nothing comes of it. The play ends with an obscene epilogue spoken by Pandarus, who laments the fact that pimps are never appreciated once their job is done:

> Full merrily the humblebee doth sting
> Till he hath lost his honey and his sting;
> And being once subdu'd in armed tail,
> Sweet honey and sweet notes together fail.
> (V, 10, 42–45)

For material on the siege of Troy, to which Chaucer had paid little attention, Shakespeare draws upon several medieval and Renaissance works: John Lydgate's *Troy Book* (c. 1412–1420); William Caxton's *Recuyell of the Historyes of Troy* (1475); and, in particular, George Chapman's translation of the *Iliad* (1598), which was to inspire Keats's famous sonnet.[49] In his handling of the love affair he relies heavily upon the Chaucerian tradition for details of plot and characterization. Shakespeare, however, telescopes the action, which in Chaucer's narrative poem unfolds in a leisurely fashion. Chaucer's Criseyde turns to Diomedes only after his persistent wooing; Shakespeare's heroine (who had been considerably debased by writers after Chaucer) is unfaithful within three days. Moreover, Shakespeare's Diomedes, unlike his counterpart in Chaucer, drops all pretense of loving Cressida and leaves her in no doubt as to what he is after. The characters in the love plot, including Pandarus, have been coarsened. In this respect they resemble the Greek and Trojan warriors, who have fallen off considerably from their legendary stature.

In a play in which disintegration is a major theme, it is appropriate that the structure of the drama should itself be disjointed.[50] The action keeps shifting, in nightmarish fashion, back and forth between different characters, different camps, different themes. Particularly puzzling is the inconclusive ending, which brings "neither the reconciliations of comedy nor the purifying calamities of tragedy."[51] Troilus, we have seen, chases Diomedes over the battlefield but does not achieve either the satisfaction of victory or the martyrdom of heroic defeat. At no point is Cressida redeemed through genuine love, nor does she ever suffer punishment or remorse. Achilles does not display the valor of a true soldier, and the Trojan War reaches no clear-cut decision. Echoing in the memory is the cynical evaluation of Thersites, a licensed fool in the tradition of Touchstone and Feste, who appears in the extraordinary role of choric commentator. "Lechery, lechery! still wars and lechery! Nothing else holds fashion" (V, 2, 195–196).[52] This is an extreme view, to be sure, but one vividly reinforced by the overpowering sense of futility that frustrates all nobility in the play and leaves a bitter taste of "the pettiness of evil; the squalor and meanness and triviality of betrayal."[53] The gigantic war initiated on account of Menelaus and Paris seems, to Thersites and to many playgoers and readers, nothing more than a fight between a cuckold and cuckold-maker over a whore, "a good quarrel to draw emulous factions and bleed to death upon" (II, 3, 78–80).

   Troilus and Cressida has often been interpreted as a tragedy;[54] it was indeed so classified by the editors of the Folio. But the title pages of the 1609 Quarto call it a history, and the epistle to the reader refers to it as a comedy. Although these discrepancies may not be significant, they serve to emphasize the enigmatic quality of what is perhaps Shakespeare's most bewildering play.

   If one accepts in broad outline the theory that *Troilus and Cressida* is a satire, much of the apparent chaos may be resolved into a consistent pattern.[55] The philosophic position from which events are examined is summed up in the play's most famous speech, Ulysses' lecture to the Greek leaders on "degree" (I, 3, 75–137). In order for the universe to function properly, each component must fill its prescribed role in a clearly defined hierarchy. This is a doctrine set forth in the Middle Ages by Thomas Aquinas and others and expanded by Anglican theologians like Richard Hooker (see p. 23). When degree, "the ladder to all high designs" (I, 3, 102), is upset, general anarchy ensues. Sons strike down their fathers, waters overflow their shores, and right and wrong become indistinguishable. Harmony and discipline are subverted by discord and license; reason is dominated by will:

> Then everything includes itself in power,
> Power into will, will into appetite;
> And appetite, an universal wolf,
> So doubly seconded with will and power,
> Must make perforce an universal prey,
> And last eat up himself.
>
> (I, 3, 119–124)[56]

Troy, he continues, cannot be conquered because the Greeks have neglected "degree"; Achilles and Patroclus sit in their tent and, exalting their personal wills, heap derision upon their lawful commanders:

> The general's disdain'd
> By him one step below, he by the next;
> That next by him beneath. So every step,
> Exampled by the first pace that is sick
> Of his superior, grows to an envious fever
> Of pale and bloodless emulation.
>
> (I, 3, 129–134)

Critics have rightly observed that the speech, in its dramatic context, contains elements of irony and even self-parody and that Ulysses, a clever schemer, is invoking military expediency rather than moral principles.[57] Nevertheless, the ideas presented in the speech provide a standard by which virtually every character in the play, including Ulysses, may be judged. As S. L. Bethell points out, we may accept Ulysses' moral judgments without searching into his own moral conduct.[58]

Although a number of critics, notably G. Wilson Knight,[59] have idealized Troilus and the Trojans as exemplars of intuition and emotion as opposed to the intellectual and rational values that are expounded (if not practiced) by Ulysses, it seems that they, like the Greeks, are dominated by will. In the memorable debate in the Trojan camp on the Greek demand for the return of Helen, Troilus sides with Paris. "Let Helen go" (II, 2, 17), Hector urges, convinced that there is no good reason to keep her. But Troilus heatedly replies that Trojan honor is at stake:

> Fie, fie, my brother!
> Weigh you the worth and honour of a king
> So great as our dread father in a scale
> Of common ounces? Will you with counters sum
> The past-proportion of his infinite?
> And buckle in a waist most fathomless
> With spans and inches so diminutive
> As fears and reasons? Fie, for godly shame!
>
> (II, 2, 25–32)[60]

One is reminded of the impetuous Hotspur in *1 Henry IV* when Troilus repudiates logic as an impediment to manhood and honor. Reason, he declares, makes the liver pale with fear. As for Hector's contention that Helen is not worth the staggering cost in human life that her continued presence in Troy demands, Troilus, who has been identified with the creative imagination,[61] answers that worth is not an absolute but a matter of individual judgment. "What is aught but as 'tis valu'd?" (II, 2, 52). The prophetess Cassandra comes on stage to sound the cry of doom. "Troy burns, or else let Helen go" (II, 2, 112). Nevertheless, Troilus and Paris persist in demanding that Helen remain, and their foolish counsel prevails.

Most startling of all, the noble Hector acquiesces in what he knows is an improper decision. Throughout the debate he acknowledges the rule of reason and maintains that ethical decisions cannot be based upon private whim. He tells Troilus that there are objective standards for determining the worth of Helen or of anything else:

> But value dwells not in particular will;
> It holds his estimate and dignity
> As well wherein 'tis precious of itself
> As in the prizer. 'Tis mad idolatry
> To make the service greater than the god;
> And the will dotes that is attributive
> To what infectiously itself affects
> Without some image [evidence] of th' affected merit.
>   (II, 2, 53–60)

Troilus and Paris are superficial young men (unfit, Aristotle said, to hear moral philosophy). Hector declares that the laws of nature and of nations require Helen's return to Menelaus:

>   If this law
> Of nature be corrupted through affection,
> And that great minds, of partial indulgence
> To their benumbed wills, resist the same,
> There is a law in each well-ord'red nation
> To curb those raging appetites that are
> Most disobedient and refractory.
> . . . .
>   Thus to persist
> In doing wrong extenuates not wrong,
> But makes it much more heavy.
>   (II, 2, 176–188)

This is Hector's opinion "in way of truth" (II, 2, 188–189). But his own will grows "benumbed," and in a spectacular about-face he allows his considered judgment to be overruled. Without offering any adequate explanation he resolves to keep Helen and save his "honor." By sacrificing moral law to this cheaper expedient, Hector demonstrates that his reason, too, can be corrupted. His open-eyed endorsement of will, which is in turn activated by personal appetite, inevitably leads to national disaster. "Thus," as Norman Council observes, "not only has the war outgrown its cause, but also the demand for honour has outgrown the war."[62]

Thus, in dealing with the Greeks as well as the Trojans, Shakespeare strips away human pretensions concerning love and war.[63] The war is fought over a trivial woman, as Diomedes bitterly informs Paris:

For every false drop in her bawdy veins
A Grecian's life hath sunk; for every scruple
   [minute portion]
Of her contaminated carrion weight
A Troyan hath been slain. Since she could speak,
She hath not given so many good words breath
As for her Greeks and Troyans suff'red death.
                 (IV, 1, 69–74)

The pattern is repeated on a lower level in the affair of Troilus and Cressida. On the morning after the consummation of their lust, they part from each other with a cynicism in shocking contrast with the tone of the analogous scene in *Romeo and Juliet*. Whereas the earlier lovers make a desperate effort to forestall the moment of separation, Troilus can hardly wait to get away. "Dear, trouble not yourself; the morn is cold . . . . I prithee now, to bed . . . . You will catch cold, and curse me" (IV, 2, 1–14). Cressida's reply (with its sexual innuendo) attests to a lifetime of such experiences:

               Prithee tarry.
You men will never tarry.
O foolish Cressid! I might have still held off,
And then you would have tarried.
                 (IV, 2, 15–18)

Meanwhile, Pandarus is on the scene with his leering interrogation, which Cressida enjoys:

Pandarus: How now, how now? How go maidenheads? Here, you maid! where's my cousin Cressid?
Cressida: Go hang yourself, you naughty mocking uncle! You bring me to do—and then you flout me too.
Pandarus: To do what? to do what? Let her say what. What have I brought you to do?
Cressida: Come, come, beshrew your heart! You'll ne'er be good Nor suffer others.
Pandarus: Ha, ha! Alas, poor wretch! a poor chipochia [fool; perhaps knob of stick—used obscenely]! hast not slept to-night? Would he not (a naughty man) let it sleep? A bugbear take him!
                 (IV, 2, 23–34)

Bearing in mind that "do" had a distinct sexual connotation in Shakespeare's day, we can appreciate the implications of Cressida's remark "Things won are done; joy's soul lies in the doing" (I, 2, 313). The dramatist has fashioned a thoroughly ugly world in which love, like war, is a kind of game pursued for ignoble ends. Degree, to quote

Ulysses, is "suffocate," and chaos—physical as well as moral—"follows the choking" (I, 3, 125–126).

No one emerges unblemished. It is disturbing that even Ulysses should fall a willing victim to the same kind of moral vacuity that poisons the other characters in the play.[64] In his attempt to get Achilles into a fighting mood by building up Ajax's reputation, Ulysses argues that man is worth only as much as others choose to esteem him, a relativistic position very similar to that taken by Paris and Troilus regarding Helen.[65] "What, are my deeds forgot?" (III, 3, 144) the young warrior asks. Yes, Ulysses replies:

> Time hath, my lord, a wallet at his back,
> Wherein he puts alms for oblivion,
> A great-siz'd monster of ingratitudes.
> Those scraps are good deeds past, which are devour'd
> As fast as they are made, forgot as soon
> As done.

(III, 3, 145–150)

No matter that what Ajax does today is less than what Achilles did yesterday; in order to keep pace with the fickle crowd's thirst for novelty, Achilles must continually seek public approbation. Once again Ulysses' time metaphor is striking:

> For Time is like a fashionable host,
> That slightly shakes his parting guest by th' hand,
> And with his arms outstretch'd as he would fly
> Grasps in the comer. The welcome ever smiles,
> And farewell goes out sighing. Let not virtue seek
> Remuneration for the thing it was!

(III, 3, 165–170)[66]

In taking this pragmatic line, Ulysses joins just about everyone else in setting policy above principle. How fittingly ironic it is that Achilles is finally roused to action, not through any sense of obligation either to his country or to himself, but out of a wild desire to avenge the death of Patroclus. Thus Ulysses' "policy," in the words of Thersites, "is not prov'd worth a blackberry" (V, 4, 13).

In *Troilus and Cressida,* as in *All's Well that Ends Well* and *Measure for Measure,* Shakespeare takes conventional narrative and dramatic situations and proceeds to complicate matters by introducing characters who refuse to respond in the conventional ways. We might like to see a demure Helena and an amiably contrite Bertram; a more tolerant Isabella; a sedate Cressida, a romantic Troilus, a consistently upright Hector, an Achilles who remains heroic. But Shakespeare does not choose to present so simplistic a view of humanity. *Troilus and Cressida* is the most difficult of the problem plays, largely because it conforms the least to our comfortable expectations. As one critic has observed, this deeply reflective play stands as Shakespeare's "classic monument to ambiguity, a tragedy deliberately thwarted by the savagery of its comic insight."[67]

NOTES

1. For a different grouping, see Ernest Schanzer's *The Problem Plays of Shakespeare* (1963) (New York: Schocken, 1965), which includes only *Julius Caesar, Measure for Measure,* and *Antony and Cleopatra.*
2. Frederick S. Boas, *Shakspere and His Predecessors* (1896; reprint ed., New York: Haskell House, 1968), p. 345. A good survey of attitudes since 1920 toward the problem plays is Michael Jamieson, "The Problem Plays, 1920–1970: A Retrospect," *Shakespeare Survey* 25 (1972):1–10.
3. John Dover Wilson, *The Essential Shakespeare* (Cambridge: Cambridge University Press, 1932), p. 115; William W. Lawrence, *Shakespeare's Problem Comedies* (1931), 2d ed. (New York: Ungar, 1960); G. Wilson Knight, "The Third Eye: An Essay on *All's Well that Ends Well,*" in *The Sovereign Flower* (London: Methuen, 1958), pp. 93–160, and "The Philosophy of *Troilus and Cressida*" and "*Measure for Measure* and the Gospels," in *The Wheel of Fire,* 5th rev. ed. (Cleveland: World Publishing, Meridian Books, 1957), pp. 47–96; E. M. W. Tillyard, *Shakespeare's Problem Plays* (Toronto: University of Toronto Press, 1950); A. P. Rossiter, "The Problem Plays," in *Angel with Horns* (New York: Theatre Arts Books, 1961), pp. 108–128; R. A. Foakes, *Shakespeare: The Dark Comedies to the Last Plays: From Satire to Celebration* (London: Routledge & Kegan Paul, 1971), p. 94; H. B. Charlton, *Shakespearian Comedy* (London: Methuen, 1938), pp. 208–265.
4. Hardin Craig, *An Interpretation of Shakespeare* (New York: Citadel, 1948), p. 221. See also Peter Ure, *William Shakespeare: The Problem Plays* (London: Longmans, 1961), p. 7.
5. See Schanzer, *Problem Plays,* pp. 187–191.
6. There are several good essays in Robert Ornstein, ed., *Discussions of Shakespeare's Problem Comedies* (Boston: Heath, 1961).
7. On the text and date, see the New Cambridge *All's Well That Ends Well,* eds. A. Quiller-Couch and John Dover Wilson (Cambridge: Cambridge University Press, 1929), pp. vii–xii, 101–113; W. W. Greg, *The Shakespeare First Folio* (Oxford: Clarendon, 1955), pp. 351–353; and the New Arden edition, ed. G. K. Hunter, 3d ed. (Cambridge: Harvard University Press, 1959), pp. xi–xxv.
8. On sources, see the New Arden edition, pp. xxv–xxix; Kenneth Muir, *Shakespeare's Sources* (London: Methuen, 1957), pp. 97–101; Geoffrey Bullough, *Narrative and Dramatic Sources of Shakespeare,* 8 vols. (New York: Columbia University Press, 1957–1975), 2: 375–396.

9. On the literary and intellectual background of the King's speech, see Muriel C. Bradbrook, "Virtue is the True Nobility: A Study of the Structure of *All's Well That Ends Well*," *Review of English Studies,* n.s. 1 (1950): 289–301. The argument is summarized in her *Shakespeare and Elizabethan Poetry* (London: Chatto & Windus, 1951), pp. 162–170.

10. The relationship between parents and children has been seen as an important theme of the play; see John Arthos, "The Comedy of Generation," *Essays in Criticism* 5 (1955):97–117.

11. Parolles has always been a huge comic success in the theater. See Jules Rothman, "A Vindication of Parolles," *Shakespeare Quarterly* 23 (1972): 183–196 and Foakes, *Dark Comedies to Last Plays,* pp. 7–17.

12. Robert Grams Hunter, *Shakespeare and the Comedy of Forgiveness* (New York: Columbia University Press, 1965), p. 112.

13. See Joseph G. Price, *The Unfortunate Comedy: A Study of All's Well That Ends Well and Its Critics* (Toronto: University of Toronto Press, 1968), p. 152.

14. Clifford Leech, "The Theme of Ambition in *All's Well That Ends Well*," *ELH* 21 (1954): 20.

15. See Tillyard, *Shakespeare's Problem Plays,* pp. 108 ff., 113–114 and William B. Toole, *Shakespeare's Problem Plays: Studies in Form and Meaning* (The Hague: Mouton, 1966), pp. 122–157.

16. Edward Wilson, ed., *Shaw on Shakespeare* (London: Cassell, 1961), p. 10.

17. Mark Van Doren, *Shakespeare* (New York: Holt, 1939), p. 215.

18. The sexual implications of this passage are noted by Hunter, *Shakespeare and the Comedy of Forgiveness,* p. 253, n. 12.

19. On the links with the late plays, see G. K. Hunter, in the New Arden edition, pp. lv–lvi.

20. See, for example, R. L. Smallwood, "The Design of *All's Well That Ends Well*," *Shakespeare Survey* 25 (1972): 45–61; Albert Howard Carter, "In Defense of Bertram," *Shakespeare Quarterly* 7 (1956): 21–31; and Francis G. Schoff, "Claudio, Bertram, and a Note on Interpretation," *Shakespeare Quarterly* 10 (1959): 11–23. Schoff warns agains entangling Bertram's character in the pleasurable working out of the plot.

21. Price, *The Unfortunate Comedy,* is a full study of the critical and theatrical history of the play.

22. B. Ifor Evans, *The Language of Shakespeare's Plays,* 2d ed. (London: Methuen, 1959), p. 134.

23. Robert Y. Turner, "Dramatic Convention in *All's Well That Ends Well*," *PMLA* 75 (1960): 497–502.

24. Josephine Waters Bennett, "New Techniques of Comedy in *All's Well That Ends Well*," *Shakespeare Quarterly* 18 (1967): 337–362.

25. See Harold S. Wilson, "Dramatic Emphasis in *All's Well That Ends Well*," *Huntington Library Quarterly* 13 (1949–1950): 217–240.

26. On the text and date, see E. K. Chambers, *William Shakespeare: A Study of Facts and Problems,* 2 vols. (Oxford: Clarendon, 1930), 1: 452–457; Greg, *The Shakespeare First Folio,* pp. 354–356; the New Cambridge edition, eds. A. Quiller-Couch and John Dover Wilson (Cambridge: Cambridge University Press, 1922; 1950), pp. vii, 97–113; the New Arden edition, ed. J. W. Lever (Cambridge: Harvard University Press, 1965), pp. xi–xxxv; and J. W. Lever,

"The Date of *Measure for Measure*," *Shakespeare Quarterly* 10 (1959): 381–388.

27. See Bullough, *Sources,* 2:399–530; Muir, *Shakespeare's Sources,* pp. 101–109; New Arden edition, pp. xxxv–lv, 151–200.

28. See Ernest Schanzer, "The Marriage-Contracts in *Measure for Measure*," *Shakespeare Survey* 13 (1960):81–89. The issue is also discussed in Schanzer's *Problem Plays,* pp. 75–79. Claudio and Juliet are similarly "married."

29. On this point, see L. C. Knights, "The Ambiguity of *Measure for Measure*," *Scrutiny* 10 (1941–1942): 222–233. Knights argues that the issue is left confused and ambiguous. In the same issue of *Scrutiny* (pp. 234–247), F. R. Leavis ("The Greatness of *Measure for Measure*") replies that Shakespeare makes the issue genuinely complex and not ambiguous.

30. David Lloyd Stevenson, *The Achievement of Shakespeare's Measure for Measure* (Ithaca, N.Y.: Cornell University Press, 1966), p. 45.

31. Leavis, "The Greatness of *Measure for Measure*."

32. The role of justice and equity in the play is well analyzed by W. Gordon Zeeveld, *The Temper of Shakespeare's Thought* (New Haven: Yale University Press, 1974), pp. 159–184.

33. Herbert Weil, Jr., "Forms and Contexts in *Measure for Measure*," *Critical Quarterly* 12 (1970): 55–72 and "The Options of the Audience: Theory and Practice in Peter Brook's *Measure for Measure*," *Shakespeare Survey* 25 (1972): 27–35.

34. Mary Lascelles, *Shakespeare's Measure for Measure* (London: University of London, The Athlone Press, 1953), p. 135.

35. See Lever, in the New Arden edition, pp. xliv–li.

36. Lawrence, *Shakespeare's Problem Comedies,* pp. 102–112; Clifford Leech, "The 'Meaning' of *Measure for Measure*," *Shakespeare Survey* 3 (1950): 66–73; D. R. C. Marsh, "The Mood of *Measure for Measure*," *Shakespeare Quarterly* 14 (1963): 31–38; Jocelyn Powell, "Theatrical *Trompe l'oeil* in *Measure for Measure*," in *Shakespearian Comedy,* eds. Malcolm Bradbury and David Palmer, Stratford-upon-Avon Studies 14 (London: Edward Arnold, 1972), pp. 181–209; Lascelles, *Shakespeare's Measure for Measure,* pp. 144–147; Josephine Waters Bennett, *Measure for Measure as Royal Entertainment* (New York: Columbia University Press, 1966), pp. 79–104; Stevenson, *Achievement of Measure for Measure,* pp. 134–166; Lawrence W. Hyman, "The Unity of *Measure for Measure*," *Modern Language Quarterly* 36 (1975): 3–20; G. Wilson Knight, "*Measure for Measure* and the Gospels"; Roy W. Battenhouse, "*Measure for Measure* and Christian Doctrine of the Atonement," *PMLA* 61 (1946): 1029–1059; R. W. Chambers, "The Jacobean Shakespeare and *Measure for Measure*," *Proceedings of the British Academy* 23 (1937), reprinted in his *Man's Unconquerable Mind* (London: Oxford University Press, 1939), pp. 277–310; Nevill Coghill, "Comic Form in *Measure for Measure*," *Shakespeare Survey* 8 (1955): 14–27.

37. Stevenson, *Achievement of Measure for Measure.* See also Schanzer, *Problem Plays,* pp. 96–112 and Lever, in New Arden edition, p. lxix. Both Stevenson (p. 20) and Lever suggest that *measure* in the title of the play means "moderation," or "avoiding extremes," and is hence a criticism of Angelo and Isabella.

38. See Muriel Bradbrook, "Authority, Truth and Justice in *Measure for Measure,*" *Review of English Studies* 17 (1941): 385–399.

39. The bed trick has been seen as a positive act of substitution, of giving oneself for someone else; see James Black, "The Unfolding of *Measure for Measure,*" *Shakespeare Survey* 26 (1973):119–128.

40. Powell, "Theatrical *Trompe l'oeil* in *Measure for Measure.*"

41. Foakes, *Dark Comedies to Last Plays,* pp. 17–31.

42. See, for example, Albert S. Cook, "Metaphysical Poetry and *Measure for Measure,*" *Accent* 13 (1953): 122–127 and Stevenson, *Achievement of Measure for Measure,* p. 11.

43. See Jonathan R. Price, "*Measure for Measure* and the Critics: Towards a New Approach," *Shakespeare Quarterly* 20 (1969): 179–204, also notable for its survey of critical opinion.

44. For additional studies, see George L. Geckle, ed., *Twentieth Century Interpretations of Measure for Measure* (Englewood Cliffs, N.J.: Prentice-Hall, 1970).

45. The structure of the play may be a result of Shakespeare's trying to please both a private and a public audience; see Robert Kimbrough, *Shakespeare's Troilus and Cressida and Its Setting* (Cambridge: Harvard University Press, 1964), pp. 10–24, 47–74, and passim.

46. See Nevill Coghill, *Shakespeare's Professional Skills* (Cambridge: Cambridge University Press, 1964), pp. 78–97; J. M. Nosworthy, *Shakespeare's Occasional Plays: Their Origin and Transmission* (New York: Barnes & Noble, 1965), pp. 61–85.

47. On the text, see Greg, *The Shakespeare First Folio,* pp. 338–350; the New Cambridge edition, ed. Alice Walker (Cambridge: Cambridge University Press, 1957), pp. ix–x, 122–134; the New Variorum edition, eds. Harold N. Hillebrand and T. W. Baldwin (Philadelphia: Lippincott, 1953), pp. 321–349; Peter Alexander, "*Troilus and Cressida,* 1609," *Library,* 4th ser. 9 (1929): 267–286. On the date, see the New Cambridge edition, p. xxxviii; the New Variorum, pp. 362–368.

48. Walker (New Cambridge edition, pp. xliii–xlv) is uncertain as to Shakespeare's firsthand debt to Chaucer.

49. See Robert K. Presson, *Shakespeare's Troilus and Cressida and the Legends of Troy* (Madison: University of Wisconsin Press, 1953), especially pp. 137–141; New Cambridge edition, pp. xxxviii–xlvi (skeptical regarding Shakespeare's direct acquaintance with Homer); New Variorum edition, pp. 419–449; Muir, *Shakespeare's Sources,* pp. 78–96; Bullough, *Sources,* 6: 83–221.

50. This point has been convincingly made in two major studies: Una Ellis-Fermor, " 'Discord in the Spheres': The Universe of *Troilus and Cressida,*" in *The Frontiers of Drama,* 2d ed. (London: Methuen, 1964), pp. 56–76 and Arnold Stein, "*Troilus and Cressida:* The Disjunctive Imagination," *ELH* 36 (1969): 145–167. See also Richard D. Fly, " 'Suited in Like Conditions as Our Argument': Imitative Form in Shakespeare's *Troilus and Cressida,*" *Studies in English Literature, 1500–1900* 15 (1975): 273–292 and Judah Stampfer, *The Tragic Engagement: A Study of Shakespeare's Classical Tragedies* (New York: Funk & Wagnalls, 1968), pp. 131–184.

51. Lawrence, *Shakespeare's Problem Comedies,* p. 160.

52. For a brief but perceptive commentary on Thersites, see Foakes, *Dark Comedies to Last Plays,* pp. 57–58.

53. M. C. Bradbrook, "What Shakespeare Did to Chaucer's *Troilus and Criseyde,*" *Shakespeare Quarterly* 9 (1958): 311–319.

54. See, for example, Coghill, *Shakespeare's Professional Skills,* pp. 78–127 and Brian Morris, "The Tragic Structure of *Troilus and Cressida,*" *Shakespeare Quarterly* 10 (1959): 481–491.

55. See especially Oscar J. Campbell's two important studies: *Comicall Satyre and Shakespeare's Troilus and Cressida* (San Marino, Calif.: The Huntington Library, 1938), pp. 185–234 and *Shakespeare's Satire* (New York: Oxford University Press, 1943), pp. 98–120. See also Walker in the New Cambridge edition, pp. x–xxxvii. Similarly, R. A. Foakes views the play not as a tragedy but as a "heroic farce"; see his "*Troilus and Cressida* Reconsidered," *University of Toronto Quarterly* 32 (1962–1963): 142–154.

56. See David Kaula, "Will and Reason in *Troilus and Cressida,*" *Shakespeare Quarterly* 12 (1961): 271–283.

57. See especially W. R. Elton's subtle analysis, "Shakespeare's Ulysses and the Problem of Value," *Shakespeare Studies,* ed. J. Leeds Barroll, 2 (1966): 95–111. See also Ure, *William Shakespeare: The Problem Plays,* pp. 37–38.

58. S. L. Bethell, *Shakespeare and the Popular Dramatic Tradition* (Durham, N.C.: Duke University Press, 1944), p. 122.

59. Knight, "The Philosophy of *Troilus and Cressida.*" See also Terence Hawkes, *Shakespeare and the Reason* (New York: Humanities, 1965), pp. 74–82 and Coghill, *Shakespeare's Professional Skills,* pp. 109–110.

60. On this speech and its implications for the play as a whole, see Willard Farnham, "Troilus in Shapes of Infinite Desire," *Shakespeare Quarterly* 15 (1964): 257–264. On war and honor in the Trojan plot, see Kimbrough, *Troilus and Cressida and Its Setting,* pp. 112–137.

61. Winifred M. T. Nowottny, " 'Opinion' and 'Value' in *Troilus and Cressida,*" *Essays in Criticism* 4 (1954): 282–296. For a reply to Nowottny, see Frank Kermode, "Opinion, Truth and Value," *Essays in Criticism* 5 (1955): 181–187.

62. Norman Council, *When Honour's at the Stake: Ideas of Honour in Shakespeare's Plays* (London: Allen and Unwin, 1973), p. 85.

63. See Derick R. C. Marsh, "Interpretation and Misinterpretation: The Problem of *Troilus and Cressida,*" *Shakespeare Studies,* ed. J. Leeds Barroll, 1 (1965): 182–198.

64. This point is effectively made by Rossiter, *Angel with Horns,* pp. 144–146.

65. Nowottny (" 'Opinion' and 'Value' in *Troilus* and *Cressida*") takes a different view. She argues that Ulysses believes that honor is conferred by others while Troilus believes it to be of a man's own making.

66. Norman Rabkin has shown how Time creates serious problems for value and moral action in both the Troilus-Cressida plot and the Achilles plot; see his *Shakespeare and the Common Understanding* (New York: Free Press, 1967), pp. 31–57. See also Ure, *William Shakespeare: The Problem Plays,* pp. 41–42.

67. J. C. Oates, "The Ambiguity of *Troilus and Cressida,*" *Shakespeare Quarterly* 17 (1966): 142–150.

10
Tragedy

Othello
King Lear
Macbeth

"If Shakspere had died at the age of forty," Edward Dowden observes in his classic study, "it might have been said, 'The world has lost much, but the world's chief poet could hardly have created anything more wonderful than *Hamlet.*' " But *Hamlet,* he continues, is "only the point of departure in Shakspere's immense and final sweep of mind."[1] In this chapter we consider three later tragedies of transcendent artistic and intellectual significance: *Othello, King Lear,* and *Macbeth.* Each of these works explores man's complex interrelationship with the forces of evil.

It is a truism that dramatic literature usually incorporates some form of conflict between good and evil, and Shakespeare's plays are no exception. Many of the comedies contain "bad" characters, like Don John in *Much Ado about Nothing* or Duke Frederick in *As You Like It,* who make life difficult for the "good" people. The histories are often propelled by fierce hatreds, personal and ideological, such as those that fester in the soul of Richard III as he marches inexorably toward the throne. And the earlier tragedies, at least *Titus Andronicus* and *Hamlet,* abound in villains ranging from Aaron the Moor, whose depravity is almost comic, to King Claudius, who has elevated treachery to the level of a fine art.

Nevertheless, it is with Claudius that one detects a new emphasis in the presentation of evil. This development is more evident in *Othello, King Lear,* and *Macbeth.* In the earlier plays villainy is mainly physical and external. It is lodged in an identifiable person or group until such time as it is either forcibly put down or neutralized by a felicitous burst of last-minute repentance. But in *Hamlet* and, especially, the three tragedies to be discussed here, evil looms much larger. Iago, Goneril and Regan, Edmund, Macbeth and Lady Macbeth are not simple villains created to generate a few hours of anxiety in the theater, but larger-than-life embodiments of a spiritual disease that poisons the whole universe.[2]

OTHELLO

The First Quarto of *Othello* was printed in 1622; the Folio text, some 160 lines longer, appeared in 1623. Some editors maintain that both texts were derived independently from authoritative sources. Others believe that the Folio represents Shakespeare's original version and that the Quarto is a careless transcript of the play as cut for performance. According to a third view, the Folio text is Shakespeare's own revision, after performance, of the 1622 Quarto. Although the Folio text is generally superior, the modern editor must sometimes adopt a particular Quarto reading as more reliable. *Othello* was performed, probably for the first time, on November 1, 1604, but there are possible echoes of the play in the bad First Quarto of *Hamlet,* a hypothesis that, if valid, would perhaps date the play late 1602 or early 1603.[3]

The story, which comes directly from Giraldi Cinthio's "Tale of the Moor" in a prose collection known as the *Hecatommithi* (1565),[4] is terrifying in its simplicity. Othello, a noble Moor who commands the Venetian military forces, is induced by his ensign Iago to suspect his wife Desdemona of adultery with his friend Cassio. In the grip of this delusion, the hero plunges ingloriously from sublime happiness to degradation, puts out the light that is his divine Desdemona, and finally, overwhelmed at the realization of what he has done, takes his own life. How Shakespeare manages to transform an Italian melodrama into a poetic tragedy has been discussed in an earlier chapter (see p. 58). Let it merely be noted here that Shakespeare, in reworking Cinthio's tale, expunges any suggestion that Othello's jealousy may have a rational basis.

The plot is superbly constructed,[5] with virtually every element skillfully exploited by Iago so as to hasten the final catastrophe. Knowing those with whom he deals, Iago can predict and control their reactions. It is easy to persuade the lovesick Roderigo that Desdemona will tire of her husband and that Cassio will then be the only obstacle to his enjoyment of her. At Iago's instigation, this desperate young fool provokes Cassio into a drunken brawl culminating in the latter's dismissal as Othello's lieutenant. Iago can now count on Cassio's desire to regain his honor. "My reputation, Iago, my reputation!" (II, 3, 265). The stage is set for Cassio, acting on what seems sound advice from Iago, to petition Desdemona to intercede on his behalf with Othello. Meanwhile, Iago recognizes that Cassio's good looks and easy manner can be used to sow the seed of mistrust:

> He hath a person and a smooth dispose
> To be suspected—fram'd to make women false.
> (I, 3, 403–404)

Desdemona is certain not to refuse Cassio's request; she is, in Iago's words, "of so free, so kind, so apt, so blessed a disposition she holds it a vice in her goodness not to do more than she is requested" (II, 3, 325–328). And, of course, "honest Iago"[6] has credit with everyone, especially the credulous Othello:

> The Moor is of a free and open nature
> That thinks men honest that but seem to be so;
> And will as tenderly be led by th' nose
> As asses are.
>
> (I, 3, 405–408)

Somewhat obscure at first, Iago's strategy becomes explicit, built as it is upon the strengths and weaknesses of his unwitting victims and confederates:

> For whiles this honest fool [Cassio]
> Plies Desdemona to repair his fortunes,
> And she for him pleads strongly to the Moor,
> I'll pour this pestilence into his ear—
> That she repeals him for her body's lust;
> And by how much she strives to do him good,
> She shall undo her credit with the Moor.
> So will I turn her virtue into pitch . . . .
>
> (II, 3, 359–366)

Out of Desdemona's goodness he does indeed "make the net / That shall enmesh them all" (II, 3, 367–368).[7]

Iago knows how to take advantage of any circumstance that comes his way. He can overhear a casual remark and put it to devastating use, as when Desdemona expresses her surprise at Othello's reluctance to invite Cassio for dinner:

> What? Michael Cassio,
> That came a-wooing with you, and so many a time,
> When I have spoke of you dispraisingly,
> Hath ta'en your part—to have so much to do
> To bring him in?
>
> (III, 3, 70–74)

When Desdemona leaves the stage, Iago converts this innocent piece of information into something sinister:

> *Iago:* Did Michael Cassio, when you woo'd my lady,
>   Know of your love?
> *Othello:* He did, from first to last. Why dost
>   thou ask?

Iago: But for a satisfaction of my thought;
    No further harm.
Othello: Why of thy thought, Iago?
Iago: I did not think he had been acquainted
    with her.
Othello: O, yes, and went between us very oft.
Iago: Indeed?

(III, 3, 94–101)

Near the end of the council chamber scene, in which Desdemona publicly attests to her love for Othello, her father Brabantio sounds an angry
warning:

Look to her, Moor, if thou hast eyes to see.
She has deceiv'd her father, and may thee.

(I, 3, 293–294)

One would be inclined to dismiss this outburst as the vindictive rhetoric
of an embittered old man, except that in a later scene, when Othello's
faith is beginning to waver, Iago recalls the admonition and adds some
embellishments of his own:

She did deceive her father, marrying you;
And when she seem'd to shake and fear your looks,
She lov'd them most.
. . . .
She that, so young, could give out such a seeming
To seel her father's eyes up close as oak . . . .

(III, 3, 206–210)

Iago's opportunism is nowhere better illustrated than in the incident
of the handkerchief. At a critical juncture in the play, with Othello
misinterpreting Desdemona's interest in Cassio but lacking "ocular proof"
(III, 3, 360) of her infidelity, Iago happens upon a phenomenal piece of
luck. Desdemona, rebuffed in the act of soothing a pain in Othello's
forehead (an allusion to the cuckold's horns traditionally imputed to
the deceived husband), chances to drop a handkerchief he had once
given her as a love token. The handkerchief is retrieved by Iago's wife
Emilia, who unquestioningly surrenders it to him, not knowing that he
intends to "lose" it in Cassio's lodging and report to Othello that he has
seen Cassio wiping his beard with it. When Desdemona cannot produce
the handkerchief on demand, Othello grows more suspicious. The web
tightens. Cassio finds the handkerchief and, ignorant of its history, asks
his mistress, the courtesan Bianca, to copy it for him. Iago stations Othello
in a hiding place from which he can see but not hear distinctly; then he
proceeds to banter Cassio concerning Bianca. When he hears Cassio's

ribald laughter, Othello assumes that Desdemona is the subject of their conversation and burns with rage. The plan succeeds beyond Iago's fondest dreams, for, while Othello looks on, Bianca herself unexpectedly enters and returns the handkerchief to Cassio. The case against Desdemona now seems conclusive. "She gave it him," Iago is quick to point out, "and he hath giv'n it his whore" (IV, 1, 186–187). Iago urges Othello to strangle Desdemona that very night in "the bed she hath contaminated." "Good, good!" Othello replies. "The justice of it pleases" (IV, 1, 220–222).

As the play unfolds, we appear to be learning a great deal about Iago from what he says, what he does, what he professes to believe. Most would agree that he is cynical. Love, he tells Roderigo, "is merely a lust of the blood and a permission of the will" (I, 3, 339–340); and he jestingly remarks to Desdemona that a truly deserving woman, if such exists, is only fit "to suckle fools and chronicle small beer" (II, 1, 161). He confides to Roderigo that, whatever show of love and duty he may exhibit, his ultimate loyalty is to himself. He prefers to remain elusive:

> For when my outward action doth demonstrate
> The native act and figure of my heart
> In compliment extern, 'tis not long after
> But I will wear my heart upon my sleeve
> For daws to peck at. I am not what I am.
> (I, 1, 61–65)

Many critics have called attention to the fact that Iago's language is cold, colorless, and prosaic. Unlike Othello, who fills his speech with rich and romantic imagery, Iago rarely uses images at all. When he does, it is often for the purpose of arousing disgust in others. He informs Brabantio of Desdemona's marriage by means of animal images that reek of sexuality. "Even now, now, very now, an old black ram / Is tupping your white ewe" (I, 1, 88–89). "You'll have your daughter cover'd with a Barbary horse" (I, 1, 111–112). "I am one, sir, that come to tell you your daughter and the Moor are now making the beast with two backs" (I, 1, 116–118). Iago later employs the same tactics when preparing Othello to accept circumstantial rather than direct evidence. "Would you, the supervisor, grossly gape on?" he asks. "Behold her topp'd?" (III, 3, 395–96). Desdemona and Cassio will hardly let anyone see them "bolster" (III, 3, 399):

> It is impossible you should see this,
> Were they as prime as goats, as hot as monkeys,
> As salt as wolves in pride . . . .
> (III, 3, 402–404)

We have ample opportunity to observe Iago in action and to admire the techniques of one who is surely the most fascinating villain in dramatic literature.[8]

Yet we know very little. At the end of the play, when the enormity of Iago's evil is at last revealed, Othello asks the inevitable question: "Will you, I pray, demand that demi-devil / Why he hath ensnar'd my soul and body?" Everyone on the stage and in the audience awaits the answer, and it comes—a stone wall:

> Demand me nothing. What you know, you know.
> From this time forth I never will speak word.
> (V, 2, 301–304)

Iago either does not know or will not say *why*. Nevertheless, it is tempting to peck away in search of some adequate explanation for his behavior. For many, in fact, Iago's motivation has become the focus of the play.[9]

Several scholars have examined Iago against the background of Elizabethan dramatic tradition. In a well-known study published in 1915, E. E. Stoll refers to the convention of "the calumniator credited," whereby the hero "unpsychologically believes whatever the slanderer (and the poet) would have him believe." Bernard Spivack sees Iago as descending from the medieval morality Vice that contends against the forces of good for possession of the human soul. Paul Siegel takes the position that Iago is a devil in the service of the Prince of Darkness who is determined to drive Adam (Othello) out of Paradise. In contrast, Tucker Brooke's "romantic Iago" stumbles into diabolism by accident; he is simply a warmhearted and exuberant boy whose mischief making gets out of hand. Harley Granville-Barker considers Iago a "shoddy creature," the "melodramatic actor in real life." In a similar vein, Richard Flatter writes of Iago's "raving hunger for self-aggrandisement" and "passion for play-acting." Among actors and directors, one finds a corresponding range of approaches to the character of Iago. José Ferrer (in the 1943 Theatre Guild production, with Paul Robeson as Othello) played him with swashbuckling good humor. Frank Finlay, in counterpoint to Laurence Olivier's titanic Othello for the National Theatre (1963), portrayed Iago on stage, and later on screen, as a quietly efficient soldier, resentful of Cassio's promotion and determined to get even with the higher-ups.[10] The Iago in the Orson Welles film version (1950) seemed less a human being than a disembodied, malevolent whisper. The diversity is indeed remarkable.[11]

Iago is often explained according to one or another of his avowed motives. To Roderigo he expresses indignation that Cassio, an "arithmetician" and a "Florentine" at that (I, 1, 19–20), was Othello's choice to be lieutenant. But this complaint seems forgotten by the time Iago utters his first soliloquy, in which he suggests that his wife may be committing adultery with Othello:

> I hate the Moor;
> And it is thought abroad that 'twixt my sheets
> 'Has done my office. I know not if't be true;
> Yet I, for mere suspicion in that kind,
> Will do as if for surety.
>
> (I, 3, 392–396)

Coleridge, in a celebrated phrase, characterizes this speech as "the motive-hunting of a motiveless malignity,"[12] an observation applying with equal force to a later soliloquy (II, 1, 295–321), in which Iago reaffirms his "suspicion" of Emilia and Othello but mentions for the first and only time two fresh considerations. First, he claims that he himself loves Desdemona, partly out of lust but partly out of a hunger for revenge against the man who, in his fancy, may have dishonored him:

> And nothing can or shall content my soul
> Till I am even'd with him, wife for wife.
>
> (II, 1, 307–308)

Second, he says parenthetically that Emilia may also be involved in a sexual relationship with Cassio.[13] As Robert B. Heilman has commented, "Iago's case is too good; as a hunter of motives he has bagged more than the legal limit." In the words of Nevill Coghill, he is "entertaining a fantasy in order to feed a passion."[14]

Without diminishing Iago's stature as a dramatic character, one should recognize that his motivation is not the central issue of the play. It is probable that Shakespeare's contemporaries would have accepted the fact of an out-and-out villain on the stage without feeling the urge to psychologize him "to the last inch of his human similitude."[15] Moreover, to motivate Iago would be in a sense to excuse him, and a justifiable Iago— no less than a corruptible Desdemona—would create a different kind of drama. Most important, the hero is not Iago but Othello. If Iago were precisely characterized, we might be distracted from the play's moral and artistic center, "the tragedy of a free and lordly creature taken in the toils, and writhing to death."[16] This does not mean that Iago is a mere abstraction; on the contrary, Shakespeare brings him vividly to life and endows him with a wealth of human characteristics. However, he refuses to delve into the origins of Iago's actions. His depravity is assumed; it is the starting point of the drama. "Here, upon the earth, evil is."[17] That is all we know and, as far as this tragedy is concerned, all we need to know.

Once we accept the basic premise that Iago represents evil incarnate and inexplicable, we are free to move on to a question of far greater interest and significance: What is there in Othello that renders him peculiarly vulnerable to the machinations of a demidevil? Some would claim that Othello is just a barbarian with an undeveloped mind.[18] But the answer is not that simple.

At first Othello exhibits exceptional self-control, as evidenced in his somewhat smug response to Iago's report that Brabantio intends to annul his marriage to Desdemona:

> Let him do his spite.
> My services which I have done the signiory
>   [the Venetian state]
> Shall outtongue his complaints.
>   (I, 2, 17–19)

He reacts to Brabantio and his band of armed followers politely, though not without a trace of irony:

> Keep up your bright swords, for the dew will rust them.
> Good signior, you shall more command with years
> Than with your weapons.
>   (I, 2, 59–61)

In the presence of the Duke and the Senators, Othello delivers what purports to be "a round [plain] unvarnish'd tale" of his courtship. To Desdemona he had spoken of fierce battles and narrow escapes; of being captured, sold into slavery, and set free; of travels to faraway places, where he saw "hills whose heads touch heaven," cannibals called "Anthropophagi," and "men whose heads / Do grow beneath their shoulders" (I, 3, 90, 128–145). As one critic has observed, "we seem to hear the voice of a Renaissance explorer, if not an Odysseus."[19] In this fantastic mixture of fact and fable, it is again possible to detect a tone of thinly veiled condescension. (This point was deftly underscored in Olivier's performance by a patronizing glance cast toward Brabantio at the mention of men whose heads "grow beneath their shoulders.") Othello, during the early scenes, appears quite pleased with his ancestry, his heroic accomplishments, his part in the forthcoming war, and, above all, his success in gaining the sympathy and love of a beautiful young Venetian gentlewoman.

The marriage of Othello and Desdemona, incongruous though it may seem to Brabantio, makes sense psychologically. Othello appeals to Desdemona's sense of adventure, which has no outlet in Venice and certainly cannot be satisfied by Roderigo or the other "wealthy curled darlings" of her nation (I, 2, 68). In requesting the Duke's permission to accompany Othello to Cyprus, Desdemona declares that she married him because she admired his courage and wanted to share in his destiny:

> That I did love the Moor to live with him,
> My downright violence, and storm of fortunes,
> May trumpet to the world. My heart's subdu'd
> Even to the very quality of my lord.
> I saw Othello's visage in his mind,
> And to his honours and his valiant parts
> Did I my soul and fortunes consecrate.
>   (I, 3, 249–255)

If Othello answers to Desdemona's craving for excitement, she in turn gives him promise of a serenity that he had never before known. She is his "fair warrior" (II, 1, 184), a phrase that suggests Othello's "unmetaphoring" of literary love conventions.[20] After their reunion at Cyprus following a severe storm at sea, he is thankful that she has brought tranquillity to his own tempestuous life:

>   O my soul's joy!
> If after every tempest come such calms,
> May the winds blow till they have waken'd death!
> . . . .
>   If it were now to die,
> 'Twere now to be most happy; for I fear
> My soul hath her content so absolute
> That not another comfort like to this
> Succeeds in unknown fate.
>   (II, 1, 186–195)

In a famous passage in his speech to the Senate, Othello gave a brief but touching explanation of what he perceives to be the secret of their mutual attraction:

> She lov'd me for the dangers I had pass'd.
> And I lov'd her that she did pity them.
>   (I, 3, 167–168)

The lovers are well matched. Even Iago grudgingly admits that the Moor is graced with "a constant, loving, noble nature" and will prove "a most dear husband" to Desdemona (II, 1, 297–300).

In transporting Othello and Desdemona to Cyprus, Shakespeare casts additional light on their relationship and enriches our understanding of the moral and psychological patterns of the play. As we have seen, the move affords Desdemona the opportunity to demonstrate her loyalty to her husband and her willingness to assume bold risks to prove her devotion. Then, too, the removal from her familiar environment isolates her during her ordeal. Finally, in what Alvin Kernan describes as the "symbolic geography" of the play, Cyprus stands as an insecure Christian outpost on the frontier of barbarism. It is an uneasy middle ground between civilization, represented by "The City" Venice and Desdemona, and ancient chaos, identified with the Turks, Iago, and the savage origins of Othello himself. In the psyche of Othello, a "barbarian" and convert to Christianity, these polar forces are maintained in precarious balance.[21]

Although Othello and Desdemona genuinely love each other, there are serious obstacles to their continued happiness: discrepancy in age, difference in race, utter dissimilarity in culture.[22] Othello, an alien who is tolerated but not accepted in Venetian society, must to some extent regard Desdemona as a prize to which he may not be legitimately entitled. Nor can he escape the fear that his good fortune will one day be revoked. It was unnatural, Brabantio tells him, for "a maid so tender, fair, and happy" to run away "to the sooty bosom / Of such a thing as thou" (I, 2, 66–71), and the insult is repeated before the full Senate:

> And she—in spite of nature,
> Of years, of country, credit, everything—
> To fall in love with what she fear'd to look on!
> (I, 3, 96–98)

Iago later picks up the same theme, pointing out to Othello that Desdemona may some day have second thoughts, especially when she compares him to her own countrymen:

> Not to affect many proposed matches
> Of her own clime, complexion, and degree,
> Whereto we see in all things nature tends—
> Foh! one may smell in such a will most rank,
> Foul disproportion, thoughts unnatural—
> But pardon me—I do not in position
> Distinctly speak of her; though I may fear
> Her will, recoiling to her better judgment,
> May fall to match you with her country forms,
> And happily [perhaps] repent.
> (III, 3, 229–238)

Othello has tried to reassure himself. "For she had eyes, and chose me" (III, 3, 189). But the doubts, which Brabantio brought to the surface and Iago slyly nurtured, do not go away:

> Haply [perhaps], for I am black
> And have not those soft parts of conversation
> That chamberers [gallants; lovers] have, or
>   for I am declin'd
> Into the vale of years (yet that's not much),
> She's gone.
>   (III, 3, 263–267)

"O curse of marriage," he exclaims, "That we can call these delicate creatures ours, / And not their appetites!" (III, 3, 268–270).

The troubles besetting Othello seem to converge in a major problem, his fear that he may not be sexually adequate. Othello finds himself in the well-established literary tradition of the older man in love with a young woman, and whether he chooses to do so or not, he is virtually forced by the circumstances of the drama to view his marriage to Desdemona as a test of virility. Othello himself raises the issue when, supporting Desdemona's plea that the Duke let her go with him to Cyprus, he insists that he is not motivated by lust. He acknowledges, in fact, that his sexual drive is no longer potent:

> Vouch with me heaven, I therefore beg it not
> To please the palate of my appetite,
> Nor to comply with heat—the young affects
> In me defunct—and proper satisfaction;
> But to be free and bounteous to her mind.
>   (I, 3, 263–267)

Reinforcing Othello's sexual insecurity, according to the controversial Polish critic Jan Kott, is his awareness that Desdemona unconsciously generates a strong current of eroticism. "Desdemona is sexually obsessed with Othello, but all men—Iago, Cassio, Roderigo—are obsessed with Desdemona."[23] One need not subscribe to all the details of Kott's interpretation to agree that the play best succeeds in reading and in performance if its erotic quality is taken into account.

It is interesting in this connection that Shakespeare makes a point of delaying the consummation of the marriage. On his wedding night Othello is summoned to the Senate and dispatched forthwith to war, occasioning the Duke's observation that the bridegroom is obliged to "slubber [soil] the gloss" of his new fortunes (I, 3, 227–228). In Cyprus, after a prolonged separation from Desdemona, Othello again anticipates the delights of married love:

> Come, my dear love.
> The purchase made, the fruits are to ensue;
> That profit's yet to come 'tween me and you.
>   (II, 3, 8–10)

But he is interrupted by the raucous fighting of Cassio and Montano. A moment ago they were friends, "like bride and groom," Iago notes in a suggestive image, "devesting [undressing] them for bed" (II, 3, 180–181). The frustrated Othello for the first time loses his equanimity:

> Now, by heaven,
> My blood begins my safer guides to rule,
> And passion, having my best judgment
> collied [darkened],
> Assays to lead the way. If I once stir
> Or do but lift this arm, the best of you
> Shall sink in my rebuke.
> (II, 3, 204–209)

With quiet restored and Cassio regretfully demoted, Othello at last leads Desdemona to bed. The emotional tension created by the drinking scene is real, however, and it does not augur well for their happiness.[24]

One ever marvels at the artistry of the process by which Othello is induced to drink Iago's poison. With the half-whispered, "Ha! I like not that" (III, 3, 35), muttered as Cassio takes embarrassed leave of Desdemona (could it be *Cassio* stealing away "so guilty-like?" [III, 3, 39]), Iago launches his teasing insinuations. "Indeed?" "Honest, my lord?" "Think, my lord?" "I dare be sworn I think that he is honest" (III, 3, 101–125). Far be it from Iago to disturb Othello's peace of mind by uttering his thoughts. Nor will he damage anyone's reputation:

> Good name in man and woman, dear my lord,
> Is the immediate jewel of their souls.
> Who steals my purse steals trash; 'tis something,
> nothing;
> 'Twas mine, 'tis his, and has been slave to
> thousands;
> But he that filches from me my good name
> Robs me of that which not enriches him
> And makes me poor indeed.
> (III, 3, 155–161)

Iago speaks on several levels simultaneously. "Good name," or reputation (so important to Cassio), obviously alludes to Othello's estimate of his friend's trustworthiness. But "good name" also bears upon Desdemona's chastity, Othello's sexual honor as a husband, and Iago's good standing with everybody else in the play.[25] Othello is thoroughly bewildered by this verbal legerdemain, especially because, like much of Iago's commentary, the speech has a deceptive ring of moral sincerity. Taking advantage of his victim's confusion, Iago abruptly introduces

the subject of jealousy, which he depicts metaphorically as a fabled
creature that might have inhabited Othello's distant past:

> O, beware, my lord, of jealousy!
> It is the green-ey'd monster, which doth mock
> The meat it feeds on.
>
> (III, 3, 165–167)

Iago plays effectively on the outsider's unfamiliarity with the sexual
mores of Venetian women:

> I know our country disposition well:
> In Venice they do let heaven see the pranks
> They dare not show their husbands; their best conscience
> Is not to leave't undone, but keep't unknown.
>
> (III, 3, 201–204)

To this presumably expert testimony, Othello can only respond with a
pathetic "Dost thou say so?" (III, 3, 205).

After securing Desdemona's handkerchief, Iago can afford to be more
daring. To quote G. Wilson Knight, he even "filches something of
Othello's style and uses it himself":[26]

> Look where he comes! Not poppy nor mandragora,
> Nor all the drowsy syrups of the world,
> Shall ever medicine thee to that sweet sleep
> Which thou ow'dst [possessed] yesterday.
>
> (III, 3, 330–333)

What unhinges Othello most in this scene is Iago's account of Cassio's
fictitious dream (an episode that Verdi's opera *Otello* re-creates with
wonderful sensuality in the passage beginning "Era la notte").[27] Realizing
that he cannot make Othello an eyewitness to Desdemona's nonexistent
adultery, Iago conjures up an explicit vision of sexual intercourse:

> In sleep I heard him say, "Sweet Desdemona,
> Let us be wary, let us hide our loves!"
> And then, sir, would he gripe and wring my hand,
> Cry "O sweet creature!" and then kiss me hard,
> As if he pluck'd up kisses by the roots
> That grew upon my lips; then laid his leg
> Over my thigh, and sigh'd, and kiss'd, and then
> Cried "Cursed fate that gave thee to the Moor!"
>
> (III, 3, 419–426)[28]

Othello finds the recital maddening, cries out for Cassio's blood, and confirms his oath of revenge with a magnificent image drawn from his vast geographic knowledge:

> Like to the Pontic sea,
> Whose icy current and compulsive course
> Ne'er feels retiring ebb, but keeps due on
> To the Propontic and the Hellespont;
> Even so my bloody thoughts, with violent pace,
> Shall ne'er look back, ne'er ebb to humble love,
> Till that a capable and wide revenge
> Swallow them up.
>
> (III, 3, 453–460)

This overpowering "temptation scene" is crowned by a hideous ritual. Othello kneels and swears vengeance "by yond marble heaven"; Iago likewise kneels and pledges himself to Othello's service, "what bloody business ever"; and the two enter into a pact reminiscent of Dr. Faustus selling his soul to Mephistophilis.[29] "I greet thy love," says Othello. "Now art thou my lieutenant." Iago replies, "I am your own for ever" (III, 3, 460–479).

Othello's subsequent deterioration is appalling. He makes lewd puns. "Lie with her? lie on her?—We say lie on her when they belie her.—Lie with her!" (IV, 1, 35–36). He strikes Desdemona in public, and when the Duke's emissary Lodovico bids him call her back, he plays obscenely with the word *turn:*

> Ay! You did wish that I would make her turn.
> Sir, she can turn, and turn, and yet go on,
> And turn again.
>
> (IV, 1, 263–265)

Moreover, Othello begins to fill his imagination and speech with Iago-like references to animals and copulation: "goats and monkeys" (IV, 1, 274); "a cistern for foul toads / To knot and gender [breed] in" (IV, 2, 61–62); "summer flies ... in the shambles [slaughterhouse], / That quicken even with blowing" (IV, 2, 66–67). His most loathsome act is to visit Desdemona as though he were a customer in a brothel (IV, 2). Nothing is more malicious than his sarcastic apology upon hearing Desdemona's denial of wrongdoing:

> I cry you mercy then.
> I took you for that cunning whore of Venice
> That married with Othello.
>
> (IV, 2, 86–90)

One is reminded of what Ophelia says of Hamlet after the similarly brutal "Get thee to a nunnery" scene: "O, what a noble mind is here o'erthrown!" (*Hamlet,* III, 1, 158).

As a further symptom of his distorted sense of reality, Othello commits murder in the name of justice. "It is the cause, it is the cause, my soul" (V, 2, 1), he soliloquizes as he enters Desdemona's bedchamber. He does not want to shed her blood or scar her lovely skin. "Yet she must die, else she'll betray more men" (V, 2, 6). This statement, in its "vague, unique altruism,"[30] betokens Othello's determination to justify the horror he is about to perpetrate. When he bends down to kiss Desdemona in her sleep, he softens for a moment, but he is quickly recalled to his solemn obligation:

> O balmy breath, that dost almost persuade
> Justice to break her sword! One more, one more!
> Be thus when thou art dead, and I will kill thee,
> And love thee after.
>
> (V, 2, 16–19)

Like a priest, he bids her think of "any crime / Unreconcil'd as yet to heaven and grace" (V, 2, 26–27). "Think on thy sins" (V, 2, 40). "Take heed of perjury; thou art on thy deathbed" (V, 2, 51). Desdemona's unwavering assertion of innocence serves only to intensify his anger:

> O perjur'd woman! thou dost stone my heart,
> And mak'st me call what I intend to do
> A murther, which I thought a sacrifice.
>
> (V, 2, 63–65)

To add ironic emphasis to Othello's tragic wrongheadedness, Desdemona remains faithful to the very end. While preparing for bed that night, she had recalled (IV, 3, 41–57) the melancholy "Willow Song," a popular ballad sung by her mother's maid Barbary while the poor soul was dying of unrequited love; and in repeating the song, Desdemona had introduced a line not in the original, then corrected herself: "Let nobody blame him; his scorn I approve" (IV, 3, 52). Desdemona's last utterance is a poignant falsehood, intended, like the earlier interpolation, to exonerate the man who has misjudged and forsaken her:

> *Emilia:* O, who hath done this deed?
> *Desdemona:* Nobody—I myself. Farewell.
>   Commend me to my kind lord. O, farewell!
>
> (V, 2, 123–125)[31]

Othello misses the point. "She's like a liar gone to burning hell!" he exclaims. " 'Twas I that kill'd her" (V, 2, 129–130). About Desdemona's death Dr. Johnson has spoken definitively: "It is not to be endured."[32]

At long last, however, decency is partially restored to the world that Iago has corrupted. Iago goads Roderigo into a fight with Cassio, hoping that the two will kill each other and thereby relieve him of the threat of disclosure. But the plan miscarries when Cassio receives only a slight wound. Iago, who has always succeeded in inciting others to do his dirty work, is reduced to the ignominy of murdering Roderigo in the dark. The dying Roderigo becomes the first person to see through Iago's facade. "O damn'd Iago! O inhuman dog!" (V, 1, 62). To complete the exposure of Iago, Emilia, who knows how the handkerchief was lost, grasps the extent of her husband's villainy and summons the courage to unmask him, even though he will take her life for this act. "O, lay me by my mistress' side" (V, 2, 237), she implores, and, in a gesture strange for one professing to be so worldly, she dies with an echo of the "Willow Song" on her lips.

And what effect does all this have on Othello? His initial reaction is a frenzy of grief and self-pity:

Whip me, ye devils,
From the possession of this heavenly sight!
Blow me about in winds! roast me in sulphur!
Wash me in steep-down gulfs of liquid fire!
O Desdemona, Desdemona! dead!
O! O! O!

(V, 2, 277–282)

"An honourable murderer," he calls himself. "For naught did I in hate, but all in honour" (V, 2, 294–295).[33] One begins to think that Othello has learned nothing from his shattering experience, especially when he instinctively lapses into his old complacency. "I have done the state some service, and they know't," he begins. But he realizes that he cannot at this awful moment rest on past laurels. "No more of that" (V, 2, 339–340). The remainder of this speech, just before his suicide, consists of a heartbreaking admission of error. As in his address to the Senate about the wooing of Desdemona, the imagery is drawn from an exotic world, but the tone is more humble:

Speak of me as I am. Nothing extenuate,
Nor set down aught in malice. Then must you speak
Of one that lov'd not wisely, but too well;
Of one not easily jealous, but, being wrought,
Perplex'd in the extreme; of one whose hand
(Like the base Indian) threw a pearl away

Richer than all his tribe; of one whose subdu'd eyes,
Albeit unused to the melting mood,
Drop tears as fast as the Arabian trees
Their med'cinable gum.

(V, 2, 342–351)

Belatedly, Othello has acquired a measure of wisdom.

Helen Gardner believes that Othello has no real flaw and that the play merely shows that there is always something in the nature of our temporal existence that defeats even the noblest of us.[34] But according to a number of critics, Othello's downfall stems from excessive pride, which leads the self-righteous hero to arrogate unto himself the godlike function of sitting in judgment.[35] Moreover, the value justice, which Othello mistakenly thinks he represents and enforces, is said to come into well-nigh irreconcilable conflict with an equally cogent value, love. Justice demands evidence, like a handkerchief or some other tangible proof; love requires an absolute "intuitive belief which is irrelevant to justice, as justice to it."[36] How, we ask, could Othello have resisted Iago? "The answer would seem to be, By an affirmation of faith which is beyond reason, by the act of choosing to believe in Desdemona."[37] In choosing not to believe, Othello casts away a pearl of infinite richness.

KING LEAR

Few of Shakespeare's plays pose as many textual problems as does *King Lear*. The First Quarto, called the Pied Bull Quarto (from the sign hung outside the shop of the printer Nathaniel Butter), was published in 1608; a reprint (Q2), mistakenly dated 1608, appeared in 1619. Both texts are probably memorial reconstructions of a performing version. As noted previously (see p. 41), the printing of Elizabethan books generally continued during the process of proofreading, and for that reason there are many textual differences among the twelve surviving copies of Q1 as well as between Q1 and Q2. The Folio (F) version (1623), which omits some 300 lines of Quarto text but adds about 100, is generally considered superior to the two Quartos, although one cannot say precisely how it evolved. The present-day consensus has been stated by G. I. Duthie, editor of the New Cambridge *King Lear:* "All we can be sure of, I think, is that at certain points F depends, directly or indirectly, on edited pages of a Q1, at other points on edited pages of a Q2, with the editing reflecting the text of an official prompt-book, and with a certain element of inefficiency and error in the editing to be taken account of."[38] Modern editors tend to follow the Folio text, modified by readings from the First and Second Quartos.

King Lear was composed some time between 1603 and 1606. Shakespeare draws heavily upon Samuel Harsnett's *Declaration of Egregious Popish Impostures,* which was entered in the Stationers' Register on March 16, 1603. We know from the entry for *King Lear* itself (November 26, 1607) that a performance took place at court on December 26, 1606. An older play, *The True Chronicle History of King Leir,* possibly dating from 1594 or earlier, was entered in the Stationers' Register on May 8, 1605; and many scholars believe that it was revived at this time to capitalize on the success of Shakespeare's new play. Moreover, if *Macbeth,* which probably came later, was written by the summer of 1606, it is likely that *King Lear* was completed at least a year or so earlier. It has been argued that Gloucester's comment about "these late eclipses in the sun and moon" (I, 2, 112) refers to actual phenomena in the fall of 1605, but such allusions need not be to specific events. All in all, the winter of 1604–1605 seems a plausible date for the play.[39]

The story of Lear and his daughters, which is derived from ancient British history and legend, begins in the fairy-tale realm of "once upon a time." The old King of Britain announces that he will divide his kingdom among his three daughters, giving the largest share to the one who declares she loves him most. The two older daughters, Goneril and Regan, proclaim their devotion with unrestrained eloquence. But the youngest, Cordelia, who is Lear's favorite, states simply that she loves him according to her bond as a daughter, "no more nor less" (I, 1, 95). Lear becomes so furious that he disinherits Cordelia (who is accepted in marriage by the King of France) and confers all his possessions upon Goneril and Regan, along with their respective husbands, the Duke of Albany and the Duke of Cornwall. He also banishes the Earl of Kent for urging him to reconsider, but this faithful lord assumes a disguise so as to remain in his country and serve his king.

When Cordelia departs for France with her husband, Lear is left at the mercy of Goneril and Regan. Almost immediately he suffers indignities at the hands of his elder daughters, whose cruelty is abetted by Cornwall. They plan to reduce Lear's retinue, and when he protests that Cornwall has placed his servant (the disguised Kent) in the stocks, he receives from Regan a chilly reply: "I pray you, father, being weak, seem so" (II, 4, 204). Enraged by his daughters' inhumanity as well as by his own powerlessness, Lear, accompanied by his Fool, rushes out into a wild storm, and Regan orders the doors shut against him. As he stands on the heath, exposing himself to the wind and the rain, Lear goes mad. Eventually he is reunited with Cordelia near Dover, where she has come with an invading army from France. When the British forces defeat the French, Lear and Cordelia are captured and imprisoned. Shortly thereafter, with Cornwall dead and with Goneril having poisoned Regan and taken her own life, an order for the deaths of Lear and Cordelia is rescinded. But it is too late. Lear enters carrying the body of Cordelia, then dies himself.

Shakespeare does not merely retell the story of Lear. With inspired artistic invention, he introduces a subplot (adapted from the episode of the blind Paphlagonian King, in book 2, chapter 10, of Sir Philip Sidney's *Arcadia* [1590]) that tells the story of another foolish old man. The Earl of Gloucester is persuaded by his illegitimate son Edmund that his lawful son, the virtuous Edgar, intends to kill him and take over his lands. Edgar has to flee for his life, adopting the disguise of "Poor Tom," beggar and lunatic. Midway through the play, the two plots converge. Lear takes refuge from the storm in a hovel occupied by "Poor Tom"; and Gloucester, disobeying Cornwall's command that the King not be succored in any way, seeks Lear out in his meager shelter and leads him to a farmhouse, where he and his companions—the disguised Kent, the Fool, and "Poor Tom" (whom Gloucester, of course, does not recognize)—will find warmth and comfort. When Cornwall learns from Edmund about this act of kindness, he has Gloucester arrested and, cheered on by Regan, puts out his eyes. At last Gloucester is aware of Edmund's true nature. Blind and despondent, he places himself under the tutelage of Edgar (still in disguise) and, like Lear, is led to Dover. Eventually Gloucester's spirits are restored. When Edgar at last reveals his identity, Gloucester's heart, we are told, " 'Twixt two extremes of passion, joy and grief, / Burst smilingly" (V, 3, 198–199).

Although the tale of Lear and his daughters first appeared in complete form in Geoffrey of Monmouth's *History of the Kings of Britain* (c. 1136) and was well known to Elizabethan audiences, Shakespeare's most immediate source was the aforementioned play *The True Chronicle History of King Leir*. He also seems to have used versions found in John Higgins's 1574 edition of *The Mirror for Magistrates,* Holinshed's *Chronicles* (1578; 1587), and book 2, canto 10, of Edmund Spenser's *Faerie Queene* (books 1–3 published 1590). In addition, he may have been acquainted with the real-life experience of Sir Brian Annesley, two of whose daughters in 1603 tried to have him declared insane so as to gain control of his estate while a third daughter (named Cordell) successfully protected his interests. In any case, Shakespeare departs significantly from his literary sources, most notably in the ending. In the old play the King returns to the throne, and he and his daughter presumably live happily ever after.[40] He also refuses to follow the irrelevant sequence presented in the other versions wherein the King regains the throne, rules peacefully until his death, and is succeeded by Cordelia, who reigns as Queen for several years before committing suicide for reasons having nothing to do with her father's travails. Shakespeare's

Cordelia is killed in prison, and the impact of her death, on Lear as well as on an audience, is stupendous.

King Lear has echoes of other specific works, in particular, Harsnett's *Declaration,* an attack upon Jesuit exorcists, from which Shakespeare borrows numerous verbal details, including the names of the devils invoked by "Poor Tom"; and John Florio's translation (1603) of Montaigne's *Essays* (which may be responsible for more than 100 words that are part of the play's vocabulary). In speaking of sources, however, one should look beyond identifiable works to note the important fact that Shakespeare incorporates into *King Lear* several archetypal themes from folk literature, medieval romance, and the morality play. Lear's spiritual pilgrimage corresponds to the Abasement of the Proud King; Kent in the stocks suggests the emblematic situation of Virtue Locked Out, the Messenger of the King (or of God) Turned Away, or Honesty Left to Freeze; and, as Alfred Harbage observes, Lear's position in the opening scene calls to mind the symbolic figure sometimes known in medieval and early Renaissance drama as Mankind, Everyman, or *Genus Humanum* flanked by opposing forces, "vices or flatterers on the one hand, virtues or truth-speakers on the other."[41]

Unlike the older play, which requires seven scenes to introduce characters and establish motivation, *King Lear* begins immediately, cutting away virtually the entire past history of the principal actors in the tragedy.[42] After a brief conversation in which Gloucester, with jovial but simpleminded sensuality, recalls the "good sport" of his bastard son's "making" (I, 1, 22–23), Lear strides imperiously onto the stage and springs his surprise. It seems that he has already decided how to divide his kingdom. But driven by vanity and the need to bolster his image as the all-powerful father and king, he forces his daughters to compete in a public expression of filial love. Goneril plays the game according to Lear's plan:

> Sir, I love you more than words can wield the matter;
> Dearer than eyesight, space, and liberty;
> Beyond what can be valued, rich or rare;
> No less than life, with grace, health, beauty, honour;
> As much as child e'er lov'd, or father found;
> A love that makes breath poor, and speech unable.
> Beyond all manner of so much I love you.
>
> (I, 1, 56–62)

Regan endorses everything Goneril says and goes even further:

> Only she comes too short, that I profess
> Myself an enemy to all other joys

Which the most precious square of sense possesses,
And find I am alone felicitate
In your dear Highness' love.

(I, 1, 74–78)

The Witch in "Snow White" gazes into the looking glass and repeats, "Mirror, mirror, on the wall, / Who's the fairest one of all?" Lear goes through a similar narcissistic ritual, and, turning to Cordelia for what he thinks will be the climactic outpouring of flattery, he, like the Witch, is taken aback by an unexpected answer:

> *Lear:*   Now, our joy,
>   Although the last, not least; to whose young love
>   The vines of France and milk of Burgundy
>   Strive to be interest; what can you say to draw
>   A third more opulent than your sisters? Speak.
> *Cordelia:* Nothing, my lord.
> *Lear:* Nothing?
> *Cordelia:* Nothing.
> *Lear:* Nothing can come of nothing. Speak again.
>   (I, 1, 84–92)[43]

In the words of Grigori Kozintsev, the outstanding Soviet director of Shakespearean films, "an avalanche can start with the almost imperceptible movement of a single stone."[44]

"Nothing can come of nothing." This simple maxim, which can be traced back as far as Aristotle, is rich in meanings that reverberate throughout the play. Lear, who believes that love can be measured in words and that both are convertible into real estate, makes it clear that he expects some quid pro quo: If Cordelia says nothing, she gets nothing. But he also unwittingly foreshadows one of the play's crucial developments: the disintegration into nothingness of his very identity as a king and as a man. The Fool later takes up the refrain. After Kent has dismissed as "nothing" some of his doggerel, the Fool jests at Lear's expense:

> *Fool:* Can you make no use of nothing, nuncle?
> *Lear:* Why, no, boy. Nothing can be made out of nothing.
> *Fool:* [to Kent] Prithee tell him, so much the rent of his land comes to.
>   He will not believe a fool.
>   (I, 4, 143–149)

"Now thou art an O without a figure," the Fool later tells him. "I am better than thou art now: I am a fool, thou art nothing" (I, 4, 211–214).[45]

Gloucester's downfall also starts with "nothing." Edmund, a robust villain who renounces all morality and worships a malign Nature that sanctifies the individual will,[46] hurriedly puts away a forged letter in which Edgar allegedly broaches a plot against his father's life:

> *Gloucester:* Why so earnestly seek you to put up that letter?
> *Edmund:* I know no news, my lord.
> *Gloucester:* What paper were you reading?
> *Edmund:* Nothing, my lord.
> *Gloucester:* No? What needed then that terrible dispatch of it into your pocket? The quality of nothing hath not such need to hide itself. Let's see. Come, if it be nothing, I shall not need spectacles.
>
> (I, 2, 28–36)

Unlike Lear, who is tragically self-deceived, Gloucester is simply the victim of a trick. But he pays a terrible price for his error. In what must be the most horrible scene in all drama, Gloucester is literally blinded. Cornwall gouges out one eye and then, to satisfy Regan's desire for symmetry ("One side will mock another. Th' other too!" [III, 7, 71]), completes the task. "Out, vile jelly!" he exclaims. "Where is thy lustre now?" (III, 7, 83–84). Regan turns upon Gloucester with an appalling sneer:

> Go thrust him out at gates, and let him smell
> His way to Dover.
>
> (III, 7, 93–94)

"You cannot see your way," Gloucester is told by a kindly servant who escorts him to the heath. Gloucester answers:

> I have no way, and therefore want no eyes;
> I stumbled when I saw.
>
> (IV, 1, 17–19)

It is not surprising that Gloucester should come to regard man as a pawn in some grotesque cosmic game:

> As flies to wanton boys are we to th' gods.
> They kill us for their sport.
>
> (IV, 1, 36–37)

But Gloucester, who had been tricked by Edmund into committing a ghastly error, is redeemed from consuming despair through an extraordinary ruse perpetrated by Edgar. In a daring scene that haunts the imagination, "Poor Tom" leads his blind father to what the old man thinks is an enormously high cliff from which he expects to plunge to certain death. Edgar gives a graphic description of the "abyss":

Come on, sir; here's the place. Stand still. How fearful
And dizzy 'tis to cast one's eyes so low!
The crows and choughs [jackdaws] that wing the midway air
Show scarce so gross as beetles. Halfway down
Hangs one that gathers sampire [an aromatic plant]—dreadful trade!
Methinks he seems no bigger than his head.
The fishermen that walk upon the beach
Appear like mice . . . .

. . . .

　　　　　　　　　　　　　The murmuring surge
That on th' unnumb'red idle pebble chafes
Cannot be heard so high. I'll look no more,
Lest my brain turn, and the deficient sight
Topple down headlong.

                                                    (IV, 6, 11–24)

After renouncing the world and then falling forward in a swoon,
Gloucester is convinced by Edgar, now assuming yet another identity,
that he has indeed dropped from a great height and miraculously survived:

Hadst thou been aught but gossamer, feathers, air,
So many fadom down precipitating,
Thou'dst shiver'd like an egg; but thou dost breathe;
Hast heavy substance; bleed'st not; speak'st; art sound.
Ten masts at each [one on top of the other] make not the altitude
Which thou hast perpendicularly fell.
Thy life's a miracle.

                                                    (IV, 6, 49–55)

Having in effect performed the suicidal act and emerged unharmed,
Gloucester is prepared to bear affliction patiently; and if he suffers a
relapse, Edgar can rekindle his spirit:

What, in ill thoughts again? Men must endure
Their going hence, even as their coming hither;
Ripeness is all.

                          (V, 2, 9–11)

"And that's true too," Gloucester replies.

The Gloucester story, it has been cogently argued, is a didactic illustration of the main action; it simplifies, verbally and visually, the difficult
issues raised in the drama of Lear.[47] In fact, Alvin Kernan sees the
movement of the play as a whole symbolized in the Dover scene, with
its image of precipitous descent.[48] If Lear's journey toward self-discovery
is far more complex, it is chiefly because his sins and his sufferings,
unlike those of Gloucester, come from inside himself.[49] Still hoping to

manage the "authorities / That he hath given away" (I, 3, 17–18), Lear fails to understand that he is embarked upon progressive self-diminution. When Goneril cuts the number of his retainers from one hundred to fifty, he determines to live with Regan, only to learn that the latter will permit him a mere twenty-five. As in the opening scene, Lear measures feeling by arithmetical standards. Goneril, he reasons, must be the more devoted daughter:

> Thy fifty yet doth double five-and-twenty,
> And thou art twice her love.
>   (II, 4, 262–263)

Hence he is shocked when Goneril and Regan reverse the old competitive game and launch their relentless ritual of substraction:

> *Goneril:*   Hear me, my lord
>   What need you five-and-twenty, ten, or five,
>   To follow in a house where twice so many
>   Have a command to tend you?
> *Regan:*   What need one?
>   (II, 4, 263–266)

In an impassioned response, Lear appears to sense for the first time that values cannot be expressed in sheerly quantitative terms:

> O, reason not the need! Our basest beggars
> Are in the poorest thing superfluous.
> Allow not nature more than nature needs,
> Man's life is cheap as beast's. Thou art a lady:
> If only to go warm were gorgeous,
> Why, nature needs not what thou gorgeous wear'st,
> Which scarcely keeps thee warm. But, for true need—
> You heavens, give me that patience, patience I need!
>   (II, 4, 267–274)

Threatening these "unnatural hags" (II, 4, 281) with unspecified revenges, Lear exits dramatically into the storm. "I shall go mad!" he shouts (II, 4, 289).

The storm, especially when viewed in conjunction with Lear's growing madness, serves a number of dramatic functions. For one thing, by providing a poetic symbol for the King's inner turmoil, it reinforces the Renaissance notion of man as a microcosm, a little world whose physical and psychological condition is reflected in the macrocosm, or great world (see pp. 25–26). This point is made clear in the anonymous Gentleman's description of Lear as he contends with the elements, tears at his white hair, and "strives in his little world of man to outscorn / The to-and-fro-conflicting wind and rain" (III, 1, 4–15). Lear's madness is thus intensified so as to assume superhuman proportions.

A second purpose of the storm is to convey Lear's feeling that all the normal relationships which ought to prevail in an orderly world have broken down and that the heavens themselves are demonstrating their sympathy with his plight.[50] For Lear, the storm, like the cruelty of his daughters, is "unnatural," and his view of Nature as a beneficent moral force is antithetical to the sentiments endorsed by Edmund.[51] Gloucester had earlier expressed his belief that the eclipses in the sun and the moon betoken Nature's displeasure at the erosion of man's proper social relationships:

> Love cools, friendship falls off, brothers divide. In cities, mutinies; in countries, discord; in palaces treason; and the bond crack'd 'twixt son and father .... We have seen the best of our time.
>
> (I, 2, 115–123)

Out on the heath, Lear, in poetry of unsurpassed strength, proclaims that the skies are torn asunder by the inhumanity of Goneril and Regan, and he calls down upon his head a cataclysm that will engulf himself, his daughters, and the entire universe:

> Blow, winds, and crack your cheeks! rage! blow!
> You cataracts and hurricanoes, spout
> Till you have drench'd our steeples, drown'd the cocks [weathercocks]!
>
> (III, 2, 1–3)

He bids the thunder "strike flat the thick rotundity o' th' world"[52] and spill out at once all "germains," or seeds of life, "that make ingrateful man!" (III, 2, 6–9). One thinks of that diverting song in *As You Like It* (II, 7, 174–190). "Blow, blow, thou winter wind," Amiens had sung. "Thou art not so unkind / As man's ingratitude." When Lear voices this feeling, however, the tone and style are infused with the impotent rage of "a poor, infirm, weak, and despis'd old man" (III, 2, 20):

> Rumble thy bellyful! Spit, fire! spout, rain!
> Nor rain, wind, thunder, fire are my daughters.
> I tax not you, you elements, with unkindness.
> I never gave you kingdom, call'd you children,
> You owe me no subscription [allegiance]. Then let fall
> Your horrible pleasure.
>
> (III, 2, 14–19)

Perhaps the most profound effect of the storm is to set the stage for Lear's regeneration. When Kent pleads with him to enter the hovel, Lear insists that the Fool go first while he himself remains outside to pray for mankind:

> Poor naked wretches, wheresoe'er you are,
> That bide the pelting of this pitiless storm,
> How shall your houseless heads and unfed sides,
> Your loop'd and window'd [i.e., full of holes] raggedness, defend you
> From seasons such as these? O, I have ta'en
> Too little care of this! Take physic, pomp;
> Expose thyself to feel what wretches feel,
> That thou mayst shake the superflux to them
> And show the heavens more just.
>
> (III, 4, 28–36)

When he finds "Poor Tom" shivering naked in the hovel, Lear feels that he is in the presence of quintessential man:

> Is man no more than this? Consider him well. Thou ow'st the worm no silk, the beast no hide, the sheep no wool, the cat no perfume. Ha! Here's three on's [three of us: Kent, the Fool, and Lear] are sophisticated! Thou art the thing itself; unaccommodated [unburdened by the commodities of civilization] man is no more but such a poor, bare, forked animal as thou art.
>
> (III, 4, 107–113)

"Poor Tom" has been called "the providence or guardian spirit that shows Lear the end of his journey to find his own nature."[53] In this encounter of king and beggar, a focal point of the play, a "heroic image of power" confronts "an ironic image of powerlessness."[54] Lear symbolically completes his spiritual identification with "Poor Tom" by tearing at his own clothes. This gesture may have recalled for Shakespeare's audience the many Doomsday paintings depicting all human beings as naked before God.[55] "Off, off, you lendings! Come, unbutton here" (III, 4, 113–114). If clothes, particularly the robes of kingship, have concealed Lear's identity even from himself, nakedness now becomes an aid to understanding and to self-knowledge.[56] As Nicholas Brooke has said, "This is at once the rock bottom from which reconstruction can begin and the utter deprivation in which sanity has no meaning."[57]

Once he has exposed himself to the afflictions of common humanity, Lear can rise to a new level of awareness. With "Poor Tom" and the Fool sitting as judges, he brings his daughters to "trial" in the farmhouse, addressing himself not merely to his own injuries but to the very metaphysics of evil. "Then let them anatomize Regan," he orders. "See what breeds about her heart. Is there any cause in nature that makes these hard hearts?" (III, 6, 80–82). In a later scene in which he speaks "reason in madness" (IV, 6, 179), Lear acknowledges the painful truth that his daughters had "flatter'd me like a dog, and told me I had white hairs [i.e., wisdom] in my beard ere the black ones were there . . . . They told me I was everything. 'Tis a lie—I am not ague-proof" (IV, 6, 98–107). He brings a passionate indictment against his former world, where "a dog's obey'd in office," where the beadle lusts hotly after the very whore whose back he lashes, and where "robes and furr'd gowns hide all" (IV, 6, 163–176). In such a life, he says, there is no happiness:

> *Lear:*   We came crying hither;
>   Thou know'st, the first time that we smell the air
>   We wawl and cry. I will preach to thee. Mark.
> *Gloucester:* Alack, alack the day!
> *Lear:* When we are born, we cry that we are come
>   To this great stage of fools.
>
>   (IV, 6, 182–187)

This comment recalls an earlier exchange between the King and the Fool. "Dost thou call me fool, boy?" Lear had asked and received a sardonic reply: "All thy other titles thou hast given away; that thou wast born with" (I, 4, 162–164). The Fool, like his predecessors Touchstone and Feste, is privileged to criticize his master with impunity. But in *King Lear* Shakespeare transforms the Fool into an almost mystical being whose vision transcends that of the ordinary court jester of the Renaissance. The Fool is in the tradition of the prophetic madman who sees and speaks truth, which he knows, to quote Enid Welsford's classic study, "not by ratiocination but by inspired intuition."[58]

It is the Fool who consistently perceives the comic potentialities in Lear's situation and who attempts, as G. Wilson Knight has said, "to direct the hero's mind to the present incongruity."[59] He hammers away at Lear's stupidity for having divested himself of the kingdom. The Fool cuts an egg in the middle, eats up the meat, and displays the two "crowns" that remain. "Thou hadst little wit in thy bald crown when thou gav'st thy golden one away" (I, 4, 177–179). The Fool has been full of songs, he tells Lear, "ever since thou mad'st thy daughters thy mother . . . gav'st them the rod, and put'st down thine own breeches" (I, 4, 187–190). Pointing to Lear, he calls him a "sheal'd [shelled] peascod" (I, 4, 219). Dr. Johnson has glossed this phrase with remarkable insight. Lear, he notes, is "now a mere husk, which contains nothing. The outside of a king remains, but all the intrinsic parts of royalty are gone: he has nothing to give."[60] The Fool regularly calls attention to Lear's propensity for self-pity. The King cries pathetically, "O me, my heart, my rising heart! But down!"—and is at once deflated by a bitter joke:

Cry to it, nuncle, as the cokney did to the eels when she put 'em i' th' paste [pastry pie] alive. She knapp'd [rapped] 'em o' th' coxcombs with a stick and cried "Down, wantons, down!"

(II, 4, 122–126)

When Lear tears at his clothes, the Fool reminds us that there is an element of absurdity in the gesture. "Prithee, nuncle, be contented! 'Tis a naughty night to swim in" (III, 4, 115–116).

A key moment in the play occurs when Lear, having begun to notice signs of studied neglect on the part of Goneril, asks the overwhelming question: "Who is it that can tell me who I am?" The Fool's answer, "Lear's shadow," like the question itself, is rich in ambiguity (I, 4, 250–251). Lear is really asking two questions: Who am I? Who can tell me who I am? In answer to the first question, "Lear's shadow" alludes to the King's present insubstantiality. But the second question has two answers. For one thing, it implies that only Lear himself, however diminished he may be, can resolve the problem of his own identity. At another level, we are to understand that it is the Fool, "Lear's shadow," who answers the King at that very instant. Thus an indestructible bond unites Lear with his alter ego the Fool. In the first half of the play, the devastating irony of the Fool is essential if we are to place Lear and his suffering in proper perspective. Moreover, as Granville-Barker astutely observes, it is "dramatic craft at its best to leave Lear in adversity this one fantastic remnant of royalty."[61]

But the Fool's cleansing invective can carry Lear only so far. In order to be restored to sanity and in a sense to be reborn, Lear must emerge from the nothingness into which his suffering has driven him and discover what love really means. The Fool, having finished his work, mysteriously disappears from the play. It is now time for Lear to join Cordelia at Dover and to rebuild with her the relationship he had defiled.

Shakespeare prepares the way with consummate artistry. From a messenger Kent learns of the gentleness with which Cordelia received the news of Lear's misery:

Patience and sorrow strove
Who should express her goodliest. You have seen
Sunshine and rain at once: her smiles and tears
Were like, a better way [similar, but more lovely].
(IV, 3, 18–21)

Then, after a few brief exclamations, she drowned her outcries in a flood of tears before withdrawing to complete her lamentation in private:

There she shook
The holy water from her heavenly eyes,

And clamour moisten'd. Then away she started
To deal with grief alone.

                    (IV, 3, 31–34)

In the next scene we see Cordelia herself getting ready to fight, not for
conquest, but for redress of Lear's grievances:

                    O dear father,
            It is thy business that I go about.
            Therefore great France
            My mourning and important tears hath pitied.
            No blown ambition doth our arms incite,
            But love, dear love, and our ag'd father's right.
            Soon may I hear and see him!

                    (IV, 4, 23–29)

The speech is especially effective because of its unmistakable allusion to
the words of Jesus in the Gospel of Luke (2:49): "Knew ye not that I
must go about my father's business?"[62] Shortly thereafter comes the
scene of Gloucester's "suicide" and redemption, and this episode helps
set the stage for Lear's long-awaited meeting with Cordelia.

The reunion of father and daughter in *King Lear* is the first in Shakespeare's great series of reconciliations that are so important in his last
works.[63] To the accompaniment of soothing music, Lear (like Pericles;
see pp. 413–414) awakens from a deep sleep during which he has been
arrayed in fresh garments, an event of particular significance in light of his
earlier physical and spiritual nakedness. He believes Cordelia to be a
heavenly spirit inaccessible to one like himself:

            You do me wrong to take me out o' th' grave.
            Thou art a soul in bliss; but I am bound
            Upon a wheel of fire, that mine own tears
            Do scald like molten lead.

                    (IV, 7, 45–48)

In language of rare simplicity that at the same time is rich in symbolic
overtones ("I am mainly ignorant what place this is"; "I know not
where I did lodge last night"), he seeks forgiveness, while Cordelia, as
before, says very little, except to ask for his blessing:

Cordelia: O, look upon me, sir,
            And hold your hands in benediction o'er me.
            No, sir, you must not kneel.
Lear: Pray, do not mock me.

I am a very foolish fond old man,
Fourscore and upward, not an hour more nor less;
And, to deal plainly,
I fear I am not in my perfect mind.
Methinks I should know you, and know this man
    [i.e., the doctor];
Yet I am doubtful; for I am mainly ignorant
What place this is; and all the skill I have
Remembers not these garments; nor I know not
Where I did lodge last night. Do not laugh at me;
For (as I am a man) I think this lady
To be my child Cordelia.
Cordelia: And so I am! I am!
                    (IV, 7, 57–70)

"Man . . . lady . . . child . . . Cordelia"—an intensely beautiful progression from "nothing" to the one imperishable good in Lear's new life. Lear persists in acknowledging his errors; Cordelia responds with quiet but fervent reassurance:

Lear: Be your tears wet? Yes, faith. I pray weep not.
  If you have poison for me, I will drink it.
  I know you do not love me; for your sisters
  Have, as I do remember, done me wrong.
  You have some cause, they have not.
Cordelia: No cause, no cause.
Lear: Am I in France?
Cordelia: In your own kingdom, sir.
Lear: Do not abuse me.
Doctor: Be comforted, good madam. The great rage
  You see is kill'd in him; and yet it is danger
  To make him even o'er [fill in] the time he has lost.
  Desire him to go in. Trouble him no more
  Till further settling.
Cordelia: Will't please your Highness walk?
Lear: You must bear with me.
  Pray you now, forget and forgive. I am old and foolish.
                  (IV, 7, 71–84)

Having taken us to such heights of sublimity, what can Shakespeare do next? At first he holds out hope. In the last scene, Lear invites Cordelia to enter with him into captivity, where they can rise above the worldly values he no longer prizes:

We two alone will sing like birds i' th' cage.
When thou dost ask me blessing, I'll kneel down

And ask of thee forgiveness. So we'll live,
And pray, and sing, and tell old tales, and laugh
At gilded butterflies, and hear poor rogues
Talk of court news; and we'll talk with them too—
Who loses and who wins; who's in, who's out—
And take upon 's the mystery of things,
As if we were God's spies; and we'll wear out,
In a wall'd prison, packs and sects of great ones
That ebb and flow by th' moon.

                                    (V, 3, 9–19)

Lear's language, which in the middle of the play had been filled with unclean and repulsive animal imagery, is in this speech "connected, musical and gentle."[64] Another seemingly encouraging sign is that Edmund is now moved to perform an act of decency. Dying of a wound received in a fight with Edgar, the villain reverses his order for the execution of Lear and Cordelia. But this last-minute conversion serves chiefly as a dramatic expedient whereby Shakespeare would "taunt us with a revival of hope, only to double the shock of the final catastrophe."[65]

"Enter *Lear,* with *Cordelia* [dead] in his arms" (V, 3, 257). Here we are assaulted by the ultimate horror—a visual image of crushing power that has been aptly described as "a secular *Pieta*."[66] It is followed by Lear's roar into which all the anguish of humanity is compressed: "Howl, howl, howl, howl!" (V, 3, 257). He pleads for respite from the inevitable: "Cordelia, Cordelia! stay a little" (V, 3, 271). There is nothing for Lear now but to die himself. His last speech, so striking in its utter plainness, is remarkable for several reasons: the curious, affectionate reference to Cordelia as his "poor fool," which may be interpreted as a sign of Lear's intuitive awareness that she shares with the Fool in the miracle of his regeneration; the terrible word *never* repeated five times; the mysterious request "Pray you undo this button," yet another hint of undressing which shows, in the words of Josephine Bennett, that "the act of a madman, performed with violence in Act III, is repeated in gentleness and humble gratitude"; and the final ineffable cry "Look there, look there!" spoken in what Bradley takes to be Lear's unbearable joy in the illusion that Cordelia still lives:

And my poor fool is hang'd! No, no, no life!
Why should a dog, a horse, a rat, have life,
And thou no breath at all? Thou'lt come no more,
Never, never, never, never, never!
Pray you undo this button. Thank you, sir.
Do you see this? Look on her! look! her lips!
Look there, look there!

                                    (V, 3, 305–311)[67]

"Look up, my lord," Edgar says as Lear is dying, but Kent intervenes:

> Vex not his ghost. O, let him pass! He hates him
> That would upon the rack of this tough world
> Stretch him out longer.
>   (V, 3, 312–315)

How does one respond to the ending of *King Lear?* For many play-goers and readers, the reaction of Dr. Johnson provides the best description of their own feelings: "I was many years ago so shocked by Cordelia's death, that I know not whether I ever endured to read again the last scenes of the play till I undertook to revise them as an editor." Indeed, Nahum Tate's notorious version of *King Lear,* which held the stage from 1681 until 1838, has a happy ending wherein Lear regains his sanity and abdicates in favor of Cordelia and Edgar (the two are married, the King of France having been omitted from the play).[68] Without attempting to defend Tate's "improvements" on artistic grounds, one can sympathize with the craving for poetic justice that lay behind his efforts. As Michael Goldman observes, Tate and Dr. Johnson both felt the essential quality of *King Lear,* "that it is nearly or perhaps wholly unbearable."[69] There is, after all, nothing in dramatic literature— not even the death of Desdemona—more outrageous to our moral sensibilities than that single heartbreaking tableau "Enter *Lear,* with *Cordelia* [dead] in his arms."

Some critics have sought a measure of consolation from this disturbing dramatic experience. The play, Bradley insists, is so beautiful that at the end we feel "not depression and much less despair, but a consciousness of greatness in pain, and of solemnity in the mystery we cannot fathom." L. C. Knights believes that *King Lear,* for all the suffering it encompasses, moves steadily toward a positive affirmation, an "affirmation *in spite of everything.*" G. Wilson Knight sees *Lear* as a "play of creative suffering" through which "Mankind are working out a sort of purgatory." Several scholars (among them J. K. Walton, Paul Jorgensen, and Winifred Nowottny) argue that although Lear may not be redeemed through suffering, he at least struggles toward a new understanding of himself and his world. By concentrating on the spiritual growth of Albany, who is changed from a negative personality into a strong and viable force for good, Leo Kirschbaum maintains that the play is not totally dark. Robert Heilman perceives in *King Lear* a pervasive religious pattern that pulls together all the other major themes, such as sight, clothes, nature, reason, and madness. For J. C. Maxwell, *King Lear* is "a Christian play about a pagan world," with paganism gradually fading during the course of the action. Finally, the play has been read by Paul Siegel and Irving Ribner (among others) as a Christian

allegory, whereby Cordelia's coming from her exalted place in another
country to suffer for Lear's sake is interpreted as a miracle, "a redemption," says Siegel, "analogous to the redemption of mankind, for which
the Son of God had come down to earth."[70]

Other critics take issue with these rather optimistic interpretations.
The claim that *King Lear* is a Christian play has been most effectively
challenged by Roland Frye and William Elton. Frye concludes that *King
Lear* is a "secular drama set in a pre-Christian and explicitly pagan
world" and that the hero's suffering by no means implies that he achieves
salvation in the Christian sense. Elton's exhaustive study shows, among
other things, that the Christian God who clearly presides over the action
in the old *Leir* play and dispenses justice to the righteous and to the
wicked has been deliberately omitted from Shakespeare's tragedy. Therefore, in contrast with *Hamlet,* which Elton characterizes as "a Chris-
tianized version of the pre-Christian Amleth story," *King Lear* becomes
"a paganized version of a Christian play." According to D. G. James,
evil—although it too is destroyed—gets the initiative in the play while
virtue is denied all "efficacy and power over the course of events." J.
Stampfer suggests that "*King Lear* is Shakespeare's first tragedy in which
the tragic hero dies unreconciled and indifferent to society." Lear and
Cordelia die to no purpose whatsoever, thereby releasing "the most
private and constricting fear to which mankind is subject, the fear that
penance is impossible . . . that we inhabit an imbecile universe." For Jan
Kott, whose existentialist approach greatly influenced Peter Brook's 1962
production of *King Lear* for the Royal Shakespeare Company starring
Paul Scofield (as well as the subsequent film), the play is absurd in the
style of Samuel Beckett. The established values of the Middle Ages and
the Renaissance have disintegrated. "All that remains at the end of this
gigantic pantomime, is the earth—empty and bleeding."[71]

King Lear, like *Hamlet,* is inexhaustible. As one scholar has observed,
"Any critic of the play willing to find a unifying thematic assertion in
it—that men learn through suffering, that they do not, that the gods
are just, or unjust, or heedless, or random, or absent, or imaginary, or
anything else—can find a counterassertion, if he will look for it."[72] Hence
the student of *King Lear* would do well to proceed on the assumption that
this great work makes no simple, definitive statements; that its characters
are not to be explained according to ordinary psychology but are to be
experienced as extreme and irreconcilable forces. As Bernard McElroy
comments, "the middle ground, the only natural habitat of compromise,
has been eliminated with respect to all characters and virtually all
issues."[73] Feelings and attitudes are everywhere displayed on a gigantic
scale: the outlandish animalism of Goneril and Regan; the total cynicism
and opportunism of Edmund; the hyperbolic cruelty of Cornwall;

Gloucester's inordinate gullibility; Edgar's superhuman patience; Kent's unlimited loyalty; Cordelia's angelic kindness;[74] and, of course, Lear's apocalyptic rage and transcendent remorse, ecstasy, and grief. In such a context the monumental painfulness of the denouement remains perfectly consistent with Shakespeare's artistic design.

If *King Lear* conveys one meaning above others, then perhaps it is this: Man enters wawling and crying upon "this great stage of fools" and (like Job) must endure all the joy and all the anguish that this tough and infinitely perplexing world has to offer—until such time as he can be stretched out on the rack no longer. And what does he finally have to show for his life? Only that he has lived. "Ripeness is all," Edgar tells his aged father, and his remark is quite different in emphasis from "the readiness is all" that Hamlet speaks to Horatio. Ripeness is the theme that is quietly sounded in the very last lines of the play, lines assigned to Albany in the Quarto but to Edgar in the Folio:

> The weight of this sad time we must obey,
> Speak what we feel, not what we ought to say.
> The oldest have borne most; we that are young
> Shall never see so much, nor live so long.
> (V, 3, 323–326)

MACBETH

The only authoritative text of *Macbeth* is that in the First Folio (1623). The play, one of the shortest in the canon, seems to have been printed from a promptbook, and it contains many errors and obscurities that have led a number of scholars to conclude that the text was rehandled, initially through abridgment (possibly by Shakespeare himself) and later through interpolation (perhaps by someone else). There is no external evidence that lines or scenes have been cut, nor would any critic be likely to maintain that anything important is missing. As Mark Van Doren observes, "The brevity of *Macbeth* is so much a function of its brilliance that we might lose rather than gain by turning up the lost scenes of legend."[75] The question of interpolation is more vexing. At one time or another many passages and scenes (including, oddly enough, the scene with the Porter) have been regarded as the work of a collaborator or reviser, but nowadays only three passages are generally thought spurious (III, 5; IV, 1, 39–43; IV, 1, 125–132). These involve the witches, with Hecate the speaker in two of the three passages. The problematic lines have unmistakable links with Thomas Middleton's play *The Witch,* probably written in 1610–1611 (some four years after the presumed date of *Macbeth*); but scholars disagree as to whether Middleton himself is their author. That these three passages differ in style from the Shakespearean witch scenes is not disputed. Beyond that, however, one cannot safely venture. "The change of tone," Professor Greg cautiously points out, "is evident: whether it implies a difference of authorship each reader must judge for himself."[76]

The earliest known performance is reported by Dr. Simon Forman, an astrologer, who saw *Macbeth* staged at the Globe on April 20, 1611, and summarized what he remembered of it in his manuscript *The Booke of Plaies,* which also contains his notes on *Cymbeline, The Winter's Tale,* and a play about Richard II that does not seem to be Shakespeare's. But *Macbeth* must have been on the boards several years before 1611. There are possible allusions to the Ghost of Banquo in at least two plays acted in 1607, one of them *The Knight of the Burning Pestle* by Francis Beaumont and John Fletcher. Furthermore, scholars are by and large convinced that *Macbeth,* at least in its present form, was influenced by the succession of James VI of Scotland to the English throne in 1603, when he began his reign as James I. For one thing, the play reflects the King's profound interest in Scottish history, especially his pride in tracing his ancestry back to Duncan, Malcolm, and, more directly, Banquo. The King was also an authority on demonology, having written a book on that subject, and would have relished a play that featured the activities of witches. Furthermore, the curious tribute (IV, 3, 146–159) to the English King Edward, whose royal touch could miraculously cure "the evil" (scrofula), is often interpreted as alluding to a similar power attributed to James. In addition, the Porter's humorous commentary on equivocators (II, 3, 9–13) is usually seen as an allusion to the jesuitical equivocation used by Father Henry Garnet during his trial (March 28, 1606) for complicity in the Gunpowder Plot (1605) to blow up the King and the Parliament. On the basis of such facts and inferences, Henry Paul has suggested that the first performance of *Macbeth* took place on August 7, 1606, at Hampton Court, where James was entertaining King Christian IV of Denmark. Although some details of Paul's exhaustive and illuminating study have been questioned, the consensus is that *Macbeth* was probably written in 1606 and was indeed presented at court, perhaps after an initial trial at the Globe.[77]

The play is chiefly derived from two incidents recounted in Holinshed's *Chronicles:* the assassination (c. 1040) of Duncan, King of Scotland, by Macbeth and several coconspirators, including Banquo; and the earlier murder of King Duff by four servants of Donwald, acting at the behest of their master, while the King was a guest of Donwald and his wife. Shakespeare had also apparently seen Holinshed's account of King Kenneth, who, having killed his nephew, was haunted by a mysterious voice promising divine punishment, after which he passed a sleepless and terrifying night. To supplement Holinshed, Shakespeare may have consulted William Stewart's *Buik of the Chronicles of Scotland,* a long manuscript poem of unknown date, and two Scottish histories in Latin—one by John Leslie, the other by George Buchanan. For the scenes involving the witches, Shakespeare may have used Reginald Scot's *Discovery of Witchcraft* (1584) and King James's *Daemonologie* (1597). Finally, there are earlier works by Shakespeare himself in which one may discern some of the emotional components of *Macbeth;* an obvious example is *Richard III*. G. Wilson Knight has written persuasively about Macbeth's links with Brutus, and Muriel Bradbrook is among those critics who find in *The Rape of Lucrece* (in Tarquin's feelings before the crime and Lucrece's feelings after it) a foreshadowing of Macbeth's complex reaction to his own infamous behavior.[78]

As usual, Shakespeare makes significant changes in adapting Holinshed's story of Macbeth to the stage. First of all, Shakespeare's Duncan is old and saintly rather than young and weak as he is portrayed in the *Chronicles*. Moreover, according to Holinshed, Macbeth had a bona fide grievance against Duncan for having cheated him of his claim to the succession. By emphasizing Duncan's virtue and stripping Macbeth of any justification for the murder, Shakespeare intensifies the hero's guilt and thereby directs attention to moral and psychological issues. In the second place, the murder of Duncan, as previously noted, is treated by Holinshed as a political affair involving others besides Macbeth. Shakespeare's Macbeth commits a private crime, which, except for the vital collaboration of Lady Macbeth, he performs in utter secrecy. Banquo is no longer Macbeth's accessory, not simply because Shakespeare has to preserve the good name of King James's purported ancestor, but because the murderer and his wife must be isolated from the human community. Other alterations point in the same direction. According to Holinshed, Macbeth ruled successfully for ten years between the murders of Duncan and Banquo. Shakespeare compresses the murders into a short span, omits any reference to Macbeth's good qualities as king, and turns him into an out-and-out tyrant. It is noteworthy that two of the greatest scenes in the play, both entirely original with Shakespeare, are concerned with guilt: the banquet scene (III, 4), at which Banquo's Ghost makes his unforgettable appearance; and the sleepwalking scene (V, 1), in which the demented Lady Macbeth is haunted by the specter of Duncan's blood on her hands. As a result of these changes, Macbeth and his wife emerge as the most flawed of Shakespeare's tragic figures. They are progressively revealed to us,[79] and we are permitted to share in the loneliness of two souls caught up in the unrelenting agony that their sins have created.

Macbeth has been described as "Shakespeare's most profound and mature vision of evil."[80] The evil in the play is generated before the appearance of any human being. The atmosphere is immediately established by the three unearthly hags who seem to materialize out of the mist:

1st Witch: When shall we three meet again
  In thunder, lightning, or in rain?
2nd Witch: When the hurlyburly's done,
  When the battle's lost and won.

               (I, 1, 1–4)

The witches are already threatening the disruption of natural order. As L. C. Knights observed, they would disjoin thunder from lightning and offer them as alternatives; and the word *hurlyburly,* occurring in the context of the battle that will paradoxically be both "lost and won," suggests a game of "metaphysical pitch-and-toss" played with good and evil.[81] Having entered into a compact with Satan, the witches are themselves the embodiment of all that is perverted. At the same time, they can stir up perversions in the hearts of men. "Fair is foul, and foul is fair," they proclaim (I, 1, 10), and the moral confusion is echoed in Macbeth's opening words: "So foul and fair a day I have not seen" (I, 3, 38).[82]

Unlike the Ghost of Hamlet's father, who imparts information and instruction to Hamlet, the witches simply plant their seed in Macbeth's consciousness, knowing that it will take root and sprout. First they tell Macbeth something he already knows, that he is Thane of Glamis; next they tell him something he does not know but will learn shortly, that he has been named Thane of Cawdor; finally they announce an alluring prospect for an unspecified future time: "All hail, Macbeth, that shalt be King hereafter!" (I, 3, 50). Macbeth, considerably impressed by the accuracy of the witches' prophecy, stands rapt:

          Two truths are told,
As happy prologues to the swelling act
Of the imperial theme.

            (I, 3, 127–129)

His mind half yields to a horrid suggestion that makes his heart knock against his ribs, an image that crystallizes in the unspeakable word *murder:*

My thought, whose murther yet is but fantastical [imaginary],
Shakes so my single state of man [i.e., strength; equilibrium]
    that function [normal activity]
Is smother'd in surmise and nothing is
But what is not.

            (I, 3, 139–142)

His nature, in the words of his wife, may indeed be "too full o' th' milk of human kindness / To catch the nearest way." But he would wrongly win without actually playing false (I, 5, 17–23). He needs only the right partner to goad him into action.

Lady Macbeth is one of the wonders of the dramatic world, and there will always be differences of opinion as to how she should be portrayed on the stage. In the eighteenth century Sarah Siddons, whose interpretation has become legendary, played her as a "fiendlike queen" (V, 8, 69) of commanding strength. On the other hand, Ellen Terry's masterful performance (1888) reflected her conviction that Lady Macbeth is frail, sensitive, and "womanly."[83] In any case, it seems that Lady Macbeth's chief function, at least in the early stages of her husband's criminal career, is to act as a "gadfly."[84] Once Macbeth is properly launched, she recedes in importance and reappears near the end to add poignancy to his desolation. Meanwhile, Shakespeare's delineation of their partnership, from its strangely ecstatic beginnings to its eventual dissolution, remains an artistic triumph of the highest order. Theirs is a "deep, 'long-engrafted' and instinctive relationship."[85]

Before the murder, Macbeth displays a well-reasoned fear of resorting to assassination. He realizes (I, 7, 1–28) that an act is never "done [completed] when 'tis done [performed]," and although he would "jump the life to come," he must still face temporal punishment in this life:

> But in these cases
> We still have judgment here, that we but teach
> Bloody instructions, which, being taught, return
> To plague th' inventor. This even-handed justice
> Commends th' ingredience of our poison'd chalice
> To our own lips.
>
> (I, 7, 7–12)

The phrase "poison'd chalice" suggests that Macbeth's mind is drifting into a consideration of spiritual retribution, an idea reinforced a few lines later in a much discussed image:

> Besides, this Duncan
> Hath borne his faculties so meek, hath been
> So clear in his great office, that his virtues
> Will plead like angels, trumpet-tongu'd, against
> The deep damnation of his taking-off;
> And pity, like a naked new-born babe,
> Striding the blast, or heaven's cherubin, hors'd
> Upon the sightless couriers of the air,
> Shall blow the horrid deed in every eye,
> That tears shall drown the wind.
>
> (I, 7, 16–25)[86]

It is worth noting that the opening lines of this famous soliloquy "If it were done when 'tis done, then 'twere well / It were done quickly" may echo Jesus's words to Judas (John 13:27): "That thou doest, do quickly.[87] If this is so, then we have additional confirmation of the fact that Macbeth senses from the start that the murder of Duncan will bring on his own "deep damnation." Nevertheless, he is impelled along his bloody path as though he had no genuine will to resist.

All Macbeth needs is the initial push, and that is supplied by his wife. But Lady Macbeth must arouse herself, no less than Macbeth, to the task. Her desperate invocation to the spirits of darkness to unsex her and fill her "from the crown to the toe, top-full / Of direst cruelty" (I, 5, 41–55) reveals, in Bradley's words, her "determination to crush the inward protest."[88] She would have night cloak her villainy from her eyes:

> Come, thick night,
> And pall [wrap] thee in the dunnest [darkest] smoke of hell,
> That my keen knife see not the wound it makes,
> Nor heaven peep through the blanket of the dark
> To cry "Hold, hold!"
>
> (I, 5, 51–55)[89]

She repeatedly hammers away at her husband. If he loves her, he will behave like a man:

> *Macbeth:*   Prithee peace!
>   I dare do all that may become a man.
>   Who dares do more is none.
> *Lady Macbeth:*   What beast was't then
>   That made you break this enterprise to me?
>   When you durst do it, then you were a man;
>   And to be more than what you were, you would
>   Be so much more the man.
>
> (I, 7, 45–51)

She would tear the sucking babe from her breast and dash out its brains had she so sworn, as he has sworn to kill Duncan. "If we should fail?" Macbeth asks. "We fail?" she repeats. "But screw your courage to the sticking place, / And we'll not fail" (I, 7, 59–61).[90] On the murder night she needs drink to sustain her resolve. "That which hath made them [Duncan's grooms] drunk hath made me bold" (II, 2, 1). She cannot, we shall see, continue at that intense pitch.

Shakespeare manages the murder itself in a way to evoke maximum suspense and horror: the "dagger of the mind, a false creation" (II, 1, 38), which seems to beckon Macbeth toward the door to Duncan's room, a dagger that suddenly displays huge drops of blood on its blade and handle; the stylized language as Macbeth, as if in a trance, awaits the ringing of the bell ("Now o'er the one half-world / Nature seems dead" [II, 1, 49–64]); Lady Macbeth's momentary fright at the shrieking of the owl; those ghastly words "He is about it" (II, 2, 4) spoken by Sarah Siddons in a chilling whisper as she placed her ear against the door.[91] The conversation immediately following the murder prolongs the mood of suspended animation:

Lady Macbeth: My husband!
Macbeth: I have done the deed. Didst thou not hear a noise?
Lady Macbeth: I heard the owl scream and the crickets cry.
    Did not you speak?
Macbeth: When?
Lady Macbeth: Now.
Macbeth: As I descended?
Lady Macbeth: Ay.

(II, 2, 14–18)

To quote from a classic essay (1823) by Thomas De Quincey, "another world has stepped in"; the normal operations of the world in which we live have been temporarily interrupted by "the awful parenthesis" introduced by the murderer and his wife.[92]

After the murder, Macbeth experiences what has been called a state of "neurotic self-alienation"[93] that contrasts sharply with the incredible poise of his wife. He tells her of a voice that cried "God bless us" and of another that replied "Amen," but he could not join in the prayer:

But wherefore could not I pronounce "Amen?"
I had most need of blessing, and "Amen"
Stuck in my throat.

(II, 2, 31–33)

He fears (II, 2, 36–37) that "the innocent sleep," the "sleep that knits up the ravell'd sleave of care," will no longer be his. The voice in the chamber dooms him, in Bradley's penetrating comment, "as if his three names gave him three personalities to suffer in":

Still it cried "Sleep no more!" to all the house;
"Glamis hath murther'd sleep, and therefore Cawdor
Shall sleep no more! Macbeth shall sleep no more!"

(II, 2, 41–43)[94]

"To know my deed, 'twere best not know myself," he laments (II, 2, 73). He does, in truth, seem detached from his own body, especially from those bloody hands:

What hands are here? Ha! they pluck out mine eyes!
Will all great Neptune's ocean wash this blood
Clean from my hand? No. This my hand will rather
The multitudinous seas incarnadine [stain blood-red],
Making the green one red.

(II, 2, 59–63)

Lady Macbeth has no patience with one who thinks "so brainsickly of things." "Go get some water," she bids him, "and wash this filthy witness from your hand . . . . A little water clears us of this deed . . . . Get on your nightgown . . . . Be not lost / So poorly in your thoughts" (II, 2, 45–72 passim).

The structure of the drama from this point on has been likened to a St. Andrew's (X-shaped) cross, "with Macbeth moving along one diagonal, Lady Macbeth along the other."[95] As he wades deeper into blood, Macbeth leaves his wife far behind. He performs the superfluous murder of Duncan's two grooms, whose faces Lady Macbeth had smeared with blood, and there is no reason for believing that her faint upon hearing the news is not genuine (it is not Shakespeare's practice to introduce a major piece of dissimulation without letting his audience know either in advance or soon after). Macbeth is tormented by a gnawing insecurity. "O, full of scorpions is my mind," he tells her (III, 2, 36). (In medieval and Renaissance thought the scorpion was an emblem of treachery and fear.)[96] He plans the murder of Banquo and his son Fleance because the witches had prophesied that Banquo would beget a line of kings.[97] When Lady Macbeth questions her husband, he puts her off: "Be innocent of the knowledge, dearest chuck, / Till thou applaud the deed" (III, 2, 45–46). He cannot share with her his terror at the report that Fleance has escaped, and Banquo's Ghost, who sits in Macbeth's place at the table, is for him alone to see.[98] Not the least of his agonies is the knowledge that he must be increasingly separated from the woman with whom he had dared everything.

Now Macbeth, "cabin'd, cribb'd, confin'd, bound in / To saucy doubts and fears" (III, 4, 24–25), resolves independently to revisit the witches, who tease him with ambiguous warnings. "Beware Macduff" (IV, 1, 71), says the First Apparition they conjure up, *an Armed Head*. The Second Apparition, *a Bloody Child,* is more reassuring:

Be bloody, bold, and resolute; laugh to scorn
The pow'r of man, for none of woman born
Shall harm Macbeth.

(IV, 1, 79–81)

His fears are allayed; but to "make assurance double sure" (IV, 1, 83), he determines to kill Macduff anyway. The Third Apparition, *a Child*

Crowned, with a tree in his hand, promises that Macbeth will not be vanquished until Birnam Wood comes to Dunsinane Hill (IV, 1, 86–94). After Macduff flees to England to join Duncan's son Malcolm in revolt, Macbeth in an excess of ruthlessness orders the slaughter of Lady Macduff and her children. But in the words of the Scottish nobleman Angus, Macbeth begins to feel "his secret murthers sticking on his hands" (V, 2, 17), a reminder of stains left by Duncan's blood. Macbeth's title, Angus continues, hangs about him loosely, "like a giant's robe / Upon a dwarfish thief" (V, 2, 21–22).[99] The "fiend of Scotland," as Macduff calls him (IV, 3, 233), has defiled the realm.

While Macbeth, once started, quickly abandons himself to his most depraved impulses, Lady Macbeth finds herself unequal to the burden of sustained inhumanity and suffers an overwhelming revulsion. Her breakdown is superbly depicted in the incomparable sleepwalking scene, as she tries to wash away the blood by rubbing her hands:

> Out, damned spot! out, I say! One; two. Why then 'tis time to do't. Hell is murky . . . . Yet who would have thought the old man to have had so much blood in him?
>
> (V, 1, 39–45)

"She speaks in spurts," says John Russell Brown, "to relapse into silences that may be more frightening than her words."[100] Her monologue, with occasional interjections by the Doctor and Waiting Gentlewoman who look on, is a remarkable example of stream of consciousness; and the images in her dream, which is actually experienced rather than recounted, grow out of images that recur throughout the play.[101] "The Thane of Fife [Macduff] had a wife," Lady Macbeth says. "Where is she now?"

> What, will these hands ne'er be clean? No more o' that, my lord, no more o' that! You mar all with this starting . . . . Here's the smell of the blood still. All the perfumes of Arabia will not sweeten this little hand . . . . Wash your hands, put on your nightgown, look not so pale! I tell you yet again, Banquo's buried. He can not come out on's grave.
>
> (V, 1, 47–71)

She had comforted Macbeth with "What's done is done" (III, 2, 12); her final words are a comfortless "What's done cannot be undone. To bed, to bed, to bed!" (V, 1, 75–76). "More needs she the divine than the physician," the Doctor sadly reflects; "God, God forgive us all!" (V, 1, 82–83).

In the meantime, Macbeth, stunned by the rebellion of his outraged countrymen, realizes the dreadful future that looms before him:

> I have liv'd long enough. My way of life
> Is fall'n into the sere, the yellow leaf;

And that which should accompany old age,
As honour, love, obedience, troops of friends,
I must not look to have; but, in their stead,
Curses not loud but deep, mouth-honour, breath,
Which the poor heart would fain deny, and dare not.

(V, 3, 22–28)

When news reaches him of Lady Macbeth's death (probably at her own hands), he has neither the time nor the energy to mourn her properly. "She should have died hereafter," he wearily observes; "there would have been a time for such a word" (V, 5, 17–18). At this point he delivers what could well be a funeral elegy for himself as well as his wife. In these lines, which are among the most famous in all literature, Macbeth acknowledges that the glory for which he sold his soul is meaningless:

To-morrow, and to-morrow, and to-morrow
Creeps in this petty pace from day to day
To the last syllable of recorded time;
And all our yesterdays have lighted fools
The way to dusty death. Out, out, brief candle!
Life's but a walking shadow, a poor player,
That struts and frets his hour upon the stage
And then is heard no more. It is a tale
Told by an idiot, full of sound and fury,
Signifying nothing.

(V, 5, 19–28)[102]

No sooner has Macbeth given expression to his disillusion than the Messenger arrives to report that Birnam Wood is indeed moving toward Dunsinane. Of course, this phenomenon can be explained rationally: The Scottish and English soldiers who oppose Macbeth are carrying boughs before them as camouflage. To Macbeth, however, it indicates that the witches have deceived him by practicing "th' equivocation of the fiend, / That lies like truth" (V, 5, 43–44). At this moment one ought to recall the words of the Porter during the knocking at the gate—"hell gate," he rightly imagines (II, 3, 2)—after Duncan's murder, for, like so much of Shakespeare's so-called comic relief, the earlier episode sheds light upon a crucial theme of the tragedy:

Knock, knock! Who's there, in th' other devil's name? Faith, here's an equivocator, that could swear in both the scales against either scale; who committed treason enough for God's sake, yet could not equivocate to heaven. O, come in, equivocator!

(II, 3, 8–13)

Himself an equivocator who used a false face to hide his false heart, Macbeth is a victim of delusive hopes that have been negated by unspoken conditions. Equivocation is again in evidence when Macbeth, confident that no one born of woman can harm him, learns that his archenemy Macduff "was from his mother's womb / Untimely ripp'd" (V, 8, 15–16). He repudiates the witches:

> And be these juggling fiends no more believ'd,
> That palter [equivocate] with us in a double sense,
> That keep the word of promise to our ear
> And break it to our hope!
>
> (V, 8, 19–22)[103]

Although he now knows that he is doomed, Macbeth hurls himself into the fight. "Lay on, Macduff," he proclaims with all the courage he can muster, "and damn'd be him that first cries 'Hold, enough!'" (V, 8, 33–34).

Macbeth is the only criminal among Shakespeare's major tragic heroes, and it is easy to condemn him out of hand. In this play, to quote Maynard Mack, Jr., everything is designed "to dramatize king killing in all its moral, political, metaphysical, and symbolic horror."[104] For an Elizabethan audience, the killing of a king would have been viewed as a form of parricide. (This interpretation is supported in a different context by those Freudian critics who see Macbeth as a hostile son to Duncan and, later, a bad father to Banquo and Macduff.)[105] But Duncan is not just a king. As noted earlier, he is almost a saint. To Macbeth's powerful imagination, his blood is "golden," an apparent allusion to the alchemical concept of tincture, whereby Duncan's soul would have the power to transmute base substances into a purer state:

> Here lay Duncan,
> His silver skin lac'd with his golden blood,
> And his gash'd stabs look'd like a breach in nature
> For ruin's wasteful entrance.
>
> (II, 3, 117–120)[106]

The "breach in nature," to which Macbeth refers, is manifest in the upheavals that accompany Duncan's murder: chimneys blown down; screams of death in the air; an unnatural darkness that enshrouds the earth; Duncan's horses suddenly turning wild, breaking from their stalls, and eating each other. "Macbeth's crime," G. Wilson Knight observes in his perceptive essay, "is a blow against nature's unity and peace, a hideous desecration of all creative, family, and social duties, all union and concord."[107] It is not surprising that the murder of Duncan and its consequences are often seen as being "profoundly impregnated with the central tragedy of the Christian myth"[108] and that Macbeth has been placed alongside such personages as Cain, Judas, and Satan himself. There is no doubt that Macbeth becomes a tyrant of the worst sort, and he goes to his death without formal repentance.

Yet Shakespeare manages to evoke sympathy for this unregenerate murderer. Clifford Davidson is surely correct in objecting to present-day critics who admire Macbeth's character, a tendency he likens to the "sentimental and wrongheaded admiration of past critics for Milton's Satan."[109] It is important, however, that we preserve the distinction between sympathy and admiration. Without morally approving of Macbeth, who incidentally never seeks such approval, one may nevertheless suffer with him and, indeed, even identify with him. In Macbeth (as in Raskolnikov, the tormented murderer-hero of Dostoevski's *Crime and Punishment*) we sense the awesome potentiality for evil that is part of the human condition. But we also experience through Macbeth (and Raskolnikov) a powerful reaction against the very criminality to which we may one day surrender. As Robert Heilman has written, "We accept ourselves as murderers, so to speak, because we also feel the strength of our resistance to murder."[110] There must surely be something noble in one who can rise out of his sin—if not like Raskolnikov to repentance, then at least to an unflinching self-awareness. Such a perception may be crushing, but it proceeds from a wisdom of which only a great spirit is capable.

In a quotation from John Donne, who understood spiritual agony, Peter Alexander has perhaps captured the essence of *Macbeth*. "Thou knowest this man's fall, but thou knowest not his wrastling; which perchance was such that almost his very fall is justified and accepted of God."[111] Rather than seek a villain, we might come closer to Shakespeare's intention by recalling the Doctor's simple words at the end of the sleep-walking scene: "God, God forgive us all!"

NOTES

1. Edward Dowden, *Shakspere: A Critical Study of His Mind and Art,* 6th ed. (London: Kegan Paul, 1882), p. 222.
2. For a valuable bibliographical guide to these plays and to *Hamlet,* see Edward Quinn et al., *The Major Shakespearean Tragedies: A Critical Bibliography* (New York: Free Press, 1973), pp. 77–145 (*Othello*), 147–209 (*King Lear*), 211–277 (*Macbeth*).
3. On the date and textual problems, see E. K. Chambers, *William Shakespeare: A Study of Facts and Problems,* 2 vols. (Oxford: Clarendon, 1930), 1: 457–463; W. W. Greg, *The Editorial Problem in Shakespeare,* 3d ed.

(Oxford: Clarendon, 1954), pp. 108–111; W. W. Greg, *The Shakespeare First Folio: Its Bibliographical and Textual History* (Oxford: Clarendon, 1955), pp. 357–374; the New Cambridge *Othello,* eds. Alice Walker and John Dover Wilson (Cambridge: Cambridge University Press, 1957), pp. 121–135; the New Arden *Othello,* ed. M. R. Ridley, 7th ed. (Cambridge: Harvard University Press, 1958), pp. xv–xlv, 199–237; Nevill Coghill, *Shakespeare's Professional Skills* (Cambridge: Cambridge University Press, 1964), pp. 164–202; E. A. J. Honigmann, *The Stability of Shakespeare's Text* (Lincoln: University of Nebraska Press, 1965), pp. 100–120; Kenneth Muir, "The Text of *Othello*," *Shakespeare Studies,* ed. J. Leeds Barroll, 1 (1965): 227–239.

4. See Kenneth Muir, *Shakespeare's Sources* (London: Methuen, 1957), pp. 122–140; Geoffrey Bullough, *Narrative and Dramatic Sources of Shakespeare,* 8 vols. (New York: Columbia University Press, 1957–1975), 7: 193–265. See also the succinct discussions in Harley Granville-Barker, *Prefaces to Shakespeare,* 2 vols. (Princeton: Princeton University Press, 1946–1947), 2: 3–9; and in the New Arden edition, pp. 237–246.

5. Dissenting from this view is H. A. Mason, who argues that the play was hastily written and is badly constructed. See *Shakespeare's Tragedies of Love* (London: Chatto & Windus, 1970), pp. 59–162.

6. William Empson counts fifty-two uses of the words *honest* and *honesty* in the play. See "Honest in *Othello*," in *The Structure of Complex Words* (London: Chatto & Windus, 1951), pp. 218–249.

7. On the mingled strengths and weaknesses of Iago's victims, see J. K. Walton, " 'Strength's Abundance': A View of *Othello*," *Review of English Studies,* n.s. 11 (1960): 8–17.

8. On language and imagery, see G. Wilson Knight, "The *Othello* Music," in *The Wheel of Fire,* 5th rev. ed. (Cleveland: World Publishing, Meridian Books, 1957), pp. 97–119; Wolfgang Clemen, *The Development of Shakespeare's Imagery* (Cambridge: Harvard University Press, 1951), pp. 119–132; F. E. Halliday, *The Poetry of Shakespeare's Plays* (London: Duckworth, 1954), pp. 147–151.

9. For a systematic review of the major schools of interpretation, see Stanley Edgar Hyman, *Iago: Some Approaches to the Illusion of His Motivation* (New York: Atheneum, 1970). These schools, says Hyman, see Iago as stage villain, Satan, artist, latent homosexual, or Machiavel.

10. "If I take it on," Olivier is quoted as saying, "I don't want a witty, Machiavellian Iago. I want a solid, honest-to-God N.C.O." See Kenneth Tynan, ed., *Othello: The National Theatre Production* (London: Rupert Hart-Davis, 1966), p. 2.

11. Elmer Edgar Stoll, *Othello: An Historical and Comparative Study* (New York: Gordian Press, 1967), pp. 5–9; Bernard Spivack, *Shakespeare and the Allegory of Evil* (New York: Columbia University Press, 1958), especially pp. 3–150, 415–453; Paul N. Siegel, *Shakespearean Tragedy and the Elizabethan Compromise* (New York: New York University Press, 1957), pp. 119–141; Tucker Brooke, *Essays on Shakespeare and Other Elizabethans* (New Haven: Yale University Press, 1948), pp. 46–56; Granville-Barker, *Prefaces,* 2: 98–112; Richard Flatter, *The Moor of Venice* (London: Heinemann, 1950), pp. 17, 23.

12. Samuel Taylor Coleridge, *Shakespearean Criticism,* ed. Thomas Middleton Raysor, rev. ed., 2 vols. (London: Dent, 1960), 1: 44.

13. Iago has been said to have an insatiable sexual hunger while suffering from psychic impotence. See Warren Staebler, "The Sexual Nihilism of Iago," *Sewanee Review* 83 (1975): 284–304.

14. Robert B. Heilman, *Magic in the Web: Action and Language in Othello* (Lexington: University of Kentucky Press, 1956), p. 33; Coghill, *Shakespeare's Professional Skills,* p. 146. See also Donald A. Stauffer, *Shakespeare's World of Images* (New York: Norton, 1949), p. 174.

15. Spivack, *Shakespeare and the Allegory of Evil,* p. 3.

16. Dowden, *Shakspere,* p. 230.

17. Ibid., p. 226.

18. See especially Albert S. Gérard, " 'Egregiously an Ass': The Dark Side of the Moor. A View of Othello's Mind," *Shakespeare Survey* 10 (1957): 98–106. That Othello is emotionally a primitive is also argued by H. B. Charlton, *Shakespearian Tragedy* (Cambridge: Cambridge University Press, 1948), pp. 113–140.

19. Reuben A. Brower, *Hero and Saint: Shakespeare and the Graeco-Roman Heroic Tradition* (New York: Oxford University Press, 1971), p. 5.

20. This point is ably developed by Rosalie L. Colie, *Shakespeare's Living Art* (Princeton: Princeton University Press, 1974), pp. 148–167.

21. Alvin Kernan, "Introduction to *Othello,*" in *The Complete Signet Classic Shakespeare,* ed. Sylvan Barnet (New York: Harcourt Brace Jovanovich, 1972), pp. 1090–1095.

Interestingly, Othello (unlike Aaron in *Titus Andronicus*) does not conform to the Renaissance stereotype of the Moor. See Eldred Jones, *Othello's Countrymen: The African in English Renaissance Drama* (London: Oxford University Press, 1965), pp. 1–26, 86–109. See also K. W. Evans, "The Racial Factor in *Othello,*" *Shakespeare Studies,* ed. J. Leeds Barroll, 5 (1969): 124–140.

22. Charlton (*Shakespearian Tragedy,* pp. 113–140) shows how Shakespeare, in adapting Cinthio's tale, emphasized Othello's differences from the Venetians. See also the interesting account of an interview with the actor Paul Robeson, perhaps the first black to play Othello in a major production, in Marvin Rosenberg, *The Masks of Othello* (Berkeley: University of California Press, 1961), pp. 151–152.

23. Jan Kott, *Shakespeare Our Contemporary,* trans. Boleslaw Taborski (Garden City, N.Y.: Doubleday, Anchor Books, 1966), p. 118.

24. The drinking scene and the two clown scenes (III, 1, 1–32 and III, 4, 1–23) have been skillfully analyzed as microcosms of the play as a whole; see Robert A. Watts, "The Comic Scenes in *Othello,*" *Shakespeare Quarterly* 19 (1968): 349–354.

25. On some aspects of reputation in *Othello,* see Brents Stirling, *Unity in Shakespearian Tragedy* (New York: Columbia University Press, 1956), pp. 111–138. Madeleine Doran sees the theme as an attack on Othello's reputation, which he must try to clear at the end; see "Good Name in *Othello,*" *Studies in English Literature, 1500–1900* 7 (1967): 195–217.

26. Knight, "The Othello Music," p. 117.

27. On the play and the opera, see Winston Dean, "Verdi's *Otello:* A Shakespearian Masterpiece," *Shakespeare Survey* 21 (1968): 87–96.

28. For the psychoanalytic view that Iago's account of the "dream" is itself a dream reflecting his own homosexual love for Othello, see Martin Wangh, "*Othello:* The Tragedy of Iago," *Psychoanalytic Quarterly* 19 (1950): 202–212, reprinted in Melvin D. Faber, ed., *The Design Within: Psychoanalytic Approaches to Shakespeare* (New York: Science House, 1970), pp. 155–168. For a summary of psychoanalytic interpretations of the play, see Norman N. Holland, *Psychoanalysis and Shakespeare* (New York: McGraw-Hill, 1964), pp. 246–258.

29. See Siegel, *Shakespearean Tragedy and the Elizabethan Compromise,* p. 127. A pioneering study offering a Christian interpretation of *Othello* (as well as *Hamlet* and *Macbeth*) is Kenneth O. Myrick, "The Theme of Damnation in Shakespeare's Tragedies," *Studies in Philology* 38 (1941): 221–245. See also S. L. Bethell's important essay, "The Diabolic Images in *Othello,*" *Shakespeare Survey* 5 (1952): 62–80.

   For an illuminating analysis of III, 3 as a whole, in which Othello's train of thought (not Iago's) is shown as governing the scene's movement, see Bernard McElroy, *Shakespeare's Mature Tragedies* (Princeton: Princeton University Press, 1973), pp. 115–131.

30. G. R. Elliott, *Flaming Minister: A Study of Othello as Tragedy of Love and Hate* (Durham, N. C.: Duke University Press, 1953), p. 213.

31. Irving Ribner, *Patterns in Shakespearian Tragedy* (London: Methuen, 1960), p. 112, goes so far as to interpret Desdemona's speech as "an assumption of Othello's guilt parallel to that of Christ for the sins of mankind." On Desdemona as Christ, see also Siegel, *Shakespearean Tragedy and the Elizabethan Compromise,* pp. 132–134. For answers to the Christianizers of the play, see Edward L. Hubler, "The Damnation of Othello: Some Limitations on the Christian View of the Play," *Shakespeare Quarterly* 9 (1958): 295–300 and Robert H. West, "The Christianness of *Othello,*" *Shakespeare Quarterly* 15 (1964): 333–343.

32. Arthur Sherbo, ed., *Johnson on Shakespeare,* Vols. 7 and 8 of The Yale Edition of the Works of Samuel Johnson (New Haven: Yale University Press, 1968), p. 1045.

33. On the love-honor conflict in *Othello,* see John Arthos's subtle discussion, "The Fall of Othello," *Shakespeare Quarterly* 9 (1958): 93–104.

34. Helen Gardner, "*Othello:* A Retrospect, 1900–67," *Shakespeare Survey* 21 (1968): 1–11.

35. See G. R. Elliott, *Flaming Minister,* p. xxvii; Helen Gardner, "The Noble Moor," *Proceedings of the British Academy* 41 (1956): 189–205, reprinted in Anne Ridler, ed., *Shakespeare Criticism: 1935–1960* (London: Oxford University Press, 1963), pp. 348–370; Robert Hapgood, "The Trials of Othello," in *Pacific Coast Studies in Shakespeare,* eds. Waldo F. McNeir and Thelma N. Greenfield (Eugene: University of Oregon Books, 1966), pp. 134–147. But J. K. Walton argues that it is Othello's modesty, not his pride, that is the source of his tragedy; see " 'Strength's Abundance': A View of *Othello.*"

36. Winifred M. T. Nowottny, "Justice and Love in *Othello,*" *University of*

Toronto Quarterly 21 (1952): 330–344 (quotation from p. 335).

37. Ibid., p. 334.

38. The New Cambridge *King Lear,* eds. George Ian Duthie and John Dover Wilson (Cambridge: Cambridge University Press, 1960), pp. vii–xiv, 122–139 (quotation from p. 129). See also Chambers, *William Shakespeare,* 1: 463–470; Greg, *The Shakespeare First Folio,* pp. 375–388; and the New Arden *King Lear,* ed. Kenneth Muir, 8th ed. (Cambridge: Harvard University Press, 1952), pp. xv–xx. On Shakespeare's "second thoughts" as reflected in textual differences, see Honigmann, *The Stability of Shakespeare's Text,* pp. 121–128.

39. See the New Arden *King Lear,* pp. xx–xxvi and the New Cambridge *King Lear,* pp. ix–xiv.

40. Tracing the folk and oral traditions behind the play, Alan R. Young shows how Shakespeare deliberately cheats the audience of the expected happy ending. See "The Written and Oral Sources of *King Lear* and the Problem of Justice in the Play," *Studies in English Literature, 1500–1900* 15 (1975): 309–319.

41. See the Pelican *King Lear,* ed. Alfred Harbage, rev. ed. (Baltimore: Penguin, 1970), p. 21 and Maynard Mack, *King Lear in Our Time* (Berkeley: University of California Press, 1965), pp. 45–80. On Shakespeare's indebtedness to specific sources, see Muir in the New Arden *King Lear,* pp. xxvi–xliii, 221–256; W. W. Greg, "The Date of *Lear* and Shakespeare's Use of Earlier Versions of the Story," *The Library* 20 (1940): 377–400; Muir, *Shakespeare's Sources,* pp. 141–166; Bullough, *Sources,* 7: 269–420.

42. On this point, see D. G. James, *The Dream of Learning: An Essay on The Advancement of Learning, Hamlet and King Lear* (Oxford: Clarendon, 1951), pp. 99–104 and McElroy, *Shakespeare's Mature Tragedies,* pp. 164–172 passim.

43. The rituals of the first scene and their implications for the play as a whole are examined by William Frost, "Shakespeare's Rituals and the Opening Scene of *King Lear,*" *Hudson Review* 10 (1958): 577–585. The structure of the scene is ably analyzed by Mark Rose, *Shakespearean Design* (Cambridge: Harvard University Press, 1972), pp. 35–39. For an interesting reading of the scene, one that is somewhat more sympathetic to Lear, see A. P. Riemer, *Darker Purpose: An Approach to Shakespeare's King Lear* (Sydney, Australia: The English Association, 1968), pp. 18–23.

44. Grigori Kozintsev, *Shakespeare: Time and Conscience,* trans. Joyce Vining (New York: Hill & Wang, 1966), p. 52.

45. On the Fool and "nothing," see Nicholas Brooke, *Shakespeare: King Lear* (London: Edward Arnold, 1963), pp. 23–26. Brooke (pp. 18–55) gives a brilliant scene-by-scene analysis of the action.

46. See Robert B. Heilman, *This Great Stage: Image and Structure in King Lear* (Baton Rouge: Louisiana State University Press, 1948), pp. 123–130 and John F. Danby, *Shakespeare's Doctrine of Nature: A Study of King Lear* (London: Faber, 1949), pp. 31–43.

For a harsh review of Heilman's important book, see W. R. Keast, "Imagery and Meaning in the Interpretation of *King Lear,*" *Modern Philology* 47 (1949): 45–64, reprinted as "The 'New Criticism' and *King Lear,*" in *Critics and Criticism: Ancient and Modern,* ed. R. S. Crane (Chicago: University of Chicago Press, 1952), pp. 108–137.

47. See Bridget Gellert-Lyons, "The Subplot as Simplification in *King Lear,*" in *Some Facets of King Lear: Essays in Prismatic Criticism,* ed. Rosalie L. Colie (Toronto: University of Toronto Press, 1974), pp. 23–38. The essays in this collection are extraordinarily good.

48. See Alvin Kernan, "Formalism and Realism in Elizabethan Drama: The Miracles in *King Lear,*" *Renaissance Drama* 9 (1966): 59–66.

49. Paul A. Jorgensen, *Lear's Self-Discovery* (Berkeley: University of California Press, 1967), pp. 12–43, examines the play against a substantial background of Renaissance literature dealing with the classical theme *nosce teipsum* ("know thyself"). See also Rolf Soellner, *Shakespeare's Patterns of Self-Knowledge* (Columbus: Ohio State University Press, 1972), pp. 3–40, 281–326.

50. That Lear's view is limited is argued by Harold Skulsky, "*King Lear* and the Meaning of Chaos," *Shakespeare Quarterly* 17 (1966): 3–17.

51. Several scholars have discussed the dual concept of nature in *King Lear.* See Heilman, *This Great Stage,* pp. 115–130; Danby, *Shakespeare's Doctrine of Nature,* pp. 15–53; and Russell A. Fraser, *Shakespeare's Poetics in Relation to King Lear* (Nashville, Tenn.: Vanderbilt University Press, 1966).

52. In its context this line could refer not only to the roundness of the globe but to the roundness of the womb in pregnancy, a reading that is reinforced by the curse of sterility Lear had called down upon Goneril (I, 4, 297–311). On this point (and the speech as a whole), see George W. Williams, "The Poetry of the Storm in *King Lear,*" *Shakespeare Quarterly* 2 (1951): 57–71.

53. Northrop Frye, *Fools of Time: Studies in Shakespearean Tragedy* (Toronto: University of Toronto Press, 1967), p. 106.

54. See Stephen J. Brown, "Shakespeare's King and Beggar," *Yale Review* 64 (1975): 370–395. Edgar's repulsiveness has been appropriately emphasized; see Michael Goldman, "The Worst of *King Lear,*" in *Shakespeare and the Energies of Drama* (Princeton: Princeton University Press, 1972), pp. 94–108 (Edgar discussed on pp. 97–98).

55. See Mary Lascelles, "*King Lear* and Doomsday," *Shakespeare Survey* 26 (1973): 69–79.

56. On the clothes imagery, see Heilman, *This Great Stage,* pp. 67–87 and Maurice Charney, " 'We Put Fresh Garments on Him': Nakedness and Clothes in *King Lear,*" in *Some Facets of King Lear,* pp. 77–88.

57. Brooke, *Shakespeare: King Lear,* p. 35.

58. Enid Welsford, *The Fool: His Social and Literary History* (London: Faber, 1935), p. 267. See also Robert Hillis Goldsmith, *Wise Fools in Shakespeare* (East Lansing: Michigan State University Press, 1955), pp. 11, 60–67, 95–99. See also William Empson, "Fool in *Lear,*" *The Structure of Complex Words,* pp. 125–157.

59. Knight, "*King Lear* and the Comedy of the Grotesque," in *The Wheel of Fire,* p. 165.

60. Sherbo, ed., *Johnson on Shakespeare,* p. 670.

61. Granville-Barker, *Prefaces,* 1: 309.

62. See S. L. Bethell, *Shakespeare and the Popular Dramatic Tradition*

(Durham, N.C.: Duke University Press, 1944), pp. 67–68. See also Brower, *Hero and Saint*, pp. 406–409. On other biblical echoes, see Rosalie L. Colie's eloquent essay, "The Energies of Endurance: Biblical Echo in *King Lear*," in *Some Facets of King Lear,* pp. 117–144. Professor Colie calls particular attention to the Book of Job.

63. See Glynne Wickham, "From Tragedy to Tragi-Comedy: *King Lear* as Prologue," *Shakespeare Survey* 26 (1973): 33–48.

64. See Clemen, *The Development of Shakespeare's Imagery*, p. 152.

65. See John D. Rosenberg, "King Lear and His Comforters," *Essays in Criticism* 16 (1966): 135–146 (quotation from p. 138). For a different view, that Edmund's conversion attests to his belated recognition of the power and divinity of love, see Knight, "The *Lear* Universe," in *The Wheel of Fire*, p. 206.

66. Helen Gardner, "*King Lear,*" John Coffin Memorial Lecture, March 2, 1966 (London: University of London, 1967), pp. 27–28.

67. See Josephine Waters Bennett, "The Storm Within: The Madness of Lear," *Shakespeare Quarterly* 13 (1962): 155 and A. C. Bradley, *Shakespearean Tragedy,* 2d ed. (London: Macmillan, 1905), p. 291. Lear's "Look there," says Phyllis Rackin, is a "creative delusion," an act of faith analogous to other illusions and delusions in the play, particularly the delusions Edgar perpetrates on Gloucester. See "Delusion as Resolution in *King Lear,*" *Shakespeare Quarterly* 21 (1970): 29–34.

68. See Sherbo, ed., *Johnson on Shakespeare*, p. 704. On Tate's *King Lear,* see Hazelton Spencer, *Shakespeare Improved: The Restoration Versions in Quarto and on the Stage* (1927) (New York: Ungar, 1963), pp. 241–252 and T. D. Duncan Williams, "Mr. Nahum Tate's *King Lear,*" *Studia Neophilologica* 38 (1966): 290–300.

69. Goldman, *Shakespeare and the Energies of Drama*, p. 102.

70. Bradley, *Shakespearean Tragedy*, p. 279; L. C. Knights, *Some Shakespearean Themes and An Approach to Hamlet* (Stanford, Calif.: Stanford University Press, 1966), pp. 74–109 (quotation from p. 109); Knight, *The Wheel of Fire*, p. 195; J. K. Walton, "Lear's Last Speech," *Shakespeare Survey* 13 (1960): 11–19; Jorgensen, *Lear's Self-Discovery;* Winifred M. T. Nowottny, "Lear's Questions," *Shakespeare Survey* 10 (1957): 90–97; Leo Kirschbaum, "Albany," *Shakespeare Survey* 13 (1960): 20–29; Heilman, *This Great Stage;* J. C. Maxwell, "The Technique of Invocation in *King Lear,*" *Modern Language Review* 45 (1950): 142–147; Siegel, *Shakespearean Tragedy and the Elizabethan Compromise,* p. 186; Ribner, *Patterns in Shakespearian Tragedy*, p. 135.

71. Roland Mushat Frye, *Shakespeare and Christian Doctrine* (Princeton: Princeton University Press, 1963), pp. 36–37, 119–120; William R. Elton, *King Lear and the Gods* (San Marino, Calif.: The Huntington Library, 1966), especially pp. 63–71; James, *The Dream of Learning*, p. 110; J. Stampfer, "The Catharsis of *King Lear.*" *Shakespeare Survey* 13 (1960): 1–10 (quotations from pp. 7, 10); Kott, "*King Lear* or *Endgame,*" in *Shakespeare Our Contemporary,* p. 147. (A similar existentialist view is that of Morris Weitz, "*King Lear* and Camus's *L'Etranger,*" *Modern Language Review* 66 [1971]: 31–39, although Weitz argues for man's worth in a morally indifferent universe.) See also John D. Rosenberg, "Lear and His Comforters"; Nicholas Brooke, "The Ending of *King Lear,*" in *Shakespeare: 1564–1964,* ed. Edward A. Bloom (Providence,

R. I.: Brown University Press, 1964), pp. 71–87; and Brooke, *Shakespeare: King Lear,* pp. 36–60.

72. Marvin Rosenberg, *The Masks of King Lear* (Berkeley: University of California Press, 1972), p. 5. Similarly, S. L. Goldberg, *An Essay on King Lear* (Cambridge: Cambridge University Press, 1974), stresses the futility of any simple moralistic reduction of the experience of the play. See especially pp. 155–192.

73. McElroy, *Shakespeare's Mature Tragedies,* p. 167; see also pp. 153 ff.

74. It should be noted that Roy W. Battenhouse, one of the critics who views *King Lear* from the perspective of Christian theology, sees Cordelia as initially guilty (like her father) of "boastful self-righteousness," and he argues that she too must develop from a character who employs legalistic reasoning to one who can act out of Christian compassion. See his *Shakespearean Tragedy: Its Art and Its Christian Premises* (Bloomington: Indiana University Press, 1969), pp. 282–286. Granville-Barker, *Prefaces,* 1: 303, had made a similar point: "It will be a fatal error to present Cordelia as a meek saint. She has more than a touch of her father in her. She is as proud as he is, and as obstinate, for all her sweetness and her youth."

75. Mark Van Doren, *Shakespeare* (New York: Holt, 1939), p. 252. Similarly, Francis Fergusson notes that the plot itself "imitates a desperate race." See "*Macbeth* as the Imitation of an Action," *English Institute Essays, 1951,* ed. Alan S. Downer (New York: Columbia University Press, 1952), pp. 31–43 (quotation from p. 38).

76. Greg, *The Shakespeare First Folio,* p. 391. On textual problems, see also Chambers, *William Shakespeare,* 1: 471–476; the New Cambridge *Macbeth,* ed. John Dover Wilson (Cambridge: Cambridge University Press, 1947), pp. xxii–xlii, 87–91; and the New Arden *Macbeth,* ed. Kenneth Muir, 9th ed. (Cambridge: Harvard University Press, pp. xi–xiv, xxiv–xxxvi. J. M. Nosworthy believes Shakespeare to be the sole author and sole reviser. See *Shakespeare's Occasional Plays: Their Origin and Transmission* (New York: Barnes & Noble, 1965), pp. 8–31.

77. Henry N. Paul, *The Royal Play of Macbeth* (New York: Macmillan, 1950), especially pp. 1–14, 317–331. See the New Arden *Macbeth,* pp. xiv–xxiv, 200–201.

78. Knight, "Brutus and Macbeth," in *The Wheel of Fire,* pp. 120–139; M. C. Bradbrook, "The Sources of *Macbeth,*" in *Shakespeare Survey* 4 (1951): 35–48. On sources in general, see the New Arden *Macbeth,* pp. xxxvii–xliv, 170–199, 201–202; Muir, *Shakespeare's Sources,* pp. 167–186; Bullough, *Sources,* 7: 423–527. There is a useful edition of relevant materials from Holinshed, one that borrows its title from the venerable compilation of W. G. Boswell-Stone: Richard Hosley, ed., *Shakespeare's Holinshed* (New York: Putnam, 1968), with pp. 9–28 devoted to *Macbeth.* For a valuable discussion of Holinshed and the Scottish historians, see Paul, *The Royal Play of Macbeth,* pp. 183–225.

79. See John Russell Brown, *Shakespeare: The Tragedy of Macbeth* (London: Edward Arnold, 1963), p. 61.

80. Knight, "*Macbeth* and the Metaphysic of Evil," in *The Wheel of Fire,* p. 140.

81. L. C. Knights, "How Many Children Had Lady Macbeth?" in *Explorations*

(London: Chatto & Windus, 1946), pp. 18–19. The amusing title of the essay is intended as a parody of some of the critics in the Bradley tradition, who approach Shakespeare's characters as though they were real.

82. On the witches, see Walter Clyde Curry, *Shakespeare's Philosophic Patterns* (Baton Rouge: Louisiana State University Press, 1937), pp. 53–93; Willard Farnham, *Shakespeare's Tragic Frontier: The World of His Final Tragedies* (Berkeley: University of California Press, 1950), pp. 93–99; Brown, *Shakespeare: Macbeth,* pp. 17–22; Arthur R. McGee, "Macbeth and the Furies," *Shakespeare Survey* 19 (1966): 55–67; Clifford Davidson, *The Primrose Way: A Study of Shakespeare's Macbeth* (Conesville, Ia.: Westbury, 1970), pp. 32 ff.; and Paul, *The Royal Play of Macbeth,* pp. 255–274.

Madeleine Doran has suggested that the witches must be taken both literally and symbolically, not just for decoration, "but for the evocation of tragic wonder." See "That Undiscovered Country: A Problem concerning the Use of the Supernatural in *Hamlet* and *Macbeth*," *Philological Quarterly* 20 (1941): 413–427 (quotation from p. 426).

83. Ellen Terry, "The Pathetic Women," in *Four Lectures on Shakespeare,* ed. Christopher St. John (New York: Blom, 1969), pp. 160–162. For a fascinating stage history, which includes documentation of Siddons's performance, see Dennis Bartholomeusz, *Macbeth and the Players* (Cambridge: Cambridge University Press, 1969). See also Ronald Watkins and Jeremy Lemmon, *Macbeth: In Shakespeare's Playhouse* (London: David & Charles, 1974), a line-by-line reconstruction of the play in performance.

84. Harley Granville-Barker, *More Prefaces to Shakespeare* (Princeton: Princeton University Press, 1974), p. 73.

85. Brown, *Shakespeare: Macbeth,* p. 41.

86. The speech is ably discussed by G. R. Elliott, *Dramatic Providence in Macbeth* (Princeton: Princeton University Press, 1958), pp. 59–60. On the implications of the "naked babe," see Cleanth Brooks, "The Naked Babe and the Cloak of Manliness," in *The Well Wrought Urn: Studies in the Structure of Poetry* (New York: Reynal, 1947), pp. 32–49.

87. See Roy Walker, *The Time is Free: A Study of Macbeth* (London: Dakers, 1949), p. 53.

88. Bradley, *Shakespearean Tragedy,* p. 370.

89. On the eroticism of this speech, which is said to have a "ferocious sexual undertone," see Wilbur Sanders, *The Dramatist and the Received Idea: Studies in the Plays of Marlowe and Shakespeare* (Cambridge: Cambridge University Press, 1968), p. 268.

90. "We fail" has stimulated considerable discussion. Defending the question mark in the Folio text, Dover Wilson (New Cambridge *Macbeth,* p. 116 n.) sees her remark as "a scornful echo of his question." Sarah Siddons, on the other hand, spoke the word as an exclamation ("We fail!") in "a quietly fatalistic tone." See Bartholomeusz, *Macbeth and the Players,* p. 110.

91. The sensationalism of this scene is demonstrated by Paul A. Jorgensen, *Our Naked Frailties: Sensational Art and Meaning in Macbeth* (Berkeley: University of California Press, 1971), pp. 59–69. On Siddons's interpretation, see Bartholomeusz, *Macbeth and the Players,* pp. 111–112.

92. Thomas De Quincey, "On the Knocking at the Gate in *Macbeth*," re-

printed in *Shakespeare Criticism: A Selection,* ed. D. Nichol Smith, 2d ed. (London: Oxford University Press, 1946), pp. 331–336 (quotations from pp. 335, 336). The knocking at the gate has been interpreted as a climactic portent of death. See John Webster Spargo, "The Knocking at the Gate in *Macbeth:* An Essay in Interpretation," in *Joseph Quincy Adams Memorial Studies,* eds. James G. McManaway, Giles E. Dawson, Edwin E. Willoughby (Washington, D.C.: The Folger Shakespeare Library, 1948), pp. 269–277.

93. Soellner, *Shakespeare's Patterns of Self-Knowledge,* p. 348.

94. Bradley, *Shakespearean Tragedy,* p. 356.

95. Alan Hobson, *Full Circle: Shakespeare and Moral Development* (London: Chatto & Windus, 1972), p. 132.

96. See Dennis Biggins, "Scorpions, Serpents, and Treachery in *Macbeth,*" *Shakespeare Studies,* ed. J. Leeds Barroll, 1 (1965): 29–36.

97. Banquo's role is not clear. Leo Kirschbaum (dissenting from Bradley) sees him not as a complex character but simply as a foil to Macbeth. See "Banquo and Edgar: Character or Function?" *Essays in Criticism* 7 (1957): 1–8.

98. For a good analysis of the banquet scene (III, 4), see J. P. Dyson, "The Structural Function of the Banquet Scene in *Macbeth,*" *Shakespeare Quarterly* 14 (1963): 369–378. See also Maynard Mack, Jr., *Killing the King: Three Studies in Shakespeare's Tragic Structure* (New Haven: Yale University Press, 1973), pp. 138–148.

99. The play abounds in images of ill-fitting "borrowed robes" (I, 3, 108) and "strange garments" (I, 3, 144); see Caroline F. E. Spurgeon, *Shakespeare's Imagery and What It Tells Us* (New York: Macmillan, 1935), pp. 326–327.

100. Brown, *Shakespeare: Macbeth,* p. 56.

101. On this point, see Marjorie B. Garber, *Dream in Shakespeare* (New Haven: Yale University Press, 1974), pp. 115–117.

102. Roy Walker (*The Time Is Free,* pp. 192–194) has noted a number of biblical echoes in this speech, particularly from Psalms and the Book of Job. For a subtle reading of the speech, one that stresses Macbeth's disengagement from humanity, see John Lawlor, "Mind and Hand: Some Reflections on the Study of Shakespeare's Imagery," *Shakespeare Quarterly* 8 (1957): 180–193 (especially pp. 186–190).

103. See Frank L. Huntley, "*Macbeth* and the Background of Jesuitical Equivocation," *PMLA* 79 (1964): 390–400.

104. Mack, *Killing the King,* p. 149.

105. See Ludwig Jekels, "The Riddle of Shakespeare's *Macbeth,*" *Imago* 5 (1917), reprinted in *Psychoanalytic Review* 30 (1943): 361–385. For a summary of the psychoanalytic literature on *Macbeth,* see Holland, *Psychoanalysis and Shakespeare,* pp. 66–69, 95–97, 219–230.

106. See W. A. Murray, "Why Was Duncan's Blood Golden?" *Shakespeare Survey* 19 (1966): 34–44.

107. G. Wilson Knight, "The Milk of Concord: An Essay on Life-themes in *Macbeth,*" in *The Imperial Theme: Further Interpretations of Shakespeare's Tragedies including the Roman Plays,* 3d ed. (London: Methuen, 1951), p. 142.

108. Walker, *The Time Is Free,* p. 55. See also Siegel, *Shakespearean Tragedy*

and the Elizabethan Compromise, pp. 142–160; Davidson, *The Primrose Way,* especially pp. 8–15; Elliott, *Dramatic Providence in Macbeth;* Glynne Wickham, "Hell-Castle and Its Door-Keeper," *Shakespeare Survey,* 19 (1966): 68–74. For a useful survey of twentieth-century scholarship and criticism, see G. K. Hunter, "*Macbeth* in the Twentieth Century," *Shakespeare Survey* 19 (1966): 1–11.

109. Davidson, *The Primrose Way,* p. 81. See also Helen Gardner, "Milton's 'Satan' and the Theme of Damnation in Elizabethan Tragedy," *English Studies, 1948. Essays and Studies,* n.s. 1 (1948): 46–66.

110. Robert B. Heilman, "The Criminal as Dramatic Hero: Dramatic Methods," *Shakespeare Survey* 19 (1966): 12–24 (quotation from p. 14).

111. Peter Alexander, *Shakespeare's Life and Art* (London: Nisbet, 1939; reprint ed., New York: New York University Press, 1961), p. 173.

11
The Last Tragedies

Antony and Cleopatra

Coriolanus

Timon of Athens

This chapter is devoted to what is considered Shakespeare's final sequence of tragedies: *Antony and Cleopatra, Coriolanus,* and *Timon of Athens*.[1] All three plays (like *Julius Caesar*) are derived from Thomas North's translation (1579) of Plutarch's *Lives*. None of the three— not even *Antony and Cleopatra*, which ranks among Shakespeare's very greatest accomplishments—has achieved the kind of popularity enjoyed by the so-called big four (*Hamlet, Othello, Kink Lear,* and *Macbeth*). Indeed, *Coriolanus* is seldom performed, and *Timon of Athens* remains virtually unknown to playgoers and readers alike. Nevertheless, these are major works that reveal important facets of Shakespeare's mind and art.

ANTONY AND CLEOPATRA

The only text of *Antony and Cleopatra* is that in the First Folio (1623). It is a good one that may have been printed from Shakespeare's manuscript. An *Antony and Cleopatra,* presumably Shakespeare's, was entered in the Stationers' Register on May 20, 1608. This was probably a so-called blocking entry, intended to prevent publication of the play by an unauthorized party and to keep a valuable stage property from falling into the hands of a rival company. There is reason to think that Shakespeare's play had a substantial effect on revisions in the 1607 edition of Samuel Daniel's *Tragedy of Cleopatra*, which was first published in 1594 and frequently reprinted. Because no Shakespearean influence has been detected in earlier editions of Daniel's play, including a version printed as late as 1605, it has been argued that 1606 or 1607 would be a plausible date for *Antony and Cleopatra*. But the evidence is inconclusive.[2]

Shakespeare's principal source is "The Life of Marcus Antonius" in

North's *Plutarch* (1579), which includes most of the incidents that occur in the play. As indicated earlier (see pp. 56–57), much of North's language and imagery finds its way into Shakespeare, notably in the wonderful description of Cleopatra in her barge on the river Cydnus (II, 2, 196–223). But the debt to Plutarch extends beyond details of plot or even explicit verbal reminiscences. One of the very few writers before the Renaissance to treat the lovers with any degree of sympathy (Chaucer portrays Cleopatra favorably in his *Legend of Good Women*), Plutarch had appreciated the "paradoxical nobility"[3] inherent in those two extraordinary personages who "kiss'd away / Kingdoms and provinces" (III, 10, 7–8), and he accordingly created an atmosphere congenial to Shakespeare's own dramatic instincts. In addition to North's *Plutarch,* Shakespeare seems to have used Appian of Alexandria's *Civil Wars* (translated in 1578), chiefly to clarify the motivation of Antony's wife Fulvia and brother Lucius, who made war against Octavius Caesar while Antony was in Egypt (II, 2, 41–44). Shakespeare probably consulted an early edition of the previously mentioned *Tragedy of Cleopatra,* and it has been proposed that he also drew upon Daniel's poem, the *Letter from Octavia to Marcus Antonius* (1599).[4] There are several analogues that Shakespeare could have found helpful, among them *Marc Antoine,* a French play by Robert Garnier, written in 1578 and translated by Mary Sidney, Countess of Pembroke, in 1590. The story of Antony and Cleopatra was indeed familiar to Shakespeare and his contemporaries.[5]

But as is often the case with a Shakespearean play, *Antony and Cleopatra* encompasses a variety of themes and attitudes not always traceable to specific passages or works. For example, Eugene Waith has identified in Antony certain qualities associated with Hercules, a type of warrior-hero more completely exemplified in *Coriolanus*. Reuben Brower sees the play as "an imaginative sequel to the *Aeneid:* what might have happened had Aeneas stayed in Carthage and not fulfilled his fate." Janet Adelman also discusses the lovers' kinship with Dido and Aeneas. In addition, she notes their affinities with the Venus and Mars of literary tradition, especially the cosmic transsexuality implicit when they wear each other's clothing (II, 5, 22–23) and on a number of more serious occasions seem metaphorically to exchange sexual roles.[6] However one may choose to assess the importance of this or that classical influence, the fact remains that the play reflects a rich cultural ancestry.

The splendor of *Antony and Cleopatra,* like the person of its bewitching heroine, beggars all description. The action ranges back and forth between Rome, Athens, Alexandria, and countless other places with a swiftness that must be the despair of realistic stage designers; and the canvas is crowded with some thirty-four characters, the very lowliest of whom seem to speak poetry of unsurpassed grandeur.[7] The play may lack the quality of brooding mystery that permeates the four great tragedies preceding it. In fact, it has been observed that here, perhaps for the only time in Shakespeare's career as a dramatist, "tragedy is taken lightly, almost playfully."[8] Nevertheless, *Antony and Cleopatra* compensates in spaciousness and variety.

The plot is deceptively simple. Marcus Antonius, along with Lepidus and Octavius Caesar, is a member of the triumvirate that governs Rome after the defeat of Cassius and Brutus at the Battle of Philippi (see *Julius Caesar,* V, 1–3). Instead of consistently meeting his military and political obligations, however, Antony carouses in Alexandria with his beloved Cleopatra, Queen of Egypt, who had been mistress to Julius Caesar in her "salad days," when she was "green in judgment" (*Antony and Cleopatra,* I, 5, 73–74). Antony is eventually defeated in battle by the young Octavius (who had disposed of the ineffectual Lepidus), and, learning that Cleopatra has presumably killed herself, he falls upon his sword. But Cleopatra, who had sent this false news of her death to mollify Antony's anger over her possible faithlessness and to test his love, has in reality taken refuge in her sepulcher lest she be captured by Octavius and put on display in Rome. Antony, fatally wounded, is carried to the sepulcher to die in Cleopatra's arms. Although Cleopatra goes through the motions of a reconciliation with Caesar, who does indeed want her as his trophy, she manages to commit suicide by applying asps to her breast and arm. Caesar is now compelled to recognize the incandescent love that has cheated him of complete triumph:

> She shall be buried by her Antony.
> No grave upon the earth shall clip [embrace] in it
> A pair so famous. High events as these
> Strike those that make them; and their story is
> No less in pity than his glory which
> Brought them to be lamented.
>
> (V, 2, 361–366)

The central theme is the conflict raging in Antony's soul between public and private values;[9] between Rome and Alexandria; between the apparently irreconcilable claims of duty, as represented by Octavius Caesar, and love, which is supremely embodied in Cleopatra. Rosalie Colie has brilliantly demonstrated how this conflict is even reflected in the play's opposing rhetorical styles: the clear and direct Attic style employed in Rome and the florid, magniloquent Asiatic style associated with Egypt and adopted by the lovers. Style becomes an aspect of morality, a way of life.[10]

For many critics the moral issue is clear-cut: Antony, a man of enormous ability, throws himself away on a courtesan par excellence. This view was forcefully stated by George Bernard Shaw:

After giving a faithful picture of the soldier broken down by debauchery, and the typical wanton in whose arms such men perish, Shakespear finally strains all his huge command of rhetoric and stage pathos to give a theatrical sublimity to the wretched end of the business, and to persuade foolish spectators that the world was well lost by the twain.[11]

But W. K. Wimsatt, Jr., argues that a literary work may portray "immoral" choices or passions in a manner so attractive that they become, if not more "moral," at least "more understandable, more than a mere barren vileness, a filthy negation." *Antony and Cleopatra* "presents these choices in all their mature interest and capacity to arouse human sympathy."[12] Throughout the play, Shakespeare shifts from one moral perspective to the other. In *Othello, King Lear,* and *Macbeth* (complex though these works may be) good and evil, right and wrong, are clearly defined; in *Antony and Cleopatra* we are confronted at virtually every turn with ambivalence and paradox.[13]

The moral ambiguities command attention in the very first scene, which some critics regard as a microcosm of the whole play.[14] As the scene opens, Antony's friend Philo is deploring the fact that "the triple pillar of the world" has been "transform'd / Into a strumpet's fool" (I, 1, 12–13):

Nay, but this dotage of our general's
O'erflows the measure. Those his goodly eyes
That o'er the files [ranks] and musters of the war
Have glow'd like plated [in armor] Mars, now bend, now turn
The office and devotion of their view
Upon a tawny [dusky] front. His captain's heart,
Which in the scuffles of great fights hath burst
The buckles on his breast, reneges all temper [gives up all self-control]
And is become the bellows and the fan
To cool a gypsy's lust.

(I, 1, 1–10)[15]

At that moment, Antony and Cleopatra enter with their attendants and begin an antiphonal chant celebrating a love that defies measurement on any mortal scale:

Cleopatra: If it be love indeed, tell me how much.
Antony: There's beggary in the love that can be reckon'd.
Cleopatra: I'll set a bourn [boundary] how far to be belov'd.
Antony: Then must thou needs find out new heaven, new earth.

(I, 1, 14–17)

They are interrupted by news from Rome that Cleopatra sarcastically bids Antony hear. Perhaps his dear wife Fulvia is angry, or possibly

Octavius, "the scarce-bearded Caesar" (I, 1, 21), has sent orders that must be obeyed:

> Do this, or this;
> Take in that kingdom, and enfranchise [set free] that.
> Perform't, or else we damn thee.
>
> (I, 1, 22–24)

But Antony, continuing to speak in the cosmic imagery that suggests the expansiveness of his love, would prefer not to hear the messengers:

> Let Rome in Tiber melt and the wide arch
> Of the rang'd [aligned; perhaps far-ranging] empire fall! Here is my space.
> Kingdoms are clay; our dungy earth alike
> Feeds beast as man. The nobleness of life
> Is to do thus [*embracing*]; when such a mutual pair
> And such a twain can do't, in which I bind,
> On pain of punishment, the world to weet [know]
> We stand up peerless.
>
> (I, 1, 33–40)

"Excellent falsehood!" declares Cleopatra, an expert like Antony at the game of love. After they leave, Philo again expresses his displeasure:

> Sir, sometimes when he is not Antony
> He comes too short of that great property
> Which still should go with Antony.
>
> (I, 1, 57–59)

Some critics would interpret the first scene, and all that follows, as a vindication of Philo's judgment.[16] But if Antony and Cleopatra overstate their case, Philo likewise overstates his; and, as Bradley says, "the truths they exaggerate are equally essential."[17]

Throughout the play Antony appears to fluctuate between the two opposing loyalties. At first he resolves to free himself from Cleopatra. "These strong Egyptian fetters I must break," he asserts, "or lose myself in dotage" (I, 2, 120–121). When he learns that Fulvia is dead, he surprises his detractors by leaving the "Epicurean cooks" who tie him up "in a field of feasts" (II, 1, 23–24), returning to Rome, and apologizing to Octavius Caesar for his riotous behavior. The two join forces against young Pompey, and to cement their alliance, Antony marries Caesar's sister Octavia. The fact that Octavia is "of a holy, cold, and still conversation" (II, 6, 131) does not bode well for the marriage, but Antony tries. "I have not kept my square," he confesses; "but that to come / Shall all be done by th' rule" (II, 3, 6–7). Although a Soothsayer

warns him that he should hurry back to Egypt, Antony participates in
the lavish drinking party aboard Pompey's galley off Misenum, where a
peace treaty is ostensibly confirmed between Pompey and the triumvirate.
He then departs with Octavia for Athens. Cleopatra had noticed earlier
that Antony "was dispos'd to mirth; but on the sudden / A Roman
thought hath struck him" (I, 2, 86–87). For the time being Rome has
him more or less under control.

Soon, however, Antony is back in Alexandria, in part because he is
angry with Caesar, but also because he cannot long resist the charms of
his "serpent of old Nile" (I, 5, 25). From this point on, he grows increasingly unstable. Rejecting sound advice, he engages Caesar's armies
by sea rather than land. Why? "For that he dares us to't" (III, 7, 30).
At the historic Battle of Actium (in northwest Greece) the entire
Egyptian fleet turns back in cowardly flight. Antony, "like a doting
mallard" (III, 10, 20), shamefully follows but almost immediately suffers
prodigious remorse:

Hark! the land bids me tread no more upon't!
It is asham'd to bear me! Friends, come hither.
I am so lated [lost in darkness] in the world that I
Have lost my way for ever.
                         (III, 11, 1–4)

His heart was tied to Cleopatra's rudder, and she towed him after her
(III, 11, 56–58). But then his anger dissolves:

Fall not a tear, I say. One of them rates
All that is won and lost. Give me a kiss.
Even this repays me.
                         (III, 11, 69–71)

Before long he is preparing for his last battle with an orgy of feasting
and drinking in honor of Cleopatra's birthday. "Come, / Let's have one
other gaudy night" (III, 13, 182–183). In an unprecedented display of
magnanimity, he sends a rich treasure to his friend Enobarbus, who has
finally deserted him to join Caesar. Antony wins an initial victory near
Alexandria (IV, 7–8), but the Egyptians once again abandon the field,
perhaps, he suspects, because his "triple-turn'd whore" has sold him out
(IV, 12, 13). When he learns of Cleopatra's "death," he looks forward
to joining her in some lovers' Elysium:

          I come, my queen . . . . Stay [wait] for me.
Where souls do couch on flowers, we'll hand in hand
And with our sprightly port [lively, perhaps also
     ghostly, bearing] make the ghosts gaze.

Dido and her Aeneas shall want troops [followers],
And all the haunt be ours.

(IV, 14, 50–54)

His courage temporarily failing him, Antony asks his servant Eros to run him through. But Eros kills himself instead, and Antony is ashamed:

Thrice nobler than myself!
Thou teachest me, O valiant Eros, what
I should, and thou couldst not. My queen and Eros
Have by their brave instruction got upon me
A nobleness in record. But I will be
A bridegroom in my death and run into't
As to a lover's bed.

(IV, 14, 95–101)

After evoking this superb image, Antony proceeds to botch his suicide and lingers half-comically until he is at last carried to Cleopatra.

It seems that for Antony, as one critic has said, "every failure in action has set against it a magnificent gesture or speech; each such gesture is followed by another failure."[18] These incongruities are an integral part of his tragic greatness. Antony is caught between Rome and Egypt, between the worlds of public service and private feeling; unlike Caesar and Cleopatra, he cannot make a simple choice. If he continually reverses himself, it is because he genuinely wants to assimilate both modes of living. Public and private values may be mutually incompatible, but intellectually and emotionally Antony finds them both necessary. As Julian Markels demonstrates in his excellent study, Antony resolves his conflict "by striving equally toward both values and rhythmically making each one a measure and condition of the other .... Antony weighs his alternatives only by living them."[19] It is part of his nature to be in constant motion, as he explains to Eros in a profound metaphor:

Sometimes we see a cloud that's dragonish;
A vapour sometime like a bear or lion,
A tower'd citadel, a pendent rock,
A forked mountain, or blue promontory
With trees upon't that nod unto the world
And mock our eyes with air. Thou hast seen these signs;
They are black Vesper's pageants [evening sights] ....
That which is now a horse, even with a thought
The rack dislimns [the mist blurs], and makes it indistinct
As water is in water ....
My good knave Eros, now thy captain is
Even such a body. Here I am Antony;
Yet cannot hold this visible shape, my knave.

(IV, 14, 2–14)

That Antony cannot hold one visible shape is his chief weakness; it is also his greatest strength.[20]

A major factor in Antony's dilemma is his disillusion with the low standard of morality that prevails in Rome. It may be true that Rome was extolled in Elizabethan tradition and that Octavius Caesar (later the Emperor Augustus) was hailed as the ideal Roman conqueror.[21] Nevertheless, there is something undeniably sordid in the way Shakespeare's Romans, including Caesar, indulge in large and small political intrigues. During the feast on Pompey's galley, Menas secretly offers to cut the cable and then, when the boat is at sea, kill the triumvirs, thereby making his friend Pompey "lord of all the world" (II, 7, 67). Pompey objects, not because he is outraged at the notion of murdering his guests, but because he would have hoped for Menas to do the deed first and tell him about it afterward:

> Repent that e'er thy tongue
> Hath so betray'd thine act. Being done unknown,
> I should have found it afterwards well done,
> But must condemn it now.
>
> (II, 7, 83–86)

Scarcely has the treaty with Pompey been concluded when Caesar wages new wars against him, imprisons Lepidus, and belittles Antony. Later, Caesar deals deviously with Cleopatra, whom he wishes to entice away from Antony. On a lower level, a Roman officer refuses to win too decisive a victory against the Parthians lest he incur Antony's envy: "Better to leave undone than by our deed / Acquire too high a fame when him we serve's away" (III, 1, 14–15). In this play one does not find the Roman virtues of a Marcus Cato or a Brutus, "but the treacheries and back-stabbing of a drunken party on a pirate's barge."[22] Bradley discerns in *Antony and Cleopatra* the kind of "cold and disenchanting light" that Shakespeare in *Troilus and Cressida* chooses to cast on the heroes of the Trojan War. His Romans "are no champions of their country like Henry V . . . . Their aims . . . are as personal as if they were captains of banditti; and they are followed merely from self-interest or private attachment." No wonder, then, that we should "turn for relief from the political game to those who are sure to lose it; to those who love some human being better than a prize . . . to the lovers, who seem to us to find in death something better than their victor's life."[23]

In Cleopatra, who has been praised as "Shakespeare's most amazing and dazzling single personification,"[24] Antony finds a warmth and excitement completely alien to the Roman temperament as exhibited in Caesar. For one thing, she is incredibly high-spirited, whether exchanging bawdy sexual innuendoes with her attendants or planning to amuse herself during Antony's absence:

Give me mine angle! we'll to th' river. There,
My music playing far off, I will betray
Tawny-finn'd fishes. My bended hook shall pierce
Their slimy jaws; and as I draw them up,
I'll think them every one an Antony,
And say, "Ah, ha! y'are caught!"

(II, 5, 10–15)

Charmian reminds her of a wager she once made with Antony about her angling, and Cleopatra relishes the memory of her diver hanging a salt fish on her hook:

That time? O times!
I laugh'd him out of patience; and that night
I laugh'd him into patience; and next morn
Ere the ninth hour I drunk him to his bed,
Then put my tires [headdresses] and mantles on him, whilst
I wore his sword Philippan [from the Battle of Philippi].

(II, 5, 18–23)

But she can be bitter, as in "Fulvia perchance is angry" (I, 1, 20) or in her jeering question to Antony, "What says the married woman?" (I, 3, 20). When he protests that his love is honorable, Cleopatra mockingly agrees:

So Fulvia told me.
I prithee turn aside and weep for her;
Then bid adieu to me, and say the tears
Belong to Egypt.

(I, 3, 75–78)

Yet her love for Antony is all-consuming. "Give me to drink mandragora ... That I might sleep out this great gap of time / My Antony is away" (I, 5, 4–6). With an impatience not unlike that of Rosalind in *As You Like It,* who demands that Celia tell her "in one word" a thousand and one things about Orlando, Cleopatra bombards Charmian with questions:

Where think'st thou he is now? Stands he, or sits he?
Or does he walk? or is he on his horse?
O happy horse, to bear the weight of Antony!
Do bravely, horse! for wot'st thou [do you know] whom thou mov'st?
The demi-Atlas of this earth, the arm
And burgonet [helmet] of men.

(I, 5, 19–24)

"The demi-Atlas of this earth" is another of those tremendous images of the macrocosm that raise the lovers and their love to superhuman heights.[25] In her glorious vision of an Antony transfigured by death, Cleopatra evokes a giant who commands the universe itself:

> His face was as the heav'ns, and therein stuck
> A sun and moon, which kept their course and lighted
> The little O, the earth . . . .
> His legs bestrid the ocean: his rear'd arm
> Crested the world. His voice was propertied
> As all the tuned spheres, and that to friends;
> But when he meant to quail and shake the orb,
> He was as rattling thunder. For his bounty,
> There was no winter in't; an autumn 'twas
> That grew the more by reaping. His delights
> Were dolphin-like: they show'd his back above
> The element they liv'd in. In his livery
> Walk'd crowns and crownets. Realms and islands were
> As plates [coins] dropp'd from his pocket.
>
> (V, 2, 79-92)[26]

If love can inspire Cleopatra to unsurpassable eloquence, it can also unleash her ferocious temper. Heaven help the poor Messenger who brings her news of Antony's marriage to Octavia. Cleopatra showers him with gold for reporting that Antony is well; pounces upon his qualifying phrase "But yet," which she likens to a "jailer" bringing forth "some monstrous malefactor" (II, 5, 52–53); and, when the full truth is out, strikes him, mauls him, and draws a knife. Next time he knows enough to choose his words more carefully:

> *Cleopatra:* Is she as tall as me?
> *Messenger:*   She is not, madam.
> *Cleopatra:* Didst hear her speak? Is she shrill-tongu'd or low?
> *Messenger:* Madam, I heard her speak. She is low-voic'd.
> *Cleopatra:* That's not so good [That's a bad quality]!
>   He cannot like her long.
> *Charmian:* Like her? O Isis! 'tis impossible.
> *Cleopatra:* I think so, Charmian. Dull of tongue, and dwarfish!
>   What majesty is in her gait? Remember,
>   If e'er thou look'dst on majesty.
> *Messenger:*   She creeps!
>   Her motion and her station are as one.
>   She shows a body rather than a life,
>   A statue than a breather.
>
> (III, 3, 14–24)

Cleopatra is relieved. "There's nothing in her yet" (III, 3, 27). How old does he guess Octavia to be? He cagily replies, "She was a widow . . . and I do think she's thirty." Is her face long or round? "Round even to faultiness." A round face, Cleopatra notes with satisfaction, is a sign of foolishness; so is a low forehead, which Octavia also has. From the Messenger's account, Cleopatra is convinced that Octavia is nothing. "The man hath seen some majesty, and should know" (III, 3, 30–45 passim). Indeed he has.

Thus Cleopatra is everything: coquette, enchantress, wit, deceiver, fierce-tongued shrew, golden-voiced queen—all this, and at the same time a woman in love, "commanded," she tells us, "by such poor passion as the maid that milks / And does the meanest chares" (IV, 15, 73–75). The imagery describing her covers a vast range of human attributes: "Egyptian dish" (II, 6, 134); "witch" (IV, 12, 47); "ribald-rid nag" (III, 10, 10); "nightingale" (IV, 8, 18); "royal wench" (II, 2, 231); "most noble Empress" (V, 2, 71); "day o' th' world" (IV, 8, 13); "Eastern star" (V, 2, 311); and, as she says just before her death, "fire and air" (V, 2, 292), two of the four elements of the universe.[27]

The most rhapsodic tribute to Cleopatra comes from the plain-speaking soldier Enobarbus, a character almost entirely original with Shakespeare.[28] With a marvelous blend of genuine admiration and tongue-in-cheek humor, Enobarbus describes her first meeting with Antony. Enobarbus speaks the lines immediately after Antony's marriage to Octavia has been arranged, thereby vividly reminding us of Cleopatra's magic at the precise moment when Antony would seem to be free of it. But that is not all. Observe the following image of Cleopatra in her barge:

> On each side her
> Stood pretty dimpled boys, like smiling Cupids,
> With divers-colour'd fans, whose wind did seem
> To glow the delicate cheeks which they did cool,
> And what they undid did.
>
> (II, 2, 206–210)

Although the lush decoration may be in the vein of Shakespeare's early poetry (like *Venus and Adonis*), the pleasant fantasy of the wind glowing what it is meant to cool hints at the paradox of Cleopatra's nature: the power to transmute faults to virtues; to hop forty paces through the street, lose her breath, speak pantingly, and thereby "make defect perfection" (II, 2, 233–236); to exert so great a spell that the holy priests must bless her even "when she is riggish [wanton]" (II, 2, 244–245). How can Antony, or any other man, resist?

Age cannot wither her nor custom stale
Her infinite variety. Other women cloy
The appetites they feed, but she makes hungry
Where most she satisfies; for vilest things
Become themselves [are attractive] in her ....
                    (II, 2, 240–244)

As one scholar has written of these immortal lines, "The tribute is so impressive because, confining himself entirely to the level of lust, Enobarbus can project Antony's transcendentalism while reveling in the sensual."[29] How typical, incidentally, of Shakespeare's artistry that a skeptic like Enobarbus should rise to such poetry, that this man of sense should long remain loyal though reason sits in the wind against him, and that, finally, when Antony has treated him so generously after his desertion, he should die in a ditch sentimentally, "by moonlight, of a broken heart."[30]

Early in the play Enobarbus laughed at Cleopatra's "celerity in dying"; he has seen her "die twenty times" on occasions less momentous than Antony's departure, and he thinks there must be "mettle [good material] in death, which commits some loving act upon her" (I, 2, 146–149). This little joke, with its probable double-entendre (dying in Elizabethan language frequently alludes to the sexual climax),[31] ironically forecasts Cleopatra's make-believe death, but it comes nowhere near anticipating the dignity of the lovers' genuine deaths. "I am dying, Egypt, dying," Antony gasps as he is heaved aloft to Cleopatra in her sepulcher (IV, 15, 41), the setting thereby providing us "with a metaphor of elevation for Antony's death, which is accompanied by a corresponding heightening of style."[32] Having lived "the greatest prince o' th' world" (IV, 15, 54), he assures her that he now dies nobly:

Not cowardly put off my helmet to
My countryman—a Roman by a Roman
Valiantly vanquish'd.
                    (IV, 15, 56–58)

Cleopatra reacts to his death with some of the grandest poetry in the play:

The crown o' th' earth doth melt. My lord!
O, wither'd is the garland of the war,
The soldier's pole [standard] is fall'n! Young boys and girls
Are level now with men. The odds [superiority] is gone,
And there is nothing left remarkable
Beneath the visiting moon.
                    (IV, 15, 63–68)

Her imagery has been brilliantly analyzed by Derek Traversi. "The crown o' th' earth" suggests Antony's extraordinary royalty; "melt" connotes impermanence but at the same time bestows a kind of softness on Antony's death; "soldier's pole" is the standard of war, but in the context of "crown" and "boys and girls," it may subtly allude to May Day, "when youthful love and the renewed life of spring meet annually in triumph." Traversi would have us balance these joyful associations against Cleopatra's "corresponding depths of desolation" and thereby experience something of the enormous emotional range that her speech encompasses.[33] "Our lamp is spent, it's out!" (IV, 15, 85), she laments. All that is left is to die "after the high Roman fashion / And make death proud to take us" (IV, 15, 87–88).

Cleopatra's death could easily have been an anticlimax, coming as it does after the exaltation of her reunion with the dying Antony. But the last scene is among Shakespeare's most original creations. One may be surprised by its tone; for, as Mark Van Doren has written, "the scene is great and final, yet nothing in it seems to be serious."[34] In this respect it may be said to capture perfectly the essential tragicomic mood of this complex work.

Shakespeare prepares for her death with an interesting meeting between Caesar and Cleopatra during which her treasurer Seleucus reveals that she is withholding from her inventory half of what she should be surrendering (V, 2, 111–175). Some believe that she has no intention of staying alive without Antony and that, in collusion with Seleucus, she is trying to deceive Caesar into thinking otherwise (the suggestion is found in Plutarch). Others maintain that Cleopatra, ever the shrewd opportunist, still envisions the possibility of being left in Egypt and wants to be ready for any contingency.[35] In either case, when the interview is over, Cleopatra knows that Caesar cannot be trusted. "He words me, girls, he words me, that I should not / Be noble to myself!" (V, 2, 191–192). She loathes the prospect of being exhibited to the Roman mob, celebrated in scurvy ballads, and (the anachronistic allusion to the Elizabethan playhouse is most amusing) impersonated by some adolescent boy actor:

> The quick comedians
> Extemporally will stage us and present
> Our Alexandrian revels. Antony
> Shall be brought drunken forth, and I shall see
> Some squeaking Cleopatra boy my greatness
> I' th' posture of a whore.
>
> (V, 2, 216–221)

Her course is clear: Let her have her best clothes, for she is "again for Cydnus, / To meet Mark Antony" (V, 2, 228–229). She obtains the basket of figs, along with the asps, from a rustic clown whose language is in the tradition of Dogberry and other Shakespearean low-comedy specialists. "But I would not be the party that should desire you to touch him [i.e., the asp], for his biting is immortal [i.e., mortal]. Those that do die of it do seldom or never recover" (V, 2, 245–248). After he grimly wishes her "joy o' th' worm" (V, 2, 261, 281), she transforms his "immortal" into her own radiant play on words:

> Give me my robe, put on my crown. I have
> Immortal longings in me. Now no more
> The juice of Egypt's grape shall moist this lip.
> Yare [quick], yare, good Iras; quick. Methinks I hear
> Antony call.
>
> (V, 2, 283–287)

When Iras dies quietly, Cleopatra realizes that death can be like "a lover's pinch, / Which hurts, and is desir'd" (V, 2, 298–299). She must be quick about it, she says half-seriously, lest Iras get to Antony first and he "spend that kiss / Which is my heaven to have" (V, 2, 305–306). The deadly asp is transmuted. "Dost thou not see my baby at my breast, / That sucks the nurse asleep?" (V, 2, 312–313). There is a wonderful moment as Charmian prepares to follow Cleopatra in death. Plutarch had referred to Charmian as "halfe dead, and trembling, trimming the Diademe which Cleopatra ware upon her head."[36] Shakespeare turns this insignificant detail into Charmian's unforgettably simple, "Your crown's awry. / I'll mend it, and then play—" (V, 2, 321–322). This is a gesture of love, to be sure; but at the same time it presents a striking visual image that gently underscores Cleopatra's imperfections and ever so slightly diminishes the solemnity of the occasion.

When it is all over, one almost envies the tragic lovers, for if they have lost the world, they have conquered eternity. "My desolation does begin to make / A better life," Cleopatra declares. "'Tis paltry to be Caesar" (V, 2, 1–2). And the triumphant "sole sir o' th' world" (V, 2, 120), looking down at the dead queen, sounds just the right note:

> But she looks like sleep,
> As she would catch another Antony
> In her strong toil of grace.
>
> (V, 2, 349–351)[37]

CORIOLANUS

Coriolanus, like *Antony and Cleopatra,* originally appeared in the First Folio (1623) in a text probably derived from the author's foul papers. The unusually elaborate stage directions (for example, *"They all shout and wave their swords, take him up in their arms and cast up their caps"* [I, 6, 75]) suggest that Shakespeare may not have gone to London with the manuscript but sent detailed instructions for staging.[38] No performance has been recorded before 1681, when Nahum Tate, the so-called improver of *King Lear* (see p. 339), produced his revision, in which the last act becomes a Senecan nightmare in the style of *Titus Andronicus,* complete with attempted rape, suicide, mutilation, and insanity.[39]

The play seems to have been written some time between 1605 and 1609–1610; 1605 is the date of William Camden's *Remaines of a Greater Worke Concerning Britaine,* one of the sources of Menenius Agrippa's "fable of the belly" (I, 1, 99–159), and 1609 or 1610 is the date of Ben Jonson's *Epicœne,* which contains a possible allusion to the line "He lurch'd all swords of the garland" (II, 2, 105). All in all, the early part of 1608 is generally accepted as a reasonable date. It has been argued that the play reflects Shakespeare's concern with the Northamptonshire peasant revolt of 1607, which may have posed a direct threat to his personal holdings,[40] and the image of "the coal of fire upon the ice" (I, 1, 177) has been taken by some scholars as a reference to the great frost of 1607–1608, when the Thames was frozen over.[41]

The play tells the story of a fifth-century B.C. Roman patrician, Caius Marcius, called Coriolanus for his heroic victory over the Volscians inside their city Corioles. Coriolanus's unconcealed contempt for the plebeians and their spokesmen, the tribunes, brings about his banishment, whereupon he finds sanctuary with the Volscians and their general, Tullus Aufidius. So intensely does Coriolanus now hate his native land that he joins his longtime foe Aufidius in war against Rome. But with revenge in his grasp, Coriolanus relents at the behest of his mother Volumnia, who has led to his tent a deputation consisting of herself, Coriolanus's wife Virgilia and son Young Marcius, and their neighbor Valeria. Although Rome is spared, Aufidius has been provided with an excuse to destroy Coriolanus. After Coriolanus is killed by Volscian conspirators acting in concert with Aufidius, he is accorded a solemn burial.

Shakespeare's principal source is Plutarch's "Life of Caius Marcius Coriolanus," in North's 1579 translation, with additional material probably drawn from Livy's *Roman History,* translated in 1600 by Philemon Holland. Although he follows Plutarch closely, Shakespeare makes significant changes. In Plutarch, we are presented with an elemental political struggle between the patricians and the plebeians. Plutarch's analysis of the hero's character is also rather simple: Coriolanus, brought up by his widowed mother, was improperly taught, hence "so chollericke and impacient, that he would yeld to no living creature: which made him churlishe, uncivill, and altogether unfit for any mans conversation."[42]

But Shakespeare depicts a complex Coriolanus, whose tragedy "is not that of a noble spirit ruined by lack of education," but that "of a noble spirit ruined by something in itself which education cannot touch, or at least does not touch."[43] Shakespeare's Coriolanus is also enriched by several extremely subtle personal relationships not found in Plutarch: with his mother, for example, who is scarcely mentioned in the source except for the big moment in which she pleads with her son that Rome not be burned; with his wife and son, who have brief but important roles in the play; with his enemy Aufidius, whom he both loves and hates; and with Menenius, who appears in no less than thirteen scenes, whereas Plutarch had given him nothing to do beyond delivering his "fable of the belly."[44]

Both Plutarch and Livy include the fable; but it is fairly certain that Shakespeare also made use of other versions of the parable in Sir Philip Sidney's *Apology for Poetrie* (1595), the previously noted *Remaines* of William Camden, and, especially, William Averell's *Mervailous Combat of Contrarieties*.[45] The fable occurs early in *Coriolanus* and serves as a focal point for many of the play's key issues: political, philosophical, and even personal.

As the play opens, the Roman Citizens, armed with staves, clubs, and other weapons, are enraged at the Senate and are threatening to kill Caius Marcius, that "very dog to the commonality" (I, 1, 27–28), in order to have corn at their own price (I, 1, 10–11). Into this incipient mutiny steps Menenius Agrippa, like Marcius a patrician, but "one that hath always lov'd the people" (I, 1, 52–53). To calm the plebeians, Menenius tells them a story: Once upon a time all the members of the body decided to rebel against the belly, accusing it of remaining idle and taking in all the food while they are hard at work performing the necessary bodily functions. The belly answered with its alimentary version of Ulysses' speech on degree:

> And fit it is,
> Because I am the storehouse and the shop
> Of the whole body. But, if you do remember,
> I send it through the rivers of your blood
> Even to the court, the heart, to th' seat o' th' brain,
> And, through the cranks and offices of man,
> The strongest nerves and small inferior veins
> From me receive that natural competency
> Whereby they live.
>
> (I, 1, 136–144)

"How apply you this?" asks one of his listeners, and Menenius answers with a full measure of political paternalism:

The senators of Rome are this good belly,
And you the mutinous members. For, examine
Their counsels and their cares, disgest [digest] things rightly
Touching the weal o' th' common, you shall find
No public benefit which you receive
But it proceeds or comes from them to you,
And no way from yourselves.

(I, 1, 151–159)

Menenius then turns to a plebeian, whom he addresses as "the great toe of this assembly" (I, 1, 159) and a "rascal" (worthless deer) that is in no condition to run yet leads the others "to win some vantage" for himself (I, 1, 163–164):

But make you ready your stiff bats and clubs.
Rome and her rats are at the point of battle;
The one side must have bale [harm].

(I, 1, 165–167)

Several points should be made about the fable. For one thing, it enunciates the familiar Renaissance doctrine that there is a divinely appointed order which must not be violated on the personal or social level lest the individual or the state itself come to grief.[46] At the same time, the fable paradoxically conveys "the condition of the social organism from which the hero's tragedy will spring" and "reveals a patrician caste unreasonably contemptuous of the rest of society."[47] In this connection, Maurice Charney observes that the plebeians are associated in the play with images of feeding or with ignoble animals (rascals, rats, and, later, hares, curs, crows, asses, wolves, and even the Hydra, that nine-headed serpent slain by Hercules).[48] Thus it has been said that Menenius, for all his "veneer of wit and policy," suffers from the same kind of intransigence that plagues Coriolanus, an unyielding sense of superiority rooted in class prejudice.[49] The only difference is that Menenius and the other patricians are on occasion willing to mask their true feelings; Coriolanus is not.

When Marcius enters, he speaks to the plebeians with a savagery that all but undoes whatever good Menenius may have accomplished with his fable:

What's the matter, you dissentious rogues
That, rubbing the poor itch of your opinion,
Make yourselves scabs?

(I, 1, 168–170)[50]

Their affections are "a sick man's appetite, who desires most that / Which would increase his evil" (I, 1, 182–183). Whoever depends upon their favors "swims with fins of lead" (I, 1, 184):

> Hang ye! Trust ye?
> With every minute you do change a mind
> And call him noble that was now your hate,
> Him vile that was your garland.
>   (I, 1, 185–188)

If not for the Senate, they "would feed on one another" (I, 1, 190–192). Marcius welcomes the imminent war with the Volscians, for some of the rabble may be killed off. "Then we shall ha' means to vent / Our musty superfluity" (I, 1, 229–230). When a Senator orders the plebeians to their homes, Marcius reaches new heights of invective:

> Nay, let them follow.
> The Volsces [Volscians] have much corn. Take these rats thither
> To gnaw their garners [granaries]. Worshipful mutiners,
> Your valour puts well forth [looks good].
>   (I, 1, 252–255)

But in the midst of these tirades, Marcius can picture another troop of plebeians who, having been granted the privilege of electing tribunes, excitedly threw their caps in the air, "as they would hang them on the horns o' th' moon" (I, 1, 217). This is scarcely the sort of image one would expect from an angry young man, nor is his description of Virgilia's friend Valeria, whom his mother brings to help turn away his wrath:

> The moon of Rome, chaste as the icicle
> That's curded by the frost from purest snow
> And hangs on Dian's temple!
>   (V, 3, 65–67)

In both cases, and in others as well, he achieves "sudden, momentary flights from the immediate and actual," evidence that in his soul there may lie hidden an "instinctive longing for poetry of living."[51] Be that as it may, his habitually abrasive style does not endear him to the Roman masses.

Ironically enough, it is the war against the Volscians, in which Coriolanus displays unbelievable heroism, that precipitates his confrontation with the plebeians. First, when his soldiers run away while he risks his life, even to the point of being shut in alone within the gates of Corioles, he erupts in denunciations:

> But for our gentlemen,
> The common file (a plague! tribunes for them!),
> The mouse ne'er shunn'd the cat as they did budge
> From rascals worse than they.
>
> (I, 6, 42–45)

Second, it is one thing to refuse a share of the spoils of war; he cannot, he says, make his heart consent to a "bribe" to pay his sword (I, 9, 37–38). But it is quite another to turn aside well-deserved praise:

> I have done
> As you have done—that's what I can; induc'd
> As you have been—that's for my country.
> He that has but effected his good will [done his best]
> Hath overta'en mine act.
>
> (I, 9, 15–19)

The Roman general Cominius has a grasp of his people's psychology; they are entitled to the ritual of honoring their hero:

> You shall not be
> The grave of your deserving. Rome must know
> The value of her own.
>
> (I, 9, 19–21)

"Too modest are you," Cominius continues; "More cruel to your good report than grateful / To us that give you truly" (I, 9, 52–54). In short, the more Coriolanus is extolled, the more he insists that these "acclamations hyperbolical" (I, 9, 50) offend him. He thereby, perhaps inadvertently, gives the impression of insolence and ingratitude.

As a crowning irony, Coriolanus is asked to stand for the consulship, which he does not want:

> Know, good mother,
> I had rather be their servant in my way
> Than sway with them in theirs.
>
> (II, 1, 218–220)

Custom obliges him to don the gown of humility, show his wounds to the citizens, and ask nicely for their "voices," or votes. The tribunes Brutus and Sicinius, anxious to discredit him and augment their own power, hope that he will find it loathsome to "beg their stinking breaths" (II, 1, 252). Indeed, Coriolanus would prefer to forgo the traditional ceremony. "It is a part," he protests, "that I shall blush in acting" (II, 2, 148–149):

To brag unto them, "This I did, and thus!"
Show them th' unaching scars which I should hide,
As if I had receiv'd them for the hire
Of their breath only!

                                        (II, 2, 151–154)

His conduct fulfills the tribunes' fondest expectations. When Menenius
urges him to speak to the citizens "in wholesome manner," Coriolanus
obliges. "Bid them wash their faces / And keep their teeth clean" (II,
3, 66–67). He sarcastically pleads for their "worthy voices," the sardonic
"here come moe [more] voices" becoming for him a synecdoche[52] that,
to quote D. J. Gordon, "reduces their whole reality to this one function or
attribute."[53] He addresses them as though they were nothing more than
ravenous mouths:

Your voices! For your voices I have fought;
Watch'd for your voices; for your voices bear
Of wounds two dozen odd; battles thrice six
I have seen and heard of; for your voices have
Done many things, some less, some more. Your voices!
Indeed I would be consul.

                                        (II, 3, 132–138)

"To my poor unworthy notice," one of the plebeians afterwards observes,
"he mock'd us when he begg'd our voices" (II, 3, 166–167). Nevertheless, his preeminence is recognized; Coriolanus passes the test.

No sooner has he been endorsed by the plebeians than the tribunes
goad them into revoking their "voices." Needless to say, Coriolanus
lashes out, particularly at the tribunes, whom he justly accuses of
fostering a plot to undermine the authority of the nobility. He denounces
the tribune Sicinius, "this Triton [sea demigod] of the minnows" (III,
1, 89). In time, he warns, the rabble will break open the locks of the
Senate itself "and bring in the crows / To peck the eagles" (III, 1,
138–139). The tribunes call for his arrest and death, but the mob is
temporarily pacified by Menenius's promise that the general will appear
at the Forum to answer charges.

Coriolanus comes to the Forum well rehearsed by Menenius and
especially by his mother, whose acquiescence may seem inconsistent
with what we know of her character (see below). In any case, her
"stage directions"[54] are explicit:

Go to them, with this bonnet in thy hand;
And thus far having stretch'd it (here be with them),
Thy knee bussing [kissing] the stones (for in such business
Action is eloquence, and the eyes of th' ignorant

More learned than the ears), waving thy head,
Which often, thus, correcting thy stout heart,
Now humble as the ripest mulberry
That will not hold [endure] the handling—say to them
Thou art their soldier, and, being bred in broils [fights],
Hast not the soft way which, thou dost confess
Were fit for thee to use, as they do claim,
In asking their good loves . . . .

(III, 2, 73–84)

Although he would, in his mother's words, rather follow his enemy "in a fiery gulf / Than flatter him in a bower" (III, 2, 91–92), Coriolanus resolves to go through with the distasteful performance:

I'll mountebank [win by trickery, like a carnival confidence man] their loves,
Cog [cheat] their hearts from them, and come home belov'd
Of all the trades in Rome.

(III, 2, 132–134)

But thanks to the manipulations of the tribunes, he cannot pull it off. When they denounce him as a traitor, Coriolanus proclaims that he would not buy the people's mercy "at the price of one fair word" (III, 3, 90–91). In an outburst of pride and scorn, he accepts, and reverses, banishment:

You common cry of curs, whose breath I hate
As reek o' th' rotten fens, whose loves I prize
As the dead carcasses of unburied men
That do currupt my air, I banish you!
(III, 3, 120–123)

He turns his back on Rome. "There is a world elsewhere" (III, 3, 135). This is a climactic moment, although, as L. C. Knights has suggested, Coriolanus had cut himself off from his society well before his official banishment.[55]

The "world elsewhere" would seem at first glance to mean the Volscian camp,[56] where Coriolanus joins his redoubtable foe to fight against his "cank'red country" (IV, 5, 96). But, in reality, Coriolanus departs from Rome "a lonely dragon" (IV, 1, 30), condemned to inhabit a private world that is essentially of his own making. What Coriolanus discovers, writes G. K. Hunter, is not at all "like Lear's world of introspective anguish and revaluation; it is only the same Roman political world, at a certain geographical remove, and equally resistant to the monomaniac individual."[57] Or, in the more sympathetic language of Eugene Waith, the world of Coriolanus is not that of the

Romans or the Volscians. "It is a world of absolutes—the world . . . of heroes."[58] To underscore the fundamental sameness of Rome and Antium, Shakespeare shows us how rudely Aufidius's servants first receive the disguised Coriolanus. "Here's no place for you" (IV, 5, 8). "Has the porter his eyes in his head that he gives entrance to such companions? Pray you get out" (IV, 5, 12–14). "Where dwell'st thou?" one asks. "Under the canopy [the heavens]," he replies. "Where's that?" "I' th' city of kites and crows" (IV, 5, 40–45). But after his identity is revealed and Aufidius embraces him, the servants change their tune. "By my hand, I had thought to have stroken him with a cudgel—and yet my mind gave me his clothes made a false report of him." "Nay, I knew by his face that there was something in him." "Would I were hang'd but I thought there was more in him than I could think" (IV, 5, 155– 166). These remarks resemble those of the Roman plebeians when they learn that the man they have banished is on the march against their city:

> *1. Citizen:*   For mine own part,
>   When I said banish him, I said 'twas pity.
> *2. Citizen:* And so did I.
> *3. Citizen:* And so did I; and to say the truth, so did very many of us. That
>   we did, we did for the best; and though we willingly consented to his
>   banishment, yet it was against our will.
>
>   (IV, 6, 139–145)

"With every minute you do change a mind," Coriolanus had scolded, "and call him noble that was now your hate" (I, 1, 186–187).

Thus the conflict of classes continues on a different battleground, and there are no easy solutions. For the nineteenth-century critic William Hazlitt, a devout liberal, Shakespeare's ugly moral "is that those who have little shall have less, and that those who have much shall take all that others have left. The people are poor; therefore they ought to be starved."[59] On the other hand, R. W. Chambers sees Shakespeare's criticism as focusing on the tribunes rather than the common people, who are portrayed as warmhearted and forgiving.[60] It appears, however, that Shakespeare does not take sides but chooses to depict a battle in which each side understands the other but neither understands itself.[61] Coriolanus persists in fighting the battle to the end, although his temperament does not permit him to win. "His nature is too noble for the world," Menenius says. "He would not flatter Neptune for his trident / Or Jove for's power to thunder" (III, 1, 255–257). In this total refusal to compromise principles that are essentially sound, "you have," in the words of A. P. Rossiter, "a tragic clash: the basis of a political tragedy, not a Tudor morality."[62]

But *Coriolanus* is more than a play about politics; it achieves a masterful integration of political and personal issues. The tragedy of Coriolanus the public figure is inextricably bound up with his family relationships, particularly the remarkable relationship with his mother Volumnia, who is one of Shakespeare's most interesting characters.[63]

Volumnia, an iron-nerved patriot, has played an active role in the formation of the boy-hero who is her son. "If my son were my husband," she says to Virgilia, who broods because Coriolanus is at war, "I should freelier rejoice in that absence wherein he won honour than in the embracements of his bed where he would show most love" (I, 3, 2–6). When Virgilia (whose gentleness has been eloquently expounded by John Middleton Murry)[64] recoils at Volumnia's picture of Coriolanus returning with "bloody brow" (I, 3, 37), the mother sternly rebukes the wife:

> Away, you fool! It more becomes a man
> Than gilt his trophy. The breasts of Hecuba
> When she did suckle Hector, look'd not lovelier
> Than Hector's forehead when it spit forth blood
> At Grecian sword, contemning.
>
> (I, 3, 42–46)

She is pleased that her grandson "had rather see the swords and hear a drum than look upon his schoolmaster" (I, 3, 60–61), and she listens in delight to Valeria's revealing story about Young Marcius playing with a butterfly:

> I saw him run after a gilded butterfly; and when he caught it, he let it go again, and after it again, and over and over he comes, and up again; catch'd it again; or whether his fall enrag'd him or how 'twas, he did so set his teeth and tear it! O, I warrant, how he mammock'd [mutilated] it!
>
> (I, 3, 66–71)

"One on's father's moods" (I, 3, 72), Volumnia happily notes. She is ecstatic that Coriolanus comes home wounded in the shoulder and left arm, adding two more wounds to the twenty-five he previously boasted. As G. Wilson Knight has observed, Volumnia counts her son's wounds "as a miser his coins."[65]

In view of this rigid code of honor, it may come as a surprise that Volumnia (as was discussed earlier) should urge her son to appear in the Forum and speak to the people with sweet words that do not reflect his true feelings:

> Now, this no more dishonours you at all
> Than to take in a town with gentle words
> Which else would put you to your fortune and

> The hazard of much blood.
> I would dissemble with my nature where
> My fortunes and my friends at stake requir'd
> I should do so in honour.
>   (III, 2, 58–64)

Dissemble in honor? Coriolanus is appalled, but after considerable vacillation he agrees, in part because he cannot resist her appeal, perhaps unfair, to his obligation as a son:

> I prithee now, sweet son, as thou hast said
> My praises made thee first a soldier, so,
> To have my praise for this, perform a part
> Thou hast not done before.
>   (III, 2, 107–110)

After this plea and a subsequent scolding when he momentarily changes his mind again, Coriolanus complies:

>   Pray be content.
> Mother, I am going to the market place.
> Chide me no more.
>   (III, 2, 130–132)

Oscar James Campbell, who interprets *Coriolanus* as an experiment in tragical satire, finds the hero at this point reduced to the status of a frightened and whimpering child, "ridiculously eager to pacify an irate parent."[66] But that is not the whole story.

This scene (III, 2) serves several dramatic functions. First, it confirms one's earlier impression that there is something childlike, but not unappealing, about this ferocious young Hercules. In the midst of celebrating his spectacular victory at Corioles, he requests clemency for a poor Volscian who had treated him kindly; but when asked for his name, Coriolanus, with the impetuosity of a Hotspur, draws a blank. "By Jupiter, forgot! / I am weary; yea, my memory is tir'd" (I, 9, 89–90), thus bringing an end to a generous natural impulse.[67] And there is authentic tenderness in his greeting to Virgilia upon his return from Corioles:

>   My gracious silence, hail!
> Wouldst thou have laugh'd had I come coffin'd home
> That weep'st to see me triumph? Ah, my dear,
> Such eyes the widows in Corioles wear
> And mothers that lack sons.
>   (II, 1, 192–196)

Second, the scene attests to the effectiveness of Coriolanus's education: He has imbibed his mother's lessons about honor beyond her expectations, perhaps even beyond her intentions. Moreover, it reveals that Volumnia's pride in her son's valor primarily revolves around the glory he brings to her and the family and, more significantly, to Rome. One senses a bloodless detachment in her feelings toward Coriolanus. She may be a mother, but before all else she is a Roman concerned with the pragmatic question of her city's survival at any cost. The episode also contributes to Coriolanus's disillusionment by undermining his image of an ideal Rome, where there should be no place for the hypocrisy he actually perceives and in which he is now forced to participate.[68] Finally, and most important, the exchange between Coriolanus and Volumnia exposes the hero's vulnerability to family feeling, a flaw perhaps, but one that, paradoxically, is a major component of his greatness as well as his humanity. These varied strands all commingle here and prepare us for the unforgettable final meeting between mother and son that, ironically, determines the destiny of Rome.

Even as the three women and Young Marcius approach the Volscian tent, Coriolanus, who has rejected the suits of Cominius and Menenius, struggles against his better instincts:

> I melt and am not
> Of stronger earth than others. My mother bows,
> As if Olympus to a molehill should
> In supplication nod; and my young boy
> Hath an aspect of intercession which
> Great Nature cries "Deny not."
>
> (V, 3, 28–33)

He will remain firm, "as if a man were author of himself / And knew no other kin" (V, 3, 36–37). But he begins to feel "like a dull actor" who has forgotten his part (V, 3, 40–41), a marvelous image that recalls his earlier disastrous performance in the Forum and also reflects his fundamental uncertainty as to the many identities he has assumed: son, husband, father, Roman hero and patriot, traitor, avenger. He kneels before his mother, only to be raised up. When she in turn kneels, Coriolanus lifts her to her feet:

> What is this?
> Your knees to me? to your corrected son?
> Then let the pebbles on the hungry beach
> Fillop [strike] the stars! Then let the mutinous winds
> Strike the proud cedars 'gainst the fiery sun,

Murd'ring impossibility [i.e., making anything possible], to make
What cannot be, slight work!

(V, 3, 56–62)

Volumnia entreats, cajoles, and scorns, again laying stress upon her
contribution to his glorious career and his cruel ingratitude:

> There's no man in the world
> More bound to's mother; yet here he lets me prate
> Like one i' th' stocks. Thou hast never in thy life
> Show'd thy dear mother any courtesy,
> When she (poor hen), fond of no second brood,
> Has cluck'd thee to the wars, and safely home
> Loaden with honour.

(V, 3, 158–164)

Finally, she prepares to go, having accused Coriolanus of renouncing
family and country:

> This fellow had a Volscian to his mother;
> His wife is in Corioles, and this child
> Like him by chance. Yet give us our dispatch.
> I am hush'd until our city be afire.
> And then I'll speak a little.

(V, 3, 178–182)

After a long pause comes his reply, "one of the great speaking silences
in Shakespeare"[69] and, as Maurice Charney notes, "one of the rare
physical contacts between Coriolanus and another human being in
the play":[70]

> *He holds her by the hand, silent.*
> *Coriolanus:*   O mother, mother!
> What have you done? Behold, the heavens do ope,
> The gods look down, and this unnatural scene
> They laugh at. O my mother, mother! O!
> You have won a happy victory to Rome;
> But for your son—believe it, O believe it!—
> Most dangerously you have with him prevail'd,
> If not most mortal to him.

(V, 3, 182–189)

He is right. Having betrayed the Volscians, Coriolanus has to die.
As was the case when he was manipulated by the tribunes into a fit of
temper, his last outburst is deliberately provoked, this time by Aufidius,
who derisively calls him a "boy of tears" (V, 6, 100):

Cut me to pieces, Volsces. Men and lads,
Stain all your edges on me. Boy? False hound!
If you have writ your annals true, 'tis there,
That, like an eagle in a dovecote, I
Flutter'd your Volscians in Corioles.
Alone I did it. Boy?

(V, 6, 111–116)

What follows is overwhelming in its brutality. "Kill, kill, kill, kill, kill him!" (V, 6, 131). We witness for perhaps the only time in Shakespeare what Bradley calls "the instantaneous cessation of enormous energy,"[71] and it is terrible to behold. And then we have the "simple, barbarous tableau" of Aufidius standing on him, "an ironic reversal of Volumnia's heroic vision of her son: 'He'll beat Aufidius' head below his knee / And tread upon his neck' " (I, 3, 49–50).[72]

It has been suggested by one scholar that Coriolanus exhibits throughout the play the kind of integrity and sense of honor that Renaissance writers would have associated with the high-minded or magnanimous man as set forth by Aristotle and that his death illustrates a tragic irony "in which the shoddy and the second-rate are seen to inherit the earth."[73] Whether or not one concurs in this judgment, it is difficult to observe Coriolanus's downfall without feeling regret. This "public hero without a public," as he has been designated, has found in dishonorable Rome "neither his Eternal City without nor his paradise within."[74] Volumnia, who is a part of that Rome, may pass across the stage in splendid triumph. But she has rejected (rather, exploited) family ties while Coriolanus has warmly embraced them. There is something tainted in her victory, something fine in his failure.[75]

TIMON OF ATHENS

The Life of Timon of Athens appears in the First Folio (1623), where it follows *Romeo and Juliet,* a position originally intended for the much longer *Troilus and Cressida,* which was temporarily withdrawn for reasons that may have involved problems of copyright. This circumstance, together with the impression on the part of most scholars that the text in its present form is probably an unrevised draft, has led to speculation that the inclusion of *Timon of Athens* in the Folio was an afterthought, although there is no evidence to support this conjecture. The text has rough spots: so-called ghost characters who are mentioned but do not appear; an announcement (IV, 3, 356) that "yonder comes a poet and a painter," although they arrive almost 200 lines later; confusing admixtures of blank verse, prose, and couplets; Shakespeare's apparent inconsistency regarding the value of the talent, an ancient money unit;[76]

and, perhaps more important, signs that several characters, including at times the hero himself, may not be fully integrated into the total dramatic structure.

It used to be fashionable to explain the play's irregularities on the basis of divided authorship; in fact, Francelia Butler, in her exhaustive survey of *Timon* criticism, includes an elaborate table showing how from 1839 to 1924 nine different editors and scholars parceled out individual acts and scenes among Shakespeare and other dramatists.[77] By the early 1930s, however, the proponents of divided authorship had defeated their purpose. As H. J. Oliver, the New Arden editor, has observed, "They began with the desire to explain the presence in the play of 'inferior' work and almost without exception ended up by assigning to Shakespeare's alleged collaborator some of the best scenes in the play . . . as well as parts that were crucial in the plot."[78] Nowadays, just about everybody credits Shakespeare as sole author, and except for a few scholars who accept the Folio text as substantially complete, the consensus is that he did not finish revising the play.

There is no reliable clue as to the date of composition. Many scholars (notably Bradley) have commented on its close relationship to *King Lear:* Sir Walter Raleigh (the scholar, not the explorer) considered *Timon* "a first sketch"; Dover Wilson, "the still-born twin"; and Coleridge, "an after vibration."[79] Thus if one inclines to an earlier date, 1605 or 1606 makes sense, that is, before *King Lear* or between *King Lear* and *Macbeth.* On the other hand, *Timon* has affinities with *Antony and Cleopatra* and *Coriolanus,* as well as with the last plays. Chambers would place it between *Coriolanus* and *Pericles* and would have us believe that Shakespeare was close to a mental breakdown when he wrote it; Clifford Leech sees *Timon* as "not the last and least of the tragedies but the doubtful harbinger of the romances"; Muriel Bradbrook suggests that the play is "an experimental scenario for an indoor dramatic pageant" that was probably staged as a court show late in 1609 when Shakespeare's company moved into its new theater.[80] There is no actual record of a performance during Shakespeare's lifetime. Shakespeare may have been acquainted with an anonymous academic play known as the old *Timon,* but that play cannot be dated either. One can do little beyond proposing 1604–1609 as a possible date for the play.[81]

The story of Timon is found in a digression in Plutarch's "Life of Marcus Antonius," which Shakespeare knew in North's translation (1579). He also drew upon Plutarch's "Life of Alcibiades," which parallels that of Coriolanus. It seems that Shakespeare was familiar with Lucian's *Dialogue of Timon* in Latin, Italian, or French (there was no English version in his day). Willard Farnham has shown that Lucian introduced into the Timon legend the theme of beasthood, which figures prominently in many Renaissance treatments of the story and is a powerful element in Shakespeare's drama. Shakespeare may have adapted some of the details of the old *Timon:* the character of Flavius, the loyal steward; the banquet for Timon's false friends (III, 6); Timon's burial of the gold (IV, 3, 45). Finally, he could have modeled Apemantus after Diogenes, the cynical philosopher in John Lyly's play *Campaspe* (1584).[82]

Because *Timon of Athens* is unusual and relatively unfamiliar, it is necessary to examine the plot rather closely. In the first half of the play, Timon, an extravagantly generous Athenian, pours benefits upon the scores of friends who cultivate him. In addition to maintaining an almost perpetual open house, he performs numerous individual acts of munificence. For example, he ransoms Ventidius from prison and bids him come for further assistance. " 'Tis not enough to help the feeble up," he explains, "but to support him after" (I, 1, 107–108); and he provides a dowry so that his servant Lucilius can marry the woman he loves:

> This gentleman of mine hath serv'd me long.
> To build his fortune I will strain a little
> For 'tis a bond in men.
>
> (I, 1, 142–144)

Apemantus, whose scurrilous commentary reminds one of Thersites in *Troilus and Cressida,* knows that Timon is surrounded by flatterers. In a striking echo of Matthew 26:23 ("And he answered and said, He that dippeth his hand with me in the dish, the same shall betray me"),[83] Apemantus predicts that Timon will be destroyed by those who profess to love him:

> O you gods, what a number of men eats Timon, and he sees 'em not! It grieves me to see so many dip their meat in one man's blood; and all the madness is, he cheers them up too. ... The fellow that sits next him now, parts bread with him, pledges the breath of him in a divided draught [a shared drink], is the readiest man to kill him.
>
> (I, 2, 39–50)

But Timon is oblivious of any danger. "Methinks I could deal kingdoms to my friends / And ne'er be weary" (I, 2, 226–227).

Timon does not know (and will not listen when his steward Flavius tries to tell him) that his bounty has been sustained only by borrowing and that his extensive landholdings have been placed in pawn. When he at last realizes that his creditors are clamoring for their money, he is confident. "I am wealthy in my friends" (II, 2, 193), he proclaims as he dispatches his servants to seek the help of acquaintances whom he has freely supplied in the past. Flavius is doubtful:

> Ah, when the means are gone that buy this praise,
> The breath is gone whereof this praise is made.

Feast-won, fast-lost. One cloud of winter show'rs,
These flies are couch'd [lie hidden].

(II, 2, 178–181)

"Feast-won, fast-lost," with its pun on *fast,* is a remarkably compact phrase. In broken verse that re-creates the rhythms of actual speech, Flavius goes on to report how the Senators have already turned him down:

They answer in a joint and corporate voice,
That now they are at fall, want treasure, cannot
Do what they would, are sorry: you are honourable;
But yet they could have wish'd—they know not what—
Something hath been amiss—a noble nature
May catch a wrench—would all were well! 'tis pity—
And so, intending other serious matters,
After distasteful looks and these hard fractions [broken sentences],
With certain half-caps and cold-moving nods
They froze me into silence.

(II, 2, 213–222)

Timon is not discouraged. Surely his friends, like Ventidius, who has inherited a large estate since Timon redeemed him from prison, will respond favorably.

In a series of superb satirical vignettes, Timon's so-called friends refuse him. First Lucullus: "One of Lord Timon's men? A gift, I warrant" (III, 1, 4–5). But when informed that Timon needs money "nothing doubting" a favorable answer, Lucullus quickly declines, not without moralizing: "La, la, la, la! 'Nothing doubting,' says he? Alas, good lord! a noble gentleman 'tis, if he would not keep so good a house" (III, 1, 20–24). This is no time to lend, he asserts, "especially upon bare friendship without security." Then, to add insult to injury, he hands Timon's servant three paltry coins, with instructions to forget the interview: "Good boy, wink at me and say thou saw'st me not" (III, 1, 45–48). Next to be approached is Lucius. When Timon's servant enters, he perks up in expectation of some new gift:

Servilius: May it please your honour, my lord hath sent—
Lucius: Ha! What has he sent? I am so much endeared to that lord! He's
ever sending . . . . And what has he sent now?

(III, 2, 33–38)

But when the reason for the visit is made known, Lucius regrets that he has no ready money. "And tell him this from me, I count it one of my greatest afflictions, say, that I cannot pleasure such an honourable gentleman" (III, 2, 60–63). Observing the encounter are three Strangers, who comment on this display of ingratitude in the manner of a chorus: "Religion groans at it" (III, 2, 83). Another friend, Sempronius, comes up with a novel excuse. When told that Lucullus and Lucius, and even Ventidius, "have all been touch'd and found base metal" (III, 3, 6), he is insulted that Timon did not ask him first. "Who bates mine honour shall not know my coin" (III, 3, 26).

Besieged by bill collectors and stripped of his illusions, Timon explodes in rage. "Cut my heart in sums!" "Tell [count] out my blood!" "Tear me, take me, and the gods fall upon you!" (III, 4, 93, 95, 100). He invites his friends to one final feast, which they eagerly attend, persuaded that Timon's fortune is intact after all. "The swallow follows not summer more willing than we your lordship" (III, 6, 31–32). A banquet of covered dishes is brought in, and after an ironic prayer that "the meat be beloved more than the man that gives it" (III, 6, 85–86), Timon orders the feast to begin. "Uncover, dogs, and lap" (III, 6, 95). The dishes contain nothing but warm water, which he hurls in the faces of his guests as he utters a scathing denunciation:

> May you a better feast never behold,
> You knot of mouth-friends! Smoke and lukewarm water
> Is your perfection. This is Timon's last!
> Who, stuck and spangled with your flatteries,
> Washes it off and sprinkles in your faces
> Your reeking villainy.
>
> (III, 6, 98–103)

Timon drives them out and embraces misanthropy. "Burn house! Sink Athens! Henceforth hated be / Of Timon man and all humanity!" (III, 6, 114–115). Outside the wall girdling those "wolves" (IV, 1, 2), Timon calls down upon the city a curse that in its intensity is akin to Lear's:

> Matrons, turn incontinent!
> Obedience fail in children! Slaves and fools,
> Pluck the grave wrinkled Senate from the bench
> And minister in their steads! To general filths
> Convert o' th' instant, green virginity!
> Do't in your parents' eyes! Bankrupts, hold fast!
> Rather than render back, out with your knives
> And cut your trusters' throats! Bound servants, steal!
> Large-handed robbers your grave masters are
> And pill [pillage] by law. Maid, to thy master's bed!
> Thy mistress is o' th' brothel. Son of sixteen,
> Pluck the lin'd crutch from thy old limping sire;
> With it beat out his brains!
>
> (IV, 1, 3–15)

Like Lear, he welcomes exile:

Timon will to the woods, where he shall find
Th' unkindest beast more kinder than mankind.
The gods confound (hear me, you good gods all)
Th' Athenians both within and out that wall!
And grant, as Timon grows, his hate may grow
To the whole race of mankind, high and low!
Amen.

                                        (IV, 1, 35–41)

Thus ends the first phase of his career. "A dedicated beggar to the air," Timon, "with his disease of all-shunn'd poverty, / Walks, like contempt, alone" (IV, 2, 13–15). But Flavius and the Servants, "all broken implements of a ruin'd house" (IV, 2, 16), resolve not to desert him. Decency is not totally dead, although Timon seems unaware of this.

In the second part of the play, Timon, who now dwells in a cave in the woods, has a series of visitors. Each serves as the occasion for a fresh display of his misanthropy. First comes the Athenian captain Alcibiades, banished by the Senate in a great scene (III, 5), because he pleaded for a comrade who had been sentenced to death. Learning that Alcibiades is making war against Athens, Timon is happy to supply him with gold (which he found, symbolically, while digging for roots). "Let not thy sword skip one" (IV, 3, 110), he urges. Timon also bestows gold upon two whores who accompany Alcibiades, on condition that they "consumptions sow / In hollow bones of man" (IV, 3, 151–152). Apemantus is the next to arrive, but Timon does not respect his cynicism because, unlike his own, it does not spring from the disillusionment of one who "had the world as my confectionary" (IV, 3, 260). "Why shouldst thou hate men?" Timon asks. "They never flatter'd thee. What hast thou given?" (IV, 3, 269–270). Timon is then visited by three thieves, to whom he freely offers gold, along with an ironic demonstration that thievery is the basic law of nature: The sun robs from the sea; the moon snatches her "pale fire" from the sun; the sea takes from the moon; and the earth "feeds and breeds by a composture stol'n / From gen'ral excrement." Let the bandits steal everything, especially from Athens. "Nothing can you steal / But thieves do lose it" (IV, 3, 438–451). Timon would even repudiate Flavius, his next visitor, but he relents when the steward weeps compassionately:

                              I do proclaim
One honest man. Mistake me not—but one!
No more, I pray—and he's a steward.
How fain would I have hated all mankind,
And thou redeem'st thyself! But all save thee
I fell with curses.

                                        (IV, 3, 503–508)

But as if to justify Timon's misanthropy, the steward is followed by the Poet and the Painter, who expect their flattery to be rewarded; Timon drives them away.

Of particular interest is Timon's last encounter, a meeting with two Senators who have come to entreat him to return to Athens to help beat back Alcibiades. But Timon has arrived at a state of renunciation:

> My long sickness
> Of health and living now begins to mend,
> And nothing brings me all things. Go, live still.
> Be Alcibiades your plague, you his,
> And last so long enough!
>
> (V, 1, 189–193)

He will, however, do Athens the kindness of showing a means of escape from Alcibiades, whereupon in a gesture of overwhelming bitterness he calls attention to a tree soon to be cut down:

> Tell Athens, in the sequence of degree
> From high to low throughout, that whoso please
> To stop affliction, let him take his haste,
> Come hither ere my tree hath felt the axe,
> And hang himself.
>
> (V, 1, 211–215)

After offering this counsel, Timon (who here has been compared to the allegorical figure of Despair in Edmund Spenser's *Faerie Queene,* book 1, canto 9)[84] announces that he will die by the sea:

> Timon hath made his everlasting mansion
> Upon the beached verge of the salt flood,
> Who once a day with his embossed [foaming] froth
> The turbulent surge shall cover.
>
> (V, 1, 218–221)

In regal isolation, Timon goes into his cave for the last time. "Sun, hide thy beams! Timon hath done his reign" (V, 1, 226). In the final scene, just after Alcibiades has agreed to spare Athens and confine his revenge to those who have been his and Timon's enemies, word reaches the city that Timon is indeed dead. Alcibiades reads the epitaph:

> Here lies a wretched corse, of wretched soul bereft.
> Seek not my name. A plague consume you wicked caitiffs left!
> Here lie I, Timon, who alive all living men did hate.
> Pass by, and curse thy fill; but pass, and stay not here thy gait.
>
> (V, 4, 70–73)

As one may infer from the foregoing summary, *Timon of Athens* is a strange play; it is stylistically uneven, episodic in structure, and generally lacking in subtle characterization even in the portrait of the hero. On one point concerning this controversial play there is little, if any, disagreement: Athens is depicted as ripe for destruction, "a city where virtue has ceased to rule in high places, a city ready for the fate of 'Sodom and Gomorra.' "[85] *Radix malorum est cupiditas* (the root of all evils is avarice).

The extent to which Timon may be responsible for the general corruption has been fiercely debated. G. Wilson Knight, an extravagant admirer of the play, sees Timon as "the flower of human aspiration," one whose generosity may lack wisdom but not grandeur, an idealist whose only "fault" is his "essential love, essential nobility, unmixed with any restraining faculty of criticism." In contrast, Oscar Campbell criticizes the hero for being unable to distinguish servile adoration from discriminating praise, fawning sycophants from true friends. J. C. Maxwell advances the provocative view that Timon cannot overcome the materialism of Athens but "can only outbid it in its own currency of gold"; by continually giving without demanding anything in return, he actively, though perhaps unknowingly, contributes to the dehumanization of his fellow Athenians. Maxwell cites the perceptive comment of Flavius, who is certainly sympathetic to his master: "For bounty, that makes gods, does still mar men" (IV, 2, 41).[86] Timon himself, at least in the beginning, does not regard his philanthropy as wrong. "No villanous bounty yet hath pass'd my heart," he tell Flavius. "Unwisely, not ignobly, have I given" (II, 2, 182–183), and from time to time others in the play support this estimate. "Poor honest lord, brought low by his own heart," Flavius laments, "undone by goodness!" (IV, 2, 37–38). Of course, the combination of goodness and unwisdom may prove as dangerous as deliberate wickedness.

If Timon the Bountiful has tragic potentialities, Timon the Man Hater sometimes borders on absurdity. As Harry Levin observes, "Other tragic heroes have undergone worse tribulations than bankruptcy, and have not arrived at so wholesale a condemnation of their fellow men."[87] His speech to Alcibiades' harlots betrays such an obsession with filth and disease that several critics have taken him to be suffering from insanity. The encounter between Timon and Apemantus degenerates into the crudest sort of name-calling:

Apemantus: Thou art the cap of all the fools alive.
Timon: Would thou wert clean enough to spit upon.
Apemantus: A plague on thee! thou art too bad to curse.
Timon: All villains that do stand by thee are pure.

Apemantus: There is no leprosy but what thou speak'st.
Timon: If I name thee.

(IV, 3, 363–368)

This invective seems to come straight out of Shakespeare's plays of the 1580s or early 1590s (could parts of *Timon* possibly have been written much earlier than we think?), for it surely does not belong in the same artistic world as *Macbeth* or *Antony and Cleopatra*. "Here," Una Ellis-Fermor writes, "is that rarest of all weaknesses in Shakespeare's work, an element which is not wholly functional; a character which does not convince us, upon inspection, that, given its nature and these events, the resultant action presented to us is inevitable."[88] It has been argued that such defects are attributable to the fact that *Timon* is unfinished; or, conversely, Shakespeare may have left the play unfinished because he could not get around its intrinsic deficiencies.

Without taking the position that the play as we know it is complete or consistently satisfying, one may suggest that *Timon of Athens* can perhaps best be understood, not as a tragedy in the general mold of *Othello* or *King Lear*, but as a boldly experimental work. The exact nature of the experiment has been variously defined. Reference has been made previously to its links with the dramatic pageant and with Shakespeare's last plays (see chapter 12). But there are other traditions in which *Timon* may be placed. A. S. Collins has shown that it contains elements of the medieval morality play. Observe, for example, how personal names are often replaced by abstractions or types: Poet, Painter, Three Strangers, Thieves, Senators. And even the named characters (Lucullus, Lucius, Sempronius) are essentially caricatures rather than individuals. O. J. Campbell interprets the play as a tragical satire and notes its affinities with Ben Jonson's *Volpone* (1606), in which the human vultures gathering around the hero's supposed deathbed constitute successive illustrations of a single vice, greed. According to Alice Birney, Timon experiences the satiric catharsis of hatred and censure, as opposed to the tragic catharsis of pity and terror. Maurice Charney, in an illuminating introductory essay to the play, calls it a "dramatic fable."[89] In any case, the play is built upon unusual structural principles and what is, for Shakespeare, a different method of characterization.[90]

Within the limits (self-imposed, it should be stressed) of this radical experiment in dramatic form, Shakespeare achieves a high degree of success. It is not difficult to see how particular episodes in *Timon* contribute to our perception of the hero and of his vision of the world. For example, when the Poet and the Painter moralize on the fickleness of Fortune, they are depicting an old medieval theme of great relevance to Timon:

When Fortune in her shift and change of mood
Spurns down her late beloved, all his dependants,
Which labour'd after him to the mountain's top
Even on their knees and hands, let him slip down,
Not one accompanying his declining foot.

                                    (I, 1, 84–88)

Yet these so-called artists turn out to be as meretricious as the rest of
Timon's false friends. Thus they call attention to the deceitfulness of
appearances in this world and at the same time exemplify the very fraud
they denounce.[91] Apemantus is a foil for Timon's unreflective idealism,
a frightening illustration of what the hero may (and indeed does) become
once the fragile basis of that idealism has been destroyed. Although one
should take Apemantus's remarks with a grain of salt, he points to a
flaw in Timon's character: "The middle of humanity thou never knewest,
but the extremity of both ends" (IV, 3, 300–301). And the role of
Flavius is to demonstrate that Timon's misanthropy should be qualified,
that goodness, no less than evil, is a positive force in the world.[92]

Timon is best understood if he is measured against Alcibiades, who,
although he has also been wronged by an ungrateful Athens, refuses
(like Coriolanus) to reduce his city to ashes. While Timon withdraws
from Athens and the world even to the extent of committing spiritual
(and perhaps physical) suicide, Alcibiades returns to root out the long-
festering corruption. One may wish that Alcibiades were a more fully
developed character, but his role in the overall design seems clear enough.
Shakespeare establishes him as a symbol of regeneration and gives him
the final speech:

                    Bring me into your city,
        And I will use the olive, with my sword,
        Make war breed peace, make peace stint war, make each
        Prescribe to other, as each other's leech [physician].
        Let our drums strike.

                                    (V, 4, 81–85)

Alcibiades can forgive; Timon cannot.[93]

In recent years *Timon of Athens* has begun to receive the recognition
it so richly deserves. G. Wilson Knight has given it unrestrained praise.
"For this play is *Hamlet, Troilus and Cressida, Othello, King Lear,*
become self-conscious and universal; it includes and transcends them
all."[94] Most of us are not prepared to go that far, but at least we should
acknowledge that *Timon of Athens,* whatever its weaknesses, is an
extraordinarily powerful and original work, altogether worthy of the
incomparable dramatist who created it.

NOTES

1. The date of *Timon of Athens* may be earlier; see below.
2. On the text, see E. K. Chambers, *William Shakespeare: A Study of Facts and Problems,* 2 vols. (Oxford: Clarendon, 1930), 1: 476–478; the New Cambridge *Antony and Cleopatra,* ed. John Dover Wilson (Cambridge: Cambridge University Press, 1950), pp. 124–130; W. W. Greg, *The Editorial Problem in Shakespeare,* 3d ed. (Oxford: Clarendon, 1954), pp. 147–148; the New Arden *Antony and Cleopatra,* ed. R. H. Case (1906), rev. M. R. Ridley, 9th ed. (Cambridge: Harvard University Press, 1954), pp. vii–xix; W. W. Greg, *The Shakespeare First Folio: Its Bibliographical and Textual History* (Oxford: Clarendon, 1955), pp. 398–403. On the date, see (in addition to the New Cambridge edition, pp. vii–x, and the New Arden edition, pp. xxvi–xxxii) Arthur M. Z. Norman, "*The Tragedie of Cleopatra* and the Date of *Antony and Cleopatra,*" *Modern Language Review* 54 (1959): 1–9.
3. Willard Farnham, *Shakespeare's Tragic Frontier: The World of His Final Tragedies* (Berkeley: University of California Press, 1963), pp. 139–148 (quotation from p. 139).
4. Ibid., pp. 172–173. See also Geoffrey Bullough, *Narrative and Dramatic Sources of Shakespeare,* 8 vols. (New York: Columbia University Press, 1957–1975), 5: 237–238.
5. On the Cleopatra legend before Shakespeare, see (in addition to Farnham [*Shakespeare's Tragic Frontier,* pp. 139–174] and Bullough [*Sources,* 5: 215–449]) Franklin M. Dickey, *Not Wisely but Too Well: Shakespeare's Love Tragedies* (San Marino, Calif.: The Huntington Library, 1957), pp. 144–176. See also Kenneth Muir, *Shakespeare's Sources* (London: Methuen, 1957), pp. 201–219.
6. Eugene M. Waith, *The Herculean Hero in Marlowe, Chapman, Shakespeare and Dryden* (New York: Columbia University Press, 1962), pp. 113–121; Reuben A. Brower, *Hero and Saint: Shakespeare and the Graeco-Roman Heroic Tradition* (New York: Oxford University Press, 1971), p. 351; Janet Adelman, *The Common Liar: An Essay on Antony and Cleopatra* (New Haven: Yale University Press, 1973), pp. 78–101. See also Raymond B. Waddington, "*Antony and Cleopatra:* 'What Venus did with Mars,'" *Shakespeare Studies,* ed. J. Leeds Barroll, 2 (1966): 210–227.
7. In *All for Love* (acted 1677, published 1688), John Dryden's superb adaptation of *Antony and Cleopatra,* there are only twelve characters and five scenes (all set in Alexandria). Dryden adheres strictly to the classical unities, with all the action taking place on the last day of the lovers' lives.
8. G. Wilson Knight, "The Transcendental Humanism of *Antony and Cleopatra,*" in *The Imperial Theme: Further Interpretations of Shakespeare's Tragedies including the Roman Plays* (London: Oxford University Press, 1931), p. 203.
9. See Julian Markels, *The Pillar of the World: Antony and Cleopatra in Shakespeare's Development* (Columbus: Ohio State University Press, 1968); A. P. Riemer, *A Reading of Shakespeare's Antony and Cleopatra* (Sydney,

Australia: Sydney University Press, 1968), p. 110; Robin Lee, *Shakespeare: Antony and Cleopatra* (London: Edward Arnold, 1971), p. 31.

10. Rosalie Colie, "*Antony and Cleopatra:* The Significance of Style," *Shakespeare's Living Art* (Princeton: Princeton University Press, 1974), pp. 168–207.

11. Edwin Wilson, ed., *Shaw on Shakespeare* (London: Cassell, 1962), p. 204. For more recent condemnations of the lovers, see Laurens J. Mills, *The Tragedies of Shakespeare's Antony and Cleopatra* (Bloomington: Indiana University Press, 1964); Dickey, *Not Wisely but Too Well,* pp. 177–202.

12. W. K. Wimsatt, Jr., "Poetry and Morals: A Relation Reargued," *Thought: Fordham University Quarterly* 23 (1948): 281–299 (quotation from p. 295).

13. Among the many scholars who have emphasized the paradoxes and ambiguities in the play, the following may be noted: Adelman, *The Common Liar,* especially pp. 24–39; Lee, *Shakespeare: Antony and Cleopatra;* Benjamin T. Spencer, "*Antony and Cleopatra* and the Paradoxical Metaphor," *Shakespeare Quarterly* 9 (1958): 373–378; Stephen A. Shapiro, "The Varying Shore of the World: Ambivalence in *Antony and Cleopatra,*" *Modern Language Quarterly* 27 (1966): 18–32.

14. See, for example, Riemer, *Reading of Antony and Cleopatra,* pp. 29–31 and Lee, *Shakespeare: Antony and Cleopatra,* pp. 29–31.

15. William Blissett sees dramatic irony in the play even in Philo's first words. See "Dramatic Irony in *Antony and Cleopatra,*" *Shakespeare Quarterly* 18 (1967): 151–166.

16. See Dickey, *Not Wisely but Too Well,* pp. 179–183 and Mills, *Antony and Cleopatra.* Brents Stirling, in *Unity in Shakespearian Tragedy* (New York: Columbia University Press, 1956), pp. 157–192, detects an "ethical void" in Antony and argues that the play has stature but the protagonist does not.

17. A. C. Bradley, "Shakespeare's *Antony and Cleopatra,*" in *Oxford Lectures on Poetry,* 2d ed. (London: Macmillan, 1909), p. 293.

18. Lee, *Shakespeare: Antony and Cleopatra,* p. 14.

19. Markels, *The Pillar of the World,* pp. 9, 21.

20. Markels (ibid., pp. 167–169) has a fine analysis of this speech.

21. See J. Leeds Barroll, "Shakespeare and Roman History," *Modern Language Review* 53 (1958): 327–343.

22. Wimsatt, "Poetry and Morals," p. 294.

23. Bradley, "Shakespeare's *Antony and Cleopatra,*" p. 291.

24. Knight, "The Diadem of Love: An Essay on *Antony and Cleopatra,*" in *The Imperial Theme,* p. 289.

25. On the world images in the play, see Caroline F. E. Spurgeon, *Shakespeare's Imagery and What It Tells Us* (New York: Macmillan, 1935), pp. 350–354; Knight, *The Imperial Theme,* pp. 206–218; and Maurice Charney, *Shakespeare's Roman Plays: The Function of Imagery in the Drama* (Cambridge: Harvard University Press, 1963), pp. 80–93.

26. This speech has been seen as part of the world-as-a-stage motif, with morality play overtones, which is said to provide a unifying theme for the play. See Thomas B. Stroup, "The Structure of *Antony and Cleopatra,*" *Shakespeare Quarterly* 15: 2 (Spring 1964): 289–298.

27. These and other images are cited by Wolfgang H. Clemen, *The Develop-

ment of Shakespeare's Imagery (Cambridge: Harvard University Press, 1951), p. 167.

28. Enobarbus is (among other things) "Shakespeare's translation of the chorus of Renaissance neo-classical drama into dramatic character." See Elkin Calhoun Wilson, "Shakespeare's Enobarbus," in *Joseph Quincy Adams Memorial Studies,* eds. James G. McManaway, Giles E. Dawson, Edwin E. Willoughby (Washington, D.C.: The Folger Shakespeare Library, 1948), pp. 391–408 (quotation from p. 407).

29. J. L. Simmons, *Shakespeare's Pagan World: The Roman Tragedies* (Charlottesville: University Press of Virginia, 1973), p. 139. On the dimpled boys image and its implications, see Adrien Bonjour, "From Shakespeare's Venus to Cleopatra's Cupids," *Shakespeare Survey* 15 (1962): 73–80. One may also consult two other excellent commentaries on the speech: Charney, *Shakespeare's Roman Plays,* pp. 116–120 and Knight, *The Imperial Theme,* pp. 256–258.

30. Harley Granville-Barker, *Prefaces to Shakespeare,* 2 vols. (Princeton: Princeton University Press, 1946–1947), 1: 453.

31. According to Philip J. Traci, *The Love Play of Antony and Cleopatra: A Critical Study of Shakespeare's Play* (The Hague: Mouton, 1970), pp. 153–160, the entire movement of *Antony and Cleopatra* seems to correspond to that of the love act itself.

32. Charney, *Shakespeare's Roman Plays,* p. 135.

33. Derek Traversi, *Shakespeare: The Roman Plays* (Stanford, Calif.: Stanford University Press, 1963), p. 184.

34. Mark Van Doren, *Shakespeare* (New York: Holt, 1939), p. 280. See also David Daiches, "Imagery and Meaning in *Antony and Cleopatra,*" *English Studies* 43 (1962): 343–358.

35. The first view has been defended by Dover Wilson; see the New Cambridge edition, pp. xxxiv–xxxv. For the argument against Cleopatra's collusion with Seleucus, see Brents Stirling, "Cleopatra's Scene with Seleucus: Plutarch, Daniel, and Shakespeare," *Shakespeare Quarterly* 15 (1964): 299–311.

36. Bullough, *Sources,* 5: 316.

37. At stake in the last scene, one critic has sensitively written, is "the honesty of the imagination and the superiority of its truths to the facts of imperial conquest"; see Robert Ornstein, "The Ethic of the Imagination: Love and Art in *Antony and Cleopatra,*" in *Later Shakespeare,* eds. John Russell Brown and Bernard Harris, Stratford-upon-Avon Studies 8 (London: Edward Arnold, 1966), p. 32. For a survey of recent criticism, see J. C. Maxwell, "Shakespeare's Roman Plays: 1900–1956," *Shakespeare Survey* 10 (1957): 1–11.

38. See Granville-Barker, *Prefaces,* 2: 295–297. It is possible, says Granville-Barker, that the famous *"He holds her by the hand, silent"* (V, 3, 182; see below), about which critics continue to wax so eloquent, occurs in the text only because Shakespeare was not personally present at rehearsals to give oral directions. What a lucky accident!

39. On the text, see Chambers, *William Shakespeare,* 1: 478–480; Greg, *The Shakespeare First Folio,* pp. 404–407; and the New Cambridge *Coriolanus,* ed. John Dover Wilson (Cambridge: Cambridge University Press, 1960), pp.

130–137. On Tate's adaptation, see Hazelton Spencer, *Shakespeare Improved: The Restoration Versions in Quarto and on the Stage* (1927) (New York: Ungar, 1963), pp. 265–272.

40. E. C. Pettet, "*Coriolanus* and the Midlands Insurrection of 1607," *Shakespeare Survey* 3 (1950): 34–42.

41. On the date, see Chambers, *William Shakespeare*, 1: 479–480; Dover Wilson, in the New Cambridge edition, pp. ix–xi; and Bullough, *Sources*, 5: 453–454.

42. Bullough, *Sources*, 5: 506.

43. Farnham, *Shakespeare's Tragic Frontier*, pp. 217–218.

44. On Shakespeare's use of Plutarch, as well as his divergences, see Bullough, *Sources*, 5: 453–495; Farnham, *Shakespeare's Tragic Frontier*, pp. 208–212; Hermann Heuer, "From Plutarch to Shakespeare: A Study of *Coriolanus*," *Shakespeare Survey* 10 (1957): 50–59; and H. D. F. Kitto, "Shakespeare: *Coriolanus*," in *Poiesis: Structure and Thought* (Berkeley: University of California Press, 1966), pp. 373 ff. For a useful study of the literary and political traditions behind the play, see Clifford Chalmers Huffman, *Coriolanus in Context* (Lewisburg, Pa.: Bucknell University Press, 1971).

45. See Muir, *Shakespeare's Sources*, p. 224.

46. See Kitto, *Poiesis*, pp. 377–378.

47. Traversi, *Shakespeare: The Roman Plays*, p. 210.

48. Charney, *Shakespeare's Roman Plays*, pp. 143–157, 163–169; see also J. C. Maxwell, "Animal Imagery in *Coriolanus*," *Modern Language Review* 42 (1947): 417–421. Spurgeon (*Shakespeare's Imagery*, pp. 347–349) sees the body as the central symbol in *Coriolanus*. See also Clemen, *The Development of Shakespeare's Imagery*, pp. 154–158.

49. See R. F. Hill, "*Coriolanus*: Violentest Contrariety," *Essays and Studies 1964* (London: The English Association, 1964), pp. 12–23.

50. Michael Goldman writes of the physical element in Coriolanus's relationship with the mob. See "Coriolanus and the Crowd," in *Shakespeare and the Energies of Drama* (Princeton: Princeton University Press, 1972), pp. 109–123.

51. Una Ellis-Fermor, "Coriolanus," in *Shakespeare the Dramatist and Other Papers* (New York: Barnes & Noble, 1961), p. 74.

52. A synecdoche is a familiar rhetorical figure whereby the part may be taken for the whole.

53. D. J. Gordon, "Name and Fame: Shakespeare's Coriolanus," in *Papers Mainly Shakespearian*, ed. G. I. Duthie (Aberdeen, Scotland: University of Aberdeen Press, 1964), p. 44.

54. Charney (*Shakespeare's Roman Plays*, pp. 169–176) writes persuasively about the acting imagery.

55. L. C. Knights, *Some Shakespearean Themes and An Approach to Hamlet* (Stanford, Calif.: Stanford University Press, 1966), p. 143.

56. The more recent stage history of *Coriolanus*, says Ralph Berry, has shown a shift in emphasis to the Volscian scenes. See "The Metamorphosis of *Coriolanus*," *Shakespeare Quarterly* 26 (1975): 172–183.

57. G. K. Hunter, "The Last Tragic Heroes," in *Later Shakespeare*, eds. Brown and Harris, p. 16.

58. Waith, *The Herculean Hero,* p. 137. See also Millar MacLure, "Shakespeare and the Lonely Dragon," *University of Toronto Quarterly* 24 (1954–1955): 109–120 and Brower, "The Deeds of Coriolanus," in *Hero and Saint,* pp. 354–381.

59. William Hazlitt, *Characters of Shakespeare's Plays,* ed. Sir Arthur Quiller-Couch (London: Oxford University Press, 1916; 1955), p. 56. That Shakespeare was catering to the aristocratic tastes of his Jacobean audience has been argued by J. L. Simmons, *"Antony and Cleopatra* and *Coriolanus,* Shakespeare's Heroic Tragedies: A Jacobean Adjustment," *Shakespeare Survey* 26 (1973): 95–101.

60. R. W. Chambers, "The Expression of Ideas—Particularly Political Ideas—in the Three Pages, and in Shakespeare," in *Shakespeare's Hand in the Play of Sir Thomas More,* eds. Alfred W. Pollard et al. (Cambridge: Cambridge University Press, 1923), pp. 142–187.

61. See D. J. Enright, *"Coriolanus:* Tragedy or Debate?" *Essays in Criticism* 4 (1954): 1–19.

62. A. P. Rossiter, *"Coriolanus,"* in *Angel with Horns and Other Shakespeare Lectures* (New York: Theatre Arts Books, 1961), p. 243.

63. Inevitably, critics with a psychoanalytic orientation have been attracted to the Coriolanus-Volumnia relationship. See, for example, Charles K. Hofling, "An Interpretation of Shakespeare's *Coriolanus,"* *American Imago* 14 (1957): 407–435 and Robert J. Stoller, "Shakespearean Tragedy: *Coriolanus,"* *Psychoanalytic Quarterly* 35 (1966): 263–274, both of which are reprinted in Melvin D. Faber, ed., *The Design Within: Psychoanalytic Approaches to Shakespeare* (New York: Science House, 1970), pp. 287–305, 327–339. For a more literary treatment of the mother-son relationship, one that answers D. J. Enright (see n. 61), see I. R. Browning, "Coriolanus: Boy of Tears," *Essays in Criticism* 5 (1955): 18–31.

64. John Middleton Murry, "A Neglected Heroine of Shakespeare," in *Countries of the Mind* (London: Collins, 1922), pp. 31–50.

65. Knight, "The Royal Occupation: An Essay on *Coriolanus,"* in *The Imperial Theme,* p. 173.

66. Oscar James Campbell, *Shakespeare's Satire* (New York: Oxford University Press, 1943), p. 212.

67. For some interesting comments on this episode, see Kitto, *Poiesis,* pp. 382–383.

68. See Ellis-Fermor, *Shakespeare the Dramatist,* pp. 60–77.

69. Brower, *Hero and Saint,* p. 370.

70. Charney, *Shakespeare's Roman Plays,* p. 194. For an excellent analysis of the entire scene (V, 3), see Traversi, *Shakespeare: The Roman Plays,* pp. 270–282.

71. A. C. Bradley, *"Coriolanus,"* in *Proceedings of the British Academy, 1911–1912* (London: Humphrey Milford, Oxford University Press, 1913), p. 469, reprinted in *Studies in Shakespeare: British Academy Lectures,* ed. Peter Alexander (London: Oxford University Press, 1964), pp. 219–237 (quotation from p. 232).

72. See Charney, *Shakespeare's Roman Plays,* p. 179.

73. Rodney Poisson, "Coriolanus as Aristotle's Magnanimous Man," in *Pacific Coast Studies in Shakespeare*, eds. Waldo F. McNeir and Thelma N. Greenfield (Eugene: University of Oregon Books, 1966), pp. 210–224 (quotation from p. 224).

74. J. L. Simmons, *Shakespeare's Pagan World: The Roman Tragedies*, p. 30.

75. For a reasoned, sympathetic view of Coriolanus, see H. J. Oliver, "Coriolanus as Tragic Hero," *Shakespeare Quarterly* 10 (1959): 53–60.

See James E. Phillips, ed., *Twentieth Century Interpretations of Coriolanus* (Englewood Cliffs, N.J.: Prentice-Hall, 1970)—a good collection.

76. Terence Spencer, "Shakespeare Learns the Value of Money: The Dramatist at Work on *Timon of Athens*," *Shakespeare Survey* 6 (1953): 75–78.

77. Francelia Butler, *The Strange Critical Fortunes of Shakespeare's Timon of Athens* (Ames: Iowa State University Press, 1966), pp. 39–41.

78. The New Arden *Timon of Athens*, ed. H. J. Oliver, 3d ed. (Cambridge: Harvard University Press, 1959; 1963), p. xxii. See also Chambers, *William Shakespeare*, 1: 480–484; Una Ellis-Fermor, "*Timon of Athens:* An Unfinished Play," *Review of English Studies* 18 (1942): 270–283, reprinted in *Shakespeare the Dramatist*, pp. 158–176; Greg, *The Shakespeare First Folio*, pp. 408–411; the New Cambridge *Timon of Athens*, ed. J. C. Maxwell (Cambridge: Cambridge University Press, 1957), pp. ix–xiv, 87–97; the Pelican *Timon of Athens*, ed. Charlton Hinman (Baltimore: Penguin, 1964), pp. 21–23, 127.

79. A. C. Bradley, *Shakespearean Tragedy*, 2d ed. (London: Macmillan, 1905), pp. 245–247, 326–327, 443–445; Sir Walter Raleigh, *Shakespeare* (London: Macmillan, 1907), p. 115; John Dover Wilson, *The Essential Shakespeare* (Cambridge: Cambridge University Press, 1932), p. 131; Samuel Taylor Coleridge, *Coleridge's Shakespearean Criticism*, ed. T. M. Raysor, rev. ed., 2 vols. (London: Dent, 1960), 1: 211 (see also 1: 98).

80. Chambers, *William Shakespeare*, 1: 483; Clifford Leech, "*Timon* and After," *Shakespeare's Tragedies and Other Studies in Seventeenth Century Drama* (London: Chatto & Windus, 1950), p. 124; M. C. Bradbrook, *The Tragic Pageant of Timon of Athens: An Inaugural Lecture* (Cambridge: Cambridge University Press, 1966), pp. 2, 36, and passim, reprinted in *Shakespeare the Craftsman*.

81. See the New Cambridge edition, pp. xi–xiv; the New Arden edition, pp. xl–xlii; Butler, *Critical Fortunes of Timon*, pp. 170–173; and, particularly for the relationship between Shakespeare's play and the old *Timon*, James C. Bulman, Jr., "The Date and Production of *Timon* Reconsidered," *Shakespeare Survey* 27 (1974): 111–127.

82. Farnham, *Shakespeare's Tragic Frontier*, pp. 50–67; the New Cambridge edition, pp. xiv–xxii; the New Arden edition, pp. xxxii–xl; Bullough, *Sources*, 6: 225–345.

83. See Maxwell's note to I, 2, 45–48, in the New Cambridge edition, p. 113.

84. See Bradbrook, *The Tragic Pageant of Timon of Athens*, p. 27. Despair bids the Red Cross Knight, as well as other knights who fall into his clutches, to commit suicide.

85. John W. Draper, "The Theme of *Timon of Athens*," *Modern Language Review* 29 (1934): 28. It has been suggested that the play satirizes the

extravagance of the court of James I; see Alice Lotvin Birney, *Satiric Catharsis in Shakespeare: A Theory of Dramatic Structure* (Berkeley: University of California Press, 1973), pp. 126–127.

86. G. Wilson Knight, "The Pilgrimage of Hate: an Essay on *Timon of Athens*," in *The Wheel of Fire: Interpretations of Shakespearean Tragedy*, 5th rev. ed. (Cleveland: World Publishing, Meridian Books, 1957), pp. 210, 218; Campbell, *Shakespeare's Satire*, p. 186; J. C. Maxwell, "*Timon of Athens*," *Scrutiny* 15 (1947–1948): 198, 201.

87. Harry Levin, "Shakespeare's Misanthrope," *Shakespeare Survey* 26 (1973): 89–94.

88. Ellis-Fermor, *Shakespeare the Dramatist*, p. 175.

89. A. S. Collins, "*Timon of Athens*: A Reconsideration," *Review of English Studies* 22 (1946): 96–108; Campbell, *Shakespeare's Satire*, pp. 168–197; Birney, *Satiric Catharsis*, pp. 122–140; Maurice Charney, in *The Complete Signet Classic Shakespeare* (New York: Harcourt Brace Jovanovich, 1972), pp. 1367–1374.

90. This point is convincingly made by E. A. J. Honigmann, "*Timon of Athens*," *Shakespeare Quarterly* 12 (1961): 3–20.

91. On the Poet and the Painter, see W. M. Merchant, "*Timon* and the Conceit of Art," *Shakespeare Quarterly* 6 (1955): 249–257.

92. Irving Ribner, in *Patterns in Shakespearian Tragedy* (London: Methuen, 1960), pp. 148–149, interprets Flavius as a Christ symbol offering salvation to Timon.

93. On Alcibiades and the theme of forgiveness, see David Cook, "*Timon of Athens*," *Shakespeare Survey* 16 (1963): 83–94.

94. Knight, *The Wheel of Fire*, p. 236.

12
Romances

Pericles
Cymbeline
The Winter's Tale
The Tempest

The plays to be discussed in this chapter constitute, along with *Henry VIII,* Shakespeare's last known works for the stage. It is therefore inevitable that critics continue to search these plays diligently for possible clues as to the bard's ultimate philosophy of life and art. There is little agreement, however, concerning the meaning of *Pericles, Cymbeline, The Winter's Tale,* and *The Tempest;* and not even their convenient designation as romances has gone unchallenged.[1]

The four romances are essentially fairytales, peopled, by and large, with characters from the improbable world of Bluebeard and Cinderella: fantastic creatures who defy the kind of solemn analysis customarily reserved for a Hamlet or a Macbeth.[2] The plays are crowded with melodramatic incidents that attest to Shakespeare's virtuosity and craftsmanship even as they reflect a deliberate disregard for verisimilitude. In all but *The Tempest* there are abrupt changes of scene encompassing a huge geographic range, and in two instances, *Pericles* and *The Winter's Tale,* we encounter a gap of many years in the middle of the story that virtually splits the action in two. Shakespeare makes extensive use of familiar motifs from folklore and myth: exiled rulers, wicked queens, storms at sea, husbands separated from wives and parents from children, young princes and princesses growing up in strange lands and often unaware of their royal lineage, recognitions and reconciliations. The plays abound in theophanies, interventions of gods and goddesses in human affairs.[3] It would seem that Shakespeare, having brought English drama to unsurpassable peaks in comedy, history, and tragedy, chooses to close out his career by exploring some of the most conventionalized and unrealistic fictions he can find.[4]

What is one to make of Shakespeare's predilection for romance in his twilight years? According to Lytton Strachey, the playwright was by then simply bored with people, real life, and drama—"bored, in fact, with everything except poetry and poetical dreams." In contrast, Frank Kermode sees the romances as the works of a master experimenting with his medium. F. E. Halliday links the romances with Shakespeare's personal life: the renewal of ties with Stratford, the marriage of his daughter Susanna, and the birth of his granddaughter Elizabeth—occasions that lend reinforcement to the father-daughter relationship at the heart of these plays. Ashley Thorndike's view is that Shakespeare was imitating the successful example of his younger contemporaries Francis Beaumont and John Fletcher, whose tragicomedies (notably *Philaster*) were attracting large audiences. (Some, like Richard Proudfoot, maintain that Beaumont and Fletcher were imitating Shakespeare.) G. E. Bentley believes that the romances were designed for sophisticated playgoers at the Blackfriars (see pp. 11–12). Carol Gesner and Hallett Smith explain Shakespeare's interest in the genre on the basis of the popularity of Greek romance. On the one hand, Tillyard discerns in the final plays a fulfillment of the tragic pattern of "prosperity, destruction, and re-creation." On the other hand, E. C. Pettet would emphasize the "broad line of continuity between the comedies and the romances." John P. Cutts interprets the romances as devastating images of man's delusion and self-interest, with the principal characters all hiding behind masks of innocence and benevolence. In a significant study, G. Wilson Knight contends that the last plays transcend the tragedies and embody Shakespeare's supreme mystical vision; they are not "pleasant fancies" but "parables of a profound and glorious truth." But D. G. James thinks that the plays reflect Shakespeare's failure to create a secular mythology to replace Christianity.[5]

It is clear that the mystery of the last plays has not been solved. Yet, without diminishing their stature, one may endorse Philip Edwards's sensible suggestion: "We can probably afford some fallow years in discussions concerning the seriousness of the Romances; at least until the manner in which they may be said to be serious has been rather more carefully defined."[6] If more attention were directed to the formal requirements of the genre itself and to the emotional response that romances were expected to arouse in an Elizabethan audience, Edwards believes that we might be in a better position to interpret the last plays of Shakespeare.[7]

PERICLES

Of the thirty-seven plays commonly assigned to the Shakespeare canon, only *Pericles* is missing from the First Folio (1623). The play was certainly popular, having been published six times (with Shakespeare's name on the title page) between 1609 and 1635. The Fourth Quarto (1619) was part of the effort of Thomas Pavier and William Jaggard to issue an unauthorized edition of the dramatist's works (see p. 37). But it was not until the second issue of the Third Folio (1664) that *Pericles,* along with six plays now considered apocryphal, was added to the celebrated collection of Heminge and Condell. The play is excluded from most eighteenth-century editions of Shakespeare. Since 1790, however, it has appeared regularly with the other thirty-six plays.

Many ingenious explanations have been offered for the omission of *Pericles* from the First Folio, but the simplest and now most commonly accepted reason is that the Folio editors did not regard it as substantially Shakespeare's work. It is not clear whether he was sole author, collaborator, or reviser, and no attempt will be made here to elucidate the tangled question. Suffice it to say that Shakespeare is usually credited with Acts III–V. If there was a coauthor, the candidates are Thomas Heywood, John Day, William Rowley, and George Wilkins. *Pericles* resembles Wilkins's *Painfull Adventures of Pericles Prince of Tyre* (1608), but we cannot be sure which work came first. Wilkins's novel is based upon Laurence Twine's *Patterne of Paynfull Adventures* (1576?) and a lost play, possibly by Shakespeare, of which the 1609 Quarto may be a reported version. Be that as it may, *Pericles* is usually dated between 1606 and 1608.[8]

The story goes back at least as far as the fifth-century Latin tale of Apollonius of Tyre, particularly as told by the poet John Gower in his *Confessio Amantis* (1390), a huge collection of *exempla* (moralized tales) illustrating the Seven Deadly Sins.[9] Gower himself appears as Chorus and narrator in *Pericles,* reviewing the action and supplying necessary links between scenes, like the Chorus in *Henry V.* Moreover, in his appearances Gower generally speaks in octosyllabic couplets reminiscent of the plodding style of the *Confessio Amantis.* On several occasions his speeches are accompanied by dumb shows, which present parts of the action in pantomime.

Whether Shakespeare or somebody else wrote the Gower passages (the evidence is inconclusive), this reincarnation of the old medieval poet contributes substantially to the play's atmosphere. By representing the authority of an ancient literary tradition, Gower puts us in an uncritical frame of mind so that we can accept the impossibilities of the story.[10] He speaks in a dreamlike tone of strange things that happened long before his own time, and Francis Berry, commenting on how the part should be staged, suggests that he come forward (downstage) and direct the audience to look back (upstage), thereby emphasizing spatially the different degrees of "pastness" that our experience of the play must involve.[11] Gower also parcels out foreknowledge in such a way as to control our responses to the twists and turns of the plot. He guarantees that we maintain emotional distance from the characters; almost everything that happens is filtered through this human screen.

Pericles contains enough material to stock half a dozen plays. Antiochus, King of Antioch, decrees that his daughter's suitors must solve the riddle he propounds or, should they fail, forfeit their lives. Pericles, Prince of Tyre, tries his hand and is successful. But inasmuch as the answer to the riddle reveals that Antiochus and his daughter live in incest, he realizes that his life is in danger and escapes to Tyre, with the King's hired assassin in close pursuit. Still not safe, he sets out for Tharsus, a city plagued by famine; by bringing relief to its inhabitants, he incurs the gratitude of the governor Cleon and his wife Dionyza. Pericles continues his flight, but he is soon caught up in a storm at sea and cast ashore at Pentapolis, which is ruled by the good King Simonides. The hero enters a tournament and wins, his victory culminating in a happy marriage with the King's daughter Thaisa. Later, Pericles learns that Antiochus and his daughter have been stricken dead by a fire from heaven and that the citizens of Tyre are impatient for the return of their sovereign. As the so-called non-Shakespearean portion of the play comes to an end, Pericles is sailing for Tyre. With him is Thaisa, who is about to give birth to their first child.

At the beginning of Act III, the point at which Shakespeare appears to take command, Pericles and Thaisa are beset by another tempest. Thaisa seems to die in childbirth, and because the sailors insist that the winds will not abate until the ship is emptied of its dead, Pericles has his wife's body placed in a chest and hurled overboard. At the same time, fearful lest his infant daughter, appropriately named Marina, be unable to withstand the long voyage, he leaves her in Tharsus in the care of Cleon and Dionyza. Meanwhile, the chest is washed ashore at Ephesus, where Thaisa is revived by a saintly physician, Lord Cerimon, a forerunner of Prospero in *The Tempest*.[12] Years later we find the family still separated: Pericles reigns in Tyre; Thaisa, believing her husband dead, is a votaress in the temple of Diana at Ephesus; Marina has matured into radiant young womanhood in Tharsus.

Through an incredible sequence of events, the family is ultimately reunited. Dionyza, jealous because Marina outshines her own daughter, orders her murdered. At the last minute, however, Marina is abducted by pirates and sold to a brothel keeper in Mytilene. Placed in the brothel, the chaste Marina preaches to the customers and succeeds in winning them over to virtue, numbering among her converts no less a personage than Lysimachus, the governor of Mytilene. The bawds and panders, who stand to lose money as a result of her annoying purity, are glad to let her go. Removed from the brothel, Marina gains a reputation as an outstanding teacher of music and needlework. While all this is happening to Marina, Pericles returns to Tharsus to reclaim his daughter. Told that she is dead, the despondent father begins the voyage back to Tyre. Again he encounters a storm and, coincidentally, is driven by the winds to Mytilene. When Lysimachus observes Pericles in a state of profound melancholy, he suggests that the king may be cured by a certain maiden who possesses unusual gifts. Marina is sent for, and in a scene recalling the reconciliation of Lear and Cordelia, Pericles gradually recognizes her. After being lulled to sleep by mysterious music, he has a vision of the goddess Diana, who bids him visit her shrine in Ephesus and recount his adventures. He obeys, and when the high priestess Thaisa hears his story, she knows he is Pericles. Husband and wife joyously embrace. They announce the betrothal of Lysimachus and Marina, who will reign in Tyre. Moreover, word having arrived that Simonides is dead, Pericles and Thaisa succeed to his throne in Pentapolis. In the Epilogue, Gower tells us that when the citizens of Tharsus learned of the cursed plot against Marina, they burned Cleon and Dionyza to death in their palace.

The foregoing summary has been made somewhat detailed, partly because *Pericles* is rarely read or acted and also because in this play, more perhaps than in any other in the canon, the story is paramount. In fact, in its loose structure *Pericles* more closely resembles romantic narrative (like Sidney's *Arcadia*) than drama.[13] Clifford Leech addresses himself to the problem of structure by distinguishing two modes of representing time in Shakespeare's last plays. On the one hand, there is the notion of "crisis," emphasizing "the decisive happening, the moment of truth and of choice, beyond which there is no going back, no recurrence of what preceded that special point of time." At the opposite extreme is the idea of time as a "cycle," whereby today repeats yesterday and foreshadows tomorrow. If *Macbeth* and the other tragedies belong in the first category, *Pericles* exemplifies the second. It "has the character of a novel in which the hero's fortunes are traced from an early moment in his life to a convenient halting-place some years later."[14] The dramatist strings together a series of events in the life of the protagonist, with almost no attempt to develop a chain of causality or to raise those perennial Shakespearean questions about the interrelationships between situation and character. Although it has been argued that Pericles should have recognized the ugly reality beneath the fair appearance of Antiochus's daughter, we do not feel at any point in the action that a crucial choice has been consciously made or that some inevitable process has been set in motion.

The episodic quality of *Pericles* is part of the artistic design in that it serves to reinforce a major theme of the play: man's inability to control

the ebb and flow of his destiny. This idea is stated in its simplest form
when Gower observes that the hero is tossed about from one shore to
another as Fortune decrees:

> All perishen of man, of pelf,
> Ne aught escapen but himself;
> Till fortune, tir'd with doing bad,
> Threw him ashore, to give him glad.
>   (II, Prologue, 35–38)

Individual responsibility, however, does not lose its meaning. Through the
events themselves and through Gower's running commentary, the play
repeatedly demonstrates that the wicked are finally punished and the
good rewarded. Man must come to acknowledge his essential weakness
and refrain from criticizing the inscrutable workings of Providence. This
doctrine, which contains elements of Stoicism and Christianity, is regularly
affirmed by Pericles—for example, when he deposits Marina in Tharsus
after the supposed death of Thaisa:

> We cannot but obey
> The powers above us. Could I rage and roar
> As doth the sea she lies in, yet the end
> Must be as 'tis.
>   (III, 3, 9–12)

Several critics have identified the main theme of the play as "patience
in adversity."[15] By resigning himself to the unalterable while at the same
time living as virtuously as he can, Pericles passes a severe test of faith and
earns the right to a happy ending for himself and his loved ones. And
in the process he comes to recognize the value of life.[16]

In a play that dwells upon the vicissitudes of life on earth, it is appropriate that the central metaphor should be bound up in the experience
of the sea voyage and the storm. Such images lend themselves to allegorical interpretation; and in *Pericles,* as in the other romances, they seem
to represent at one level the power (perhaps even the cruelty) of nature,
which compels our submission. We cannot forget, however, that the very
tempest that oppresses Pericles and appears to destroy Thaisa is the
cradle of Marina, an agent of limitless benevolence. Even Pericles,
crushed by tragedy, can envision a special role for "this fresh new sea-
farer" (III, 1, 41), and he welcomes her into the world:

> Now mild may be thy life!
> For a more blusterous birth had never babe;
> Quiet and gentle thy conditions! for
> Thou art the rudeliest welcome to this world

That ever was prince's child. Happy what follows!
Thou hast as chiding a nativity
As fire, air, water, earth, and heaven can make,
To herald thee from the womb.
....
                      Now the good gods
Throw their best eyes upon't!
                           (III, 1, 27–37)

In a later scene Marina, carrying a basket of flowers to commemorate the death of her nurse Lychorida, reflects upon the circumstances that attended her birth:

                Ay me, poor maid,
Born in a tempest when my mother died!
This world to me is like a lasting storm,
Whirring me from my friends.
                (IV, 1, 18–21)

Lysimachus employs the metaphor in the brothel. "Is she not a fair creature?" the Bawd asks. "Faith," Lysimachus replies, "she would serve after a long voyage at sea" (IV, 6, 47–49). In its context, of course, the remark is mild ribaldry, but its function in the larger structure of the play cannot be overlooked.[17]

Although the play is uneven, there are individual scenes that rank with Shakespeare's finest achievements. Among these is the tremendous opening of Act III, in which Pericles' voice rings out in a magnificent prayer for calm seas (a passage that recalls Lear battling the storm):

Thou god of this great vast, rebuke these surges,
Which wash both heaven and hell; and thou that hast
Upon the winds command, bind them in brass,
Having recall'd them from the deep! O, still
Thy deaf'ning dreadful thunders; gently quench
Thy nimble sulphurous flashes!
....
                     The seaman's whistle
Is as a whisper in the ears of death,
Unheard.
                (III, 1, 1–10)

A moment later the nurse enters carrying the infant:

Here is a thing too young for such a place,
Who, if it had conceit [thought], would die, as I
Am like to do. Take in your arms this piece
Of your dead queen.
                (III, 1, 15–18)

At first, Pericles cries out in anguish at having had his precious gift snatched away by the gods, but he soon recovers his composure and bestows upon Thaisa a poignant burial at sea:

> A terrible childbed hast thou had, my dear;
> No light, no fire. Th' unfriendly elements
> Forgot thee utterly; nor have I time
> To give thee hallow'd to thy grave, but straight
> Must cast thee, scarcely coffin'd, in the ooze.
>   (III, 1, 57–61)

Whatever questions remain concerning the authorship of Acts I and II, the first scene of Act III bears the Shakespearean stamp.[18]

The climax, however, is the reunion of father and daughter. The cycle is complete, for the overt incest with which the play began undergoes a sublime transformation.[19] "Tell thy story," Pericles bids Marina (V, 1, 135):

>   Yet thou dost look
> Like Patience gazing on kings' graves and smiling
> Extremity out of act.
>   (V, 1, 138–140)

As he realizes that Marina stands before him, Pericles declares to his faithful friend Helicanus that his ecstasy is sweet almost beyond endurance. He conveys this feeling through the familiar sea metaphor, now transfigured into a symbol of intense joy:

> O Helicanus, strike me, honour'd sir,
> Give me a gash, put me to present pain,
> Lest this great sea of joys rushing upon me
> O'erbear the shores of my mortality
> And drown me with their sweetness. O, come hither,
> Thou that beget'st him that did thee beget;
> Thou that wast born at sea, buried at Tharsus,
> And found at sea again! O Helicanus,
> Down on thy knees, thank the holy gods as loud
> As thunder threatens us. This is Marina.
>   (V, 1, 192–201)

Then fresh garments, heavenly music that betokens a physical and spiritual regeneration, and soothing sleep:

> *Pericles:* Give me my robes. I am wild in my beholding.
>   O heavens bless my girl! But hark, what music?
>   Tell Helicanus, my Marina, tell him

O'er, point by point, for yet he seems to doubt,
How sure you are my daughter. But what music?
Helicanus: My lord, I hear none.
Pericles: None?
    The music of the spheres! List, my Marina.
Lysimachus: It is not good to cross him. Give him way.
Pericles: Rarest sounds! Do ye not hear?
Lysimachus: Music, my lord? I hear.
Pericles: Most heavenly music!
    It nips [enraptures] me unto list'ning, and thick slumber
    Hangs upon mine eyes. Let me rest. [*Sleeps.*]
                      (V, 1, 224–236)

Not surprisingly, critics have detected religious overtones in *Pericles*. The play seems to recall the Book of Job, and scholars have established links with the medieval miracle and morality tradition (for example, a lost miracle play on the martyrdom of St. Eustace).[20] But Shakespeare's vision, for all its metaphysical implications, remains essentially secular. "*Pericles*," in the words of Donald Stauffer, "is not an abstract preachment, but an embodied intuition."[21]

CYMBELINE

The earliest mention of *Cymbeline* occurs in Dr. Simon Forman's *Book of Plaies* (see p. 342), which contains an account of a performance he attended some time before September 8, 1611 (the date of his death). This fact, together with the play's compressed style (a characteristic of Shakespeare's late works), has led scholars to date *Cymbeline* around 1609 or 1610. The only text is that printed in the 1623 Folio. Despite the argument that the Vision (V, 4, 30–122) may have been interpolated by somebody else, there is little doubt of Shakespeare's exclusive authorship.[22]

In sheer quantity of episode *Cymbeline* probably surpasses all other Shakespearean plays. The final scene features some two dozen surprises, recognitions, and recoveries of lost identity. The atmosphere is saturated with folkloristic elements, many of them melodramatic: a foolish king, a wicked stepmother-queen, an attempted poisoning, a misjudged wife, a headless corpse, an exiled lord, and kidnapped princes living as primitives. All this is played against a background of war between ancient Britain and Rome, spiced with intrigue of the sort Shakespeare's audiences would have ascribed to Renaissance Italy. Few readers can keep the threads disentangled, let alone recall the complicated process by which they are finally woven together.

One may distinguish three separate plots. First, there is the material involving Cymbeline himself, who presumably became King of Britain in 33 B.C. and ruled for thirty-five years. This part of the drama can be traced back to Geoffrey of Monmouth's *History of the Kings of Britain* (c. 1136), which also introduced Lear and his daughters into our literature. But Shakespeare probably drew upon Holinshed's *Chronicles,* with supplementary details from "The Complaint of Guiderius" in the *Second Part of the Mirrour for Magistrates* (1578) and from several tragedies in John Higgins's 1587 edition of the *Mirrour*. The second ingredient is the chastity wager, a popular folktale almost certainly adapted from Boccaccio's story of Bernabò of Genoa and his wife Zinevra (*Decameron*, 2. 9) and augmented with episodes from a fifteenth-century German narrative translated into English as *Frederick of Jennen* (1518, c. 1520, c. 1560). The third story, concerning Belarius and the kidnapped princes, may have been derived from two anonymous old romantic plays: *The Rare Triumphs of Love and Fortune,* performed in 1582 and printed in 1589, and *Sir Clyomon and Sir Clamydes,* published in 1599 but probably written in the 1580s.[23]

The historical material, though important thematically, takes relatively little space in the play. Cymbeline, King of Britain, refuses to pay the annual tribute rightfully due Augustus Caesar. He is strongly encouraged in this act of defiance by his evil Queen and his loutish stepson Cloten. In denying the tribute demanded by the Roman ambassador Caius Lucius, Cymbeline provokes a war with Rome. At the end of the play, with the Queen and Cloten both dead, the King agrees to pay the debt, even though he has vanquished Lucius's army on the battlefield. This noble act dramatizes the marriage of British and Roman qualities believed by Elizabethans to have contributed to England's greatness. In his concluding speech Cymbeline heralds the dawn of a glorious era:

> Laud we the gods;
> And let our crooked smokes climb to their nostrils
> From our blest altars. Publish we this peace
> To all our subjects. Set we forward. Let
> A Roman and a British ensign wave
> Friendly together.
>
> (V, 5, 476–481)[24]

While this national drama is unfolding, our attention is focused upon the wager plot, which Shakespeare takes great pains to develop. Cymbeline's daughter Imogen, ignoring her father's wish that she marry Cloten, chooses instead the poor but worthy Posthumus Leonatus, an orphan who has lived in the British court since childhood. Before being banished, Posthumus bestows his bracelet upon Imogen in exchange for her gift of a diamond ring. In Rome Posthumus meets the cynical

Italian Iachimo, who asserts that every woman—even Imogen, whose
virtue the young husband has been extolling—has her price: "If you buy
ladies' flesh at a million a dram, you cannot preserve it from tainting"
(I, 4, 147–148). Disregarding Philario's advice, Posthumus allows himself to be manipulated into wagering his ring against ten thousand
ducats that Imogen will withstand Iachimo's attempt at seduction. Armed
with a letter of introduction from Posthumus, Iachimo is to visit her and
return with proof that he has enjoyed her "dearest bodily part" (I, 4, 162).

   The encounter between Iachimo and Imogen is one of the highlights of
the play. Enraptured by Imogen's outward and inward beauty, Iachimo
at first tries to win her over by slandering Posthumus. The "Britain
reveller" (I, 6, 61), he says, defiles himself with harlots while his incomparable wife languishes at home. Iachimo insists that he himself
could never betray so divine a creature to feed on garbage:

> Had I this cheek
> To bathe my lips upon; this hand, whose touch,
> Whose every touch, would force the feeler's soul
> To th' oath of loyalty; this object, which
> Takes prisoner the wild motion of mine eye,
> Fixing it only here; should I (damn'd then)
> Slaver with lips as common as the stairs
> That mount the Capitol; join gripes with hands
> Made hard with hourly falsehood—falsehood, as
> With labour; then lie peeping in an eye
> Base and illustrious as the smoky light
> That's fed with stinking tallow: it were fit
> That all the plagues of hell should at one time
> Encounter such revolt.
>   (I, 6, 99–112)

Let Imogen get back at Posthumus by giving herself to Iachimo, who truly
appreciates her:

> Should he make me
> Live like Diana's priest, betwixt cold sheets,
> Whiles he is vaulting variable ramps [harlots],
> In your despite, upon your purse? Revenge it!
>   (I, 6, 132–135)

Imogen, whose chastity and absolute trust in her husband mark her as
the ideal Elizabethan woman,[25] denounces this "saucy stranger" for
behaving as if he were in a brothel (I, 6, 151–152) and threatens to
expose him to her father, whereupon Iachimo craftily changes his tune.

He has merely been testing her, he says, and he is delighted to find that she is a perfect mate for her irreproachable husband:

> Blessed live you long,
> A lady to the worthiest sir that ever
> Country call'd his! and you his mistress, only
> For the most worthiest fit! Give me your pardon.
> (I, 6, 159–162)

Imogen accepts his explanation and agrees to keep in her bedroom overnight a trunk containing valuables that Iachimo tells her have been entrusted to his care.

While Imogen sleeps, Iachimo, on one of those rare occasions in Shakespearean drama when even the audience is taken by surprise, creeps out of the trunk and notes the most intimate details of her room and person. This accomplished villain suffers a momentary pang of conscience, likening himself to Tarquin, who ravished the chaste Lucrece:

> Our Tarquin thus
> Did softly press the rushes ere he waken'd
> The chastity he wounded. Cytherea [Venus],
> How bravely thou becom'st thy bed! fresh lily,
> And whiter than the sheets! That I might touch!
> But kiss; one kiss! Rubies unparagon'd,
> How dearly they do't! 'Tis her breathing that
> Perfumes the chamber thus.
> (II, 2, 12–19)

He removes her bracelet, carefully observes a mole on her left breast, and steals back into the trunk. This figurative assault on Imogen's virtue is in part continued into the early morning, when Cloten vulgarly tries to "penetrate" (II, 3, 14) her with music (ironically, the gentle aubade "Hark, hark! the lark at heaven's gate sings" [II, 3, 22–30], familiar in Schubert's graceful setting). But Imogen sleeps on.

When Posthumus is confronted with Iachimo's circumstantial evidence, particularly the bracelet and the description of the mole, he is convinced of Imogen's infidelity. "Will you hear more?" the cunning Iachimo asks, knowing full well that he has nothing further to impart. "Spare your arithmetic," Posthumus replies; "never count the turns" (II, 4, 141–142). If Iachimo sometimes utilizes the techniques of Iago, Posthumus can explode in a manner that reminds us briefly of Othello:

Iachimo: I'll be sworn—
Posthumus: No swearing.
   If you will swear you have not done't, you lie;

> And I will kill thee if thou dost deny
> Thou'st made me cuckold.
> *Iachimo:*   I'll deny nothing.
> *Posthumus:* O that I had her here, to tear her limbmeal!
> I will go there and do't, i' th' court, before
> Her father. I'll do something—   [*Exit.*]
>   (II, 4, 143–149)

Iachimo then disappears from view until almost the end of the play. This is a superb dramatic touch, a remarkable example of Shakespeare's ability to exploit what Bertrand Evans has termed "discrepant awareness," whereby the audience shares a piece of special knowledge unavailable to the participants. In this instance Iachimo has the only key to the truth so that, during the three acts he is off the stage, "the evil sown by him has wild growth, while we bear alone and helplessly the secret of its origin."[26]

After railing bitterly against all women, Posthumus sends a letter to his servant Pisanio ordering him to kill Imogen, who at the same time receives a letter urging her to meet her husband at Milford Haven in Wales. "O, for a horse with wings!" (III, 2, 50), the ecstatic heroine proclaims:

>   If one of mean affairs
> May plod it in a week, why may not I
> Glide thither in a day?
>   (III, 2, 52–54)

Pisanio, like her, must be longing to see Posthumus. "O, not like me!" she quickly corrects herself. "For mine's beyond beyond" (III, 2, 57–58). When she learns the real purpose of the journey to Milford Haven, Imogen courageously bids Pisanio make haste with the execution. Her resignation recalls the last gasp of the dying Desdemona ("Commend me to my kind lord") :

> Do thou thy master's bidding. When thou seest him,
> A little witness my obedience. Look!
> I draw the sword myself. Take it, and hit
> The innocent mansion of my love, my heart.
> Fear not! 'Tis empty of all things but grief.
> Thy master is not there, who was indeed
> The riches of it. Do his bidding, strike!
>   (III, 4, 67–73)

At Pisanio's suggestion, however, Imogen disguises herself as a boy, Fidele, and plans to attach herself to Lucius in order to get to Rome and be near Posthumus. Earlier, the Queen, hoping to eliminate Posthumus and Imogen and thereby insure Cloten's succession to the throne, had asked the physician Cornelius for a box of poison and had passed it on to Pisanio, leading the servant to believe it was a restorative drug. Pisanio now gives it to Imogen, but the audience knows that the box contains a harmless sleeping potion that Cornelius had substituted because he was suspicious of the Queen. Imogen (Fidele) accepts the drug and proceeds to wander about the Welsh countryside for several days. At last she stumbles into a mountain cave, where she finds food and shelter.

At this point we turn to the third major plot. Some twenty years ago the King's two sons, Guiderius and Arviragus, disappeared. Cymbeline is unaware that they were abducted by Belarius, a faithful lord whom he had unjustly exiled. When we first meet the young princes, they have been living all this time in the mountains of Wales with their supposed father, Belarius, and are ignorant of their true identity. Douglas Peterson describes their Welsh abode as a "golden world," but J. C. Maxwell notes the humorous detachment in Shakespeare's presentation of the pastoral element in *Cymbeline*.[27] With a flair for rationalizing that could have been inherited from the banished Duke in *As You Like It,* Belarius expounds the "advantages" of rustic simplicity over courtly sophistication:

> O, this life
> Is nobler than attending for a check [rebuke],
> Richer than doing nothing for a bribe,
> Prouder than rustling in unpaid-for silk.
> (III, 3, 21–24)

But the boys are not satisfied. In a striking image, Guiderius complains that the old man is at least able to speak from experience that has been inaccessible to the two brothers:

> We poor unfledg'd
> Have never wing'd from view o' th' nest, nor know not
> What air's from home.
> (III, 3, 27–29)

Arviragus, who is more poetic, supports his brother:

> What should we speak of
> When we are old as you? When we shall hear
> The rain and wind beat dark December, how
> In this our pinching cave shall we discourse
> The freezing hours away?
> (III, 3, 35–39)

When the two go off to hunt, Belarius delightedly notes that the princely spark shines within them even though they have no idea that King Cymbeline is their father. They respond eagerly to Belarius's tales of war and heroism, demonstrating that despite their humble surroundings, royal blood still flows through their veins and confers upon them an instinctive civility.[28]

It is in keeping with the laws of romance that the cave inhabited by Belarius, Guiderius, and Arviragus should be the very one where Imogen seeks refuge. The princes are taken with Fidele, not knowing that the handsome lad is their sister. Shakespeare indulges in some of those typical pleasantries that hark back to Rosalind-Ganymede and Viola-Cesario. "Were you a woman, youth," Guiderius confides, "I should woo hard but be your groom" (III, 6, 69–70). "I'll love him as my brother," says Arviragus (III, 6, 72). The irony unwittingly spoken by Imogen is even more to the point:

> Would it had been so that they
> Had been my father's sons! Then had my prize
> Been less, and so more equal ballasting
> To thee, Posthumus.
> (III, 6, 76–79)

That is, if Guiderius and Arviragus were indeed her brothers, they would displace her in the succession and thus mitigate the social inequality that threatens her relationship with Posthumus.

Complications now follow thick and fast. Left alone, Imogen swallows the drug Pisanio gave her and falls into a deathlike sleep, not unlike Juliet's. Meanwhile, Cloten has dressed himself in Posthumus's clothes and set out for Milford Haven, intending to rape Imogen and kill her husband. But in the course of a quarrel in front of Belarius's cave, he is beheaded by Guiderius. Shortly thereafter, Guiderius and Arviragus discover the sleeping Imogen and, believing her dead, lay her in a simple grave strewn with flowers. While burying their beloved Fidele, they recite their famous dirge:

> Fear no more the heat o' th' sun
>   Nor the furious winter's rages;
> Thou thy worldly task hast done,
>   Home art gone, and ta'en thy wages.
> Golden lads and girls all must,
> As chimney-sweepers, come to dust.
> (IV, 2, 258–263)

Derek Marsh, in his detailed study of the play, speaks of the dirge as a "poem of acceptance," an acknowledgment of the finality of death[29] (although one notes that the context—Fidele is, after all, alive—is far from serious). After the brothers complete their obsequies and leave, Imogen awakens to find the headless body of Cloten. Recognizing the garments worn by the corpse, she assumes that the dead man is Posthumus and falls in a faint. Lucius enters with his Roman troops and, impressed with this evidence of loyalty on the part of Fidele, invites the young page into his service. Imogen accepts the offer.

While Imogen is casting her lot with Lucius, Guiderius and Arviragus repudiate their life of inaction and resolve to join the war against Rome. At the same time, Posthumus, persuaded that Pisanio has killed Imogen, adopts the disguise of a peasant so that he, too, might fight for Britain. Belarius and the princes turn defeat into victory, an achievement described in the compact phrase "a narrow lane, an old man, and two boys!" (V, 3, 52). And Posthumus also distinguishes himself in battle, although he is bitterly disappointed at not having lost his life:

> I, in mine own woe charm'd,
> Could not find Death where I did hear him groan
> Nor feel him where he struck. Being an ugly monster,
> 'Tis strange he hides him in fresh cups, soft beds,
> Sweet words; or hath moe ministers than we
> That draw his knives i' th' war. Well, I will find him.
> (V, 3, 68–73)

In order to hasten his death, Posthumus identifies himself to the Britons as a Roman and is taken into captivity. While in prison awaiting hanging, he has a vision in which Jupiter makes a cryptic promise that he will again be happy:

> When as a lion's whelp shall, to himself unknown, without seeking find, and be embrac'd by a piece of tender air; and when from a stately cedar shall be lopp'd branches which, being dead many years, shall after revive, be jointed to the old stock, and freshly grow; then shall Posthumus end his miseries, Britain be fortunate and flourish in peace and plenty.
> (V, 4, 138–145)

At last, with virtually all the characters assembled in Cymbeline's tent and bearing their individual pieces of vital information, the labyrinthian plot is disentangled. Imogen, still disguised as Fidele, notices that Iachimo is wearing the ring she gave Posthumus; and the villain, now repentant, confesses his grand deception. Posthumus is reunited with his Imogen, who throws her arms around him. "Hang there like fruit, my soul," he says to her, "till the tree die!" (V, 5, 263–264). Belarius discloses the strange history of Guiderius and Arviragus, whereupon Cymbeline em-

braces his long lost sons. "O Imogen," the King tells his daughter, "thou
hast lost by this a kingdom." "No, my lord," she replies; "I have got
two worlds by't" (V, 5, 372–374). The Soothsayer interprets Jupiter's
baffling oracle. The "lion's whelp" is Posthumus *Leo-natus* ("one born of
the lion"). Thanks to an even more ingenious bit of Latin wordplay, the
"piece of tender air" (*mollis aer*) by which he is embraced turns out
to be Imogen, "this most constant wife" (*mulier*, "woman") (V, 5, 446–
449). The "stately cedar" is Cymbeline; the "lopp'd branches" that
revive after being dead for many years are, of course, Guiderius and
Arviragus. "Pardon's the word to all," Cymbeline announces (V, 5, 422),
a fitting motto for *Cymbeline* as indeed for the other Shakespearean
romances.

The play has had its detractors, among them two formidable critics:
Samuel Johnson and George Bernard Shaw. Dr. Johnson finds *Cymbeline*
totally implausible:

> To remark the folly of the fiction, the absurdity of the conduct, the
> confusion of the names and manners of different times, and the impossibility
> of the events in any system of life, were to waste criticism upon unresisting
> imbecillity, upon faults too evident for detection, and too gross for
> aggravation.[30]

Shaw, who habitually disparages Shakespeare, comments more strongly:

> [Cymbeline] is for the most part stagey trash of the lowest melodramatic
> order, in parts abominably written, throughout intellectually vulgar, and
> judged in point of thought by modern intellectual standards, vulgar, foolish,
> offensive, indecent, and exasperating beyond all tolerance. There are moments
> when one asks despairingly why our stage should ever have been cursed
> with this "immortal" pilferer of other men's stories and ideas, with his
> monstrous rhetorical fustian, his unbearable platitudes, his pretentious reduc-
> tion of the subtlest problems of life to commonplaces against which a
> Polytechnic debating club would revolt.[31]

In a less flamboyant vein, other readers, while admiring Imogen's nobility
and much of the poetry, feel that the play's structure is loose and that
the characters are conceived and developed in the sketchiest of psychological terms.

In recent years *Cymbeline* has been more highly esteemed as critics
have altered their view of Shakespeare's aims and methods. No longer
are they put off by the general lack of dramatic realism. Arthur Kirsch
believes that in *Cymbeline* Shakespeare deliberately explores the techniques and implications of the coterie drama of the private theaters:
discontinuous characterizations, flamboyant villains that are not to be

taken too seriously, tragicomic shifts from sorrow to joy, and so on.[32]
It is now generally acknowledged that, whatever larger questions it may
raise, *Cymbeline* is a stunning performance by a master dramatist who
positively flaunts his expert technique. In the words of Harley Granville-
Barker, Shakespeare provides an example of "the art that rather displays
art than conceals it," saying in effect to his wide-eyed audience, " 'Ladies
and gentlemen, this is an exhibition of tricks, and what I want you to
enjoy among other things is the skill with which I hope to perform
them.' "[33] We know from the start that the Queen's poison is not really
poison and that the headless body Imogen discovers is not really the
body of Posthumus. In fact, her overly meticulous proof that it is her
husband's corpse seems to constitute what a recent editor has termed "a
deliberate touch of deflating comedy":

A headless man? The garments of Posthumus?
I know the shape of's leg; this is his hand,
His foot Mercurial, his Martial thigh,
The brawns of Hercules; but his Jovial face—
Murther in heaven? How? 'Tis gone.
(IV, 2, 308–312)[34]

In this speech, as elsewhere in the play, Shakespeare exploits to the hilt
the conventions of romance, but he does so from an ironic perspective
that allows neither himself nor his audience to become emotionally
involved.[35]

Yet Shakespeare touches upon important issues in *Cymbeline*. Reference
was made earlier to the allegorical significance of the conflict between
Britain and Rome, together with the eventual reconciliation of the two
cultures into a single national tradition. It is in the erratic soul of
Cymbeline himself that the battle has to be fought and resolved. As a
king and as a man Cymbeline displays poor judgment (witness his
persecution of Belarius, Posthumus, and Imogen, as well as his nearly
fatal deception at the hands of the Queen and Cloten). His spiritual
blindness generates the kind of atmosphere in which evil may flourish
and go undetected. It can thus be said that Cymbeline creates the moral
setting for Iachimo's diabolical scheming and Posthumus's grievous loss
of faith. Before the conventional happy ending of romance can be
achieved in Cymbeline's Britain, corruption must be duly expunged.[36]
The Queen and Cloten are beyond the pale. But the other sinners
(Cymbeline, Iachimo, and Posthumus) experience contrition and therefore deserve to be forgiven.

Some would go beyond these general suggestions to interpret *Cymbeline* in more specific historical and theological terms. Several critics have
reminded us that the historical Cymbeline reigned when Christ was born

and that this event, though not mentioned, colors the entire play and accounts for the transcendental peace at the ending. Moreover, it has been said, the spirit of the Nativity has been skillfully incorporated into a panegyric to James I, as well as a celebration of English nationalism in general.[37] William Thorne, who sees *Cymbeline* as a development of ritualistic folk drama (in particular, the Mummers' Play of Saint George), believes that the theme of regeneration is central to Shakespeare's play.[38] Other critics are more thoroughly allegorical. For example, they equate Jupiter with the Christian God who exercises firm control over all that happens, regardless of how desperately we appear to be floundering. Imogen is viewed as the embodiment of feminine transcendentalism and is thus cast in a mystical role akin to that of the Virgin Mary. Cloten is often seen as a caricature of Posthumus, an alter ego whose death symbolizes the death of the sinful hero, the prerequisite for his subsequent rebirth in Imogen's arms. Posthumus's development during the play has accordingly been described as the "pagan equivalent to Christian regeneration."[39] Few works have evoked such an abundance of metaphysical speculation and, conversely, few have produced such a wealth of rebuttal that insists upon our reading *Cymbeline* as essentially neither more nor less than an entertaining romance.[40]

Perhaps the problem lies with Shakespeare himself, who in this instance may have failed to achieve a fully satisfactory integration of comedy, romance, and theology. The play has been called an experimental romance in which realism gets in the way.[41] But it can be successful, provided that we heed J. C. Maxwell's advice not to be bent on proving it a masterpiece.[42] Whatever its imperfections, *Cymbeline* boasts phenomenal craftsmanship, poetry of the highest order, and one of Shakespeare's most vibrant and attractive heroines.

THE WINTER'S TALE

The Winter's Tale, like *Macbeth* and *Cymbeline*, is mentioned in Dr. Simon Forman's *Book of Plaies*. Forman saw it at the Globe on May 15, 1611. An account book of the Revels Office, discovered in 1842 and probably genuine, records a performance by the King's Men on November 5, 1611. These facts, together with stylistic evidence pointing to Shakespeare's latest period, would establish 1610 or 1611 as a likely date of composition. The only text, a good one, is that printed in the 1623 Folio.[43]

The main source is Robert Greene's prose romance *Pandosto: The Triumph of Time* (1588), reprinted in 1607 with a new title, *Dorastus and Fawnia*. Minor sources include Greene's cony-catching pamphlets (1592) and two narrative poems (derived from *Pandosto*) by Francis

Sabie: *The Fisherman's Tale* (1595) and *Flora's Fortune* (1595).[44] In the play Leontes, King of Sicilia, becomes jealous of his guest and childhood friend Polixenes, King of Bohemia, suspecting him of adultery with his wife Hermione. Leontes asserts that Polixenes is the father of Hermione's unborn child and that the Prince of Sicilia, Mamilius, is not his own son. Polixenes flees, accompanied by the trusted Sicilian lord Camillo, whereupon Leontes, more convinced of his wife's guilt, orders that she be arrested and that Mamilius be taken from her. Hermione gives birth to a daughter in prison, but when the Lady Paulina presents the infant to the King, hoping to soften his heart, he explodes: "This brat is none of mine" (II, 3, 92). He instructs Antigonus, Paulina's husband, to throw the child into the fire, then, as a mild concession, bids him instead take the infant to some remote place and expose it to the elements. Meanwhile, Leontes sends messengers to the oracle at Delphi to solicit a verdict on Hermione and convenes a court of justice where she may be indicted and convicted. The oracle vindicates the Queen:

> Hermione is chaste; Polixenes blameless; Camillo a true subject; Leontes a jealous tyrant; his innocent babe truly begotten; and the King shall live without an heir, if that which is lost be not found.
>
> (III, 2, 133–137)

But Leontes repudiates the oracle and orders the trial to continue, a stirring climax to a highly dramatic scene:

> There is no truth at all i' th' oracle!
> The sessions shall proceed. This is mere falsehood!
> (III, 2, 141–142)

At that very instant, as if for retribution, Mamilius dies. The Queen falls in a swoon as Paulina utters a poignant cry:

> This news is mortal to the Queen. Look down
> And see what death is doing.
> (III, 2, 149–150)

Hermione is carried out, and a moment later Paulina returns to inform Leontes that she is dead. The grief-stricken King vows to do penance for the rest of his life.

The trial scene is followed by one of the most peculiar episodes in all Shakespeare. Antigonus, who set sail with the infant before Leontes' repentance, arrives at the stormy seacoast of Bohemia (which has no seacoast except in Shakespeare's unconventional geography) and places tiny Perdita ("the lost one") on the shore. He then must execute the arresting stage direction *"Exit, pursued by a bear"* (III, 3, 58). An old shepherd comes on stage and discovers the baby. He is soon joined by his son, who describes how the ship and its crew were destroyed in the storm and, in gruesome counterpoint, how Antigonus was eaten by the bear:

> I have not wink'd since I saw these sights. The men are not yet cold under water, nor the bear half din'd on the gentleman—he's at it now . . . . I'll go see if the bear be gone from the gentleman, and how much he hath eaten. They are never curst but when they are hungry. If there be any of him left, I'll bury it.

> (III, 3, 106–109, 133–136)

The two men take the child home. " 'Tis a lucky day, boy," the father says, "and we'll do good deeds on't" (III, 3, 142–143). Thus ends the first part of *The Winter's Tale*.

To bridge the gap between Acts III and IV, Shakespeare introduces Time as his choric commentator.[45] Sixteen years have elapsed. While Leontes continues his penitential life in Sicilia, Perdita has grown into a lovely young woman in Bohemia, where she lives as the daughter of the shepherd who found her. She is in love with Polixenes' son Florizel, Prince of Bohemia, and he with her, despite her misgivings about their apparent difference in rank. During a sheepshearing festival, they are visited by King Polixenes and Camillo, who have come in disguise in order to ferret out more information on the romance. Although Polixenes is impressed with Perdita's naturalness and beauty, he nevertheless finds the match unacceptable and, angrily disclosing his true identity, threatens to punish the lovers if they continue their relationship. But Florizel cannot give Perdita up, and with the help of Camillo, who yearns to see his homeland again, the Prince and Perdita depart for Sicilia. At the same time, the old shepherd, fearful of the King's wrath, determines to inform Polixenes that he is not Perdita's father and prepares to produce as evidence to that effect the rich garments and jewels found with her sixteen years ago. On the way to the King's palace, however, he is intercepted by Autolycus, a combination of peddler, pickpocket, and confidence man, who tricks the shepherd and his son into boarding the ship bearing the lovers to Sicilia. The ship arrives in Sicilia, with Polixenes and Camillo in close pursuit.

With the major characters gathered in Leontes' court, we fully expect to witness the long-awaited reunion of Leontes and Perdita. But Shakespeare has a surprise or two in store for us. First of all, the reunion of father and daughter takes place offstage, as though Shakespeare were reluctant merely to repeat what he had already brilliantly dramatized in *Pericles*. Then, with little if any forewarning, we are the happy victims of an astounding coup de theatre. In Paulina's keeping is a statue of Hermione, said to have been carved by the Italian master Julio Romano (historically, a disciple of Raphael), and Perdita is eager to see this supposedly perfect likeness of her mother. When the statue is unveiled, Leontes is struck by its resemblance to the dead Queen, although Hermione "was not so much wrinkled" (V, 3, 28). At a signal from Paulina, Hermione descends from the pedestal and embraces Leontes. She has, of course, been alive all the time, a fact known only to Paulina. Leontes begs forgiveness, indicates that the widowed Paulina should marry Camillo, and bestows his blessing upon the forthcoming marriage of Florizel and Perdita.[46]

Throughout the play we are kept somewhat at a distance from Leontes. In the first part he displays certain elements of the stock comic tyrant; in the second, he is the stock penitent.[47] Some critics, like Nevill Coghill, believe that he was jealous all along; while others maintain that jealousy (which comes slowly in *Pandosto*) comes upon him suddenly, like a visitation from the gods, and that its nature, to quote Tillyard, "is that of an earthquake or the loss of the 'Titanic' rather than of rational human psychology." A third view, ingeniously argued by William Matchett, is that Shakespeare skillfully misleads the audience into temporarily suspecting Hermione so as to make Leontes' jealousy dramatically convincing.[48] In any case, Leontes' catastrophe unfolds with enormous speed and intensity.

Early in the play Polixenes recalls to Hermione how he and Leontes played together as children:

> We were, fair queen,
> Two lads that thought there was no more behind
> But such a day to-morrow as to-day,
> And to be boy eternal.
>
> (I, 2, 62–65)

But this reminiscence of an earlier pastoral paradise is from one minute to the next contaminated by superstition and obsession.[49] When Hermione, chaste but at the same time warmly feminine, engages Polixenes in gently ribald banter (I, 2, 38–86) as she takes his hand and urges him to prolong his visit, Leontes notes the "paddling palms and pinching fingers" (I, 2, 115) and begins to build a crazy tissue of conjectures:

> Is whispering nothing?
> Is leaning cheek to cheek? Is meeting noses?
> Kissing with inside lip? stopping the career
> Of laughter with a sigh?—a note infallible
> Of breaking honesty!—horsing foot on foot?

Skulking in corners? wishing clocks more swift?
Hours, minutes? noon, midnight? and all eyes
Blind with the pin and web [cataract] but theirs—theirs only,
That would unseen be wicked? Is this nothing?
Why, then the world and all that's in't is nothing;
The covering sky is nothing; Bohemia nothing;
My wife is nothing; nor nothing have these nothings,
If this be nothing.

(I, 2, 284–296)[50]

One may drink, he reasons, not knowing that his cup contains a venomous spider and remain unharmed; but if he is afterward shown the horrible creature, he will become violently ill. "I have drunk, and seen the spider" (II, 1, 45).[51]

Thus the Sicilian court, as depicted in the first three acts, is enveloped in an atmosphere as poisoned as that of *King Lear* or *Othello*. "Come, and lead me to these sorrows" (III, 2, 243–244), Leontes says as he goes into mourning for Mamilius and Hermione; and when he speaks these words, we feel as if we have been present at the finale of a five-act tragedy.[52] But the Bohemia of Act IV introduces a miniature pastoral romance in the spirit of *As You Like It* and leads to the comic de-nouement. To be sure, there are clouds in Bohemia. As Francis Berry points out, an audience sees the young lovers through the darkened lens of their parents' tragic experience in the first part.[53] Moreover, Polixenes' sudden cruelty to Perdita, filtered though it may be through the softening magic of a pastoral setting, provides an uncomfortable echo of Leontes' earlier eruption.[54] Nevertheless, Sicilia and Bohemia become the focus of some of the play's major thematic contrasts: court and country, winter and summer, art and nature, age and youth, death and resurrection.[55]

The tone of *The Winter's Tale* changes drastically, oddly enough during the very scene in which Antigonus meets his bizarre death (III, 3). Antigonus has to die so that the evidence that Perdita is alive can be completely destroyed.[56] But Shakespeare artfully pre-pares us for his death as well as for the shift in mood. By setting Antigonus's disaster on the nonexistent seacoast of a remote Bohemia, he reduces its impact and, in effect, transfers it to the realm of fantasy. When the mariner warns Antigonus that Bohemia is famous for its man-eating beasts, the audience is alerted to dangers but comforted by the realization that they are of the sort encountered in fairytales rather than real life. When Antigonus discloses that Hermione appeared in a dream with instructions to leave the infant in Bohemia and name it Perdita, we can infer that a special providence is presiding over its destiny and that all will be well. Of course, we are touched when Antigonus lays his bundle down and bids Perdita farewell:

Weep I cannot,
But my heart bleeds; and most accurs'd am I
To be by oath enjoin'd to this. Farewell!
The day frowns more and more. Thou'rt like to have
A lullaby too rough.

(III, 3, 51–55)

But, curiously, this tender speech is followed by the incongruous sound
of hunters and dogs in the chase. In this context Antigonus makes his
celebrated exit pursued by a bear, and in Coghill's words, "the tale,
hitherto wholly and deeply tragic, turns suddenly and triumphantly to
comedy."[57]

Thus, by steadily diluting the seriousness of Antigonus's death, Shakespeare paves the way for our casual acceptance of it. This reaction is
reinforced when the shepherd's son tells about the event in a style both
grim and ludicrous. The old man's response to his son's grisly narrative
establishes a mood of optimism:

Heavy matters, heavy matters! But look thee here, boy. Now bless thyself!
thou met'st with things dying, I with things newborn. Here's a sight for thee.

(III, 3, 115–118)

His remarks crystallize the meaning of this complex scene and of the play
as a whole; for, as suggested earlier, *The Winter's Tale* is organically unified around the carefully developed contrast between "things dying" and
"things newborn." As F. R. Leavis has noted, this theme is enriched "by
the concrete presence of time in its rhythmic processes, and by the
association of human growth, decay, and rebirth with the vital rhythms
of nature at large."[58] It is fitting that the agent of rebirth should turn
out to be the exiled Perdita, "a seed sowed in winter and flowering in
summer,"[59] and that this radiant heroine should flourish in the idyllic
setting of the Bohemian countryside.

Notwithstanding her royal birth, Perdita emerges as a symbol of the
pure and the natural. When put to the test by Polixenes and Camillo, she
unabashedly stands her ground, notably in the great floral scene (IV,
4). As queen of the sheepshearing festival, she distributes flowers to each
according to the recipient's age. Apologizing for not having any autumnal
flowers for the two visitors, she offers rosemary and rue, which retain
their beauty and fragrance throughout the winter. Polixenes suggests that
she graft flowers, arguing (in ironic contradiction to his view of the
Florizel-Perdita romance) that one may crossbreed a noble bud with
one of inferior quality, thereby improving upon nature. But Perdita refuses to usurp the function of "great creating nature" (IV, 4, 88):

I'll not put

The dibble [tool] in earth to set one slip of them;

No more than, were I painted, I would wish
This youth should say 'twere well, and only therefore
Desire to breed by me.

                              (IV, 4, 99–103)

The speech has a healthy sexuality reminiscent of Hermione, underscored
a moment later when Perdita longs for some spring flowers to strew
upon Florizel.[60] "What, like a corse [corpse]?" Florizel asks. Perdita
answers with a freshness born of love, physical as well as spiritual:

No, like a bank for love to lie and play on;
Not like a corse; or if—not to be buried,
But quick [alive], and in mine arms.

                              (IV, 4, 129–132)

Florizel then pays her one of the most exquisite compliments in all
literature. His chief metaphor is chosen from royalty, although neither
he nor Perdita as yet knows that what he says is literally true:

                                          What you do
Still betters what is done. When you speak, sweet,
I'd have you do it ever. When you sing,
I'd have you buy and sell so; so give alms;
Pray so; and for the ord'ring your affairs,
To sing them too. When you do dance, I wish you
A wave o' th' sea, that you might ever do
Nothing but that; move still, still so,
And own no other function. Each your doing,
So singular in each particular,
Crowns what you are doing in the present deed,
That all your acts are queens.

                              (IV, 4, 135–146)

Polixenes senses that Perdita's bearing "smacks of something greater
than herself" (IV, 4, 158), and Camillo compresses her refinement and
rusticity into an incisive image, "the queen of curds and cream"
(IV, 4, 161).[61]

    In the floral interlude, as previously noted, Perdita rejects Polixenes'
concept of a corpse strewn with flowers and alludes to the power of her
love to requicken the dead. This is indeed her effect upon Leontes; the
anonymous Third Gentleman who witnessed the reunion of father and
daughter implies that the King experienced a spiritual transformation:

There might you have beheld one joy crown another, so and in such manner
that it seem'd sorrow wept to take leave of them; for their joy waked in
tears. . . . Our king, being ready to leap out of himself for joy of his found

daughter, as if that joy were now become a loss, cries, "O, thy mother, thy mother!" then asks Bohemia [Polixenes] forgiveness; then embraces his son-in-law; then again worries he his daughter with clipping [embracing] her.

(V, 2, 47–59)

Like other Shakespearean heroines—Helena (in *All's Well that Ends Well*), Marina, and Imogen—Perdita personifies the redemptive force of the young. Leontes is made to live again.

The death-rebirth theme is most compellingly expressed in the spectacular final scene, in which the supposed statue of Hermione comes to life. Although her resurrection is accompanied by what is meant to be a rational explanation, the fact remains that whenever *The Winter's Tale* is performed, those in the theater who do not know how the story ends are electrified at that moment when Hermione steps down into Leontes' arms. Nowhere else in all his works does Shakespeare make such a point of keeping the audience in the dark.

In retrospect we can see that Shakespeare has prepared us for the statue scene.[62] Before Perdita's return to Sicilia, Paulina extracts from Leontes a promise that she herself will choose his new wife in the unlikely event that he should decide to marry:

> She shall not be so young
> As was your former; but she shall be such
> As, walk'd your first queen's ghost, it should take joy
> To see her in your arms.

(V, 1, 78–81).

So perfect is Julio Romano's statue of Hermione, the Third Gentleman says, "that they say one would speak to her and stand in hope of answer" (V, 2, 109–110). "Comes it not something near?" Paulina asks Leontes as she unveils the statue. The King grows more agitated:

> Her natural posture!
> Chide me, dear stone, that I may say indeed
> Thou art Hermione; or rather, thou art she
> In thy not chiding; for she was as tender
> As infancy and grace.

(V, 3, 23–27)

Paulina threatens to draw the curtain again, for Leontes is carried away almost to the point that he thinks the statue is alive. "I could afflict you farther," she tells him. "Do, Paulina!" he beseeches:

> For this affliction has a taste as sweet
> As any cordial comfort. Still methinks

> There is an air comes from her. What fine chisel
> Could ever yet cut breath? Let no man mock me,
> For I will kiss her.
>
> (V, 3, 75–80)

The tension is unbearable, for the audience no less than for the agonized Leontes.

But we are also prepared spiritually to accept the miracle of Hermione's return.[63] At the climactic moment of the drama, Paulina calls upon the spectators—those in the audience as well as on the stage—to participate in a communal act of faith that will dissolve the barrier between the unreal and the real, between art and nature, between the dead and the living.[64] "Dear life redeems you," Paulina announces (V, 3, 103). Hermione descends, and Leontes ecstatically embraces her:

> O, she's warm!
> If this be magic, let it be an art
> Lawful as eating.
>
> (V, 3, 109–111)

But, significantly, it is only at Paulina's words "Our Perdita is found" that Hermione breaks her long silence:

> You gods, look down,
> And from your sacred vials pour your graces
> Upon my daughter's head!
>
> (V, 3, 121–123)

Art can go only so far. The finest chisel of a Julio Romano cannot cut breath in dead stone. Such a miracle can be wrought only through love.

As one might expect, *The Winter's Tale* has stimulated a number of religious interpretations. Leontes' jealousy, according to S. R. Maveety, is "a manifestation of his fallen nature," with Acts IV and V constituting a "'comic' allegorical presentation of Christian salvation." J. A. Bryant, Jr., advances the more controversial view that there are scriptural analogues to the various characters: Hermione corresponds to Jesus Christ, the incarnation of divine grace; Mamilius, who dies suddenly, is the Jewish church, and Perdita stands for the true church that is the vehicle for salvation; Leontes symbolizes the Jew whom St. Paul (Paulina in the play) wants to see saved.[65] (Even Autolycus, the irrepressible balladmonger and thief, has been described as a parody of the good Samaritan.)[66]

Without denying the validity of an allegorical approach, one may cite Roland M. Frye's strictures concerning the most extreme arguments

of the Christian allegorical school. The plays, he says, "make no encompassing appeal to theological categories" but rather dramatize "uni-
versally human situations within a temporal and this-worldly arena."
At the same time, they "attest to [Shakespeare's] theological literacy and
to his uncanny ability to adapt his impressive religious knowledge to
dramatic purposes."[67] This desire to infuse a secular story, even a fairy-
tale, with religious significance helps account for the trick Shakespeare
plays on us in the statue scene. Writing a play for a secular audience, he
did not want to resort to an actual miracle. But, in the words of Alfred
Harbage, he succeeds in creating "the atmosphere of a miracle, the atmosphere of a resurrection, and this would have been impossible had he
employed his usual method of withholding no facts from the audience."[68]

One should also remember that the subtitle of Greene's *Pandosto*
is "The Triumph of Time," and perhaps the key to Shakespeare's bittersweet comedy is to be found in the venerable figure who appears with his
traditional hourglass to slide over the gap of sixteen years:

> I, that please some, try all, both joy and terror
> Of good and bad, that makes and unfolds error,
> Now take upon me, in the name of Time,
> To use my wings.
>
> (IV, 1, 1–4)

His speech, like the action to which it is linked, suggests that *The
Winter's Tale* does not celebrate the Christian myth of immortality so
much as the complex role of all-powerful Time within this life. It brings
both sickness and healing, sin and repentance, death and the possibility
of renewal. The exquisite joy of the last scene balances but cannot erase
the tragic fact that Hermione and Leontes have lost sixteen precious
years.[69]

THE TEMPEST

When Heminge and Condell issued the Folio in 1623, they printed
The Tempest for the first time, placing it at the head of the collection.
The text is extraordinarily well edited, with detailed stage directions,
complete act and scene divisions, and a full list of dramatis personae (a
distinction shared with only three other plays in the Folio). The play
was performed at court November 1, 1611 (Hallowmas Night), and was
later presented on December 27, 1612, as part of the festivities honoring
the betrothal and marriage of the Prince Palatine Elector and Princess
Elizabeth, daughter of Charles I. Except for *The Comedy of Errors*,
this is Shakespeare's shortest play, inviting the speculation that the text

may have been abridged before being printed in the Folio. But the existence of an earlier version is improbable. The date is generally accepted as 1611.[70]

Although no direct source has been discovered, there are a number of literary and semiliterary works from which various elements in *The Tempest* seem to have been derived. One detects Old and New Testament echoes, as well as parallels with the *Aeneid* and Ovid's *Metamorphoses*. Carol Gesner has pointed out links with Greek pastoral romance (like Longus's *Daphnis and Chloe*), and K. M. Lea (among others) has noted the influence of the Italian commedia del l'arte, which emphasized such elements as music, magic, comic business, and love (often in the pastoral setting of a desert island).[71] From Montaigne's essay "Of Cannibals" (in John Florio's English translation [1603]) came the inspiration for Gonzalo's description of the ideal commonwealth (II, 1, 143–168). Montaigne draws comparisons between primitivism and civilization, a subject that figures prominently in the play.

The Tempest also reflects Shakespeare's knowledge of contemporary travel literature, especially accounts of actual voyages to the New World. In 1609 *The Sea-Venture,* part of a fleet of nine ships that had set sail for Virginia, was wrecked on the coast of Bermuda. Shakespeare made use of three pamphlets that reported the events of that expedition: Sylvester Jourdain's *Discovery of the Barmudas* (1610); the Council of Virginia's *True Declaration of the Estate of the Colonie in Virginia* (1610); and a letter known to Shakespeare in 1610 (though not published until 1625), William Strachey's *True Reportory of the Wrack*. Shakespeare learned much from these narratives. Not only did they furnish information about the voyages, but they contained philosophic observations on the quality of life among the savages in the New World, comments that sometimes resembled those of Montaigne. In these and other documents, as Leo Marx has brilliantly demonstrated, one finds contradictory images of the American landscape. The New World is seen as a pastoral garden and as a primitive wilderness, and both attitudes are found in Shakespeare.[72] Moreover, the documents are conducive to allegorical use in that they interpret the events of the voyage and shipwreck as manifestations of the ways of divine Providence.[73] It would be misleading, however, to lay undue stress upon this or that specific source, for *The Tempest,* even for Shakespeare, is a strikingly original work.[74]

The Tempest is one of only two plays (the other is *The Comedy of Errors*) in which Shakespeare observes the neoclassical unities of place and time. The action occurs on an island inhabited by the magician Prospero, his daughter Miranda, and his servants Ariel and Caliban; and although the plot had been set in motion twelve years earlier, the drama unfolds and reaches its conclusion in a single day. Perhaps, as some have pointed out, Shakespeare deliberately chose to emphasize the sense of the present moment, to which the past is prologue.[75] In any case, *The Tempest* moves toward its denouement with a directness and clarity not found in the other dramatic romances. Shakespeare's artistry has never been more economical.

The play begins with an exciting storm at sea. Then, having captured our attention, Shakespeare proceeds (I, 2) to a leisurely exposition of the vital antecedent action, details that Prospero imparts to Miranda as father and daughter stand on the shore and observe the distress of the passengers. D. G. James makes the interesting point that there are really two storms, representing two different orders of perception: the storm Miranda sees, a shattering experience that heralds her emergence from innocence and her initiation into an awareness of evil, and the magical tempest raised by Prospero and Ariel, a harmless affair that leaves no mark upon its victims.[76] Be that as it may, Prospero tells his tale with considerable bitterness and forces Miranda to listen. He not only narrates the past; he relives it.[77]

Twelve years ago Prospero had been Duke of Milan. However, his neglect of worldly affairs and his concentration on occult studies had enabled his brother Antonio to conspire successfully with Alonso, King of Naples, to remove him from the dukedom and cast him and his young daughter adrift at sea in a rotten boat. But the kindly Neapolitan lord Gonzalo had provided food and clothing so that the pair managed to survive and find shelter on an enchanted island. Gonzalo had also furnished Prospero with books on necromancy, as well as his magic wand and conjuring robes.

After twelve years, during which Prospero has been perfecting his art as a Neoplatonic theurgist, or beneficent magician,[78] fortune brings the conspirators (along with Gonzalo, the King's son Ferdinand, and various attendants) near the coast of the island. To punish his enemies, Prospero intercepts their ship en route back to Naples from Africa, where they had gone for the wedding of Alonso's daughter, and invokes the tempest of the opening scene. With the ship presumably destroyed and the crew believed dead, the travelers come ashore in separate groups, each assuming that the others have perished. By nightfall everything is set right. Ferdinand and Miranda have fallen in love; the conspirators for the most part repent and are forgiven; ship and crew are found intact; and everybody in the royal party, including the newly reconciled brothers, returns to Naples for the forthcoming marriage of Ferdinand and Miranda, after which Prospero will be restored as Duke of Milan. In the meantime, we have seen strange sights, heard wonderful music, and delighted in a rich assortment of episodes and characters.

Above all, *The Tempest* is a marvelous show, and that in itself should be enough. John Dover Wilson says that the play "is not . . . the subject

of argument or explanation; it is to be accepted and experienced."
"Maybe we do it wrong," Bonamy Dobrée writes, "to offer it a show of
violence in trying to extract secrets from it, the secrets it might reveal
if we fitted it less into our preconceptions, and let it quietly do its work
upon us."[79] This may be a romantic view, but it comes remarkably close
to conveying the essential spirit of the work. Nevertheless, the fantasy
continues to evoke a host of interpretations, and critics have perennially
been tempted to search for a deeper significance. Not only has *The
Tempest* generated many other works of art (for example, W. H. Auden's
poem "The Sea and the Mirror"), but as Anne Righter observes, the
best of the so-called straight criticism tends to read like creative "adaptation."[80] As with *Hamlet,* one should probably think of multiple meanings
rather than of a single meaning.

For one thing, *The Tempest* is linked with the other romances in that
it touches upon the contrast between age and youth. The storm itself,
along with Prospero's narration of Milanese intrigue (a tale that Miranda,
appropriately, finds wearisome), telescopes the uprooting of an old and
decaying way of life; the young lovers speak for the new generation, hopeful and as yet uncorrupted. At her first meeting with a man other than
her father, Miranda can envision no fairer person than this handsome
Ferdinand. Later, when she is introduced to the rest of the shipwrecked
party, her capacity to love—though she never discards Ferdinand—is
expanded so as to encompass them all:

> O, wonder!
> How many goodly creatures are there here!
> How beauteous mankind is! O brave new world
> That has such people in't!
> (V, 1, 181–184)

Her father, who knows from personal experience that this particular
group is not so beauteous, rejoins: " 'Tis new to thee." But his comment
merely qualifies Miranda's enthusiasm and places it in perspective. A
few lines later Gonzalo hails the lovers as agents of reconciliation:

> I have inly wept,
> Or should have spoke ere this. Look down, you gods,
> And on this couple drop a blessed crown!
> For it is you that have chalk'd forth the way
> Which brought us hither.
> (V, 1, 200–204)

"I say amen, Gonzalo," the now penitent Alonso declares. Ferdinand
and Miranda, who, in D. G. James's words, "represent the hope by

which we live and without which we could not bear the burden of our lives,"[81] share with the young people in the other three romances— Marina, Imogen and her brothers, Perdita—the exalted function of spiritual healers and redeemers. Dover Wilson sees this function symbolized in the game of chess that Ferdinand and Miranda play during the last-act reunions. "The ancient feud between Milan and Naples has softened into the mimic war of ivory armies who shed no blood, played out by the representatives of the two houses, united in love."[82]

The Tempest may also be read as a political play, for it explores in a number of different contexts the relationship between freedom and authority. Gonzalo envisages a mythical state, where everything would be owned in common and where there would be no need for any sort of government. One could dispense with all the trappings of so-called civilization, including work:

> For no kind of traffic
> Would I admit; no name of magistrate;
> Letters should not be known; riches, poverty,
> And use of service, none; contract, succession,
> Bourn, bound of land, tilth, vineyard, none;
> No use of metal, corn, or wine, or oil;
> No occupation; all men idle, all;
> And women too, but innocent and pure;
> No sovereignty.
>
> (II, 1, 148–156)

There would be no treason, no felony, no war, and no weapons of war. Nature would simply pour out in abundance everything required for life, and Gonzalo could rule his innocent subjects with such perfection as "t'excel the golden age" (II, 1, 167–168). Harry Levin has called attention to a basic paradox, that "in order to redistribute power, one must first possess it; and those who have possessed and tasted it . . . have proved notoriously reluctant to give it up."[83] Gonzalo himself confesses that his utopia is intended as a "kind of merry fooling" (II, 1, 177), and elsewhere in *The Tempest* Shakespeare underscores the irony of the old man's speech by holding up for our inspection a series of miniature political bodies composed of imperfect men in the real world rather than paragons from the Golden Age.

Indeed, much of the action in *The Tempest* serves as a refutation of Gonzalo's fanciful theorizing. In the very first scene the ship is a commonwealth, and as the Boatswain boldly orders Alonso below deck, he asserts that in an impatient sea the monarch must yield his authority to the mariner. "Keep your cabins! You do assist the storm . . . . Hence! What cares these roarers for the name of king? To cabin! Silence! Trouble us not!" (I, 1, 15–19). Yet when the crew and the courtiers rejoin each other safely on land, the Boatswain relinquishes his command and is once again the loyal subject. During his tenure as Duke of Milan, Prospero had made the mistake of abdicating his responsibility to govern and relying on what he thought was the inherent goodness of men. He had placed "a confidence sans bound" (I, 2, 97) in his brother. But now, having learned that Gonzalo's brand of idealism will not work, he exercises firm control over Ariel, Caliban, and Miranda. In fact, his warning to Ferdinand and Miranda about premarital sexual relations (IV, 1, 14–22), a speech some consider unduly severe, may arise out of his determination to take nothing for granted where human nature is concerned.[84] Prospero has become an effective and self-disciplined ruler.

As further evidence that Gonzalo's utopia is inadequate, Shakespeare provides examples of what Elizabethans regarded among the worst of sins, mutiny. Antonio, an august villain, plots with Sebastian, the King's brother, to kill Alonso and Gonzalo in their sleep. This constitutes a reenactment of Antonio's earlier plot against Prospero, "thus drawing it out of the past and placing it before us in the present."[85] In a harsh speech Antonio urges that Sebastian can easily be installed on the throne in Alonso's place:

> There be that can rule Naples
> As well as he that sleeps; lords that can prate
> As amply and unnecessarily
> As this Gonzalo. I myself could make
> A chough [crow] of as deep chat.
>   (II, 1, 262–266)

But thanks to the invisible Ariel, the sleepers are awakened before the villainy can be carried out. Although Shakespeare has assured us that Antonio and Sebastian will be thwarted, the fact remains that they have been bent on fratricide and regicide.[86]

On the political level Caliban serves as a kind of comic counterpart to Antonio and Sebastian.[87] Ariel submits, however reluctantly, to his master's orderly rule and ultimately earns his freedom. But Caliban remains intractable to the end. Prospero is both disappointed and angry:

> A devil, a born devil, on whose nature
> Nurture can never stick! on whom my pains,
> Humanely taken, all, all lost, quite lost!
> And as with age his body uglier grows,
> So his mind cankers.
>   (IV, 1, 188–192)

Arguing that Prospero has cheated him of the island, Caliban, who embodies "the animal qualities of physical man,"[88] deserts him and kneels before a new king, the drunken butler Stephano. "That's a brave god and bears celestial liquor" (II, 2, 121). In what seems to be a parody of Gonzalo's vision of the Golden Age, in which men will be idle, Caliban sings a wild song celebrating his grotesque concept of freedom as a regime in which he will do no work:

> No more dams I'll make for fish,
>> Nor fetch in firing
>> At requiring,
> Nor scrape trenchering, nor wash dish.
>> 'Ban, 'Ban, Ca—Caliban
>> Has a new master. Get a new man.
>> (II, 2, 184–189)

Like Antonio and Sebastian, the besotted Caliban hatches a plot to kill a ruler in his sleep. The monster's half-articulate brutality is terrifying:

> There thou mayst brain him,
> Having first seiz'd his books, or with a log
> Batter his skull, or paunch him with a stake,
> Or cut his wesand [windpipe] with thy knife. Remember
> First to possess his books; for without them
> He's but a sot, as I am, nor hath not
> One spirit to command.
>> (III, 2, 96–102)

Caliban is correct, for Prospero's books indeed distinguish him from the monster and confer on him the power to govern. Once again, however, conspiracy is frustrated by Prospero and Ariel. Authority, bolstered by intelligence and learning, has withstood the threat of rebellion.

Another major theme of *The Tempest* is the power of art, particularly as it functions in a universe that some would characterize as morally indifferent.[89] Ariel may be regarded as the force of imagination, inviting Ferdinand and the audience in the theater to join him in the world of make-believe. "Come unto these yellow sands," Ariel sings (I, 2, 375–386); and a moment later, he implicitly describes how poetry, through metaphor, transforms grim reality "into something rich and strange":

> Full fadom five thy father lies;
>> Of his bones are coral made;
> Those are pearls that were his eyes;
>> Nothing of him that doth fade
> But doth suffer a sea-change

Into something rich and strange.
Sea nymphs hourly ring his knell:
                    Ding-dong.
Hark! now I hear them—Ding-dong bell.
                    (I, 2, 396–404)[90]

To the poetic imagination nothing is lost, not even in death.

In contrast, Caliban could represent nature in its most primitive form—nature, to quote from Frank Kermode's excellent critical introduction, "without benefit of nurture; Nature, opposed to an Art which is man's power over the created world and over himself; nature divorced from grace, or the senses without the mind."[91] Yet Caliban, unappreciated though he may be (by Prospero as distinguished from Shakespeare), somehow remains in touch with the transcendent world of the supernatural.[92] He can at times produce poetry that is hauntingly beautiful:

Be not afeard. The isle is full of noises,
Sounds and sweet airs that give delight and hurt not.
Sometimes a thousand twangling instruments
Will hum about mine ears; and sometime voices
That, if I then had wak'd after long sleep,
Will make me sleep again; and then, in dreaming,
The clouds methought would open and show riches
Ready to drop upon me, that, when I wak'd,
I cried to dream again.
                    (III, 2, 144–152)

Caliban has been called "the amoral, appetitive, suffering Self in all of us."[93] We can neither accept him nor cast him out. A. D. Nuttall, in a masterful analysis, places him in that remote children's world that plays a negligible role in our adult lives, a world dimly remembered in "an intellectual half-light of bites, pinches, nettle-stings, terrors, cupboard-love, glimpses of extraordinary and inexplicable beauty."[94]

Most important, perhaps, *The Tempest* is a play about forgiveness. As his foes are being routed, Prospero is happy. "At this hour," he declares, "lie at my mercy all mine enemies" (IV, 1, 263–264). But he realizes that his responsibility as a sovereign extends beyond the exercise of power. Ariel feels sorry for the evildoers and for Gonzalo, who are imprisoned in Prospero's grove, and urges his master to take pity:

His [Gonzalo's] tears run down his beard like winter's drops
From eaves of reeds. Your charm so strongly works 'em,
That if you now beheld them, your affections
Would become tender.
                    (V, 1, 16–19)

Prospero assures Ariel that, as a human being, he is obliged to show more sympathy than a mere spirit:

> Hast thou, which art but air, a touch, a feeling
> Of their afflictions, and shall not myself,
> One of their kind, that relish all as sharply
> Passion as they, be kindlier mov'd than thou art?
>
> (V, 1, 21–24)

Then, in a crucial passage, he indicates that as a king and as a man he has passed a most difficult test. He announces that he will forgive his enemies *in spite of* his anger:

> Though with their high wrongs I am struck to th' quick,
> Yet with my nobler reason 'gainst my fury
> Do I take part. The rarer action is
> In virtue than in vengeance. They being penitent,
> The sole drift of my purpose doth extend
> Not a frown further. Go, release them, Ariel.
>
> (V, 1, 25–30)[95]

By accepting and forgiving the weaknesses of his fellow human beings, Prospero displays a quality that had been missing from his spectacular artistry: love. He thereby confirms his own humanity.[96]

Prospero obviously dominates the play, and he has inevitably attracted considerable critical attention. As noted earlier, he has been identified as a noble practitioner of white magic (in contrast with Caliban's mother, Sycorax, who practiced black magic).[97] Even more conspicuously than Duke Vincentio in *Measure for Measure,* he is the stage manager par excellence, literally and figuratively the traditional masque presenter.[98] He has often been interpreted allegorically. According to one view, which gained favor with nineteenth-century romantic critics and still has adherents, Prospero is God; and to carry the symbolism further, Ariel in some discussions becomes the Angel of the Lord, Caliban the Devil, and Miranda the Celestial Bride.[99] More commonly, however, Prospero is taken to be Shakespeare himself (or, at least, the prototype of the creative artist), with *The. Tempest* as a whole emerging as his "artistic autobiography."[100]

That Prospero is to some extent Shakespeare has been argued mainly on the basis of three great speeches in which the magician crowns his work of a lifetime and wearily renounces his art. The first is spoken as Prospero, suddenly remembering "that foul conspiracy / Of the beast Caliban and his confederates" (IV, 1, 139–140), dismisses the spirit-actors who have presented a wedding masque in honor of Ferdinand and

Miranda. Ferdinand observes that Prospero is strangely disturbed, and
Miranda replies that she has never before seen him "touch'd with anger
so distemper'd" (IV, 1, 145). Prospero reassures Ferdinand, then begins
what amounts to an elegy:

> Our revels now are ended. These our actors,
> As I foretold you, were all spirits and
> Are melted into air, into thin air;
> And, like the baseless fabric of this vision,
> The cloud-capp'd towers, the gorgeous palaces,
> The solemn temples, the great globe itself,
> Yea, all which it inherit, shall dissolve,
> And, like this insubstantial pageant faded,
> Leave not a rack [cloudy vapor] behind. We are such stuff
> As dreams are made on, and our little life
> Is rounded with a sleep.
>
> (IV, 1, 148–158)

Apart from the brief reference to Caliban, we are not told in so many
words the reason for Prospero's abrupt breaking-off of the revels. But
the episode certainly conveys a sense of what John Russell Brown calls
the "turbulence at the roots of life," based in part upon Prospero's
awareness that all his power as a king and as an artist cannot finally
keep evil under control and that, furthermore, nothing endures—not
even the artist, whose reality, like everyone else's, is illusory.[101]

In the second speech, Prospero makes a circle with his magic staff
and addresses the countless "elves of hills, brooks, standing lakes, and
groves" (V, 1, 32–33) who have assisted him in his manifold endeavors.
Some feel that Prospero's review of his magical accomplishments is a
retrospective glance at Shakespeare's own poetic achievements over his
long career:

> I have bedimm'd
> The noontide sun, call'd forth the mutinous winds,
> And 'twixt the green sea and the azur'd vault
> Set roaring war; to the dread rattling thunder
> Have I given fire and rifted Jove's stout oak
> With his own bolt; the strong-bas'd promontory
> Have I made shake and by the spurs pluck'd up
> The pine and cedar; graves at my command
> Have wak'd their sleepers, op'd, and let 'em forth
> By my so potent art.
>
> (V, 1, 41–50)

"But this rough magic," he continues, "I here abjure" (V, 1, 50–51):

> I'll break my staff,
> Bury it certain fadoms in the earth,
> And deeper than did ever plummet sound
> I'll drown my book.
>
> (V, 1, 54–57)

In drowning his book Prospero is anticipating his resumption of the practical responsibility of governing in the real world from which art offers no lasting escape. As John Dixon Hunt observes, "In a magnificent valediction to this 'so potent Art,' that celebrates its power as it admits its limitations, Prospero signals his return to humanity." "In a sense," to quote Theodore Spencer, "his temporary control of the spirit world has also been a purgation.... His wisdom makes him return to his rightful place as a governor of himself, and as a governor, through his dukedom, of other human beings as well."[102] On the autobiographical level, Shakespeare (like Chaucer, in his celebrated Retraction at the end of *The Canterbury Tales*) may have arrived at a point in his intellectual and spiritual development where even his art had to play a subordinate role.

Prospero's third major speech is the extraordinary epilogue, in which the conventional *plaudite* (a request for applause spoken by a player at the end of a performance) is transformed into a mysterious and deeply suggestive ritual. In language of remarkable simplicity, the hero, once a mighty magician but now an ordinary mortal impersonated by an ordinary actor, pleads for the support of his audience:

> Now my charms are all o'erthrown,
> And what strength I have's mine own,
> Which is most faint.
>
> (Epilogue, 1–3)

He cannot leave the island until the spectators release him with the help of their good hands and gentle breath:

> Now I want
> Spirits to enforce, art to enchant;
> And my ending is despair
> Unless I be reliev'd by prayer,
> Which pierces so that it assaults
> Mercy itself and frees all faults.
> As you from crimes would pardon'd be,
> Let your indulgence set me free.
>
> (Epilogue, 13–20)

Shakespeare thus frees the characters, himself, and his audience from illusion. Or perhaps the audience itself becomes part of the illusion as it merges its identity with that of the actor, the character he represents, and the dramatist who created the whole "insubstantial pageant" that briefly held the stage. Anne Righter likens the atmosphere to the last paintings of William Turner (1775–1851), in which the ship becomes indistinguishable from its surroundings.[103] *The Tempest* may be Shakespeare's most profound statement about the meaning of his art.

As with other interpretations, one should take the autobiographical approach with caution and restraint, for *The Tempest* defies analysis. But it does seem to embody with transcendent craftsmanship and wisdom much of what its author found worth saying in some thirty-seven comedies, histories, tragedies, and dramatic romances. Here are the great themes of love, kingship, human weakness, and divine forgiveness—all welded unobtrusively into a single unified work of art. For that reason *The Tempest* may be the most resplendent of Shakespearean miracles.

NOTES

1. See, for example, Diana T. Childress, "Are Shakespeare's Late Plays Really Romances?" in *Shakespeare's Late Plays: Essays in Honor of Charles Crow,* eds. Richard C. Tobias and Paul G. Zolbrod (Athens: Ohio University Press, 1974), pp. 44–55.

2. F. E. Halliday, *The Poetry of Shakespeare's Plays* (London: Duckworth, 1954), pp. 173–174.

3. See Kenneth Muir, "Theophanies in the Last Plays," in *Shakespeare's Late Plays,* eds. Tobias and Zolbrod, pp. 32–43.

4. Northrop Frye, *A Natural Perspective: The Development of Shakespearean Comedy and Romance* (New York: Columbia University Press, 1965), pp. 1–33.

5. Lytton Strachey, "Shakespeare's Final Period," *Books and Characters* (New York: Harcourt, 1922), p. 64; Frank Kermode, *William Shakespeare: The Final Plays* (London: Longmans, 1963), p. 8; Halliday, *Poetry of Shakespeare's Plays,* p. 168; Ashley H. Thorndike, *The Influence of Beaumont and Fletcher on Shakespeare* (Worcester, Mass.: Wood, 1901); Richard Proudfoot, "Shakespeare and the New Dramatists of the King's Men," in *Later Shakespeare,* eds. John Russell Brown and Bernard Harris, Stratford-upon-Avon Studies 8 (London: Edward Arnold, 1966), pp. 235–261; G. E. Bentley, "Shakespeare and the Blackfriars Theatre," *Shakespeare Survey* 1 (1948): 38–50; Carol Gesner, *Shakespeare and the Greek Romance: A Study of Origins* (Lexington: University of Kentucky Press, 1970); Hallett Smith, *Shakespeare's Romances: A Study of Some Ways of the Imagination* (San Marino, Calif.: The Huntington Library, 1972), pp. 1–20; E. M. W. Tillyard, *Shakespeare's Last Plays* (London: Chatto & Windus, 1938), p. 26; E. C. Pettet, *Shakespeare and the Romance Tradition* (London: Staples, 1949), p. 174; G. Wilson Knight, "Myth and Miracle," *The Crown of Life* (London: Oxford University Press, 1947),

p. 30; D. G. James, "The Failure of the Ballad-Makers," *Scepticism and Poetry: An Essay on the Poetic Imagination* (London: Allen and Unwin, 1937), pp. 205–241.

I have not seen Frances Yates, *Shakespeare's Last Plays: A New Approach* (London: Routledge & Kegan Paul, 1975).

6. Philip Edwards, "Shakespeare's Romances: 1900–1957," *Shakespeare Survey* 11 (1958): 1–18 (quotation from p. 17). Following Edwards's suggestion, Joan Hartwig has explored the plays as tragicomedies. See *Shakespeare's Tragicomic Vision* (Baton Rouge: Louisiana State University Press, 1972).

7. A useful review of four recent books on the romances is Norman Rabkin, "Shakespeare's Golden Worlds," *Modern Language Quarterly* 35 (1974): 187–198.

8. On the text, authorship, and date, see E. K. Chambers, *William Shakespeare: A Study of Facts and Problems*, 2 vols. (Oxford: Clarendon, 1930), 1: 518–528; the New Cambridge *Pericles*, ed. J. C. Maxwell (Cambridge: Cambridge University Press, 1956; 1959), pp. ix–xxv, 88–97; the New Arden *Pericles*, ed. F. D. Hoeniger (Cambridge: Harvard University Press, 1963), pp. xxiii–lxv; Kenneth Muir, "The Problem of *Pericles*," *English Studies* 30 (1949): 65–83; Philip Edwards, "An Approach to the Problem of *Pericles*," *Shakespeare Survey* 5 (1952): 25–49.

9. The question of sources is bound up with the authorship problem. In addition to the New Cambridge and New Arden editions, see Kenneth Muir, *Shakespeare's Sources* (London: Methuen, 1957), pp. 225–231; Geoffrey Bullough, *Narrative and Dramatic Sources of Shakespeare*, 8 vols. (New York: Columbia University Press, 1957–1975), 6: 349–564; and an older work, Albert H. Smyth, *Shakespeare's Pericles and Apollonius of Tyre: A Study in Comparative Literature* (Philadelphia: MacCalla, 1898), especially pp. 47–69.

10. Frye, *A Natural Perspective*, pp. 31–32.

11. Francis Berry, "Word and Picture in the Final Plays," in *Later Shakespeare*, eds. Brown and Harris, pp. 81–101. On Gower, see also Bertrand Evans, *Shakespeare's Comedies* (Oxford: Clarendon, 1960), pp. 221–245; Douglas L. Peterson, *Time, Tide, and Tempest: A Study of Shakespeare's Romances* (San Marino, Calif.: The Huntington Library, 1973), pp. 72–73; Anne Righter, *Shakespeare and the Idea of the Play* (London: Chatto & Windus, 1962), p. 193.

12. See Knight, *The Crown of Life*, p. 25.

13. See John Arthos, "*Pericles, Prince of Tyre:* A Study in the Dramatic Use of Romantic Narrative," *Shakespeare Quarterly* 4 (1953): 257–270.

14. Clifford Leech, "The Structure of the Last Plays," *Shakespeare Survey* 11 (1958): 19–30.

15. See, for example, Donald A. Stauffer, *Shakespeare's World of Images: The Development of His Moral Ideas* (New York: Norton, 1949), pp. 266–278; John F. Danby, *Poets on Fortune's Hill: Studies in Sidney, Shakespeare, Beaumont and Fletcher* (London: Faber, 1952), pp. 87–103; J. M. S. Tompkins, "Why Pericles?" *Review of English Studies*, n. s. 3 (1952): 315–324; Hoeniger, in New Arden *Pericles*, pp. lxix–xci; Gerard A. Barker, "Themes and Variations in Shakespeare's *Pericles*," *English Studies* 44 (1963): 401–414.

Dissenting from this view is Thelma N. Greenfield, "A Re-examination of the 'Patient' Pericles," *Shakespeare Studies,* ed. J. Leeds Barroll, 3 (1967): 51–61, which assesses the hero as a wily Greek traveler who knows when to retreat from misfortune. See also Peterson, *Time, Tide, and Tempest,* pp. 76–77.

16. See D. R. C. Marsh, *The Recurring Miracle: A Study of Cymbeline and the Last Plays* (Lincoln: University of Nebraska Press, 1962), p. 13–23.

17. For an elaborate working out of the symbolism, see G. Wilson Knight, *The Shakespearian Tempest,* 3d ed. (New York: Barnes & Noble, 1960) and "The Writing of *Pericles,*" in *The Crown of Life,* pp. 32–75. On the sea metaphor, see also J. P. Brockbank, "*Pericles* and the Dream of Immortality," *Shakespeare Survey* 24 (1971): 105–116.

18. For a fine analysis of III, 1, see Danby, *Poets on Fortune's Hill,* pp. 92–97.

19. See C. L. Barber, "'Thou that beget'st him that did thee beget': Transformation in *Pericles* and *The Winter's Tale,*" *Shakespeare Survey* 22 (1969): 59–67.

20. See, for example, Howard Felperin, "This Great Miracle: *Pericles,*" *Shakespearean Romance* (Princeton: Princeton University Press, 1972), pp. 143–176 and Hoeniger, in the New Arden edition, pp. lxxxviii–xci. Knight (*The Crown of Life,* p. 65) sees an analogy with St. Paul.

21. Stauffer, *Shakespeare's World of Images,* p. 275.

22. On the text and date, see Chambers, *William Shakespeare,* 1: 484–487; W. W. Greg, *The Shakespeare First Folio* (Oxford: Clarendon, 1955), pp. 412–414; the New Arden *Cymbeline,* ed. J. M. Nosworthy (Cambridge: Harvard University Press, 1955), pp. xii–xvii; the New Cambridge edition, ed. J. C. Maxwell (Cambridge: Cambridge University Press, 1960), pp. xi–xv, 125–128. The authenticity of the Vision has been elaborately defended by Knight, *The Crown of Life,* pp. 168–202; by Nosworthy, New Arden edition, pp. xxxiv–xxxvii; and by Maxwell, New Cambridge edition, pp. xi–xv. In the New Cambridge edition, pp. vii–x, Dover Wilson argues against the Vision's authenticity.

23. On the sources of *Cymbeline,* see the New Arden edition, pp. xvii–xxxvii, 197–216; Muir, *Shakespeare's Sources,* pp. 231–240; the New Cambridge *Cymbeline,* pp. xv–xxvii; and Bullough, *Sources,* 8:3–111.

24. See Knight, *The Crown of Life,* p. 139 and J. P. Brockbank, "History and Histrionics in *Cymbeline,*" *Shakespeare Survey* 11 (1958): 42–49.

25. See Carroll Camden, "The Elizabethan Imogen," *Rice Institute Pamphlet* 38, no. 1 (1951): 1–17.

26. Evans, *Shakespeare's Comedies,* p. 262.

27. Peterson, *Time, Tide, and Tempest,* p. 111; Maxwell, New Cambridge *Cymbeline,* pp. xxxvii–xxxviii.

28. On civility ("inborn gentleness") in *Cymbeline,* see W. Gordon Zeeveld, *The Temper of Shakespeare's Thought* (New Haven: Yale University Press, 1974), pp. 237–241.

29. Marsh, *The Recurring Miracle,* pp. 81–85.

30. *Johnson on Shakespeare,* ed. Arthur Sherbo, Vols. 7 and 8 of The Yale Edition of the Works of Samuel Johnson (New Haven: Yale University Press, 1968), p. 908.

31. Edwin Wilson, ed., *Shaw on Shakespeare* (London: Cassell, 1962), p. 50. Shaw wrote these words in 1896. By 1945 he had come to see merit in the play (including the last act, which he rewrote); see *Shaw on Shakespeare,* pp. 58 ff.

32. Arthur C. Kirsch, "*Cymbeline* and Coterie Dramaturgy," *ELH* 34 (1967): 285–306.

33. Harley Granville-Barker, *Prefaces to Shakespeare,* 2 vols. (Princeton: Princeton University Press, 1946–1947), 1: 466–467.

34. See Maxwell, New Cambridge *Cymbeline,* pp. xxxiv–xxxv. See also Leonard Powlick, "*Cymbeline* and the Comedy of Anticlimax," *Shakespeare's Late Plays,* eds. Tobias and Zolbrod, pp. 131–141.

35. See F. D. Hoeniger, "Irony and Romance in *Cymbeline,*" *Studies in English Literature, 1500–1900* 2 (1962): 219–228.

36. Brockbank, "History and Histrionics in *Cymbeline.*"

37. See Robin Moffet, "*Cymbeline* and the Nativity," *Shakespeare Quarterly* 13 (1962): 207–218; Emrys Jones, "Stuart *Cymbeline,*" *Essays in Criticism* 11 (1961): 84–99; Bernard Harris, " 'What's past is prologue': *Cymbeline* and *Henry VIII,*" *Later Shakespeare,* eds. Brown and Harris, pp. 203–233. For example, Milford Haven would have immediately suggested to a Jacobean audience the place where the Earl of Richmond (Henry VII) had landed in 1485 in order to wrest the throne from Richard III at the Battle of Bosworth. But Smith (*Shakespeare's Romances,* pp. 211–215) questions the topicality of the play.

38. William B. Thorne, "*Cymbeline:* 'Lopp'd Branches' and the Concept of Regeneration," *Shakespeare Quarterly* 20 (1969): 143–159.

39. Robert Grams Hunter, *Shakespeare and the Comedy of Forgiveness* (New York: Columbia University Press, 1965), p. 159. Hunter (pp. 176–184) also points out interesting parallels between *Cymbeline* and the medieval miracle play *Ostes, Roy d'Espaigne.* Among other studies that stress a theological or allegorical interpretation, see Knight, *The Crown of Life,* pp. 129–202 and Homer D. Swander, "*Cymbeline:* Religious Idea and Dramatic Design," in *Pacific Coast Studies in Shakespeare,* eds. Waldo F. McNeir and Thelma N. Greenfield (Eugene: University of Oregon Books, 1966), pp. 248–262.

40. See, for example, Irving Ribner, "Shakespeare and Legendary History: *Lear* and *Cymbeline,*" *Shakespeare Quarterly* 7 (1956): 47–52 and F. R. Leavis, "The Criticism of Shakespeare's Late Plays: A Caveat," *Scrutiny* 10 (1942): 339–345. The Leavis essay is reprinted in his book *The Common Pursuit* (London: Chatto & Windus, 1952), pp. 173–181, and is included in Anne Ridler, ed., *Shakespeare Criticism: 1935–1960* (London: Oxford University Press, 1963), pp. 132–141.

41. Nosworthy, in the New Arden edition, pp. xlviii–lxii.

42. Maxwell, in the New Cambridge edition, pp. xxvii–xlii.

43. On the text and date, see the New Cambridge edition, eds. A. Quiller-Couch and John Dover Wilson (Cambridge: Cambridge University Press, 1931), pp. vii–xii, 109–127; Chambers, *William Shakespeare,* 1: 487–490; Greg, *The Shakespeare First Folio,* pp. 415–417; the New Arden edition, ed. J. H. P. Pafford, 4th ed. (Cambridge: Harvard University Press, 1963), pp. xv–xxvii.

44. On sources, see the New Arden edition, pp. xxvii–xxxvii, 181–225; Muir,

Shakespeare's Sources, pp. 240–251; Bullough, *Sources,* 8: 115–233; E. A. J. Honigmann, "Secondary Sources of *The Winter's Tale,*" *Philological Quarterly* 34 (1955): 27–38.

45. On Time and his speech, see Fitzroy Pyle, *The Winter's Tale: A Commentary on the Structure* (New York: Barnes & Noble, 1969), pp. 71–75; David Young, *The Heart's Forest: A Study of Shakespeare's Pastoral Plays* (New Haven: Yale University Press, 1972), pp. 133–145.

46. For an excellent scene-by-scene analysis, see Pyle, *The Winter's Tale.*

47. See Joan Hartwig, "The Tragicomic Perspective of *The Winter's Tale,*" *ELH* 37 (1970): 12–36. Similarly, Paulina is in part a stock comic shrew and then a stock confessor.

48. Nevill Coghill, "Six Points of Stage-craft in *The Winter's Tale,*" *Shakespeare Survey* 11 (1958): 31–41; Tillyard, *Shakespeare's Last Plays,* p. 41; William H. Matchett, "Some Dramatic Techniques in *The Winter's Tale,*" *Shakespeare Survey* 22 (1969): 93–107.

49. See Northrop Frye, *A Natural Perspective,* p. 114; Thomas McFarland, *Shakespeare's Pastoral Comedy* (Chapel Hill: University of North Carolina Press, 1972), pp. 122–131 passim.

50. Peter Lindenbaum observes that Leontes and, in Act IV, Polixenes resent and fear the intrusion of sexuality upon their innocent world of the "boy eternal." See his "Time, Sexual Love, and the Uses of Pastoral in *The Winter's Tale,*" *Modern Language Quarterly* 33 (1972): 3–22.

51. This image is ably discussed in the context of the disease and poison images in the play; see Wolfgang H. Clemen, *The Development of Shakespeare's Imagery* (Cambridge: Harvard University Press, 1951), pp. 196–198.

52. Halliday, *The Poetry of Shakespeare's Plays,* pp. 179–180.

53. Berry, "Word and Picture," pp. 92–95. See also Felperin, *Shakespearean Romance,* pp. 232–240 passim.

54. See McFarland, *Shakespeare's Pastoral Comedy,* p. 137 and Marsh, *The Recurring Miracle,* pp. 150–154. On structural parallels between the two parts, see especially Ernest Schanzer, "The Structural Pattern of *The Winter's Tale,*" *Review of English Literature* 5:2 (April 1964): 72–82.

55. See F. David Hoeniger, "The Meaning of *The Winter's Tale,*" *University of Toronto Quarterly* 20 (1950–1951): 11–26. Carol Thomas Neely ("*The Winter's Tale:* The Triumph of Speech," *Studies in English Literature, 1500–1900* 15 [1975]: 321–338) notes contrasting styles of speech in Sicilia and Bohemia.

56. See Stanley Wells, "Shakespeare and Romance," *Later Shakespeare,* eds. Brown and Harris, p. 66.

57. Coghill, "Six Points of Stage-craft," p. 34. See also Dennis Biggins, " 'Exit pursued by a Beare': A Problem in *The Winter's Tale,*" *Shakespeare Quarterly* 13 (1962): 3–13; John Anthony Williams, *The Natural Work of Art: The Experience of Romance in Shakespeare's Winter's Tale* (Cambridge: Harvard University Press, 1967), pp. 5–9; Matchett, "Some Dramatic Techniques," pp. 98–102.

58. Leavis, "The Criticism of Shakespeare's Late Plays: A Caveat," in *The Common Pursuit,* p. 180.

59. Knight, *The Crown of Life,* p. 106.

60. On the sexuality of Hermione and Perdita, see (in addition to Lindenbaum, "Time, Sexual Love, and the Uses of Pastoral") Michael Taylor, "Shakespeare's *The Winter's Tale:* Speaking in the Freedom of Knowledge," *The Critical Quarterly* 14 (1972): 49–56.

61. On the floral scene, especially the Polixenes-Perdita debate, see Pyle, *The Winter's Tale,* pp. 80–97; Peterson, *Time, Tide, and Tempest,* pp. 169–190; McFarland, *Shakespeare's Pastoral Comedy,* pp. 132–139. Pafford (New Arden edition, pp. lx–lxi) advises against making too much of the debate.

62. See Adrien Bonjour, "The Final Scene of *The Winter's Tale,*" *English Studies* 33 (1952): 193–208; Matchett, "Some Dramatic Techniques," pp. 102–107; Michael Goldman, *Shakespeare and the Energies of Drama* (Princeton: Princeton University Press, 1972), pp. 129–130, n. 2.

63. According to John Taylor ("The Patience of *The Winter's Tale,*" *Essays in Criticism* 23 [1973]: 333–356), we have learned from the pattern of previous events in the play to remain patient and await the miraculous.

64. On this point, see (among others) Pyle, *The Winter's Tale,* pp. 3–8, 118 ff.; Robert Egan, *Drama within Drama: Shakespeare's Sense of His Art in King Lear, The Winter's Tale, and The Tempest* (New York: Columbia University Press, 1975), pp. 56–89; Righter, *Shakespeare and the Idea of the Play,* pp. 196–201; Young, *The Heart's Forest,* pp. 120–133.

65. S. R. Maveety, "What Shakespeare Did with *Pandosto:* An Interpretation of *The Winter's Tale,*" in *Pacific Coast Studies in Shakespeare,* pp. 263–279; J. A. Bryant, Jr., *Hippolyta's View: Some Christian Aspects of Shakespeare's Plays* (Lexington: University of Kentucky Press, 1961), pp. 210–216. See also S. L. Bethell, *The Winter's Tale: A Study* (London: Staples, 1947); Hunter, *Shakespeare and the Comedy of Forgiveness,* pp. 185–203; and the important essay by Knight, in *The Crown of Life,* pp. 76–128.

66. For more orthodox views of Autolycus, see Lee Sheridan Cox, "The Role of Autolycus in *The Winter's Tale,*" *Studies in English Literature, 1500–1900* 9 (1969): 283–301; and Pyle, *The Winter's Tale,* pp. 78–79.

67. Roland Mushat Frye, *Shakespeare and Christian Doctrine* (Princeton: Princeton University Press, 1963), pp. 43, 271.

68. Alfred Harbage, *William Shakespeare: A Reader's Guide* (New York: Noonday, 1963), p. 460.

69. See Inga-Stina Ewbank, "The Triumph of Time in *The Winter's Tale,*" *Review of English Literature* 5: 2 (April 1964): 83–100. See also Bonjour, "The Final Scene of *The Winter's Tale*" and Lindenbaum, "Time, Sexual Love, and the Uses of Pastoral."

70. On the text and date, see the New Cambridge *The Tempest,* eds. A. Quiller-Couch and John Dover Wilson (Cambridge: Cambridge University Press, 1921), pp. xxix–xliv, 79–85; Chambers, *William Shakespeare,* 1: 490–494; Greg, *The Shakespeare First Folio,* pp. 418–421; the New Arden edition, ed. Frank Kermode, 6th ed. (Cambridge: Harvard University Press, 1958), pp. xi–xxiv, 161–165.

71. See Carol Gesner, "*The Tempest* as Pastoral Romance," *Shakespeare Quarterly* 10 (1959): 531–539; K. M. Lea, *Italian Popular Comedy,* 2 vols. (Oxford: Oxford University Press, 1934), 1: 201–212, 2: 442–453. See also Young, *The Heart's Forest,* pp. 146–159.

72. Leo Marx, "Shakespeare's American Fable," *The Machine in the Garden: Technology and the Pastoral Ideal in America* (New York: Oxford University Press, 1964), pp. 34–72.

73. See Philip Brockbank, "*The Tempest:* Conventions of Art and Empire," *Later Shakespeare,* eds. Brown and Harris, pp. 183–201. See also Kermode, in the New Arden edition, pp. xxv–xxxiv.

74. On sources, see also Muir, *Shakespeare's Sources,* pp. 260–261; and Bullough, *Sources,* 8: 237–339.

75. See Hallett Smith, "Introduction: *The Tempest* as a Kaleidoscope," in *Twentieth Century Interpretations of The Tempest,* ed. Hallett Smith (Englewood Cliffs, N.J.: Prentice-Hall, 1969), pp. 3–4. (This is a good collection of essays.) See also *The Tempest,* ed. Anne Righter (Harmondsworth, Middlesex: Penguin, 1968), p. 15.

76. D. G. James, *The Dream of Prospero* (Oxford: Clarendon, 1967), pp. 27–44.

77. See F. D. Hoeniger, "Prospero's Storm and Miracle," *Shakespeare Quarterly* 7:1 (Winter 1956): 33–38.

78. See Walter Clyde Curry, "Sacerdotal Science in Shakespeare's *The Tempest,*" *Shakespeare's Philosophical Patterns,* 2d ed. (Baton Rouge: Louisiana State University Press, 1959), pp. 163–199. See also Robert Hunter West, *The Invisible World: A Study of Pneumatology in Elizabethan Drama* (Athens: University of Georgia Press, 1939), especially pp. 41–45. A more recent work is David Woodman, *White Magic and English Renaissance Drama* (Rutherford, N.J.: Fairleigh Dickinson University Press, 1973), pp. 73–86.

79. John Dover Wilson, *The Essential Shakespeare* (Cambridge: Cambridge University Press, 1932), p. 145; Bonamy Dobrée, "*The Tempest,*" *Essays and Studies,* n. s. 5 (1952): 13–25 (quotation from p. 25). The play, says John Russell Brown, is "unassertive"; see his *Shakespeare: The Tempest* (London: Edward Arnold, 1969), p. 43.

80. Righter, in Penguin edition, pp. 19–22, 53.

81. James, *The Dream of Prospero,* p. 171.

82. J. Dover Wilson, *The Meaning of The Tempest* (Newcastle-upon-Tyne: Literary and Philosophical Society, 1936), p. 18.

83. Harry Levin, *The Myth of the Golden Age in the Renaissance* (London: Faber, 1969), p. 188; see also pp. 125–127. On Gonzalo's paradox, see also Melvin Seiden, "Utopianism in *The Tempest,*" *Modern Language Quarterly* 31 (1970): 3–21.

84. Felperin (*Shakespearean Romance,* pp. 262–265) suggests that Prospero is purging Ferdinand of the Caliban within (Caliban having tried to rape Miranda). On the idea of control in the play, see Wells, "Shakespeare and Romance," pp. 74–75.

85. Tillyard, *Shakespeare's Last Plays,* p. 51.

86. On the means whereby Shakespeare exploits our awareness to allay anxiety, see Evans, *Shakespeare's Comedies,* pp. 316–317. McFarland (*Shakespeare's Pastoral Comedy,* pp. 146–175) writes of the impotence of evil in Prospero's paradise.

87. The name Caliban is often seen as an anagram of *cannibal.* Chambers

(*William Shakespeare,* 1: 494) derives the name from the Gypsy *cauliban,* "blackness."

88. Marsh, *The Recurring Miracle,* p. 166.

89. See Mike Frank, "Shakespeare's Existential Comedy," *Shakespeare's Late Plays,* eds. Tobias and Zolbrod, pp. 142–165.

90. Reuben Brower suggests that metamorphosis, or magical transformation, is the key metaphor of the play. See "The Heresy of Plot," *English Institute Essays, 1951,* ed. Alan S. Downer (New York: Columbia University Press, 1952), pp. 44–69 and especially "The Mirror of Analogy: *The Tempest,*" in *The Fields of Light* (New York: Oxford University Press, 1951), pp. 95–122.

91. Kermode, in the New Arden edition, pp. xxiv–xxv. On the art-nature opposition, see also Young, *The Heart's Forest,* pp. 180–191.

92. See James, *The Dream of Prospero,* pp. 113–114.

93. Egan, *Drama within Drama,* p. 95.

94. A. D. Nuttall, *Two Concepts of Allegory: A Study of The Tempest and the Logic of Allegorical Expression* (New York: Barnes & Noble, 1967), p. 140.

95. The passage may echo Montaigne's essay "Of Crueltie"; see Eleanor Prosser, "Shakespeare, Montaigne, and *the Rarer Action,*" *Shakespeare Studies,* ed. J. Leeds Barroll, 1 (1965): 261–264.

96. See Egan, *Drama within Drama,* p. 112; Peterson, *Time, Tide, and Tempest,* pp. 244–245.

97. Dissenting from this view is D'Orsay W. Pearson, who maintains that Prospero is not a beneficent theurgist but a "potentially damned sorcerer" who ultimately repents and seeks divine forgiveness. See " 'Unless I Be Reliev'd by Prayer': *The Tempest* in Perspective," *Shakespeare Studies,* ed. J. Leeds Barroll, 7 (1974): 253–282. In a somewhat similar vein, Felperin (*Shakespearean Romance,* pp. 276–277) says that Prospero learns the danger of playing God and redeems the Faustus in himself.

98. See Enid Welsford, *The Court Masque* (Cambridge: Cambridge University Press, 1927), pp. 335–349.

99. The most famous proponent of this view was Colin Still, whose book *Shakespeare's Mystery Play* (1921) was revised and reissued as *The Timeless Theme* (London: Nicholson & Watson, 1936). For a superb summary and critique of nineteenth-century allegorical interpretations, see Nuttall, *Two Concepts of Allegory,* especially pp. 1–14.

100. Knight, *The Crown of Life,* p. 225.

101. Brown, *Shakespeare: The Tempest,* p. 40 and passim. For an analysis of this speech, see Nuttall, *Two Concepts of Allegory,* pp. 146–151. See also Welsford, *The Court Masque,* pp. 342–345 and L. C. Knights, "*The Tempest,*" *Shakespeare's Late Plays,* eds. Tobias and Zolbrod, pp. 15–31.

102. John Dixon Hunt, *A Critical Commentary on Shakespeare's The Tempest* (London: Macmillan, 1968), p. 37; Theodore Spencer, *Shakespeare and the Nature of Man* (New York: Macmillan, 1942), pp. 198–199. See also James, *The Dream of Prospero,* pp. 124–153. Prospero, says James, had lived in a dream, from which he has now awakened.

103. Righter, *Shakespeare and the Idea of the Play,* p. 202. See also Goldman, *Shakespeare and the Energies of Drama,* pp. 147–150.

Postscript

The Two Noble Kinsmen

In addition to the thirty-seven plays (including *Pericles*) commonly regarded as part of the canon, Shakespeare has at one time or another been credited with the authorship of many other dramatic works.[1] Apart from his probable contribution to *Sir Thomas More* (see p. 42), he may have had a hand in *Edward III* (1595); and, having possibly shared the authorship of *Henry VIII* with John Fletcher, he may have collaborated with him on the lost *Cardenio*, acted in 1613 but known only in a questionable version published in 1728 by the editor Lewis Theobald under the title *Double Falsehood*. But the most important joint effort of the two men (excluding *Henry VIII*, which may be entirely Shakespeare's) seems to have been *The Two Noble Kinsmen*.[2]

According to the title page of the earliest text, a 1634 quarto, *Kinsmen* was acted at the Blackfriars by the King's Men and written by John Fletcher and William Shakespeare, "the memorable Worthies of their time"; and their authorship is acknowledged in the play's entry in the Stationers' Register on April 8 of that same year.[3] Although some (notably Una Ellis-Fermor) reject Shakespeare's authorship because of the play's allegedly weak characterization and its lack of sustained intellectual and emotional force, there is no compelling reason to question the 1634 attributions.[4] But scholars disagree as to the nature of the collaboration. For example, Frank Kermode sees *Kinsmen* as Fletcher's play, with incidental contributions from Shakespeare; G. R. Proudfoot believes Fletcher responsible for its final form; Philip Edwards argues that the artistic design had to be Shakespeare's.[5] The consensus is that Shakespeare wrote I; III, 1 and 2; and V, 1, 3, and 4, although, as Proudfoot sensibly reminds us, "the aim of collaborating playwrights was to write a play, not to leave to posterity clear evidence of their respective shares in it."[6] The morris dance (III, 5) is taken from Francis Beaumont's

Masque of the Inner Temple and Gray's Inn (first presented at court on February 20, 1613),[7] and there is an apparent allusion to *Kinsmen* in Ben Jonson's *Bartholomew Fair* (1614). Hence the date of composition would seem to be 1613.

The Two Noble Kinsmen is a dramatization of Chaucer's *Knight's Tale* in *The Canterbury Tales*. In the main plot, two Theban noblemen, Palamon and Arcite, while in prison together in Athens, catch sight of Emilia through their window, fall in love with her simultaneously, and become bitter enemies. Eventually Arcite is banished from Athens and Palamon escapes. When they meet in the woods outside Athens, they begin to fight, but they are interrupted by Theseus, Duke of Athens and husband of Emilia's sister Hippolyta. Because Emilia cannot decide between them, they agree to fight again in a month. The winner will marry Emilia; the loser will be executed. When the duel takes place, Arcite wins and Palamon's head is placed on the block. Just at that moment a messenger arrives with word that Arcite has been mortally injured in a fall from his horse. Before he dies, Arcite gallantly bestows Emilia upon Palamon.

As Arcite is carried out, Palamon comments upon his joyless victory:

> O cousin,
> That we should things desire which do cost us
> The loss of our desire! that naught could buy
> Dear love but loss of dear love!
> (V, 4, 109–112)

Theseus, in turn, reflects upon the inscrutability of the gods:

> O you heavenly charmers,
> What things you make of us! For what we lack
> We laugh, for what we have are sorry; still
> Are children in some kind. Let us be thankful
> For that which is, and with you leave dispute
> That are above our question.
> (V, 4, 131–136)

Chaucer's Theseus had offered Palamon similar comfort, drawing his lessons from Boethius's *Consolation of Philosophy:*

> Thanne is it wysdom, as it thynketh me,
> To maken vertu of necessitee,
> And take it weel that [what] we may nat eschue,
> And namely [particularly] that [what] to us alle is due.
> (*The Canterbury Tales*, Group A, ll. 3041–3044)[8]

In the subplot, the jailer's daughter, desperately in love with Palamon, helps him escape. Later, not finding him, she goes mad and, like Ophelia, gives vent to erotic fantasies. But she is cured and married to a longtime wooer. Her situation reinforces a major theme of the principal action: the destructive power of sexual love. Although the story of the jailer's daughter is not found in Chaucer, it too is consistent with the philosophy of *The Knight's Tale*.

NOTES

1. Lindley Williams Hubbell (*A Note on the Shakespeare Apocrypha* [Kobe, Japan: The Ikuta Press, 1972]) lists seventy-two such plays. Baldwin Maxwell discusses four: *Locrine, Thomas Lord of Cromwell, The Puritan,* and *A Yorkshire Tragedy*. See his *Studies in the Shakespeare Apocrypha* (New York: King's Crown, 1956). See also William Kozlenko, ed., *Disputed Plays of Shakespeare* (New York: Hawthorn, 1974).

2. See Kenneth Muir, *Shakespeare as Collaborator* (London: Methuen, 1960). Paul Bertram, in *Shakespeare and The Two Noble Kinsmen* (New Brunswick, N.J.: Rutgers University Press, 1965), believes (pp. 180–196) that Shakespeare had nothing to do with *Cardenio* but credits him (pp. 13–57, 197–243) with the sole authorship of *Kinsmen*.

3. See E. K. Chambers, *William Shakespeare: A Study of Facts and Problems*, 2 vols. (Oxford: Clarendon, 1930), 1: 528–532.

4. Una Ellis-Fermor, "*The Two Noble Kinsmen*" (1949), in *Shakespeare the Dramatist and Other Papers,* ed. Kenneth Muir (New York: Barnes & Noble, 1961), pp. 177–186. But Muir notes (p. 186) that by the time of her death (1958) she was not sure.

5. Frank Kermode, *William Shakespeare: The Final Plays* (London: Longmans, 1963), pp. 50–52; *The Two Noble Kinsmen,* ed. G. R. Proudfoot, (Lincoln: University of Nebraska Press, 1970), pp. xiii–xix; Philip Edwards, "On the Design of The Two Noble Kinsmen," *Review of English Literature* 5: 4 (October 1964): 89–105. Several critics have found stylistic evidence for Shakespeare's collaboration: vocabulary, images, image clusters, and so on. See Muir, *Shakespeare as Collaborator,* pp. 98–147; Marco Mincoff, "The Authorship of The Two Noble Kinsmen," *English Studies* 33 (1952): 97–115; and John P. Cutts, "Shakespeare's Song and Masque Hand in The Two Noble Kinsmen," *English Miscellany* 18 (1967): 55–85.

6. Proudfoot edition, p. xix.

7. *Kinsmen* is especially rich in formal dances, processionals, and other highly stylized spectacles. Theodore Spenser speaks of its "static pageantry." See "*The Two Noble Kinsmen*," *Modern Philology* 36 (1938–1939): 255–276.

8. In *The Works of Geoffrey Chaucer,* ed. F. N. Robinson, 2d ed. (Boston: Houghton Mifflin, 1957).

A Selected Bibliography

ANNUAL BIBLIOGRAPHIES

PMLA: Publications of the Modern Language Association of America
Shakespeare Quarterly
Annual assessments of Shakespeare studies may be found in *Shakespeare Survey* and *The Year's Work in English Studies*. *The Shakespeare Newsletter* (published six times annually) has valuable abstracts and summaries, with other useful information.

OTHER BIBLIOGRAPHIES

Bateson, F. W., ed. *Cambridge Bibliography of English Literature*. 4 vols. New York: Macmillan, 1941. (See 1: 539–608 for Shakespeare.) *Supplement*. 1957.

Berman, Ronald. *A Reader's Guide to Shakespeare's Plays: A Discursive Bibliography*. Rev. ed. Glenview, Ill.: Scott, Foresman, 1973. Selective; good annotations.

Ebisch, Walter, and Schücking, Levin L. *A Shakespeare Bibliography*. Oxford: Clarendon, 1931 (to 1929). *Supplement for the Years 1930–1935*. 1937.

Jaggard, W. *Shakespeare Bibliography*. Stratford-upon-Avon: Shakespeare Head Press, 1911.

McManaway, James G., and Roberts, Jeanne Addison. *A Selective Bibliography of Shakespeare: Editions, Textual Studies, Commentary*. Charlottesville: University Press of Virginia (for the Folger Shakespeare Library), 1975.

Quinn, Edward; Ruoff, James; and Grennen, Joseph. *The Major Shake-*

spearean Tragedies: A Critical Bibliography. New York: Macmillan
(The Free Press), 1973.
Selective guide to *Hamlet, Othello, King Lear,* and *Macbeth,* with full
summaries and sharp critical evaluations.
Smith, Gordon Ross. *A Classified Shakespeare Bibliography 1936–1958.*
University Park, Pa.: Pennsylvania State University Press, 1963.
See also the published catalogs of some of the great Shakespeare
collections: the Birmingham Shakespeare Library, the Folger Shakespeare
Library, and the Shakespeare excerpt (published in 1964) from the
British Museum Catalog of Printed Books.

SOME SIGNIFICANT BOOKS

Alexander, Peter. *Shakespeare's Life and Art* (1939). New York: New
York University Press, 1961.
Bowers, Fredson. *On Editing Shakespeare.* Charlottesville: University
Press of Virginia, 1966.
Bradley, A. C. *Shakespearean Tragedy* (1904). 2d ed. London: Mac-
millan, 1905.
Bullough, Geoffrey. *Narrative and Dramatic Sources of Shakespeare.*
8 vols. New York: Columbia University Press, 1957–1975.
Campbell, Oscar James, and Quinn, Edward G., eds. *The Reader's
Encyclopedia of Shakespeare.* New York: T. Y. Crowell, 1966.
Chambers, E. K. *The Elizabethan Stage.* 4 vols. Oxford: Clarendon, 1923.
Chambers, E. K. *William Shakespeare: A Study of Facts and Problems.*
2 vols. Oxford: Clarendon, 1930.
Clemen, Wolfgang H. *The Development of Shakespeare's Imagery.*
Cambridge: Harvard University Press, 1951.
Coleridge, Samuel Taylor. *Coleridge's Shakespearean Criticism.* Edited
by T. M. Raysor. 2 vols. Rev. ed. London: Dent, 1960.
Granville-Barker, Harley. *Prefaces to Shakespeare.* 2 vols. Princeton:
Princeton University Press, 1946–1947.
Greg, W. W. *The Shakespeare First Folio: Its Bibliographical and Textual
History.* Oxford: Clarendon, 1955.
Harbage, Alfred. *As They Liked It: An Essay on Shakespeare and
Morality.* New York: Macmillan, 1947.
Hinman, Charlton. *The Printing and Proof-Reading of the First Folio.*
2 vols. Oxford: Clarendon, 1963.
Hodges, C. Walter. *The Globe Restored: A Study of the Elizabethan
Theatre.* Rev. ed. London: Oxford University Press, 1968.
Johnson, Samuel. *Johnson on Shakespeare.* Edited by Arthur Sherbo.
2 vols. New Haven: Yale University Press, 1968.
Knight, G. Wilson. *The Wheel of Fire: Interpretations of Shakespearean*

Tragedy (1930). 5th rev. ed. Cleveland: World Publishing, Meridian Books, 1957.

Muir, Kenneth, and Schoenbaum, S., eds. *A New Companion to Shakespeare Studies*. Cambridge: Cambridge University Press, 1971.

Salingar, Leo. *Shakespeare and the Traditions of Comedy*. London: Cambridge University Press, 1974.

Sprague, Arthur Colby. *Shakespearian Players and Performances*. Cambridge: Harvard University Press, 1953.

Spurgeon, Caroline F. E. *Shakespeare's Imagery and What It Tells Us*. New York: Macmillan, 1935.

Tillyard, E. M. W. *The Elizabethan World Picture*. New York: Macmillan, 1943.

Van Doren, Mark. *Shakespeare*. New York: Holt, 1939.

Zeeveld, W. Gordon. *The Temper of Shakespeare's Thought*. New Haven: Yale University Press, 1974.

Index